C0-DAD-909

Books Listed in Table Inside Front Cover

Alexander, J. E. (Ed.) *Teaching Reading.* Boston: Little, Brown and Co., 1979.

Cunningham, P. M., Arthur, S. V., and Cunningham, J. W. *Classroom Reading Instruction K–5 Alternative Approaches.* Lexington, Massachusetts: D. C. Heath and Company, 1977.

Dallmann, M. Rouch, R. L., Char, L. Y. C., and DeBoer, J. J. *The Teaching of Reading,* 5th ed. New York: Holt, Rinehart and Winston, Inc., 1978.

Farr, R., and Roser, N. *Teaching a Child to Read.* New York: Harcourt Brace Jovanovich, Inc., 1979.

Guszak, F. J. *Diagnostic Reading Instruction in the Elementary School,* 2nd ed. New York: Harper & Row, Inc., 1978.

Hall, M. A., Ribovich, J. K., and Ramig, C. J. *Reading and the Elementary School Child,* 2nd ed. New York: D. Van Nostrand, 1979.

Harris, A. J., and Sipay, E. R. *How to Teach Reading.* New York: Longman Inc., 1979.

Hittleman, D. R. *Developmental Reading: A Psycholinguistic Perspective.* Chicago: Rand McNally and Co., 1978.

Lapp, D., and Flood, J. *Teaching Reading to Every Child.* New York: Macmillan Publishing Co., Inc., 1978.

McNeil, J. D., Donant, L., and Alkin, M. C. *How to Teach Reading Successfully.* Boston: Little, Brown and Company, 1980.

Otto, W., Rude, R., and Spiegel, D. L. *How to Teach Reading.* Reading, Massachusetts: Addison-Wesley Publishing Company, 1979.

Ransom, G. A. *Preparing to Teach Reading.* Boston: Little, Brown and Company, 1978.

Second Edition

Joanne P. Olson

Martha H. Dillner

UNIVERSITY OF HOUSTON, CLEAR LAKE CITY

Learning to Teach Reading in the Elementary School

UTILIZING A COMPETENCY-BASED INSTRUCTIONAL SYSTEM

Macmillan Publishing Co., Inc.
NEW YORK

Collier Macmillan Publishers
LONDON

Printed in the United States of America

Macmillan Publishing Co., Inc.
866 Third Avenue, New York, New York 10022

Collier Macmillan Canada, Ltd.

Library of Congress Cataloging in Publication Data

Olson, Joanne P
Learning to teach reading in the elementary school.

Includes bibliographies and index.
1. Reading (Elementary) 2. Competency based education. I. Dillner, Martha H., joint author.
II. Title.
LB1573.0543 1982 372.4'1 80-16162
ISBN 0-02-389300-1

Printing: 1 2 3 4 5 6 7 8 Year: 2 3 4 5 6 7 8 9

Preface

Learning to Teach Reading in the Elementary School is designed to introduce students to the basic skills they will need to be successful teachers of reading in the elementary school. The book is divided into eight parts.

Part One familiarizes the reader with a knowledge of the reading process. The initial chapter discusses the nature of reading. Chapter 2 introduces the participant to a basic knowledge of word identification skills. Chapter 3 illustrates the scope of the comprehension skills. Chapter 4 describes the range of study skills.

Part Two discusses several techniques by which the reading skills can be assessed and includes only one chapter, Chapter 5. Part Three presents a variety of methods commonly used to teach reading. Chapter 6 discusses the basal reader as a method for teaching reading. Chapter 7 discusses other methods such as the language experience and the individualized reading programs; Chapter 8 describes a diagnostic–prescriptive technique for the teaching of reading.

Part Four presents ways in which the teacher can manage the reading program and includes only Chapter 9, "Grouping by Achievement, Interests, and Needs." Part Five focuses on aspects needed to round out the reading program. Chapter 10 demonstrates a means by which recreational reading may be made an integral part of every program; Chapter 11 centers on teaching reading while teaching the content area materials.

Part Six focuses on teaching reading to special groups and includes Chapter 12, "Teaching Reading to the Diverse Learner," and Chapter 13, "Reading Readiness."

Part Seven, which consists of only one chapter, presents practical application of Chapters 2, 3, 4, and 13. Students are given strategies for teaching the word identification, comprehension, study, and readiness skills. Although this chapter is optimally designed to be removed from the text and incorporated into a notebook that can be used by the participant through many years of an actual teaching situation, some objectives require the participant to use a portion of these strategies immediately.

Each chapter contains objectives of two types. The first type is cognitive and is based on information given within the chapter. The second type requires the participant to put the cognitive objectives into practice by requiring that the participant complete at least one "experience" correlated with the information contained in the chapter. Although these experiences are optimally designed for a course that allows students to teach children, most of the objectives can also be assessed through peer teaching.

The authors gratefully acknowledge the many students and colleagues who helped to make this book possible. Special recognition should be given to Dr. W. Robert Houston, who introduced us to the competency-based philosophy, to Dr. Lee Mountain for her help in the early stages of the first edition, to Dr. Josephine Sobrino, Dr. Laveria Hutchinson, Dr. Peter Gingiss, and Judy Stevens, who read selected chapters, and to Emma L. Ankele and Janice Guetzow, who read the manuscript in its entirety.

J. P. O.
M. H. D.

Contents

Part Four
Managing the Reading Program

Part Five
Rounding Out the Reading Program

Part Six
Teaching Reading to Special Groups

Part Seven
Practicing Teaching Reading

Appendixes

Part One
The Reading Process

Chapter 1
Reading and Reading Instruction

Objectives 1.1

On completion of this chapter, the participant should be able to

1. Given a description of a person *reading*: (a) state whether the reading process is actually occurring and (b) defend the answer with a definition of reading that includes both word recognition and comprehension.
2. Describe the importance of reading in society today.
3. Describe the role of the teacher in reading instruction.

Experience 1 extends chapter 1 with this objective:

4. During this experience, the student will gather definitions of *reading* from at least three different people.

Information Given 1.2
Reading and Reading Instruction

The purpose of this chapter is to examine (1) the nature of reading, (2) the importance of reading in society today, and (3) the role of the teacher in instructing children to read. This review will be carried out first through an observation of a fictitious family, the Greens, and, second, through a discussion on relevant issues reflected by the family members.

THE GREEN FAMILY

The Green family consists of two adults--Mr. and Mrs. Green—and their two children--Jack and Peter. When asked if they read frequently, Mrs. Green replied, "My husband and I don't read at all. My older son, Peter, reads quite a bit. Our younger son, Jack, can read anything to us, and he's only finished grade one!"

Mrs. Green skims the paper for the grocery ads, views each carefully, and then prepares her shopping list.

Schneider Market

need $5 min. purchase and coupons

coffee
sugar

Delgado Market

milk
ground beef

Meanwhile, six-year-old Jack has located a children's book to read. He says each word carefully aloud. When he has finished, he is asked by his mother what the story was about. Jack looks surprised and confused at this question. Jack can say the words aloud, but he is unable to recall the content of what he has read.

Nine-year-old Peter comes into the house. He has just seen a bird and wants to find out what type it is. He looks in his bird book and identifies the one he saw as a cat bird from the family Mimidae. He marks this name on his Birdwatcher's Checksheet. Then Peter tells his mother about a story of two boys that he was reading the previous evening. He tells her that "They played baseball behind the school—just like we do."

Meanwhile, Mr. Green is preparing to leave for his rounds as handyman for several families in the neighborhood. He prepares the following schedule:

9 am	Flores	219 Coach Street
11 am	Pearson	4830 Triway Ct.
1 pm	McCullar	1271 Penn
3 pm	Schubb	Camerson

The Schubbs are new customers, and Mr. Green realizes that he has not recorded their street address. He consults the telephone directory and finds that the number is 1119. Before leaving the house he checks to be sure that his city map is in the truck in case he needs it to locate the Schubb house.

On arriving at the Flore's, Mr. Green finds that Mrs. Flores has left him a note:

Mr. Green,

In addition to cutting the lawn, do you have time to wash the leaded windows?

Mrs. Flores

Mr. Green reads the note and decides that he has time to perform the extra chore.

READING DEFINED

Mrs. Green made the statement that her husband and she didn't read at all and that Peter and Jack read extensively. The validity of this statement is contingent upon the definition of reading used.

Surprisingly, there is no single, accepted definition of reading. For example, definitions may range from the "visual perception of word forms and their meaning" (Harris, 1969) to "Perception and comprehension of written messages in a manner paralleling that of the corresponding spoken message" (Carroll, 1964) to "a process of thinking, evaluating, judging, imagining, reasoning, and problem solving" (NSSE, 1949).

Educators usually define *reading* in a manner similar to that used by Harris (1969), as "a process of meaning elaboration or thinking in relation to written symbols." This definition presupposes that two aspects are essential to the reading process—word recognition and comprehension. *Word recognition* is the ability to pronounce and/or give meaning to a printed symbol. *Comprehension* is the ability to understand and apply the material.

For reading to take place, some of each element—word recognition and comprehension—must be present. Word recognition is insufficient by itself for reading to take place. Comprehension cannot occur without word recognition.

On the basis of this definition of reading, look at the questions following and try to decide whether you agree or disagree with Mrs. Green's statement. Write "yes" or "no" in the blanks.

Is Mrs. Green reading when she
skims the newspaper to locate the grocery ads? ________ uses the ads to make her shopping list? ________

Is Mr. Green reading when he
uses the telephone directory to locate an address? ________ uses a map to find a house? ________ reacts to a note left by a customer? ________

Is Jack reading when he
calls the words aloud but fails to recall anything about what he has read? ________

Is Peter reading when he
uses his bird book to classify a bird? ________ compares a scene read from a book to one he has been involved with? ________

If you answered "yes" to the questions concerning the senior Greens and Peter, then you were correct. In each case the person recognized words and comprehended. You were also correct if you responded that Jack was not reading when he named the words aloud but was unable to recall anything about the story. He was recognizing the words but was not comprehending their meaning. For this reason, Jack was not reading.

IMPORTANCE OF THE DEFINITION OF READING FOR THE TEACHER

The stated or unstated definition that each teacher has of reading is important because the reading program carried on by the teacher will reflect that definition. For example, Jack's grade one teacher incompletely defined reading as "calling the words aloud correctly."

Thus, this teacher's reading program leaned heavily toward teaching the child to recognize words and to say them aloud correctly. The problem with this definition of reading is that Jack was being taught merely to recognize words and was not being taught to understand and use what he was reading.

In contrast, the teachers that Peter had for the last three years possessed a broader view of reading and believed that word recognition was nothing more than a way station to the real goal of reading—comprehension. Although they taught many word recognition skills, they also taught the comprehension skills. Since they knew that children needed many experiences to make their reading more meaningful, they planned field trips and discussion sessions to expand the children's language background, asked questions concerning inference, main idea, detail, and sequence to develop different types of comprehension skills, and taught children to organize material in an efficient manner by instructing them in note-taking, outlining, and summarizing techniques. These teachers were teaching reading in the fullest sense of the term.

IMPORTANCE OF READING TODAY

Reading is a vital skill in today's complex society. The importance of reading will be treated under the headings "Relationship to Everyday Needs" and "Relationship to Recreation."

RELATIONSHIP TO EVERYDAY NEEDS

Reading is required on a daily basis by all adults if they are to participate in modern-day society. Many everyday chores—completing tax forms, renewing a driver's license, and withdrawing money from a bank—require reading. In addition to using reading for such mundane tasks, this skill allows an individual to make informed choices. The television schedule will help a person to plan his or her evening's entertainment, the sale ads will help him or her to buy new furniture, and political announcements will aid in his or her choice of a candidate. It is possible that in today's automated world many of these tasks can be completed without the need to read. Forms may be completed with the help of a friend or an official; products of all kinds are advertised on radio and television; and politicians ordinarily offer the public ample opportunity to hear their views. However, the disadvantages of sole reliance on these sources include

1. the nonreader's dependence on other people
2. the nonreader's exposure to a minimum of viewpoints on an issue from the mass media, and
3. the nonreader's inability to make comparisons because the nonreader has available to him only one perspective at a time.

EXAMPLE

If Peter's good reading skills continue to increase, he should be able to do the chores and make the decisions required for an intelligent, complete participation in today's culture. On the other hand, if Jack's reading comprehension skills do not develop beyond where they are now, he will encounter difficulty in both competing and benefiting fully from the society in which he will be living.

RELATIONSHIP TO RECREATION

Many types of reading-related activities can and should be enjoyable. The pleasure gleaned from vicarious reading experiences, as well as the sense of accomplishment felt in successfully putting into concrete form a written set of directions on "how to build a model," can provide many rewarding leisure time hours for young and old alike. Although this role has been important in the past, it should increase in importance for adults as the work week becomes shorter and more leisure time is available.

EXAMPLE

If Peter's reading skills continue to expand, he may continue to experience success in this area and, as such, his probability for using reading as a leisure time activity will increase. If Jack's reading skills do not develop further, he will be limited in his desire for recreational reading.

It will be difficult for Jack to enjoy a written description of an automobile race or build a model car if he cannot understand the meaning of the words he has learned to pronounce.

TEACHER'S ROLE IN READING INSTRUCTION

Several studies have indicated that the crucial factor in reading instruction is the teacher. One significant study that was highly supportive of this viewpoint was the Cooperative Research Program in First Grade Reading Instruction (Bond and Dykstra, 1967) carried out under the auspices of the U.S. Office of Education in 1964–1965. The purpose of this research was to investigate the relationship of several factors, including methodology, sex of the pupil, and amount of phonics, to success in beginning reading. The reading growth of nearly 30,000 first grade children was carefully observed. Following collection and analysis of the data, the one factor that stood out as being highly significant in children's reading success was the teacher. Findings such as this place a heavy burden on the teacher. Of all the classroom factors, it is the influence of the instructor that makes the difference between success and failure for children enrolled in his or her reading class.

SUMMARY

Reading has been defined as the ability to recognize printed symbols and to comprehend their meaning. Furthermore, reading has been shown to be an essential skill for facilitating a multitude of day-to-day tasks and promoting an easily accessible means for recreation in today's highly complex, print-oriented society. The teacher has an immense responsibility for instructing children to read, as research has shown that the teacher is the crucial factor in the learning situation.

References and Bibliography

Bond, G. L., and Dykstra, R. "The Cooperative Research Program in First Grade Reading Instruction." *Reading Research Quarterly*, 2 (Winter 1967): 1–142.

Carroll, J. B. "The Analysis of Reading Instruction: Perspectives from Psychology and Linguistics," in E. R. Hilgard, ed., *Theories of Learning Instruction*, 63rd Yearbook, Part 1, NSSE. Chicago: University of Chicago Press, 1964, pp. 336–353.

Harris, T. L. *Encyclopedia of Educational Research*. New York: Macmillan Publishing Co., Inc., 1969, p. 1075.

NSSE. *Reading in the Elementary School*, 48th Yearbook of the National Society for the Study of Education, Part II. Chicago: University of Chicago Press, 1949, p. 3.

Zintz, M. V. *The Reading Process: The Teacher and the Learner*. 3rd ed. Dubuque, Iowa: William C. Brown Company, Publishers, 1979.

Self-Check 1.3
Reading and Reading Instruction

The following questions are designed to help the participant assess his or her competence on the first three objectives stated at the beginning of this chapter. Although every effort has been made to make the self-check questions comprehensive, participants should remember that they are held responsible for meeting the objectives as stated at the beginning of this chapter.

1. Objective 1. Mrs. Walter's daughter always says "ice cream" and pats her stomach when riding past a massive roadside advertisement stating "Good food and world famous desserts at Jiffy's restaurant." Is this child reading? State why or why not and support your answer with what you believe to be a definition of the reading process.
2. Objective 2. Describe why you think reading is important in today's society.
3. Objective 3. What is the role of the teacher in reading instruction?

Chapter 1
Experience 1

Objective

During this experience, the student will gather definitions of *reading* from at least three different people.

Activity and Assessment Guide

1. Give the ages for the three people interviewed. No two should be the same age, and, if possible, there should be at least two years' difference in ages between each interviewee.

   a. Person one age: _______

   b. Person two age: _______

   c. Person three age: _______

2. Person one's definition of reading: ______________________________

   ____

   ____

3. Person two's definition of reading: ______________________________

   ____

   ____

4. Person three's definition of reading: ______________________________

____

____

* 5. Compare and contrast the definition of reading of each subject with one another; for example, did age make a difference in terms of how the person defined reading?

   a. Person one ______________________________

   b. Person two ______________________________

   c. Person three ______________________________

* 6. Compare and contrast the definition of reading of each subject with your personal definition of reading.

   a. Person one ______________________________

   b. Person two ______________________________

   c. Person three ______________________________

* 7. State what you believe to be the significant implication of this experience for the classroom teacher. ______________________________

____

____

Note: An asterisk (*) appears next to some of the questions in the experiences presented in this chapter. This indicates that these particular questions may be reacted to twice—once by the participant and once by someone who is observing the participant while he or she is completing the experience. In many cases, only the participant will react to all the questions within the experience he or she is completing. However, in some cases the instructor will request that the participant be observed by a peer, a cooperating teacher, the instructor, or some other person. In such cases, the questions with the asterisks (*) should be completed by the observer as well as the participant. The observer should write his or her reactions to these questions on a separate sheet of paper and staple them to the experience so that both responses may be given to the instructor at the same time. Throughout this text the asterisk (*) has been used to indicate portions of each experience which may or may not be reacted to by an observer. If the participant does not have an observer, these asterisks (*), but not the questions themselves, should be ignored.

In addition, in some cases the observer may have to slightly adapt the question in order to answer it. For example, in Chapter 3, Experience 1, the participant is to "briefly describe why you selected the skills that you did." The observer should describe why he or she believes those skills were selected by the observer.

Chapter 2
Word Identification Skills

Objectives 2.1

On completion of this chapter, the participant should be able to

1. Define each of the following terms:
   a. word identification skills
   b. sight word skills
   c. decoding skills
   d. configuration clues
   e. picture clues
   f. context clues
   g. phonic clues
   h. grapheme
   i. phoneme
   j. syllable
   k. morpheme
   l. morphemic clues
   m. dictionary usage

2. State the relationship among the following: word identification, sight word, and decoding skills.
3. Designate the word identification skill being used in given situations involving a child's reading (such as the example in 4).
4. Given any of the word identification skills, compose an original example of a child's use of that skill in a reading situation. Your example might read, "Donna is reading and comes to the word radiate, which she does not recognize on sight. She divides radiate into syl-

lables, places the accent, names the parts, and blends them to arrive at the word's pronunciation. She has used phonic clues."

5. Given a real or nonsense word, indicate the syllable division(s), accent, and vowel sounds. Example: Given the word mitel, indicate the syllable division, accented syllable, and the long, short, or schwa vowel sounds.
6. Given a real or nonsense word in isolation or in a sentence, correctly label appropriate word parts using the following phonic terminology: hard or soft g, hard or soft c, consonant blend or digraph, vowel digraph or diphthong, schwa, silent letter, and short or long vowel. Example: "Given the word girl, state whether its g is hard or soft."
7. State at least one limitation and one advantage of each word identification skills.

Experiences 1 and 2 extend Chapter 2 with these objectives:

8. During this experience, the participant will analyze an adult's or a child's reading and accurately identify the word identification skills used; and/or
9. During this experience, the participant will assess and teach a minimum of one word identification skill.

Information Given 2.2
Word Identification Skills

Two teacher education students spent the morning at a public elementary school observing several different reading lessons. They saw a group of first grade beginning readers using configuration clues, several members of a second grade class studying long and short vowels, the third grade class reviewing context clues, and the majority of fourth and fifth grade pupils working at an exercise on rules about affixes. While visiting the sixth grade class, whose teacher was explaining how to place accents on appropriate syllables, the prospective teachers wondered how this skill helped the pupils to read. They also had many other questions involving the overall organization of the skills that they had seen taught, as well as the meaning of terms that they had heard being used.

The purpose of this chapter is to answer questions such as these to help the participant understand the theory upon which instruction in the word identification skills is based.

ORGANIZATION OF THE WORD IDENTIFICATION SKILLS

Chapter 1 presented the concept that reading involves three interrelated types of skills: word identification skills, comprehension skills, and study skills. This chapter will focus upon the word identification skills, Chapter 3 upon the comprehension skills, and chapter 4 upon the study skills.

Word Identification Skills Defined: The word identification skills are those that aid the reader in pronouncing and/or gaining meaning from the printed page. The two major categories of word identification skills are sight word skills and decoding skills.

Sight Word Skills Defined: Sight word skills allow the reader to pronounce a word immediately upon sight. For example, when Hamilton instantly and accurately pronounces the word picture, he is using his sight word skills.

Decoding Skills Defined: Decoding skills aid the reader in pronouncing and/or attaching meaning to written words not recognized upon sight. For example, when Rachel sees a word that she does not immediately recognize on sight, she must use decoding skills to pronounce the word. The decoding skills include the following categories of subskills: configuration clues, picture clues, context clues, phonic clues, morphemic clues, and dictionary usage.

The next section, "Content of the Word Identification Skills," defines and explains the content of both the sight word skills and all components of the decoding skills. Figure 2.1 summarizes the relationship between the two categories of word identification skills.

CONTENT OF THE WORD IDENTIFICATION SKILLS

This section discusses the word identification skills in detail. Assessments and teaching procedures are described in Chapter 14, "Teaching Word Identification, Comprehension, Study, and Readiness Skills." Assessment procedures are given so that the teacher can determine whether or not the child knows the skill before being taught it, as well as whether or not the child learns the skill after it has been taught. A variety of teaching procedures are

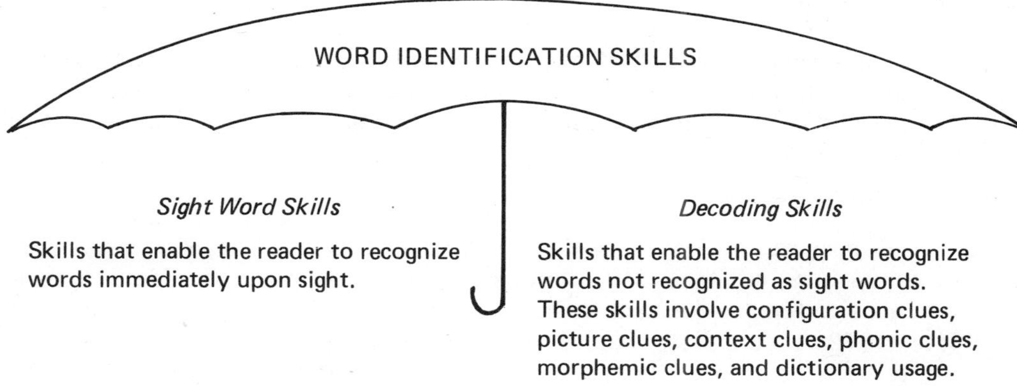

Figure 2.1. Relationship Between the Word Identification Skills.

included so that the teacher may select those that are most suited to the needs of the pupil.

SIGHT WORD SKILLS

Sight word skills enable the reader to recognize words immediately upon sight. Therefore, words that a reader can identify in this manner are part of his or her *sight vocabulary.* For example, without the use of decoding skills, Paul knows his name immediately when he sees it. Thus, the word Paul is in his sight vocabulary.

To test his or her sight word skills, the reader may view the word owl. If the reader can read the word accurately and immediately, he or she is using his or her sight word skills, and owl is part of his or her sight vocabulary.

Most programs of reading instruction specify the words that children are expected to learn as part of their sight vocabularies. In addition to these words, individual teachers will often add those that are important to their pupils, such as the names of the children, school, city, county, and state.

Basic sight vocabulary lists may serve as an aid in teaching sight word skills. Examples of such lists include the Dolch list (1936), the Kucera-Francis list (1967), and the Fry list (1972). Studies of frequently occurring words have been used as the basis for choosing the word included on these lists, which are overlapping. Therefore, teachers often use one of these lists to ensure that their pupils know as sight words those that occur frequently in their reading materials. Table 2.1 presents one such list.

Most people recognize as sight words the majority of the words that they encounter. Since this is the most rapid way to read, the decoding skills described later in this chapter should be used only when a word is not recognized as a sight word.

DECODING SKILLS

Decoding skills are those that help the reader to recognize words that are not known as sight words and include configuration clues, picture clues, context clues, phonic clues, morphemic clues, and dictionary usage. Discussions of each of these follow.

Configuration Clues

Configuration clues include elements such as word length, word shape, double letters, capital letters, hyphens, apostrophes, position of letters, repetition of letters, and characteristics of individual letters (Ives, Bursuk, and Ives, 1979) that aid the reader in pronouncing or gaining meaning from a printed word not in his or her sight vocabulary. For example, the reader who remembers how the printed letters look are pronounced because there are two letter o's in the middle of the word is using the configuration clue repetition of letters to identify the word.

TABLE 2.1 The Stetson Reading-Spelling-Vocabulary Program

Level I: 225 Words for Grades 1 and 2				
Lesson 1	*Lesson 2*	*Lesson 3*	*Lesson 4*	*Lesson 5*
a	can	at	out	on
I	you	be	she	too
in	red	am	so	was
is	one	do	big	yes
me	are	no	but	will
it	for	run	did	say
go	two	all	eat	who
my	not	find	get	well
to	look	help	now	good
up	make	jump	our	that
we	come	said	ran	must
the	play	came	saw	with
see	down	four	new	black
he	blue	funny	here	where
and	away	little	three	yellow
Lesson 6	*Lesson 7*	*Lesson 8*	*Lesson 9*	*Lesson 10*
an	us	his	ride	tell
by	if	stop	soon	pull
as	off	how	they	fast
or	sit	give	went	call
of	its	had	have	best
ate	buy	any	into	know
old	cut	her	this	them
put	hot	from	what	live
fly	ten	again	like	once
ask	going	every	white	sing
has	after	over	please	made
let	just	walk	went	gave
him	take	open	pretty	think
may	were	some	under	round
there	could	when	brown	thank
Lesson 11	*Lesson 12*	*Lesson 13*	*Lesson 14*	*Lesson 15*
cold	your	far	clean	day
both	work	six	pick	seven
use	before	own	show	stand
why	first	try	long	shall
does	don't	done	kind	eight
read	green	fall	only	small
been	found	hold	hurt	house
five	these	full	much	bring
many	right	grow	carry	laugh
goes	wash	keep	drink	today
upon	sleep	warm	start	hope
very	write	draw	never	often
wish	their	about	light	then
around	would	which	better	fine
always	because	those	myself	together

Level II: 225 Words for Grades 3 and 4

Lesson 1	*Lesson 2*	*Lesson 3*	*Lesson 4*	*Lesson 5*
man	son	time	lost	back
got	few	boat	feel	lady
boy	ago	home	past	girl
men	sat	tree	hill	real
end	war	fish	mind	snow
bed	dog	kill	need	room
cry	air	mean	road	door
die	pay	fell	sent	more
way	hit	face	life	told
hat	cow	same	pass	hand
bad	set	wait	late	dark
eye	cat	wife	note	took
sun	egg	rest	fill	next
car	fat	name	miss	stay
arm	yet	side	last	book

Lesson 6	*Lesson 7*	*Lesson 8*	*Lesson 9*	*Lesson 10*
turn	near	wind	sort	night
talk	fire	shoe	most	mother
each	even	drop	such	people
head	knew	poor	cost	father
left	high	bank	ball	window
kept	felt	hour	flew	school
farm	town	part	wear	another
hard	land	week	half	picture
baby	than	hear	able	thought
love	king	bird	idea	nothing
gone	step	milk	might	husband
food	city	ship	woman	morning
move	care	wood	thing	herself
year	swim	glad	cause	brought
sick	sure	body	watch	something

Lesson 11	*Lesson 12*	*Lesson 13*	*Lesson 14*	*Lesson 15*
water	still	music	stick	month
horse	hair	table	whole	reach
marry	ready	river	guess	color
money	until	chair	paper	class
while	story	young	alone	dress
happy	world	wrong	sound	plant
catch	fight	close	floor	cover
friend	along	change	great	church
winter	learn	street	leave	finish
garden	sister	should	hundred	office
almost	enough	dinner	himself	bridge
happen	ground	summer	person	being
doctor	brother	wonder	matter	reason
outside	children	clothes	figure	country
anything	beautiful	teacher	different	already

Level III: 225 Words for Grades 5 and 6

Lesson 1	*Lesson 2*	*Lesson 3*	*Lesson 4*	*Lesson 5*
dig	box	rich	dive	won
dry	met	sail	wake	hid
fit	bury	trip	place	sad
top	chop	blow	shut	bread
fix	save	else	trap	short
hop	push	hide	rain	since
hug	onto	woke	kiss	point
lay	dead	wild	nice	alive
oh	drew	shot	plow	crash
pop	easy	swam	none	treat
row	ever	pray	pour	steal
tip	grab	lean	quite	shine
bit	join	hunt	seen	chase
yell	lock	grew	born	dirty
burn	paid	blew	cook	spell

Lesson 6	*Lesson 7*	*Lesson 8*	*Lesson 9*	*Lesson 10*
crawl	awful	spill	twenty	front
dance	below	fifty	family	wrote
faint	touch	guide	strong	began
hurry	steep	float	master	quite
kick	slept	shout	letter	brave
okay	drove	smart	eleven	tired
knock	fifth	later	afraid	twelve
scare	guard	maybe	anyway	either
silly	sharp	plain	behind	o'clock
stuck	foggy	giant	eighty	arrest
sixty	threw	other	forget	broken
allow	slide	quiet	hungry	decide
count	loose	spring	inside	polite
dream	snowy	minute	lovely	really
eaten	asleep	across	mostly	golden

Lesson 11	*Lesson 12*	*Lesson 13*	*Lesson 14*	*Lesson 15*
break	broke	nobody	ashamed	bright
build	paint	operate	electric	famous
climb	smoke	pretend	everything	thousand
drive	throw	quietly	sometimes	horrible
field	tight	anywhere	fifteen	musical
beside	bought	everyone	though	scream
caught	wander	except	downstairs	seventeen
wicked	course	through	American	understand
sleepy	listen	worried	married	Indian
stupid	paddle	yourself	scratch	animal
launch	careful	downtown	surprised	terrible
anybody	without	fourteen	special	probably
against	company	practice	thirsty	interesting
suppose	believe	scary	finally	eighteen
	purple	swallow	gotten	disappointed

As a test of skill in using configuration clues, the reader may examine the word house. If the reader uses word length, word shape (the word house is shaped like a house with a chimney), position of letters, and/or characteristics of individual letters to identify this word, then use of its configuration clues was made.

Configuration clues when used in isolation quickly become extremely limited. For example, when the reader learns a second word with two letter o's in the middle, such as book, or another word that has a "house" shape, such as horse, he or she can no longer depend on configuration clues alone to decode these words. However, developing skill in the use of configuration clues is important because, when used in conjunction with other decoding skills, configuration clues are helpful to the reader.

Picture Clues

Decoding skills include the use of pictures that help the reader to pronounce and/or attach meaning to written words not recognized immediately. For example, Mary encounters the word Doberman in a written sentence, but she is unable to attach meaning to the word until she refers to the drawing of a Doberman that accompanies the sentence. Therefore, she has used a picture clues to decode the new word.

If a reader can immediately ascertain the meaning of a written term, then there is no need for a picture clue. Therefore, the use of nonsense words accompanied by pictures provides an effective technique to test a reader's expertise in this decoding skill. For example, the reader may look at the nonsense term efabido and view the following picture.

If using the illustration aids in understanding the nonsense term efabido, then the reader possesses skill in using picture clues to decode new words.

In addition to aiding in the understanding of meaning, picture clues help the reader to pronounce a word that is recognized verbally in print. For example, although she knew the meaning of the spoken word, Ada was not able to pronounce the written word potpourri. However, after referring to an appropriate illustration, she immediately recognized the printed word potpourri as the spoken word potpourri.

Context Clues

Using context clues involves applying knowledge of surrounding words as an aid in pronouncing or giving meaning to an unrecognized word. This particular decoding skill is the one most helpful to all readers, since through its use the meanings of unknown words can be deduced without having to glance from the printed page. Although context clues aid primarily in understanding meaning, they are also helpful in pronouncing words whose context brings to mind the familiar spoken word. For example, even though the written word bell is not in Jimmy's sight vocabulary, he uses his knowledge of the other words in the following sentence to surmise its meaning: "When the school bell rang, I knew I was late."

Types of Context Clues:

Most content area textbooks contain several different *types of context clues.* Some of the most common are as follows:

1. A *definition* of a term may be directly stated: "An artery, a thick muscular tube that carries blood away from the heart, in one of the three kinds of tubes through which blood flows."
2. An *implication* of the term from the general context of the passage may suggest the meaning: "Air passes from the nose or mouth into the windpipe where rings of hard material keep the windpipe from squeezing shut when you breathe."
3. Several *examples* might illustrate the meaning: "Some food is classified as *roughage*, for example, celery and leafy vegetables."
4. The use of *contrast* may provide meaning: "The *veins*, unlike the arteries, do not carry blood away from the heart."
5. The *expectancy* of meaning might help the student: If a child were reading about digestion, he or she might expect to see such terms as *swallow*, *dissolve*, *change*, and *saliva.*

Teachers can encourage children to use context to help them recognize words in two ways. First, before the children are assigned to read any content area material, the topic should be discussed so that the children will have heard many of the words before they actually read them. Second, teachers should show children the various types of context clues, such as the five just listed, and then encourage them to look for such clues when they encounter unknown words.

Readers may test their own skill in using context clues by reading the following sentence: "The two police officers rushed to the crime scene in their prowl car." If the readers did not know the meaning of the term prowl car before reading this sentence, context clues should have helped them in ascertaining that prowl car is synonymous with police car.

Phonic Clues

Phonic clues include the decoding tools, sound-symbol correspondence, and syllabication. Discussion for each of these decoding aids follows.

Sound–Symbol Correspondence

Unless a word is recognized on sight or through the use of configuration, picture, or context clues, the reader will probably attempt to identify the word by relating its printed letters (graphemes) to their corresponding spoken sounds (phonemes). Graphemes include consonants such as b, d, and f; consonant combinations such as sh and ch; vowels such as a and e; and vowel combinations such as ou and oi.

When attempting to pronounce an unrecognized word or syllable, the pupil usually first identifies the graphemes or grapheme groups corresponding to single phonemes and then pronounces each phoneme individually before blending all the phonemes to pronounce the entire word. For example, Marie encounters the word thin, which she has never seen in print and does not recognize on sight. First, she identifies the graphemes, th/i/n. Then, she pronounces the phonemes, th as in thick, i as in it, and n as in no. Finally, she blends the phonemes to pronounce the complete word thin.

Readers may test their skill in the use of sound–symbol correspondence by examining the nonsense word ko. If the readers are able to identify the graphemes k and o and to pronounce and correctly blend the phonemes k as in kite and o as in go, then they possess skill in using sound–symbol correspondence to decode unrecognized words.

Instruction in the identification of graphemes and the pronunciation of phonemes involves teaching the reader to recognize all the following:

1. *the common single consonant sounds*, such as b (bat), d (dog), f (fat), h (hat), j (jump), k (king), l (lamp), m (man), n (nip), p (pat), q (u) (queen), r (rest), s (sick), t (test), v (very), w (was), x (box), y (you), and z (zoo).
2. *the common double consonant sounds* of c and g, referred to as hard c and g (cat, girl) and soft c and g (city, gem).
3. *the consonant blends*, which are formed when two or more consonants occur together producing two or more sounds, such as bl (blend), sp (spell), cr (crux), cl (clue), and spr (spring).
4. *the consonant digraphs*, which are formed when two consonants occur together producing only one sound that is totally different from either of the consonants, such as ph (digraph), the (the), ch (chair), wh (when), and sh (cash).
5. *the common silent consonants*, which have no sound in the spoken word, such as b (limb), g (benign), and k (knit).
6. *the vowel diphthongs*, which occur when two vowels are adjacent and two sounds are heard, including oi (oil), ou (blouse), ow (how), and oy (boy).
7. *the vowel digraphs*, which occur when two vowels are adjacent but only one sound is heard, as in ai (wait), ay (bay), ea (eat), ee (meet), and oa (oat).
8. *the schwa sound*, which occurs in unaccented syllables and has a brief "uh" sound, as in a (account), e (fatten), i (pencil), o (reckon), and u (discuss).

9. *the controlled vowels*, whose sounds are influenced by consonants, such as r (as in far, fir, for, and fur), w (as in claw and yew), and ll (as in all).
10. *the common short vowel sounds and the situations under which they usually occur*, for example, in accented syllables (lemon, strategy) and one-syllable words ending in a consonant (hat, set, mix, stop, nut).
11. *the common long vowel sounds and the situations under which they usually occur*, for example in accented syllables and one-syllable words ending in the vowel itself (no, me, pi), ending in silent e (mate, bite), or containing a vowel digraph (neat, wait).

Syllabication

The reader attempting to pronounce a multisyllabic word by using the phonic clue syllabication as a decoding tool usually (1) identifies the syllables, (2) decides which syllable is accented, (3) pronounces each syllable, and (4) blends the syllables to form the word (adapted from Bond and Tinker, 1973, pp. 316-318). For example, Palmer encounters the word obfuscate, which he has never seen in print and, thus, does not recognize. Using his syllabication skills, he (1) identifies the syllables (ob/fus/cate), (2) decides which syllable is accented (fus), (3) pronounces the syllables (ob as in obtuse, fus as in fuss, and cate as in indicate), and (4) blends the syllables to pronounce the word. Since he recognizes the word when he hears himself pronounce it, his skill in syllabication allows him to pronounce the word.

Readers may test their own syllabication skills by attempting to pronounce a word not in their sight vocabularies. For example, if they do not immediately recognize the printed word constrainedly, they might (1) identify its syllables (con/strain/ed/ly), (2) identify its accented syllable (strain), (3) pronounce each syllable (con as in confuse, strain as in strainer, ed as in bunted, and ly as in jelly), and (4) blend the syllables to pronounce the word, "constrainedly." If the readers are able to pronounce the word correctly, then they possess sufficient syllabication skills.

Before pupils can benefit from instructional activities designed to develop syllabication skills, they must have learned the:

1. *Definition of a Syllable.* A syllable is the part of a word that is pronounced with a single, uninterrupted sounding of the voice. For each vowel sound there is one and only one syllable. For example, even though the word measure has four vowels, it has only two vowel sounds and, hence, consists of two syllables (meas/ure).
2. *Generalizations for Dividing Words into Syllables.* (1) When two consonants (similar or dissimilar) occur between two vowels, the word is divided into syllables between the two consonants (sum/mer, for/ty); (2) when a single consonant occurs between two vowels, the word is usually divided into syllables between the first vowel and the consonant (ho/tel); (3) consonant blends or digraphs

occurring between two vowels are treated as a single consonant (con/stant, go/pher); (4) prefixes and suffixes often form separate syllables (un/like, jump/ing).

3. *Generalizations for Accenting Syllables.* (1) When the first syllable of a word is not a prefix, it is usually accented (syl'/la/ble), (2) when the first syllable of a word is a prefix, the second syllable is usually accented (pre/des'/tine).
4. *Generalizations for Pronouncing Syllables.* Unless a syllable is recognized immediately, the printed letter must be related to the spoken sound through the use of sound–symbol correspondence, described previously.

Limitations of Phonic Clues

Sound–symbol correspondence and syllabication may serve as valuable decoding tools. However, unless the reader possesses the skills necessary to carry out the analytic procedure, the usefulness of phonic clues is limited. Furthermore, phonic clues are limited by the following:

1. Grapheme by grapheme analysis is a slow process. Other decoding tools, such as context clues and picture clues, usually provide much quicker means for gaining the meaning of a word. Therefore, students should be taught to use phonic clues only when other decoding skills have not proven useful.
2. The word being analyzed must follow the phonic generalization that should apply. For example, the words wane, complete, chide, remote, and mute follow the generalization that a vowel is long in accented syllables and one-syllable words ending in silent e. However, this silent e rule does not apply to words such as mirage, here, regime, come, and sure.
3. The student must recognize the unfamiliar printed word when it is spoken. For example, using the syllabication procedure, Ben correctly pronounced the unfamiliar word obfuscate. However, unlike Palmer in the previous example, Ben did not recognize the word when he heard himself say it. Therefore, Ben was unable to tell whether or not his pronunciation was accurate or to attach meaning to the word.

Morphemic Clues

Using morphemic clues as aids in decoding an unrecognized word involves analyzing the word's various meaning-bearing parts, or morphemes, such as root words, prefixes, and suffixes, to determine word meaning. For example, the word transgress may be analyzed by identifying the prefix trans as meaning across and the root word gress as meaning go to determine the meaning of the word as to go across.

Readers may test their skill in using morphemic clues by examining a word with which they are not familiar. For example, if readers are unfamiliar with the word monograph, they might attempt to identify it by breaking the word into its morphemes and then interpreting the meanings of each (the prefix mono, meaning one and the root graph, meaning write) to deduce the meaning of the entire word (a written record of a single topic).

As exemplified by the previous example, to be able to use morphemic clues effectively as decoding tools, the reader must have a wide knowledge of the meanings of

1. *root words*, such as trees, jumping, bicycle, automobile, and telegraph;
2. *prefixes*, such as adhere, depose, and misjudge;
3. *suffixes*, such as respectable, performance, careful, and Billy.
4. *inflectional endings*, indications of plurality including (snakes, brushes), possession (Jane's), tense (jumped, fallen), and comparison (taller, tallest), and
5. *contractions*, such as aren't, I've, she'll, and we'd. (Ives, Bursuk, and Ives, 1979)

Dictionary Usage

Dictionary usage as a decoding technique involves finding the unrecognized word in a dictionary, pronouncing the word according to its diacritical markings, and ascertaining the word's appropriate meaning. For example, Lee encountered the word appendices, which he did not recognize on sight and was unable to decode using configuration, picture, context, phonic, or morphemic clues. He, therefore, used his dictionary to decode appendices by locating the word in the dictionary, using its diacritical markings to determine its pronunciation and choosing its appropriate meaning from those listed.

Although dictionary usage is a valuable tool to be used throughout a person's reading career, its major limitation is that it is an extremely slow process and, as such, is inefficient as a major decoding skill.

Readers may test their own dictionary skills by analyzing the following sentence: "Winnie's spoonbread was memorable." If the readers can locate spoonbread in the dictionary, pronounce it correctly using the diacritical markings, and identify its precise meaning in this sentence, then they possess adequate dictionary skills.

THE WORD IDENTIFICATION SKILLS COMBINED

Although the word identification skills have been discussed separately in this chapter, during the reading process they are used in combination. For example, Karl read the sentence "The clatter reverberated through the canyon" and recognized all the words as sight words except reverberated. Using context clues Karl guessed that reverberated might be synonymous with echoed. However, since Karl did not recognize the meaning of any of its morphemes, he could not use morphemic clues to confirm his guess. Therefore, he used phonic clues instead to divide reverberated into syllables (re/ver/ber/a/ted). Then he used his knowledge of graphemes and phonemes to pronounce the syllable re. Since he could already pronounce the other syllables, Karl did not have to use phonic clues to pronounce them. Next, he blended the syllables to correctly pronounce the entire word. However, he did not recognize the spoken word and, thus, was unable to attach any meaning to it other than that which he had already gained through context clues. Karl felt that it was essential that he know the exact meaning of the word. Therefore, he used his dictionary skills to locate its meaning.

Readers may test their own skill in using a combination of word identification skills by reading the following sentence. While doing so, readers should mentally note the word identification skills they are using.

"At sunset the vespertine racoon raided the trash cans."

While reading this sentence, did the readers recognize all the words as sight words or was there any word on which they needed to use decoding skills? If so, which ones were used?

SUMMARY

The purpose of learning and using the word identification skills is to develop the ability to pronounce and/or give meaning to printed words. These skills may be categorized into two main groups: (1) sight word skills, which are used by the reader to identify words recognized immediately, and (2) decoding skills, which are used by the reader to identify words not recognized immediately by using configuration, picture, context, phonic, and morphemic clues and the dictionary. In combination, all the word identification skills are used throughout a reader's lifetime.

References and Bibliography

Bond, G. L., and Tinker, M. A. *Reading Difficulties: Their Diagnosis and Correction.* 3rd ed. New York: Appleton-Century-Crofts, 1973.

Bormuth, J. "The Cloze Readability Procedure." *Elementary English* 45 (May 1968): 429-436.

Clymer, T. "The Utility of Phonic Generalizations in the Primary Grades." *Reading Teacher* 16 (January 1963): 252-258.

Dillner, M. and Olson, J. *Personalizing Reading Instruction in Middle, Junior, and Senior High Schools.* New York: Macmillan Publishing Co., Inc. 1977.

Dolch, B. W. *Dolch Basic Sight Words.* Champaign, Ill.: Garrard Press, 1936.

Durkin, D. *Strategies for Identifying Words.* Boston: Allyn & Bacon, Inc., 1976.

Fry, E. *Reading Instruction for Classroom and Clinic.* New York: McGraw-Hill Book Company, 1972.

Hall, M. A., and Ramig, C. J. *Linguistic Foundations for Reading.* Columbus, Ohio: Charles E. Merrill Publishing Company, 1978.

Ives, J., Bursuk, L. Z., and Ives, S. *Word Identification Techniques.* Chicago: Rand McNally & Company, 1979.

Karlin, R. "Evaluation for Diagnostic Teaching," in W. H. MacGinitie, ed., *Assessment Problems in Reading.* Newark, Dela.: International Reading Association, 1973, pp. 8-13.

Kucera, H., and Francis, W. N. *Computational Analysis of Present-Day American English.* Providence, R.I.: Brown University Press, 1967.

Mazurkiewicz, A. J. *Teaching About Phonics.* New York: St. Martin's Press, Inc., 1976.

Stetson, E. *The Stetson Reading–Spelling–Vocabulary Program.* Houston: Educational Services, 1981.

Stetson, E. *Reading–Spelling–Vocabulary Program Placement Test* (Forms A and B). Houston: Educational Services, 1979.

Wardhaugh, R. "Linguistics and Phonics," in R. B. Ruddell et al., eds., *Resources in Reading–Language Instruction.* Englewood Cliffs, N.J.: Prentice-Hall, Inc., 1974.

Self-Check 2.3
Word Identification Skills

The following questions are designed to help the participant assess his or her competence on the first seven objectives stated at the beginning of this chapter. Although every effort has been made to make the self-check questions comprehensive, participants should remember that they are held responsible for meeting the objectives as stated at the beginning of this chapter.

1. Objective 1. Define each of the following terms: a. word identification skills, b. sight word skills, c. decoding skills, d. configuration clues, e. picture clues, f. context clues, g. phonic clues, h. grapheme, i. phoneme, j. syllable, k. morpheme, l. morphemic clues, and m. dictionary usage.
2. Objectives 2. What is the relationship among word identification, sight word, and decoding skills?
3. Objective 3. Jeff is reading and comes to the words I love you that he recognizes immediately. What word identification skill is he using?
4. Objective 4. Compose original examples of a child's use of a. sight word skills, b. configuration clues, c. picture clues, d. context clues, e. phonic clues, f. morphemic clues, and g. dictionary skills.
5. Objective 5. Mark the syllable division and accent for the nonsense word umma. Indicate whether each vowel is long (L), short (S), schwa (SCH), or silent (SI).
6. Objective 6. Fill in the following blanks with as many words from the following list as possible. As you place a word in the appropriate category, underline the designated part. Words may be used more than once.

space found planet meat thin go germ coma sigh

a. hard g ____________________

b. soft g ____________________

c. hard c ____________________

d. soft c ____________________

e. consonant blend ____________________

f. consonant digraph ____________________

g. vowel diphthong ____________________

h. vowel digraph ____________________

i. short vowel ____________________

j. long vowel ____________________

k. schwa ____________________

l. silent consonant ____________________

7. Objective 7. State at least one limitation and one advantage of each of the following word identification skills: a. sight word skills, b. configuration clues, c. picture clues, d. context clues, e. phonic analysis, f. morphemic analysis, and g. dictionary usage.

Chapter 2
Experience 1

Objective

During this experience, the participant will analyze an adult's or a child's reading and accurately identify the word identification skills used.

1. Examine the Checklist for Administrator and Copy for Subject (Figure 2.2) in this experience carefully so that you will understand your task. Remember that this activity is designed to familiarize you with the various word identification skills. It is not intended to serve as a definitive evaluation of the subject's use of these skills.
2. Before you begin this experience, examine the dictionary that you will use to be sure that (1) the word Andalusian is included in the dictionary, (2) its pronunciation is shown, and (3) at least two of its meanings are given. If Andalusian does not meet these criteria, locate another word in your dictionary that does. Then underline that word in a written sentence and substitute your sentence for the one in box 7 of the Copy for Subject.
3. The wording in the instructions to the subject is designed for a child of elementary school age. You should, therefore, modify the wording appropriately if you are working with an adult.
4. If the subject becomes frustrated with a task, move to the next box. If the subject continues to be frustrated, stop the activity.

Activity and Assessment Guide

1. Introduce the task to the subject by saying, "I am going to show you some words and I want you to tell me what they are. Don't worry if you don't know them. Some of them are not even real words. You just figure them out as best you can."
2. Hand the Copy for Subject that you have torn out of this book to your subject.
3. Follow the directions for administration on your copy of Checklist for Administrator.

Checklist for Administrator

Directions for box 1 on Copy for Subject: Say to the subject, "Read the word in box 1 aloud." Place a check mark beside the following phrase that best describes the subject's response.

______ responded immediately and accurately

______ did not respond immediately and accurately

Directions for box 2 on Copy for Subject: Say to the subject, "Tell me what word in box 2 means."

Did the subject arrive at a correct response after seeing the picture clue? (circle one) yes no

Directions for box 3 on Copy for Subject: Say to the subject, "Read the sentence in box 3. What word goes in the blank?" Place a check mark beside the following phrase that best describes the subject's response.

______ provided a verb that makes sense in the sentence

______ provided a word that does not make sense

______ did not respond

Directions for box 4 on Copy for Subject: As you point to box 4, say to the subject, "This is not a real word, but read it as best you can." Place a check mark beside the following phrase that best describes the subject's response.

______ subject pronounced naib entirely correctly; that is, n as in noon, ai as in nail, and b as in tub

______ subject did not pronounce naib entire correctly; that is, the subject pronounced (fill in the blanks)

n as in ______

a as in ______

i as in ______

b as in ______

FIGURE 2.2. Copy for Subject

1.
look

2.
abegfah

3.
The boy ________________.

4.
naib

5.
unpeckness

6.
matricide

7.
The <u>Andalusian</u> appeared.

4. Directions for box 5 Copy for Subject: Point to box 5 and say to the subject, "Read the word in box 5."

   a. Place a check mark beside the phrase that best describes the subject's response.

      _______ subject pronounced the word correctly; that is, un as in undo, peck as in peck, ness as in business

      _______ subject pronounced the word incorrectly

   b. If the subject pronounced the word correctly, proceed directly to instructions for box 6. If the subject pronounced the word incorrectly, do the following before proceeding to box 6.

      (1) Ask the subject to draw lines at the end of the first, second, and third syllables. Place a check mark beside the phrase that most closely matches the subject's response.

      _______ un / peck / ness (correct)

      _______ other (show) ______________________________

      (2) Ask the subject which syllable is accented. Place a check mark beside his or her response.

      _______ peck (correct)

      _______ un

      _______ ness

      (3) Ask the subject, "How would you pronounce the first part?" Pause. "The second part?" Pause. "The last part?" Place check marks beside the responses that best match the subject's.

      _______ un as in undo (correct)

      _______ peck as in peck (correct)

      _______ ness as in business (correct)

      _______ Other (specify) ______________________________

      ____

      (4) Say to the subject, "Blend the sounds to make a word." Mark the subject's response.

      _______ unpeckness (correct)

      _______ other (specify) ______________________________

5. Directions for box 6 on Copy for Subject: Point to box 6 and say to the subject, "What is the meaning of the word in box 6?"

   a. Place a check mark beside the phrase that best describes the subject's response.

      _______ subject gave the correct meaning of the word; that is, *act of killing one's mother*

______ subject did not give the correct meaning of the word

b. If the subject gave the correct meaning of the word, proceed directly to instructions for box 7. If the subject could not give the correct meaning of the word, do the following before proceeding to box 7.

(1) Ask the subject to draw a line between the two meaningful units. Place a check mark beside the phrase that most closely matches the subject's response.

______ matri/cide (correct)

______ other (specify) ______________________________

(2) Ask the subject, "What is the meaning of the first part?" Pause. "The second part?" Place a check mark beside the response that best matches the subject's.

______ *matri*, meaning *mother*, and *cide*, meaning *to kill* (correct)

______ other (specify) ______________________________

6. Directions for box 7 on Copy for Subject: Ask the subject to pronounce and give the meaning of the underlined word in the sentence in box 7.

a. Mark the subject's response.

______ word was correctly pronounced and defined

______ word was not correctly pronounced and defined

b. If the subject was *unable* to pronounce and define the word, ask the subject to look up the word in your dictionary, to pronounce it, and to find the correct meaning to fit the sentence. Mark the results.

______ subject *was* able to locate word in dictionary

______ subject *was not* able to locate word in dictionary

______ subject *was* able to use diacritical markings to arrive at correct pronunciation

______ subject *was not* able to use diacritical markings to arrive at correct pronunciation

______ *subject was* able to locate appropriate meaning

______ subject *was not* able to locate appropriate meaning

Participant's Follow-up *

* 1. (Box 1) Subject used sight word skills? (circle one) yes no Why or why not? ____

____

* 2. (Box 2) Subject used picture clue? (circle one) yes no Why or why not?__________

____

* 3. (Box 3) Subject used context clues to correctly deduce an appropriate word? (circle one) yes no Why or why not? __________

____

* 4. (Box 4) Subject used sound/symbol correspondences to correctly pronounce *naib*? (circle one) yes no If any difficulties were encountered, where did they occur? __________

____

* 5. (Box 5) Subject used phonic clues to correctly pronounce *unpeckness*? (circle one) yes no If any difficulties were encountered, at which step did they occur?__________

____

* 6. (Box 6) Subject used morphemic clues to correctly give meaning of *matricide*? (circle one) yes no If any difficulties were encountered, at which step did they occur?__________

____

* 7. (Box 7) Subject used the dictionary to pronounce and define the underlined word? (circle one) yes no If no, describe any difficulties that the subject encountered. __________

____

8. Write a brief summary of your feelings about the child's reaction to this experience. __________

____

9. State what you believe to be the significant implications of this experience for you as a future classroom teacher.

____

____

*See Chapter 1, Experience 1 for an explanation of the asterisk.

Chapter 2
Experience 2

Objective

During this experience, the participant will assess and teach a minimum of one word identification skill.

Note: Participant should refer to Chapter 15, "Teaching Word Identification, Comprehension, Study, and Readiness Skills," for appropriate assessment and teaching activities. Information on lesson planning is included in Appendix E.

Activity and Assessment Guide:*

* 1. Which specific word identification skill do you intend to teach? (for example, hard and soft sounds of *g*)

____

* 2. Describe the assessment activity that you plan to use to measure the pupil's knowledge of this skill before you teach your lesson.

____

____

____

____

* 3. Describe the instructional techniques that you intend to use during this lesson. ______________________________

____

____

____

* 4. Describe the assessment activity that you plan to use to measure the pupil's knowledge of this skill after you teach your lesson.

5. Write a brief summary of your feelings about the child's reaction toward this strategy and the amount of learning that took place.

6. State what you believe to be the significant implications of this experience for you as a future classroom teacher.

*See Chapter 1, Experience 1 for an explanation of the asterisk.

Chapter 3
Comprehension Skills

Objectives 3.1

On completion of this chapter, the participant should be able to

1. Define the term "reading comprehension."
2. Differentiate between and give examples of models of reading that view the process as "total" and models of reading that view the process as "separable subskills."
3. Define, differentiate among, and give examples of the twelve subskills of comprehension presented in this chapter.
4. Discuss the relationship between cognitive development of the child and the type of comprehension skills that may most effectively be taught.
5. Describe a technique for teaching comprehension skills that uses a set of increasingly simplified questioning strategies.

Experiences 1, 2, and 3 extend Chapter 3 with these objectives:

6. During this experience, the participant will locate, describe, and react to strategies for teaching the comprehension skills.
7. During this experience, the participant will design and use a questioning strategy for teaching one of the comprehension skills.
8. During this experience, the participant will design and teach a lesson on a comprehension skill using a strategy other than a questioning strategy.

Information Given 3.2
Comprehension Skills

Susie read the following sentence to herself silently, "The kite was up in the sky," and envisioned her kitty in a box in the cargo section of a plane. However, when Ms. Yohannan, the third grade teacher, read the sentence aloud for the class, Susie's mental image changed completely. Her incorrect pronunciation of just one word had led to a drastically different interpretation of the sentence. Paul had never heard of a flying object called a kite and did not understand the sentence even when he heard every word correctly read aloud to him. Both Brian and Fred correctly decoded every word and knew the meaning of each. But their interpretations of the total message were not alike. Fred visualized a diamond-shaped object on a string floating lazily in the sky. Brian pictured a box-shaped object that he and his father were wildly chasing down the beach.

For these four children, the following assumptions concerning reading comprehension might be made: (1) Susie's understanding was affected by the incorrect decoding of a single word, that is "kitty" for "kite"; (2) Paul's understanding was impaired because he did not have the concept of "kite" in his background; (3) Fred's interpretation of the meaning was based on his limited experience with kites; and (4) Brian's comprehension extended far beyond the author's intended message. His familiarity with many types of kites, his joyful attitude toward the hobby, and his innate creativity stimulated images not presented by the literal message of the sentence.

READING COMPREHENSION DEFINED

Comprehension of printed material depends upon the characteristics of both the material and the reader. All the children in the example had their reading comprehension affected by factors such as decoding ability, knowledge of the vocabulary presented, familiarity with the concepts, and cognitive development.

Reading comprehension is a term used to identify those skills needed to understand and apply information contained within written material. The process is difficult to define precisely because it *is* influenced by a great many factors. There are numerous theories about the process of comprehension that take these various different factors into consideration. For example, a study by Geyer (1972) found that as many as seventy-seven models of reading have been proposed. Most of the currently cited models of reading may be placed in one of two general categories: (1) those in which the components are fused together and have no individual identity within the larger entity labeled as the "reading process," that is, reading is considered to be a "total" process; and (2) those in which the components are parts that function in association with other parts but can easily be detached from them, that is, the reading process is composed of a combination of separable subskills.

Both these categories—reading as a "total process" and reading as a composite of "separable subskills"—will be discussed in more detail in the following paragraphs.

READING VIEWED AS A TOTAL PROCESS

Researchers such as Thorndike (1973) believe that reading is thinking and that efforts to increase comprehension should concentrate on improving thinking skills. He considers separate subskills to be hypothesized units that research has failed to validate.

Beery (1967) suggests that skills exist but cannot be used in isolation. A reader does not read just to get the main idea or details but, rather, uses skills in combination, shifting from skill to skill as he or she gains understanding. The difficulty of the reading matter and its development by the author affect the reader's strategies as he or she develops and rejects hunches concerning interpretation.

Goodman (1973) describes reading as a psycholinguistic process in which thought and language are interrelated but are not the same. The reader may experience cycles of reflective thinking in response to the printed words; these cycles should not be considered part of the reading process itself any more than following directions after having read them can be considered part of the reading process. Reading is information processing. The reader interacts with the graphic input as he or she seeks to reconstruct a message encoded by the writer. The reader concentrates his or her total prior experience and learning on the task, drawing on his or her experiences and the concepts that he or she has attained as well as on the language competence that he or she has achieved. Success in comprehension, according to another study by Goodman (1966), is based on the extent to which the reader's reconstructed message agrees with the writer's intended message.

Smith (1973), also a psycholinguist, states that reading is both a visual and a nonvisual activity in which two types of information are involved. The visual type comes from in front of the eyeball, that is, the printed page; the nonvisual type comes from behind the eyeball, that is, the brain. Nonvisual information is what the reader already knows about reading, language, and the world in general. Furthermore, there is a trade-off between the visual and the nonvisual. The more the brain knows, the less visual information is required to identify a letter, word, or meaning, and vice versa. Unfortunately, there is a severe limitation to the amount of visual information that can be processed. Hence the reader with a limited experiential background who relies primarily on visual information for meaning will quickly overload his or her system and not be able to adequately interpret the printed page.

Separable Subskills Defined

A second category of theories about reading comprehension suggests that separate subskills or tasks may be identified that, when used singly or in combination, lead to an understanding of written materials. Considerable research over the past thirty years does seem to verify the existence of separable, distinguishable skills. One significant work in reading comprehension was done by Davis (1968). He constructed test items to measure eight comprehension skills and then employed a uniqueness-analysis technique to analyze his data as he claimed that "highly refined statistical techniques must be employed if tiny amounts of variance unique to each skill" are to be detected (Davis, 1968, p. 509). The eight major components of reading comprehension that he felt were separable were (1) recalling word meaning, (2) drawing inferences about the meaning of a word from context, (3) finding answers to questions answered explicitly or in paraphrases, (4) weaving ideas in context, (5) drawing inferences from the context, (6) recognizing a writer's purpose, attitude, tone, and mood, (7) identifying a writer's techniques, and (8) following the structure of a passage.

Other researchers have identified similar skills. Although not all researchers have identified exactly the same skills, it does appear that specific comprehension skills are identifiable (Spearritt, 1972; Peters and Peters, 1976).

Separable Subskills Organized for Teaching Purposes

Regardless of the specific skills identified, when the comprehension skills are grouped to facilitate their being taught to children, they are usually placed in one of three major classification systems: unit length, taxonomical ordering, or an aggregate of skills.

Unit length stresses teaching techniques that include first the understanding of words, then sentences, and then paragraphs and longer units. The meaning of each unit depends, in part, on the meanings of the words that surround it. For example, first a child must understand that the word "run" has various meanings before he or she can comprehend its intended interpretation in a sentence. Furthermore, the child must understand the meaning of the word "run" in the sentence to make the entire paragraph comprehensible; that is, the word "run" will have a different meaning if the other words in the sentence are concerned with a baseball game than if the rest of the sentence is describing a horse race. Likewise, the sentence "Jones made a run" has a different meaning if the entire paragraph is concerned with a "tie" baseball game than if the total paragraph is describing a yearly list of baseball statistics. Some of the better-known reading authorities who discuss reading comprehension in terms of unit length are Carver (1973) and Bond and Tinker (1973).

Taxonomical ordering involves dividing skills into hierarchial groups. Although there may be no differentiation in the difficulty of the skills within each group, every group in the hierarchy is considered to be more difficult than the one preceding it. Each group of skills is designed to be taught before succeeding ones can be understood. For example, the skill "recognizing details" in the grouping "literal comprehension" would have to be taught before the skill "classifying details" in the group "reorganization." Some reading authorities who discuss reading comprehension in terms of taxonomical grouping are Barrett (1972) and Smith (1969).

The aggregate of skills classification system presents skills in a single fashion, but a hierarchy through which one *must* progress to learn subsequent skills is not delineated. For example, although "understanding main ideas" is placed earlier on the list than is "grasping sequence of time, place, ideas, or steps," it is not stated that "main idea" *must* be learned before "sequence" may be understood. Both Thomas and Robinson (1972) and Klausmeier (1976) classify comprehension skills into categories to simplify conflicting terminology related to comprehension. One category is not presumed to be better or more advanced than any other.

VIEW OF COMPREHENSION PRESENTED IN THIS TEXT

Both the "total" and "subskills" approach to understanding reading comprehension contain theoretically sound views, and this text attempts to combine aspects of each. Comprehension is viewed as a "total" process that becomes easier to teach if it can be divided into some sort of manageable units or subskills. To keep the comprehension process as "total" as possible, the following list of subskills has been kept small. The varying viewpoints presented in the preceding section of this text support the notion that there is no one definition of reading comprehension or no one agreed-upon list of comprehension subskills. Hence the twelve subskills given are not presented as a dogmatic view of the comprehension subskills. Rather, they represent a grouping of units that should be easily understood by the classroom teacher and that, when used in total, would seem to encompass most of the aspects of the thinking process needed to produce a flexible, critical reader.

TWELVE SUBSKILLS OF COMPREHENSION

1. Gaining Word Meaning
2. Identifying Details
3. Identifying Main Ideas
4. Identifying Sequence
5. Identifying Cause–Effect Relationships
6. Making Inferences
7. Making Generalizations and Conclusions
8. Identifying Tone and Mood
9. Identifying Theme
10. Identifying Characterization

11. Identifying Fact, Fiction, and Opinion
12. Identifying Propaganda

Though separate subskills are delineated, it is recognized that there is no clear division among the subskills. They are listed in a loosely arranged hierarchy under the assumption that in most cases a reader will have to understand the skills first presented on the list before he or she can understand the skills presented near the end of the list. For example, a reader will probably have to be able to "identify pertinent details" (skill 2) related to a "cause–effect" incident before he or she can recognize the "cause–effect" relationship (skill 5). Additionally, it is recognized that each reading skill makes sense to the reader only in terms of his or her individual background, word perceptions, and sum total of experiences that he or she brings with him or her to the printed page. Hence the teaching of each skill should include any background experiences that are needed by each child to understand the message intended by the author.

STRATEGIES FOR TEACHING THE COMPREHENSION SKILLS

Research indicates that effective questioning strategies may be used as a tool to enhance children's thinking (Piaget, 1967; Taba and Elzey, 1964). Since there is an obvious relationship between reading comprehension and thinking, it would be reasonable to incorporate questioning strategies into instruction in reading comprehension. Good questions can identify students in need of specific skill instruction, provide a means for teaching particular skills, and reinforce any skills already known. It is important to recognize the distinction between these three purposes—(1) assessment, (2) reinforcement, and (3) instruction—when designing questions for reading comprehension.

Questions That Assess and Reinforce

A student who knows how to use a skill such as main idea may be identified by his or her correct response to the *assessment* question, "What is this story about?" For the student who already possesses the assessed reading skill, *reinforcement* questions such as "How did you know that was the main idea?" can strengthen the child's competence with the skill. Similar *reinforcement* questions can also raise the child's level of sophistication in interpreting what is read by providing him or her with practice on the application of that skill.

Questions That Assess and Instruct

The student who responds incorrectly to the assessment questions cannot learn the skill unless the teacher is able to recognize what background information a student needs to correctly respond to the assessment question. Then the teacher needs to construct questions specifically designed to teach that skill. One means of simplifying a question and guiding a student's thinking toward the correct response is to ask the student to find support for statements that express possible alternatives for the correct answers. A teacher might ask, "What is the moral of the story about the race between the turtle and the rabbit?" The child responds, "I don't know." At that point, the teacher rephrases the question and asks, "Which of the following statements represent the moral of the story: (1) Turtles should not race rabbits; (2) Some good can result from the worst situation; or (3) Persistence may be worth more than talent."

The process of guiding a student's thinking toward the correct response by asking the child to react to possible answers to the question originally posed is based on the premise that an instructional sequence does exist that can move children along some sort of continuum toward independence. When designing instruction, the teacher should begin the questioning process with the most difficult question, that is, the assessment question, and then move directly toward the simplest. The purpose of the assessment question is to determine whether the student needs instruction or simply reinforcement on the skill. It is more intellectually stimulating for the student and time saving for the teacher to instruct pupils on those skills in which they need instruction rather than on all skills whether they know them or not. An example of a five-step continuum for teaching comprehension skills through questioning appears in Table 3.1. Each of the five steps of the procedure contains a short description, an illustration, and the rationale behind the questioning procedure for that step.

PRESENTATION AND DISCUSSION OF THE TWELVE COMPREHENSION SUBSKILLS

To better understand the comprehension subskills and the strategies presented for teaching each, the following aspects should be noted: (1) questioning sequence, (2) skill load and cognitive development, (3) learning principles, and (4) format for presentation of each subskill.

Sequence

It should be pointed out again that the questions in this strategy are in order of most difficult toward most simple. The process models the sequence of teaching the skill. As soon as students are able to respond correctly to a question, they may be assumed to know that skill and need not be asked to respond to the remainder of the questions in the sequence. Step 5 in Table 3.1 suggests that, if children have not yet responded correctly by that point in the sequence, the teacher should attempt to formulate other contexts that might be more familiar to the child rather than to just "tell" the answers.

Cognitive Development and Skill Load

Although twelve skills are delineated, younger children should not be expected to learn all twelve. As children mature, their ability to reason also

TABLE 3.1 Questioning Strategy That May Be Used to Teach Comprehension

Description	*Illustration*	*Rationale*
1. Step 1 Ask assessment question.	1. What is the meaning of the word "hail?"	1. Straightforward assessment of skill.
2. Step 2 Provide reference to passage read.	2. Look at this sentence and see if you can tell me the meaning of the word "hail."	2. Meaning is best interpreted in terms of total context.
3. Step 3 a. Construct list of alternative responses. b. If incorrect response is received, go to step 4. c. If correct response is received, compliment the child and ask the child to explain how he or she arrived at the correct answer. d. If the child is unable to do this, show him or her at least one means for doing so.	3. In this sentence, does the word "hail" mean (a) lump of ice, (b) to call loudly to, or (c) to be healthy? Good, "hail" does mean lump of ice. How did you figure that out? You probably figured that out because of the surrounding words. See, here is the word "frozen" and here is the word "hit."	3. It is easier to recognize the correct response than it is to reproduce it. The ability to verbalize the strategy used provides the student with a model that he or she can use independently in future situations.
4. Step 4 a. Place the word or skill in a context more familiar to the child and make the correct response more obvious. b. If incorrect response is received, go to step 5. c. If correct response is received, compliment the child and ask the child to explain how he or she arrived at the correct answer. d. If the child is unable to do this, show him at least one means for doing this. e. Finally, ask the child to answer the question originally posed in step 1.	4. If I said "The hail pitted Dad's car last winter," what would the word "hail" mean? Very nice. Hail does mean lump of ice. How did you figure that out? You probably figured that out because of the surrounding words. See here is the word "pits" and here is the word "winter." Now can you tell me if the word "hail" means the same in the story we just read?	4. The ability to associate the skill with words and ideas already known provides meaningful background and helps the child understand and conceptualize the skill.
5. Step 5 a. Tell the child the correct response expected in step 4. Describe the strategy to arrive at the correct response. b. Ask the child to use the word or skill in a sentence or two of his or her own. c. Finally, ask the child to answer the question originally posed in step 1. d. If incorrect response is received, construct a new context for the skill and repeat steps 4 and 5.	5. In the above sentence, the word "hail" would mean small, roundish lump of ice caused by a thunderstorm. We can tell this through context. That is, the other words in the sentence indicate to us that hail is hard (it pits) and it probably is formed when it is cold (last winter). Can you make up a sentence in which you use the word "hail?" Good. Now look back at the story and tell me if the word means the same there. (If the child responds incorrectly, the teacher says something like, "Let me try another sentence with you. If I said, the hail storm . . . , etc.").	5. Because the student had to be told the correct response and was not able to arrive at the correct response on his or her own. The only way that he or she can demonstrate that this strategy has been internalized is to provide the teacher with feedback. Applying the skill in terms of his or her own experience indicates to the teacher that the skill has been, at least partially, understood by that particular child.

matures. This growth has been thoroughly described by Piaget (1967) in his theory of cognitive development. In short, Piaget states that there are five stages through which one passes as he or she develops the ability to think. Although all normal children go through all states, they do not all do so at the same age. For example, most first graders can correctly respond to the question, "What type of animal is Lassie?" (The correct response is "a dog." A child in an earlier stage of cognitive development might reply "a horsie" because to him or her all animals with four legs are horses.) Likewise, most sixth graders would be able to correctly respond to the question, "What is the moral found in the story about King Midas?" (Children of this age group are normally at the stage where they can see hidden assumptions and use verbal generalizations or rules.) Since there is such a wide variation in the age level at which children reach the various stages of cognitive development, there is no hard and fast rule for when teachers should present each skill to each child. However, a general listing of the order in which each skill should be presented will be discussed in Chapter 8 under the heading "Scope and Sequence of Skills." Although first graders would seldom be expected to learn about the "theme" of the story, the skill is included because it is one of the skills that the child should be able to use before he or she completes elementary school. Many children have been overly acquainted with the skills presented early on the list and almost never presented with the critical reading skills located near the end of the list. The goal of the elementary teacher should be to guide his or her pupils toward those higher-level skills. All earlier skills should be presented and reinforced with that in mind. Since the earlier skills are prerequisite to the later ones, any child who can correctly use the latter five types of skills does not need instruction on the earlier skills.

Learning Principles

The focus on questioning strategy is to help children to associate the reading skill with words and ideas that they already possess. This process incorporates the psycholinguistic notions discussed earlier in this chapter; that is, reading is information processing in which the reader draws upon the experiences and concepts that he or she has attained as well as upon the language competence that he or she has achieved (Goodman, 1973). A simplistic example of the effect of background experiences can be illustrated by asking a very immature child to tell the meaning of the word "oldest." A six- or seven-year-old might say, "Oldest is like I'm oldest and Eric is youngest." A more mature child would be more abstract and might say something resembling, "Oldest relates to age. The oldest member of a family is the person who has lived the longest." Immature children must translate things into immediate and concrete terms to understand them. The best way for the teacher to provide this translation, particularly for young children, is to relate new skills to the child's known background. Hence, before reading a story about a "raccoon," a teacher might bring in pictures of a raccoon, a raccoon cap, or a pet raccoon. An older child might gather information through merely listening to a description of a raccoon; a younger child would do better by being placed in a situation in which he or she could touch and see a "real" raccoon.

Format for Skill Presentation

In the following section, each of the twelve comprehension skills are described. Reading skills are usually directly taught during reading class, but they must be used by the child in any subject area in which he or she is required to do some reading. Research indicates that children do not apply needed reading skills simply because they were presented in reading class. The content area teacher must directly point out the reading skills needed for that subject area lesson if the teacher wants to make certain that the child applies the needed skill (Serra, 1953; Johnson, 1952). Hence examples from various "content area" classes as well as from "reading class" are given in the following section of this text.

Throughout the presentation of the twelve skills, theoretical viewpoints supporting the illustrated techniques are discussed. Theory is presented in this format under the assumption that the technique utilized at that particular point in the illustration represents an important educational premise that should be emphasized. For example, when "gaining word meaning" is described, the rationale behind the specific strategy illustrated in the example is discussed. Hence the reader of this textbook is encouraged to look for these theoretical viewpoints while reading through the following section.

After each skill is described, a question that can be used to assess a child's competence with that skill is given. To simplify the examples, all questions have been based on pages 2 and 3 of the book *Josita's Dancing Cleaners* (Walborn, 1975) shown in Figure 3.1. However, teachers would not ordinarily assess all twelve comprehension skills over the same lesson. Rather, a teacher would tend to assess two or three skills at a time to assure the teacher of a current diagnosis. If assessments were done on all twelve skills en masse, the results would likely be outdated by the time the children were actually presented a lesson on those skills. For example, the teacher might determine that the child did not know six of the twelve skills. By the time the teacher was able to design a lesson on the sixth skill, the child has learned the skill already. Additionally, the skill being assessed often depends on the type of material being presented. A story about "Honest Abe" might lead to lesson on character development; an article about the current energy crisis might be used to teach a lesson on propaganda.

Josita waved good-by to her friends after school and walked three blocks to Mango Street. On the corner stood a two-story building with a large palm tree in front. Josita's mother and father worked in the cleaning shop on the first floor of the building. A large sign hung outside.

Page 2

Josita stopped in front of the shop's big glass window and looked in. Her mother was behind the counter. Her father was in the back, working the big clothes presser. PUFF went the presser!

Josita knocked on the window and waved. Then she pulled open the door and went inside. A little bell over the door rang, and her father looked up from his work.

"Josita, you are late today. Please try to be quick and get here on time. This is not called Pronto Cleaners for nothing!"

Josita said, *"Lo siento,"* which means "I'm sorry."

From Marla Walborn, *Josita's Dancing Cleaners*, Macmillan, Inc. 1975. Reprinted by permission.

Page 3

Figure 3.1 Excerpt from *Josita's Dancing Cleaners.*

CHAPTER 15: TEACHING ACTIVITIES RELATED TO COMPREHENSION

Chapter 15 of this text suggests several types of activities that may be used to teach each of the twelve comprehension skills. The first type of activity presented for each skill is a set of increasingly simplified questions of the type illustrated in Table 3.1. For the purpose of illustration, all the questions have been based upon the excerpt from *Josita's Dancing Cleaners* shown in Figure 3.1. Ordinarily, the teacher does not attempt to teach all twelve skills over the same lesson. Usually, skills are taught one or two at a time, which gives each skill a chance to be learned thoroughly before proceeding toward skills that might be based on an earlier skill; for example, the teacher would make certain that the child knew how to apply "sequence" before asking him or her to learn "cause and effect."

Additionally, related activities that might also be used to teach each reading skill are described. While research does indicate that appropriate questioning can teach comprehension, other teaching devices such as worksheets, audiovisual materials, learning centers, games, and similar activities should also be used to provide effective learning experiences. Whenever possible, the activities presented in this section are designed to be fun. This is done under the assumption that, if an activity is fun for the child, the child will want to complete it and hence will obtain the practice needed to learn the skill. In all cases, the activities described are meant to be as relevant as possible to the child's background. While a dull exercise using material in a context that is of little interest to a child might teach the child the skill of "sequence," the child will learn it more easily and retain it longer if the content is fun and/or focused on topics that he or she wants to read about. Children of various ages and backgrounds find different activities fun and/or relevant. Means for locating activities and interests appropriate to the diverse ages and backgrounds will be discussed in Chapter 11 under the heading "Interest Inventories."

One extremely useful source of teaching materials worthy of special note at this point is the newspaper. This material is highly effective, relatively inexpensive, and readily available. Its content is diverse enough to appeal to readers of any grade level. Additionally, since adults read the newspaper, children find it motivating, particularly if they are "pretending to be grown up" or are older, remedial readers who become embarrassed when asked to read materials that appear too "babyish."

Activities for using the newspaper as a teaching tool, as well as many other similar type devices, will be presented throughout Chapter 15.

1. GAINING WORD MEANING

If children do not know the correct definition of the words that they are reading, they will be unable to accurately interpret the intended message. Few words may be defined in isolation, since meaning is almost always dependent upon the way in which the word is used in context. Hence word study should help students to recognize that most words have more than one meaning and that the meaning can only be determined by its use in a sentence or paragraph.

Denotative meaning, connotative meaning, figurative language, and certain *unique features* of American English are factors that should be considered when teaching word meaning.

DENOTATIVE MEANING

Denotative meaning refers to the literal meaning of a word. For example, if one were to look up the word *see* in the dictionary, the denotative meaning given would be "to get knowledge or an impression of through the eyes and the sense of sight" (*Webster's*, 1957, p. 1319). However, many words, including the word *see*, have more than one literal or denotative meaning. A second denotative meaning for the word *see* is given as "to escort, accompany, attend to" (*Webster's*, 1957, p. 1319). Denotative meaning can become varied through word usage or because the same group of letters originally represented different ideas that were incorporated into the English language. For example, the word *will* is derived from the Anglo-Saxon word *willa* and has come to have many meanings including wish, legal document, and self-control. On the other hand, the word *sewer*, meaning "one who stitches," is derived from the Anglo-Saxon word *siwian*, whereas *sewer*, meaning a "conduit for water," is derived from the Old French word *sewiere.*

If a word has multiple meanings, one spelling but two sounds, such as tear-tear, it is usually called a *homograph* (Greek: homo = same; graph = write). However, if a word has multiple meanings, one spelling and only one sound, such as saw-saw, it is usually called a *homonym* (Greek: homo = same; nym = name). Examples of *homographs* include *present, lead, read, bow, wind, live*, and *close.* Examples of *homonyms* include *iron, buggy, duck, seal, punch*, and *pound.* (Weiss and Hunt, 1973).

Words that sound alike but are spelled differently are called *homophones* (Gk: homo = same; phone = sound) and should be presented to the child when he or she is being taught the concept of multiple meanings of words. Although words such as "pair" and "pear" are entirely different words, unless they are *heard in context*, the intended word form may not be identified correctly. Beginning readers who accurately sound out the word may still not recognize which word they have decoded until they look at its use in the sentence. For example, the sound of the sentence, "Hand me a pair" conveys two possible meanings. However, the sound of the sentence conveys only one reasonable meaning if the sentence becomes "Hand me a pair of gloves." Examples of words that often sound alike to children at the primary level include wood–would; see–sea; our–hour; which–witch; here–hear; no–know; right–write; and ate–eight (Weiss and Hunt, 1973).

CONNOTATIVE MEANING

Words that have emotional overtones are said to be *connotative*. Aside from their literal meanings, these words carry a second interpretation. For example, *skinny* tends to connote a negative meaning, whereas *slender* tends to connote a positive meaning. Many connotative meanings can only be understood in terms of the total context and are not usually defined as such in the dictionary. For example, the word *fat* in the sentence "That was a *fat* hamburger" has a different connotation than it does in the sentence "Susy was a *fat* housewife." The multiple meanings due to the emotional overtones can confuse the child who doesn't fully understand the range of connotative meanings carried by a particular word. For example, a child might overhear, "That pro football team plays dirty!" Depending on the tone of the speaker and the weather, the meaning could be "plays in the mud," "plays according to unfair schemes," or "takes advantage of all opportunities and should be applauded."

FIGURATIVE LANGUAGE

Figurative language is used to convey a more exact impression through the use of tropes such as *idioms, metaphors, similes, personifications,* and *hyperboles. Idioms* are expressions whose total meanings cannot be derived literally from each word. For example, "toss the salad" does not make sense literally, but only as a figure of speech. *Metaphors* are statements that compare two objects that are different. For example, "Bobby was a mountain of a boy." *Similes* are statements that use like or as to make the comparisons. For example, "Bobby was as brown as a bear." *Personifications* are statements that attribute human characteristics to things that are not human. For example, "The dog politely asked to go out." An *hyperbole* is an extravagant exaggeration of a statement for effect. For example, "At the picnic a million ants ate my sandwich." Since young children tend to take everything quite literally, these tropes need to be discussed by the teacher whenever they occur. Often, figurative language that seems almost blatantly obvious to the teacher will be utterly confusing to the child. For example, a child who is told that he is ". . .as cute as a bug's ear" is likely to try and locate the ears on a mosquito for comparison's sake.

CERTAIN UNIQUE FEATURES OF THE AMERICAN LANGUAGE

As the child gets a little older, often new words become more meaningful and are more easily learned if the child is taught the origin of the words. One of the distinctive traits of American English is its large capacity for taking in new words and phrases from outside sources as well as simply manufacturing them out of its own materials (Mencken, 1937). These two aspects—*borrowing* and *coining*—will be discussed briefly in the following paragraphs.

Borrowing

Latin and Greek were the languages of learning for many centuries. Thus much terminology used today was developed from these languages. As a result, many of the technical terms found in the various content areas are derived from Latin and Greek. For example, in social studies the word *democracy* is derived from two Greek words that mean "rule" and "people," while the word *transoceanic* comes from two Latin words that mean "across" and "outer sea." In science the word *dinasaur* is made by combining two Greek words that mean "terrible" and "lizard," while the word *sonic* comes from the Latin word for "sound." In math the word *perimeter* is derived from two Greek words for "around" and "measure," while the word *circumference* is composed of Latin words meaning "around" and "carry." In English the word *simile* comes from the Latin word "similis" meaning "like," and *pseudonym* comes from the Greek word meaning "false."

Sometimes words are borrowed almost directly from other languages rather than derived from common roots. For example, in social studies or English the words *barbecue, burro, lariet,* and *bonanza* come directly from the Spanish. In science the words *alcohol* and *talcum* come from the Arabic. Other words in common use in all content areas include *avenue, ballet, garage* (French); *albino, marmalade, molasses* (Portuguese); *presto* (Italian); *tea* (Chinese); *camel, cinnamon, sapphire* (Hebrew); and *tycoon* (Japanese).

Words have commonly been added to the American language through the names of people or places. For example, the word *maverick* derived from the rancher, Samuel A. Maverick, a man who did not bother to brand his calves. Hence unbranded calves in his area came to be known as mavericks. Later the meaning extended to apply to anyone who was of an independent turn of mind. Other words that have entered the American language in a similar manner include *mesmerize, Braille, hygiene, atlas,* and *sadism.*

Coining

Another characteristic of the American language is to invent, or "coin," new terms. One kind of coining that fabricates new words by joining parts or syllables of others is termed *blending.* For example, *splatter* is made from *splash* and *spatter.* In science the blends *altimeter* (altitude, barometer) and *minicam* (miniature, camera) are used. In social studies such blends as *fem lib* (feminine, liberation) and *Gerrymander* (Elbridge Gerry, salamander) are common.

Making words by cutting large ones into smaller ones is called *clipping* and is another commonly used Americanism for creating new words. Some common examples of *clipping* include *ad, grad, flu, champ, gas, quotes,* and *tarp.*

Coining also includes the development of *acryonyms,* words formed usually by joining the beginning letters of other words. Words such as *O.K., N.G.,* and *P.D.Q.* have been traced back to the colonial days of the American Republic (Mencken, 1937). Contemporary acronyms are particularly used in social studies where *NATO, UNESCO, UN,* and *HEW* often appear. In science such acronyms as *DNA, RNA,* and *LSD* are commonplace.

Sometimes new words have been created by using old ones in new ways. For example, the *fox* is usually considered as a clever animal. The term *fox* is now often extended to humans who have done a particularly clever act, as in "You are a real fox!" Similarly adapted words are *dog* and *turkey*.

ASSESSMENT QUESTION

One technique for determining if the child knows the word meaning is to ask a question such as "What does the word *pronto* mean?"

2. IDENTIFYING DETAILS

This skill requires the location and recall of specifically stated facts. Typical details that children are often asked to locate and remember are names of characters and descriptions of the setting. Identifying details requires basically concrete-level concepts and is prerequisite to constructing higher-level abstract concepts. As children become older, assignments that focus primarily upon the correct identification of many details may be viewed by children as meaningless memory exercises. Children often do not understand the relationship between the details and the total content unless this is directly told to them. Teachers should point out to students why they need to locate the details. Knowing the designated purpose for identifying the details cannot only facilitate the child's ability to locate the relevant facts but should also make the task more meaningful to him or her. For example, if children are reading to compare the good witch with the wicked witch in the folk tale, "Sleeping Beauty," they should be shown that they need to locate facts that reflect characteristics of each witch. After understanding the reason for knowing the facts, the comprehension skill of "identifying characterization," requiring higher-level thinking, becomes the reader's focus. Facts located are not thought of as isolated, meaningless bits of information but, rather, are put into their proper perspective and become important in terms of higher-level tasks.

The ability to identify appropriate details is basic to all other skills in reading. It is impossible to formulate a main idea if the supporting facts cannot be found. For example, locating a cause–effect relationship requires finding the detail that shows cause and the one that shows effect. To identify fact and opinion requires locating items in the material that reflect fact or opinion.

Various techniques can be used to help students learn to select and recall those details that are appropriate to their purpose for reading. Primary among these is telling students *why* they are being asked to look for a particular item. For example, the teacher may ask students to read a paragraph, such as the one presented here, being careful to look for details that will help them describe some of the reasons why the dinosaur became extinct.

Scientists are not sure why dinosaurs became extinct, but they have several different theories. Some scientists believe that, during the time of the dinosaurs, the climate changed, becoming too cold and dry for the dinosaurs to live. Others believe that new kinds of plants developed which could not be eaten by the plant-eating animals. As the plant-eating dinosaurs died, the flesh-eating dinosaurs could no longer find food, and they died too. There is also a possibility that dinosaur eggs laid on the ground were eaten in large numbers by other types of animals. (Piltz and Van Bever, 1970, p. 322)

Students might pick up key details, such as "too cold and dry" or "could no longer find food," that would help them to make generalizations about why dinosaurs became extinct. This technique is very helpful to students who feel that they have to know *all* the facts and have not yet learned to distinguish which ones are relevant to which purposes. Furthermore, *global* learning of this nature promotes better retention of facts. In other words, having a purpose for obtaining the details provides the reader with a format for putting all the details into an integrated whole. If the teacher wants his or her pupils to learn and remember details concerning the extinction of the dinosaur, the teacher should tell the children to look for these necessary facts while reading.

ASSESSMENT QUESTION

One technique for determining whether a child knows how to identify important details is to ask him a question such as, "What was the street that Josita was walking toward?"

3. IDENTIFYING MAIN IDEAS

Identifying main ideas involves conceptualizing the central thought of a sentence, paragraph, or longer unit. The main idea is distinct from the facts presented. It is often similar to the label of a category, expressing a relationship or common characteristic. Sometimes it is stated directly in a topic sentence, an introduction, or a conclusion. Sometimes the main idea must be inferred. It is a general, rather than a specific, idea (Gerhard, 1975). The following excerpts from a third grade science textbook illustrate two different types of main ideas:

> Some dinosaurs lived on land. Others were fishlike and swam in the sea. There were even flying dinosaurs. Some dinosaurs were only as large as chickens. Others were nearly seventy feet long and weighed many tons. (Main idea is inferred—there are many types of dinosaurs.) (Mallinson et al., 1975, p. 54)
>
> Some green plants get water from the soil. Water enters the plant through its roots. The water then moves up through the stem of the plant. Then it moves into the leaves. Plants use more water than you might think. A tree may use as much as 500 gallons of water in one summer day. (Main idea is stated directly in the first sentence.) (Mallison et al., 1975, p. 64)

To identify the main idea of a passage, a reader must be able to locate relevant details and then synthesize and interpret these details in terms of the total message. Locating relevant details is a prerequisite skill. Additionally, other related skills, such as identifying sequence or cause–effect relationships, are often needed to formulate the main idea (Otto, Peters, and Peters, 1977).

ASSESSMENT QUESTION

One technique for determining whether or not a child knows how to identify main ideas is to ask a question such as "What is the main idea of *Josita's Dancing Cleaners*?"

4. IDENTIFYING SEQUENCE

Identifying sequence insolves aspects of both time and space. Time, or chronological order, requires that the child locate and recall the order of incidents or actions as they occur within a particular selection. For example, a child might read about how a bean plant grows and how it might look at various stages in its development. Clue words such as *first*, *second*, *additionally*, *furthermore*, and *finally* can help a child to identify chronological order. Spatial sequence requires that a child locate details as they occur from space to space or area to area. For example, a child might be asked to draw a picture of a bean plant. The child would probably begin with the roots, then draw the stem, and end with the top of the plant. Clue words such as *clockwise*, *horizontal*, *parallel*, *reverse*, *upright*, and *easterly* can help a child learn to identify spatial order.

Clark (1971) indicates that very young children use temporal order in speech as the only indicator of sequence. That is, a child who hears the sentence "He went to the store after he ate lunch" would interpret the sequence as first he went to the store then he ate lunch. The child would do this because this is the order in which the words occur in the sentence. Additionally, Pearson (1977) found that the logical relationship between two events seems to affect the young child's understanding of sequence. The sentence "He took a nap and later went to the movies" is more difficult to understand than "He got on his bike and then pedaled down the street." The events in the first sentence are reversible while the events in the second are not. Because of this trait, Pearson and Johnson (1978) suggest that teaching activities dealing with chronological sequence begin with irreversible events. Predictably ordered sets of events should be gradually introduced. At about the age of ten, reversible, arbitrary events may be introduced.

Pearson and Johnson (1978) also indicate that, by the time children reach third or fourth grade, they should be given instruction in paraphrasing so that they will become aware that many sets of syntactic structures can be used to communicate the same relationship between two events: For example, (1) First he went to the store, then he sat down; (2) He sat down after he went to the store; (3) Before he sat down, he had gone to the store.

Questions with "when," "what happened next," "what happened after," and the like can be helpful in teaching this skill.

ASSESSMENT QUESTION

One technique for determining whether or not a child knows how to identify sequence is to ask a question such as "What is the first thing that Josita does in the story? The second? The third?"

5. IDENTIFYING CAUSE-EFFECT RELATIONSHIPS

Identifying cause-effect relationships requires students to recognize reasons for certain occurrences or reactions. This skill is dependent upon the ability to use and understand a sequence of events. Children need to be directly shown the difference between time order (He ate too much dinner and then had a nap) and causal relationships (Because he ate too much dinner, he needed a nap). Close inspection of the sequence of events, that is, what follows or normally precedes a situation, is often essential to determining the cause and/or effect of the action. For example, a child might see the following sentence in his or her science book: "A person should never clean his or her ear with a hairpin because it can puncture the eardrum." To learn the intended lesson, the child must note the relevant details related to cause (hairpin to clean ears) and effect (puncture eardrum). The child must also note the sequence to know which detail is the cause and which is the effect. Questions beginning with "why" and "how" often help a child to focus on this relationship.

The skill of identifying cause-effect relationships is a prerequisite to many other reading skills. For example, most inferences and generalizations require that the student understand a cause-effect relationship before the skill may be applied.

ASSESSMENT QUESTION

One technique for determining whether or not a child can identify cause-effect relationships is to ask questions such as "Why did Josita's father look up from his work?"

6. MAKING INFERENCES

To make an inference, readers must locate and understand the relationship among details related to an unstated message. The inference provides the readers with information that the author has intended for them, even though they must uncover it for themselves. Teachers can facilitate this process by constructing questions that focus the child's attention upon (1) key words in the passage, (2) possible implications in the meaning of those words beyond what is directly stated, and (3) inferences that might be made about people or situations from descriptions of their belongings, surroundings, or actions. For example, the social studies text might state "Since the senator was not yet thirty-five, he could not accept the nomination for president of the United States." The key words, "not yet thirty-five" and "could not accept the nomination" do not directly tell the reader that a person must be at least thirty-five to be president, but they do imply this. Children who could correctly interpret the implication would make the intended inference.

ASSESSMENT QUESTION

One technique for determining whether or not a child can make inferences is to ask a question such as "In which country do you think Josita lived?"

7. MAKING GENERALIZATIONS AND CONCLUSIONS

Making a generalization is a process whereby one reaches a judgment applicable to a whole class, often on the basis of experiences with a limited number of the class (English and English, 1958). This skill requires the reader to conceptualize connections among facts that are directly stated and facts that are inferred. For example, the child must make a generalization to put the correct word in the following:

Scavengers eat dead things (directly stated *fact*).

Humans eat fried chicken (inferred *fact* that fried chicken is not alive).

Humans are (generalization of directly stated *fact* and inferred *fact*).

Some reading specialists distinguish between the skill of making generalizations and the skill of making conclusions. They do this by stating that conclusions are a type of generalization—one that is based solely on facts. For example, a first grader would be making a conclusion in the following example:

Dogs mean more than one dog (*fact* that "s" makes dog plural).

Cats mean more than one cat (*fact* that "s" makes cat plural).

Adding an "s" must mean more than one (*fact* one + *fact* two = *conclusion*).

In the example that uses the word "scavenger," the generalization would have been labeled a conclusion if the second statement was "Humans eat dead things." Since both skills may be incorporated under the broad heating of "generalizations," the distinction between the two does not have to be made if the teacher does not wish to do so. Teachers who work with young children will probably prefer to use the general heading.

The skill of making generalizations and conclusions is required of children in all content areas. For example, in math children are asked to "identify everyday objects such as a circle, rectangle, and square in mathematical terms" (kindergarten); in science children are asked to "describe why the color of clothing is important in different climates" (grade three); in social studies children are directed to "list all the countries whose residents currently speak Spanish and then write a statement about how powerful Spain may have been in the past" (grade five).

Fraenkel (1973) suggests a sequence of questions to help children make generalizations and conclusions. The teacher first locates at least two different passages that discuss a topic about which he or she thinks that the children should make a generalization. Then questions designed to show children similar aspects of content that they previously believed to be unrelated are asked. Examples of Fraenkel's technique and sample responses are as follows:

1. *Fraenkel's first question:* Ask the reader to describe the situation presented in each piece of reading material.
   a. Sample question: "Tell me what you read about in each story."
   b. Sample response: "I read a story about Fido and a story about Fuzzy."
2. *Fraenkel's second question:* Ask the reader to describe any differences that the reader sees.
   a. Sample question: "What differences were there in the two stories?"
   b. Sample response: "One story was about a pet cat. The other story was about a pet dog."
3. *Fraenkel's third question:* Ask the reader to account for the differences.
   a. Sample question: "Why would a cat be a pet in one story and a dog be a pet in a second story?"
   b. Sample response: "Because pets can be all sorts of animals."
4. *Fraenkel's fourth question:* Ask the reader to describe other situations in which differing conditions exist.
   a. Sample question: "Can you think of situations in which pets are not cats or dogs?"
   b. Sample response: "Yes I know a lady who has a pet rat, a pet snake, and a pet gold fish. I think I was right before when I said that pets can be all types of animals."

ASSESSMENT QUESTION

One technique for determining whether or not a child can make generalizations and conclusions is to ask a question such as "Can you make a generalization about owning a cleaning shop?"

8. IDENTIFYING TONE AND MOOD

Tone and mood are created by an author to help convey his or her ideas and are particularly important in the content areas of language arts and social studies. Tone is defined differently by various authors, but it is most often described as the characteristics of a writer's style by which he or she expresses his or her attitudes toward his or her subject matter, his or her readers, or both. Tone is not attitude itself but, rather, the quality of the author's writing style that puts forth his or her attitude. Tone may be described by many adjectives including serious, unsympathetic, solemn, or sympathetic.

Finally all but one of the twelve fairies had announced their gifts. As the last one stood up to speak, in walked another guest. She was a wicked fairy who had not been invited to the feast to celebrate the baby's birth. She was very angry. (tone: ominous, fateful) ("Sleeping Beauty," p. 295)

Children can be taught to recognize tone by being shown how words such as "wicked" and "angry" in the example have a connotative meaning as well as a literal meaning that helps convey the tone.

Identifying mood requires that the child be made aware of the emotional overtones in what is being read. Mood may be thought of as the atmosphere of a work, that is, the total of all the material's characteristics that creates a prevalent feeling in the reader. The mood of a work may create emotions such as gloom, cheer, sadness, happiness, joy, or grief. The following excerpt from a grade five social studies text illustrates the mood of happiness.

. . . The neighborhood was close-knit. Although the houses were a half-mile to a mile apart, the people know one another well and, in time of trouble, came running to offer their help. On Sundays wagons and buggies carried whole families to church. Some Sundays the neighbors spent more time talking than they did *in* church. (tone: pleasant; mood: happiness) (Prunty and Fincher, 1971, p. 285)

Children can be taught the concept of mood by being asked such questions as "How did this passage make you feel?" They can be shown how phrases such as "close-knit," "came running," and "time talking" contribute to the feeling that the author wanted them to know that the people liked each other and were happy.

In addition to being able to recognize words that contribute to the tone and mood, children need to be shown other elements in a passage that might contribute to these skills. The general impressions that are gained from picture clues, details, main ideas, and cause–effect relationships should be discussed. For example, the general impression created by the illustrations and speech in the cartoon "Beetle Bailey" might be compared with that of "Dick Tracy." Additionally, paragraphs from their textbooks may be presented in such a manner that the children react in the fashion the author wanted them to. The following excerpt from *The Big Wave* by Pearl Buck (1947) is taken from a sixth grade basal reader.

"May the gods save us," Kino heard his father mutter. The bell began to toll again, deep and pleading. Ah, but would the people hear it in the roaring wind? Did they know what was about to happen? Their houses had no windows toward the sea. (tone: ominous; mood: suspense)

After reading this, the child should be asked questions such as "Do you think the author wants us to laugh? How does this make you feel about Kino? Do you feel sad? Frightened? Lonesome?" The child would need to know the literal and connotative meanings of key words (e.g., "deep and pleading," "roaring"), the sequence of events (e.g., Father had explained tidal waves that had occurred before to his son), and the cause–effect relationships (e.g., There had been a volcano erupt earlier that day that would tend to disrupt the natural state of nature). All these factors contribute to the general impression created by the passage.

Younger children need to be guided carefully to learn to distinguish between subtle differences in various tones and moods. A young child can easily distinguish between happiness and sadness or seriousness and lightheartedness. However, distinctions between closely related moods, such as embarrassment and fear, would be more difficult for the child to make. This is particularly true when the author develops mood through inference rather than through direct statement, as in "After the ribbon was tied on his tail, the dog pulled loose from him and hid under the table." It would not be uncommon to have equally as many children label the mood as fear as label it embarrassement.

Most stories written for young children are fairly straightforward and concrete. For example, the tone and mood of the following poem by Robert Louis Stevenson (1885) should be obvious to elementary level children of any age. This particular poem is often read in the first grade.

> The world is so full
>   of a number of things,
> I'm sure we should all
>   be as happy as kings.
> (tone: lighthearted; mood: happiness)

When children reach the upper elementary level, they are usually introduced to more sophisticated devices for creating tone and mood. Satire, parody, and sarcasm all tend to diminish a subject by making it ridiculous and evoking toward it attitudes of amusement, contempt, or scorn. The older children can understand how such devices use humor as a weapon rather than as an end in itself. The following excerpt from *Charlie and the Chocolate Factory* by Roald Dahl (1964) is used to teach fifth graders how to recognize satire.

> "Here we go!" cried Mr. Wonka, hopping up and down with excitement. "This is the testing room for my very latest and greatest invention—Television Chocolate!" (p. T-374).

To recognize the satirical tone, children need to locate the words that spoof advertising techniques ("latest and greatest") as well as the incongruous conclusions ("Television Chocolate" refers to chocolate that is transported to the buyer through his or her television set).

ASSESSMENT QUESTION

One technique for determining whether or not a child can identify tone and mood is to ask a question such as "How do you think the author wanted you to feel after you read *Josita's Dancing Cleaners*?"

9. IDENTIFYING THEME

Theme and main idea are similar but not the same skill. In both cases, the reader must conceptualize the central thought of a sentence, paragraph, or longer unit. However, to identify the theme, the reader must go beyond the main idea and locate an abstract—usually "Universal Truth." In most cases, the reader needs to understand the main idea before he or she can identify the theme. Theme is more than the main idea and often describes a code of conduct that is presented to the reader as a model of preferred behavior. The skill of identifying themes is often first presented to children in the form of a parable, fable, or nursery rhyme. For example, the fable "King Midas" demonstrates the concepts that material possessions are not the most important things in life. Similarly, "The Three Little Pigs" contains both a main idea (three pigs go out in the world to seek their fortunes and encounter a big, bad wolf) and a theme (if you do it right, it may take longer, but you're better off in the long run). Though first graders are usually asked questions about details and sequence, they are presented with many such stories that do have themes and are asked such questions as "Do you think that the third little pig was smart to make his house out of bricks? Why?" Such questions help prepare the child for understanding theme when he or she is mature enough to be taught this concept.

In nonfiction, particularly in the content areas of social studies and science, the theme may be openly stated. For example, a science unit might be focused around the theme of "pollution control." All information included in the unit would support this theme. Hence the respiratory system, digestive system, and auditory system might be described in terms of the effect of pollution on breathing, eating, and listening. Awareness of the theme by the child would help him or her to put the facts presented into meaningful organization. The central theme of "pollution control" would provide the child with a "handle" for learning all the facts and "tying them" together.

In fiction, often the theme is not stated directly, and the child needs to be shown how to use his or her other reading skills to help determine the theme. The ability to identify main idea, inference, generalizations, conclusions, and tone and mood are particularly important in recognizing theme.

Abstract concepts such as theme are difficult for young children to grasp. Piaget (1967) supports this in his theory of cognitive development as he describes traits of the "concrete development stage," ages 7 through 11. However, Piaget also indicates that children can be taught higher-level thinking skills through careful questioning. While first and second graders would not be mature enough to verbalize theme, they can usually recognize it if it is presented in fairly obvious terms. Hence the first or second grade teacher might want to begin with step 3 in the continuum given in this text rather than with step 1.

Additionally, as the skills become more sophisticated, the technical terms that describe them need to be defined for the child. Hence the teacher should make certain that the child understands what he or she is being asked to do when he or she is asked to tell the theme, for example, asking "Do you know what I mean by theme? Do you know what I mean when I ask for the moral of the story? How about when I ask for the lesson to be learned?" Questions that begin with "What do you think the author wanted us to learn?" and "What is the lesson we are being taught in this story?" facilitate the child's ability to understand the concept of theme.

ASSESSMENT QUESTION

One technique for determining whether or not a child can identify theme is to ask a question such as "What is the theme of the story? What lesson is the author trying to teach us?"

10. IDENTIFYING CHARACTERIZATION

To identify characterization, the child must be able to interpret everything that the author has written about a person. Four means by which a writer describes a character to the reader are (1) by what the character says, (2) by what the character does, (3) by what others say about the character, and (4) by what the author says about the character. Children usually have little trouble with interpreting the character when the author is describing him or her. Since the author normally "speaks the truth," the author's description can usually be accepted as valid. That is, if the author stated that "Paul was a pleasant fellow," it is probably true, whereas, if another character stated that "Paul was a pleasant fellow," it might be only in terms of that person's perception. Hence children need to be made aware that, when characters are developed by the other three techniques cited, they should be evaluated in light of the situation presented. Children should also be shown how to predict future behavior of individuals based on their past actions. If Thomas Edison was creative as a child, he would probably continue to be creative as an adult.

The older child should be shown that inconsistency in a character can leave the story open to criticism and decrease its credibility. For example, a story in which the bully magically becomes a hero is not as believable as a story in which the bully gets into trouble because of his or her personality traits.

Understanding characterization is important in many content areas, particularly in language arts and social studies. Understanding that George Washington could "not tell a lie" when he cut down a cherry tree helps the child to understand why Washington acted as he did while he was president.

Prerequisite reading skills to identifying characterization include identifying details (her hair was red), making inferences (she had to stoop over to walk in the door to the house), identifying cause–effect relationships (when she stared at people, they shivered in their boots), and making generalizations (all the previous clues indicate the character was a tall, red-haired tyrant).

Teachers can show children how to interpret character by asking leading questions such as "What did he say? What kinds of people usually say that? What did he do? Do you know anybody who does that type of thing? How did other people feel about him? Why do you think they felt that way? How is he described in the story?"

ASSESSMENT QUESTION

One technique for determining whether or not a child can identify characterization is to ask questions such as "What type of person do you think Josita's father was?"

11. IDENTIFYING FACT, FICTION, AND OPINION

Children need to be made aware that material may be fact, fiction, or opinion. Often, children think that everything that appears in print is the truth. Extremely young children have trouble discriminating fact from fiction and must be directly told that "This is a made-up story and never really happened." The teacher can help pupils learn this discrimination by pointing out details that affect a story's credibility and by asking children to react to those details. For example,

> What is that dog doing? Yes, he is cooking his own dinner. Do you think a dog can really cook his own dinner? No, dogs can't cook can they? Sometimes stories have make-believe things in them just to make them more fun to read.

As youngsters get older, they can be taught to discriminate between fact and fiction in works that are not so obviously fictitious. Asking children to focus on key details and to evaluate those details in light of reality can help in this discrimination process. For example,

> Do you think that a boy who has never ridden a horse before can become rodeo champion in two weeks? Yes, it could happen, but do you think this is typical? Do you think this really happened in this story? What other clues do we have that this story is probably not true?

Children should also be made aware of the varying locations of each type of material in the library. Books located in the "fiction" section contain fictionalized events and/or people even though they may be based on some truth. On the other hand, books selected from the "nonfiction" section contain only factual material. For example, books selected from the nonfiction science section of the library should depict only true facts about animals.

Children often have trouble discriminating truth from fiction in historical fiction. These stories, based on true characters and events, can confuse a child by the addition of fictitious material. For example, the following excerpt is taken from a child's reader:

> To General Washington she said, "Mary's going to help carry food to the soldiers."
> The General smiled. "That's fine," he said. He took Mary to the window, and together they looked out at the snow-covered log house. (Anastasio, 1973, p. 199)

This story is intended to be read by third grade children. Since George Washington is a real person, some third graders may accept all the facts in the story as true. All such literature must be discussed by the teacher so that children realize that, even though some of the characters are based on real people, the story itself may not be true.

In learning to discriminate fact from opinion, children should be shown how clue words reflect the ideas of a particular person. Some of these clue words include *perhaps*, *I think*, *maybe*, *one possibility*, my *beliefs suggest*, and *in my opinion*. All these words indicate the point of view of the author and help to identify the work as opinion. Other words that indicate personal involvement are personal pronouns such as *I* and *my*.

Fact, fiction, and opinion are all found in most types of current periodicals as well as in other kinds of mass media. Often, newspaper or magazine editors will provide clues to the truthfulness by introducing a selection with phrases such as "A short story by . . ."; "A factual account by . . ."; "A commentary by . . .". In some cases, children need to be told that some written material is by its nature intended to be fact, fiction, or opinion; that is, an editorial cartoon reflects an opinion, the lovelorn column reflects an opinion, most children's cartoons are fictitious, and news on the front page is usually fact.

Many children as well as many adults accept as fact materials that have the following traits: (1) anything that is written down, (2) anything with which they agree, (3) any logically developed position, and (4) frequently repeated positions. Instead of accepting as fact materials that have these traits, children should be taught to examine such aspects as copyright dates, different versions of the same account, and the author's qualifications. For example, the teacher might have children compare a textbook account of landing on the moon with one presented in a science fiction story. For example, a 1969 account of landing on the moon by astronaut Neil Armstrong could be discussed along with an excerpt from *From the Earth to the Moon* written in 1865 by Jules Verne.

A similar procedure could be used to teach older children to discriminate between fact and opinion. Letters from the lovelorn column could be analyzed and rewritten from various points of view. For instance, a letter from a child discussing how mean his older brother was to him could be rewritten as though it were (1) completely objective, (2) from the older brother, and (3) from the parents. Words used to indicate the different points of view could be compared and analyzed.

Prerequisite reading skills include the ability to recognize and to evaluate relevant details (chickens do not talk), to identify the main idea (turtles do not beat rabbits in races) and the sequence (two weeks is not long enough to grow from a baby into an adult), to locate cause–effect relationships (if someone cuts his or her finger, it should bleed), to make inferences (since he called his neighbor a "creep," his opinion of the neighbor must not be a good one), and to make generalizations (since this is in the food section of newspaper, it is probably a valid recipe). Since some reading skills require more sophistication than do others, teachers should always keep in mind the age of the child when asking him or her to make these discriminations. Most children can use relevant details in material written on their instructional level to help them classify material as fact, fiction, or opinion. However, some of the higher-level reading skills are not so easily utilized by the young child. For example, while an older child might recognize something as an opinion by the tone, the younger child might not be able to identify the tone and hence miss the fact that the words express an opinion. For example, Carl Sandburg's verse, "I sit in a chair and read the newspapers. Millions of men go to war, acres of them are buried. . ." (1920) might be accepted as fact by the first grader. The sixth grader should have little trouble recognizing the tone and hence the opinion expressed.

ASSESSMENT QUESTION

One technique for determining whether or not a child can identify fact, fiction, and opinion is to ask a question such as "Look at the story, *Josita's Dancing Cleaners*, and see if you think any opinions are expressed."

12. IDENTIFYING PROPAGANDA

To identify propaganda, children need to recognize varying types of persuasive devices. The Institute for Propaganda Analysis has described seven categories into which most propaganda techniques may be placed (Burns and Roe, 1976).

1. *Name Calling*—Uses words that contain negative connotations so that the reader will associate those traits with the person or ideas being discredited. For example, "The brand X recording is *shrill*" (instead of having a *pleasing tone*); "The senator's bill may have a *cancerous* effect upon our nation" (instead of *harmful*).

2. *Glittering Generalities*—Uses words that are generally positive in connotation and that are vague enough to make it impossible to

determine where the speaker really stands. For example, "The Senator promises *justice*!" (How will this be done?); "Brand X *charms* your hands" (How is a hand charmed?).

3. *Transfer*—Uses words that symbolize a particular trait or concept for purposes other than those for which they were intended. The reader is supposed to transfer the implications associated with the person or traits being described. For example, "*Baseball, hot dogs, apple pie*, and Senator Jones" (he must be an integral part of America); "Brand X is the detergent in the bottle with an *angel* on the front" (it must be good for your hands).

4. *Plain Folks*—Uses comparisons with ordinary people to convince the reader that the person or product is good for the common person. For example, "People like you and me need a car that is economical yet has style" (you are just like me, and I have a car like this); "Senator shares his lunch with newsboy" (the senator is just like everybody else)

5. *Testimonial*—Uses the endorsement of a famous or admired person in the hope that the reader will want to emulate that person. For example, "Bruce Gender, Olympic Star, always eats Cornies for breakfast" (if it's good enough for Bruce, it ought to be good enough for you); "Movie star Helen Haw would like to say a word about the senator" (if Helen likes the senator, you ought to too).

6. *Card Stacking*—Uses only evidence that supports the person or idea being presented. Points that discredit opposing evidence may also be given, while points that oppose his or her cause are ignored. For example, "Energy wastes decreased while he was mayor" (fails to mention that the winter was unseasonably warm and little fuel was needed to heat homes); "This special diet drink will enable you to lose five pounds in two weeks" (fails to mention that you must eat only five hundred calories a day while you are drinking the diet drink).

7. *Bandwagon*—Uses phrases indicating that all people with whom the reader might identify are supporting the person or idea being presented. For example, "All the best athletes wear brand X jogging shoes" (if you want to be a "best" athlete, you better buy these shoes); "Blue-collar workers united to support Senator Smith" (since you are a blue-collar worker, you also should support Smith).

Today, propoganda permeates almost all aspects of a child's life. Propaganda techniques are most obvious in such things as advertisements and editorials. The following cartoon illustrates the type of propoganda techniques which might be "typically" read by the elementary age child.

Figure 3.2 Cartoon Illustrating "Typical" Propaganda Technique.

However, children also need to be made aware that persuasive devices may be used in less apparent materials including their own textbooks. Though math and science are usually presented in an objective manner, other content areas such as language arts and social studies may be written more subjectively. For example, the following excerpt is taken from a fifth grade social studies text:

> As the British advanced, the Americans inflicted heavy losses upon them and, as before, retreated. When Cornwallis' army reached the third line of the American army, the Americans fought stubbornly, then slowly retreated into the surrounding woods. (Prunty and Fincher, 1971, p. 117)

The American soldiers are pictured in a very positive light. Words such as *slowly retreated*, rather than *fled* or *ran away*, and *fought stubbornly*, rather than *battled* or were *engaged in a skirmish*, are devices that help create the intended tone.

Frances Fitzgerald (1979) analyzed American history books used in the schools and stated

> History textbooks for elementary and secondary schools are not like other kinds of histories. They serve a different function, and they have their own traditions, which continue independent of academic history writing . . . they are written not to explore but to

instruct—to tell children what their elders want them to know about their country. (February 26, 1979, p. 65)

. . . the publisher . . . has a social-studies series for the elementary grades which devotes endless pages to showing that people of the most exotic nationalities, races, creeds, and cultures are all very nice and just as human as American boys and girls. The messages that children must receive are thus rather confusing: love everyone in the elementary grades, fight Communism in junior high, and face endless intractable problems in high school. (March 5, 1979, p. 90)

To react critically to both the mass media and material within their own textbooks, children should be taught to do the following:

1. *Examine the author's purpose.*
   Example 1: Why did the author draw this cartoon about Drink-Pop? (Teacher uses excerpt from newspaper, television, or the like.)
   Example 2: Why would the author want to picture our forefathers in a very positive light? (Teacher uses excerpt from social studies similar to example given about the American soldiers fighting Cornwallis.)
2. *Examine the writer's competence.*
   Example 1: Who made up this Drink-Pop cartoon? Why should we believe him when he says it is good for us?
   Example 2: The authors are professors in geography, political science, and education at various universities. They probably know facts about geography, political science, and education. Do you think they know about the American Revolution?
3. *Consider their own background of experiences and familiarity with the topic.*
   Example 1: Have I ever tasted Drink-Pop? Have I ever tasted a similar beverage made by the same company?
   Example 2: Have I ever heard of Cornwallis before? Is the battle always depicted in these same terms?
4. *Note any propaganda techniques used.*
   Example 1: Does the cartoonist use any of the seven devices discussed earlier? Yes, he uses bandwagon because he says "all kids like Drink-Pop." He also uses glittering generalities because he tells us that "Drink-Pop is good for you" without explaining what he means by "good."
   Example 2: Does the author use any propaganda devices? Yes, he uses card stacking. All we see is the good side of the American soldiers. The authors tell us that they "slowly retreated" and "fought stubbornly." The American soldiers were probably less brave occasionally and perhaps not all the American soldiers "fought stubbornly" during the battle described.
5. *Decide to accept or reject ideas offered or delay decision until more data is available.*
   Example 1: I will delay decision on "Drink-Pop" until after I taste it for myself. I will delay decisions on how good it is for me until I investigate the facts more.
   Example 2: I need to know more about the battle with Cornwallis before I can evaluate the American soldiers.
   (based on Dillner and Olson, 1977, p. 56)

Since children cannot critically evaluate material beyond their experiential backgrounds, the teacher may need to provide prereading activities to expand their backgrounds. For example, a filmstrip on the American Revolution or a discussion of the reasons behind it would help them evaluate the excerpt. This type of background expansion is essential if the teacher is asking children to evaluate materials based primarily on their personal experiences. For example, a child would not understand the "transfer" technique used to portray a particular brand of tissue as especially soft unless he or she understood that a baby's skin symbolized a very tender surface.

Furthermore, because children cannot be expected to evaluate material that they are not cognitively mature enough to interpret, analyzing content area textbooks is often delayed until the upper elementary level. For example, young children tend to see things as either black or white. As children get older, they are able to cognitively deal with the fact that things are not all good or all bad; that is, the American soldiers could have had some cowardly moments and would still be the kind of people worthy of our respect.

When children are being presented with examples of persuasion, it is wisest to begin with those examples that affect their immediate lives, such as frequently shown television commercials. When showing a young child the seven types of persuasive strategies, it is probably best to deal with one or two at a time. As the child gets older, he or she will have less difficulty in dealing with and differentiating among all seven types all at one time.

ASSESSMENT QUESTION

One technique for determining whether or not a child can identify propaganda is to ask questions such as "Can you find an example of propaganda in *Josita's Dancing Cleaners*?"

Table 3.2 illustrates questions that might be asked in step 1 of the questioning strategy for each of the twelve comprehension skills.

SUMMARY

This chapter discussed the following ten important premises:

1. Comprehension may be divided into *subskills* to break down the process into more manageable and, hence, teachable units.
2. As soon as children are old enough to learn them, they should be taught the names of the subskills. They need to understand the terms so they can communicate effectively with their teachers. For example, they would have to know what the term "theme" meant before they could complete an activity that asked them to identify theme.
3. Skills are taught a few at a time. Their presentation is based upon

prerequisite skills that must be learned first as well as upon the nature of the material to be read.

4. Although comprehension may be broken down into subskills, these skills *must* be taught with constant regard to the "total" nature of comprehension. The association among the various reading skills and the ideas and words already possessed by the child should be pointed out to the child. This association incorporates the psycholinguistic viewpoint that reading is always interpreted in terms of the reader's own experiences.
5. Reading comprehension and thinking are similar. Since questioning has been proven to increase thinking skills, this same strategy may be used to increase reading comprehension.
6. Questions can be designed so that they are on a continuum from simple to complex. To maximize the teaching effectiveness of the questioning process, the teacher should try to reword and simplify questions that the child is unable to answer correctly rather than to just tell the child the intended response. The questioning continuum can be useful as a model for the teacher in designing simpler questions.
7. The focus of the questioning should be to teach the child a strategy for learning the skill as well as the skill itself. This is the only way for a child to learn to be an independent reader. For example, instead of telling a child that "John Doe was evil and this is a character trait," the teacher would show the child how character traits may be identified in four different ways. Hence the child not only would learn about the personality traits of John Doe but would also learn about a technique for identifying the character traits of persons about whom he or she had not yet read.
8. Relevant lessons which are fun are useful in helping a child to internalize a reading skill. Games and activities of this nature can provide the child with needed reinforcement because the child will *want* to practice the skill. The newspaper is a particularly good source for these activities.
9. Children of all ages cannot learn all twelve subskills. Some of the skills are too complex for the very young child. The teacher should always be aware of the cognitive development of each child when teaching the skills. In general, the older the child, the higher the level of abstraction that can be made. Since the skills toward the end of the list tend to be more complex than the skills near the beginning of the list, the youngest elementary children will probably not be able to learn skills such as "theme" until their ability to reason becomes more mature.
10. Since children have to read not only their reading textbooks but textbooks in other subjects as well, examples have been given of how reading skills should be emphasized in all content areas. Although most reading skills will be presented initially in reading class, the teacher should reinforce the skills whenever possible during content area instruction.

TABLE 3.2 An Overview of the Twelve Comprehension Skills

	Skill	*Definition*	*Sample Assessment Question*
Most Simple	1. Gaining word meaning	Interpreting intended meaning	What does the word *pronto* mean?
	2. Identifying details	Finding one or more specifically stated pieces of information	What was the name of the street that Josita was walking toward?
	3. Identifying main ideas	Identifying the central thought of a selection	What is the main idea of the story?
↑	4. Identifying sequence	Determining the order in which components occur or are placed	What is the first thing Josita did in the story? The second? The third?
	5. Identifying cause–effect relationships	Determining the reasons for the occurrence of an event or action	Why did Josita's father look up from his work?
	6. Making inferences	Formulating images not directly presented in the written material	In which country do you think Josita lived?
toward	7. Making generalizations and conclusions	Inferring the relationship between separate situations or events	Can you make a generalization about owning a cleaning shop?
	8. Identifying tone and mood	Recognizing the author's attitude and the emotion he or she intends for the reader to feel	How do you think the author wanted you to feel after you read the story?
↑	9. Identifying theme	Recognizing the moral or abstract concept that the work is intended to clarify to the reader	What is the theme of the story? What lesson is the author trying to teach us?
	10. Identifying characterization	Determining the personality traits and feelings of a character in a selection	What type of person do you think Josita's father was?
	11. Identifying fact, fiction,	Determining which passages represent actual conditions and which passages reflect the personal feelings of the author	Look at the story and see if you think any opinions are expressed.
Most Complex	12. Identifying propaganda	Determining if any bias exists in passage	Can you find an example of propaganda in *Josita's Dancing Cleaners*?

References and Bibliography

Anastasio, Dina. "Mary of Valley Forge," in *Never Give Up*. New York: Holt, Rinehart and Winston, 1973, pp. 194-207.

Barrett, Thomas C. "Taxonomy of Reading Comprehension," *Reading 360 Monograph*. Lexington, Mass: Ginn and Company, 1972.

Beery, Althea. "Clustering Comprehension Skills to Solve Problems," in J. Allen Figurel, ed. *Forging Ahead in Reading*. Newark, Dela.: International Reading Association, 1968, pp. 109-111.

Bond, G. L., and Tinker, M. A. *Reading Difficulties: Their Diagnosis and Correction*. 3rd ed. New York: Appleton-Century-Crofts, 1973.

Buck, Pearl. *The Big Wave* (1947). New York: The John Day Co., Publishers, 1948.

Burns, Paul C., and Roe, Betty. *Teaching Reading in Today's Elementary School*. Chicago: Rand McNally & Company, 1976.

Carver, Ronald. "Reading as Reasoning: Implications for Measurement," in W. MacGinitie, ed., *Assessment Problems in Reading*. Newark: Dela.: International Reading Association, 1973, pp. 44-56.

Clark, E. V. "On the Acquisition of the Meaning of 'Before' and 'After'." *Journal of Verbal Learning and Verbal Behavior* 10 (June 1971): 266-275.

Dahl, Roald. *Charlie and the Chocolate Factory*, New York: Knoff, 1964.

Davis, F. B. "Research on Comprehension in Reading." *Reading Research Quarterly* 3 (Summer 1968): 499-545.

Dillner, Martha, and Olson, Joanne. *Personalizing Reading Instruction in Middle, Junior, and Senior High Schools*. New York: Macmillan Publishing Co., Inc., 1977.

Ekwall, Eldon. *Locating and Correcting Reading Difficulties*. Columbus, Ohio: Charles E. Merrill Publishing Company, 1970.

English, Horace B., and English, Ava Champney. *A Comprehensive Dictionary of Psychoanalytical Terms*. New York: David McKay Co., Inc., 1958.

FitzGerald, Frances. "Rewriting American History: I." *The New Yorker*, February 26, 1979, pp. 41-77.

FitzGerald, Frances. "Rewriting American History: II." *The New Yorker*, March 5, 1979, pp. 40-91.

FitzGerald, Frances. "Rewriting American History: III." *The New Yorker*, March 12, 1979, pp. 48-106.

Fraenkel, J. R. *Helping Students Think and Value: Strategies for Teaching the Social Studies*. Englewood Cliffs, N.J.: Prentice-Hall, Inc., 1973.

Gerhard, Christian. *Making Sense: Reading Comprehension Improved Through Categorizing*. Newark, Dela.: International Reading Association, 1975, p. 154.

Geyer, John. "Comprehensive and Partial Models Related to the Reading Process." *Reading Research Quarterly* 7 (Summer 1972): 541-587.

Goodman, Kenneth. "Analysis of Oral Reading Miscues: Applied Psycholinguistics," in Frank Smith, ed., *Psycholinguistics and Reading*. New York: Holt, Rinehart and Winston, 1973), pp. 158-176.

Goodman, Kenneth. "A Psycholinguistic View of Reading Comprehension," in G. Schick and M. May, eds., *New Frontiers in College-Adult Reading: Fifteenth Yearbook of the National Reading Conference*. Milwaukee: National Reading Conference, 1966, pp. 188-196.

Herr, Selma. *Learning Activities for Reading*. 2nd Edition. Dubuque, Iowa: William C. Brown Company, Publishers, 1973.

Johnson, M. E. "The Vocabulary Difficulty in Content Subject in Grade Five." *Elementary English* 29 (May 1952): 277-280.

Klausmeier, Herbert J. "Instructional Design and Teaching of Concept," in Joel Levin and Vernon Allen, ed., *Cognitive Learning in Children: Theories and Strategies*. New York: Academic Press, Inc., 1976.

Mallison, George C. and Jacqueline B., and Feravolo, Rocco. *Science: Understanding Your Environment—Level Three*. Dallas: Silver Burdett, 1975.

Mencken, H. L. *The American Language*. New York: Alfred A. Knopf, Inc., 1937.

Otto, Wayne, Peters, Nathaniel, and Peters, Charles. *Reading Problems: A Multidisciplinary Perspective.* Reading, Mass.: Addison-Wesley Publishing Co., Inc., 1977, p. 256.

Pearson, David. "Children's Comprehension of Sequential Relations among Events," unpublished paper. Minneapolis, University of Minnesota, 1977.

Pearson, David and Johnson, Dale. *Teaching Reading Comprehension.* New York: Holt, Rinehart and Winston, 1978.

Peters, Charles W. and Nathaniel A. "A Systematic Approach to Predicting Reading Performance at the Secondary Level," in Miller, Wallace and McNinch, George, eds., the *Twenty-fifth Yearbook of the National Reading Conference, 1976* Hattiesburg, Miss: Univ. of Southern Mississippi Press, pp. 121-128.

Piaget, J. *Six Psychological Studies.* A. Tenzea and D. Elkind, Trans., New York: Random House, Inc., 1967.

Piltz, Albert, and Van Bever, Roger. *Discovering Science 5.* Columbus, Ohio: Charles E. Merrill Publishing Company, 1970.

Prunty, Merle, and Fincher, E. B. *Lands of Promise: Western Hemisphere: Setting and Settlement.* New York: Macmillan Publishing Co., Inc., 1971.

Serra, M. C. "The Concept Burden of Instructional Materials." *Elementary School Journal* 53 (1953): 508-512.

Smith, Frank. *Psycholinguistics and Reading.* New York: Holt, Rinehart and Winston, 1974.

Smith, Nila B. "The Many Faces of Reading Comprehension." *Reading Teacher* 23 (December 1969): 249-259.

Taba, H., and Elzey, F. F. "Teaching Strategies and Thought Processes." *Teachers College Record* 65 (1964): 524-534.

Thomas, E. L., and Robinson, H. A. *Improving Reading in Every Class.* Boston: Allyn & Bacon, Inc., 1972.

Thorndike, Robert. "Reading as Reasoning." *Reading Research Quarterly* 9 (Winter 1973): 135-147.

Sandburg, Carl. "Smoke" (1920) in Carl Sandburg, *Smoke and Steel,* New York: Harcourt, Brace, 1920.

Spearritt, Donald. "Identification of Subskills of Reading Comprehension by Maximum Likelihood Factor Analysis." *Reading Research Quarterly* 8 (Fall 1972): 92-111.

Stevenson, Robert Lewis. "A Happy Thought," *A Child's Garden of Verse.* London: Longman, Green and Company, 1885.

Verner, Zenobia. *Newsbook of Reading Comprehension Activities.* Houston: Clayton Publishing Company, 1978.

Walborn, Maria. *Josita's Dancing Clearners.* New York: Macmillan Publishing Co., Inc., 1975.

Webster's New World Dictionary of the American Language: College Edition. New York: William Collins World Publishing Co., Inc., 1957, p. 1319.

Weiss, Bernard and Hunt, Lyman. *Time to Wonder: Level 13: The Holt Basic Reading System. Teacher's Edition.* New York: Holt, Rinehart and Winston, Inc., 1973.

Additional References

"Beetle Bailey"
"Charlie Brown"
"Dick Tracy"
"Fred Bassett"
"King Midas"
"Marmaduke"
"Three Little Pigs"
"Sleeping Beauty"

Self-Check 3.3
Comprehension Skills

The following questions are designed to help the participant assess his or her competence on the first five objectives stated at the beginning of this chapter. Although every effort has been made to make the self-check questions comprehensive, participants should remember that they are held responsible for meeting the objectives as stated at the beginning of this chapter.

1. Objective 1. Define the term "reading comprehension."
2. Objective 2. Differentiate between and give examples of models of reading that view the process as "total" and models of reading that view the process as "separable subskills."
3. Objective 3. Define, differentiate among, and give examples of the twelve subskills of comprehension presented in this chapter.
4. Objective 4. Discuss the relationship between cognitive development of the child and the type of comprehension skills that may most effectively be taught.
5. Objective 5. Describe a technique for teaching comprehension skills that uses a set of increasingly simplified questioning strategies.

Chapter 3

Experience 1

Objective

During this experience, the participant will locate, describe, and react to strategies for teaching the comprehension skills.

Activity and Assessment Guide

1. Several means for teaching each of the comprehension skills are located in Chapter 14. Space is given for you to skim those strategies and then briefly jot down at least two ways in which to teach four of the comprehension skills. The strategies that you select should be appropriate to the needs of the children with whom you will most probably be working. If you have located strategies from another source, you may use them instead of the ones supplied in Chapter 15.

   a. Gaining Word Meaning

      (1) ____________________

      (2) ____________________

   b. Identifying Details

      (1) ____________________

      (2) ____________________

c. Identifying Main Ideas

(1) ____________________

(2) ____________________

d. Identifying Sequence

(1) ____________________

(2) ____________________

e. Identifying Cause–Effect Relationships

(1) ____________________

(2) ____________________

f. Making Inferences

(1) ____________________

(2) ____________________

g. Making Generalizations and Conclusions

(1) ____________________

(2) ____________________

h. Identifying Tone and Mood

(1) ____________________

(2) ____________________

i. Identifying Theme

(1) ____________________

(2) ____________________

j. Identifying Characterization

(1) ____________________

(2) ____________________

k. Identifying Fact, Fiction, and Opinion

(1) ____________________

(2) ____________________

l. Identifying Propaganda

(1) ____________________

(2) ____________________

* 2. Look over the skills that you have selected and briefly describe why you selected the skills that you did. ______________________________

____

* 3. Select one of the strategies that you have chosen and describe at least two ways in which it is appropriate to the age of the child with whom you will most probably be working. ______________________________

____

* 4. State what you believe to be the significant implications of this experience for the classroom teacher. ______________________________

____

*See Chapter 1, Experience 1 for explanation of the asterisk.

Chapter 3
Experience 2

Objective

During this experience, the participant will design and use a questioning strategy for teaching one of the comprehension skills.

Activity and Assessment Guide

1. What skill do you intend to teach? Be specific, for example, chronological sequence.
2. What reading material do you intend to use as the basis of your questioning strategy? Be specific, for example, name of author, title of work, date of publication, name of publisher, and exact page number. (If possible, attach a photostat of the material to this sheet.)
3. Write out questions for each of the five steps and attach them to this sheet of paper.
4. Write out the child's responses to the steps that you asked him or her on the appropriate lines provided. If you did not have to proceed through all five steps, write the words "did not ask" in the space provided.

   a. Child's response to step 1 ______________________________

   ____

   b. Child's response to step 2 ______________________________

   ____

c. Child's response to step 3 ______________________________

____

d. Child's response to step 4 ______________________________

____

e. Child's response to step 5 ______________________________

____

* 5. Write a brief summary of your feelings about the child's reaction towards this strategy and the amount of learning that took place.

____

____

* 6. State what you believe to be the significant implications of this experience for the classroom teacher. ______________________________

____

____

*See Chapter 1, Experience 1 for explanation of the asterisk.

Chapter 3
Experience 3

Objective

During this experience, the participant will design and teach a lesson on a comprehension skill using a strategy other than a questioning strategy.

Activity and Assessment Guide

1. What skill do you intend to teach? Be specific, for example, the "bandwagon" approach of the propaganda techniques. ____________________

   ____

2. Describe the assessment activity that you plan to use before teaching the lesson so that you can assess the student's knowledge of the skill.

   ____

   ____

3. Describe the techniques that you intend to use to instruct the students in this skill. ____________________

   ____

   ____

   ____

   ____

   ____

4. Describe the assessment activity that you plan to use after teaching your lesson so that you can assess the student's knowledge of that skill.

____

____

* 5. Write a brief summary of your feelings about the child's reaction toward this strategy and the amount of learning that took place.

____

____

6. Attach a copy of your lesson plan to this sheet.

* 7. State what you believe to be the significant implications of this experience for the classroom teacher. __________________________

____

____

*See Chapter 1, Experience 1 for explanation of the asterisk.

Chapter 4
Study Skills

Objectives 4.1

On completion of this chapter, the participant should be able to

1. Define the term "study skills."
2. Define, differentiate among, and give examples of the twelve study skills presented in this chapter.
3. Discuss the relationship between the age of the child and the type and amount of study skills that may be taught most effectively to him or her.
4. Describe an assessment technique for each of the twelve study skills.

Experiences 1 and 2 extend Chapter 4 with these objectives:

5. During this experience, the participant will locate, describe, and react to strategies for teaching the study skills.
6. During this experience, the participant will design and teach a lesson on one of the study skills.

Information Given 4.2
Study Skills

On the first day of the new school year, Miss Jones, the new teacher located the school by holding the map of the area to coincide with the direction in which she was heading; Mark, a fourth grader, copied verbatim a passage out of the encyclopedia for his science report on "respiration"; and Jane, a kindergarten child, colored with her red crayon instead of her blue as directed.

The new teacher was having difficulty utilizing her "map reading" skills, Mark was having difficulty applying "note-taking" skills, and Jane needed to learn the skill of "following directions."

These situations illustrate the use of the study skills of reading. The ability to interpret and retain information from various materials requires that the child do more than just recognize the words and comprehend the basic meaning. The child must be able to follow directions, utilize a variety of organizational skills, and read in a manner appropriate for which the material has been assigned. These skills are necessary so that the child can use reading to learn and are labeled the "study skills" of reading. In this text, the study skills involved in helping a child read to learn have been divided into the following twelve categories:

1. Following Directions
2. Scheduling Time
3. Adjusting Rate to Purpose
4. Using a Study Technique
5. Using Aids within Books
6. Using Maps, Graphs, and Tables
7. Using Locational Aids in the Library
8. Using Reference Materials
9. Using Materials Appropriate to Purpose
10. Organizing Information
11. Recalling Information
12. Evaluating Information

This list is presented as one that can easily be understood by the classroom teacher and that contains skills needed by the child to read efficiently. Though most reading experts include much the same listing of skills, the categories and labels might vary from authority to authority. For example, Ruddell (1974) includes a category labeled "reading in content areas: math, science, social studies." Cooper et al. (1979) list "evaluating information" as one of the comprehension skills. Garland (1978) has condensed the twelve skills listed in this text into only six categories.

Despite the lack of agreement over the names and classification of components within the study skill categories, major authorities appear to agree that these skills are of primary importance in helping children to read with greatest efficiency. However, elementary teachers sometimes get so involved in teaching the word identification and comprehension skills that they spend little time in preparing the children to use their study skills when asked to read independently (Otto, Rude, and Spiegel, 1979). Furthermore, even when teachers show children how to use the various study skills during reading class, children probably will not learn these skills through teacher instruction alone. If an instructor wishes a child to acquire these skills, he or she must prepare study skill exercises and then provide supervised practice during which children are required to follow the proper procedures (Fry, 1972).

Although twelve study skills are delineated, younger children should not be expected to learn all twelve. For example, while children of all ages should be taught how to "recall information," most children are not presented with the skill of "note-taking" or use of the *Reader's Guide* until they have acquired the necessary prerequisite skills and maturity to be able to learn them.

When the child progresses through school, the amount of reading for information as well as the number of study skills that the child is expected to use increases. As the amount of time that he or she is required to devote to school work increases, the amount of teacher time in showing the child strategies for understanding the material decreases. For example, a first grade child may be carefully shown how to overview material and anticipate its contents (using a study strategy). However, a fourth grade child is likely to be given his or her assignment and merely told to read it. Hence the older child is likely to have more need of the study skills with less direct instruction.

In the following section, each of the twelve study skills is described and examples from various content areas are given. After each skill is described, an assessment question is given to illustrate how the teacher can determine whether or not a child knows the skills before he or she begins to teach the skill to the child. All questions have been based on pages 2 and 3 of the book *Josita's Dancing Cleaners* (Walborn, 1975) reproduced on page 49 of this text. Usually, the teacher will not assess or teach all twelve skills over the same lesson but, rather, will tend to present one or two skills at a time. This will give each skill a chance to be learned thoroughly before the child proceeds toward skills that might be based on an earlier skill; for example, the teacher would make certain that the child knew how to "follow directions" before asking him or her to "organize information." Additionally, the skill taught usually depends upon the type of material being presented. If a child were reading about the "Old South," he or she would probably be taught map-reading skills; if the child were reading a math book, he or she would probably be taught how to read graphs.

Throughout the presentation of the twelve skills, theoretical viewpoints supporting the illustrated technique are often discussed. Theory is presented in this format under the assumption that the technique utilized at this particular point in the illustration represents an important educational premise that should be emphasized. For example, when "using a study technique" is described, the rationale behind the specific strategy illustrated in the example is discussed. Hence the reader of this textbook is encouraged to look for these theoretical viewpoints while reading through the following section.

CHAPTER 15: TEACHING ACTIVITIES RELATED TO STUDY SKILLS

Chapter 15 suggests several types of activities that may be used to teach each of the twelve study skills. While the teaching of the study skills during reading class is necessary, research indicates that direct instruction throughout the content areas should also be used if the child is to learn to use the skills independently in all his or her school work (Serra, 1953; Johnson, 1952). Hence examples for reading class as well as for various content area classes are given.

FOLLOWING DIRECTIONS

Following directions is one the most basic of all the reading skills. When entering school, a child must be able to first understand and adequately complete instructions if he or she is to learn any of the other skills. Even a simple task such as "Write your name" requires this skill. Before the child can read, most important instructions in school must be given orally. Hence one of the first means to teach directions orally is to make the child understand that the directions will be given only once. Teachers sometimes foster poor listening and direction-following habits by repeating directions several times. The child quickly learns that he or she does not have to pay attention the first time as the instructions will be repeated.

As the child matures and learns to read, he or she must learn to depend more upon written instructions. One technique that the teacher may use to increase the child's skill in following written instruction is to gradually increase the complexity of instructions given to the children. For example, the teacher may begin by giving the children one-step instructions. Soon two-step instructions are given. Finally, instructions requiring three or more steps are constructed. For example, "Close your books" (one step); "Close your books and get out your pencils" (two steps); "Close your books, get out your pencils, and write your name on your paper" (three steps).

ASSESSMENT QUESTION

One technique for determining if the child knows this skill is to ask the child to complete a task that requires that he or she follow directions; for example, "Draw one line under the name Josita and two lines under the name of her father."

SCHEDULING TIME

Adults as well as children tend to have trouble completing tasks because they do not organize their schedule to allow them enough time to complete needed tasks. Though very young children do not have homework, learning to schedule time can begin as early as the first or second grade. This study skill is usually introduced by the teacher, who requests that the children's parents help them keep a diary of their activities for several days. Then the teacher goes over the diary with the children and they discuss "best times" to do their homework.

As the children mature and become more independent readers, the teacher can require that the children keep their own diary of activities. Often, just by keeping a diary, the children are able to determine for themselves that they have not allowed themselves sufficient time to complete their assignments.

There are two major ways in which children can gain time to do their homework: (1) do the job in less time than usual or (2) use small blocks of time that are usually wasted. By keeping a diary, a child can be helped to locate many blocks of wasted time and taught to use them more efficiently.

ASSESSMENT QUESTION

One technique for determining whether or not the child knows how to schedule time is to ask the child to fill in a chart with the time that he or she spent studying the previous day. Those children whose charts reflected time slots saved for studying have some idea of how to schedule study time.

ADJUSTING RATE TO PURPOSE

Children need to learn that everything they read is read for a particular purpose. The efficient reader can read at a variety of speeds and can use rate flexibly, according to the demands of the situation. Depending on the nature of the material and the reader's purpose, the mature reader may use a rate varying from under fifty words per minute to over a thousand words per minute. The rate at which a child reads depends upon (1) the purpose for which he or she is reading, (2) the difficulty of the material being read, and (3) his or her familiarity with the topic.

A study conducted by Smith (1961) indicates that good readers do attempt to adjust their reading techniques to the purpose for which they are reading. However, the same study supports the contention that most students have had little, if any, direct guidance in reading for different purposes. Thus students need to be taught to approach a written selection in light of their purpose for reading.

The teacher's task of building purposes for reading can be facilitated through close inspection of his or her purposes for having students read the material and then informing the students of these purposes. For example, during a social studies lesson, the teacher might believe that it is important that his or her students be able to answer several specific questions about the "Old South" and to understand the cause-effect relationships between the economy of the "Old South" and the development of the cotton gin. Hence the teacher should communicate these purposes to the children before they are asked to read the assignment. Discussion after the reading should show the students how to locate cause-effect relationships. Students reading this assignment ought to be told to read this at a *slow, careful rate.*

On the other hand, if the teacher wanted the children to read the social studies chapter to find the specific date when the cotton gin was developed, their purpose for reading would be different. To efficiently meet this second purpose, the children should be shown how to use the *scanning* technique.

The various rates that should be used by children may be grouped into the five following categories: (1) textbook reading rate, (2) slow, careful rate, (3) rapid reading rate, (4) skimming, and (5) scanning (Dillner and Olson; 1977).

The *textbook reading rate* is the rate typically used when a child is asked to read continuous running material such as that found in science or social studies books. This rate is slow enough so that the child can pay attention to the main points and details and can retain much of what is read.

The *slow, careful rate* is often used when a child is asked to read his or her textbooks to complete a specific task. For example, a child reading a word problem in his or her math book would have to read each word carefully to be able to solve the problem.

The *rapid reading rate* is typically used by a child who is reading a very easy book. This rate is often used when the material read is not intended to be retained. For example, if an excerpt in a science book gave a short interesting paragraph about the life of a prominent scientist, the child might read it rapidly and with understanding, but not be expected to recall it for later testing. Much recreational reading is done at this rapid rate. However, there are times when a child will want to read more slowly than he or she is capable of reading simply because the recreational material is interesting.

Skimming is used when the child is asked to rapidly overview a paragraph or other segment of written material to get a general impression of it. In textbook reading, this usually involves such tasks as reading titles or subtitles written in heavy print, italicized words, and initial sentences in paragraphs. For example, a teacher might tell the children that he or she will give them only a minute or two to glance through tomorrow's science lesson to make some guesses about the main idea. At the end of the specified time period, the children are directed to close their books and briefly list what they believe the main idea to be.

Scanning is used when a child is asked to locate a specific detail or look for answers to particular questions. For example, if asked to locate the date of the discovery of polio vaccine, the child should be shown how to scan the chapter for the date.

Two other factors involved in determining the child's reading rate are the difficulty of the material and the child's familiarity with the topic. For example, most children would probably find the concepts involved in understanding "democracy" more difficult than the concepts involved in understanding what motivated Columbus to sail to America. Hence the first topic would be read at a slower rate than the second. However, if a child were familiar with the topic of "democracy," he or she might be able to read that textbook material as rapidly as the information concerning Columbus.

Children need to be made aware of the various purposes for reading and the rates that are appropriate to each. They also must be taught that rate and purpose may vary within a particular assignment. For example, if a child was asked to compute the area of a rectangle and he or she did not know how, the child might "scan" the chapter to find the formula. Once he or she found it, the child might slow down and read the text at a slow, careful rate to interpret the formula and apply it to the word problem. Likewise, if asked to tell details about Lincoln's life, the child might read very rapidly over information that he or she already knew about Lincoln and then slow down and carefully read any new information that he or she encountered about the president.

One method of teaching children about reading rates and the advantages of using them appropriately is to present students with hypothetical situations and then have them discuss the appropriate reading rate. For example,

> You are to read this story about Washington to obtain an overview of the type of life lived by a person during the revolution. Your purpose is the overview, not specific facts.
>
> You are to read this section about Washington to determine what type of person he was. No other questions will be asked about the rest of the information given in the chapter.
>
> You are to read this story about Washington to determine how you feel the author of the textbook felt about Washington.

Assuming that the social studies text was very readable, students would probably read the first selection at a *rapid rate* because no retention of facts was required. The second selection should be read *very rapidly*, while *scanning* for details about Washington. The third situation ought to be read *very slowly* and *carefully* to analyze each word and to determine from word choice the tone and mood of the author as a clue to his or her feelings about Washington.

ASSESSMENT QUESTION

One technique for determining whether or not the child knows how to adjust rate to purpose is to ask a question such as "Read this paragraph for me and locate the part where Josita talks to her father. Now read this paragraph for one minute, then turn it over, and tell me what the 'gist' of the paragraph is." If the child adjusts his or her rate according to the different purposes, the child probably knows this skill.

USING A STUDY TECHNIQUE

This skill shows children how to organize their study strategies. For example, a child should be shown how to open his or her textbook and complete the following steps: (1) first skim over the materials in boldface; (2) read the questions at the end of the chapter; (3) finally go back and actually read the material. A number of such strategies have been designed by reading authorities. Most of these are activities that direct the child to follow a series of steps to approach study-type reading tasks in an organized manner. In most cases, the strategies include instructions to survey the material to be read and to formulate questions regarding the data before actually reading the material. The children are then shown how to assess their understanding of the content after reading the material. Often, these series of steps are given labels arranged in the form of an acronym that provides the child with a mnemonic device for remembering the steps and their order. The forerunner of most of the study techniques was the SQ3R method (survey, question, read, recite, and review) developed by Robinson in 1946. Others include Spache and Berg's (1966) PQRST (preview, question, read, summarize, and test) and Pauk's (1974) OK4R (overview, key ideas, read, recall, reflect, and review). The procedures, practices, and repetition that are built into study systems such as these lend themselves to the theoretical support of many of the sound principles of learning psychology.

The SQ3R method can be used to illustrate the strategy behind most of the other techniques. It also demonstrates how the student may use the strategy in cases in which the teacher has not set specific purposes for reading the chapter.

Students who are taught to use the SQ3R method are encouraged to follow these steps:

1. *Survey*—Take five to ten minutes to overview the chapter about to be read. Read introductory material, words in italics, words in large type, headings of various sizes that show the subordination and organization of ideas, and the final summary. Note: By providing them with "advance organizers" (Ausubel, 1960), this step helps students to understand the author's format and main points. Gestalt psychology views surveying as a procedure that facilitates the selection of relevant stimuli, making reading a process of integrating the relevant parts into a new whole.
2. *Question*—Look through the text again and formulate questions concerning what is to be read. Change subheadings and topic sentences into questions. For example, the heading "Damage Caused by Air Pollution" can be changed into the question, "What kind of damage is caused by air pollution?" Note: This step helps students to focus and add specific purpose to their reading by aiding them in selecting relevant stimuli, as does the survey step (Gestalt).
3. *Read*—Complete this step immediately after the questions are formulated and before going on to another section. Read thoroughly to find the answers to the questions and record the answers. Note: Recording may be in any form that allows students to review the answers to their questions without being able to see the answer when they read the question. For instance, students may divide their notebook page lengthwise and write the question on one side and the answer on the other, or they may write the question on one side of an index card and the answer on the opposite side. Some students find underlining the answer in the text or making marginal notes sufficient.
4. *Recite*—Immediately after reading a chapter, go back to your questions and try to answer them. Look away from the answer and try

to respond correctly to the question. If the answer is incomplete, reread appropriate sections of the chapter. Note: Skinnerian psychologists explain the worth of the recitation in terms of reward caused by immediate feedback. However, the amount of recitation needed will depend on the nature of the material read. If the material is not meaningfully involved (e.g., spelling words), almost all the study time needs to be spent on recitation. If the material is well organized and storylike (e.g., a literature selection), much less time needs to be spent on recitation.

5. *Review*—Take a second look at the chapter at a later time to gain new insights into the material. Self-test a few times between the first recitation and the final review for the examination. Possibly skim over the headings in the book to reformulate the outline of each chapter and then attempt to answer the questions. Reread the answers to be sure that nothing has been forgotten. All the material to be covered on the examination should be gone over during the final pre-examination review.

Ideally, these strategies should be an integral part of the teaching of all content areas and should be presented to the students along with a specific purpose for reading. For example, the teacher might determine that his or her purpose for asking students to read a chapter in the health book is to answer the question, "What is a communicable disease?"

Then the teacher might show the students the SQ3R study strategy by doing the following:

1. Teach the students to survey the chapter, looking for italics, headings, boldface, and other typographical clues that would assist them in locating sections concerning communicable diseases.
2. Show students how to transform typographical clues into questions that are related to their purpose of determining what a communicable disease is. For example, the title "Certain Kinds of Bacteria Are Harmful" might be made into the question "Can certain kinds of bacteria cause communicable diseases?"
3. Teach students how to go back and read the identified sections with their questions in mind and how to record their answers.
4. Instruct students to pause after reading all the material on diseases and try to recite the answers to all the questions that they formulated as well as to the original question. If they cannot, tell them to reread appropriate sections.
5. Teach students to review by repeating steps 1 through 4 if necessary and by surveying key points, reciting their answers, and rereading to judge their accuracy immediately prior to the examination.

Authorities differ on the age of the child at which these skills should be introduced. Ransom (1978) suggests that readiness for the SQ3R skills may be taught as early as kindergarten. She states, "As they look or listen only to picture books, we help them skim the pictures, ask questions, look at the picture more carefully, and recite meanings or summaries" (pp. 396–397).

Other authorities suggest that these sets of skills are best taught when the child reaches the intermediate level. ". . . students in fourth and fifth grades, and even third can learn to use the SQ3R when dealing with content-area materials. Students must be taught early that they must be active participants in reading and that they should read content-area materials differently from the way in which they read narrative material. Too often secondary-school teachers must overcome their students' concept that all reading is done essentially the same way and at the same rate. Instruction in the elementary grades can help prevent those" (Otto, Rude, and Spiegel, 1979, pp. 204–205).

The authors of this text believe that readiness for learning a study strategy may be presented as early as first grade. However, the teacher needs to carefully guide the child toward independent use of a study technique by directly telling the child to follow the steps that he or she has been previously led through by the teacher. For example, in first grade the teacher might state, "Let's see what we are going to read about today. Let's look at the pictures before we begin to read. Here's a picture of a lion, on the next page is a picture of a tiger, on the next page is a picture of a zebra. Where do we find all these animals? Where do you think this story takes place?"

Later in the school year, to help the child toward independence in his or her reading skills, the teacher might say, "Now you are going to read this story on your own. What's the first thing you should do? Yes, that's right, we should look over the story first to get an idea of what it is about before we read it."

If the child has been presented with study strategy in this manner, by the time he or she reaches the intermediate level, the child should be able to use an effective study strategy with little teacher guidance.

ASSESSMENT QUESTION

One technique for determining whether or not the child knows how to use a study technique is to ask him or her to complete a task such as the following: "Read this chapter through for me as though you were studying for a test." If the child uses a study technique, such as the SQ3R, then he or she probably knows this skill.

USING AIDS WITHIN BOOKS

Most books, and in particular, content area textbooks are written in a manner that helps the reader to interpret them. However, many times children are never taught how to use these aids effectively. These aids may be divided into six major categories: (1) using locational aids within books such as indexes, tables of contents, and chapter heading and subheadings, (2) using footnotes; (3) using glossaries; (4) using typographical aids to meaning such as bold print and italicized words; (5) using illustrations other than maps, graphs, and tables, and (6) using paragraph clues as aids to study.

The reading of maps, graphs, and tables located within books could also be considered as part of the study skill, "Using Aids within Books." However, in this text, reading maps, graphs, and tables has been considered under a separate heading under the rationale that a child can learn skills more easily if his or her focus is made more specific. This is not considered to be the "only way" to categorize the study skills, but rather is considered as one means to try and make the skills as manageable as possible in order to facilitate good teaching. Hence discussion of study skill number 6, "Using Maps, Graphs, and Tables" follows the presentation of study skill number 5, "Using Aids within Books."

Using locational aids within books includes the use of the index, table of contents, and chapter headings and subheadings.

An index may be used to locate information on a given topic. If students are to use an index successfully, they must be able to select key words that may be listed, locate the index, find the key words in the index, and then locate them as headings of information in the text. For example, a child might be trying to solve a word problem concerning the amount of square yards of carpet needed to carpet a room. The child would use a math book as a reference and locate information by finding the index and then looking for key entries such as *area* and *square.* The child might note any cross-entries, such as "See rectangle," and refer to them if necessary.

Tables of contents and chapter headings and subheadings may also be used to ascertain the location of textual information. For example, a child might want to know more about the metric system. The table of contents in his or her math book might indicate a chapter devoted to measurement. The child could then turn to this chapter and use its headings and subheadings to locate information on the metric system.

Using footnotes is a skill often neglected by the elementary age child. Footnotes are often found in literary materials in which reference to aspects mentioned within the text are explained. For example, a child reading a story about Scotland Yard might find the term explained in a footnote at the bottom of the page. A child who does not understand the purpose of footnotes may ask for help when the answer to his or her question is actually available already.

Using glossaries is similar to using dictionaries. However, the child needs to be made aware of the fact that only terms that the authors feel the reader might not know are described in a glossary. Hence the child should understand the convenience as well as the limitedness of this textbook aid. Often, children forget that their textbook contains a glossary. Perhaps the best technique for teaching children to use their glossaries is to give them assignments in which they are required to use it. For example, the term Scotland Yard defined in a footnote could be looked up in the glossary. A child might be asked questions such as "Is the definition the same in both places? Why do you think that the word may not be found in the glossary?"

Using typographical aids to meaning includes such devices as words in boldface and italicized terms. Children should be taught the words in boldface or italics are presented in such a fashion because the author of the textbook thought the words were particularly important. Children might be encouraged to look over their reading assignment for such words before they begin to actually read it. This type of previewing of important terms will help them to gain a general idea of what the material is about before they begin to read it.

The size of print can provide a good review or introduction to outlining skills. The child should know that the largest type usually represents a roman numeral, the next largest type a subheading under that roman numeral, and so forth. A good way to teach the importance of typographical aids is to ask the children to outline their textbook chapter using only size of type. Children can then be asked to compare subheadings on their outlines with the relative importance of ideas presented.

Content area textbooks contain many *illustrations* other than maps, graphs, and tables that children should use to help them interpret the material being read. A social studies text might contain a photograph of the skyline of Atlanta or a flow chart showing the steps taken to enable the Hoover Dam to supply electric power to Nevada. A health textbook might contain a drawing that shows the correct way to brush one's teeth. A math book often pictures geometric figures such as prisms and cylinders. Figure 4.1 is taken from a fourth grade science book and illustrates how electricity flows. The reader is also given an illustration of a car on a road so that the analogy can help him or her understand the flow of electricity. However, children need to have these illustrations pointed out to them and many times must have them explained. Too often, children ignore important illustrations when reference to them would enable them to better interpret the concept about which they have been reading.

Figure 4.1 Diagram to illustrate flow of electricity by comparing it with flow of traffic. Rockcastle et al., 1975.

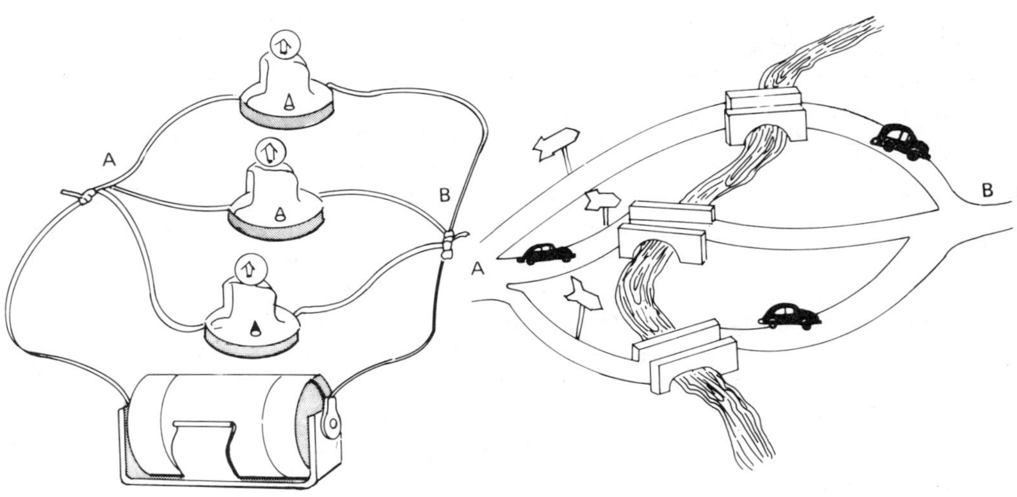

Using paragraph clues can aid the child in studying the material. Understanding the organization of paragraphs requires children to determine the author's organization so that they may more easily locate and understand what they read. Several types of paragraph organization have been described by a variety of authors. The four most common patterns include cause-effect, comparison-contrast, enumeration, and chronology. The following paragraphs illustrate these patterns, and key words for each pattern are delineated.

The following paragraph illustrates cause-effect organization.

Along streams and beaches you often can see rocks that have been worn and dissolved. Pebbles in streams usually become smooth and rounded. This is because they get bumped and scraped against one another by the running water. Pebbles on beaches are rounded by the motion of the waves. (Rockcastle et al., 1975, p. 28)

The key words in this paragraph that indicate a cause-effect organization are *because* and *by*. Other key terms that signal a cause-effect paragraph are *as a result, therefore, hence, for this reasons*, and *consequently*.

The following paragraph illustrates a comparison-contrast format.

Some valleys have very steep sides, and are called canyons or gorges. Others have sides that are not so steep. Many valleys are so nearly flat that people may live in one and never know it. (Rockcastle et al., 1975, p. 18)

Key terms in this paragraph type are *some*, *others*, and *many*. Other key words that give clues to this format are *like*, *although*, *however*, *but*, *on the other hand*, and *whereas*.

A third paragraph type is enumerative.

Does meat also bring you energy from the sun? When you eat meat, you are eating animals that ate plants, or animals that ate animals that ate plants. Beef cattle eat grass that stores energy from the sun. So do sheep. Pigs and chickens eat corn. Many fish eat insects that may have eaten parts of plants. So some of the sun's energy is stored in these animals. (Rockcastle et al., 1975, p. 166)

Sometimes paragraphs with enumerative formats are signaled by key words such as *additionally*, *also*, *besides*, and *another*.

A fourth common paragraph structure is chronological.

Valleys and basins. When it first falls, rainwater often washes over the whole surface of the ground. Then it usually runs into little gullies and from these into larger valleys. The water flows as brooks, creeks, and rivers along the bottoms of these valleys. All of these are streams. The water in most streams flows to the sea. (Rockcastle et al., 1975, p. 18)

Key signals in this format are when, first, and then. Other frequently used signal words are *in the meanwhile*, *by*, *eventually*, *next*, *after*, and *finally*.

Other paragraph structures that have been described include Karlin's transitional (1972), Pauk's problem-effect-solution (1974), and Smith's substantiated fact (1961).

One way to teach students to understand the organization of paragraphs is to locate paragraphs that provide examples of the formats just described. After reading the paragraphs in class, the students can analyze their structural formats. For example, after giving introductory instruction, the teacher might present a paragraph such as the following, taken from a fourth grade science book.

> Limestone or marble gets worn by pebbles and sand moved by water. Besides, it is also slowly dissolved by the water. Sometimes underground water even makes caverns in these rocks. (Rockcastle et al., 1975, p. 28)

After reading the paragraph, students should be able to (1) evaluate its format (cause-effect), (2) tell what is being acted upon (types of rocks), and (3) list the cause–effect relationships (rocks worn by pebbles, sand, and water).

ASSESSMENT QUESTION

One technique for determining whether or not the child knows how to use the aids within his or her textbook is to ask questions that would indicate use of textbook aids. For example, to assess a child's knowledge of italics, the teacher could ask, "Do you see any italicized words in the story? Why do you think they are there?"

USING MAPS, GRAPHS, AND TABLES

Maps, graphs, and tables are found extensively in all content areas in the elementary curriculum. For example, a unit on "Cities" might include a *map* of the United States showing where the densest population centers are located; a *chart* showing the cost of living in the various parts of the country; and a *graph* showing the amount of industry in selected cities. All these illustrations contain information about cities. However, each of these illustrations is used for different purposes, and children need to be made aware of these purposes to learn best how to interpret maps, graphs, and tables.

Maps involve an understanding of projections, distortions, distance, directions, latitude, and reading a key. Children learning how to read maps should first be able to understand the concepts of symbols. Even realistic symbols such as small pictures of people are still abstract and can be confusing to the young child. Furthermore, to use the grid to locate specific cities or to determine the distance from one place to the next, the child must also be taught appropriate locational and measurement skills.

Graphs require an understanding of how numbers can be pictured and that they may be shown in picture, circle, bar, or line formats. All contain similar elements and are designed to present information in a compact manner. Picture graphs should be taught first as they are the simplest to understand. Most young children are initially made aware of picture graphs through classroom charts. For example, each book read by a child might be represented by a small picture of a book placed on a piece of posterboard. Circle graphs are somewhat more difficult to understand, and their primary purpose is to show the parts into which a whole has been divided.

For example, the health text might picture the amount of food that should be eaten daily as indicated in Figure 4.2. Bar graphs are often used to

Figure 4.2. Circle graph.

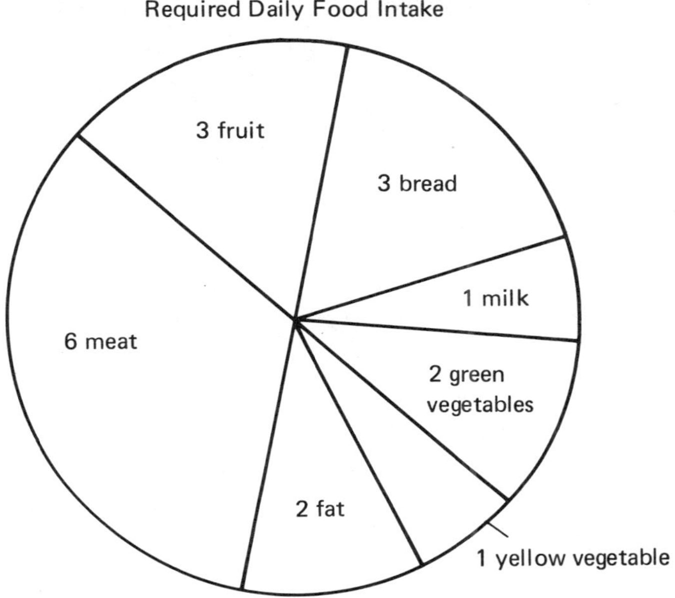

represent how one variable relates to another. For example, the science book might have a bar graph such as that in Figure 4.3 concerning the relationship

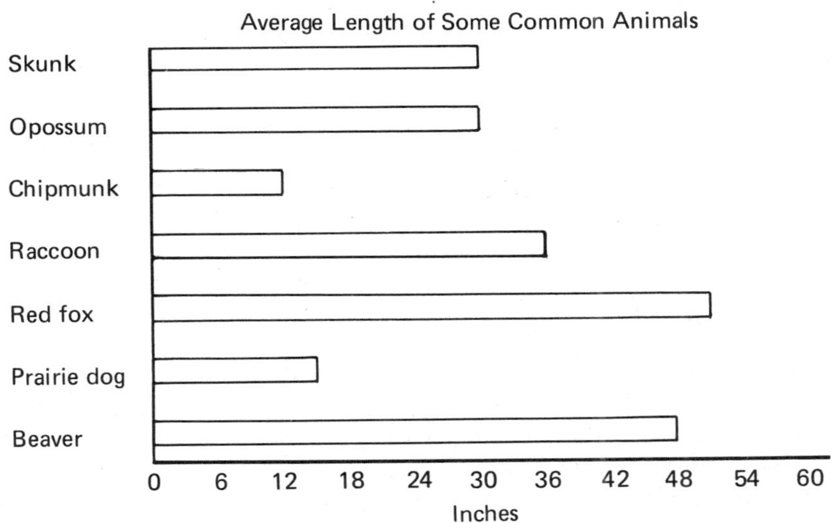

Figure 4.3. Bar graph. (Nicols et al., 1974.)

between certain animals and their lengths. Line graphs have the same purpose as do bar graphs but use points connected by lines to show relationships. An example of a line graph adapted from a fourth grade science book is given in Figure 4.4.

Figure 4.4. Line graph. (Adapted from Rockcastle et al., 1975, p. 221.)

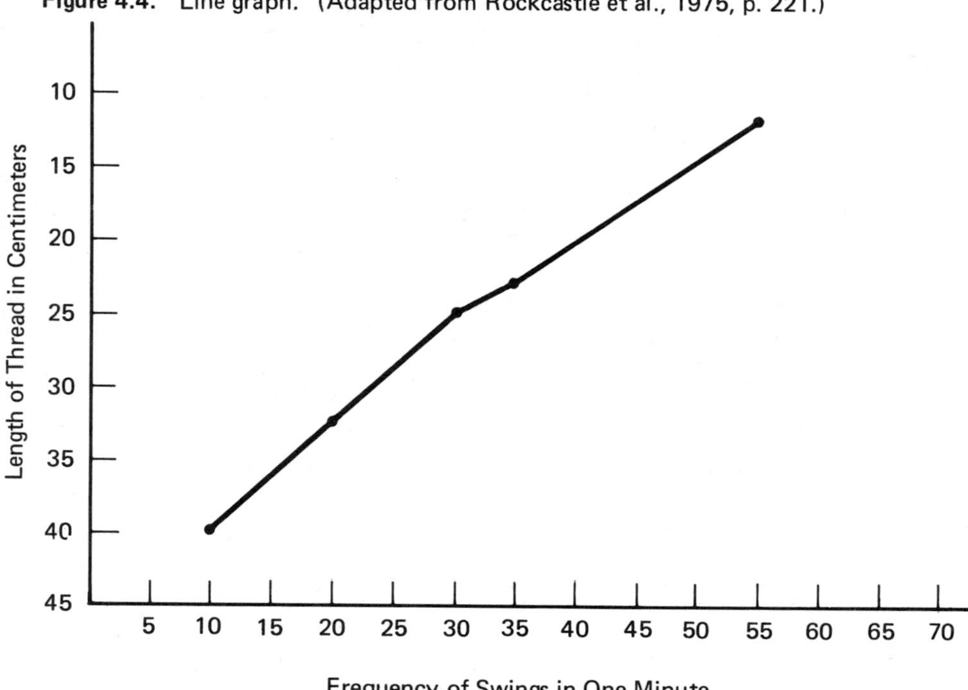

All graphs contain the same elements, and children should be given the following directions concerning all four types: (1) always read the titles, (2) look for the scale of measure or legend, (3) note what types of relationships are being presented, and (4) identify the relationships shown by the graph.

Tables are usually a listing of facts and information. They are helpful in showing comparisons between facts as well as in helping the reader to locate specific facts. Tables may be used to illustrate information that has three dimensions. For example, a table might contain (1) the names of cities, (2) temperature of each, and (3) the temperature of each over a given time period.

The approach to reading a table is similar to that of reading a graph. The following steps should be taken: (1) read the title; (2) look at the headings of the various columns and note any subheadings; (3) read the details in the vertical and horizontal columns of the chart; (4) begin to draw some conclusions about the information contained. Commonly used graphs include timetables and those used in describing the weather in various parts of the country.

ASSESSMENT QUESTION

One technique for determining whether or not a child knows how to read maps, graphs, and tables is to ask questions that require their use. For example, to assess a child's knowledge of map reading, the teacher could ask a question such as "Here is a map that I drew of Josita's trip to the cleaners. Can you show me the northwest corner of the town?"

USING LOCATIONAL AIDS IN THE LIBRARY

Locating information in the library requires using the *Reader's Guide*, the card catalogue, and the library call system.

The *Reader's Guide to Periodical Literature* is a guide that indexes by author and subject all the articles in each issue of more than one hundred magazines. Children should be made aware that many topics that they wish to locate are best described in magazines rather than in books. For example, any extremely current topic is usually not found in book format. Teachers can help children to learn the purpose for this index by giving children a list of contemporary events and asking the children to locate sources that describe those events. Even very young children can be shown how descriptions of a current movie that they want to see is not yet in books but can be found in magazines articles indexed in the *Reader's Guide*.

The *card catalogue* contains cards arranged alphabetically with material filed by author, subject, and title. Each card contains the full name of the author, publisher, copyright date, and a call number. Children can be introduced to the use of the card catalogue through helping the teacher to develop a card catalogue for books located in the classroom. Children could be encouraged to bring books from home that could be filed "temporarily" in the classroom card catalogue.

Children need to be shown that libraries have a *call system* to help readers locate materials quickly. Most libraries use either the Dewey decimal system or the Library of Congress system.

The Dewey decimal system classifies all books except fiction into ten main divisions. The classes are from 000 to 999 and are arranged on the shelves in this order. The Library of Congress system divides books into twenty classes and uses a combination of letters and numbers to identify the classes. Younger children are best introduced to only the system used in their school library. Children may be given meaningful practice using a classification system by helping them to place the books in their own classroom into the system used in the library.

ASSESSMENT QUESTION

One technique for determining whether or not a child knows how to use the locational aids in the library is to ask questions that require the child to use the locational aid. A sample question that could be used to assess the use of the card catalogue is "If you wanted to find the entire story about Josita, what type of card or cards could you look for in the card catalogue?"

USING REFERENCE MATERIALS

One of the most used portions in any library is the reference section. Children need to be shown that materials found in this section contain brief articles on almost everything. A partial list of reference materials includes dictionaries, encyclopedias, atlases, almanacs, yearbooks, directories, newspapers, magazines, *Reader's Guide to Periodical Literature*, thesaurus, audio-video recordings, and microfilm or microfiche copies of assorted materials.

Almost all reference materials have unique features, and hence each must be learned separately. Though the most commonly used references, that is, the telephone directory, the dictionary, and the encyclopedia, are usually introduced to the child early in the school curriculum, many older children, and even adults, do not know how to use these references correctly. For example, many persons fail to use the index that accompanies the "yellow pages" of the telephone directory. It is not uncommon to hear someone state "There is no taxi in this town" because the person looked for a heading of "taxi" rather than "transportation—public."

ASSESSMENT QUESTION

One technique for determining whether or not a child knows how to use reference materials is to ask a question such as "If you wanted to find out what city Josita lived in, where could you look to find more information about the cities in the United States that contained a lot of Spanish-speaking people?"

USING MATERIALS APPROPRIATE TO PURPOSE

Once students have located material relevant to a topic, they need to determine whether or not it is suitable for their purposes. Sometimes children will bring in an article from a "pulp" magazine as support for some research assignment in class. Discussion of why information in the article may not be appropriate to the given task can help the child to learn to select better sources for future research. The appropriateness of material depends on the nature of the task for which the material is being used and the needs of the reader.

To help children analyze appropriateness, the teacher should show the children how publication data and bibliographical information on the writer can help them to evaluate the material. For example, a book on first aid dated 1950 and written by a high school student would probably not be an appropriate source for writing a research paper about food poisoning. A more current book, containing the most modern treatment written by a medical doctor, would seem to be a much better resource.

One technique content area that teachers can use to aid their students in judging the appropriateness of materials for a given purpose is to ask each child to locate at least one reference on a given topic. If each child is given the same topic (e.g., "dinosaurs"), the purpose of each child's source can then be compared. The teacher could ask questions such as "What type of information does the book contain? Does a look at the index, table of contents, headings, and subheadings indicate that this book is a fantasy and not a factual account of dinosaurs? What is the expertise of the writer? Did the writer get this information through research? Is the writer a well-known archeologist? Is the writer a novelist hoping to make money?"

After the children have responded to these questions, the teacher can help the children match up the articles they have chosen with a set of purposes given to them by the teacher. Some of these purposes might include (1) building a scale model of a dinosaur for science class, (2) describing dinosaurs to a younger child, (3) satisfying a casual curiosity about dinosaurs, or (4) simply reading an interesting story about dinosaurs.

Another aspect of selecting materials appropriate to a given purpose is the needs of the reader. For example, a book intended to explain drug abuse to adults would not be appropriate for a fourth grade child being asked to make a report on aspirin. Likewise, a sixth grade child who reads above level should not select a second grade book on rocks for a presentation at the science fair. Children who read below grade level may have to use material that is written for another age group to complete their tasks independently. Sometimes this material may not be appropriate to the information needed by the poor reader. In such a case, the teacher might help the child locate materials about the given topic in texts designed particularly for the older child who does not read as well as he or she ought to.

ASSESSMENT QUESTION

One technique for determining whether or not a child knows how to select materials appropriate to his or her purpose is to ask questions such as "If you wanted to find out more about a cleaning shop, what type of book would you select?"

ORGANIZING INFORMATION

As the child progresses through school, the amount of information that he or she is expected to learn continues to increase. To facilitate learning the massive amount of facts being disseminated, the child needs to be shown how to organize the information in some meaningful manner. The skill of organizing information requires children to select an appropriate method of recording information that is pertinent to their purpose. For example, if a child wanted to know how snakes shed their skin and had located a paragraph that described the process in detail, the child might *outline* that paragraph. If the child was to retell the short story, "How the Leopard Got Its Spots," he or she might take notes on it first. If the child wanted to find out which containers were used to hold perishable foods and which containers were used to hold nonperishables, he or she might *classify* the information. If the child was interested in only the main points of the settlement of the disagreement between the Pilgrims and the Indians, he or she might *summarize* the story of the first Thanksgiving. If the child wanted to note similarities between respiration in fish and respiration in mammals, he or she might *make a chart* comparing the two.

Outlining is used when the reader wishes to note main points and details and to organize the order and relationships among them. For example, students providing a broad outline of a book might list the chapter headings and perhaps one or two main topics under each heading. If they were outlining a chapter, they might list the chapter subheadings and one or two important points under each. To outline a paragraph, they might state the main idea and the important details. An example of how a child might outline a paragraph from a "typical" science text could be:

Learning About Teeth

I. Appearance
   A. White
   B. Many Shapes
II. Texture
   A. Hard
   B. Sharp

Note-taking is used to record pertinent facts without necessarily attempting to order them. The format of the notes should vary according to the purpose for which they are being taken. For example, if the student's purpose were to list details, the notes might appear as follows.

Learning About Teeth

1. white
2. sharp
3. many shapes
4. hard

A comparison between the samples of note-taking and outlining illustrates the difference between the two skills. Since the purpose of the note-taking was simply to list details, the child did not attempt to impose much structure upon the notes. However, if his or her purpose in taking notes was to organize the information and order the relationships between details, he or she would probably have taken notes in an outline format. Outlining, by definition, implies ordering of information in a certain fashion; note-taking does not. Though notes are often taken in outline format, the structure of the notes is determined by purpose, and much note-taking is not in outline format. Examples of ways to teach several different types of note-taking formats are given in Chapter 15 of this text.

Classifying requires the reader to find items of information that can be placed into appropriate categories. For example, a child might read grocery ads and classify pertinent merchandise in groups labeled dairy products, produce, and paper products.

Summarizing, like note-taking and outlining, requires the selection of main points. The final product of summarizing is better not recorded as sentence fragments but, rather, as a complete sentence or as a paragraph made up of complete sentences. After reading the following paragraph, a student might summarize it as shown.

Messages are carried to the brain by sensory nerves. Special places on the brain receive sensory messages from all parts of the body. For example, messages travel over the sensory nerves from the eyes to the seeing or vision center. There are also centers for hearing, touching, tasting, and smelling. (Richmond and Pounds, 1977, p. 56)

Summary

The brain contains centers for all the senses.

Comparison and contrast is used by students when their purpose for reading is to note similarities (compare) and differences (contrast). Thus a child might read about carbohydrates and then produce notes like the following.

Name	*Contains Starch*	*Contains Little If Any Starch*
Rice	X	
Potato	X	
Milk		X
Apple		X

Children learn basic organizational skills as early as kindergarten. Most readiness materials require that children complete tasks such as "identify like objects by similar characteristics" or "organize articles by shape." *Note-taking* is usually the last skill to be taught and is seldom presented before the child reaches the intermediate grade levels.

ASSESSMENT QUESTION

One technique for determining whether or not a child knows how to organize information efficiently is to ask him or her to complete a task that requires an identified organizational skill. For example, for the skill of outlining, the teacher could ask, "Would you outline *Josita's Dancing Cleaners*?"

RECALLING INFORMATION

Children are constantly being asked to recall information either in formal testing situations or simply in response to some classroom questions or tasks.

There are certain things that a teacher can do to help a child absorb and retain information in a manner that can be easily recalled. Some of the most common strategies include the principles of association, recitation, repetition, and organization.

Association is the process that enables a child to relate new information to previously acquired knowledge. For example, if a child is being taught about friction, he or she might be reminded of the difference between walking on a wet street and a dry one. If the teacher can help the child associate the rain that causes slipping with a lubricant to reduce contact between objects, the child can remember the concept of friction more easily. Likewise, a child studying about events immediately prior to World War II could be reminded that the popular television show, "The Waltons," takes place during that same period in history. Young children should constantly be made aware of the association between what they are learning and past knowledge. For example, the first grade teacher might say, "Can you show me the word 'look'? Remember, it looks as if it has two eyes."

Recitation refers to the practice of responding to a question about something that one has read. This may be done silently or orally, and the questions may be constructed by the child as well as by the teacher or textbook author. For example, if a child is studying for a test in which he or she is expected to spell ten words correctly, he or she might look at each word and then close his or her eyes and spell it to himself or herself. This type of activity helps the child to remember by making him or her actively react to what he or she is trying to learn.

Repetition is the process of rereading and restudying something that someone is trying to remember. For example, a child might read a chapter in a social studies book three times to remember it. Another child might try to memorize by repeatedly saying the names of the first six presidents to himself or herself. All commercially published readers contain words that are repeated over and over to help the child learn them.

Some of the techniques for teaching *organization* have been discussed earlier in this chapter under the heading of "Organizing Information." This process can help a child to recall information by providing the child with a "chain of events" or an "entry point" to related data. For example, one child might have difficulty remembering the names of the nine planets in isolation. However, by listing them in sequential order from the sun outward, the child is able to visualize and recall the names of each of them. Another student might have difficulty remembering the names of various countries that colonized America. By drawing a chart that places each important explorer with a country, the child is able to recall the needed information. Reading material presented to young children is usually done in such a manner that the children can use organizational skills to help them remember important concepts. For example, a first grade child might be taught the names of various animals by being asked to place them in categories according to size or color.

All these principles are incorporated into the SQ3R strategy discussed earlier under the heading, "Using a Study Technique." The letter "S" (survey) provides *organization* and helps memory by giving the child a "whole" look at what is to be read before he or she reads it. The letter "Q" (question) requires that the child make up questions about what he or she is going to read and forces the child to make *associations* with previous knowledge that should be confirmed or rejected during the first "R" (reading) step. The second "R" (recite) emphasizes the principle of *recitation*, and the third "R" (review) emphasizes the principle of *repetition*.

One term commonly associated with recalling information is mnemonics, which means "aiding the memory" and usually refers to a variety of popularized memory-improvement techniques. Typically, the strategies include such devices as the use of acrostics (Every good boy does fine), rhymes (i before e except after c), verbal mediators (principal is your pal), and visual imagery (when reading about digestion try to picture the path of the food through the body). Research indicates that these mnemonic devices are helpful in educational settings (Higbee, 1979). All the devices include some or all four principles discussed earlier in this section of the text.

For example, a child might decide to use the acrostic HOMES to remember the Great Lakes. Hence the child would probably follow the following steps: Match each letter with the name of a lake (*association*). Say the name of each lake aloud as the child matches it with the appropriate letter (*recitation*). Repeat the recitation aloud several times until the child feels that he or she can remember it (*repetition*). Look at the word HOMES and attempt to recall which lake each letter stands for (*organization*).

Sometimes children know information but are unable to recall it in a manner acceptable to the teacher in a testing situation. Following directions incorrectly is a common cause for poor test performance. For example, a child who matches pairs of *synonyms* when asked to match *antonyms* will most likely fail that portion of the test. Teachers should teach children to follow test directions correctly before the children are asked to take the tests. For instance, the teacher might provide each child in class with the same copy of an old test. Each child could be told to read the directions silently and underline key words. Next children could confer with a neighbor to see if both underlined the same words. Then the teacher can summarize key words by listing them on the board. Words most likely to appear on an objective test include alike, antonym, synonym, eliminate, opposite, related, one best, not alike. Those commonly found on an essay test include clarify, compare, contrast, describe, discuss, explain, delineate, summarize, and list. Finally, the teacher might discuss how misunderstanding of any of the words could change a test answer so that it would be incorrect.

Children can be helped to recall information during a testing situation by asking them to follow certain strategies. Although there are many more, some of the most common include (1) when children come to a question that they cannot answer, they should skip it and go on to the next question (sometimes later test questions will stimulate *associations* that will help them to remember the correct answer); (2) children should read over all possible responses to a multiple-choice question before they mark their answer (often the first reasonable-sounding choice is not the correct one); (3) when children are writing an essay test, they should look over all the questions first and determine how much time to spend on each question before they begin to write any answers (sometimes children spend too much time on questions that they find difficult and never get to questions to which they know the answers); (4) before children begin to answer an essay question, they should make a short outline of what they want to say (the *organization* will help them to remember and will improve their ability to be understood by the person grading the test).

ASSESSMENT QUESTION

One technique for determining whether or not a child is able to recall information efficiently is to ask questions such as "Without looking back, can you tell me the name of Josita's father's shop? How were you able to remember that? Do you have a technique for helping you remember?"

EVALUATING INFORMATION

Evaluating information requires the child to determine the relevance, significance, and adequacy of information that he or she is reading. This skill contains all the aspects of the comprehension and study skills discussed earlier in this text. In particular, the child must be able to identify fact, fiction, opinion, and propaganda to react critically to what he or she has read. Although evaluation includes many facets, the most common are (1) the relationship between a child's personal feelings and what he or she is reading, (2) the purpose of an author in writing a given piece of material, (3) the completeness and accuracy with which a topic has been discussed, and (4) the literacy worth of what has been written.

Young children usually do not have the experience or knowledge to evaluate information too critically because much evaluation is based upon a comparison of what the child already knows with what has been read. However, young children can be made aware of certain factors that affect the relevance of the material. For example, a first grade child might be encouraged to describe his or her personal feelings concerning a character's actions. Then the teacher can discuss how one's own feelings affect whether one likes a certain story or not.

Older children can be asked to bring movie reviews to class. The children analyze the reviews for opinions expressed by the critic on the worth of the movie. After they locate the critic's opinion, they must state their own opinion of the worth of the movie. The teacher then asks the children to meet in small groups to compare the critic's values with their own. Discussion should focus on such aspects as the reader's own value system, code of ethics, and moral code. The teacher should point out that disagreement with the value system of another does not mean that one system is "right" and the other "wrong" but that it does affect how one views the worth and acceptability of a given piece of writing.

By becoming aware of the various purposes of authors, children can learn to evaluate information more critically. A child might be asked to read a passage about the care of pets in a health book and in a language arts book. The teacher can ask questions such as "Is the purpose of each author the same? Do you think that they both want to inform? entertain? persuade? Why would they want to do that? Which author is the closest to the truth? How do you know that?"

Children should be asked to determine the thoroughness, accuracy, and completeness of material to make a judgment on its validity. The teacher can help the children to learn this skill by requesting that they each locate an article that they believe to be factual. Each child then brings his or her article to class and is asked to trade with a partner. The partner reads the article and reacts to the thoroughness with which the author has covered the topic. For example, one youngster might bring in an article on new safety devices that have been developed for automobiles. The partner reads the article and asks questions such as "How does the author prove that the new device is any safer than existing ones? How many concrete details are given concerning the need for new safety devices? Who developed the safety devices and what is their expertise in the area? Does the authority include any irrelevant information?"

As children gain more maturity, they can learn to evaluate the literary worth of a given piece of material. For example, the fifth grade teacher might locate several descriptions of Huck Finn. One could be written by Samuel Clemens, one by an author who has adapted the novel to make it simpler, and one by a cartoonist who created a comic book version. The children could be asked to meet in small groups to compare the three versions. After a given amount of time, they should be asked to select which version they believe is of the "best literary quality." The teacher should help summarize the group evaluations by comparing such aspects as word choice and imagery that make one selection "better" than another.

ASSESSMENT QUESTION

Children may be assessed on their competence with this skill by being asked questions such as "For what purpose do you think the author wrote *Josita's Dancing Cleaners*? Do you think that the story presents an accurate view of a cleaning shop? Why or why not?"

Table 4.1 illustrates a question that might be asked to assess each of the twelve study skills.

SUMMARY

This chapter has presented the skills needed to use reading to learn. Although each study skill has been discussed and presented as it might be taught in reading class, special emphasis has been put on teaching children these skills while presenting them their content area lessons.

TABLE 4.1 The Study Skills of Reading

Skill	*Definition*	*Sample Assessment Question*
1. Following directions	Act in the manner recommended by printed or written instructions (trace, circle, etc.);	Draw one line under the name Josita and two lines under the name of her father
2. Scheduling time	organizing study sessions to allow time to complete needed tasks	Fill in the chart with the time you spent studying last night
3. Adjusting rate to purpose	Reading flexibly by first establishing a purpose for reading and then skimming, scanning, or carefully reading the material as required by the task	Read this paragraph and locate the part where Josita talks to her father; then tell me what she said
4. Using a study technique	Using a strategy such as SQ3R to gain as much information as possible	Read this chapter for me as though you were studying it for a test
5. Using aids within books	Using the index, table of contents, footnotes, chapter headings, glossaries, typographical aids, illustrations, and paragraph organization as clues to studying	Do you see any italicized words in the story? Why do you think they are there?
6. Using maps, graphs, and tables	Maps usually involve distance and directions; graphs require picturing numbers; tables are usually a listing of facts and information	Here is a map I drew of Josita's trip to the cleaners. Can you show me the northwest corner of the town?
7. Using locational aids in the library	Using the reader's guide, card catalogue, and the library call system	If you wanted to find the entire story about Josita, what type of card or cards could you find about it in the card catalogue?
8. Using reference materials	Using dictionaries, telephone books, encyclopedias, a *Who's Who*, a thesaurus, a world almanac, and the like	If we wanted to find out what country Josita lived in, where could we look to find more information about the various Spanish-speaking countries?
9. Using materials appropriate to purpose	Being able to match various reading materials with the needs of the reader	If you wanted to find out more about a cleaning shop, what type of book would you want to use to help you the most?
10. Organizing Information	Note-taking, classifying, summarizing, outlining, comparing, contrasting	Would you outline *Josita's Dancing Cleaners* for me?
11. Recalling information	Memorization; test taking	Without looking back, can you tell me the name of Josita's father's shop? How did you remember that?
12. Evaluating information	Determining the relevance, significance, and adequacy of the information	For what purpose do you think the author wrote *Josita's Dancing Cleaners*? Do you think the story presents an accurate view of a cleaning shop? Why or why not?

Reference and Bibliography

Aaron, Ira, David, Charles, and Schelly, Joan. *Flying Hoofs.* Glenview, Ill.: Scott, Foresman and Company, 1978.

Ausubel, D. P. "The Use of Advance Organizers in the Learning and Retention of Meaningful Verbal Material." *Journal of Educational Psychology* 51 (Oct. 1960): 267-272.

Cooper, David, Warnicke, Edna, Ramstad, Peggy and Shipman, Dorothy. *The What and How of Reading Instruction.* Columbus, Ohio: Charles E. Merrill Publishing Company, 1979.

Dedrick, Nelle, Lindop, Esther, Tiegs, Ernest, and Adams, Fay. *Our People.* Lexington, Mass.: Ginn and Company, 1979.

Dedrick, Nelle, Lindop, Ester, Tiegs, Ernest and Adams, Fay. *Our People: Workbook.* Lexington, Mass.: Ginn and Company, 1979.

Dillner, Martha, and Olson, Joanne. *Personalizing Reading Instruction in the Middle, Junior, and Senior High Schools.* New York: Macmillan Publishing Co., Inc., 1977.

Evertts, Eldonna, Junt, Lyman, Weiss, Bernard, and Bartlett, Elsa. *People Need People.* New York: Holt, Rinehart and Winston, 1973.

Fry, E. E. *Reading Instruction for Classroom and Clinic.* New York: McGraw-Hill Book Company, 1972.

Garland, Colden. *Developing Competence in Teaching Reading.* Dubuque, Iowa: William C. Brown Company, Publishers, 1978.

Higbee, Kenneth. "Recent Research on Visual Mnemonics: Historical Roots and Educational Fruits." *Review of Educational Research* 49 (Fall 1979): 611–629.

Indrisano, Roselmina. "Reading: Specialized Skills" in Pose Lamb and Richard Arnold, eds., *Reading: Foundations and Instructional Strategies.* Belmont, Calif: Wadsworth Publishing Co., Inc., 1976, pp. 419-431.

Johnson, M. E. "The Vocabulary Difficulty in Content Subject in Grade Five." *Elementary English* 29 (May 1952): 277-280.

Karlin, R. *Teaching Reading in High School.* 2nd ed. Indianapolis: The Bobbs-Merrill Co., Inc., 1972.

Nichols, Eugene, Anderson, Paul, Dwight, Frances, Flournoy, Frances, Kalin, Robert, Schluep, John, and Simon, Leonard. *Holt School Mathematics.* New York: Holt, Rinehart and Winston, 1974.

Otto, Wayne, Rude, Robert, and Spiegel, Dixie Lee. *How to Teach Reading.* Menlo Park, Calif.: Addison-Wesley Publishing Co., Inc., 1979.

Pauk, W. *How to Study in College.* 2nd ed. Boston: Houghton Mifflin Company, 1974.

Ransom, Grayce. *Preparing to Teach Reading.* Boston: Little, Brown and Company, 1978.

Richmond, Julius B., and Pounds, Elenore. *You and Your Health.* Glenview, Ill.: Scott, Foresman and Company, 1977.

Robinson, F. P. "Study Skills for Superior Students in Secondary School." *The Reading Teacher* 15 (September 1961): 29–33, 37.

Rockcastle, Verne, Salamon, Frank, Schmidt, Victor, and McKnight, Betty. *STEM: Elementary School Science.* Menlo Park, Calif.: Addison-Wesley Publishing Co., Inc., 1975.

Ruddell, Robert. *Reading Language Instruction: Innovative Practices.* Englewood Cliffs, N.J.: Prentice-Hall, Inc., 1974.

Serra, M. C. "The Concept Burden of Instructional Materials." *Elementary School Journal* 53 (May 1953): 508-512.

Smith, H. K. "Research in Reading for Different Purposes." in J. Allen Figurel, ed. *Changing Concepts of Reading Instruction: Proceedings of the International Reading Association. New York:* Scholastic Book Services, 1961, pp. 119–122.

Spache, G. D., and Berg, P. D. *The Art of Efficient Reading.* New York: Macmillan Publishing Co., Inc., 1966.

Walborn, Marla. *Josita's Dancing Cleaners.* New York: Macmillan Publishing Co., Inc., 1975.

Self Check 4.3
Study Skills

The following questions are designed to help the participant assess his or her competence on the first four objectives stated at the beginning of this chapter. Although every effort has been made to make the self-check questions comprehensive, participants should remember that they are held responsible for meeting the objectives as stated at the beginning of this chapter.

1. Objective 1. Define the term "study skills."
2. Objective 2. Define, differentiate among, and give examples of the twelve study skills presented in this chapter.
3. Objective 3. Discuss the relationship between the age of the child and the type and amount of study skills that may be taught most effectively to him or her.
4. Objective 4. Describe an assessment technique for each of the twelve study skills.

Experiences 4.4
Study Skills

Chapter 4
Experience 1

Objective

During this experience, the participant will locate, describe, and react to strategies for teaching the study skills.

Activity and Assessment Guide

1. Several means for teaching each of the study skills are located in Chapter 15 of this text. Space is given for you to skim those strategies and then briefly jot down at least two ways in which to teach four of the study skills. The strategies that you select should be appropriate to the needs of the children with whom you will most probably be working. If you have located strategies from another source, you may use them instead of the ones located in Chapter 15.

   a. Following Directions

      (1) ______________________________

      (2) ______________________________

   b. Scheduling Time

      (1) ______________________________

      (2) ______________________________

c. Adjusting Rate to Purpose

(1) ______________________________

(2) ______________________________

d. Using a Study Technique

(1) ______________________________

(2) ______________________________

e. Using Aids within Books

(1) ______________________________

(2) ______________________________

f. Using Maps, Graphs, and Tables

(1) ______________________________

(2) ______________________________

g. Using Locational Aids in the Library

(1) ______________________________

(2) ______________________________

h. Using Reference Materials

(1) ______________________________

(2) ______________________________

i. Using Materials Appropriate to Purpose

(1) ______________________________

(2) ______________________________

j. Organizing Information

(1) ______________________________

(2) ______________________________

k. Recalling Information

(1) ______________________________

(2) ______________________________

l. Evaluating Information

(1) ______________________________

(2) ______________________________

* 2. Look over the skills that you have selected and briefly describe why you selected the skills you did. ______________________________

____

* 3. Select one of the strategies that you have chosen and describe at least two ways in which it is appropriate to the age of the child with whom you will most probably be working. ______________________________

____

* 4. State what you believe to be the significant implications of this experience for the classroom teacher. ______________________________

____

*See Chapter 1, Experience 1 for explanation of the asterisk.

Chapter 4
Experience 2

Objective

During this experience, the participant will design and teach a lesson on one of the study skills.

Activity and Assessment Guide

1. What skill do you intend to teach? Be specific, for example, "skimming" technique of study skill 3, adjusting rate to purpose.__________

   ____

2. Describe the assessment activity that you plan to use before teaching the lesson so that you can assess the child's knowledge of the skill.

   ____

   ____

3. Describe the techniques that you intend to use to instruct the students in this skill. ______________________________

   ____

   ____

   ____

   ____

4. Design a lesson including your techniques and attach that lesson plan to this sheet.
5. Describe the assessment activity that you plan to use after teaching your lesson so that you can assess the student's knowledge of that skill.

____

____

* 6. Write a brief summary of your feelings about the child's reaction toward this strategy and the amount of learning that took place. ________

____

____

* 7. State what you believe to be the significant implications of this experience for the classroom teacher. ____________________

____

____

*See Chapter 1, Experience 1 for explanation of the asterisk.

Part Two
Assessing Reading Skills

Chapter 5 Determining Students' Reading Levels

Objectives 5.1

On completion of this chapter, the participant should be able to

1. Given any grade level one through six, state why the teacher ought to diagnose the reading level of each member of the class.
2. Describe two factors that complicate the teacher's task of choosing reading materials on the appropriate difficulty level.
3. Describe the way in which a classroom teacher might make the use of the results of a standardized reading survey test. What advantages and limitations do standardized reading survey tests have that would cause them to be used in this manner?
4. Describe the way in which a classroom teacher might make use of the results of a word list test. Delineate the advantages and limitations that word list tests have that cause them to be used in this manner.
5. Identify and correctly transcribe the oral reading errors made by a child.
6. Accurately score reading of the oral portion of an informal reading inventory and a set of answers to the questions following silent reading comprehension selection.
7. Given a set of test scores, state the student's instructional level.
8. Describe one method by which a teacher might administer an informal reading inventory.
9. Describe the way in which a classroom teacher might make use of an informal reading inventory. Delineate what advantages and limitations informal reading inventories have that would cause them to be used in this manner.

10. Prepare a given selection for use as a cloze passage.
11. Evaluate the construction, administration, and scoring of a cloze passage.
12. Describe the way in which a classroom teacher might make use of the cloze testing procedure. What advantages and limitations does the cloze procedure have that would cause it to be used in this manner?

Experiences 1 and 2 extend Chapter 5 with these objectives:

13. The participant will administer, score, and interpret the results of an informal reading inventory.
14. The participant will administer, score, and interpret the results of a cloze procedure.

Information Given 5.2
Determining Students' Reading Levels

Children vary widely in their abilities to read. At any grade level, the child who has the most developed reading skills will read significantly better than the child who has the least developed reading skills.

If a class of grade three children were tested, their scores would probably appear similar to those in Table 5.1, which indicates the grade level at which each child reads. According to this test, Blanche, whose name appears first on the list, made the highest score in class. Her score of 6.3[1] (sixth grade, third month) indicates that she has the ability to function in reading material for grade six students. Ruth scored on the 1.4 (first grade, fourth month) level, lower than any of her classmates. Her score indicates that she has the necessary reading skills to learn from reading material designed for first grade students.

A careful study of Table 5.1 indicates that although the majority of the children in the class read on grade level, a few children read well above or well below that level. Thirteen children appear to be reading at the grade level in which they are placed. These children are functioning on the grade three level.

Table 5.2 shows the range of reading abilities that might typically be found at all grade levels between grades one and six. A wide range of reading ability is evident at every level. If the least competent reader in grade one is reading at a grade one level and the most competent reader is reading at a grade three level, then the difference is two years. This disparity of reading levels that differentiates the child with the highest score from the child with the lowest score increases throughout the grades until by grade six variances of ten or more years are not uncommon.

[1]The figure preceding the *period* denotes grade. The figure following the *period* denotes the number of months the child has completed in that grade.

TABLE 5.1 Reading Levels for a Grade Three Class

Name	*Grade Scores*
Blanche	6.3
Starlet	6.1
Alice	5.2
Rita	4.8
Myrna	4.6
William	4.3
Carol	3.9
Michael	3.9
Kingsley	3.9
Gordon	3.7
Lewis	3.5
Sanford	3.5
Jay	3.3
Jerry	3.3
Robert	3.3
Louis	3.2
Dale	3.2
Charles	3.1
John	3.0
Armstrong	2.8
Heather	2.4
Sigworth	2.2
Lionel	2.1
Kenneth	1.9
Ruth	1.4

This range of reading abilities indicates why the teacher who wishes maximum growth in reading for children must use materials on a variety of reading levels. The instructor who is assigned to teach the children in the grade three class portrayed in Table 5.2 will need to instruct from materials ranging from the grade one through grade five levels.

TABLE 5.2 Typical Range of Reading Ability for Each Grade Level

Grade	*Reading Level for Child with Highest Score*	*Reading Level for Child with Lowest Score*	*Difference (in years)*
1	3	1	2
2	4	1	3
3	5	1	4
4	7	1	6
5	9	1	8
6	11	1	10

Teachers who instruct from materials that are not on a child's reading level decrease their chances for success, particularly when the materials used are above the child's reading level. The child who can't understand the material fails to progress. If a child is reading at first grade level and is being instructed from a grade three book, the materials will simply be too difficult for him or her with his or her insufficient background of reading skills.

When material is used that is below a child's reading level, the child may profit from being exposed to the material but will likely learn few new skills. For example, if a child is reading at a grade five level but is being instructed from a grade three book, even though he or she might enjoy the stories, maximum growth of that child's reading skills will not be facilitated. Therefore, it is incumbent upon the teacher to discern the reading level of each child who is being instructed so that materials at the child's reading level are selected, thereby encouraging rapid progress.

Unfortunately, even after the teacher has correctly determined the student's reading level, the task of choosing material at this appropriate level may be complicated by nonstandardized labeling procedures. That is, even though two books might bear the same grade level designation, they often vary widely in reading difficulty. Furthermore, the difficulty levels of material found within any one instructional book may be diverse. Studies have found that books leveled for use in grade three contained material ranging in difficulty from the grade two to the grade six level (Bradley and Ames, 1978; Eberwein, 1979). Thus teachers must exercise extreme care in the selection and use of classroom materials.

METHODS FOR FINDING THE STUDENT'S INSTRUCTION LEVEL

To find the appropriate reading instruction level for each child, the teacher needs to use all available information. This information may include the teacher's own records of observations of the child's class performance in relation to reading as well as data pertinent to reading instruction recorded in the student's permanent file. In addition, the teacher may employ procedures designed specifically to measure reading achievement such as standardized reading survey tests, word list tests, informal reading inventories, placement tests, and the cloze procedure.

STANDARDIZED READING SURVEY TESTS

Gronlund (1976) defines a standardized test as one that has a fixed set of test items, that has specific directions for administration and scoring, and that has been given to representative groups of individuals for the purpose of establishing norms. Norms are the average scores made by members of representative groups at various age and grade levels that make it possible to compare one person's test score with those of other individuals whose characteristics are known. Thus it is possible to administer a standardized reading test to a student in the sixth grade and to compare his or her performance with that of a typical sixth grader in the norm population (Dillner and Olson, 1977).

Standardized reading survey tests are designed to give an overview of the general reading ability of the student. They are usually administered in a group situation and take about one class session (i.e., forty-five to fifty minutes) to complete. Results are ordinarily given in terms of two or three subskills, which include measures of vocabulary, comprehension, accuracy, and sometimes rate (Dillner and Olson, 1977).

Some frequently used standardized reading survey tests may be purchased from major publishing companies and include the *Gates–MacGinitie Reading Tests* (1972), the *Iowa Tests of Basic Skills* (Hieronymus and Lindquist, 1974), and the *Metropolitan Achievement Test* (Durost, Bixler, and Wrightstone, 1971).

Advantages and Limitations of Standardized Reading Survey Tests

Advantages of standardized reading survey tests include the following: (1) They allow teachers to compare, through the use of norms, the achievement levels of the students with those of other pupils of the same age or grade level. (2) They are objective. The teacher's personal feelings toward a student are not reflected in the test scores. (3) The teacher, having limited resources, may benefit from the research that has resulted in establishing procedures for the administration, scoring, and interpretation of the scores of standardized reading survey tests (Dillner and Olson, 1977).

Limitations of standardized reading survey tests include the following: (1) Grade level norms indicate only a rough approximation of the level on which the pupil should be instructed (Bradley and Ames, 1978). Thus, the grade level designated by the results of a standardized test may actually be too high or too low for instructional purposes (Burgett and Glaser, 1973). (2) While tests do indicate the number of errors made, most do not reveal the cause of the error. Hence, the teacher must be aware that standardized reading survey test scores may not be entirely attributable to a child's ability to read. For example, a student's test-taking skills, vision, hearing, general physical condition, or emotional state at the time of testing may cause the child to make errors and thus are factors that need to be considered. (3) Teachers are often limited by school policy as to which standardized tests they may administer. Usually, school systems have a plan for administering specific tests in given grades and do not encourage teachers to administer other standardized tests of their choice.

Uses for Standardized Reading Survey Tests

The classroom teacher may find standardized reading survey tests useful in a number of ways that include (1) providing an estimate of the range of reading abilities in a given class (Strang, 1967), (2) identifying students in need of special reading instruction (Strang, 1967), and (3) providing a source of information regarding the approximate reading level of each child.

WORD LIST TESTS

Word list tests are reading tests that assess the student's ability to read words presented in lists. Such tests measure the child's sight word skills, phonic skills, and morphemic analysis skills. However, they do not test other word identification skills, such as the use of context clues or dictionary usage. Likewise they do not assess comprehension skills.

Whether commercially published or teacher made, word list tests are comprised of a series of graded word lists usually ranging from grade one to grade twelve. The list on each level might contain as few as ten or as many as twenty words. The test is administered by asking the student to orally read the lists in succession beginning at a level at which the teacher expects the child to make few errors. The teacher stops the student when his or her errors exceed the amount designated as a cutoff point.

Typical of word list tests are teacher-made tests, which the teacher constructs by randomly selecting words from the new vocabulary presented at various levels of the intructional material from which the child may be instructed, and commercially published tests such as those by Ekwall (1979), Silvaroli (1976), and Jastak (1965).

Word list tests are used to find an approximate level at which to begin administering other reading tests. Although some systems have been devised for determining the instructional reading level based on the results of a word list test (LaPray and Ross, 1969, Froese, 1976), most educators agree that word list tests alone should not be used to determine the level at which a child should be instructed (Ekwall, 1979; Marzano et al., 1978; Pikulski, 1974).

INFORMAL READING INVENTORIES

In addition to standardized reading survey tests and word list tests, informal reading inventories may also be used by teachers to assess the reading levels of their pupils (Betts, 1946). Although specific individual formats and details of administration may vary widely, all informal reading inventories consist of a series of graded reading selections ranging from the least difficult to the most difficult material that the pupil being tested might be expected to read. Much like the word list test, the informal reading inventory is administered by asking the student to read material on progressively more difficult levels until their amount of reading errors exceeds the number determined as a cutoff point. Thus, an informal reading inventory may be administered by asking a child to read the first selection on any given level aloud and to read the second selection to himself or herself. After having read the second reading selection, the child is asked to answer the comprehension questions that follow. Following this, the teacher may read selected passages aloud, and the student may answer the questions that follow. This procedure is continued until the level that is appropriate for the child can be determined from his or her responses.

Scoring an Informal Reading Inventory

A student's total number of oral reading errors may be simply listed by the teacher, or the teacher may record each student's incorrect responses on the actual oral reading selection, if one copy per student is available. Of course, any system that is convenient may be used. A typical method of marking errors, based on Gray's (1963) system, is the following:

1. *Word added:* Write in the inserted word above the place where it occurred (cried ^loudly all).
2. *Word omitted:* Draw a circle around the omitted word ((young)).
3. *Word changed:* Write the change above the intended word (puppy ^dog).
4. *Teacher pronounced word:* Write the letter "T" above the word that the teacher pronounced for the student after the student hesitated for five to ten seconds (night ^T).

The following sentence further illustrates Gray's marking system:

The (young) puppy ^dog cried ^loudly all night ^T.

When scoring the informal reading inventory, the teacher should be aware that the following are not to be counted as errors: (1) *mispronunciations* due to dialect or individual speech patterns (Goodman and Burke, 1973); (2) *spontaneous corrections* in which the child corrects himself or herself immediately (Gray, 1963); (3) the second and succeeding errors on the same word; and (4) mispronunciations of proper nouns or very rare words. Lack of fluency or extremely poor rate are not counted as errors but should be noted as weaknesses since either of these may invalidate the results of an informal reading inventory.

After the student has either orally or silently read a selection or has listened to it being read to him or her, the child is asked to answer the comprehension questions following the selection. The student is given credit for a correct answer for any response that appears to adequately answer the question. Half-points may be given so that a student could answer five and a half out of ten questions correctly and thus obtain a score of 55 per cent.

Interpreting the Results of an Informal Reading Inventory

The four levels of reading that can be determined from the results of an informal reading inventory are the independent level, the instructional level, the frustration level, and the capacity level (Betts, 1946).

The *independent level* is that level at which the child can read material with no teacher guidance. The highest level at which the child reads at least 99 per cent of the words correctly and answers at least 90 per cent of the comprehension questions correctly represents the independent level. Fluency and rate should be excellent. This is the level at which most of the child's recreational reading materials should be written.

The *instructional level* is that level at which the child can read material with teacher guidance. The highest level at which the child reads correctly at least 95 per cent of the words in the reading selections read orally and answers at least 75 per cent of the comprehension questions asked following oral or silent reading of the selection correctly represents the instructional level. Fluency and rate of oral reading and rate of silent reading should be acceptable. The instructional level is usually about one year above the independent level and is the level at which most of the materials used to instruct the child in reading should be written.

The *frustration level* is that level at which the child cannot read material even with teacher guidance. The lowest level at which the child reads fewer than 95 per cent of the word correctly or answers fewer than 75 per cent of the comprehension questions correctly represents the frustration level. Material written on a more difficult level than the child's instructional level may be considered to be on the child's frustration level. Children should not be required to read material written on their frustration level.

The *capacity level* is the highest level at which students can understand material that is read aloud to them. The highest level at which the child can answer 75 per cent of the comprehension questions correctly after the selection has been read to him or her represents the capacity level. Instructional materials written at this level may be used only if they have been adapted into a format to which the student will listen. This level is sometimes considered to be the student's "potential" reading level, as the student understands the words and concepts but is unable to recognize them in print.

Varying the Administration of an Informal Reading Inventory

Because the informal reading inventory is not a standardized test, there is much room for variation in administration. In addition, although it is labeled as an individual test, some of the administration may be done in a group situation. Means for both a group administration and an individual administration are described in the following paragraphs.

Group Administration of an Informal Reading Inventory.

Oral Reading: In the oral reading situation, the teacher often gives the class an assignment that frees him or her for the entire period. Then the teacher asks students to come to the teacher's desk individually and read the grade level passage aloud (i.e., if the class were grade six, the passage read would also be grade six). As each student reads, the teacher tallies all errors. If the student is able to read the passage successfully, the teacher asks the child to read progressively more difficult passages until the child reaches the level at which he or she makes more than 5 per cent errors. Conversely, if the student is unable to read the grade level selection successfully, the teacher asks him or her to read progressively less difficult selections until a level is found at which he or she makes fewer than 5 per cent errors (Dillner and Olson, 1977).

Silent Reading: After the teacher has determined the oral reading levels of all the students, he or she gives each student the passage and comprehension questions correlated with the highest level at which the student made less than 5 per cent oral errors. That is, if the student's oral reading level is grade six, the student is asked to read a grade six passage and then answer in writing the questions that follow. If the student is able to answer the questions successfully, the teacher gives the student more difficult selections until the student reaches the point at which he or she is unable to answer 75 per cent of the questions successfully. Conversely, if the student is unable to answer 75 per cent of the comprehension questions accurately, the teacher gives the student selections and questions on progressively easier grade levels until the student reaches the level on which he or she can answer 75 per cent of the comprehension questions successfully (Dillner and Olson, 1977).

Individual Administration of an Informal Reading Inventory

Oral Reading: Administering an informal reading inventory to individuals is very similar to administering it to groups. However, the teacher often starts at a level about two grades below the one at which the student is expected to function or begins at the one at which he or she thinks the student has a reasonable chance for success. Then the teacher gives the student progressively harder passages until the student reaches the level at which he or she makes more than the allowable number of errors. For example, if the student were a sixth grader who appeared to be at grade level, the teacher would begin with the fourth grade level passage. If the student were a fifth grader who appeared to be at the third grade level, the teacher would begin with the first grade level passage (Dillner and Olson, 1977).

Silent Reading: The student is first given the silent reading passage that is one level below the highest level oral passage that he or she read successfully. Then the teacher gives the student progressively easier or harder passages until the teacher can determine the highest level at which the student makes more than the allowable number of errors when he or she responds orally to the comprehension questions asked orally by the teacher. This procedure is continued until the appropriate instructional level can be determined from the child's responses (Dillner and Olson, 1977).

Listening: The teacher reads to the student the silent reading passage that is one level above the highest level silent passage at which he or she answered with an allowable number of errors. The student then attempts to answer orally the comprehension questions asked orally by the teacher. This procedure is continued with easier or harder passages until the teacher can determine the highest level at which the student makes more than the allowable number of errors. Through assessment of the student's listening skills, the teacher may determine the student's "capacity" level or that level at which the student is capable of reading, providing that the student had no difficulties with word identification.

Advantages and Disadvantages of Teacher-Made and Commercially Published Informal Reading Inventories

Teacher-Made Informal Reading Inventories

Informal reading inventories may be constructed by teachers or other school personnel using materials from which children in their class or school will be instructed. The principal *advantage* of a teacher-made informal reading inventory is that it is based on the instructional materials to be used and as such is an excellent indicator of the book in which the child should be placed (Pikulski, 1974). The *disadvantages* of such an inventory are that a teacher who is inexperienced in test construction might select a passage that is not typical for that book or might design comprehension questions that are too easy or too difficult for children reading on that level.

Commercially Published Informal Reading Inventories

Examples of commercially published informal reading inventories available include the *Indiana Test of Basic Skills* (Gallant, 1975), the *Classroom Reading Inventory* (Silvaroli, 1976), the *Analytical Reading Inventory* (Woods and Moe, 1977), and the *Ekwall Reading Inventory* (1979). The major *advantage* of commercially published informal reading inventories is that they usually have been field tested and are therefore less prone to error. The major *disadvantage* of commercially published inventories is that they are not necessarily based on the materials that are to be used in the classroom. Thus, a discrepancy may exist between the results of these tests and the actual appropriate level of materials. For example, because of nonstandardized labeling procedures discussed previously in this chapter, the results of the commercial informal reading inventory may indicate that the child should be instructed from fourth grade materials, while the correct level of the given set of material to actually be used may be third grade.

An informal reading inventory has been included in Appendixes A, B, C, and D of this book. Detailed suggestions for administering, scoring, and interpreting the results of this test are given in the following section in the context of Miss Plum's grade four class.

Miss Plum's Testing Procedure

Miss Plum is a bright, creative, grade four teacher. It is the end of September and school has been in session three weeks. Miss Plum knows that she will have to select basal reader materials for her class, so she has decided to find the reading level of each class member.

Preparation of Test Materials for Oral Reading

Miss Plum locates Appendixes A and B, which contain the necessary materials for testing oral reading. She discovers that Appendix A, "Teacher's Copy of Oral Reading Selections," is ready for use and that each level includes instructions for administration and scoring. She then proceeds to prepare Appendix B, "Pupil's Copy of Oral Reading Selections," for use by tearing it from the book along the perforated line. She now has a copy of the test to hand to the student.

Administration of Oral Reading Selections

Miss Plum takes each child to a quiet place in the classroom and asks the child to read aloud. She uses any information she has such as the child's age, grade placement, or school history to decide the level at which the child should begin the test. The first child whom Miss Plum tests is David. She knows only that David is in grade four and that, from classroom observation, he appears to be an average student. She asks him to read the grade four selection first. The second child whom Miss Plum tests is Peter. From a perusal of school records and having worked with Peter for the last three weeks, Miss Plum is aware that Peter is a weak reader. She asks Peter to begin with the 3:1 (grade three, first semester) selection. The third child whom Miss Plum tests is Dan. Again, from observation and school records, Miss Plum believes that Dan is an above-average student. She has Dan begin reading on a fifth grade level.

As each child reads, Miss Plum listens very carefully to ascertain whether the child omits, adds, or mispronounces any words—all of which are counted as errors. Miss Plum does not include as errors spontaneous corrections in which the child corrects himself or herself immediately, mispronunciations of proper nouns or very rare words, or words that the child pronounces "differently" due to speech or dialectic differences. If a child cannot say a word, Miss Plum tells the child the word and, of course, counts that word as an error. If a child misses the same word several times, Miss Plum scores this as only one error.

When David reads, he makes four errors on the first selection that he was asked to read—grade four. Because this is fewer than the five errors allowed, Miss Plum then tests him on the next most difficult selection—that equal in difficulty to the average grade five reader. On this selection, David makes six errors—more than the allowed 5 per cent. Thus, Miss Plum is led to believe that, on the basis of this test, David's oral reading score is grade four. Table 5.3 shows David's oral reading score and the scores of the other children tested.

Miss Plum then proceeds to test Peter. She asks Peter to read the 3:1 selection first. He makes ten errors at this level. Then, Miss Plum tests him at the next easiest level—the 2:2 (grade 2, second semester) level—where he makes eight errors. Miss Plum finally asks Peter to read the selection at the 2:1 (grade 2, first semester) level. Peter is successful in that he makes only five errors.

Miss Plum continues to test the remainder of her class in the same manner, trying the children out in easier and more difficult selections until the highest level at which each child makes 5 per cent or less errors is ascertained.

As Miss Plum tests all the children in her class, she finds that she can speed up the testing process in two ways. While some children are reading orally to her, it becomes quickly apparent that the child is going to make

TABLE 5.3 Oral Reading Scores
Portion of Miss Plum's Grade Four Class

Name	*Grade 6*		*Grade 5*		*Grade 4*		*Grade 3:2*		*Grade 3:1*		*Grade 2:2*		*Grade 2:1*		*Grade 1*		*Primer*	
	Oral	*Silent*	*Oral*	*Silent*	*Oral*	*Silent*	*Oral*	*Silent*	*Oral*	*Silent*	*Oral*	*Silent*	*Oral*	*Silent*	*Oral*	*Silent*	*Oral*	*Silent*
David			6		(4)													
Peter									10		8		(5)					
Dan	6		(ok)															
Jane									not ok		not ok		(4)					
Ronnie					not ok						8		(4)					

Note:
Column marked oral is for recording errors in oral reading.
Column marked silent is for recording errors in silent reading comprehension.
Circle in oral reading column indicates oral reading score, i.e., highest level on which child made 5 per cent or less errors.

many more or many fewer than the 5 per cent errors allowed. Miss Plum does not have these children read the entire selection. For example, after Dan had read the first few sentences of the grade five selection, it was obvious that he was going to make less than 5 per cent errors. Miss Plum simply marked his score "ok" and did not have him read the entire selection. On the grade six selection, Dan made six errors. Hence he passed the oral reading portion of the test at the grade five level. Conversely, Jane needed help on three out of the first six words at the grade 3:1 selection, so Miss Plum simply marked her score as "not ok" at that level. Jane proceeded to have extreme difficulty with the 2:2 selection, and again Miss Plum had her read only a portion of this selection. On the 2:1 selection Jane made four errors and therefore passed the oral reading portion of the test on the 2:1 level.

Miss Plum also found that she could reduce the time required to administer the oral portions by not testing each child at every level but by skipping levels at which she was sure that the child would be successful or not successful. For example, after Miss Plum had tested Ronnie at the grade four level and had found his reading to be very weak, she skipped down to the 2:2 level at which he did better but still made eight errors. Ronnie scored less than the allowable 5 per cent errors on the 2:1 level where he made only four errors.

Miss Plum proceeds using these shortcuts until all the children in her class have been tested on the oral reading section of the test.

Preparation of Test Materials for Silent Reading Comprehension

Miss Plum is now ready to test the children on the silent reading comprehension portion of the test. Miss Plum discovers that Appendix C, "Teacher's Copy of the Silent Reading Selections and Comprehension Questions", is ready for her use and contains information regarding administration and scoring. To prepare Appendix D, "Student's Copy of Silent Reading Comprehension Selections and Comprehension Questions," for use, Miss Plum removes the copies from the book. Each child in the class reads three silent reading selections and answers the accompanying comprehension questions—the level above his or her oral reading score, the level that represents his or her oral reading score, and the level immediately below his or her reading score. For example, David's oral reading score is grade four. David, therefore, completes the grade 5, 4, and 3:2 silent reading levels. Likewise, Peter's score is level 2:1. Peter completes the 1, 2:1, and 2:2 reader levels.

Administration of the Silent Reading Comprehension Selections

Miss Plum gives each child in her class the three silent reading selections on the levels she has deemed appropriate for him or her. She instructs the child to read the story on one sheet carefully, then turn the sheet over and answer the questions without looking back at the selection. Miss Plum tells the child that, upon finishing the first selection and set of questions, the child should proceed in the same manner with the second and third selections.

Miss Plum grades the papers, counting as errors any answers she would consider incorrect if the child made that response in a workbook. Miss Plum then records the number of errors each child made on the same score sheet as that which contains the oral reading scores for each child. Table 5.4 is a cumulative table showing the errors that each child made in oral reading and in silent reading comprehension.

Interpreting the Results of the Test

Miss Plum now proceeds to interpret the test results. From Table 5.4, it appears that the highest level at which David passed both the oral and silent reading portions of the test is grade four. Thus David should be instructed from a grade four book. Peter shows a different pattern. He makes only three errors on the most difficult set of silent reading comprehension tests that Miss Plum gives him. It is possible that Peter can comprehend on a level higher than 2:2. Miss Plum makes a note to test him using the silent reading selections on progressively higher levels until she can identify the highest level at which he can answer 75 per cent of the comprehension questions accurately. Tentatively, she places him at a grade 2:1 level—being aware of the fact that his ability to name the words is weaker than his ability to understand what he has read. Dan shows a problem opposite to that of Peter. Although Dan can call the words accurately on the grade five level, he could only pass the silent reading comprehension test on the grade four level. Miss Plum places him at a grade four level and is cognizant of the fact that his oral reading is superior to his ability to understand what he has read. Miss Plum proceeds to analyze the remainder of her class in the same manner, tentatively assigning each child to a level for instruction, noting those cases in which children need further testing, and recording each pupil's particular strength or weakness in either oral reading or silent reading comprehension.

Advantages of the Informal Reading Inventory

The advantages of the informal procedure are that (1) informal reading inventories can be used to determine the student's reading levels; the instructional level is normally used to determine placement in the correct reading instruction material; (2) they may be administered and interpreted by the classroom teacher; (3) they may be administered within a short time span; and (4) because they are informal tests, the teacher does not normally require administrative approval before administering them.

PLACEMENT TESTS

A fourth procedure that may help teachers to assess the reading achievements of their pupils is placement tests, which have been designed by the publishers of some reading instructional materials to help the teacher determine which level of a series of instructional materials is appropriate for a given child. Although placement tests from different publishers may vary in content and format, they are often informal reading inventories based on the materials from which the child is to be instructed.

TABLE 5.4 Oral Reading and Silent Reading Comprehension Scores Portion of Miss Plum's Grade Four Class

Name	*Grade 6*		*Grade 5*		*Grade 4*		*Grade 3:2*		*Grade 3:1*		*Grade 2:2*		*Grade 2:1*		*Grade 1*		*Primer*	
	Oral	*Silent*	*Oral*	*Silent*	*Oral*	*Silent*	*Oral*	*Silent*	*Oral*	*Silent*	*Oral*	*Silent*	*Oral*	*Silent*	*Oral*	*Silent*	*Oral*	*Silent*
David			6	5	[(4)]	[(3)]		0										
Peter									10		8	3	[(5)]	[(2)]		1		
Dan	6	8	(ok)	5	[ ]	[(3)]												
Jane									not ok		not ok	8	(4)	7	[ ]	[(3)]		
Ronnie					not ok						8	(3)	[(4)]	[3]		2		

Rectangle indicates level at which child should be instructed.
Circle in silent reading column indicates highest level at which child scored 75 percent or better on comprehension questions.
Circle in oral reading column indicates highest level at which child pronounced 95 per cent or more words correctly.

Placement tests have several advantages. First, because the inventories are based on the materials from which the child is to be instructed, they are usually quite accurate in defining the child's instructional level. Second, they have the following advantages relating to test construction: (1) Usually, they have been prepared by educators skilled in test construction. (2) They contain appropriate selections and comprehension questions. (3) They have been field tested. (4) They usually contain guidelines for administration and scoring.

Therefore, if placement tests are available, they are probably one of the best measures that a teacher can use to match the children with materials of the appropriate reading levels.

CLOZE PROCEDURE

The cloze procedure is another method used by teachers to determine the instructional reading levels of their pupils. This procedure is designed with the express purpose of determining whether a specific set of materials is appropriate for a given child. Thus, cloze procedure methodology, like the informal reading inventory, is based on the premise that, if the teacher wishes to determine whether or not the students can read a given set of materials, it is necessary to first try them out in that particular material.

Because cloze tests are relatively easy to construct, they are usually teacher made and are based on passages selected from the material to be used in the classroom. Students are asked to read passages drawn from the text under consideration from which usually every fifth word has been deleted. The students' responses are then analyzed to determine if the material under consideration is appropriate.

Construction of a Cloze Procedure

Cloze tests are constructed as follows (Bormuth, 1968; Earle, 1976):

1. Carefully choose from the text under consideration a section of about three hundred words that appear typical of the text.
2. Leave the first sentence intact. That is, do not make any changes in it (Earle, 1976).
3. Beginning with any of the first five words in the second sentence, delete every fifth word and replace these words with blanks of uniform length until the passage contains fifty blanks (Bormuth, 1968; Rankin and Culhane, 1969).
4. In addition to the last sentence that contains blanks, include within the passage the succeeding sentence from which no deletions have been made (Earle, 1976).

An example of one such passage ready to be used as a cloze test is shown in Figure 5.1.

REMEMBER THE MAINE!

On Tuesday, February 15, 1898, the battleship U.S.S. *Maine* rocked gently at her mooring in Havana harbor, where she had been anchored for three weeks. Night had ______and Captain Charles Sigsbee, ______of the *Maine*, stood______ the bridge railing, looking______ over the moon-dappled______.He had just finished______nightly inspection tour of______guard posts to make______that everything was shipshape.

______was a hard-working______ ______who was sharply aware______ the reasons which had______him to Cuba. The______was in a state ______turmoil. Bands of rebellious ______, fighting to free Cuba______ the rule of Spain,______attacking, ambushing, and killing______ throughout the country. Spanish ______were hunting down the ______and cruelly stopping them. ______turbulent condition had existed______Cuba for years. American______had long been with______ rebels, known as *insurrectos*. American consul, Fitzhugh Lee, ______not call upon Washington ______help, however, until January 12, 1898.______that date a bloody ______in Havana endangered the ______and property of American ______living there. In response______ Lee's request, the Navy______had sent the *Maine*______the light cruiser *Montgomery*______Havana on what was______termed a "good will"______.

The two American ships______ January 25, and were warmly______ by Spanish authorities. Since______ the *Maine* had spent______quiet weeks during which______were no further riots.______ Sigsbee could not have______that the night of ______15 would be different from ______other nights that had______ since the *Maine's* arrival.

______a mile or so______the *Maine's* bow the______of Havana glittered and shone with a thousand tiny lights. Faint snatches of music from waterfront cafes drifted across the harbor.

Figure 5.1. Three Hundred Word Passage Readied for Cloze Test (Reprinted by permission of the Macmillan Co., from *Into New Worlds* by Marion Gartler, 1970, p. 269.)

Administration of a Cloze Test

Explain the task to the students as follows:

1. First read the entire passage in which the words have been removed.
2. Return to the beginning of the passage and fill in the blanks with what you believe to be the missing words.
3. Take as much time as you need. There is no time limit.

Earle (1976) advocates the use of practice exercises prior to the cloze testing procedure if students are not familiar with this technique. Practice exercises might be based on relatively easy selections of about fifty words in length from which every *n*th word has been deleted. Students' answers are discussed following completion of the practice exercises, which may be continued until the students understand the procedure.

Scoring a Cloze Test

Students are given credit only for responses that are identical to those in the original text. While misspelled words are accepted as correct, synonyms are not. This scoring procedure simplifies grading and makes it more objective. Furthermore, research studies (McKenna, 1976) that have investigated the crediting of synonyms have found that this policy rarely improves students' scores significantly.

Calculate the score using the formula (Number of correct responses/number of possible correct responses) × 100. For example, if the student makes twenty correct responses out of a possible fifty, the student's score would be 40 per cent: (20/50) × 100.

Interpretation of Cloze Test Scores

Cloze test scores may be used to discern whether material is on the child's independent, instructional, or frustration level. Bormuth (1968) suggests that (1) a score greater than 58 per cent indicates that the material is on the child's independent level, (2) a score of 44 per cent to 57 per cent indicates that the material is on the child's instructional level, and (3) a score below 44 per cent indicates that the material is on the child's frustration level.

Locating a Typical Passage

Because materials within most texts vary widely in difficulty, a typical passage should be located for the cloze test. To locate a typical passage, about twelve passages selected from all parts of the intended instructional material are prepared as cloze passages. Each passage is then completed by at least thirty students. If one class is used, each student can complete all twelve passages; if three classes are used, each student can complete four passages. After the percentage score for each test paper has been calculated, the average percentage score for each passage is found. Sample results are shown as follows.

Passage	*Average Score* (%)
1	49.2
2	50.0
3	43.8
4	39.0
5	86.0
6	32.6
7	68.2
8	68.4
9	52.4
10	58.6
11	45.2
12	56.1
Overall total	650.1
Average	54.1

Next, the average score for all passages combined is figured by totaling the averages for each passage and then dividing by the number of passages. In the example, the total for the averages shown is 650.1 and number of passages is 12, resulting in an average score of 54.1.

The passages whose average score most closely resembles the average for all passages is probably the most representative and should be used as the test selection. In the example, passage 9, with an average score of 52.4 per cent, most closely resembles the average score for all passages of 54.1 per cent. In the future, passage 9 and only passage 9 should be used to determine the independent, instructional, and frustration level for each student.

Advantages and Limitations of the Cloze Procedure

Cloze passages have the following *advantages:* (1) They are based on materials from which the child is to be instructed. (2) They are designed to indicate whether a given set of materials is on the child's independent, instructional, or frustration level. (3) They can be constructed, administered, and scored by the classroom teacher. (4) They can be administered in a short time span. (5) They do not normally require administrative approval.

Cloze passages have the following *disadvantages:* (1) They lack the advantages associated with test construction by professionals, including choice of appropriate test selections and field testing. (2) Most authors do not recommend their use prior to grade four. (3) Norms are based on the deletion of every fifth word. Children may find filling in so many blanks too formidable a task (Karlin, 1973). (4) There is some question as to the accuracy of the cloze procedure. Although one research study (Ransom, 1968) found that a cloze test gave results similar to teacher-made informal reading inventory, other studies such as that by Pikulski and Pikulski (1977) found that the cloze procedure tended to overestimate the reading levels of the subjects. Another study by Tomas (1979) indicated that the cloze procedure was invalid for selections of a literary nature.

Hence, as with all assessment measures, the cloze scores should be used with caution. The results are meant to serve as guidelines; they are not meant to be rigid labels.

SUMMARY

Students at each grade level show a wide range of reading achievement. The teacher's role is to determine the reading level of each student in a class so that appropriate instructional materials may be selected for him or her. Diagnosing a student's reading level may include observing the student in class and studying his or her standardized survey test score. These sources will give general information about the student's reading achievement.

Word list tests can be used as an indication of the level at which to begin further testing. If the teacher uses an appropriate marking system to label types of error, the informal reading inventory can give more exact information on the child's reading level, especially if such inventories are based on the materials from which instruction might be given. Placement tests also are an excellent source of information as to the instructional level on which to place children. The cloze technique may also be used to ascertain whether a specific level of material is appropriate for a given student.

References and Bibliography

Betts, E. A. *Foundations of Reading Instruction.* New York: American Book Company, 1946.

Bader, L. A. *Reading Diagnosis and Remediation in Classroom and Clinic.* New York: Macmillan Publishing Co., Inc., 1980.

Bormuth, J. "The Cloze Readability Procedure." *Elementary English* 45 (April 1968): 429-436.

Bradley, J. M. and Ames, W. S. "You Can't Judge a Basal by the Number on the Cover." *Reading World* 17 (March 1978): 175-183.

Buros, O. K., ed. *Reading Tests and Reviews.* Highland Park, N.J.: Gryphon Press, 1968.

Burgett, R. E., and Glaser, N. A. "Appraising the Revised Standardized Reading Test." *Elementary English* 50 (January 1973): 71-74.

Dillner, M., and Olson, J. *Personalizing Reading Instruction in Middle, Junior, and Senior High Schools.* New York: Macmillan Publishing Co., Inc., 1977.

Durost, W. N., Bixler, H. H., Wrightstone, J. W., Prescott, G. A., and Balow, I. H. *Metropolitan Achievement Test.* New York: Harcourt Brace Jovanovich, Inc., 1971.

Durrell, D. D. *Durrell Analysis of Reading Difficulty.* New York: Harcourt Brace Jovanovich, Inc., 1955.

Earle, R. A. *Teaching Reading and Mathematics.* Newark, Dela.: International Reading Association, 1976.

Eberwein, L. D. "The Variability of Readability of Basal Reader Textbooks and How Much Teachers Know About It." *Reading World* 18 (March 1979): 259-272.

Ekwall, E. E. *Ekwall Reading Inventory.* Boston: Allyn & Bacon, Inc., 1979.

Ekwall, E. E. "Informal Reading Inventories: The Instructional Level." *The Reading Teacher* 29 (April 1976): 662-665.

Froese, V. "Functional Reading Levels: From Graded Word Lists?" *The Alberta Journal of Educational Research* 22 (December 1976): 325-329.

Gallant, R. "Indiana Test of Basic Skills" in R. Gallant, *Handbook in Corrective Reading: Basic Tasks.* Columbus, Ohio: Charles E. Merrill Publishing Company, 1976, pp. 107-153.

Gartler, M. *Into New Worlds.* New York: Macmillan Publishing Co., Inc., 1970.

Gates, A., and MacGinitie, W. H. *Gates–MacGinitie Reading Tests.* New York: Teachers College Press, 1972.

Goodman, Y., and Burke, C. *Reading Miscue Inventory.* New York: Macmillan Publishing Co., Inc., 1973.

Gray, W. S. *Gray Oral Reading Test.* Indianapolis: The Bobbs-Merrill Co., 1963.

Hieronymus, A. N., and Lindquist, E. F. *Iowa Tests of Basic Skills.* Boston: Houghton Mifflin Company, 1974.

Gronlund, N. E. *Measurement and Evaluation in Teaching.* New York: Macmillan Publishing Co., Inc., 1976.

Jastak, A. *Wide Range Achievement Test.* rev. ed. New York: The Psychological Corporation, 1965.

Johnson, M. S., and Kress, R. A. *Informal Reading Inventories.* Newark, Dela.: International Reading Association, 1965.

Karlin, R. "Evaluation for Diagnostic Teaching," in W. H. MacGinitie, ed., *Assessment Problems in Reading.* Newark, Dela.: International Reading Association, 1973, pp. 8–13.

LaPray, M., and Ross, R. "The Graded Word List: Quick Gauge of Reading Ability." *Journal of Reading* 12 (January 1969): 305–307.

Marzano, R. T., Larson, J., Tish, G., and Vodehnal, S. "The Graded Word List Is Not a Shortcut to an IRI." *The Reading Teacher* 31 (March 1978): 647-653.

McKenna, M. "Synonymic versus Verbatim Scoring of the Cloze Procedure." *Journal of Reading* 20 (November 1976): 141–143.

Pikulski, J. "A Critical Review: Informal Reading Inventories." *The Reading Teacher* 28 (November 1974): 141–151.

Pikulski, J. J. and Pikulski, E. C. "Cloze, Maze, and Teacher Judgment." *The Reading Teacher* 30 (April 1977): 776–770.

Rankin, E. F. and Culhane, J. "Comparable Cloze and Multiple-Choice Comprehension Test Scores." *Journal of Reading* 13 (December 1969): 193–198.

Rupley, W. H., and Blair, T. R. *Reading Diagnosis and Remediation.* Chicago: Rand McNally & Company, 1979.

Salvia, J., and Ysseldyke, J. E. *Assessment in Special and Remedial Education.* Boston: Houghton Mifflin Company, 1978.

Silvaroli, N. J. *Classroom Reading Inventory.* 2nd ed. Dubuque, Iowa: William C. Brown Company, Publishers, 1976.

Strang, R. *Diagnostic Teaching of Reading.* 2nd ed. New York: McGraw-Hill Book Company, 1969.

Tomas, D. "Don't Cloze Students Out of Literary Discourse." *Epistle* 5 (Winter 1979): 27–32.

Valmont, W. J. "Creating Questions for Informal Reading Inventories." *The Reading Teacher* 25 (March 1972): 509–512.

Woods, M. L., and Moe, A. J. *Analytical Reading Inventory.* Columbus, Ohio: Charles E. Merrill Publishing Company, 1977.

Self-Check 5.3
Determining Students' Reading Levels

The following questions are designed to help the participant assess his or her competence on the first twelve objectives stated at the beginning of this chapter. Although every effort has been made to make the self-check questions comprehensive, participants should remember that they are held responsible for meeting the objectives as stated at the beginning of this chapter.

1. Objective 1. Why should a Grade 2 teacher diagnose the reading level of each class member?
2. Objective 2. What two factors complicate the teacher's task of choosing reading materials on the appropriate difficulty level?
3. Objective 3. How might a classroom teacher make use of the results of a standardized reading survey test? What advantages and limitations do standardized reading survey tests have that would cause them to be used in this manner?
4. Objective 4. How might a classroom teacher make use of the results of a word list test. What advantages and limitations do word list tests have that would cause them to be used in this manner?
5. Objective 5. What errors did the child make while reading this sentence?

T way beside
Meg's blond hair flew ^ out behind her as she rode (away).

6. Objective 6. A self-check of the participant's ability to score the oral portion of an informal reading inventory is not possible. However, the student should review the section titled *Scoring an Informal Reading Inventory* in this chapter.

   A child answered the questions based on the 3:1 level of the silent reading selection of the informal reading inventory found in the Appendixes of this book. What is the child's score? 1. Pierre 2. seven 3. fished 4. boat 5. His mother worked in a bakery. 6. unload the fish 7. make models 8. in the morning 9. in a town where there were lots of visitors 10. yes
7. Objective 7. Keith made the following scores on an informal reading inventory.

Levels	*Number of Oral Reading Errors*	*Number of Silent Reading Comprehension Errors*
Primer	0	0
1	1	1
2:1	2	3
2:2	3	5
3:1	5	6

   There were 100 words in each oral reading selection and 10 questions following each silent reading selection. What is Keith's instructional level?
8. Objective 8. How might a teacher administer an informal reading inventory?

9. Objective 9. How might a teacher use an informal reading inventory? What advantages and limitations does an informal reading inventory have that would cause it to be used in this manner?
10. Objective 10. Using any book at your disposal, prepare a selection for use as a cloze passage.
11. Objective 11. Mr. Joseph is using the cloze procedure to determine whether a book is appropriate for his students. He leafs through the book until he finds a passage of about three hundred words. Then, leaving the first sentence intact, he begins deleting every fifth word until he has created fifty blanks of equal length. During the next class day, he has each student fill in the blanks. He then has the students exchange papers and has them correct each others papers. He then collects them and marks each paper according to the following criteria: 75 per cent or better is marked independent level, 50–75 per cent is marked instructional level, and 49 per cent and below is marked frustration level.

    What, is anything, is Mr. Joseph doing correctly? What, if anything, is he doing incorrectly?
12. Objective 12. How might a classroom teacher make use of the results of the cloze testing procedure? What advantages and limitations does the cloze procedure have that would cause it to be used in this manner?

Chapter 5
Experience 1

Objective

The participant will administer an informal reading inventory and score and interpret its results.

Activity and Assessment Guide

1. State the name and grade for the child tested.

   Name ____________ Age ____________ Grade ____________

2. Circle the child's instructional level and record his or her test results on the chart.

Name	6		5		4		3:2		3:1		2:2		2:1		1		P	
	O	S	O	S	O	S	O	S	O	S	O	S	O	S	O	S	O	S

3. State the level on which you would instruct the child tested and record any special strengths and/or weaknesses noted during testing.

Name	Instructional Level	Strengths and/or Weaknesses
____________________	____________	________________

* 4. At what level was testing of oral reading begun?____________Why?

____

* 5. At what level was testing of oral reading terminated?__________Why?

____

* 6. Was child told not to look back when answering silent reading comprehension questions? ____________Why?______________________

* 7. At what level was testing of silent reading terminated?____________

Why?____

* 8. Does further testing need to be done?____________Why or why not?

____

* 9. Do you believe that the test results are accurate?____________Why or why not?____

10. Write a brief summary of the child's reaction toward this experience.

____

____

11. State what you believe to be the significant implications of this experience for you as a future classroom teacher.____________________

____

____

*See Chapter 1: Experience 1 for an explanation of the asterisk.

Chapter 5
Experience 2

Objective

The student will administer a cloze test and score and interpret its results.

Activity and Assessment Guide

1. State the name and grade for each child tested.

Name	*Grade*
______________________	_________
______________________	_________
______________________	_________
______________________	_________

2. From what book was material chosen?

   Name of book ____

   Author ____

   Publisher ____

3. Attach a copy of the selection prepared for the cloze test.
4. Why was this selection in particular chosen? ____________________

   ____

5. Record the results of the cloze test. Indicate whether the passage was on the instructional, frustration, or independent level for each child.

Name	*Raw Score*	*% Score*	*Level*
__________	__________	__________	__________
__________	__________	__________	__________
__________	__________	__________	__________
__________	__________	__________	__________
__________	__________	__________	__________

* 6. Do you believe that your test results are accurate?_______________Why or why not?____

____

* 7. Write a brief summary of the child's reaction toward this strategy._____

____

____

8. State what you believe to be the significant implications of this experience for you as a prospective classroom teacher.____________________

____

____

*Question may be answered by an observer.

Part Three
Methods of Teaching Reading

Chapter 6 Basal Reader Approach

Objectives 6.1

On completion of this chapter, the participant should be able to

1. Describe a delineation of reading levels and related vocabulary loads that are typically found in a current basal reader series.
2. Describe and discuss at least three generalizations that can be made about a basal reader series.
3. Describe the three basic components ordinarily found within each level of a basal reader series.
4. Explain the purpose of at least five different supplementary materials that could be found within a particular basal reader program (i.e., various types of correlated reading tests, self-help dictionaries, introductory story cards, word and sentence building cards, spirit duplicating master stencils, little paperback storybooks, filmstrips, skill games, cassette story tapes, and the like).
5. Compare the strengths and weaknesses of using a basal reader series.
6. Given a demonstration of one step of a five-step basal reader lesson, identify the step being taught.
7. Differentiate between a five-step basal reader lesson and a five-step daily lesson plan.

Experience 1 extends Chapter 6 with this objective:

8. During this experience, the participant will develop and teach at least one step of a basal reader lesson.

Information Given 6.2
Basal Reader Approach

A teacher education student walked into a first grade classroom and noticed many different things. Labels with the words "chair," "table," "desk," and "pencil" were pasted on all the representative articles. The majority of the children were sitting at their desks, and it appeared that they were working independently on some sort of reading-related task. Some youngsters were drawing pictures, others were printing words on worksheets, and still others were reading silently. The teacher, Miss Daisy, was in the far corner of the room surrounded by ten pupils. She held up a plastic model of a pony and asked, "What letter does the word 'pony' begin with?" The children responded in unison with the sound of the letter *p*. She replied, "Good," and wrote the letter *p* on the chalkboard. Then she stated, "Now repeat the name of the letter *p* with me as I write it again." As she printed the letter *p*, the first graders said *p* in unison.

This observation stimulated several questions from the teacher education student. How did Miss Daisy know to present the letter *p* at that time? Why did she use the word "pony"? How did she know to use a word beginning with *p*, such as "pony," rather than a word ending with *p*, such as "hop"? Where did she get the idea of putting labels all over the classroom furniture? How was she able to determine which individual lesson to give to each child? How was she able to develop activities to keep twenty other six-year-olds busy and in their seats while she was working with her group of ten?

With these questions still fresh in her mind, the teacher education student walked down the hall into Mr. Rough's fourth grade classroom. She noticed that all the children were sitting in their seats and listening to Mr. Rough discuss how to read maps. After his ten-minute talk, the class broke into small groups. Some youngsters brought workbooks dealing with "using the index" and sat down with Mr. Rough, others completed exercises dealing with locating Africa on a blank map, and still others were reading a story entitled "Fred Sails to Egypt" in a hardback book. One youngster was listening to a tape recording and watching slides while filling out a worksheet on beginning consonants. A girl was listening to a record while reading a story that seemed to relate to the story about "Fred Sails to Egypt" but was much simpler in vocabulary and sentence structure. One of the fourth graders walked up to the teacher education major and asked her the meaning of the word "plateau." She told him and then was immediately asked by another boy to pronounce a word to which he pointed. The word he was having trouble with was "come." She was amazed that the first boy couldn't figure out the word "plateau" as the meaning was given at the bottom of the page. The second boy's inability to pronounce the word "come" indicated to her that he didn't even know his basic sight vocabulary and was probably a non-reader. She got up and continued to walk around the room. She noticed that some of the youngsters had finished reading the hardback books and were reading library-type books at their desks. One child was reading a very sophisticated book about Egyptian culture.

This classroom scene stimulated even more questions than had the first grade classroom. How was the teacher, Mr. Rough, able to provide for the obvious wide range of reading achievement? The skills emphasized seemed to be more concerned with study-type reading than with the word recognition skills emphasized in the first grade. Was this typical, and was direct instruction in word recognition no longer given in the fourth grade? Where did all the library-type books come from? Where did the teacher get the tape recording of the skill lessons that the one boy was working on? How did the record and the story that it illustrated fit into the total lesson taught by the teacher?

The answers to all these questions are provided by the companies that produced the materials used by the two teachers. Both Mr. Rough and Miss Daisy were using a basal reading approach to teaching reading in their classrooms. This approach is used today by over 95 per cent of the primary school teachers, grades one to three, and over 80 per cent of the intermediate school teachers, grades four to six.

Several major companies publish basal reader series, and millions of dollars have been invested in research and development by each company that publishes this approach to teaching reading. Most basal reader series follow a similar pattern, yet have individual characteristics. The careful development and presentation of sequenced skill development have over the years helped teachers to teach thousands of youngsters how to read.

Typically, about 350 to 400 different words are presented in the first three grades and between 1,500 and 2,500 in the intermediate grades. Since the words are cumulative, a youngster should know at least 6,000 different words by the time he or she finishes grade six. Basal reader materials are arranged to parallel the grade level designations found traditionally in most elementary schools and range from extremely simple picture-word relationships at the readiness level to rather sophisticated concept development at the fifth and sixth grade levels.

A "typical" basal reader grade level designation and corresponding vocabulary load is described in Table 6.1.

Most series arrange their materials into at least eleven different reading levels. The series shown in Table 6.1 can be described in terms of the following eleven reading levels: (1) level one—readiness; (2) level two—preprimer; (3) level three—primer; (4) level four—first reader; (5) level five—first half of grade two; (6) level six—second half of grade two; (7) level seven—first half of grade three; (8) level eight—second half of grade three; (9) level nine—grade four; (10) level ten—grade five; (11) level eleven—grade six.

GENERALIZATIONS CONCERNING BASAL READERS

Although the exact words used to teach reading and the amount and type presented at each level vary from publisher to publisher, several generalizations may be made about all basal reader series. (1) They usually consist of a

TABLE 6.1 Grade Level Designation and Vocabulary Load for a "Typical" Basal Reader Series

Grade Level Designation	*New Words Presented*	*Cumulative Words*
K: readiness	15	15
1: preprimer 1	24	39
preprimer 2		
preprimer 3	103	142
primer	192	334
first reader	173 .	507
2: second reader (2:1)	300	807
second reader (2:2)	350	1,157
3: third reader (3:1)	450	1,607
third reader (3:2)	450	2,057
4: fourth reader	600	2,657
5: fifth reader	2,000	4,657
6: sixth reader	2,000	6,657

sequence of books containing reading materials of increasing difficulty that teach all the reading skills in an orderly fashion. (2) The vocabulary used in creating stories in the series is carefully selected and limited to words in print that are thought to be already known to the children in listening or speaking situations. (3) The number of new words presented in each succeeding reading selection is carefully controlled and based on the premise that children learn to read best through a planned continuum of introducing and maintaining vocabulary. (4) The number of words per sentence is carefully controlled. (5) Most of the stories in the series are primarily narrative and are based on concepts that are believed to be familiar to the child. (6) The series view themselves as capable of being a "total program" and as such consist of a great variety of sequenced, integrated components.

Each of these generalizations will be discussed in turn.

A SEQUENCE OF BOOKS

Basal reader series usually consist of a sequence of books containing reading materials of increasing difficulty that teach all the reading skills in an orderly fashion. Each developmental step grows out of the preceding steps and at the same time serves as a foundation for the ones following. The materials are carefully scaled in difficulty and are arranged in a sequential pattern. As demonstrated in Table 6.1, there may be as many as six different books in the first grade, two in the second, and two in the third. In subsequent grades there is usually only one reader for each grade. Some series extend through grade nine, but most stop at grade six.

In Miss Daisy's class, many of the children were already into their first hardback book, the primer. Others were at various levels in the paperback preprimers. Although she did have six books that the first graders could get through by the end of the year, her range at the point of the observation was from readiness to primer, and as such she was already using five different books. Mr. Rough's class ranged in reading ability from readiness to grade nine. Although his grade level text was the fourth grade reader, he used materials from the other levels to supplement his program and provide for the individual reading differences that existed in his classroom. Since he had a reading range of thirteen years, the sequential characteristic of the basal helped him provide each youngster in the classroom with material of an appropriate reading level.

The skills developed for Miss Daisy's class were entirely different in focus from those designed for Mr. Rough's. Some of Miss Daisy's students needed practice with prereading skills. Their backgrounds were such that either their immaturity or their lack of experience had not yet enabled them to have the skills to even begin to learn to read. These children were provided with basal reader material written on a readiness level and were taught such basic skills as left-to-right progression, letters of the alphabet, and visual discrimination between letters such as *b* and *d*. Once the readiness skills had been mastered, the youngsters moved to the preprimer, where they began to learn the basic sight words (see Table 2.1 for list).

On the other hand, by the time the pupils entered Mr. Rough's fourth grade class, they were expected to know all the basic reading skills, and emphasis in their basals switched from word recognition skills to comprehension and study skills. In other words, the emphasis switched from "learning to read" in the first three grades to "reading to learn" in the next three grades.

CONTROLLED SELECTION OF WORDS

The vocabulary used in creating the stories in the series is carefully selected and limited to words in print that are thought to be already known to the children in listening or speaking situations. These words are selected from a variety of sources, and each basal reader often differs in its source of basic words.

In his classroom, Mr. Rough was using a series different from Miss Daisy's. The series Mr. Rough used had obtained its basic list through examination and research on library books that had been designated as popular with primary age readers. Although over 85,000 words were used in the books, after inflected and compounded forms were eliminated, only 2,500 different words were identified. Further analysis of these words revealed that about 200 words made up as much as 70 per cent of the contents of the childrens' books. Therefore, the core vocabulary of that particular series was based on those 200 words. The series used by Miss Daisy based its core vocabulary on the words most frequently used by children in speaking situations.

It is typical for each series to select its own base for identifying words to be used for its core vocabulary. As a result, there is little overlap in words found in series published by different companies. George Spache cites Selma Herr's recent survey of twelve different basal readers, which reveals that only 600 words were used in common out of a total of approximately 12,000 words. Of the words in common, only 206 were introduced at the same grade level in more than one basal reader series (Spache, 1973). These overlapping words were the most frequently used words in the English language and consisted primarily of prepositions, conjunctions, verbs, and adverbs. The "sight vocabulary" words discussed in Chapter 2 are usually included in this category. The basal used by Miss Daisy and the basal used by Mr. Rough taught words such as *he*, *I*, *you*, *we*, *go*, *will*, *on*, and *to* in the first few stories. While they bind the content together, many of the words are meaningless by themselves, and both basal series tried to introduce the words in a meaningful context.

CONTROLLED PRESENTATION OF WORDS

The number of new words presented in each succeeding reading selection is carefully controlled and based on the premise that children learn to read best through a planned continuum of introducing and maintaining vocabulary. The basal readers vary from one to another in *number* of new words presented in each story. Miss Daisy's series limited new words introduced in each story to one or two. For example, when the authors of that particular series were writing the stories, a tale about Susie riding to school on her pony was to be included. A check on the words revealed that "riding, "school," and "pony" were all new words. The authors believed that three new words were too many for that age reader to include on one page. To overcome a stilted story due to a limited introduction of words, Miss Daisy's basal included picture clues to add interest to the reading and help the children understand the words. Therefore the child's book contained a large colored picture of Susie riding to school on her galloping pony above the caption "The pony runs." This picture was intended to add motivation, introduce one of the new words, and prepare the way for other words to be introduced in a later part of the reader.

The authors also believed that each new word needed to be reinforced (in subsequent lessons) according to an established pattern. For example, when Miss Daisy presented the word "pony" in lesson 1, the word "pony" was used six times in the story that accompanied lesson 1, four times in the story that accompanied lesson 2, and three times in the story that accompanied lesson 4. The word was periodically reinforced throughout the whole series according to a systematic scheme determined by the authors.

The authors of the primary level of Mr. Rough's series had a little different philosophy from Miss Daisy's. They knew that the average first grader has been shown to be able to use accurately and/or understand about 4,000 different words (Chall, 1967). They felt that children could assimilate at least seven or eight new words per story if the words were carefully chosen and many picture clues were included.

Mr. Rough's series differed from Miss Daisy's in the pattern of repetition used to reinforce each word used. For example, had his series been teaching the word "pony," it would have repeated the word in a similar fashion, but not in exactly the same manner.

Although there is some commonality, in general, the choice of words selected, the number of words introduced per story, and the sequence of word repetition and reinforcing exercises are based on the philosophy and research of the various authors of the series. As a result these aspects are often quite different from series to series.

CONTROLLED NUMBER OF WORDS

The number of words per sentence is carefully controlled. The authors of most basals have carefully considered research results that reveal that short, simple sentences are easier to read than long, complex ones. A great many of the sentences in both Miss Daisy's and Mr. Rough's readers are of the "Look! Look! Look! The pony runs!" variety.

NARRATIVE STORIES AND FAMILIAR CONCEPTS

Most of the stories in the series are primarily written in narrative style and are based on concepts that are believed to be familiar to the child. Traditionally, basal reader series have placed strong emphasis on stories that they believed would be of universal appeal to youngsters regardless of their various environments. It has not been uncommon for a series to create a family and maintain it throughout a series. Recent complaints about overemphasis on the "typical middle-class family" culture have caused the content of the more recently written series to reflect a variety of different cultures.

Miss Daisy's series was an example of what used to be standard in basal readers. The principal characters were children who lived comfortably in their suburban houses, their mothers were housewives, their fathers were employed, and the boys and girls always had pets. Mr. Rough's series was a new edition of an older series rewritten specifically to relate to the needs of inner-city children. The stories centered around characters who were members of a minority group and whose activities took place, for the most part, on the streets of a large city.

A "TOTAL PROGRAM"

The series view themselves as capable of being a "total program" and as such consist of a great variety of sequenced, integrated components. Although series vary in skill emphasis from one to another based on the philosophies of the authors, most cover all the reading skills in some manner. The series used by Miss Daisy placed heavy emphasis upon a phonetic approach to word recognition to learn to read. However, it did not ignore the other word recognition skills and comprehension-building activities. The stories used by Mr. Rough were based on a linguistic approach to learning to read. The authors of this series stressed reading as one of the communication processes and focused much of the instruction on oral language development activities.

While Miss Daisy's series had some activities involving oral language development, most oral work focused more on sounding out words in print rather than involvement in activities designed to develop and extend the oral language. On the other hand, Mr. Rough's series had some lessons on the phonic approach to word recognition, but it focused more on the ability to distinguish different sounds needed to understand various dialects rather than on unlocking words with phonic skills. Miss Daisy's approach was based on the theory that the initial stage in reading should emphasize teaching children to master the alphabetic sound code; Mr. Rough's approach was based on the theory that children learn to read best when meaning is emphasized from the start.

Both series did cover all the approaches to teaching word recognition skills, comprehension skills, and study skills. As such, both series could be considered somewhat eclectic. Although many skills were introduced in isolation, after a child had mastered a variety of approaches, the manuals encouraged the teachers to help the child use a combination of skills to unlock unknown words and glean meaning out of what was read.

COMPONENTS OF A BASAL READER SERIES

On each of the levels, from readiness to grade six, shown in Table 4.1, there are usually four types of materials. The first three types may be described as the basic teaching components of the series and include (1) a teacher's manual that explains the philosophy of the program, telling in detail how to teach each selection and suggesting skill activities and other related ideas, (2) a pupil's book that contains the stories to be read by the children, and (3) a pupil's workbook that includes exercises in reading to be completed by the children. In addition to these, there are (4) supplementary materials that are available from the publishers to reinforce and expand the skills presented in the basic components.

THE TEACHER'S MANUAL

Had the teacher education major looked at the teacher's manual that accompanied the basal reader series Miss Daisy used, she would have noticed such specific suggestions to the teacher as: Now hold up the model of the pony and ask, "What is this a model of?" Now ask, "What letter does the word *pony* begin with?" The instructions are obviously precise, but the authors of the manual anticipated that Miss Daisy would deviate a bit from the lesson and supplement it with her own ideas. For example, if Johnny had a pony, Miss Daisy should have varied from the example in the teacher's manual and asked the children about the type of pet Johnny owned. This would have added to the motivation to read the story and related the study of words to concrete objects relevant to the needs and interests of the children in her particular classroom. Although the series used by Mr. Rough differed from the series used by Miss Daisy in using the word "pencil" instead of "pony" to introduce the initial consonant *p*, the instructions in the teacher's manual were just as precise.

When Mr. Rough selected his series, one of the things he liked the most was that the teacher's edition was well organized and easy to follow. Reproductions of the student book were within his teacher's edition in close proximity to the teaching suggestions, and at the end of each unit the authors listed a variety of supplementary reading material and activities for enriching the children's experiences.

THE PUPIL'S BOOK AND WORKBOOK

The pupil's books used by both teachers contained only the stories to be read by the children. The questions they were to answer after their reading, as well as coordinated skill-building exercises on words contained in the story, were bound separately in the pupil's workbook designed to accompany the story in the child's reader. Both publishers had gone to great expense to make certain that the stories and workbooks were attractively illustrated and printed in a size type that was easy on young eyes. Although the workbook was made to be written in and hence was consumable, the publishers tried to make the readers durable enough to last through the rough handling of many different children.

The pupil's books used by both teachers were organized around a unit theme. For example, Miss Daisy's first reader was organized around the theme "Animals and Americans." All the stories in that level concerned the relationship between Americans and animals. In the first reader there were ten basic units. Each unit extended the theme of Americans and animals. The first unit contained stories about cowboys and horses. The second unit contained stories about children in the suburban area of a large city and the types of pets they owned. Each unit in the first reader extended the theme in a like manner.

Regardless of the series used, it is characteristic of the basal reader publisher to provide the teacher with clear-cut, precise directions and materials for teaching each skill. As long as the teacher followed the basic structure of skill presentation, he or she could be assured that the children in his or her classroom would be systematically acquainted with all the reading skills.

For example, a child in Mr. Rough's class might read a story about Egypt. The teacher's manual would help Mr. Rough formulate questions about the word recognition and comprehension skills involved in the story itself. The manual would also suggest exercises for developing additional skills. The youngsters would read the story, guided through it by Mr. Rough and his teacher's manual, and then do follow-up coordinated exercises in the workbook. Thus, while the workbook might be teaching and reinforcing map-reading skills, the content of the workbook exercise material would concern Egypt in an attempt to tie all the skills in with the content of the story.

SUPPLEMENTARY MATERIALS

In addition to the traditional three types of components of a basal reader series, publishers of basal series usually offer a variety of instructional resource materials and other teaching aids. Most publishers supplement their basic reading program with some or all of the following.

Various Types of Correlated Reading Tests: Some tests are *placement tests* designed to help the classroom teacher decide at which level basal each child should be working. Some are *achievement tests* designed to measure the success with which the pupils meet the objectives set at each level of the program. Others are *diagnostic tests* designed to measure specific skill aspects such as ability in using syllabication to gather meaning from a word.

Basic Teaching Aids: Most series make available to the classroom teacher pictures, introductory story cards, self-help dictionaries, and duplicating materials to supplement words and skills presented in the lessons. Some series have developed very elaborate means for presenting these aids and have produced a vast array of materials and manipulative devices including (1) plastic objects that represent words children have learned, (2) plastic panels of recessed letter shapes that children can match with plastic letters, and (3) three-dimensional flash cards for practice in sight vocabulary and other learnings.

Supplementary Teaching Aids: In addition to these aids, many of the series produce filmstrips, games, and recordings that are correlated with the stories and are designed to provide motivation or additional practice on skills introduced. Some of these aids include (1) bingo-type games in which the children make moves when they have accurately responded to words or letters, (2) listening labs, which give the children a chance to hear the stories they are to read or provide additional practice on skills previously presented by the teachers, (3) various types of filmstrips that sometimes retell a story, sometimes expand it, and at other times teach specific reading skills within the story itself (i.e., sound within words, the meanings of words, word order, and the like), and (4) reading skill labs that are often cardboard boxes filled with skill-building stories and accompanying exercises. The boxes are usually accompanied by their own comprehensive battery of diagnostic tests and are designed to meet the needs of pupils who are deficient in one or more of the basic reading skills. Ordinarily, they require a minimum of teacher participation and are primarily a self-teaching, self-directing, and self-scoring activity.

Correlated Extension Activities: Many of the series try to make provisions for slow and superior groups of children through additional support materials. In most cases this is done by means of a series of books on a variety of subjects and reading levels. They are often accompanied by a teacher's manual that helps the teacher to extend ideas from the basal lesson to the extension activity. These books are primarily written for the enjoyment of the pupil and often are paperbacks. (More recent publications of this kind have focused on multicultural aspects to give the reader a better understanding of the culture in which he or she lives and the culture in which others live.) In other cases this extension material is in the form of filmstrips or reading labs, as discussed under "Supplementary Teaching Aids."

SELECTION OF A BASAL READER SERIES

In deciding to use a basal reader series, the teacher must weigh the advantages against the disadvantages. By identifying ways in which the effectiveness of a series is limited, the teacher can adapt it so as to expand its usefulness. A summary of all the characteristics discussed show some of the following pros and cons of the basal series:

Advantages

1. Continuity of skill development from level to level is assured if the same series is used.
2. Gradual introduction to carefully selected words according to a set formula facilitates the child's maximum chance to learn.
3. Carefully developed materials and manuals reduce teacher preparation time.
4. Wide variety of supplementary materials provides multitudes of activities for recreational reading as well as needed skill building.

Disadvantages

1. Content may stress type of culture that is meaningless or dull to the reader.
2. Emphasis is on groups rather than the individual.
3. Story content can be shallow and unimaginative due to strict vocabulary control.
4. Schools may not be able to afford extensive available supplementary material or to keep the series updated.
5. Teacher may use the basal as the only method of teaching reading rather than using it as a flexible tool to help teach reading.
6. No self-selection.
7. Pacing determined by publisher.

LESSON PLANNING USING THE BASAL READER SERIES

Basal reader series present reading skills through the use of stories. Each story is usually presented in the following five steps.

THE BASAL READER LESSON

Step 1: Preparation

Included in this step are (1) motivation—interest the child in reading the story. Make the story as relevant to the needs and interests of the children as possible. If the story is about an "ookpik" and someone has one, methods for caring for the toy might be discussed before the story is read. (2) new words—develop meanings of new words by building concept readiness for them through discussion. Determine whether or not the child knows the word in print by listening to him or her pronounce the word. If the child pronounces the word correctly, determine whether or not the child knows the meaning. It's no fun to read about a correctly pronounced "ookpik" if one does not know what an "ookpik" is. (3) concept development—extend the child's background knowledge through use of new words or through story content with which he is unfamiliar. The concepts involved in "ownership" may not be new to all children, but they may be new to some. In addition, the concept of "ownership" may be extended to cover the new concepts, such as "sharing" or "possession is nine tenths of the law."

Step 2: Silent Reading

Step 2 includes more than just asking the students to read the story. (1) Youngsters should not be asked to read unless they are given a definite purpose for reading the story. Ask questions to give a purpose for reading to the pupils. They should be made aware before they read that they will be asked to answer the questions. (2) After the story is read, the purpose for which the story was read can be assessed by asking the pupils to answer the questions that they were asked before they read. The discussion technique described in step 3 is a good way to do this.

Step 3: Oral Reading and Discussion

Step 3 is the follow-up to the silent reading to assess whether or not the pupils understand the new words, concepts, and ideas presented in the story that they just read. Suggested procedures for conducting an effective lesson include the following:

1. Remind the children of their purpose for reading. The technique of giving purpose to all oral reading helps the youngsters to remember that reading means gaining meaning from the printed page, not just a parroting back of an isolated set of words.

2. Ask a specific question related to the purpose for which the story was read and ask the pupils to find the passage in the story that answers the question. This passage should then be read orally by the pupil who locates it. Never "Round Robin" read. This is the outdated practice of asking each child in a circle to read aloud, in turn, a particular sentence. Each child reads his or her sentence according to his or her sequence in the circle. If the teacher thinks back to when he or she was asked to do this, the teacher might remember all the "tricks" used by youngsters when this method is employed; that is, read ahead and find the sentence so that it can be pronounced correctly when one's turn comes, and study it long enough to be able to read it correctly to the teacher. In the meantime, the pupil can read another book, or in other ways completely ignore the rest of the oral reading.

3. Involve as many children as possible. If the same youngsters always locate the correct sentence, and the teacher is concerned that the others are not getting a chance to read orally, the teacher can ask one child to locate the sentence and then ask another to read the sentence that was located for

a different purpose. This technique gives all the youngsters a chance to read orally. For example, the teacher is discussing the story with the children building on questions that he or she asked them prior to silent reading. Johnny says that the boy in the story was "happy" Mary says that he was "sad." The teacher can then say, "Read the part from the book to prove your point." The other children *do not* just listen. They actively try to find the part in the story where the boy reflects either "happiness" or "sadness." After Mary reads the correct sentence, one might ask a less capable reader to read the sentence aloud reflecting a sad tone of voice. Almost all the questions found in the teacher's manual can be used in this manner to create purposes and increase participation. Note: Many more specific questioning techniques for increasing pupil response are found in Chapter 10.

Step 4: Follow-up

Step 4 includes all the individual tasks that youngsters need to do after they have finished their reading and discussion. Some youngsters who are above grade level might be working on sophisticated expansion of skills; other youngsters who are at grade level may be expanding the skills learned in the lesson of the day; and still other youngsters who are reading below grade level may be doing lessons to help them "catch up" in the skills in which they are the least proficient. Step 4 also encompasses the following:

1. Teaching a new skill. If the youngsters have learned about soft *g* but do not know the soft *c* sound, then the group can be taught the new skill at this time.

2. Practicing a skill already taught either in the current lesson or in a previous lesson. While the youngsters go on to learn the *c* sound, those who don't know the hard and soft *g* sound well enough to proceed may be asked to practice this skill.

3. Both learning a new skill and practicing an old one may be done at the same time in this step. The teacher might first review with the pupils the fact that *g* has two sounds before introducing the new sounds of *c*. The teacher then lets the youngsters compare the two sounds of *c* to the two sounds of *g* just taught.

Step 5: Extension Activities

Step 5 includes many activities designed to reinforce skills already taught. There is a definite difference between teaching a skill and reinforcing it. A youngster can play a game to reinforce or practice a skill that he or she already knows. The child should not play a game to learn a skill. The teacher must first teach the youngster that *c* has two sounds before asking him or her to play a hopscotch game in which he or she jumps on the *c* words that have a hard *c* sound. Step 5 includes all those activities designed to reinforce and extend the reading skills previously taught. Components could include the following:

1. *Supplementary reading.* This could be practice in reading for pleasure on a topic of interest to the pupil or reading related to the basal story just read.

2. *Dramatization.* This involves making a play out of an incident in the story and presenting it to the rest of the class.

3. *Rereading for different purposes.* Although the pupil may have understood the basic concepts the first time he or she read the story, the child may be asked to read it again to determine what kind of person the main character was or to suggest background music for those working on the dramatization activity. If the child is a very poor reader, the child may have read it the first time just to decode the words. The child may need to read it again for the idea.

4. *Creative activities such as art or writing.* Youngsters can be asked to draw pictures of the main characters or the setting of the story. They can be asked to make collages illustrating the feelings of one of the characters when his Daddy told him that he could not play with the pony any more. They can be asked to write a description of a character or summarize a story.

Some basals put step 4 before step 2. Others combine steps 2 and 3 into one step. The description given here is simply a representative example of the kinds of lessons usually suggested in the teacher's manual that accompanies the basal reader series.

TEACHER'S LESSON PLANS

All teachers should plan lessons carefully before teaching reading to their classes. Although the teacher's manuals are quite helpful in delineating skills and methods for teaching each story, the teacher must adapt the lessons to suit the needs of the class. The five-step lesson plan recommended for classroom teachers contains (1) a behavioral objective that describes what the pupils should be able to do after they complete the lesson; (2) preassessment, which diagnoses which pupils already know the skills to be taught. If the youngsters can already do the skills, they should be given other skills to learn or be used as a resource person for the group; (3) a list of materials that are needed to teach the lesson; (4) procedures that describe how the instructor intends to teach the lesson. If the teacher reuses this lesson with another group, this will help the instructor remember that he or she "played a popular song" to introduce the concept of vanity to the fifth graders. It then can be reused without rethinking through the entire process. In addition, writing out a procedure before one teaches enables the teacher to ask colleagues to make suggestions for possible improvement in the classroom situation; and (5) postassessment, which delineates how one measures the pupils to see if one's objective was achieved. This step may well be the most important. It forces the teacher to evaluate whether or not his or her teaching has been successful; that is, were his or her objectives met? This indicates whether or not the material should be retaught. If the objective has been reached, then the teacher should proceed to new material.

The behavioral objective step forces the teacher to focus on the learner rather than on his or her own performance as a teacher. It helps the teacher to think in terms of skills. A behavioral objective describes outcomes or performances that the children should accomplish as a result of their participation in the reading lesson. Teaching reading by objectives helps the teacher to clarify his or her thinking about desired pupil learnings, plan instruction to achieve this learning, and determine to what extent the child has learned the reading skills. When writing objectives, the teacher must describe desired reading performance in terms of an observable act and in terms of the student. In other words, an objective would be "the child will list . . ." *not* "the teacher will list . . .". Verbs that can help the teacher in planning reading lessons based on observable behavior are recite, identify, differentiate, solve, construct, list, compare, contrast, predict, design, teach, remake, describe, define, analyze, select, demonstrate, present, and the like. Verbs that are not helpful because they are not specific enough are "know" (How does the teacher determine "know?" If the child lists, or defines, or predicts, the child shows the teacher what he or she must do to prove that the child knows); "appreciate" (What must the child do to show the teacher that he or she "appreciates"? If the child analyzes a story read or constructs a book report, the child shows the teacher what he or she can do to demonstrate "appreciation"); "enjoy" (How do we know that the child "enjoys?" If the child requests additional books, smiles when given the book, and enthusiastically asks specific questions about the book, the teacher may determine that the child has "enjoyed" what he or she had read.)

The five steps of a basal reader lesson and the five-step lesson plan are not the same. The teacher may have a five-step lesson plan for each step of a basal reader lesson. In other words, for one basal reader lesson it is possible to have five different lesson plans. The sample lesson plans below will serve to illustrate this distinction as well as to clarify the steps in both the lesson planning and the basal reader lesson. An important rule of thumb in each lesson plan is not to plan more objectives than can be evaluated in a lesson.

SAMPLE LESSON PLANS

Here are sample lesson plans using basal readers.

Sample Lesson Plan 1

(Components of Preparation Step—New Words)

Behavioral Objective: On successful completion of this lesson, students should be able to pronounce correctly the words *Edison*, *electricity*, and *laboratory* when presented with a flash card on which the words are written.

Preassessment: Hold up words *Edison*, *electricity*, and *laboratory*. Those children who can pronounce the words correctly should go on to a different lesson.

Materials: Pocket chart; flash cards with the words *Edison*, *electricity*, and *laboratory* written on them; sentence strips with the following sentences printed on them:

Thomas *Edison* lived a long time ago. He made many inventions. He was a smart man. He also worked in a *laboratory*. He loved to work with *electricity* in his laboratory.

Procedure: Hold up flash cards and ask if anyone knows the words. Tell the children they concern an American inventor who made great improvements in the telegraph and see if they can use context and background knowledge to identify words. Present words on flash cards to children by syllables. See if they can unlock words by word attack skills. Present words in sentences. Discuss meanings. Present words in a second set of sentences with key words covered. Can the children use context to help unlock unknown words? Check by removing cover.

Postassessment: Hold up the three flash cards. Those children who can pronounce the three words correctly have met the objective.

Sample Lesson Plan 2

(Components of Step 2—Purpose)

Behavioral Objective: On successful completion of this lesson, students should be able to answer the following questions after silently reading the story. "Where were the explorers? What happened to them? Why?"

Preassessment: Those children who answer the questions correctly should go on to another lesson.

Materials: Pictures of explorers; book for each child.

Procedures: Show the pictures of the explorers; discuss where they were, what happened to them, and why; have children read silently to find the answers.

Postassessment: Those children who answer all three questions correctly have met the objectives.

Sample Lesson Plan 3

(Components of Step 3—Oral Reading and Discussion)

Behavioral Objective: On successful completion of this lesson, students should have read orally expressing the appropriate feelings of Shirley, Clarice, or Parry.

Preassessment: When asked to read aloud, those children who reflect the feelings of the characters correctly should go on to another lesson.

Material: Each child should have a reader.

Procedure: Discuss possible feelings of each of the characters in the story. How do the children feel when they are treated that way? How do they sound when they feel that way? Have each child read at least one of the character's statements.

Postassessment: Those children who reflect the feelings of the characters correctly in an oral reading situation have met the objective.

Sample Lesson Plan 4

(Components of Follow-up Step—New Skill and Practice)

Behavioral Objective: On successful completion of this lesson, students should be able to divide all the words on a given list of unknown *vowel, consonant,* and *consonant-vowel* words (words that have the pattern vccv—like *rabbit*).

Preassessment: Those children who can correctly divide all the words on the given list of vccv words into syllables should go on to a different lesson.

Materials: Overhead projector; individual pocket charts; words to fit in pocket chart.

Procedure: Begin with a list of known vccv words. Ask children to listen for the number of syllables that they hear in each word and then state the dividing point. Place the words on an overhead projector. Elicit the vccv rule. Try the rule on unknown words as a group. When the group appears successful, ask them to respond as individuals. Instruct them to divide the words into syllables according to the vccv rule and then hold up the words in the pocket chart.

Postassessment: Those children who have correctly divided all the unknown vccv words in their pocket charts have met the objective.

If the distinction between lesson plans and basal reader lessons is still not clear, the following explanation might prove useful. First, a teacher might teach one step a day if the group of pupils is slow moving. This would mean one lesson plan per step. However, if the group of youngsters is fast moving, then the teacher might cover three or four steps a day. In that case, the teacher will have included those three or four steps in his or her lesson plan. Therefore, the length of the lesson plan depends on the ability of the students. For example, if the children complete steps 1, 2, and 3 in one day, then the daily lesson plan for the behavioral objective for that particular group might read: "The students will be able to make a statement and prove their point by reading from the text." This will assume that there had been adequate preparation, silent reading, and discussion before reaching this point.

The importance of thinking of basal reader lessons and lesson planning with behavioral objectives in such flexible terms is that it allows the teacher to use the basal reader lesson, the basal reader components, and the basal reader supplementary materials as tools to teach pupils reading. Lesson planning by objectives helps the teacher to keep the focus on performances that must be demonstrated by youngsters to complete objectives rather than a progression through a basal series without attention to what the child needs to do to show the teacher that he or she has indeed learned the skills.

SUMMARY

This chapter has focused upon methods and materials commonly found in the basal reader method of teaching reading. A delineation of reading levels and related vocabulary loads, the three basic components ordinarily found within each level, and the purpose of various different supplementary materials was presented. In addition, several generalizations that can be made about a basal reader series as well as its strengths and weaknesses were discussed. Finally, the relationship between a five-step basal reader lesson and a five-step daily lesson plan was discussed and illustrated.

References and Bibliography

Bond, Guy L., and Wagner, Eva Bond. *Teaching the Child to Read.* New York: Macmillan Publishing Co., Inc., 1966.

Chall, Jeanne. *Learning to Read: The Great Debate.* New York: McGraw-Hill Book Company, 1967.

Dallmann, Martha, Rouch, Roger L., Chang, Lynnette Y. C., and DeBoer, John. *The Teaching of Reading,* 5th ed. New York: Holt, Rinehart and Winston, 1978.

Durr, William, LePere, Jean, and Brown, Ruth. *Teacher's Guide for Fiesta.* Boston: Houghton Mifflin Company, 1971, p. 18.

Fry, Edward. *Reading Instruction for Classroom and Clinic.* New York: McGraw-Hill Book Company, 1972.

Guszak, Frank J. *Diagnostic Reading Instruction in the Elementary School.* 2nd ed. New York: Harder & Row, Publishers, 1978.

Harris, Larry A., and Smith, Carl B. *Reading Instruction Through Diagnostic Teaching.* New York: Holt, Rinehart and Winston, 1976.

Heilman, Arthur W. *Principles and Practices of Teaching Reading.* 4th ed. Columbus, Ohio: Charles E. Merrill Publishing Company, 1977.

Herr, Selma H. Recent Survey Cited by Spache, G. and Spache, E., *Reading in the Elementary School,* 3rd ed. Boston: Allyn & Bacon, Inc., 1973, p. 173.

Spache, George D. and Evelyn B. *Reading in the Elementary School.* 3rd ed. Boston: Allyn & Bacon, Inc., 1973.

Zintz, Miles V. *The Reading Process: The Teacher and the Learner.* 3rd ed. Dubuque, Iowa: William C. Brown Company, Publishers, 1979.

Self-Check 6.3
Basal Reader Approach

The following questions are designed to help the participant assess his or her competence on the first seven objectives stated at the beginning of this chapter. Although every effort has been made to make the self-check questions comprehensive, participants should remember that they are held responsible for meeting the objectives as stated at the beginning of this chapter.

1. Objective 1. Describe a delineation of reading levels and related vocabulary loads that are typically found in a current basal reader series.

2. Objective 2. Describe and discuss at least three generalizations that can be made about a basal reader series.
3. Objective 3. Describe the three basic components ordinarily found within each level of a basal reader series.
4. Objective 4. Explain the purpose of at least five supplementary materials that could be found within a particular basal reader program.
5. Objective 5. Compare the strengths and weaknesses of using a basal reader series.
6. Objective 6. Mrs. Richards states to the children, "Now that you have read the story, I want you to look for the answers to various questions about it which I will ask." What step of the basal reader lesson is she teaching?
7. Objective 7. Differentiate between a five-step basal reader lesson and a five-step daily lesson plan.

Chapter 6
Experience 1

Objective

During this experience, the participant will develop and teach at least one step of a basal reader lesson.

Activity and Assessment Guide

1. Attach a copy of the lesson plan that you designed to teach one of the steps of the basal reader lesson.
2. State the author, title, publisher, copyright date, grade level, and page numbers that you used to develop your lesson.

____

____

____

3. State which one of the five steps of a basal reader lesson that you developed a lesson on. ____________________
4. Did your lesson plan format contain a behaviorally stated objective? circle one yes no Briefly describe the objective.

____

5. Did your lesson plan format contain the following? (circle the appropriate response)

   a. preassessment yes no

   b. materials section yes no

   c. procedures yes no

   d. postassessment yes no

* 6. Did the children you taught show the behavior intended by the objective? (circle one) yes no Describe a behavior that indicated to you that the object was or was not met. ______________________________

____

____

* 7. Did the procedure suggested by the teacher's manual prove helpful and effective to you? (circle one) yes no Briefly explain why or why not. ______________________________

____

____

* 8. Do you have any suggestions for varying the same letter next time and for improving upon the suggestions in the teacher's manual? (circle one) yes no Briefly describe at least one suggestion. ______________________________

____

____

*See Chapter 1, Experience 1 for explanation of the asterisk.

Chapter 7
Other Approaches to Teaching Reading

Objectives 7.1

On completion of this chapter, the participant should be able to

1. Describe the four premises underlying the language experience approach to teaching reading.
2. Discuss why facility with language, background experiences, and interests should be assessed before instruction is planned.
3. Identify at least three different sources that can be used to provide experiences for stories.
4. Differentiate among the purposes for large-group dictation, small-group dictation, and individual dictation.
5. Describe at least five techniques that should be used by the teacher when transcribing an experience dictated by one or more children.
6. Describe the construction of a word bank and illustrate how at least three different reading skills can be taught through its use.
7. Differentiate between instruction given to children who already know how to read and those who do not.
8. Discuss why it is important that the teacher transcribe each child's stories regularly even if the child is also transcribing some of his or her own.
9. Discuss at least three types of records that should be kept by a teacher using the language experience approach.
10. Discuss how "learning centers" may be used.
11. Discuss the role of children's literature in a language experience approach to reading.
12. Discuss a procedure for developing critical thinking skills.

13. Discuss groups of learners for whom the language experience approach would be particularly appropriate.
14. Describe at least one advantage and one disadvantage of the language experience approach.
15. Given a description of a specific youngster, prescribe instruction using the language experience approach.
16. Given a specific reading skill, describe how it could be taught using the language experience approach.
17. Given a specific reading skill, construct at least three different lesson plans teaching that same skill to three different types of learners.
18. Given a description of a language experience program, evaluate it according to criteria given in this chapter.
19. Define what is meant by the term "individualized reading program."
20. Identify the five basic components upon which an individualized program is based.
21. Describe a five-step procedure for organizing an individualized reading program.
22. Discuss at least three factors related to instruction that should be diagnosed.
23. Discuss each of the following components related to planning instruction in an individualized program:
    a. locating materials
    b. scheduling time
    c. holding individual conferences
    d. designing lessons
    e. formulating independent activities
    f. formulating group activities
    g. formulating book-sharing situations
24. Discuss at least three different types of records that should be kept in an individualized program.
25. Describe at least one technique for facilitating an efficient management system in an individualized reading program.
26. Discuss how an individualized reading program can be incorporated into either a basal reader program or a language experience program.
27. List at least three advantages and at least three disadvantages of an individualized reading program.
28. Given a description of an individualized reading program, evaluate it according to criteria given in this chapter.
29. Briefly describe at least three methods other than basal, language experience, and individualized approaches for teaching reading.

Experiences 1, 2, and 3 extend Chapter 7 with these objectives:

30. Design and teach a lesson based upon the language experience approach.

31. The student will perform one or more of the following:
    a. design and teach a lesson for helping the child select a book
    b. conduct an individual conference
    c. construct a motivating skill-building activity
32. Design and teach a lesson in reading using a method other than the basal, language experience, and individualized approaches.

Information Given 7.2
Other Approaches to Teaching Reading

LANGUAGE EXPERIENCE APPROACH

When the teacher education major entered Mr. Weather's first grade class, she noticed that he was showing the whole group a clock that had a spinning figure on the top. He held it up and asked if any one in class knew what it was. Then he showed them how it sounded when it was wound up. It went "tick" "tick" "tick." All the children were asked if they could tick like a clock, at which point they all went "tick, tick, tick." When the big hand on the clock pointed to twelve, the figure on top of the clock, went "ring," then spun around in a circle. He asked the children if they could go "ring" and then spin. Each child said "rinnnnnnng" and then spun himself or herself around in a circle. After much similar discussion, the class wrote the following story with Mr. Weather.

Our Clock

We have a clock.
It goes tick, tick, tick.
When the big hand reaches twelve
it goes rinnnnnnng.
When the big hand reaches twelve it spins.
We like our clock!

The approach to beginning reading used by Mr. Weather can be designed by the term "language experience approach."

In this approach to teaching reading there is not a sharp distinction between teaching the skills of reading and teaching the other language art skills. The language experience approach to teaching reading unifies all the language arts and puts the primary emphasis on total communication. The child comes to school with an experiential background that becomes the beginning point in his or her formal, academic instruction in learning to read. As such, this approach uses the existing language and thinking of each individual as the basis for skill development. As each learns to read, he or she tends to think of reading in terms of the following rationale, which has been outlined by Roach Van Allen (1962):

1. What I think about, I can talk about.
2. What I say, I can write, or someone can write for me.
3. What I can write, I can read.
4. I can read what I have written, and I can also read what other people have written for me to read.

PROCEDURES FOR USING A LANGUAGE EXPERIENCE APPROACH

In establishing a reading program that relied upon this approach, Mr. Weather knew that he had to identify each child's facility with the language, interests, and background experience. Then he would use these components to build more experiences, develop greater facility with the language, and subsequently have the children compose stories that would be written down and placed into a notebook kept by the child. He therefore developed a four-step plan to help him organize his instructional procedures. These four steps included (1) identify language facility, interests, and background, (2) plan instruction around these existing elements, (3) keep accurate records of each child's progress, and (4) develop some sort of management system to give instructions to the children and make certain that each child is taught needed skills. These steps will be discussed in more detail in the following paragraphs.

STEP 1: IDENTIFY BACKGROUND EXPERIENCES, INTERESTS, AND FACILITY WITH THE LANGUAGE

When Mr. Weather's students entered his class in September, he gave them all a readiness test to determine which children seemed to be the most ready to read. In addition, since some of the youngsters could already read, he administered a test to get an estimate of the children's reading level; he found that he had a reading range from readiness to grade two. Since it had been his experience that children who could read had more facility with the language than did those who could not, he tentatively grouped his class into three levels: those who could already read; those who were ready to learn to read; and those who needed readiness activities.

Another measure of language facility was reflected informally in conversations with each child. One boy, Jeff, seemed never to stop talking, while his best friend, Pete, hardly ever said more than two words at a time. Further, when Mr. Weather talked individually with Pete, he spoke only when specifically asked to respond. Therefore, Mr. Weather assumed that Jeff had more facility with the language than Pete and would probably learn to read sooner.

In addition to noticing the children's facility with the language, Mr. Weather also noticed the topics of their conversation. This type of observation helped him to determine what kinds of experiences would appeal to them. For example, one day Mr. Weather took his class out to the children's zoo and showed them the farm animals. He felt that this type of field trip would stimulate them. On the way home most of the children chatted animatedly about the stories they were going to compose. However, one of the boys, Henry, didn't want to write about it at all. It seemed to him that it was "dumb" to write about animals because he lived on a ranch and there was really nothing worth mentioning that they had seen. On the other hand, one of the little girls, Sue, had talked constantly on the way from the zoo back to the school about all the animals she had seen. Mr. Weather was certain that she would be excited about writing a follow-up story. However, when the children sat down to dictate, all except Henry and Sue were anxious to contribute. Sue was completely uninterested. When questioned about this she merely stated, "Why write about it, I already told you all about it!" For both these children, the experience provided by Mr. Weather did not motivate them to compose a story. Both were uninterested, as they did not see the value of such talk written down.

Mr. Weather knew that he had to develop an experience for these two children where talk written down would become quite important. He asked Henry if he would like to be room monitor. The boy quite eagerly accepted. As part of his task, he was to put up signs around the room. He spent the next few days asking Mr. Weather how to write "chair," "table," "desk," "paste," and "crayons."

Sue wasn't the least bit interested in being room monitor, but she had just acquired a gerbil and told Mr. Weather all about it. Mr. Weather asked her what kind of cage it was in, and she replied that it was one her father had built. Mr. Weather told her that he would like to build a cage if she would write out a set of directions for him on how it was done. She spent the next several days dictating directions to him.

STEP 2: PLAN INSTRUCTION

When Mr. Weather took the children to the zoo, he intended it to be a stimulus activity to encourage them to write a story about their trip. However, he was also able to use it as a means to identify language facility, interests, and experiential background. As could be seen from the description, he had to adapt his plans to suit the needs of Sue and Henry, who were completely unmotivated to write about the activity. He usually tried to provide the children with experiences from a variety of sources: (1) *Field trips.* He tried to provide visits to such places as the local fire station, the candy factory, and the local post office. (2) *Audiovisual resources.* He frequently presented films, records, tape recordings, and pictures of all types. In some cases, they had been part of the supplementary material available with commercially produced programs; in other cases, he made them himself. (3) *Demonstrations and simple experiments.* These varied considerably in length and complexity. In one instance, he spent five minutes showing the children how to make a whistle by flattening a straw; in another instance, he helped the children to plant seeds and then write daily progress reports about their growth. (4) *Poems and stories.* He found that most of the children thoroughly enjoyed listening to him read. Furthermore, if he read a ghost story, the next type of story that each wanted to write would invariably be about a ghost. (5) *Their own lives.* He was usually able to persuade all the children to reveal their experiences and interests. Although Sue had not wanted to write about the zoo, Mr. Weather had no problem getting her to write about her gerbil. As soon as Sue felt that Mr. Weather was really interested in the gerbil's cage and needed the directions for building it written down, she dictated the needed instructions. (6) *Their families.* Most of the children could be encouraged to write about brothers, sisters, cousins, friends, the type of dwelling in which they lived, and so forth. (7) *Current events.* When Thanksgiving came around, almost all the children wanted to write stories about turkeys. (8) *School itself.* Mr. Weather was always amused to find himself the center of many of the stories the children wrote.

Techniques for Dictation

The use of whole-class dictation demonstrated in the story "Our Clock" served a useful purpose in initially diagnosing children and was a good means of getting the children started in reading. However, as in all reading instruction, Mr. Weather knew that an approach that met each child's special needs would be best. In this case, it meant that an individually dictated story would be more meaningful to the learner than a group-dictated story. However, Mr. Weather felt that he could also accomplish a great deal with small-group dictations, as it made more economical use of his time. Also, the group interaction would stimulate more experiences and make the children aware of how many different possible stories could be written about the same topic, such as their visit to the zoo. Therefore, Mr. Weather used all three types of situations for dictating.

Individual Dictation

When Mr. Weather met with an individual child, he tried to ascertain the child's interests first to stimulate conversation with the youngster so that he or she would have something to write about. When Pam sat with him, he knew that she and her father had gone fishing the previous weekend. Therefore, he asked her to tell him about the fishing trip. After she talked about it a bit, he helped her determine what she wanted to write down.

Since Mr. Weather's main purpose in using this approach was to make reading as meaningful and easy to understand as possible, he dictated exactly what she told him to dictate, regardless of whether or not it was "perfect" English. Therefore, when Pam told him that "Me and my daddy went fishin' last week," he transcribed the story into her notebook as "Me and my daddy went fishing last week." He made no attempt to change her "Me and my daddy" to "my daddy and I." However, he did transcribe her pronunciation of "fishin" into standard spelling, as she was learning to read and needed to know how the words she spoke usually looked when she encountered them in someone else's writing. His initial purpose was to encourage student self-expression, not to hamper the youngsters by preoccupation with adult standards of "perfect" English.

Large Group Dictation

On occasion, particularly at the beginning of the year, there would be some activity or event in which all the children were interested. In such case, Mr. Weather would compose stories with the whole class dictating sentences to him. Those children who were not yet interested in language were motivated by the obvious pleasure that their peers demonstrated during these story writing sessions. It also gave Mr. Weather an opportunity to do more informal diagnosing of interest, experiential background, and facility with the language in a more rapid manner than with small-group or individual dictations. However, regardless of group size or maturity of youngsters involved, his procedures for developing a lesson were the same. A large group dictation based on suggestions from Spache and Spache (1973) is illustrated here.

First, Mr. Weather encouraged each learner to share his or her ideas and experiences with others. Example: Several types of plants were brought to class. The students talked about which ones were edible, what they looked like, and what they felt like. Eventually, the group played a game of charades in which each member of the group guessed which plant the player was thinking about.

Second, he helped each student to clarify and summarize his or her ideas and experiences. This taught his pupils that reading matter often contained only the "heart of the discussion," not all the extraneous comments that occurred in normal speech. Example: One of the youngsters told about his grandpa's farm and all the cows. Mr. Weather acknowledged the youngster's comment about the cows, and then asked him if any plants grew on the farm, and if they did were they similar to any in the classroom. He said there were plants at the farm. They all had leaves and they all had roots just like the ones in the class.

Third, he recorded the learner's story. Example: After the class had discussed plants, Mr. Weather asked for a title for the story. The children suggested many things, but all had to do with details rather than main ideas. Mr. Weather asked the youngster whose grandpa lived on a farm to say again what he had said about how grandpa's plants were like the ones in the classroom. The child repeated his previous statement. Mr. Weather then asked if all the things that they had suggested for the story had to do with that statement. All the children agreed that was true. He asked if that would make a good idea for a title. They agreed that it would. Mr. Weather wrote out the title of the story on blank newsprint; he asked them to repeat the statements that they had suggested previously and wrote the following story with the children.

Why Plants Have Roots

All plants have roots.
Roots take in water.
All plants need water.
All plants have roots so they can get water.)

Fourth, he asked the children to share their written ideas with the whole class. Example: The class read the story that they had written together on plants. They discussed the fact that another good story could be written about plants of different colors, since carrots were orange, beans were green, and tomatoes were red. One child said he didn't like plants and was going to bring an apple to school the next day, because it was red and besides it tasted much better than a tomato. Another little boy stated that he had a red car and would prefer to show that rather than anything to do with things to eat. This caused discussion on modes of transportation and all begged the teacher to help them write a story on that topic. One girl mentioned her ice skates on which she had traveled far when she had lived in Minnesota. The rest of the youngsters had never lived in a cold climate and asked her all about skates and how to skate. She promised to bring the skates to class the next day.

Finally, Mr. Weather designed skill development and extension activities. While the youngsters were reading their stories, Mr. Weather pointed out sentence structure, word choices, sounds of words, and the like. Example: The class read the story on plants that they had written. They discussed why "roots" had an *s* on the end, why the first letter in each word that began a sentence was a large one, and why the word "every" could be substituted for "all" as it meant the same thing. Mr. Weather encouraged each child to expand his or her own language development and was careful not to write his ideas instead of the child's.

Use of a Word Bank

Each word that the child used in a group story, or in an individual story, that the child identified as known to him or her was placed on an index card and put in a personal "word bank." Since the first graders tended to spill things easily, the "word banks" were really old shoe boxes, attractively decorated, but with tight-fitting lids. Mr. Weather used this resource of individually kept words as a tool for teaching all kinds of reading skills. For example, he taught alphabetizing (first letter only, first three letters); directional sense (make sentence putting words together from left to right; select word from front of box, middle of box, back of box); categorizing (place all words referring to plants in one pile, animals in another; verbs in one pile, nouns in another); structural analysis (all words with same prefixes, suffixes together; all words with the same roots together); phonics (all words with hard *c* in one pile, soft *c* in another; all words that end in *nd* together); and vocabulary development (put all synonyms for a word in one pile, all antonyms in another; all words that look the same but are pronounced more than one way together).

Small Group Dictation Organized by Reading Level

As was mentioned earlier, when Mr. Weather assessed his class's facility with the language, he found that he had children who could already read, children who were quite ready to learn to read, and children who needed readiness activities. Therefore, he frequently divided the class into three groups and worked with them accordingly:

The group that was already reading met together and read books, shared ideas, and wrote stories. Although many of them were able to write stories on their own, Mr. Weather still regularly transcribed stories for them in both individualized and group situations, as they needed a model to see what standard spelling, punctuation, and capitalization looked like. When they were asked to dictate individually, they were usually so adept with the language that they came up one at a time and readily told Mr. Weather what they wanted him to write. While he was transcribing individual stories for the members of the group, the other children would be writing their own stories, reading their books, or building their word banks. When they were involved with a group dictation, since they already knew a great number of words, they usually met with Mr. Weather and told him what words they really wanted to learn that day. One little girl told him that she really needed to know the word "picturesque," as she had overheard her father say that their house was "picturesque." Mr. Weather helped them with the meaning and the spelling of the word, and they wrote it out and placed it in their word banks. All the teachers in the school soon knew that the children in Mr. Weather's class knew that word, as the school was "picturesque," the lunchroom was "picturesque," even the principal was "picturesque." Additionally, every story written by members of that group contained a "picturesque" something or other for the next few weeks.

While working on their word banks or while reading from books, magazines, or newspapers, these children continued to identify words that they really wanted to know. When they shared each other's stories, they would ask their peers the meaning of unknown words. As they were writing freely about all kinds of things at this time, they began to become aware that they didn't always spell words like their friends did. When Mr. Weather wrote their stories for them, he transcribed the words into standard spelling, but made no attempt to correct their spelling in the stories they wrote on their own. Since they were allowed to spell the words in any way they wished, many of their words reflected what they felt was a sound-symbol relationship rather than the standard spelling. Therefore, when Debby wrote the story about the "ded dog" of the "nabrs," Fritz was not quite sure what it meant. When Debby "translated" for him, he went to his own word bank that contained only standard spellings and showed her that when Mr. Weather wrote those words they looked like "dead" and "neighbors." This stimulated a small group discussion on the virtue of standard spelling. Thus Mr. Weather did not have to teach the children why they needed to spell in a uniform manner. They discovered it on their own, and it became quite relevant to them.

The group that was ready to read met with him in a different fashion. They knew a few words but were basically much less fluent in their speech than the group who could already read. Therefore, Mr. Weather did a great deal of total small group dictation with this group where each child had to contribute only a sentence or two instead of a total story. In addition, since these youngsters were not able to read yet, when he did meet with them for individual dictation he asked the nondictating group members to read picture books, or to illustrate their previously written stories with drawings, or to locate words that they thought they knew in available reading material, while he worked with an individual child. He had to motivate these youngsters and sometimes almost had to draw out each line of their story word by word. For example, he asked Pete what his favorite pet was. Pete replied, "A dog." He then asked Pete if he had a dog. Pete replied, "Yes." He then asked Pete to describe the dog. Pete said, "He's black." He asked him to tell more about the dog, and Pete said, "He's big." After several minutes, Mr. Weather and Pete wrote the following story:

Pete's Dog

I have a big dog.
His name is Sarge.
He is black.
He is my favorite pet.

When this group shared ideas, they talked with Mr. Weather about the words they knew. Pete told everyone that he knew the words "dog," "pet," and "black." Mr. Weather helped him to add those words to his word bank. The next time that the group met, Pete was given a magazine that he was to look through for the words "dog," "pet," and "black." Each time he found one of those three words, he cut it out of the magazine and pasted it on a large sheet of cardboard. When it came time for a group "show and tell," Pete held up his collage and showed his peers how many different ways those three words were written. Sometimes "dog" was written in black letters; sometimes it was written in red letters; sometimes it was written in quite large letters; sometimes it was written in quite small letters. The group then discussed why the word was written in so many different colors and sizes.

The group that needed readiness were, for the most part, simply not motivated by the desire to learn to read. Sue, the girl who would rather talk about gerbils than write about them, was in this group. Furthermore, many of these children lacked an attention span of over ten minutes. Therefore, when Mr. Weather worked with this group, he had to present them with activities that varied about every ten minutes or so. In addition to giving them activities to expand their experiential background, he also tried to teach them such things as visual discrimination, left to right progression, and auditory discrimination. One of the first things that Mr. Weather did with these children was to make out an index card with the name of each child on it. Every time he wanted to talk to a youngster, he would point to the name card and ask the children to tell him the name of the child whom he wanted to see. While he met with individual children for dictation, the rest of the group members were writing their own names on a huge sheet of newsprint and then drawing pictures of themselves to illustrate the names. He pointed out to each child that before the child began to write his or her name the child should begin at the left and work to the right. For some children, he had to guide their hands when they first began to print their name. Some of the more advanced children were using colored chalk and writing their last names as well as their first. During the group dictation, they wrote a story about a game they played, "Simon Says," in which Mr. Weather had attempted to teach them to follow directions. The story went

Simon Says

Simon says touch the pencil.
Simon says touch the head.
Touch the floor.
You are out!

Mr. Weather did not include quotation marks at this time, as he felt they were not ready for them.

To develop visual discrimination as well as the other readiness skills, Mr. Weather asked the children, "What color is the pencil that Simon said to touch?" "What size is the pencil?" What shape is the pencil?" Then he asked each child to draw a picture of a pencil and then use scissors to cut pictures out of magazines representing objects that were the same color as the pencil, the same shape, and the same size then paste them on three separate sheets of paper. One was marked "Color," one was marked "Size," and one was marked "Shape."

Other Types of Small Groups

It is important to note at this point that these children were not always grouped according to reading facility. Mr. Weather usually tried to group according to the interest shown by children in the various activites. This interaction of good readers and nonreaders was very important to the success of Mr. Weather's program. Many of the children who did not know left from right or the letter *d* from the letter *b* learned by watching "good readers" read their group stories.

For example, one day Georgia brought in a picture of her family's new yellow trailer. Most of the children in class gathered around to see the picture of the trailer. Not all the children remained interested, and the majority soon went back to their other activities. However, a group of six youngsters ranging in reading ability from grade two to readiness stood around the picture of the trailer. Mr. Weather took out a sheet of newsprint and asked them to write a story about the trailer.

One of the more articulate youngsters rattled off several sentences about the trailer. Mr. Weather wrote down one of these sentences and then tried to get the others to participate. Georgia, the child whose family had a new trailer and whose skills were at readiness level, was able to tell the class that the trailer was "Georgia's." Mr. Weather made that the title of the story and continued to solicit responses from *all* six children. The story they wrote was

Georgia's Trailer

Georgia has a trailer.
We saw a picture of it.
It is brand new.
The color is dark yellow.
It is very pretty.

After the story was written, Georgia was just as proud of "her" story—although she had contributed only one word—as were the rest of the children in the group. Additionally, when the youngsters read the story back to Mr. Weather, he asked Georgia to "read" the title. She easily said "Georgia's Trailer." In this manner she learned to have a successful beginning experience with reading. In a like manner, she watched the best reader in the group read from left to right as he moved his hand in a continuous motion along with the words. Furthermore, she noticed that he did not pronounce the *d* in "dark" like the *b* in "brand". To her, the *d* and *b* looked like the same letter. Therefore, she looked at the letters closely to figure out how they were different. In this manner, Georgia learned auditory and visual discrimination and left to right progression and also developed an interest in wanting to learn how to read.

STEP 3: KEEP ACCURATE RECORDS

Because the children were learning to read according to their own background and facility with language and because skills were primarily based upon stories that they had dictated, there was no precise, exact sequence or structure in which skills were presented. Therefore, it was quite important for Mr. Weather to keep accurate records. Although the word bank provided an accurate record of the amount of words each child was learning, Mr. Weather also kept track of each story he had written for the children. Each child in his class had a standard 8½" × 11" notebook in which he or she kept track of all his or her individual stories. If Mr. Weather had happened to type them, he merely pasted them into the book. In other cases, he wrote the story directly into the notebook as it was dictated. Each story was dated, so that he could keep chronological track of the stories. In addition, he left the first few pages blank, as this became the table of contents for the child's book. He also wrote only on the right-hand side of the page so that the child would have a place to illustrate the story on the left-hand side (Stauffer, 1970).

In addition, those children who were already writing their own stories kept them in a separate notebook. Mr. Weather's transcriptions of their dictations contained their ideas but reflected correct spelling, punctuation, and capitalization. Since their own stories purposely had no such restrictions, it was important to Mr. Weather to keep the two types of stories separate. They made words for their word banks only out of the words that came from the stories that Mr. Weather had transcribed. His rationale for this was to give them a resource to turn to when they did want to find out how to spell a word, punctuate a sentence, or capitalize a word. Furthermore, by keeping their own stories separate, they were able to see their own progress. It became apparent to the children at the end of a month or so that they were writing much differently from their first attempts; that they were indeed learning to read seemed to be motivating to them.

Another record that Mr. Weather kept was that of each book read by the children. Many of their experiences and much of their vocabulary were developed from the books they selected to read once they had begun to read. In fact, Mr. Weather felt that having a great number of books available for each child was paramount to the success of his program. So he provided them with as many books as he could possibly obtain from the library, the bookmobile, and his own personal resources. The type of book read was also an indication of their interests and provided Mr. Weather with data for further experiences that would appeal to each child.

STEP 4: DEVELOP A MANAGEMENT SYSTEM

Because of the unstructured nature of this approach, Mr. Weather needed to plan lessons for the children carefully and to keep track of their assignments so that they would know what they were supposed to be doing the majority of the time. His basic activities in reading included writing down dictated stories, working with children on skill development, and providing them with a variety of books and experiences in which they could actually participate to expand their interests, experiential background, and facility with the language. To do this, he divided his reading program into ten different "learning centers:" (1) reading center, (2) writing center, (3) art media center, (4) building center, (5) game center, (6) listening center, (7) publishing center, (8) talking center, (9) drama and puppetry center, and (10) seminar center. To help children locate each center, he gave it a label and placed an attractive marker with that designation in the middle of the area where that center was located. An expanded description of each of these centers and their identifying labels follows.

1. *Center R was the reading area.* Mr. Weather had placed a rug in one corner of the room so that children could lie on the floor and read if they wished. A variety of reading material was kept there. There were picture books, newspapers, magazines, and stories written by other children who wanted to "lend" them to the center for a short period of time. Since there was a range from readiness to grade two, Mr. Weather had books of many grade levels and interests in this center.

2. *Center W was the writing area.* It was at this spot where Mr. Weather did most of the dictation of the children's stories. Sometimes they came one by one; other times they met as a group.

3. *Center A was the art media area.* Mr. Weather had placed paint brushes, finger paints, paste, crayons, pieces of fabric, and old magazines and newspapers. The children were encouraged to paint, make sculptures, collages, and murals and anything else with which they could express themselves in this form.

4. *Center B was a building area.* Mr. Weather had placed hammers, nails, saws, chicken wire, papier mache supplies, clay, yarn, scissors, and construction paper in this area. This was the center the children used the most when preparing props to perform a skit.

5. *Center G was the game area.* This consisted of a variety of activities designed to extend the language. For example, the game of "Alphabet Bingo," which was located there, was played exactly like regular bingo except

that a student who could read would call out words whose initial sound began the same as the sound of pictures pasted on the game board. The child who was able to cover up all his or her pictures first won the game.

6. *Center L was the listening area.* This center was equipped with several cassette tape recorders. Mr. Weather had located many stories that children in the past had enjoyed and recorded them on tape. In addition, many commercially made tapes had been purchased and placed in the center. These recordings provided each child with opportunities to listen to well-read stories that were exciting to them. The children had quickly learned how to use the tape recorder, and even the nonreaders were able to tell the topic of each recording because of the picture clues Mr. Weather had placed on the container that held each tape. For example, tapes that contained ghost stories had ghosts on the covers as well as the word *ghost.*

7. *Center P was the publishing area.* Mr. Weather had placed an old primary typewriter, some magic markers, some ditto masters, paper of various sizes, resources of words such as high-frequency word lists, pictionaries and dictionaries, blank books for storywriting, cut headlines from pictures for children to complete stories, cartoons with comments blacked out so that children could fill them in, poems to copy and illustrate, and other similar resources. The children who came to this center created and illustrated stories for sharing with others. Many of the children copied their stories on the ditto masters and then drew an accompanying illustration. Mr. Weather ran the story off for all members of the class.

8. *Center T was the talking area.* Mr. Weather encouraged small group discussion and sharing of experiences. For example, one boy brought in a model airplane that he wanted to show to others. Since not all students wanted to see the airplane, Mr. Weather assigned Fritz and his airplane to the talking center where he became the center of discussion. This center was also widely used by the children who wanted to read their stories to one another and then discuss them. Mr. Weather encouraged this activity, as it tended to expand their background, language facility, and interests.

9. *Center D was the drama and puppetry center.* The children could use this space to act out any stories they had read or written. Mr. Weather had constructed a stage out of an old refrigerator carton. Puppets made out of socks or paper bags were available for use. There was also material available so that the children could make their own puppets and create the scenery they needed.

10. *Center S was Mr. Weather's seminar area.* There he worked with individuals or groups in developing "critical thinking" skills. This was different from the "dictation center," as it was a teacher led, questioning center based upon carefully selected, well-written literature that Mr. Weather would read aloud to the children.

DEVELOPING CRITICAL THINKING SKILLS

Mr. Weather's procedure for developing "critical thinking skills" was similar to Stauffer's (1970) teacher led directed reading–thinking activity plan.

Stauffer's three basic steps in development of this activity include (1) developing a purpose for reading, (2) developing habits of reasoning, and (3) developing habits of testing predictions. However, Mr. Weather did not divide his seminar into three steps but, rather, developed a questioning strategy that focused upon the hierarchical development of the comprehension skills at the higher than memory levels. He would begin by asking the children questions at the interpretation and translation level and then gradually build toward the application and synthesis level questions.

This activity could not be done as effectively in the children's own stories as their writing reflected relatively immature literary development. For example, one story that Mr. Weather read to the group was *Whistle for Willie*, by Ezra Jack Keats. This book is a picture story written well above the first grade reading level.

> Picture books are not to be confused with beginning reading books. Most picture story books require reading ability of at least third grade level, and are read to children by adults. They are written for the young child's interest and appreciation level and not his reading ability level. (Huck and Kuhn, 1958, p. 109)

By reading the story aloud and pointing out pictures to them, Mr. Weather was able to develop the rudimentary thinking skills needed for the comprehension skills of interpretation and translation and application and synthesis. In *Whistle for Willie*, Peter, the main character, has not yet developed the fine motor control needed to produce a whistle with which he can call his dog, Willie. No story written by a first grader could reflect the skills of the author, Keats, in presenting the story of Peter's triumph as he finally is able to whistle and Willie comes running.

When meeting with the children in the seminar, Mr. Weather tried to model purposeful reading by guiding their thinking with some carefully developed comprehension skills. He asked them, "What is the story trying to tell us?" (identifying main idea); "Can you find the picture that shows how Peter felt when he could whistle?" (identifying detail); "Which of these three pictures came first: Peter on the way to the grocery store whistling, Peter with his father's old hat on his head, or Peter whirling around and around?" (identifying sequence); "What would you do if you could not whistle?" (making inferences); "Do you think Peter will learn to whistle before the end of the story?" (making inferences); "Why do you think Peter put on his father's old hat?" (making generalizations and conclusions).

Procedure for Scheduling

At the beginning of each week, each child was given an assignment sheet that directed him or her to the learning centers. This learning center approach provided Mr. Weather with a physical structure for organizing instruction. Activities were assigned on the basis of formal and informal assessments of the child's needs and strengths and the availability of appropriate materials.

The letter designating each center was written on the child's assignment sheet, and the child was to progress through the stations in the order in which they appeared on his or her sheet. Since these children were only in the first grade, Mr. Weather knew that their attention span was not as long as that of more mature children. Therefore, he divided his hour into twenty-minute segments and scheduled children accordingly. In some cases, when the activity was such that the child could benefit from forty minutes or even sixty minutes at that same center, Mr. Weather scheduled the child at that spot for the needed amount of time. Henry's schedule for one week follows.

	Monday	*Tuesday*	*Wednesday*	*Thursday*	*Friday*
20 min.	W	R	P	R	L
20 min.	G	B	S	D	A
20 min.	T	P	D	D	T

The schedule indicates that on Wednesday Henry went to the publishing center and typed out his story. After twenty minutes, he went to Mr. Weather along with a group of other children and listened to him read the story *Nobody Listens to Andrew* by Elizabeth Guilfoile (1957). After Mr. Weather read the story he asked the following kinds of questions: "Do you think that there really was a bear in Andrew's bed? Why wouldn't anybody listen to Andrew? Do you think that this story is funny? How do you think it will end?"

After twenty minutes in his seminar with Mr. Weather, Henry went to the drama and puppetry center where he was to prepare a puppet to illustrate the bear in the bed in the story he had just listened to.

When Mr. Weather scheduled the children into different activities, he tried to arrange his own time so that he would spend the first twenty minutes of the hour dictating stories, the second twenty minutes working with various skill-building activities, and the third twenty minutes encouraging story and experience sharing. In other words, while Henry was busy on Wednesday at the publishing center, Mr. Weather was sitting with a group of children, composing a story with them. Then, after twenty minutes, Mr. Weather went to the seminar center and questioned the children about the story *Nobody Listens to Andrew*, which he had read aloud to them. When Henry left to go to the drama and puppetry center, Mr. Weather proceeded to the talking center where he encouraged the children to share their ideas and stories with one another.

Although Mr. Weather formally scheduled an hour specifically for reading every day, he felt that activities throughout the entire day lent themselves to teaching reading. For example, in science class, the children labeled plants, in math they learned the words "add" and "subtract," and in social studies they were reading about people from other countries. Therefore, though his schedule reflected only an hour a day specifically for teaching reading, he actually used every opportunity throughout the day to provide "experiences" for his children to read and write about.

SPECIAL USES OF THE LANGUAGE EXPERIENCE APPROACH

Becuase the language experience approach blends the communication skills that reflect the unique interests and maturity of each individual, this approach is often used with beginning readers of any age. This includes the teaching of reading to the culturally different and to older children who are reading below grade level as well as first grade children.

USING THE LANGUAGE EXPERIENCE METHOD WITH THE CULTURALLY DIFFERENT

Because culturally different children often come to school with a background and language patterns completely different from those of the teacher, the language experience method with its emphasis on the real experiences has been used with much success with these children.

The basic premises underlying the language experience approach that make it work for any child make it particularly effective for the culturally different child. Because the child's story is transcribed exactly as he or she dictates it, the child learns to recognize words in a familiar sentence pattern, and reading is thus easier for him or her. However, just as in the case of any child who dictates, the phonology of his or her speech is translated by the teacher to standard spelling. Therefore, the sentence "Cal get hurts" would be transcribed as "Carol get hurts." The nonstandard verb form would be left alone because it represents the speech pattern, but the standard spelling would be used for the word "Carol," as the child would need to recognize words with *r* in a medial position if he or she were going to become a good reader.

The effect of differences in experiential background can be minimized with this approach.

For example, one day Mr. Weather brought some pictures of edible foods to class. The children were to look at the pictures of apple pies, ice cream cones, and chocolate whipped creamed cake and then discuss the sensory factor of taste. One of the children, Billy Hamlett, was a recent immigrant (whose diet did not include apple pie). When asked about the picture of apple pie, he had no idea about how it would taste. So, when Billy sat with Mr. Weather to dictate his story, he was encouraged by the teacher to tell him what kinds of food he liked. Billy told Mr. Weather about the "fry bread" his mother had made the day before, and the two wrote a story about "How to Make Fry Bread."

USING THE LANGUAGE EXPERIENCE APPROACH WITH CHILDREN READING BELOW GRADE LEVEL

Often older children who have had little success in school are motivated by a language experience approach. This is possible for several reasons. First, they are working with reading material that reflects their maturity, whereas most published texts on their reading level are geared to the interests of much younger children. In addition, the presentation of such youngsters to a completely different approach from one they may have been exposed to before may give them new hope that they can indeed learn to read. Finally, the material that they write can be made quite relevant to their experiential background and needs. For example, Bruce was two years older than most of the sixth graders in Mrs. Luken's class. He read at the first grade level and barely knew any sight words. When given a basal reader on the first grade level, he refused to look at it as he considered it an insult to a boy of his age. Likewise, when Mrs. Lukens tried to find other material written on a first grade level that she considered to be of interest to him, it was unappealing to him either because it sounded too babyish or it simply was not relevant to his interests. Finally, Mrs. Lukens discovered that he knew a great deal about cars. As she had trouble with a flat tire, she asked him how to change it. Bruce told her in great detail how this could be done. She told him that she could not possibly remember all the steps in changing a tire and convinced him to write it down for her. He sat with her and dictated the directions. In a like manner, she was able to convince him to write an entire "car maintenance" manual for her. By the end of the year, his reading vocabulary had increased tremendously, and she had located several auto mechanic manuals that were written on a simple level that he began to read voluntarily.

ADVANTAGES AND DISADVANTAGES OF THE LANGUAGE EXPERIENCE APPROACH

Most children learning to read find the language experience approach quite relevant to their interests, needs, and facility with the language. However, since there is not an orderly progression of skill learning, the approach requires a great deal of coordination, planning, and skill on the part of the teacher. Additionally, as the child matures, he or she eventually outgrows his or her oral language and should not be restricted to his or her own vocabulary and experiences. Once the child has learned to read, this approach becomes less useful than other approaches to reading that are more easily used by the teacher to extend and develop the skills needed by the proficient reader.

INDIVIDUALIZED READING APPROACH

When another teacher education major walked into Mr. Poindexter's room, he immediately became aware of the fact that a variety of activities all seemed to be going on at the same time. He noticed that the teacher was discussing a book with one child while the rest of the children in class were busy with a multitude of other activities. The teacher education major walked over and listened in on Mr. Poindexter's end of the conversation.

Mr. Poindexter: Which character did you like best? Why?
Was there a person in the story you did not like? Why?
What is another title for this book?

Would you write down another ending and share it with me later?
Did you meet any new words you did not know? May I see your list?
Let's look at a page at random. Last time we had a problem with compound words, the short *i* sound, and the prefixes. Can you locate the compound words on this page? The short *i* sound words? The prefixes?
Would you like to read another book like this? By the same author? Look through our library and let me know whether you find one you think you will like.

The teacher education major walked around the room to see what the rest of the class was doing. About half the class members were reading. Some were looking at magazines, some were reading textbooks, and still others were engrossed in storybooks. A group of five was in one corner constructing paper bag puppets and formulating a skit about their story that they were going to present to the rest of the class. Sitting nearby was a trio of youngsters who were reading parts of their books aloud to one another. In the far corner of the room, one pair of students were quietly sharing their ideas about books with each other. One lone child was listening to a tape recording of a story while following along in his book. Several other children were working individually on what looked to be different sorts of worksheet activities. Others seemed to be taking skill development tests. Two little girls had made up a story based on a book that they read and were dictating it into a tape recorder. They had highly dramatized an event and were quite serious about making certain that the tapping of a pencil on the desk was an appropriate sound effect for horses' hooves.

Although the room buzzed with the sound of activity, it was essentially very quiet. The teacher education major noticed a brightly colored box containing manila folders. One boy walked up, rummaged through the box, and pulled out a folder. He made a check mark and wrote the day's date on the instruction sheet that was pasted inside the front cover. He moved his finger down the sheet, located another activity, and then went over to the file cabinet and pulled out a drawer. After some searching, he pulled out a folder marked "activity #62" and sat down at his desk to work on it.

The teacher education major had many questions to ask Mr. Poindexter, in particular about how the teacher was able to coordinate so many different activities at the same time. In a few minutes, the room cleared out as the children went to lunch. During that time, the teacher education major and Mr. Poindexter discussed the program. The procedure that the teacher education major had observed was one that Mr. Poindexter had been using for several years; he called it "an individualized reading program."

DEFINITION OF TERMS

Individualized reading is a term that has been used for more than thirty years to denote a system of teaching reading in which skill development is based on books that have been selected by the child rather than by the teacher. The plan provides for individual instruction in reading by carefully guiding each child in his or her selection of books, by developing independent study activities for the child, and by developing reading skills through frequent individual conferences. The sequence of skills developed is determined by the child's reading needs that are reflected in each of his or her individual conferences.

PROCEDURES FOR MAINTAINING AN INDIVIDUALIZED READING PROGRAM

Mr. Poindexter had based his individualized reading program on five basic components: (1) motivation, (2) self-selection of material, (3) self-pacing in instruction, (4) individual conferences, and (5) peer interaction. To put those components together in a meaningful way, Mr. Poindexter organized his instruction into five steps.

Step 1: Motivate the Children

When the children first entered his class in September, and continuously throughout the year, he made a great effort to motivate the children to want to read. The room was attractively decorated, and several bulletin boards were in the room. One bulletin board was titled "Books for Boys," another "Books about Animals," and a third, which had been made by the children, was titled "Books We Really Liked." He frequently read portions of books aloud to the class and then stopped at an exciting part of the story. He made certain that multiple copies of the books were available and then let the children read the rest of the story on their own, which they eagerly did.

Step 2: Diagnose Factors Related to Instruction

To help the children find books that would be most conducive to their learning to read, Mr. Poindexter knew that he needed some more information about the children.

Diagnose Reading Needs

Mr. Poindexter used the Informal Reading Inventory (IRI) as well as standardized tests to help him determine the reading skills of each child. Once he had obtained this information, he was able to help children choose books appropriate for their instructional level and skill needs.

Diagnose Reading Interests

To locate the interests of each child, Mr. Poindexter had constructed an interest inventory consisting of a series of questions in which he asked each child about the type of activities that the child preferred. For example, one of the questions required the child to respond to how he or she felt about reading the cartoons in the newspaper (this inventory is further discussed in Chapter 11). From this inventory, as well as from informal observation about subjects on which the children seemed to focus in their conversation and reading matter, Mr. Poindexter was able to get a fairly accurate impression of what types of reading topics would appeal to each youngster.

Analyze Other Related Factors

In September, when the children had first entered his class, Mr. Poindexter had looked at past records to determine specific academic strengths and weaknesses of each. This was helpful to him in finding materials that would add to the success of his program. For example, one of the boys had just come over from Germany the year before. His records indicated that although he could not read English very well, he was way above average in math. Mr. Poindexter knew that, if he gave that child materials containing "universal" mathematical terms such as *centimeter* and *millimeter* and many "universal" mathematical symbols such as +, −, ×, ÷, the child would probably be quite interested and would also have a chance to gain some academic experience. Further, if the English description of how to work a mathematical problem the child already knew how to do was short, he could probably figure out what it said and hence expand his knowledge of the language.

Another factor that Mr. Poindexter took into consideration was the perceptual strengths and weaknesses of some children. It seemed to him that many of the poor readers really needed to write out a word before they could have success with learning it. He also noted that group size made a difference. He had a few children who were "loners" and seemed to learn best by themselves. In addition, he had some children who seemed to need to interact with at least one other child before they could learn the concept being taught. Since he wanted his class to be truly individualized, he knew that those children who learned best with other children needed to be placed in instructional situations in which they could interact. To Mr. Poindexter, individualized instruction did not mean independent study but, rather, providing each child with the alternative for learning that would be most beneficial to him or her.

Mr. Poindexter also noted the pace at which each child learned the best. Self-pacing was an essential characteristic of his program, so he wanted to make certain that he allowed each child to progress at the pace most comfortable for him or her. Some of his weakest readers learned a skill very slowly because they needed a great deal of exposure to the skill to learn it. In the case of slow readers, Mr. Poindexter not only made a note of their learning pace, but also wrote a reminder to himself to provide them with a great deal of material on a particular skill so that they could learn it.

Another factor that was quite important to Mr. Poindexter in setting up his program was the amount of self-discipline possessed by each child. This factor was helpful to him in determining which pupils could assume partial responsibility for their own learning and subsequently be assigned several self-directed tasks.

The last related factor that Mr. Poindexter considered extremely important was the ability of each child to operate audiovisual equipment. Mr. Poindexter used supplementary media to enhance his program, and he knew that the material that could be helpful to each child was somewhat dependent upon the child's ability to use the material effectively.

Step 3: Plan Instruction

Once all the preceding factors had been identified, Mr. Poindexter proceeded to plan instruction based on them. His aim was to organize the program around the individual needs reflected by each child. He wanted to encourage the children to participate actively in decision making areas of the learning process by requiring them to select options from among a number of alternatives. Each child would be graded in terms of his or her own achievements, not in comparison with the achievements of others.

Locate Materials

A wide variety of materials was needed. Since instruction was to be based on the reading needs of each individual child, Mr. Poindexter knew that he would have to gather as much reading material as he could to provide his students with their "tools of instruction." He determined that ten books per child would be his absolute minimum to teach his children how to read. He used the results of his IRI and his interest inventory to locate books on a variety of topics. As he knew that some of his children were reading well above grade level and others far below, he tried to locate books of appropriate interests both above and below grade level. He had checked with the librarian at the public library and had obtained annotated graded lists of books written for elementary school children (see Chapter 11, on recreational reading, for these sources). While he was there, he made arrangements with the library to borrow books for several weeks at a time. Further, he encouraged his pupils to bring books from home. He also had kept his eye out all summer long for magazines and brochures that he believed would interest his pupils. One of his "best sellers" was the Children's Toy Catalogue from one of the large retail stores.

Self-selected materials was one of the basic premises on which his program was based. He tried to give the children plenty of time to select the books that they wanted to read. They were allowed to browse through the variety of books that he had available and were encouraged to sample the contents of many different books before they finally chose the one they wanted to read. Although he tried not to restrict their choice of books, he did give them guidance in their reading. Mike had read every fiction book in the library on basketball, baseball, and football. However, it seemed to Mr. Poindexter that most of the stories the boy selected were about flat, one-dimensional characters with stilted dialogue and predictable plots. He tried to get Mike to read an adventure story by Stephen Meader called *The Voyage of the Javelin*, as he felt that the author wrote a realistic story with good characterization. However, Mike would have no part of the book and wanted to stick with sports stories. Mr. Poindexter then recommended a sports story that he felt did a better job on characterization and realism than the ones Mike had previously selected. After Mike read the book, Mr. Poindexter was able to entice him to read the *Voyage of the Javelin*, as the character in the previous book about sports had been on a sailing boat and Mr. Poindexter was able to transfer the interest in sailing from the sports book to the adventure story.

To help children select books, Mr. Poindexter knew that he had to be aware of both their instructional level and independent reading level. The instructional level was obtained through the oral and silent reading technique discussed in Chapter 5. The independent level is approximately one level below the instructional level and is ordinarily considered to be the level at which the child can function by himself or herself quite comfortably without help from the teacher. In other words, if Mike's instructional level were fourth grade, his independent level would probably be third grade materials, and his free reading could comfortably be in third grade reading material.

Since Mr. Poindexter was not with the children every time that they browsed through the books looking for one to read, he taught the children the *hand technique* to help them avoid any books that would be too difficult for them. This technique consisted of having the child open a book to the middle and read about one hundred words silently; in an intermediate level book, this would be close to a half page. Each time the child encountered an unknown word the child was to fold under a finger on his or her hand. If his or her hand was a fist before the child finished reading the half page, the book was to be considered too hard and was to be put back on the shelf.

However, if the child folded under fewer than five fingers or more than two, the book was considered to be on his or her instructional level, and he or she chose it after first checking with Mr. Poindexter. But, since Mr. Poindexter wanted the children to read some books with complete freedom of choice, he told them that they could read any book they wished if two, one, or no fingers were folded under. In such a case, the book was considered to be on the child's independent level, and Mr. Poindexter knew that the child could read it with little guidance.

Schedule Time

To include time for each child to have an individual conference, to select and read books of his or her own choice, and to share books and activities with others, Mr. Poindexter knew that he would have to organize his instruction in some systematic, yet flexible, manner. He decided that he would divide his time during the reading hour into twenty-minute segments. In the first twenty minutes, he would hold individual conferences with some of the children, while the rest would be permitted to read or work in activity centers. In the second twenty minutes, he would ask the children to work on skill lessons or task groups or just read. While they were doing this, he would work with small groups with common skill needs. In the last twenty minutes, he would have some of the children present their reports to one another. While he watched this activity, the other children would be allowed to read or to continue working on group and individual projects.

Hold Individual Conferences

Mr. Poindexter's individual conferences were really the heart of his skill development program. He used the conferences for a variety of purposes. Each time that a child sat with him, Mr. Poindexter (1) assessed what skills he or she needed, (2) helped him or her select a book, (3) gave him or her instruction on a needed skill, (4) gave him or her further assignments for skill instruction, (5) postassessed him or her on needed skills to see if he or she had learned, (6) assessed his or her interests, or (7) helped him or her decide how he or she wanted to share the book with others.

When assessing what skills each child needed, Mr. Poindexter tried to evaluate both word recognition and comprehension skills. His procedure for doing this centered on the book that the child had chosen to read. For example, when assessing comprehension skills, Mr. Poindexter would ask the child to tell about the book that he or she was reading. If the child could understand the story, Mr. Poindexter felt that the child was comprehending. In addition, Mr. Poindexter tried to determine different types of comprehension skills that each child might need. He tried to ask a variety of questions that included more than just memory level skills (see Chapter 3 and 4 for description of these comprehension and study skills). For example, Bob was reading a story about a boy whose friend had just bought a new car. Mr. Poindexter asked him, "Why did the boy's friend buy a new car?" (identifying cause-effect relationship). "After reading the first chapter of this book, what do you think will happen in the second chapter?" (making generalizations and conclusions). "Read the boy's statement about the car when he first saw it exactly as you think he would have said it." (identifying characterization). "Where in the encyclopedia would you look to find out more about the geographical area in which the story took place?" (using reference materials). "Could you make me an outline of Chapter 1?" (organizing information). (See Chapters 3 and 4 for descriptions of these comprehension and study skills.)

Since Bob was not able to make generalizations or organize information, Mr. Poindexter made a note on Bob's record that he needed those skills.

Mr. Poindexter used a combination of oral and silent reading techniques to assess needed word identification skills. For example, he asked Bob to read the following sentences silently to find out what the word *postpone* meant: "There was a breath-taking wait while the equipment was checked. This final check postponed the race for an hour. Finally the gun went off and the race began." When Bob was not able to tell him, Mr. Poindexter determined that he did not know how to use context clues.

In addition, he usually asked each child to read aloud and then tried to determine from the oral reading problem if there were any recognizable word recognition skills that he or she needed. For example, when Bob came to the word "sedan," he pronounced it sed/an. Mr. Poindexter assumed that the boy needed help with the word recognition skill of "when a single consonant occurs between two vowels, the syllables usually divide after the first vowel, for example, ho/tel." (For more about this rule, see pages 21-22.) Therefore, Mr. Poindexter noted in his records that Bob needed some help with structural analysis.

Design Lessons

Once Mr. Poindexter had held his conference with each child, he was able to determine what skills he thought the youngster needed. For example, Fred had experienced great difficulty in understanding the meaning of the word *logy* in the sentence in his book that stated, "Unlike his logy brother, who just sat, Jack ran up and down the pier." Furthermore, after the use of context clues in that sentence had been explained to him, Fred was not able to locate another similar example when told by Mr. Poindexter to "turn to page 6 and look in the second paragraph from the bottom of the page." Mr. Poindexter decided that Fred needed help with following directions as well as with using context clues. He found several different basal reader workbooks on Fred's instructional level and located a number of exercises on the use of context clues and following directions. He also found a commercially made set of exercises that focused on the skill of using context clues and was accompanied by a filmstrip and an audiotape. Since this material was appropriate for Fred's skill needs, Mr. Poindexter assigned Fred these activities for the week.

In addition, Mr. Poindexter had discovered several other children who needed the skill of using context clues. Therefore, he scheduled a time for that group to get together to work on the skill. One of these children also needed the skill of following directions, so Mr. Poindexter located a game that required the skill of following directions to play and assigned that activity to Fred and the other child to do together.

An Activity Approach to Designing Lessons. Though his introduction to a skill and the teaching of that skill were usually done in a teacher-directed manner, Mr. Poindexter had discovered that the children seemed to find the activities and games more motivating and relevant than working in workbooks or on worksheets. So, when Mr. Poindexter designed his lesson, he liked to use activities and games as reinforcing activities as much as possible. For example, Fred had needed help in "following directions," so Mr. Poindexter wrote a list of directions for him on how to construct a dart board. Fred not only was given practice in following directions but he also learned the importance of why he needed to learn to follow them when his first attempt at a dart board had not been successful. Some of the activities and games that Mr. Poindexter used are described in the next discussion. It should be pointed out that he made as many activities as possible on manila folders so that game parts could be placed inside, the folder closed, and then stored in a file cabinet for easy accessibility. Furthermore, though some of the games are illustrated in terms of specific skills, he often varied the games to teach any number of different skills. For example, although the Bingo game is illustrated in terms of context clues, it was often adapted by Mr. Poindexter to teach antonyms or homonyms. It is also interesting to note that other children were able to benefit from Fred's dart board, as it is used in one of the games described here.

1. *Vocabulary Hopscotch.* He drew a hopscotch format on newsprint and used masking tape to hold it flat to the floor. Vocabulary cards that children had been studying were placed in each square. The child was to say

the word and use it correctly in a sentence as the child hopped onto the squares. If the child missed the word, the child wrote his or her name in the square and waited until it was his or her turn to try again.

Home base
Start
grandmother
ball
call
sand
dirt
clay
hill
car
box
dog

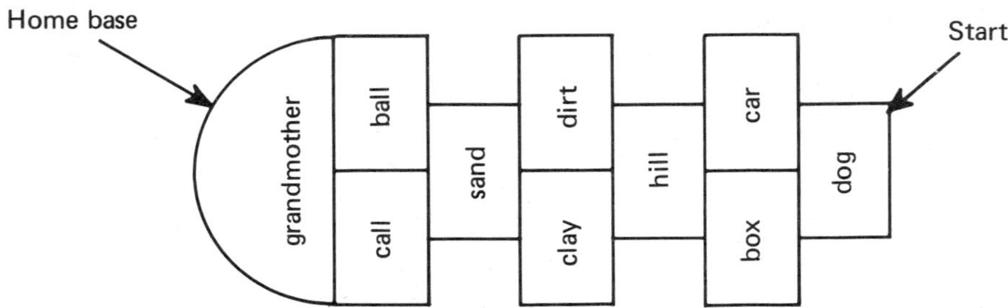

2. *Paragraph Meaning.* Three pictures all relating to the child's center of interest, but each a bit different, were pasted on a sheet of cardboard. A paragraph describing one of the pictures was pasted below the pictures. The child read the paragraph and tried to figure out which pictures belonged to the paragraph. A key on the back told the child the correct answer so that the child could check himself or herself. Paragraphs cut out of the newspaper with three related pictures was one of Mr. Poindexter's best devices for this activity.

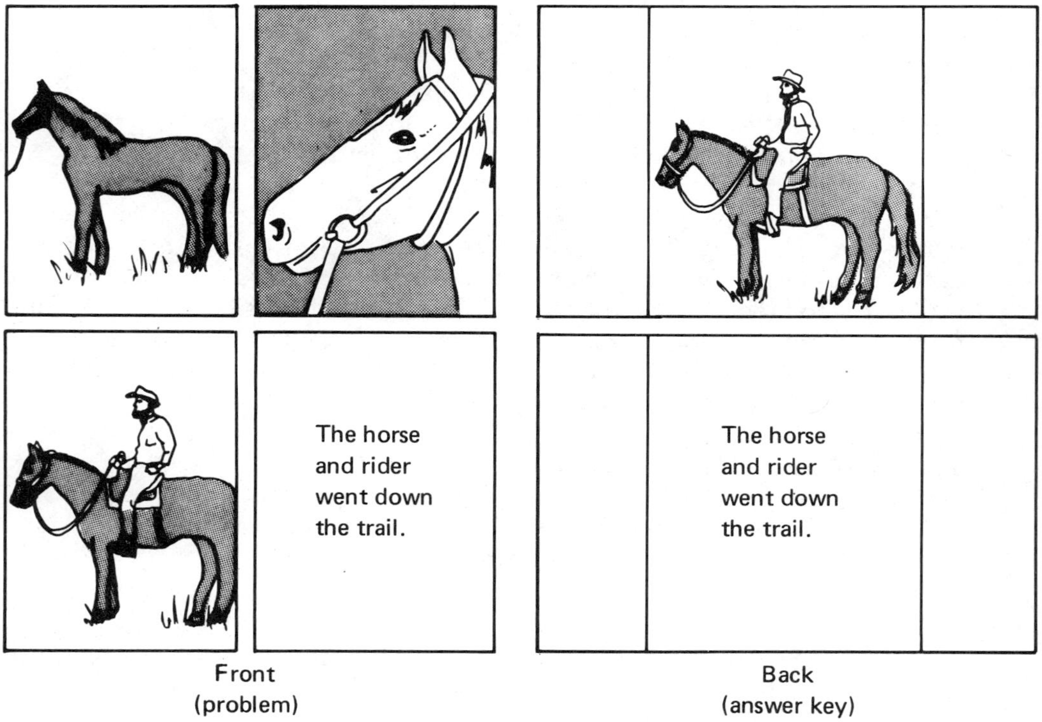

The horse
and rider
went down
the trail.
The horse
and rider
went down
the trail.
Front
(problem)
Back
(answer key)

3. *Map Game.* Mr. Poindexter obtained several city maps from the Chamber of Commerce and filling stations. He then pasted the map flat on a large piece of cardboard and made up directions for getting from school to a designated part of the city. Each child was given a different set of directions. Each child took a turn following the first instruction on his or her direction sheet; the second time around the child followed the second direction on his or her sheet; the child continued following the rest of the directions in this manner. If the child missed a direction, he or she lost his or her turn. The first child to reach the designated area was the winner.

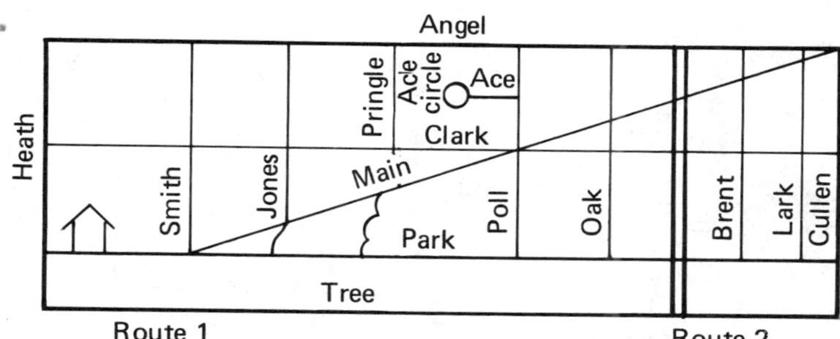

Route 1

1. North on Smith
2. East on Clark
3. South on Jones
4. Southwest on Main
5. West on Park

Route 2

1. North on Heath
2. East on Angel
3. South on Pringle
4. Northeast on Main
5. South on Oak

4. *Dart Game.* A target was made from cardboard, and vocabulary words were tacked in the circle. The children took turns throwing rubber darts at various words. Each child had to pronounce correctly the word that he or she hit, tell its meaning and the meaning of any affix, and then use it correctly in a sentence to score a point.

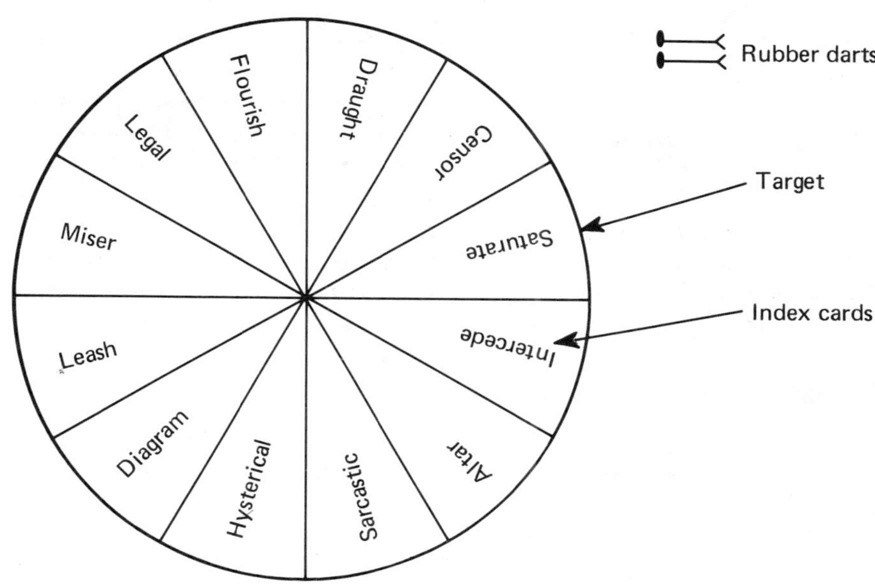

5. *Puppet Show.* Mr. Poindexter constructed a stage out of an old cardboard refrigerator box and made puppets out of old socks. He let the children act out the story just read or add a "new act" to one they particularly liked.

6. *Context Clue Bingo.* Mr. Poindexter marked off two-inch squares on the inside of an opened up manila folder. In each square he pasted synonyms of vocabulary words from a series of sentences in which the word was used in context. He prepared a folder for each youngster but placed synonyms in different orders. As he, or a student leader, read each sentence aloud, each youngster covered up the word that meant the same as the one used in context. The first student to cover up a row of words would yell "Bingo."

Develop Independent Activities

Some of the skills that the children needed were taught to them in individual situations. Part of Mr. Poindexter's philosophy, when setting up his individualized program, was to teach his pupils to be as self-directed as possible. Many of his immature students had difficulty when first assigned tasks for which they alone were responsible. Therefore, he wanted to teach them two things: (1) how to work by themselves when given a specific task and (2) how to select specific activities when given a choice of tasks. To develop this type of self-discipline, he made the assigned tasks very short and as much fun as possible. He tried to develop the children's ability to choose from among tasks by first giving them only one task or a choice between two tasks and then gradually building up to many choices. For example, Mark was quite immature and always seemed to get into trouble when given a task to do on his own. Mr. Poindexter gave him the task of "finger painting" his interpretation of the story. Mark enjoyed the activity and was able to work independently. In a few weeks, Mr. Poindexter gave Mark a choice of finger painting, making a collage out of old magazines, or writing a creative story about one of the characters in the book he was reading. Mark chose to write the creative story and was able to do this without too much direction from Mr. Poindexter. Other activities that Mr. Poindexter used to develop self-discipline, experimentation, and growth in self-directed activities were based on interests that individuals indicated they particularly liked. Some of these were block painting, collecting and labeling leaves, making model airplanes, and the like. Mr. Poindexter was able to tie in all activities to the individualized reading program because it was individualized. For example, in making the model airplane, the skills of "following directions" were particularly needed. In collecting and labeling leaves, the skills of using reference sources and the library were particularly apparent. Block painting could be used as a means to reveal some aspect of a story read or could be in itself an instructional tool, as the student followed a graph that told the exact dimensions needed to get a particular pattern on one of the blocks.

Develop Group Activities

It is obvious from Mr. Poindexter's use of activites and games to make skill development more fun that he did not equate an individualized reading program with one that consisted only of independent activities. He felt that an individualized program should be one that attempted to meet the individual needs of each child. Since he was well aware of the fact that some children learn best through interaction with other children, he frequently developed group activities. Many of these groups were extremely short-lived; they were set up for a specific purpose and disbanded as soon as the purpose was met. Among his purposes for setting up groups were the following:

Skill groups were formed whenever more than one youngster needed the same skill. For example, one day he discovered that no one in the class could use a glossary. Therefore, he held a large group discussion and demonstrated its use. This activity was enough so that all but five children were able to use the glossary. Those five were grouped together for instruction. After meeting three different times, Mr. Poindexter ascertained that they knew the skill, and he disbanded the group. Sometimes Mr. Poindexter led the group; other times he set up the group so that two students worked together in a "tutorial" capacity. In still other cases, a pair with "complementary needs" would work together. Mary might not know how to identify compound words but be good at predicting outcomes. Sue, on the other hand, might be good at identifying compound words but be poor at predicting outcomes. By working together, these two girls could both learn needed skills.

Task groups were formed for a variety of reasons. Sometimes a current event would interest children enough to want to find out more about it. At this point, Mr. Poindexter would help them to form research groups or discussion groups to look into or discuss a topic such as "noise pollution." Sometimes project groups were formed. In such a case, the students might decide that they wanted to make papier mache puppets. They would gather books on the topic, share their ideas, and then construct the puppets.

Interest groups were formed whenever more than one child wanted to read about the same topic. For example, Fred and Sue and Pete worked together in such a group. They all liked horses and were involved in a research project that illustrated the development of the quarter horse in Texas. Since Pete read at the sixth grade level, while Sue and Fred read at the third grade level, Pete did the most in gathering the necessary books and sifting through them. However, he was from New York and knew little about quarter horses. Both Fred and Sue had always lived in Texas. Fred grew up on a ranch and had ridden and raised horses most of his life. Therefore, when Pete read excerpts from the textbooks, both Fred and Sue evaluated the truthfulness of the statements. Pete was amazed that "everything the book said" was not true. They learned a great deal about evaluating the expertise of the author before believing what was written.

Develop Book-Sharing Activities

Each of the group activities noted gave children a chance to share ideas gained from reading in a meaningful way. To research or discuss the topic of "noise pollution," for example, each of the children in the group read a book of his or her own choice, on his or her instructional level. The purpose for doing so was to investigate the chosen topic. Likewise, when the project groups or interest groups met, they had read material so that they could build a papier mache puppet or discuss horses. However, in such situations many books that could be beneficial to children not in the group were not shared with those children. Mr. Poindexter knew that one way to expand the scope of his pupils' reading was to stimulate interest in books being read by their peers. For example, if Bob did not like horses, he probably would not want to be a member of that interest group and would not know anything about some of the books they were reading. However, if he had an opportunity to hear what *Misty of Chincoteague* was about, he might be very much interested in reading the book because he was from the Virginia area. Then, while reading the book, he might develop an interest in horses and read more books about that topic.

To assure his pupils this chance to expand their interests, Mr. Poindexter scheduled frequent book sharing activities. In this situation, all types of books were shared. If a child had read a horse story for the horse interest group, he or she could share that with the rest of the class. If a child read a book about the Civil War for no other reason than pure enjoyment, that child did not have to be a member of a task or interest group to share it with others.

Group book sharing activities were held in a variety of ways. In some cases, small groups or individuals elected to read part of their story to others in a "reader's theater" format. In other cases, individuals gave reports on their books to small groups of interested children. They were free to do this in any fashion they liked. Although many used oral retelling, Mr. Poindexter encouraged creative presentations such as putting on a puppet show or constructing a diorama of a scene that they would present to the group. In still other cases, students who had read the same book simply discussed it or made a group summary that they gave to the rest of the class. Some of the books had been summarized as skits, puppet shows, panel discussions, and group collages. Many times Mr. Poindexter scheduled several reports of varying types at the same time and let the children attend the ones in which they were the most interested. (Other ways to share books are discussed in Chapter 10 on recreational reading.)

Individual book-sharing activities were also conducted. Although Mr. Poindexter felt peer interaction to be an important aspect of book sharing, he tried to individualize his approach here too. He gave each child a choice of how to share his or her book. Some of the youngsters preferred to share their books with others in writing. As such, posters about the books read and written reports were tacked up all over the room. Some of the children who were quite shy requested individual conferences with Mr. Poindexter and wanted to tell only him about their book. Mr. Poindexter did allow this but tried gradually to expand their book sharing by encouraging the shy students to tell their story to one other friend. In this fashion several of the very shy children had progressed to the state where they were able to talk freely about their reading to small groups. Fred initially had wanted to talk only with Mr. Poindexter. By the end of the second month, and with gradual encouragement, Fred was in the process of making a puppet with which he could tell the class about his book.

Step 4: Keep Accurate Records

If the children were to learn the skills in some systematic manner, Mr. Poindexter knew that he needed to keep records so that he would not be reteaching a child the same skill all year long. Also he knew that, when his students were promoted at the end of the year, the next teacher would need some sort of record of each child's reading performance to continue where he left off. Furthermore, each child needed to know what task he or she was supposed to be doing. Therefore, Mr. Poindexter kept five different basic types of records for each child.

1. The first set included the facts acquired from the school's cumulative record keeping system and from informal discussions with the previous year's teacher. These records included each child's age, IQ, mental age, and general comments on his or her interests, progress, and difficulties. Recent

reading test results from both standardized and informal testing were also included. In addition, he added notes on each child's personality and needs as well as any health or family conditions that he felt might affect the child's schoolwork.

2. A second set of records was based on the results of the IRI. Data was kept on the child's instructional and independent reading levels that were obtained during the initial reading conference at the beginning of the school year.

3. In addition, Mr. Poindexter kept a record that contained an analysis of the oral and silent reading errors as observed during the IRI and subsequent special individual conferences. Since he knew that an analysis of both the oral and silent reading errors could help him to identify specific reading problems, Mr. Poindexter scheduled some special types of individual conferences whenever he felt that they were needed to assess specific types of errors. (See Chapter 5 for more information on this.)

For example, when Mr. Poindexter wanted to ascertain Harriet's current strengths and weaknesses of her reading skills, he copied two paragraphs out of the book that Harriet was reading and set up a special conference with her. When she sat with him, he asked her to read the first paragraph from the book aloud. By noting any word repetitions, insertions, gross mispronunciations, omissions, substitutions, and reversals, as well as any words that he had to help her with, Mr. Poindexter was able to identify several word identification skills with which he felt Harriet needed help. (See Chapter 5 for discussion on these various types of oral errors.)

The following sentence shows Mr. Poindexter's marking upon his copy of one of the sentences in the paragraph read aloud by Harriet.

"The little (brown) burro ran across the plateau. The boy tried to catch it, but it was too slippery for him."

Mr. Poindexter analyzed each error and made several "educated guesses" about some of the reading problems that he felt Harriet had. She probably knew how to use context clues as she substituted a word that meant the same as "burro," and her omission of the word "brown" did not affect the meaning. The fact that she repeated the word "the" twice, a basic sight word, probably indicated that she was having trouble with the next word, "plateau." The gross mispronunciation of the word "catch" most likely indicated that she needed to learn about the "ch" digraph. The fact that Mr. Poindexter had to pronounce the word "slippery" for her may have indicated that she relied primarily on context clues, and, when the context of this sentence did not give her the exact meaning, she did not try to use either structural analysis of phonic skills to figure it out. Furthermore, on closer inspection of the errors, Mr. Poindexter realized that two words she had trouble with contained consonant digraphs. He made a note to himself to provide special instruction in that skill.

Then Mr. Poindexter assessed Harriet's strengths in comprehension by asking her to read the second passage silently. After she had done so, Mr. Poindexter asked Harriet a variety of different kinds of comprehension questions. Some of the questions required very simple skills, such as identifying details; some required more complex skills, such as identifying cause-effect relationships; and some required fairly advanced skills, such as identifying theme. In this manner, he was able to keep track of the specific types of comprehension skills that Harriet seemed to need the most help with. For example, in the conference with Harriet, he asked her, "Why do you think the burro ran away from the boy?" She was unable to tell him. He determined that Harriet needed help in identifying cause effect relationships and wrote that on her record sheet. The record sheet that he used to keep track of Harriet's errors is as follows.

Pupil Harriet Cusack

Date 10/12

Book being read The Little Donkey

Oral errors

1 repetition   0 insertion   1 omission   1 substitution

1 gross mispronunciation   1 aid   0 reversal

0 pause

Comprehension errors

0 identifying detail   3 identifying cause effect relationships

1 identifying sequence   1 identifying propaganda

4. A fourth set of records that Mr. Poindexter kept included notes that he deemed adequate for judging and guiding the progress of the pupils. These included pupil cards that listed title of book read, books that had been suggested to the child, plans made for sharing the selection with other children, and plans for follow-up activities. He also noted each individual's progress in a group situation on their individual cards.

5. The final set of records that Mr. Poindexter used were those kept by the students. To complete their assigned tasks, each youngster needed to know what activities had been scheduled for him or her. Mr. Poindexter had simply taped a ditto sheet inside an individual manila folder that was kept by each child. Each time a child picked up his or her folder, the child would look inside the front cover to see what activities he or she should complete.

Tables 7.1 and 7.2 indicate the record kept by Mr. Poindexter on an individual child as well as the record of activities and assignments kept by the child. The posttest shown on Mr. Poindexter's records was usually done in terms of a set of follow-up questions on previously assigned skills. For example, in the case of Fred, one of his posttest questions would have asked him to locate a sentence containing a context clue and then tell the meaning of the given word.

TABLE 7.1 Mr. Poindexter's Record of Fred Phillips

Date	*Book*	*Skills Needed*	*Activity Assigned*	*Activity Completed*	*Posttest results*
9/30	*Blue Pony*	context clues, following directions	#32, 35, 37, 62	all completed	OK
10/7	*Blue Pony*	context clues, accent	group work with Sally and John on 10/8 at 9:00 #33, 34, 75, 77	still needs to do #75 and 77	
10/17	*Baseball Wins*	similes, make inferences	#52, 53, 55, 82, 84, 87		

Instructional level, 3:2.
Independent level, 3:1.

TABLE 7.2 Fred's Record

Activity Number	*Date Assigned*	*Date Completed*	*Person Verifying*	*Date Verified*
#32	9/30	10/5	JP	10/7
#35	9/30	10/7	JP	10/7
#37	9/30	10/5	PR	10/5
#62	9/30	10/5	JP	10/6
Group work on 10/8 9:00 with Sally and John	10/7	10/8	JP	10/8
#33	10/7			
#34	10/7			
#75	10/7			
#77	10/7			
#52	10/17			
#53	10/17			
#55	10/17			
#82	10/17			
#84	10/17			
#87	10/17			

The numbers attached to each activity in Tables 7.1 and 7.2 are explained in terms of Mr. Poindexter's management system, step 5, which follows.

Step 5: Develop a Management System

Mr. Poindexter's record-keeping system was extremely important in making the program work for him and the children. Once he had identified the skills that each child needed and had selected activities for instruction, Mr. Poindexter needed a means of organizing his activities and getting these assignments to the children in a systematic manner. The process can be termed a *management system* and is crucial to the success of a smoothly functioning individualized reading program. Although there are many possible ways to develop such a system, Mr. Poindexter wanted his to be as pupil directed as possible.

Therefore, Mr. Poindexter put emphasis on record keeping by the children. This served a dual purpose. It not only helped provide the children with a systematic means of getting information about future assignments, but it also helped them learn to keep track of their own progress.

Mr. Poindexter's use of numbers correlated with activities developed was one technique he used to make instruction giving as simple as possible for both himself and the children. Each number referred to a particular activity. Each activity was a workbook, a ditto worksheet, a game, or a set of directions especially written out for that youngster. For example, in Fred's case, activity #62 referred to a manila folder in the file cabinet in which most of the activities were kept. Inside the manila folder were directions for "how to make a dart board." Likewise, activity #32 referred to an activity in a manila folder that Mr. Poindexter had pulled out of an old basal reader workbook and that focused on the skill of using context clues. Activity #35 was a filmstrip, audiotape, and accompanying workbook also on the topic of context clues; #37 was a "Bingo" game in which he had to use correct context clues to play.

When Fred opened the front cover of his own folder and went down the list of activities that had been assigned to him, he knew that he could do them in any order he wished and, in most cases, with anyone he wished who also needed to work on that activity. From his record, it can be determined that Fred was assigned activity #62 on 9/30 and completed the dart board on 10/5. This activity was left on Mr. Poindexter's desk, who verified its completion and signed his initials to indicate this on 10/6. Fred completed the filmstrip (#35) on 10/7 and the worksheet (#32) on 10/5 and had them both verified and initialed by Mr. Poindexter while in his individualized conference. However, when Fred played the "Bingo" game (#37), he found several other boys who also had been assigned the activity as well as another boy, Paul, who had been evaluated as proficient in that skill and hence had been assigned that activity as a group leader. Paul had called out the words and, after the game was played, verified completion of the activity and signed his initials. On October 8 at 9:00, Fred met with Mr. Poindexter, Sally, and John to work on the skill of using context clues.

Although Mr. Poindexter had had much success with this management system, he had also used the "contract system" with great success. Under this method, he and his pupils had worked out a mutually acceptable amount of work for the student to meet the objective. These agreements between each pupil and Mr. Poindexter had stated (1) the learning objectives, (2) the choice of activities by which the objectives could be accomplished, (3) the criteria that had to be met for a particular grade, and (4) the method for evaluating successful completion of objectives.

The student had some freedom of choice among activities, but Mr. Poindexter retained the power of approval and based a grade upon the work. Students who had wanted to get an "A" would contract for more work than those who wanted to get a "B," those who wanted a "B" would contract for more work than those who wanted to get a "C," and so forth. Since there were always more activities and materials available in the contract than one would have to complete to receive a particular grade, the use of contracts helped develop the student's decision-making powers. In some cases, successful completion of objectives was assessed when the student showed his or her work to Mr. Poindexter in the individual conference or gave it to him to evaluate later. In other cases, this was done by giving the student the name of a peer and telling the child to have his or her lesson initialed by the peer when completed. The sample contract following shows how Mr. Poindexter would have made the assignment to Fred Phillips given earlier into a contract if he were still using this system. In this illustration, Fred has contracted for a "B." In addition, Mr. Poindexter used the same type of posttest as he used in the other management system. That is, when Fred came in for his individual conference, Mr. Poindexter posttested him on the skill of using context clues by asking him to locate a sentence containing a context clue in the book that he was reading and then tell the meaning of the word. Furthermore, Mr. Poindexter waited until the day of the conference to verify and initial most of the activities that Fred had completed to meet his "B" contract.

Contract of Fred Phillips

Name: Fred Phillips
Date began: September 30 Date ended: October 7

Objectives:

After completion of this contract, the student will be able to

1. identify all words with their meaning given by context clues in chapter four of *Blue Pony*
2. follow a given set of directions

Contract for C:

Complete two of the six activities listed on context clues and one of the four activities listed on following directions and successfully complete the posttest given by Mr. Poindexter.

Contract for B:

Complete at least four of the six activities listed on context clues and two of the four activities listed on following directions and successfully complete the posttest given by Mr. Poindexter.

Contract for A:

Complete at least five of the six activities listed on context clues and three of the four activities listed on following directions and successfully complete the posttest given by Mr. Poindexter (see Table 7.3).

TABLE 7.3 Posttest Record for Fred Phillips

Activity Number	*Date Assigned*	*Date Completed*	*Date Verified*	*Person Verifying*
#32	9/30	10/5	10/7	JP
#35	9/30	10/7	10/7	JP
#36	9/30			
#37	9/30	10/5	10/5	PR
#38	9/30	10/2	10/7	JP
#39	9/30			
#60	9/30	10/1	10/7	JP
#61	9/30			
#62	9/30	10/5	10/6	JP
#63	9/30			

Results of posttest: OK
Date of posttest: 10/7

However, regardless of what management system Mr. Poindexter used he was always aware of several things: (1) When all assignments were completed, more work was *not* to be assigned until the next individualized conference. The payoff for completing the work could be not getting more work. Therefore, those children who finished their work before their next conference were allowed to free read, play any of the available games, or participate in any other activity they wished. On occasion, the payoff for early completion of assignments or a contract was in the form of a "bonus." For example, Mike finished all the work in his contract in two days. He was particularly interested in building his model train engine, so Mr. Poindexter let him work on that for the next three days. Mike enjoyed his activity bonus and was unaware of the fact that he was actually "reading" when putting together the train engine according to the complex instructions that came with it.

Furthermore, Mr. Poindexter saved all completed contracts and assignment sheets for final evaluation for each child's progress. He found them particularly useful for parental conferences.

VARIOUS USES OF THE INDIVIDUALIZED APPROACH

INCORPORATING AN INDIVIDUALIZED APPROACH INTO A BASAL READER PROGRAM

Mr. Poindexter had been teaching for several years and knew the reading skills very well. In his talk with Mr. Poindexter, the teacher education major told him that he was not certain that he, as a first year teacher, would be able to "handle" such a program. Mr. Poindexter assured him that it could be done and took him down the hall to see Miss Yohannan's third grade class. She was a second-year teacher and was just beginning the transition from a basal reader program to that of an individualized program. She had started off in September with a basal and found it to be working quite well. However, after she felt secure about her organization and teaching of skills, she decided to partially adopt some aspects of the individualized reading program. She started with the "top" group when they had completed the grade level basal. Essentially what she did was let each child select a book that he or she wanted to read. Once a week, she sat down with each child and discussed the book with him or her. When an occasional child had problems, she pulled worksheets out of the appropriate level basal and put them in his or her folder to be completed before the next conference. Since she knew the reading levels of each child, she tried to give the children skill-building lessons taken from the appropriate basal reader level. The program seemed to be going well. The children enjoyed it, and Miss Yohannan was beginning to gather an impressive library of books and activities on various reading skills that could be used by these children as the need arose. She estimated that some of the children in her average group would finish their 3:2 basal in the middle of April. At that time, she would extend her individualized program to include those children. Furthermore, she had already decided that, when she established her program for the following year, she would try to have a completely individualized program.

INCORPORATING AN INDIVIDUALIZED READING APPROACH INTO A LANGUAGE EXPERIENCE PROGRAM

Mr. Weather used a language experience program but also utilized many of the aspects of the individualized program. As his children began to read, he gave them books on topics of their choice. Although the books expanded their backgrounds, they also were selected, for the most part, on the basis of interest. Furthermore, Mr. Weather decided that he could help his students more by setting up individual conferences with each. The focus of the conference would be the stories that they had dictated as well as the stories that they had read. In this manner, he would actually be incorporating many of the aspects of an individualized reading program into his language experience program.

ADVANTAGES AND DISADVANTAGES OF AN INDIVIDUALIZED READING PROGRAM

Miss Yohannan was particularly interested in changing to an individualized reading program because she felt that it had many advantages over her basal reader program. She knew that each child not only would be reading on his or her own level of difficulty but that the child would be reading books that were of interest to him or her. No child would be pulled along or held back by others. Additionally, skills would be taught in very relevant situations, as they would be presented as each child showed a need for them.

However, the reason that Miss Yohannan waited to change her basal program to an individualized program was that she knew it would take a great amount of work on her part and that she would have to be very knowledgeable about all the reading skills. Not only would she have to know how to teach each skill, but she would also have to know how to tell when each child needed to be presented with a particular skill. Although there was some interaction between the children, her basal reader program encouraged much more interaction, and she felt interaction between students to be extremely important. Furthermore, in many situations she knew her time would not be economically well used. For example, she might teach a skill to Joey, and then to Bobby, and then to Mike in subsequent individual conferences.

However, essentially Miss Yohannan felt that the advantages outweighed the disadvantages and that the children learned to enjoy reading in this type of approach. Therefore, she continued to plan to individualize her entire program for the next year.

OTHER APPROACHES TO TEACHING READING

Phil, a teacher education major, was telling Betty, Ann, and Glenn about the "intensified phonics" program that he had observed. He stated that the teacher had used a set of graded materials and an accompanying teacher's manual to teach reading to the children. Betty listened carefully and commented that the program sounded a lot like the basal reader program that she had observed in Mr. Rough's fourth grade classroom. Ann confused the issue further by suggesting that her observation of a "linguistics" program sounded very similar to the programs that Phil and Betty had observed. Glenn then stated that Phil and Ann must be mistaken about the names of the reading programs that they had observed because there were really only three methods for teaching reading: the basal, the language experience, and the individualized.

The discussion described here typifies the sort of confusion often encountered by beginning teachers when trying to sort out the differences among the various approaches used to teach reading. Although the three most frequently used approaches are described by the terms "basal," "language experience," and "individualized," there are other approaches. There is much overlap in all the approaches, and confusion can occur if the beginning teacher views each approach to teaching reading as completely different from all others. Most approaches have many components in common. Their differences are usually in terms of skill emphasis or presentation rather than in terms of some mutually exclusive components. To illustrate some of the many ways in which a teacher may present reading skills to his or her students, the following approaches will be described briefly: (1) intensive phonics, (2) linguistics, (3) modified alphabet, (4) programmed, (5) computer assisted, (6) diagnostic-prescriptive, and (7) eclectic.

INTENSIVE PHONICS

A phonics program is not a program for teaching reading but, rather, a set of generalizations about the relationships among letters and sounds that are taught to children. Phonics is taught with all kinds of materials and through a variety of teaching activities as a part of many programs. What most people mean by a "phonics" program is any reading program with an emphasis on teaching phonics. There are several published programs that are similar to basals because they are graded sets of materials that cover word identification, comprehension, and study skills. However, they differ from what is ordinarily thought of as a basal because of their intensive emphasis on phonics. Vocabulary words are selected on the basis of following certain phonics rules rather than on frequency of occurrence (Smith and Johnson, 1976; Farr and Roser, 1979).

LINGUISTICS

As with the phonics program, linguistics is not actually an approach but rather, an emphasis upon the relationship between language development and reading. The main emphasis is on decoding. Although there are many differences among the various types of linguistic programs, most have the following factors in common: (1) The names of the letters rather than the sounds are taught first. (2) Beginning vocabulary is almost entirely restricted to words that have consistent letter-sound relationships. (3) They present three-letter words of a consonant-vowel-consonant pattern in words that have a common spelling pattern (e.g., ban, Dan, fan, and man or bit, fit, hit, and sit). (4) They teach a few high-utility words as sight words so that meaningful sentences can be written. (5) They do not teach phonic generalizations, but they expect children to note the similarities of words containing the same spelling pattern and then develop an understanding of the relationship between spelling and sound. (6) They give ample practice in comparing words that have "minimal contrasts," that is, words that differ in only one phoneme (sound) and one grapheme (symbol) such as hit and hip, hit and pit, or hit and hat (Harris and Sipay, 1979).

MODIFIED ALPHABET

This system or medium modifies the traditional English alphabet so that many of the irregularities between the sound and the symbol that typically occur (e.g., knight, enough, ghost) will not confuse the beginning reader. One example of a modified alphabet is the Initial Teaching Alphabet (ITA), which was developed and publicized by Pitman in about 1960. ITA contains forty-four characters or sound symbols, one for each of the over forty different phonemes (sounds) in the English language. Each symbol always represents the same sound, and each sound is signaled by only one symbol. Figure 7.1 pictures all forty-four symbols in this system (Harris and Sipay, 1979; Aukerman, 1971; Pitman, 1969).

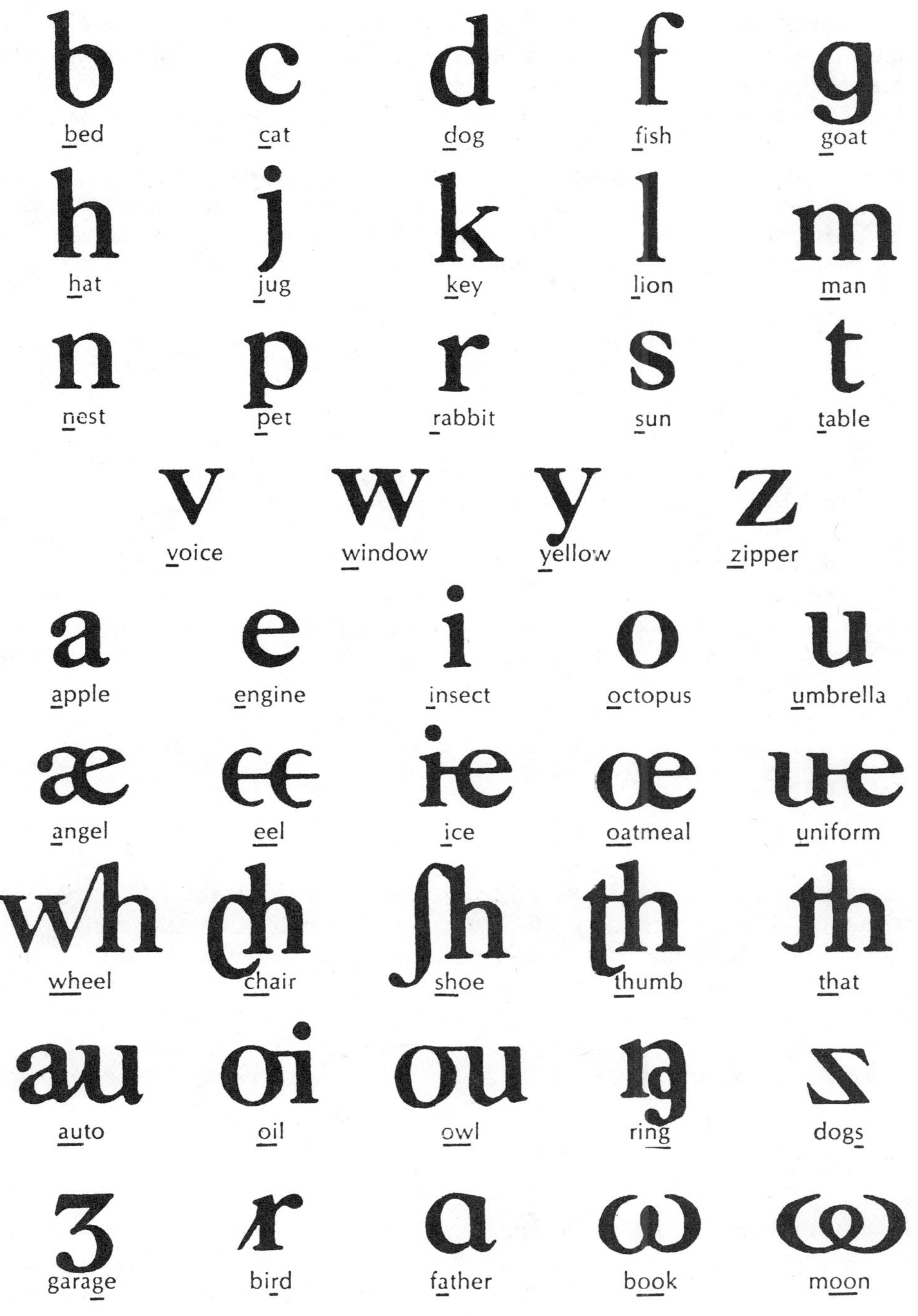

Figure 7.1. The forty-four ITA symbols and words illustrating the sounds the symbols represent. (Reprinted by permission of the Initial Teaching Alphabet Foundation, 19 West 34th Street, New York, New York 10001.)

Other modified alphabets retain the traditional letters but use colors as cues to sounds that the letters represent. One hue usually represents all letters that reflect a given sound. Hence the ee in feet, the ea in feat, and the e in he would all be printed in the same color (Harris and Sipay, 1979).

Fry (1972) has developed a diacritical marking system that tries to preserve traditional spellings of words while adding marks to aid pronunciation. This system is somewhat simpler that the diacritical marking systems found in most dictionaries, since the intention is to aid beginning readers. For example, long vowels are indicated by a bar over the printed vowel; short vowels are not marked since this is the most common use of the letters (Fry, 1972; Burns and Roe, 1976).

PROGRAMMED MATERIALS

Programmed instruction presents instructional materials in small, sequential steps, each of which is referred to as a frame. The pupil is required to respond in some way to each frame and is instantly informed of the correctness of his or her response. The child moves through the material at his or her own pace. Although a "total" reading program containing programmed materials on word identification, comprehension, and study skills may be used as the only instructional approach, this is seldom done. In most cases, other materials and methods are used in conjunction with the programmed approach. In other cases, the teacher uses programmed materials only to teach a few selected skills (Burns and Roe, 1976).

COMPUTER-ASSISTED INSTRUCTION

This approach uses a computer to administer a programmed instructional sequence. Usually, children sit in front of a small computer console in a one-to-one setting and respond in a self-paced individualized manner to each computer command. Feedback as to the correctness of the response is immediate. Again, although this could be programmed to teach all the reading skills, the computer is usually used in conjunction with other teaching approaches (Burns and Roe, 1976).

DIAGNOSTIC PRESCRIPTIVE

In this approach to teaching reading, emphasis is placed on the use of comprehensive diagnostic tests that assess the learning abilities of each child at every level of instruction. Through analysis of individual performance, a self-paced program in reading is designed for each child. Every youngster then receives a "prescription sheet" from the teacher that contains his or her lessons. The child often completes the work independently, but group instruction may be used if a common need among pupils is identified. As soon as the child demonstrates adequate competency in a skill area, he or she is moved to a more difficult set of skills designed to challenge his or her increased proficiency with them (Harris and Sipay, 1979; Dallman, 1978; Farr and Roser, 1979).

Each child's "prescription" comes from master files that contain the core materials for the entire program. These materials are both commercially produced and teacher made and may include such devices as filmstrips, records, supplementary readers, and worksheets (Dallman, 1978; Hall et al., 1979).

Plans of this type have also been called "skills management systems," "objective-based systems," and "individually prescribed systems." Because the name "individually prescribed system" is very similar to the label used in Mr. Poindexter's "individualized reading program" described earlier in this chapter, beginning teachers often confuse the two approaches. However, the two programs have major differences. An "individualized reading program" *must*, by definition, focus skill diagnosis and skill building on individual conferences and materials self-selected by each child. The "individually prescribed system" *may* include some individual conferences and self-selection of materials, but the material, for the most part, is prescribed by the teacher (Glaser, 1968; Beck and Bolvin, 1969; Scanlon, 1970).

This approach to teaching reading will be discussed in more depth in Chapter 8, "Diagnostic-Prescriptive Approach."

ECLECTIC

This term refers to any approach to teaching reading that combines desirable aspects of a number of different major approaches. For example, a teacher might organize a program that uses the skill exercises from a basal reader program along with the self-selection of books, individualized conferences, and book-sharing aspects of an individualized program. Furthermore, he or she may use the language experience approach with one of the nonreading children and supplement that child's skill building with computer-assisted instruction (Bond and Wagner, 1966).

COMPARISONS OF THE VARIOUS APPROACHES

These approaches may be viewed from a number of different perspectives to clarify their similarities and differences. One organizational perspective has been developed by Smith and Johnson (1976) who state that the basic approaches to reading instruction may be simplified by examining the sources of the child's initial reading vocabulary. The three categories that they have delineated are (1) words that the child wants to read, (2) words that occur most frequently, and (3) words that contain consistent letter-sound relationships. Each of these terms will be described briefly.

1. *Words that the child wants to read.* Approaches to this category include the individualized and the language experience approaches. Typical

words selected by a child might include "Daddy," "Marmaduke" (the name of a favorite pet), "incredible" (a word used by an older sibling), or "Well, excuse me!" (a slang term currently in vogue).

2. *Words that occur frequently in much of the reading material likely to be encountered by the child.* The basal reader belongs in this category. Typical words selected by the basal readers as "core" vocabulary include the basic sight words (e.g., come, read, live, hear). Most programmed materials, computer-assisted instructional programs, and diagnostic-prescriptive programs also base their vocabulary on frequently occurring words. However, this is not always true, as some diagnostic-prescriptive programs are used to help systematize the skills needed by children using the language experience or individualized approach.

3. *Words that contain consistent letter-sound relationships.* Approaches that belong in this category are the phonics approach, the linguistics approach, and the modified alphabet approach. For example, "pin" and "pine" might be used in a phonics approach because they reflect a phonics generalization about short and long vowels; "pin" and "pit" might be used in a linguistics approach because they reflect words of "minimal contrasts" of the cvc pattern; and "pop" might be used in a modified alphabet approach with the "p" printed in brown to illustrate to the child the consistent sound of the consonant "p."

SUMMARY

This chapter has placed most of the emphasis on descriptions of the language experience and the individualized approaches to teaching reading. However, some discussion of other approaches to teaching reading has been presented, namely, intensive phonics, linguistics, modified alphabet, programmed, computer assisted, eclectic, and diagnostic-prescriptive. A comparison of all these approaches to teaching reading shows that they may be viewed as a set of materials (programmed), a collection of specific methods (language experience), or a combination of both (basal). Each approach has unique features, and each reflects a somewhat different philosophical view of teaching reading. The teacher using programmed materials as the core probably believes in a more structured view of teaching reading than does the teacher who uses the individualized approach. But most approaches are alike in certain ways; that is, all present decoding skills to the children. The relative emphasis upon one component or another is what makes each different. The teacher must match the needs of his or her pupils with the relative merits of each approach when determining which approach to use.

References and Bibliography

Aukerman, Robert C. *Approaches to Beginning Reading.* New York: John Wiley & Sons, Inc., 1971.

Beck, Isabel, and Bolvin, John. "A Model for Non-Gradedness: The Reading Program for Individually Prescribed Instruction." *Elementary English* 46 (February 1969): 130–135.

Bond, Guy L., and Wagner, Eva Bond. *Teaching the Child to Read.* New York: Macmillan Publishing Co., Inc., 1966.

Burns, Paul C., and Roe, Betty D. *Teaching Reading in Today's Elementary School.* Chicago: Rand McNally & Company, 1976.

Dallman, Martha, Rouch, Roger, Char, Lynette, and DeBoer, John. *The Teaching of Reading.* 5th ed. New York: Holt, Rinehart and Winston, 1978.

Farr, Roger, and Roser, Nancy. *Teaching a Child to Read.* New York: Harcourt Brace Jovanovich, Inc., 1979.

Fry, Edward. *Reading Instruction for Classroom and Clinic.* New York: McGraw-Hill Book Company, 1972.

Glaser, Robert. "Adapting the Elementary School Curriculum to Individual Performances," in *Proceedings of the 1967 Invitational Conference on Teaching Problems.* Princeton, N.J.: Educational Testing Service, 1968.

Guilfoile, Elizabeth. *Nobody Listens to Andrew.* Chicago: Follet Publishing Company, 1957.

Guszak, Frank J. *Diagnostic Reading Instruction in the Elementary School.* 2nd Ed. New York: Harper & Row Publishers, 1978.

Hall, MaryAnne, Ribovich, Jerilyn, and Ramig, Christopher. *Reading and the Elementary School Child.* 2nd ed. New York: D. Van Nostrand Company, 1979.

Harris, Albert J., and Sipay, Edward R. *How to Teach Reading.* New York: Longman, Inc., 1979.

Harris, Larry A., and Smith, Carl B. *Reading Instruction Through Diagnostic Teaching* 2nd Ed. New York: Holt, Rinehart and Winston, 1976.

Heilman, Arthur W. *Principles and Practices of Teaching Reading.* 4th ed. Columbus, Ohio: Charles E. Merrill Publishing Company, 1977.

Huck, Charlotte S., and Kuhn, Doris Young. *Children's Literature in the Elementary School*, 2nd ed. New York: Holt, Rinehart and Winston, 1968, p. 109.

Keats, Ezra Jack. *Whistle for Willie.* New York: The Viking Press, Inc., 1964.

Lapp, Diane, and Flood, James. *Teaching Reading to Every Child.* New York: Macmillan Publishing Co., Inc., 1978.

Meader, Stephen. *The Voyage of the Javelin.* New York: Harcourt Brace Jovanovich, Inc., 1959.

Pitman, J., and St. John, J. *Alphabets and Reading.* New York: Pitman Publishing Corporation, 1969.

Ransom, Grayce C. *Preparing to Teach Reading.* Boston: Little, Brown and Company, 1978.

Scanlon, Robert C. "Individually Prescribed Instruction: A System of Individualized Instruction." *Educational Technology* 10 (December 1970): 44–46.

Smith, Richard, and Johnson, Dale. *Teaching Children to Read.* Reading, Mass.: Addison-Wesley Publishing Co., Inc., 1976.

Spache, George D. and Evelyn B. *Reading in the Elementary School.* 3rd ed. Boston: Allyn & Bacon, Inc., 1973.

Stauffer, Russell G. *Directing the Reading–Thinking Process.* New York: Harper & Row, Publishers, 1975.

Stauffer, Russel G. *The Language Experience Approach to the Teaching of Reading.* New York: Harper & Row, Publishers, 1970.

Van, Allen R. Comments at the U.S. Office of Education, "Conference on Beginning Reading Instruction." Washington, D.C.: Government Printing Office, November 1952.

Veatch, Jeannette. *Reading in the Elementary School.* 2nd ed. New York: John Wiley & Sons, Inc., 1978.

Zintz, Miles V. *The Reading Process: The Teacher and the Learner,* 3rd ed. Dubuque, Iowa: William C. Brown Company, Publishers, 1979.

Self-Check 7.3
Other Approaches to Teaching Reading

The following questions are designed to help the participant assess his or her competence on the first twenty-nine objectives stated at the beginning of this chapter. Although every effort has been made to make the self-check questions comprehensive, participants should remember that they are held responsible for meeting the objectives as stated at the beginning of this chapter.

1. Objective 1. Describe the four premises underlying the language experience approach to teaching reading.
2. Objective 2. Discuss why facility with language, background experiences, and interests should be assessed before instruction is planned.
3. Objective 3. Identify at least three different sources that can be used to provide experiences for stories.
4. Objective 4. Differentiate among the purposes for large group dictation, small group dictation, and individual dictation.
5. Objective 5. Describe at least five techniques that should be used by the teacher when transcribing an experience dictated by one or more children.
6. Objective 6. Describe the construction of a word bank and illustrate how at least three different reading skills can be taught through its use.
7. Objective 7. Differentiate between instruction given to children who already know how to read and those who do not.
8. Objective 8. Discuss why it is important that the teacher transcribe each child's stories regularly even if the child is also transcribing some of his or her own.
9. Objective 9. Discuss at least three types of records that should be kept by a teacher using the language experience approach.
10. Objective 10. Discuss how "learning centers" may be used.
11. Objective 11. Discuss the role of children's literature in a language experience approach to reading.
12. Objective 12. Discuss a procedure for developing critical thinking skills.
13. Objective 13. Discuss groups of learners for whom the language experience approach would be particularly appropriate.
14. Objective 14. Describe at least one advantage and one disadvantage of the language experience approach.
15. Objective 15. Ralph is repeating the first grade. He is very discouraged about his ability to read and is bored with the type of stories found in the primer. Prescribe instruction for Ralph using the language experience approach.

16. Objective 16. Mr. Gaines wants to teach his first graders how to make inferences. Describe a language experience lesson in which the comprehension skill of inferences is focused upon and taught.
17. Objective 17. Mr. Tillson wants to teach identifying main idea to three children in his "special reading" class. Sue is repeating first grade and is eight years old; Paul is in the seventh grade but is a nonreader; Heidi is in the third grade but has recently arrived from Germany and does not speak or read English very well. Construct at least three different lesson plans teaching main idea. One should focus upon Sue's needs; one should focus on Paul's needs; one should focus on Heidi's needs.
18. Objective 18. Mrs. Ryan has prepared a lesson on turkeys for a pre-Thanksgiving Day language experience story. As she begins to elicit comments about turkeys, one of the children tries to tell her about the school bus accident which happened on the way to school that morning. Mrs. Ryan tells the child "not to interrupt" and continues to elicit comments about the turkey. The rest of the children sit quietly and she cannot get them to actively participate. Evaluate this portion of Mrs. Ryan's language experience program using criteria given in this chapter.
19. Objective 19. Define what is meant by the term "individualized reading program."
20. Objective 20. Identify the five basic components upon which an individualized program is based.
21. Objective 21. Describe a five-step procedure for organizing an individualized reading program.
22. Objective 22. Discuss at least three factors related to instruction that should be diagnosed.
23. Objective 23. Discuss each of the following components related to planning instruction in an individualized program: (1) locating materials, (b) scheduling time, (c) holding individual conferences, (d) designing lessons, (e) formulating group activities, and (f) formulating book-sharing situations.
24. Objective 24. Discuss at least three different types of records that should be kept in an individualized program.
25. Objective 25. Describe at least one technique for facilitating an efficient management system in an individualized reading program.
26. Objective 26. Discuss how an individualized reading program can be incorporated into either a basal reader program or a language experience program.
27. Objective 27. List at least three advantages and at least three disadvantages of an individualized reading program.
28. Objective 28. Mr. Huggins lets each child in his fourth grade class select one book a week to read. They select books from a selection of books on the classroom shelf. However, if they can find an "acceptable" book from another source, Mr. Huggins will let them read that instead of one of the classroom books. At the end of each week, Mr. Huggins sits with the children in small groups and dis-

cusses their books. Each child is expected to read at least one book a week, but the size of the book is irrelevant to the time limit. Evaluate Mr. Huggins individualized reading program according to criteria given in this chapter.

29. Objective 29. Briefly describe at least three methods other than basal, language experience, and individualized approaches for teaching reading.

Experiences 7.4
Other Approaches to Teaching Reading

Chapter 7
Experience 1

Objective

During this experience, the participant will design and teach a lesson based on the language experience approach.

Activity and Assessment Guide

1. State the name, age, grade, and reading level of the child with whom worked. ____________________

2. Which of the following techniques did you use to gather data for the story you wrote with the child? (circle one) asked a child about an experience created an experience for the child other ____________ Briefly describe your technique. ____________________

____

3. Into which of the following categories would you fit the child with whom you worked? (circle one or more) first grader culturally dif-

ferent older child reading below grade level peer acting as child substitute other __________ Briefly describe the child. ____

____

* 4. Did the child appear to enjoy the lesson? (circle one) yes no Briefly describe the child's reaction. ______________________________

____

* 5. Did this experience give you any more ideas about what type of stories you could write with this child? (circle one) yes no Briefly describe at least one of those ideas. ______________________________

____

* 6. Carefully analyze the story you wrote with the child and then briefly illustrate how you could use the story to teach at least one of each of following skills. (Attach a copy of the story to this sheet.)

a. word identification skill ______________________________

____

b. comprehension skill ______________________________

____

c. study skill ______________________________

____

* 7. State what you believe to be the significant implications of this experience for the classroom teacher. ______________________________

____

____

*See Chapter 1, Experience 1 for explanation of the asterisk.

Chapter 7

Experience 2

Objective

During this experience, the participant will do one or more of the following: Design and teach a lesson in which he or she (1) helps a child to select a book, (2) conducts an individual conference, (3) constructs a motivating skill-building activity.

Activity and Assessment Guide

1. State the name, age, grade, and reading level of the child with whom you worked. ____

   ____

2. Did you design a lesson in which you helped a child select a book, conduct an individualized conference, or construct a motivating skill-building activity? (Attach a copy of your lesson plan to this sheet.) Briefly describe which of the activities you designed. ________________________

   ____

3. Did you use the lesson you designed in an actual teaching situation? (circle one) yes no Briefly describe the situation in which the lesson was used. ____

   ____

4. Was objective for which lesson was intended met? (circle one) yes no Briefly describe why or why not. ____________________

____

Note: Answer questions 5, 6, and 7 if you helped a child to select a book; answer questions 8, 9, and 10 if you conducted an individual conference; answer questions 11, 12, and 13 if you constructed a motivating skill-building activity.

5. Did you make certain that the book was on the child's instructional level? (circle one) yes no Briefly describe how this was done.

____

____

6. Did you motivate the child to read the book? (circle one) yes no Briefly describe techniques used to do this. ____________________

____

* 7. Was the child motivated to read the book? (circle one) yes no Briefly describe the child's reaction. ____________________

____

8. Did you use the child's book to assess comprehension skills? (circle one) yes no Briefly describe how this was done. ____________________

____

9. Did you use the child's book to assess word recognition skills? (circle one) yes no Briefly describe how this was done. ____________________

____

____

* 10. Was the child motivated to read the book? (circle one) yes no Briefly describe the child's reaction. ____________________

____

11. Did you construct an activity that matched a skill needed by the child? (circle one) yes no Briefly describe the needed skill. ____________________

____

12. Did you construct a motivating activity? (circle one) yes no Briefly describe the activity. ____________________

____

* 13. Was the child motivated by the activity? (circle one) yes no Briefly describe the child's reaction. ______________________________

____

* 14. Did this activity give you any ideas for other ways in which to help a child select a book, conduct an individualized conference, or construct another motivating skill-building activity? (circle one) yes no Briefly describe at least one of those ideas. ______________________________

____

* 15. Did this activity give you any ideas for establishing an individualized reading program in your own classroom? (circle one) yes no Briefly describe at least one of those ideas. ______________________________

____

* 16. State what you believe to be the significant implications of this experience for the classroom teacher. ______________________________

____

____

*See Chapter 1, Experience 1 for explanation of the asterisk.

Chapter 7
Experience 3

Objective

During this experience, the participant will design and teach a lesson in reading using a method other than the basal, language experience, or individualized approach.

Activity and Assessment Guide

1. State the name, age, grade, and reading level of the child with whom you worked. ______________________________
2. Did you design a lesson in which you used an approach other than the basal, language experience, or individualized approach? (Attach a copy of your lesson plan to this sheet.) Briefly describe which approach you used. ______________________________

   ____
3. Did you use the lesson you designed in an actual teaching situation? (circle one) yes no Briefly describe the situation in which the lesson was used. ______________________________

   ____

* 4. Was objective for which lesson was intended met? (circle one) yes no Briefly discuss why or why not. ______________________________

   ____

* 5. Did the child appear to enjoy the lesson? (circle one) yes no
Briefly describe the child's reaction. ____________________

____

* 6. Did this lesson give you any more ideas about other approaches to teaching reading? (circle one) yes no Briefly describe one of these ideas. ____________________

____

7. Did you have to read more information about the technique you used before you were able to design your lesson? (circle one) yes no
Briefly identify your sources by title, author, and publication date. ____

____

* 8. State what you believe to be the significant implications of this experience for the classroom teacher. ____________________

____

____

*See Chapter 1, Experience 1 for explanation of the asterisk.

Chapter 8
Diagnostic–Prescriptive Approach

Objectives 8.1

On completion of this chapter, the participant should be able to

1. State with which programs a diagnostic–prescriptive approach may be used.
2. State the advantages of a diagnostic-prescriptive approach to the skills program.
3. List six teacher tasks involved in a diagnostic-prescriptive skills program.
4. List three possible sources for scope and sequences of reading skills, state which one is preferred, and give reasons for his or her choice.
5. List three possible sources for designing test items to be used to discern which skills a child has or has not mastered.
6. State whether an assessment has the characteristics of a formal preassessment when given an objective and sample assessment.
7. State the conditions under which informal assessments may be used.
8. State the reason for preassessing only a few objectives at one time.
9. List the information that he or she thinks should be kept on a child's record in a diagnostic–prescriptive program and give reasons for the selection.
10. Describe a record-keeping system—either one given in a book or one of his or her own devising—that would record the information that should be kept on a child's record.

11. Evaluate a skill resource plan according to the criteria given in this chapter (for a skill resource plan) for diagnostic-prescriptive teaching.
12. Describe the method for scheduling diagnostic-prescriptive instruction that he or she feels is preferable. Description should include the amount of time that would lapse between preassessment and initial teaching lesson, initial teaching lesson and reinforcement lessons, between reinforcement lessons, and between the last reinforcement lesson and postassessment.

Experience 1 extends Chapter 8 with this objective:

13. During this experience the participant will teach one skill including a preassessment, an introductory activity, two reinforcement activities, and a postassessment.

Information Given 8.2
Diagnostic–Prescriptive Approach

Several elementary school reading teachers have gathered at a workshop to enlarge their knowledge of reading instruction. Two of the teachers have been asked to describe their reading programs. The first teacher to speak, Helen Yohannan, outlines her grade three reading program, which is centered on a basal reader approach. She describes her initial testing using an informal reading inventory, her methods of grouping, and her choice of material based on her test results. She also explains how she assesses each skill that the teacher's manual suggests be included at that particular time and how she decides whether to present it in her program. She concludes with the comment, "Even with a careful selection of skills, I am sure that I move on to new skills before some children have mastered the one currently being taught, omit skills that some children in a group need, and include skills in which many children are already competent. My next step will be to try to find a better way of handling the skills."

Mr. Poindexter is the next to speak. He outlines his individualized reading program by describing how he analyzes the learning needs of the children, motivates them, gives them ample opportunity to read, and follows up with conferences and activities. He describes the growth the children have shown in reading, independent study habits, and self-direction. When asked by one of the teachers present what he considers the principal weakness in his program, he answers, "I am concerned about the skills program. When a child is having a conference with me, I notice any skill weaknesses. However, I feel that many children may miss a needed skill."

The consultant for the workshop now injects the following remark, "Both Miss Yohannan and Mr. Poindexter appear to be having a problem in the same area—individualizing the skills program to meet the needs of the students. A diagnostic-prescriptive skills program that provides orderly instruction in word identification, comprehension, and study skills might be the solution for both of you. Such a program is always used in conjunction with a basal, individualized, or other program that provides copious reading opportunities. Therfore, it could be used with both the programs described."

TEACHER TASKS IN A DIAGNOSTIC-PRESCRIPTIVE SKILLS PROGRAM

When conducting a diagnostic-prescriptive skills program, the teacher has six main tasks:

Task 1: *Ascertaining a Scope and Sequence of Skills*
To begin a diagnostic-prescriptive program, the teacher needs to have a listing of reading skills (scope) to be mastered by children and the approximate level (sequence) on which they should be taught.

Task 2: *Diagnosing before Instruction (Preassessment)*
The teacher needs to perform two types of preassessment for each child: first, assess the instructional level and, second, determine the skills that are mastered and not mastered.

Task 3: *Keeping Records*
The teacher needs to record the skills mastered and not mastered for each child.

Task 4: *Designing Instructional Strategies*
For those skills that the child has not mastered, the teacher needs to plan instruction. Such instruction includes an initial teaching lesson and reinforcement lesson.

Task 5: *Diagnosing after Instruction (Postassessment)*
The teacher needs to assess children's skills after instruction has been given to assess their competence on each skill.

Task 6: *Organizing Instruction*
The teacher needs to plan and schedule assessments and teaching procedures.

Discussion of these six tasks follows.

TASK 1: ASCERTAINING SCOPE AND SEQUENCE OF SKILLS

A scope and sequence of reading skills for the elementary grades may contain the following:

1. *Scope:* A complete list of skills in reading readiness, word recognition, comprehension, and study skills for children with instructional levels of kindergarten through grade six.
2. *Sequence:* The skills should be sequenced so that the teacher will know which skills to present to children reading on a given level.

A novice in the field of reading might assume that there is one standard set of skills and one order in which to teach them. This assumption is erroneous. There are many possible listings and order of skills. The teacher who is planning on using a diagnostic-prescriptive program needs to develop a scope and sequence of skills uniquely suited to his or her own situation or to select a scope and sequence from those that have been published.

TEACHER-MADE SCOPE AND SEQUENCE OF SKILL CHARTS

Teachers may develop scope and sequence of skill charts based on published materials. One common way in which teachers do this is to identify and list the skills that are taught in the basal reader series in use in their school and that they feel are significant. Table 8.1 shows a sample for one level—the preprimer—from the Houghton Mifflin reading series. This teacher developed a scope and sequence of the skills in a behavioral objective format.

TABLE 8.1 Scope and Sequence of Skills Houghton Mifflin* PP2

Student will be able to

1. Recognize and use the contraction *isn't.*
2. Recognize and use the abbreviation *Mr.* (*Mister*).
3. Recognize and use simple compound words.
4. Recognize the sound and letter association for /ay/ and /ick/ as in bay and sick.
5. Recognize and use punctuation marks.
6. Recognize the use of a period in an abbreviation.
7. Recognize the sound and letters association for the *ing* ending.
8. Add the *ing* ending to root words.
9. Add the *ake* phonogram to initial consonants.
10. Add the *s* ending to verbs.
11. Select and name words beginning with the *pl* cluster.
12. Select and name words beginning with the *sm* cluster.
13. Name the /*s*/ sound for the *c* consonant.
14. Add the *ook* phonogram to initial consonants.
15. Select and name *w* and *y* as vowel helpers.
16. Name a comma as the punctuation following an introductory word.
17. Name the letter-sound association for /*x*/.
18. Name and say the *cr* and *fr* clusters in words.
19. Name the letter-sound association for /oa/.
20. Name and select, from printed words, the *mp* cluster.
21. Name and select, from printed words, the *sc* cluster.
22. Name and add the *un* phonogram to root words.
23. Name and add the *s* ending to nouns.
24. Name the letter-sound association for /ee/.
25. Name and select from printed words the *ck* digraph.
26. Recognize and name the apostrophe in contractions.
27. Name and write, in context, words with more than one meaning.
28. Recognize and use the comma to set off direct address.
29. Recognize elliptical sentences.

*Based on the Houghton Mifflin Reading Series, 2nd preprimer, *Lions.*

Teachers may also develop scope and sequence of skill charts based on their own knowledge of reading. For example, Mrs. Huff has taught reading for several years. She is able to list the skills that she expects children functioning on each grade level to master. Mrs. Huff has, therefore, developed her own scope and sequence of skills.

Teacher-made skill charts may be used with either individualized or basal programs and have the advantage of the teachers' becoming involved in a very personal way in deciding which skills should be included in their programs.

PUBLISHED SCOPE AND SEQUENCE OF SKILL CHARTS

Published skill charts may be found as part of published diagnostic–prescriptive skill programs or in textbooks of reading methodology.

Published Diagnostic–Prescriptive Programs

The *Wisconsin Design for Reading Skill Development* (Otto and Askov, 1972) is representative of diagnostic-prescriptive skills programs. It includes a scope and sequence of reading skills from readiness through grade six and involves the areas of word recognition, comprehension, and study skills. This scope and sequence chart lists the skills in both a brief format and in an objective format.

Published Charts in Reading Methodology Textbooks

Several textbooks on reading instruction include scope and sequence of skill charts. Representative of these are the checksheets on each level readiness through grade six, which include readiness, word recognition, comprehension, and study skills to be found in *Diagnostic Reading Instruction in the Elementary Classroom* (Guszak, 1978). These charts list the skills in a descriptive format.

Learning to Teach Reading in the Elementary School includes a scope of skills for readiness through grade six. Suggestions for sequencing skills within each level are left to the teacher who uses this scope of skills. An overview of these skills is presented in Table 15.1 of this textbook.

FORMATS FOR SKILLS CHARTS

Scope and sequence of skills lists present the skills in brief lists, in descriptive statements, as behavioral objectives, or in a combination of these formats. The lists and descriptive statements have the advantage of presenting the skills in a concise fashion so that all the skills to be mastered can be perceived at one time and the overall organization can be seen. The behavioral objective format has the advantage of specifying the exact nature of the skill to be mastered, simplifying the teacher's task of developing objectives for each lesson.

TYPES OF SKILLS

Skills vary greatly in their depth. Many skills are unitary. For example, children will either have mastered or not have mastered the ability to use context. Other skills are comprised of many subskills. For example, the skill "naming affixes" comprises many smaller skills as each affix to be learned comprises a separate subskill. Furthermore, some skills can be taught over a brief time period, whereas others require more extensive coverage. For example, the skill of "finding details" can be mastered by most children in a relatively brief period of time, whereas the skill of "word meanings" requires continuous learning experiences.

TASK 2: DIAGNOSING BEFORE INSTRUCTION (PREASSESSMENT)

The teacher needs to perform two types of preassessment for each child. First, the teacher needs to assess the instructional level; second, the teacher needs to assess specific skill needs.

ASSESSING INSTRUCTIONAL LEVEL

The procedure for finding instructional levels in a diagnostic-prescriptive program is identical to finding reading level in a basal reader program. Procedures for finding instructional level are given in Chapter 5.

ASSESSING SPECIFIC SKILL NEEDS

Assessing the specific skill needs of each child may be performed through the use of formal preassessments or informal observations.

Formal Preassessments

Formal preassessment procedures will be discussed under three headings: "Characteristics of Formal Preassessments"; "Aids for Developing Formal Preassessments"; and "Number of Skills to be Preassessed Simultaneously."

Characteristics of Formal Preassessments

Formal preassessment items must match exactly the objectives that they are designed to measure, must contain about three items per objective being assessed, and must be appropriate in difficulty level. Discussion of each of these characteristics follows.

1. The assessment item (question) must match the objective exactly. For example, if the objective reads "The student will be able to name the

word family "all" when it is encountered in unknown words," the assessment items might read

fall gall wall

and the student would be asked to name the three words.

To match the objective exactly, each word must contain the word family "all," must not be recognized as a sight word by the student, and must be scored so that the student will receive credit if he or she names the "all" sound correctly regardless of whether or not the student pronounced the initial consonants accurately.

2. About three items should be used to assess a child's skill on each objective whenever possible. If the child responds to the majority of the items correctly, then the child has probably mastered the skill. The first example comprises three items. If the child responds to two or three words accurately, then the child has probably mastered the skill. If the child responds to none or one word accurately, then the child is probably not competent in the skill.

3. The difficulty level must be appropriate. If the child is demonstrating a skill on a given instructional level, for example, fourth grade material, then the selection must be on a fourth grade level.

Aids for Developing Formal Preassessments

Unless the teacher is using a published diagnostic-prescriptive program such as the *Wisconsin Design for Reading Skill Development* (Otto and Askov, 1972), which includes assessments, it is the teacher's responsibility to design assessment items to aid in determining if a child has mastered a given skill. Teachers can usually design, from their knowledge of reading, items to measure a child's performance. However, exercises in workbooks or teacher's editions of basal readers and assessment suggestions in reading methods textbooks may prove helpful.

Exercises in Workbooks or Teacher's Editions: Questions from workbook pages or exercises presented in teacher's manuals can often be used as assessment items. Although these sources may be used with any scope and sequence of skills, they are particularly helpful with a ladder of skills that has been developed from the material from which the questions are being taken. Table 8.2 shows a way in which workbook questions and questions in a teacher's edition may be keyed to a set of objectives.

Aids Provided with a Scope and Sequence of Skills in Reading Methodology Textbooks: As suggested earlier, some textbooks in reading materials include a scope and sequence of reading skills. Many of these, such as *Diagnostic Reading Instruction in the Elementary School*, contain a chapter concerning methods of assessing specific skills (Guszak, 1978, Chapter 11). This text includes assessment suggestions for each skill discussed. Assessment suggestions for word identification and readiness skills are given in Chapter 15; assessment suggestions for comprehension and study skills are given in Chapters 3 and 4, respectively.

TABLE 8.2 Teacher's Edition and Workbook Questions to Be Used as Assessment Items for a Scope and Sequence of Skills*

Student will be able to

1. Recognize and use the contraction *isn't* (TE p. 64).
2. Recognize and use the abbreviation *Mr.* (*Mister*) (TE p. 64).
3. Recognize and use simple compound words (TE p. 66).
4. Recognize the sound and letter association for /ay/ and /lick/ as in *bay* and *sick* (TE pp. 71-72).
5. Recognize and use punctuation marks (oral).
6. Recognize the use of a period in an abbreviation (oral).
7. Recognize the sound and letters association for the *ing* ending (TE p. 91).
8. Add the *ing* ending to root words (TE p. 91).
9. Add the *ake* phonogram to initial consonants (TE p. 91).
10. Add the *s* ending to verbs (TE p. 100).
11. Select and name words beginning with the *pl* cluster (TE p. 100).
12. Select and name words beginning with the *sm* cluster (TE p. 116).
13. Name the */s/* sound for the *c* consonant (TE p. 117).
14. Add the *ook* phonogram to initial consonants (TE p. 117).
15. Select and name *w* and *y* as vowel helpers (oral).
16. Name a comma as the punctuation following an introductory word (oral).
17. Name the letter and sound association for /oa/ (TE p. 167).
18. Name and say the *cr* and *fr* clusters in words (TE p. 167).
19. Name the letter and sound association for /oa/ (TE p. 167).
20. Name and select, from printed words, the *mp* cluster (TE p. 184).
21. Name and select, from printed words, the *sc* cluster (TE p. 208).
22. Name and add the *un* phonogram to root words (TE p. 209).
23. Name and add the *s* ending to nouns (TE p. 224).
24. Name the letter and sound association for /ee/ (TE p. 232).
25. Name and select from printed words the *ck* digraph (TE p. 250).
26. Recognize and name the apostrophe in contractions (TE p. 251).
27. Name and write, in context, words with more than one meaning (simple) (TE p. 266).
28. Recognize and use the comma to set off direct address (TE p. 267).
29. Recognize elliptical sentences (TE p. 273).

*Based on the Houghton Mifflin Reading Series, 2nd preprimer, *Lions.*

Number of Skills to Be Preassessed Simultaneously

Assessments for a series of objectives should be carried out over a period of time. For example, Mr. Rimcom has forty objectives that he hopes his students reading at grade five level will be able to master by the end of the year. He does not assess the children on all forty objectives at one time. Instead, he tests the children on only enough objectives to distinguish several skills on which they need instruction. Once they have mastered these skills, he does further assessing on additional objectives. Performing a minimum of assessments at one time assures a current diagnosis. When testing is done en masse, the results are often outdated by the time that instruction is begun. For example, Yolanda's teacher tests her on sixty skills early in September. At this time, Yolanda shows difficulty with many skills including locating words in the dictionary. However, before instruction in this skill is given several months later, Yolanda learns it. Thus, her diagnosis was outdated before instruction occurred.

Informal Preassessment

Each skill does not require formal assessment for each child. Many assessments can be performed through classroom observation. For example, Miss Kerr wants to assess her students reading on the primary level on the skill "word meaning." She knows through conversations and answers to questions, and through the vocabulary portion of English tests, that three students in that group have very large vocabularies. There is no need for her to assess further these children's knowledge of word meanings.

TASK 3: KEEPING RECORDS

A diagnostic–prescriptive skills program requires records of instructional level, skills mastered, and skills to be mastered. One method of record keeping is that used by the *Wisconsin Design for Reading Skill Development* written by Otto and Askov (1972), who suggest that a card be maintained on each child. About one-quarter inch from the edge of the card are small holes beside each of which a skill is listed. When the child masters a skill, the cardboard between the hole and the edge of the card is punched out. If the teacher wishes to work with a given objective, the teacher slides a rod through the hole beside the appropriate skill. The cards of the children who have mastered that skill fall off. The cards of the children who need diagnosis or instruction are those that remain on the rod.

A second type of record keeping form can be found in Table 8.3. This form provides for a listing of the children's names and an indication of whether the child has mastered or has not mastered the skill on the preassessment and whether or not the child had mastered the skill upon completion of instruction. A key used to indicate whether a skill has been assessed or mastered is as follows:

Blank	Not assessed
√	Passed preassessment
◯	Did not pass preassessment; needs instruction
◯ with √ inside	Did not pass preassessment; has received instruction and passed postassessment

Table 8.3 shows that five children—Preston, Hans, Quentin, Rita, and Sabina—have been tested on objectives 1-6 and that all have mastered objectives 1 and 3. Additionally, Quentin, Rita, and Sabina passed the preassessment for objectives 2 and 4, as did Preston and Hans for objective 6. None of the children is competent on objective 5; all require instruction, as do Preston and Hans on objective 2 and Quentin and Rita on objective 6. Preston and Hans did not satisfactorily complete objective 4 and Sabina did not satisfactorily complete objective 6 on the preassessment. However, following instruction they appeared competent in these skills.

In the event that skills are broken into subskills, a separate chart listing each subskill should be kept. For example, Table 8.3 indicates that only Preston and Hans has mastered the skill "naming affixes." However, Table 8.4 indicates that Quentin has mastered naming prefixes but not suffixes and that Rita has mastered some of the prefixes and suffixes and requires instruction in the others, whereas Sabina could not name any of the prefixes or suffixes when first assessed but now has mastered the skill as indicated by the ⓥ in Table 8.4.

TABLE 8.3 Teacher's Checksheet of Skills to Be Mastered

		Students							
Objective	*Objective Number*	*Preston*	*Hans*	*Quentin*	*Rita*	*Sabina*			
Using context clues	1	√	√	√	√	√			
Using configuration clues	2	○	○	√	√	√			
Using picture clues	3	√	√	√	√	√			
Using spelling/sound correspondences	4	ⓥ	ⓥ	√	√	√			
Dividing words into syllables	5	○	○	○	○	○			
Naming affixes	6	√	√	○	○	ⓥ			
Blending syllables	7								

Key: Blank Not assessed
√ Passed preassessment
○ Did not pass preassessment; needs instruction
ⓥ Did not pass preassessment; has received instruction and passed postassessment

TABLE 8.4 Teacher's Checksheet of Skills to Be Mastered

	Students							
Prefixes	*Quentin*	*Rita*	*Sabina*					
ab	√	√	(√)					
dis	√	○	(√)					
pre	√	√	(√)					
re	√	○	(√)					
un	√	○	(√)					
Suffixes								
able	○	√	(√)					
er	○	○	(√)					
y	○	√	(√)					

TASK 4: DESIGNING INSTRUCTIONAL STRATEGIES

Instruction in a diagnostic-prescriptive program includes, for each skill, an initial teaching lesson and reinforcement lessons. For each objective or subobjective, there is usually one initial teaching lesson that provides for explanation and demonstration of the skill. This lesson is usually teacher directed. The initial teaching lesson is followed by sufficient reinforcement lessons to ensure mastery of the skill. Usually, two or three reinforcement lessons are sufficient for this purpose, although any number can be used if they appeared necessary. Reinforcement lessons may include explanation and demonstration or may simply provide practice in the skill to be mastered. As such, reinforcement lessons may be teacher or pupil directed. Group and individual reading games and activites may be profitably used as reinforcement lesson experiences. Contract and other instructional strategies as described in Chapter 7 may be profitably used in a diagnostic-prescriptive program.

Published diagnostic-prescriptive programs sometimes include instructional procedures in addition to objectives and assessments. Correlating instructional materials available to the teacher with the objectives is, however, the most common method of providing instructional strategies. The materials available to a teacher are analyzed to determine which can be used to help children meet an objective. If so, the materials are correlated with that objective.

References and Resource Books

This text correlates teaching procedures with each word identification skill, comprehension skill, study skill, and readiness skill described in Chapters 2, 3, 4, and 14. These teaching procedures may be found in Chapter 15, "Teaching the Word Identification, Comprehension, Study, and Readiness Skills."

Additionally, the following books describe activites for teaching reading skills.

Burns, P., and Roe, B. *Reading Activities for Today's Elementary Schools.* Chicago: Rand McNally & Company, 1979 (Box 7600, Chicago, Ill. 60680).

Ekwall, E. E. *Locating and Correcting Reading Difficulties.* 2nd ed. Columbus, Ohio: Charles E. Merrill Publishing Company, 1977 (1300 Alum Creek Dr., Columbus, Ohio 43216).

Herr, S. E. *Learning Activities for Reading.* 3rd ed. Dubuque, Iowa: William C. Brown Company, Publishers, 1976 (2460 Kerper Blvd., Dubuque, Iowa 52003).

Highley, J. *Activities Deskbook for Teaching Reading Skills.* Englewood Cliffs, N.J.: Parker Publishing Company, 1977 (West Nyack, N.Y. 10994).

Keith, J. *Word Attack Joy.* Naperville, Ill.: Reading Joy, Inc., 1976 (Box 404, Naperville, Ill. 60540).

Mallett, J. J. *Classroom Reading Games Activities Kit.* New York: The Center for Applied Research in Education, Inc., 1975 (521 Fifth Ave., New York, N.Y. 10017).

Spache, E. B. *Reading Activities for Child Involvement.* 2nd ed. Boston: Allyn & Bacon, Inc., 1976 (470 Atlantic Ave., Boston, Mass. 02210).

Thompson, R. *Energizers for Reading Instruction.* Englewood Cliffs, N.J.: Prentice-Hall, Inc., 1973 (Englewood Cliffs, N.J. 07632).

Verner, Z. *Collections: A Newsbook of Vocabulary Activities.* Houston: Clayton Publishing Company, 1979 (4384 Wheeler, Houston, Tex. 77004).

The following selection, although not strictly an activities book, includes many lists of words containing identified graphemes. These lists can be most helpful in constructing activities.

Heilman, A. W. *Phonics in Proper Perspective.* 2nd ed. Columbus, Ohio: Charles E. Merrill Publishing Company, 1976 (1300 Alum Creek Dr., Columbus, Ohio 43216).

TASK 5: DIAGNOSING AFTER INSTRUCTION (POSTASSESSMENT)

A postassessment for any objective may be identical with the preassessment or may be similar in format with different words or passages used in the question. Therefore, the information included under "Task 2: Diagnosing before Instruction (Preassessment)" applies equally well to postassessments.

Postassessments differ from preassessments in time of administration. Whereas preassessments are administered prior to instruction to determine if instruction is required, postassessments are administered pursuant to instruction to determine if the skill has been mastered or if further instruction is necessary.

The teacher must make the decision on when the postassessment should be administered. If the teacher believes that a skill has been mastered when the child can pass the postassessment one day after the last reinforcement lesson, then the postassessment should be administered at that time. However, if the teacher believes that a child is not competent in a skill unless he or she can pass the postassessment two weeks after the last reinforcement lesson, then the postassessment should be administered at that time.

TASK 6: ORGANIZING INSTRUCTION

Two steps are involved in organizing instruction: skill resource planning and scheduling instruction.

SKILL RESOURCE PLANNING

A skill resource plan for diagnostic-prescriptive instruction includes

Objectives
Materials
Preassessment
Instructional strategies
Postassessment

A lesson plan containing these five elements has been presented in Chapter 6. A major difference between lesson planning in a basal reader program and skill resource planning in a diagnostic-prescriptive program is in the instructional strategies. The teaching techniques used in a diagnostic-prescriptive program as introduced in "Task 4: Designing Instructional Strategies" should include two types of lessons—an introductory lesson and reinforcement lessons—whereas the strategies in a basal reader program, as discussed in Chapter 6, include only one or two steps of a basal reader program. A self-check for a skill resource plan for diagnostic-prescriptive instruction is given in Table 8.5.

SCHEDULING INSTRUCTION

A second major difference between lesson planning as presented in a basal reader program and skill resource planning in a diagnostic-prescriptive program is the timing of instruction. In a diagnostic-prescriptive program, the teacher needs to schedule the preassessment, the initial teaching lesson, the reinforcement lessons, and the postassessment. The amount of time that lapses between each step is at the discretion of the teacher. For example, Mr. Edwards might believe that preassessments on five objectives should be administered at the same time and that instruction on all of the objectives should begin the following week for those children who require it. He also believes that the reinforcement lessons should follow the initial teaching lesson at three-day intervals. Furthermore, he thinks that

TABLE 8.5 Self-Check for a Skill Resource Plan for a Diagnostic–Prescriptive Program

Can you answer "yes" to each of the following questions?

Objective

1. Is your objective appropriate for the instructional level of your group, that is, was it chosen from the level of a scope and sequence chart that matched the children's instructional level?

Materials

2. Is your material appropriate to the skill to be taught?
3. Is your material on the correct instructional level?

Preassessment

4. Do your questions match the objective exactly?
5. Does your assessment contain at least three parts that can be graded?
6. Are your questions of an appropriate difficulty level, that is, on the correct instructional level?

Instructional Strategies

Introductory Lesson (Initial Teaching Lesson)

7. Does your lesson help students to understand the concept by providing demonstration and explanation?
8. Does your lesson plan include techniques such as motivational activities and student participation that will make it enjoyable for students?

Reinforcement Lessons

9. Do your reinforcement lessons provide for practice on a skill that has previously been introduced?
10. Do your plans include demonstration or explanation if children appear to be in need of such instruction?
11. Do your plans include activities which will make the lesson interesting for children?

Postassessment

12. Do your questions match the objective exactly?
13. Does your postassessment contain at least three parts that can be graded?
14. Are your questions of an appropriate difficulty level, that is, on the correct instructional level?

the postassessment should be administered a week following the last reinforcement lesson. Thus, his calendar appears as shown in Table 8.6.

Alternately, Mrs. Lukens is a member of a team in a team-teaching situation. Each Monday she is assigned a group of children who have been preassessed and deemed in need of instruction on a given skill. She retains these children in her reading class through Friday. Thus, Mrs. Lukens plans her week in the following manner:

Monday	Initial teaching lesson
Tuesday	Reinforcement lesson 1
Wednesday	Reinforcement lesson 2
Thursday	Reinforcement lesson 3
Friday	Postassessment

TABLE 8.6 Mr. Edwards' Schedule

Week	*Monday*	*Tuesday*	*Wednesday*	*Thursday*	*Friday*
Week 1				Preassessment: Objectives 6–10	
Week 2	Initial teaching lesson: Objective 6—Sam, John, Pat	Initial teaching lesson: Objective 7—James, Bob, Betty, Danny, Nita	Initial teaching lesson: Objective 8—Chet, Shirley, Martha, Tom	Initial teaching lesson: Objective 9—Tom, Robert, Richard, Jacques Reinforcement lesson 1: Objective 6	Initial teaching lesson: Objective 10—Dick, Win Reinforcement lesson 2: Objective 7
Week 3	Reinforcement lesson 1: Objective 8	Reinforcement lesson 1: Objective 9 Reinforcement lesson 2: Objective 6	Reinforcement lesson 1: Objective 10 Reinforcement lesson 2: Objective 7	Reinforcement lesson 2: Objective 8	Reinforcement lesson 2: Objective 9 Reinforcement lesson 3: Objective 6
Week 4	Reinforcement lesson 2: Objective 10 Reinforcement lesson 3: Objective 7	Reinforcement lesson 3: Objective 8	Reinforcement lesson 3: Objective 9	Reinforcement lesson 3: Objective 10	Postassessment: Objective 6
Week 5	Postassessment: Objective 7	Postassessment: Objective 8	Postassessment: Objective 9	Postassessment: Objective 10	

EXAMPLE OF A TEACHER USING A DIAGNOSTIC-PRESCRIPTIVE PROGRAM

Ms. Tuck teaches a grade three class. Although most of the children in her class are doing well in a basal program, she has five children—Eartha, Sylvia, Dean, Henry, and Oscar—whom she feels need an enriched program. Therefore, she decides to add a diagnostic-prescriptive skills program to their basal program.

Ms. Tuck decided to first teach the following skills: identifying details, identifying main ideas, identifying sequence, and identifying cause-effect relationships. Ms. Tuck records the children's progress on a checksheet as shown in Table 8.7.

TABLE 8.7 Ms. Tuck's Checksheet for Diagnostic-Prescriptive Instruction

	Students							
Objective	*Eartha*	*Sylvia*	*Dean*	*Henry*	*Oscar*			
Identifying details	(√)	√	(√)	(√)	√			
Identifying main ideas	√	√	√	√	√			
Identifying sequence	○	○	○	○	√			
Identifying cause-effect relationships								

Blank Not assessed
√ Passed preassessment
○ Did not pass preassessment; needs instruction
(√) Did not pass preassessment; has received instruction and passed postassessment

On checking the records, Ms. Tuck decides that the next skill to be taught should be "sequencing." As Oscar passed the preassessment on this skill, he will not receive instruction; instruction will be given to Eartha, Sylvia, Dean, and Henry.

Ms. Tuck then constructs the following skill resource plan based on the suggestions given in Chapter 15 of this text, the resource books listed earlier in this chapter, and other materials at her disposal.

Lesson Plan for Identifying Sequence

Objective: The student will be able to sequence the main events of a story.

Materials: Basal reader, list of events on mimeo, (initial teaching lesson); cards with phrases copied from basal reader (ordered phrases); sentences written on cards, which, when sequenced, form paragraphs (sentence puzzles); illustrations and accompanying stories (reconstruct the story).

Instructional Strategies

Initial Teaching Lesson: Discuss with children their activities prior to arriving at school that morning. Then, sequence several children's activities by asking "What did you do first? Next?" When children appear to have the idea of sequence, place three sentence strips pertaining to a story with which all children are familiar on a pocket chart. Ask students to sequence the strips. Ask children to complete a worksheet that has the same type of activity, that is, sequencing three events from a known story.

Reinforcement Lesson 1: Children will work in groups of two to complete the following activities:

1. Ordered phrases (Ekwall, 1977, p. 104)
2. Sentence puzzles (Ekwall, 1977, p. 104)

Activities are self-checking. Teacher should be available to give help if needed.

Reinforcement Lesson 2: Children should complete the following activities independently:

1. Reconstruct the story (Burns and Roe, 1979, p. 127)
2. Sequence five events from a story that has been recently read

Activities should be self-checking. Teaching should give help if needed.

Postassessment: Same technique as preassessment. Use different stories.

Ms. Tuck schedules instruction on "sequencing" on her calendar in the manner shown in Table 8.8.

TABLE 8.8 Ms. Tuck's Schedule for Teaching Ascertaining Sequence

Week	*M*	*T*	*W*	*TH*	*F*
1		Initial teaching lesson: Objective 22—Eartha, Sylvia, Dean, Henry			Reinforcement lesson 1: Objective 22
2	Reinforcement lesson 2: Objective 22				
3	Postassessment: Objective 22				

Ms. Tuck continues to enrich these pupils' reading program by preassessing on appropriate skills and by providing instruction in these skills until the pupils can complete the postassessment at a satisfactory level.

SUMMARY

A diagnostic-prescriptive approach to the skills program is designed to individualize the skills program to meet the needs of all pupils. It provides orderly instruction in word identification, comprehension, and study skills and has the following sequence for each student: a. the instructional level of the student is ascertained, b. the skills in which the student should be competent or that level are delineated, c. those skills that the student has already mastered and has yet to master on this instructional level are determined by a preassessment, d. instruction is given in the skills in which the child needs to become proficient, and e. those skills that the child has studied are postassessed to ascertain his or her mastery of them. If the child has mastered them, he or she proceeds to new skills. If the child has not mastered them, he or she receives additional instruction until he or she becomes competent. Teacher tasks in a diagnostic-prescriptive approach include a. ascertaining a scope and sequence of skills, b. preassessing, c. keeping records, d. designing instructional strategies, e. postassessing, and f. organizing instruction. Because a diagnostic-prescriptive approach is focused on skills, it is always used in conjunction with a basal, individualized, or other reading instruction program that provides copious reading opportunities.

References and Bibliography

Askov, E., and Otto, W. *Teacher's Planning Guide—Study Skills. Wisconsin Design for Reading Skill Development.* Minneapolis: National Computer Systems, 1972.

Bader, L. A. *Reading Diagnosis and Remediation in Classroom and Clinic.* New York: Macmillan Publishing Co., Inc., 1980.

Burns, P., and Roe, B. *Reading Activities for Today's Elementary Schools.* Chicago: Rand McNally & Company, 1979.

Ekwall, E. E. *Locating and Correcting Reading Difficulties.* 2nd ed. Columbus, Ohio: Charles E. Merrill Publishing Company, 1977.

Guszak, F. J. *Diagnostic Reading Instruction in the Elementary School.* 2nd ed. New York: Harper & Row, Publishers, 1978.

Heilman, A. W. *Phonics in Proper Perspective.* 2nd ed. Columbus, Ohio: Charles E. Merrill Publishing Company, 1977.

Herr, S. E. *Learning Activities for Reading.* 3rd ed. Dubuque, Iowa: William C. Brown Company, Publishers, 1976.

Highley, J. *Activities Deskbook for Teaching Reading Skills.* Englewood Cliffs, N.J.: Parker Publishing Company, 1977.

Keith, J. *Word Attack Joy.* Naperville, Ill.: Reading Joy, Inc., 1976.

Mallett, J. J. *Classroom Reading Games Activites Kit.* New York: The Center for Applied Research in Education, Inc., 1975.

Mallett, J. J. *101 Make-and-Play Reading Games for the Intermediate Grades.* New York: The Center for Applied Research in Education, Inc., 1976.

Otto, W., and Askov, E. *The Wisconsin Design for Reading Skill Development: Rationale and Guidelines.* Minneapolis: National Computer Systems, 1972.

Otto, W., Rude, R., and Spiegel, D. L. *How to Teach Reading.* Reading, Mass.: Addison-Wesley Publishing Co., Inc., 1979.

Rupley, W. H., and Blair, T. R. *Reading Diagnosis and Remediation: A Primer for Classroom and Clinic.* Chicago: Rand McNally Publishing Company, 1979.

Spache, E. B. *Reading Activities for Child Involvement.* 2nd ed. Boston: Allyn & Bacon, Inc., 1976.

Thompson, R. *Energizers for Reading Instruction.* Englewood Cliffs, N.J.: Prentice-Hall, Inc., 1973.

Verner, Z. *Collections: A Newsbook of Vocabulary Activities.* Houston: Clayton Publishing Company, 1979.

Self-Check 8.3
Diagnostic–Prescriptive Approach

The following questions are designed to help the participant assess his or her competence on the first twelve objectives stated at the beginning of this chapter. Although every effort has been made to make the self-check questions comprehensive, participants should remember that they are held responsible for meeting the objectives as stated at the beginning of this chapter.

1. Objective 1. With which programs may a diagnostic-prescriptive approach be used?
2. Objective 2. What are the advantages of a diagnostic-prescriptive approach to the skills program?
3. Objective 3. What are six teacher tasks involved in a diagnostic-prescriptive skills program?
4. Objective 4. What are three places that a scope and sequence of skills may be found? Which one do you prefer? Give reasons for your choice.
5. Objective 5. What are three possible sources for designing test items to be used to discern which skills a child has or has not mastered?
6. Objective 6. Ms. Timerick wishes to assess the following objective for children reading on the first grade level: Given a list of words orally, the student will be able to identify the digraph in each word. She designs the following assessment question: The student will identify the digraph in each of five words presented orally. Does this assessment question match the characteristics of a formal preassessment? Why or why not?
7. Objective 7. Under what conditions may informal assessments be used?
8. Objective 8. Why should only a few objectives be preassessed at one time?
9. Objective 9. What information do you think should be kept on a child's record in a diagnostic-prescriptive program? Give reasons for your choice.
10. Objective 10. Describe a record keeping system which would record the information that should be kept on a child's record.

11. Objective 11. Evaluate the following skill resource plan according to criteria given in this chapter.

Objective: Given twenty words with silent consonants, the student will be able to draw a line through the silent consonants with 80 percent accuracy.

Preassessment: The student will mark out the silent consonants on the preassessment worksheet.

Instructional Strategies

Introductory Lesson: To introduce the generalizations for silent consonants, words containing silent letters are printed on the chalkboard. Have children read the words aloud and discuss in general terms if they hear all the letters in each word. Then, review the words individually and write beside each the silent letter and why it is silent, i.e., In words beginning with kn, the k is usually silent.

Reinforcement Lessons: (a) Children listen to audiotape and complete accompanying worksheet on topic of silent consonants. (b) Children complete two worksheets which stress silent consonants.

Postassessment: Same as the preassessment.

12. Objective 12. Describe a method for scheduling diagnostic–prescriptive instruction. Be sure that your description shows the amount of time that would lapse between the preassessment and introductory lesson, introductory lesson and reinforcement lessons, between reinforcement lessons, and between the last reinforcement lesson and the postassessment.

Chapter 8
Experience 1

Objective

During this experience, the participant will prepare a skill resource plan and a teacher checksheet and teach one skill including a preassessment, introductory activity, two reinforcement activities, and a postassessment.

Activity and Assessment Guide

Selection of Objective and Use of Teacher Checksheet

* 1. Did objective selected appear to be on the correct instructional level for the subjects? (circle one) yes no Why or why not?__________

____

2. Are names and objective correctly recorded on checksheet? (circle one) yes no If no, why not?____________________________

____

*Question may be answered by an observer. See Chapter 1: Experience 1 for a complete explanation.

Preassessment

* 3. Did each test question appear to assess the behavior described in the objective? (circle one) yes no If no, why not? ____________

____

4. Were there at least three assessment items? (circle one) yes no If no, why not? ____________

____

* 5. Did each test question appear to be on the correct level of difficulty? (circle one) yes no If no, why not? ____________

____

Introductory Activity

6. Did the introductory activity provide demonstration or explanation of the skill to be learned? (circle one) yes no If yes, how was it given? (teacher, audiotape, film, combination) ____________

____

* 7. What emotional reaction did subjects show to the activity? ____________

____

First Reinforcement Activity

8. Did the first reinforcement activity provide practice and any necessary explanation regarding the skill to be learned? (circle one) yes no If no, why not? ____________

____

* 9. What emotional reaction to the lesson did the subjects show? ____________

____

Second Reinforcement Activity

10. Did the second reinforcement lesson provide practice and any needed explanation regarding the skill to be learned? (circle one) yes no

If no, why not?____

* 11. What emotional reaction did the subjects show to the lesson?__________

Postassessment

* 12. Did each test question appear to assess the behavior described in the objective? (circle one) yes no If no, why not?____________________

13. Are there at least three assessment items? (circle one) yes no If no, why not?____

* 14. Did each test question appear to be on the correct level of difficulty? (circle one) yes no If no, why not?__________________________

Checksheet

* 15. Were the preassessment and postassessment results correctly recorded on the teacher's checksheet? (circle one) yes no If no, why not?____

Summary

16. Do you believe that you taught your pupils a skill? (circle one) yes no Why or why not?____

17. Do you believe that subjects felt that they had learned? (circle one) yes no Why or why not?____

18. Write a brief summary about the child's reaction toward this strategy and the amount of learning that took place.__________________________

19. State what you believe to be the significant implications of this experience for you as a future classroom teacher. ______________________________

____

____

20. Attach a copy of your skill resource plan to this sheet.

Part Four
Managing the Reading Program

Chapter 9
Grouping by Achievement, Interests, and Needs

Objectives 9.1

On completion of this chapter, the participant should be able to

1. Describe one reason why a teacher would want to use more than one basal reader series in his or her classroom.
2. State the purpose of achievement level groups.
3. Given a tally sheet of test scores for a class in grades two through six, divide the class into achievement level groups.
4. State why achievement level groups should be kept flexible.
5. State one way in which teachers can minimize the stigmatizing effect of achievement level groups.
6. State two factors that should be taken into consideration when deciding on the number of groups.
7. Evaluate a weekly schedule that shows a teacher's plans for instructing three achievement level groups in a basal reader program.
8. Describe at least one way in which achievement level groups are used in the basal reader approach, the language experience approach, and the individualized approach to teaching reading.
9. Describe at least one way in which interest groups are used in the basal reader approach, the language experience approach, and the individualized approach to teaching reading.
10. Describe at least one way in which needs groups are used in the basal reader approach, the language experience approach, and the individualized approach to teaching reading.
11. List diagnostic procedures for identifying each child's interests.
12. Describe at least two "substitutes" for the teacher that can be used to facilitate grouping.

13. Describe two basic premises involved in teaching peers to help each other.

Experiences 1 and 2 extend Chapter 9 with these objectives:

14. Given a tally sheet of test scores for a class in grades two through six, divide the class into achievement level instructional groups and plan for a week of instruction.
15. Design and teach a lesson that requires establishing needs groups, interest groups, or achievement level groups in the basal reader, language experience, or individualized approach to teaching reading.

Information Given 9.2
Grouping by Achievement, Interests, and Needs

When the teacher education major visited Mr. Rough's class, she was overwhelmed by the range of reading achievement levels she saw in the fourth grade. What she further discovered upon follow-up discussion with Mr. Rough was that the basal reader approach provided enough materials and suggestions for teaching, so that he had time to plan for reading instruction for three different reading groups each reading on a different level. Furthermore, when she looked closely at the materials in Mr. Rough's room, she noticed that he was using three different basal reader series. He used the grade five level of one of the series for his superior readers, the grade four level of a second series for his pupils who read at or just below grade level, and the 2:2 level of a third series for his pupils who read far below grade level. Mr. Rough used a variety of basal reader series so that each groups of children could have access to materials that were appropriate for them. For example, the series used with the superior readers stressed the comprehension skills, whereas the series used with the group that read well below grade level was designed for older children who were encountering reading difficulties.

Later the teacher education student saw Chuck scoop up his basal reader and leave the group he had been working with. Almost simultaneously, four other children left their various basal reader groups and met with Chuck in the far corner of the room. Mr. Rough joined the children and asked them to open their newspapers. He explained to them that they would be working on the reading skill of naming affixes, and each was to select a different article and locate as many affixes as possible in the article. He spent the next twenty minutes working with them on the skill and carefully discussed with the group members the meaning of the different suffixes and prefixes and the influences that they had on parts of speech.

The basal reader group that Chuck had left was reading above grade level, the group that Susie and Kathy had left was reading very close to grade level, and the group that Bill and Bert had left was reading below grade level. Each child had the same problem with naming affixes, and Mr. Rough had regrouped them for the purpose of working on that specific reading skill need.

This situation illustrates two of the three basic types of grouping systems that Mr. Rough used with his fourth grade class. The basal reader groups with which the children had been working originally could be described as "reading achievement" groups; the groups that they had formed for the purpose of learning how to name affixes could be described as a "reading skill needs" group. The third type grouping that Mr. Rough used was based on reading interest and could be described as a "reading interest" group.

Although achievement level groups, interest groups, and needs groups are found in most approaches to teaching reading, they will initially be described as part of a basal reader approach. Later in this chapter, each of these groups will be illustrated in terms of their use in both a language experience approach and an individualized approach to teaching reading.

USING ACHIEVEMENT LEVEL GROUPS, INTEREST GROUPS, AND NEEDS GROUPS IN THE BASAL READER APPROACH TO TEACHING READING

READING ACHIEVEMENT LEVEL GROUPS IN A BASAL READER APPROACH

A reading achievement level group is based on the reading level of the members and is often the major type of grouping used in a basal reader approach to teaching reading. Once the reading level has been ascertained, the classroom teacher can use a variety of materials in which to prescribe instruction. However, the basal reader itself is the primary tool for achievement level groups in a basal reader program.

Placing Children in the Appropriate Achievement Level Group

To place children into appropriate achievement level groups, the teacher (1) finds each child's achievement level using an assessment procedure such as the informal reading inventory, a placement test, a word list test, a standardized test, or the cloze procedure; (2) summarizes the results of the testing by listing children by achievement level; and (3) places children in groups that include children reading on similar levels. Table 9.1 and Table 9.2 show the results and summary of an informal reading inventory given to Mr. Rough's grade four class. Although a variety of groupings is possible, Mr. Rough selected grouping 1 shown in Table 9.3 as a beginning point for basal reading instruction. Mr. Rough plans to use difficult fifth grade material for his outstanding students, fourth grade materials for his second group, and materials on the 2:2 level for his weakest readers.

TABLE 9.1 Results of Informal Reading Inventory Testing of Mr. Rough's Grade Four Class

	Grade 4		*Grade 3:2*		*Grade 3:1*		*Grade 2:2*		*Grade 2:1*		*Grade 1*		*Grade P*		*Grade PP*	
Name	*Oral*	*Silent*	*Oral*	*Silent*	*Oral*	*Silent*	*Oral*	*Silent*	*Oral*	*Silent*	*Oral*	*Silent*	*Oral*	*Silent*	*Oral*	*Silent*
George	2	1														
Chuck	0	0														
Carol	5	5	4	3												
Bill	7	8			7	6	4	2								
John	2	8		6		2										
Todd	8	3	3													
Guy	5	3														
Helen	2	2														
Susie	3	1														
Diane	0	0														
Kathy	2	2														
Maragret	3	2														
Bert	7	9			8	6			4	2						
Ruth	9	4	3	2												
Pete	2	3														
Joan	3	2														
Heather	9	6	7	2	8		5									
Ross	1	3														
Mark	2	2														
Barry	3	3														
Al	7	5	5	3												
Ray	3	3														
Audrey	0	1														

TABLE 9.2 Summary by Grade Level of Results of Informal Reading Inventory Testing of Mr. Rough's Grade Four Class

Grade 4		*Grade 3:2*	*Grade 3:1*	*Grade 2:2*	*Grade 2:1*
Ross	George*	Carol	John	Bill	Bert
Mark	Chuck*	Todd		Heather	
Barry	Guy	Ruth			
Ray	Helen	Al			
Audrey*	Susie				
Pete	Diane*				
Joan	Kathy				
	Margaret				

*Outstanding at that level.

TABLE 9.3 Possible Grouping Arrangements for Mr. Rough's Grade Four Class

	Arrangement
1	Outstanding students in grade four together; instructional levels 3:2 and remainder of four together; instructional levels 3:1, 2:2, and 2:1 together.
2	Instructional level four together; instructional levels 3:2 and 3:1 together; instructional levels 2:2 and 2:1 together.
3	There are many more possibilities, as there is no one right way to group pupils.

Flexible Grouping and Methods for Reducing Group Stigma

The main criterion for placing children into basal reading groups is reading level. The range of reading skills can often help the teacher to decide how many groups into which to initially divide his or her class. The number and composition of the groups should be kept flexible. No matter how carefully children may be placed into groups, some errors will be made, and children will be placed in the wrong level group; some children will make rapid progress, and others will seem to regress in reading skill development. These differences in growth make flexible grouping a necessity.

The purpose of achievement level groups is obviously to put children of a similar level of reading achievement together to provide them with materials as close to their instructional level as possible. However, there may be a stigma or a status connected with the various reading groups into which a child is placed. Placement in a particular group may make some children feel inferior and others feel superior. An attitude of "we're all here to learn, and this is how we learn best" can help reduce the negative reactions.

Formation of groups for a variety of other purposes, which are not based on reading level alone, can help to minimize adverse effects. Both interest groups, based on each child's individual interests, and special needs groups, based on specific reading skills that span several reading levels, can be formed. The content areas often lend themselves to "group" projects for which interest groups can be formed. For example, social studies is often taught in a thematic manner with "research groups" composed of children with diverse reading abilities investigating different aspects of each theme. If a child is not always in a group composed only of the low achievers, it is easier to avoid being labeled a low achiever.

Another way to minimize the stigma of grouping is to name groups after one of the children in the group rather than by level designation, which may tend to call attention to the difference in achievement. Bobby's Group, Susie's Group, and Robin's Group call less attention to the achievement level of various groups than do group 1, group 2, and group 3 or group A, group B, and group C.

Organizing a Classroom for Different Basal Reading Levels

Since Mr. Rough had a range of about six years in reading levels in his classroom, he decided to group the children into three basic groups: those who read above grade level, those who read at grade level, and those who read below grade level. Ideally, he would have had twenty-three groups—one for each individual child in his classroom. However, he felt that he simply did not have the time or the resources to divide his class into twenty-three groups, so he tried to put together children who were most alike. He knew that "three" was not a magic number and that some teachers used five or six groups, whereas others didn't group at all. He felt that the number of groups was really a matter of how many groups the teacher felt he or she could handle and how much variance the teacher had in his or her classroom. His experiential background and his own individual needs made him decide to use three basic groups when teaching reading.

Since Mr. Rough wanted to use a different basal series with each of the three groups, he developed an organizational system that would help him do so. When he began to plan instruction for each of the three groups, he knew that he wanted to spend some time each day with each group. He actually preferred to spend most of his time with his weak readers because he felt that they needed the most help. However, he knew that this was not fair to the average or superior readers, as they too needed this help and guidance. He was also quite emphatic about making sure that each group had the opportunity to "read" each day. Mr. Rough did not regard working worksheets or group discussions as reading. He knew that to learn how to read, as well as to enjoy reading, his pupils had to actually confront the pages of print within a meaningful, relevant context. To Mr. Rough, then, reading meant letting the children react to the stories in a basal reader, the supplementary books, or any other such reading materials.

When Mr. Rough closely examined the five-step basal reader format, he realized that many of the steps did not require that he be present. Although he felt it was essential that he be with a group to motivate them to read the story and to present new words, he didn't feel that he needed to be present when they began to read silently. Likewise, since he knew oral reading and group discussion revealed much about each child's word recognition and comprehension skills, he felt that he would have to be with a group when they were working on that step but that, depending on the skill or activity being planned, he might or might not need to be with the children completing steps 4 and 5—follow-up and extension (see Table 9.4). He knew that if he were well organized he could set up a schedule for their lessons that would allow him to be with a group when they were working on a step where he was needed. Table 9.4 shows the organizational format he designed to reach each group each day as well as a list of suggestions that he wrote out for himself to make certain that he was teaching the basal reader lessons in the best possible manner.

First, he specifically set aside an hour a day to work with the basal reader achievement level groups. To work with each group each day, the hour was divided into twenty-minute segments. At the end of each twenty minutes Mr. Rough rotated skills and went to work with another group. The symbol T by the step in Table 9.4 indicates that the teacher is almost always present at that step; the symbol T/N means that the teacher does not necessarily have to be there to assure successful completion of the step.

Mr. Rough's weekly schedule is shown in Table 9.5.

READING INTEREST GROUPS IN A BASAL READER APPROACH

Another type of grouping used by Mr. Rough was based on the interests expressed by each child. These interests concerned recreational needs and in some cases other needs. He tried to help the children to select materials that would be interesting to them to provide them with practice in developing their reading skills through content that was particularly meaningful and relevant to them. The interests of the children were determined by a number of factors that Mr. Rough tried to keep in mind as he planned lessons and selected materials. Some of the factors are described further in the following paragraphs.

TABLE 9.4 Organizational Format and Teaching Suggestions

Organizational Format

1. Preparation
    - T a. Motivation
    - T b. New words
    - T c. Concept development
2. T/N Silent reading
3. Oral reading and discussion
    - T/N a. Interpretation and sharing
    - T b. Discussion
4. Follow-up
    - T a. Learn new skill
    - T/N b. Practice a new skill—the skill just learned in step 4
    - T/N c. Practice an old skill—a skill formerly learned
5. Extension
    - T/N a. Supplementary reading

T/N b. Dramatization
T/N c. Rereading for a different purpose
T/N d. Creative activities

Teaching Suggestions for Planning for Each Group

1. Teacher should work with each group each day.
2. Each group should do some reading each day.
3. Steps 1 and 2 should be completed the same day.
4. Steps 1, 2, and 3 should be included in the same week.
5. Step 3a can be completed by reading to another student or tape recorder.
6. Step 3b (Discussion) should be completed before Step 5c (Rereading for a different purpose) is introduced.
7. Step 4a should be completed before Step 4b is introduced.
8. Steps 4a and 4b should be completed the same day.
9. Step 4 may sometimes be completed out of sequence.
10. 5a, 5b, 5c, and 5d are optional.
11. Steps 5a–5d may be completed between Steps 1 and 5. (Do not have to go through all the rest to get to 5a–5d.)

TABLE 9.5 Mr. Rough's Weekly Schedule

	High Achievement Group	*Average Achievement Group*	*Low Achievement Group*
Mon.	T1 a, b, c 2 3a	5c T1 a, b, c 2	5a 5d T 3b
Tue.	5d T 3b 5c	3a 5d T 3b	T1 a, b, c 2 5b
Wed.	5a 3a T 4a, b	T 4a 4b 5a	3a T 3b 5a
Thu.	T1 a, b, c 2 4c	5a T1 a, b, c 2	5c 5d T 4a, b
Fri.	3a, b T 2b 5c	3a 4c T 3b	T 3b 4c 5d

Key

1. Preparation
   a. Motivation
   b. New words
   c. Concept development
2. Silent reading
3. Oral reading and discussion
   a. Interpretation and sharing
   b. Discussion
4. Follow-up
   a. Learn new skill
   b. Practice new skill
   c. Practice old skill
5. Extension
   a. Supplementary reading
   b. Dramatization
   c. Reread new purpose
   d. Creative activities

Recreational Interests

All the children had hobbies or topics in which they were particularly interested. Chuck loved to talk about baseball, Kathy had always wanted a pony, Susie collected dolls, and Pete had started his own "car wash" business to make money to buy a camera. Therefore, through informal observation Mr. Rough knew that interest groups on the topics of baseball, ponies, dolls, car washes, and photography would appeal to at least one child in class. However, he did not want to rely on informal observation alone to determine the interests of his pupils.

Mr. Rough used an interest inventory to help him determine the interests of his students. (See a further explanation on this instrument in Chapter 11 on recreational reading.) Completion of this questionnaire was one of the activities that he had his class do while he was busy assessing during the first week in September. His administration of this inventory varied according to the reading skills of his pupils. He had asked the majority of the children to fill out the questionnaire independently; however, his approach with the poorest readers in class differed. In that situation he had one of the best readers "interview" his small group of nonreaders and they would fill out the inventory together. He followed up on the information collected through scheduling individual conferences during which he and the child discussed many of the items in the inventory.

Other Interests

Although the primary purpose of Mr. Rough's interest inventory was designed to focus on the recreational interests of children, he also used it to help him discover other areas or topics in which he felt that the children would be interested. For example, after a long talk with one of his pupils, Mr. Rough discovered that the child, George, was interested in the field of medicine because a family member was seriously ill. Therefore, Mr. Rough assumed that books on George's achievement level that dealt with hospitals, doctors, or medical research might be of interest to him. He found several fiction books about children who had "taken over the family" after a parent had been unable to do so, some nonfiction books on fourth grade reading level that told about selecting medicine and medically related fields as a career, and several other fictional stories about boys who wanted to be doctors.

When Mr. Rough was able to talk to George individually, he helped him to select several different books. George was eager to read the material. Mr. Rough then formed an interest group based on the topic of "careers," and George became a vocal member of the group telling the other children about the responsibilities and training needed to become a modern-day doctor.

Mr. Rough knew that interest groups were formed when interest was aroused and disbanded when interest in the topic was exhausted. In addition to the group on careers, several other interest groups were meeting for a variety of purposes. One of the groups was researching the topic "communications." A story that had been read in the children's basal reader dealt with the invention of the printing press. Several of the children decided that they would like to read more about this topic and construct their own printing press. Further, they intended to write and print a newsletter using their "printing press" to run off copies for everyone in class. This group spanned the achievement and needs groups. Chuck was a member, and his task (since he was the best reader in the group and had excellent study skills as diagnosed by Mr. Rough on the scope and sequence chart) was to research the library for all references, including blueprints, books on model building, and periodicals that described how to construct a printing press. Susie Phillips wanted to be "editor" and was reading a fourth grade reading level pamphlet on how a newspaper operates. This booklet, available at no cost, had been prepared by the educational services division of the local newspaper. Bert was a very poor reader, but could read diagrams and instruction sheets dealing with model building. Therefore, his task was to figure out how to build the press once Chuck had located the appropriate diagrams.

READING SKILLS NEEDS GROUPS IN A BASAL READER APPROACH

A third type of grouping—grouping by special needs—may be defined as using specific reading skills as the basis for setting up a group; that is, groups are formed for the purpose of learning "context clues," "main idea," and the like. This type of grouping is short-lived; it is usually formed only when a reading skill need becomes apparent and is disbanded after the skill has been learned.

Chuck was in the achievement level group that was reading above grade level but was unable to pass the preassessment for affixes. Therefore, he became a member of a group on that skill that spanned achievement level groups. The group included Susie and Kathy who were members of the grade level achievement group and Bert and Bill who were members of the below grade level achievement group.

Since the purpose of this type of grouping is to teach a specific reading skill, youngsters who need work on more than one reading skill can be members of more than one reading skill needs group simultaneously. For example, Kathy belonged to both the affixes group and a second group learning how to use the card catalogue. Likewise, most of the children in the class belonged to more than one needs group at the same time.

USING ACHIEVEMENT LEVEL GROUPS, INTEREST GROUPS, AND NEEDS GROUPS IN THE LANGUAGE EXPERIENCE AND INDIVIDUALIZED APPROACH TO TEACHING READING

Both the language experience approach to teaching reading and the individualized approach to teaching reading rely upon the same three types of groups used by Mr. Rough. However, the emphasis is switched from the preponderance of achievement level groups found in the basal reader approach to a preponderance of needs and interest groups.

Teachers using the language experience approach or the individualized approach might not use basal reader materials or the accompanying placement tests; thus other informal and standardized reading tests are ordinarily used to assess reading level. Once the reading level has been diagnosed, the nature of both the language experience approach and the individualized approach requires a great deal of available reading materials for the children. Lists of books and their reading levels are available to the teacher from a variety of sources. (See Chapter 11 for suggested resources.)

The focus of both these approaches on the individual experiences or interests of each child support a diagnostic-prescriptive approach to reading that does not preclude grouping for needs. In fact, to make the most efficient use of teacher time so that individual "experience stories" can be written and "individual conferences" held, the use of grouping for similar needs is highly recommended.

Both approaches give heavy credence to the sharing of experiences, books, and ideas between the children. These groups formed for sharing can usually be thought of as the interest group variety.

Each of the three grouping techniques that have been discussed is illustrated in the following paragraphs through Mr. Weather's language experience program and through Mr. Poindexter's individualized reading program.

MR. WEATHER'S LANGUAGE EXPERIENCE APPROACH

Since Mr. Weather's pupils were first graders. he used a readiness test to diagnose their reading level. Those children who were identified as already being able to read were given the word list test to give him an estimate of their reading level. He also felt that his informal diagnosis of each child's facility with the language to be an extremely important factor in helping him to assess their reading level or readiness for reading instruction.

When Mr. Weather diagnosed his students, he found that he had a range of reading abilities from readiness to grade two. Since many of the activities he used in his teaching were related to reading level, he decided to group the children by achievement level, as follows:

Susie's Group		*John's Group*		*Rick's Group*	
(reading)		*(ready to read)*		*(need readiness)*	
Susie	(2:2)	John	Phil	Rick	Terry
Fred	(2:1)	Pat	Biff	Ruth	Nancy
Paul	(1)	Jim	Penny	Bob	Dave
Gloria	(1)	Mark	Flo	Harold	Scott
Sam	(P)	Joel	Betty	Cary	Jeff
		Kathy	Mory	Jane	Eric

Some of the group activities closely related to reading level were the way in which the stories were dictated as well as the type of experiences that Mr. Weather presented to each group. For example, the group of children who could already read would be able to use books that they would be reading as springboards for writing their own stories. Furthermore, the children who could already read could be involved in many tasks that required reading, which the other youngsters would be unable to do at first. Susie's group would be able to follow directions on a ditto sheet if they were written at the first grade level; the other groups would not be able to do this.

In addition, the children who could already read at the first grade level would be assumed to have a vocabulary that included the first seventy-five words found in the sight word list. (See Chapter 2 for a discussion of these words.) In this case, their skill-building activities would of necessity be different from those of children who could not read. For example, those children who could read would be asked to add to their word banks only those words that they encountered in a book or in another child's story that they could not read. On the other hand, the children who were unable to read would be asked to place in their word banks only words that they could read.

Additionally, these children who could already read had a much greater facility with both the written and spoken language than the nonreaders. Therefore, they would be asked, most of the time, to dictate their own individual stories. When Mr. Weather met with Susie's group, he asked the children to come up to him one at a time and dictate a story that he wrote down on a large sheet of paper for them while the rest of the children read silently. All these children were so verbal that their stories took only a few minutes or so to write. After the dictation, each child would go back to his or her desk and silently read his or her own story and underline the words that he or she did not know. Those words were then placed in his or her word bank for further reference. Some of the children in the group were already writing their stories, without dictating them to Mr. Weather. In fact, Susie had written and illustrated a "book" containing six stories all on her own.

The children who could not read, but were ready to read, dictated stories in a slightly different fashion. They wrote a group story to which each child contributed a sentence. Since their language was not as fluent as that of Susie's group, Mr. Weather spent a great deal of time in helping them to summarize their stories and to write complete sentences.

The readiness level readers needed even more careful guidance. Not only did they need help in writing, but they also needed much background experience to have ideas to write about. Mr. Weather had them begin with concrete familiar concepts, such as their own names, when helping them to write their first story.

After selecting both a comprehension and a word recognition skill, Mr. Weather preassessed each child on two skills. The results revealed that Mr. Weather would have to regroup his class for the several different types of needs groups indicated from the results of the preassessment.

Mr. Weather's constant observation of the children's use of spoken and written language not only helped him to assess their facility with the language but also gave him clues as to their interests.

In addition to these informal measures, Mr. Weather used an interest inventory to help him locate materials on the appropriate interests of the children in his class and subsequently to determine that some of the major interests that spanned the achievement levels included children who were particularly interested in (1) animals, (2) things that fly, (3) crafts, and (4) television.

The multilevel membership of the interest groups gave the children in readiness level skills a chance to enlarge their backgrounds through working with children of both the reading and beginning reader groups. Their reading and subsequent group discussions on the topics of their choice expanded their experiential background and added to their reading development. One such group that spanned achievement and skill level was that on the topic of "Things That Fly." Mr. Weather was able to find books from primer to grade 2:1 level about "things that fly." In addition, he asked the children to gather newspaper and magazine pictures for a scrapbook on "things that fly." Many of the children who had thought that birds and airplanes were the only "things that fly" had their experiential background greatly expanded by belonging to the "things that fly" group. Furthermore, the maturity shown by the children in the other two achievement level groups provided excellent models for the readiness level children in their growth in the ability to learn to read.

Mr. Weather used all three types of grouping frequently. In addition, as discussed earlier, he had arranged his classroom into various "learning" and "activity" centers (see Chapter 7). The children and their tasks at the various centers on a "typical" day are illustrated as follows:

First Twenty Minutes' Work with Achievement Level Groups

Reading Center	*Writing Center*	*Art Media Center*
Susie's Group	John's Group	Rick's Group
Read silently	Dictate group story	Extension activities concerning last story written (i.e., illustrate story)

Second Twenty Minutes' Work with Needs Group

Game Center	*Listening Center*
Context clues, second reinforcement lesson	Sequencing, second reinforcement lesson

Third Twenty Minutes' Work with Interest Groups

Building Center	*Publishing Center*	*Talking Center*
Research magazines and newspapers for pictures of "things that fly"	Animal group write story together about pets; Susie, secretary	Craft group write story about model plane; dictate into tape recorder

Drama and Puppetry Center
Television—prepare a "skit" on popular TV show

Mr. Poindexter also used all three types of groups in his sixth grade individualized program. Although his program was labeled "individualized," he wanted to use group work as much as possible to make the most efficient use of his time and hence have more opportunity to truly "individualize" instruction for those who most needed it.

When Mr. Poindexter assessed the reading achievement levels of his students, he found that he had the following achievement level groups:

Grade 9	*Grade 8*	*Grade 7*	*Grade 6*	*Grade 5*	*Grade 4*
Peggy	Sherry	Mary	Timmy	Sylvia	Chris
Phillip	Esther	Fern	Paul	Elizabeth	Sheila
		Alice	Mac	Shane	
			Helen	Rosemary	
			Biff		
			Ben		
			Lisa		
			Rorrey		

Grade 3:2	*Grade 3:1*	*Grade 2:2*	*Grade 2:1*
Scott	Andy	Jane	Robin
Fred	Marily	Brian	
	Lenn		

Some of the activities closely related to grouping by reading level were the ways in which Mr. Poindexter introduced new topics and materials to the students. For example, he used several different resources to find a multitude of books on the sixth grade level. He brought in these books and presented them to the children in "Timmy's group" and helped each child to select from among those books. Furthermore, many of the sharing ideas essential to an individualized program took place among the members reading the same grade level books. Part of his rationale for emphasizing instructional level sharing was that, if a child reading at the second grade level grew interested in a book presented at the sixth grade level, his or her interest might be killed by the difficulty that he or she would encounter when trying to read the book. Furthermore, he knew that, by the time that children reached the sixth grade, peer influence was quite high. Those children who read at the second grade level might be embarrassed to share a book written on that grade level with the other sixth graders.

Like Mr. Weather's, his program was not based on a previously established set of interests or skills but, rather, on the interests of students as reflected through the materials that each had selected to read.

As Mr. Poindexter had a range of reading achievement levels from 2:1 to grade nine, he wanted an orderly, systematic fashion in which to present the skills. A scope and sequence chart proved to be invaluable to him in providing a structured sequence of skills for his program. Like Mr. Rough, he decided to narrow his skill development down to concentrate on only two or three skills at a time. His procedure for doing this was very simple. During the individual conferences, he would preassess each child on a preselected comprehension skill, a preselected word identification skill, and a preselected study skill that he had selected from the scope and sequence chart for emphasis at that particular point in time. It made no difference what book the child was reading, as the three types of reading skills could be assessed in material of any content on any level.

Those children who did not pass the preassessment were given both group and individual exercises on that skill at their reading level. Those who did pass the skill were either preassessed on another skill or were allowed to read recreationally.

In assessing interests, Mr. Poindexter gathered data from a reading interest inventory, informal observations on the topics that the children brought up for discussion, and the content of the books that the children had selected to read in the past. From these assessments, he was able to formulate what he felt were relevant and appropriate topics for interest groups. For example, several of the boys seemed to be highly interested in cars. One of the better readers had chosen an automobile mechanics book to read; one of the average readers had chosen a fictional book about auto racing; one of the poorest readers had selected *Hot Rod* magazine; and another of the poorest readers was reading a book from a series of easy-to-read books designed for older children who were interested in cars. Therefore, Mr. Poindexter formed an interest group on "cars" for this particular group of boys.

In like fashion, he was able to set up three more interest groups. One focused on "world hunger," another on "transportation," and the third on "science fiction."

Mr. Poindexter used all three types of groups frequently. An example of a "typical" Thursday is shown as follows:

First Twenty Minutes' Work with Achievement Level Groups

Grade Levels 9–5	*Grade Levels 4–2:1*
Read silently; individual conferences with members of this group	Book-sharing and reporting time

Second Twenty Minutes' Work with Needs Group

Locating cause–effect relationships, first reinforcement lesson	Using a combination of study skills, initial teaching lesson	Applying accent rules, second reinforcement lesson

Third Twenty Minutes' Work with Interest Groups

Cars	*World Hunger*	*Transportation*	*Science Fiction*
Build a model	Write research paper	Outline procedure for making more interviews	Write their own story

TEACHER "SUBSTITUTES" TO FACILITATE GROUPING

Mr. Rough, Mr. Weather, and Mr. Poindexter all knew that, if they wanted to individualize reading instruction, they would need to have many different types of groups working on a variety of levels, needs, and interests simultaneously. They also knew that they could not be in two places at one time, that their school could not afford to buy materials so that each child would always have materials precisely designed for his or her level, needs, and interests, and that they had only so many hours in the day to plan lessons for their pupils. Therefore, all three teachers used nonprint media and student helpers as teacher "substitutes" to aid in individualizing their instruction. Although all three used these techniques to some extent, Mr. Rough used them the most and was the primary force in encouraging others to do likewise.

NONPRINT MEDIA SUBSTITUTES

Although Mr. Rough knew that it was best for him to be with all groups he had marked with a T on his organizational format and teaching suggestions, he learned over the years that there were teacher "substitutes" that he could use to help him be in two places at the same time. Some of his "substitutes" were basal reader supplementary material and tape recorders. To illustrate, one of the basal reader series had developed coordinated filmstrips and records to introduce many of their stories. Mr. Rough was able to motivate the children and introduce them to new words and concepts with the aid of the audiovisual material. This reduced his actual time with the group, as he did not have to sit with them during the filmstrip presentation. Nevertheless, he was careful to make certain that he motivated them to watch the filmstrip and that he conducted follow-up activities after the presentations before asking the children to proceed to the silent reading step.

Another useful substitute was the tape recorder. He discovered that, if he read instructions into it, the children became self-directed. They would turn it on and follow the oral instructions without even being told to do so. He found the tape recorder particularly useful during the steps where his presence was not essential. He particularly liked to ask his students to practice old skills through tape-recorded directions. This step lent itself well to that approach as the children were somewhat familiar with the skills and enjoyed the motivating introduction to the skill-building lesson that Mr. Rough always used.

STUDENT HELPERS

The children themselves were probably the most useful "substitutes" that Mr. Rough had. When using student helpers, he followed these two basic premises: (1) All students must be given some sort of preparation before giving or receiving help, and (2) all students must be able to be helpers as well as "helpees" (those receiving help). Mr. Rough knew that these two aspects of pupil aid could not be overemphasized.

Mr. Rough's basic plan was this: Before asking any youngsters to work with others, he gathered a group of "helpers" together in a small "seminar" and discussed the following issues through inductive questioning techniques: "How would you like to receive help? Do you like it when someone is "bossy" with you? How can you tell someone he is wrong without making fun of him?" Further, he included a role-playing situation in which one of the youngsters was "bossy" with another. All the "helpers" watch or participated in the role playing and then discussed how they could do it better.

Then Mr. Rough held a seminar for the "helpees"—those who were to receive the help. In this seminar, a role play similar to the one held by the "helpers" was conducted. However, the emphasis was switched from "How can you give help?" to "How can you be helpful by receiving help?" Notice that Mr. Rough did *not* emphasize how to receive help but, rather, how to give help by receiving help. Problems in a previous semester—the first time he tried this peer teaching—had convinced him that it was somehow easier for the youngster to give help than to receive it. In other words, all the children enjoyed helping other children, but no one liked to be the "learner" who needed the help. By focusing on how one could give help by the way in which one received help, Mr. Rough solved one of his major problems in the use of teacher substitutes. His seminar with the "helpees" consisted of questions such as "Would you like to help someone who acted like that? How can you tell the helper that he is not being very nice when he helps you without getting him mad at you? Could he help you at all if you wouldn't let him? How does it make him feel when he has helped you? Do you like to make people feel good? Can you help them feel good by letting them help you?" All the "helpees" participated in the role playing and then discussed how "help" could be given to the peer teacher in a better manner.

Mr. Rough didn't hold all the seminars the same day. He found it most useful to ease into the peer-teaching situation. He worked with the peer "helpers" when they were to teach the first time and, likewise, with the peer "helpees" when they were to receive help for the first time. Mr. Rough continued to hold seminars on the issues of giving and receiving help at various intervals throughout the year. While he did not plan a definite schedule for follow-up "helper" and "helpee" seminars, he watched his peer teachers closely and held seminars whenever he felt someone was "forgetting" how to help.

Mr. Rough knew from his own experience as well as from a great deal of research he had read on the topic that the low achievers seemed to benefit the most from helping other children. For example, one of Mr. Rough's pupils, Bert, was a discipline problem and a weak student. However, he enjoyed woodcraft and machinery and built models at home. Mr. Rough believed that Bert could help the interest group on "communications" to follow the complex directions on "how to build a printing press" and then help them to find the materials to build it. Therefore, Mr. Rough asked Bert to join the group when he held his first seminar for "helpers." Bert's first reaction to being given a task of helping someone was to express disbelief and a cynical attitude. However, Bert accepted the task as a valid job and proved helpful to the group in its model building. As a result, Bert no longer engaged in trouble-making activities but sought out ways in which he could be helpful to Mr. Rough.

Both Mr. Rough and Mr. Weather knew that Mr. Rough's weakest readers were learning the same skills as many of the pupils in Mr. Weather's first grade class. Therefore, the two teachers made plans for Mr. Rough's fourth graders, particularly his low-achieving fourth graders, to help Mr. Weather's first graders every Wednesday afternoon. In this way, the low achievers would be giving help while reviewing skills that they themselves needed.

Several weeks after the inception of the 'cross-age'' tutoring, both Mr. Weather and Mr. Rough evaluated its progress and concluded that the plan was successful. The attitude of the younger children toward the older fourth grade low achievers had done wonders for the fourth graders' morales. They felt knowledgeable, intelligent, and worthwhile. Additionally, they were learning necessary reading skills that they would not otherwise have wanted to learn. They felt that, if their "buddy" needed the skill, they would learn it so that they could teach it to their "first grader." Furthermore, some of the first graders who definitely needed individual one-to-one tutoring were receiving it—and they were really learning to read!

SUMMARY

To better individualize reading instruction, children may be grouped for reading classes on the bases of achievement level, interest, and needs. *Achievement level groups* are composed of children reading on or about the same reading level, *interest groups* are composed of children who have similar interests, and *needs groups* are composed of children who require instruction on a predetermined skill. Although all types of groups are used with any single approach to teaching reading, grouping by achievement level is most commonly used with a basal reader approach to teaching reading; grouping by interest is most commonly used with a language experience or individualized approach to reading instruction; and grouping by need is most often used with the diagnostic-prescriptive component of the above programs. One of the major problems in the use of instructional groups is that children must often proceed without the physical presence of the teacher. Under such circumstances, students may work independently of the teacher or may be assigned to work with such teacher substitutes as nonprint media (audiotapes or filmstrips) and student helpers.

References and Bibliography

Alexander, J. E. (ed.) *Teaching Reading.* Boston: Little, Brown and Company, 1979.

Allen, A. R., and Boraks, N. "Peer Tutoring: Putting It to the Test." *The Reading Teacher,* 32 (December 1978), 274-278.

Callahan, J. F., and Clark, L. H. *Teaching in the Elementary School.* New York: Macmillan Publishing Co., Inc., 1977.

Cunningham, P. M., Arthur S. V., and Cunningham, J. W. *Classroom Reading Instruction.* Lexington, Massachusetts: D. C. Heath and Company, 1977.

Harris, A. J. and Sipay, E. R. *How to Teach Reading.* New York: Longman Inc., 1979.

Hot Rod. Los Angeles: Trend, Inc. (periodical).

McNeil, J. D., Donant, L., and Alkin, M. C. *How to Teach Reading Successfully.* Boston: Little, Brown and Company, 1980.

Self-Check 9.3
Grouping by Achievement, Interests, and Needs

The following questions are designed to help the participant assess his or her competence on the first thirteen objectives stated at the beginning of this chapter. Although every effort has been made to make the self-check questions comprehensive, participants should remember that they are held responsible for meeting the objectives as stated at the beginning of this chapter.

1. Objective 1. Why would a teacher want to use more than one basal reader series in his or her classroom?
2. Objective 2. What is the purpose of achievement level groups?
3. Objective 3. Look at the tally sheet following (Table 9.6) and divide the class into achievement level groups.
4. Objective 4. Why should achievement level groups be kept flexible?
5. Objective 5. What is one way by which teachers can minimize the stigmatizing effect of achievement level groups?
6. Objective 6. What are two factors that should be taken into consideration when deciding on the number of groups?
7. Objective 7. Make a list of the errors that are made by the teacher whose chart is shown below.

Weekly Reading Schedule

	Dot's Group	*Frank's Group*	*Jimmy's Group*
Monday	2 3a 4b, c	5c 5d 5d	T1a T1b T1c
Tuesday	5a 5a T4a	T1a, b T1c 2	2 2 T3a, b
Wednesday	5d 5d 1a, b, c	3a T3b T4a	T4a 4b 4b
Thursday	2 T3a, b T4a	4b 4c 5a	T4c 4c 4c
Friday	4b, c T5d 5d	T5b 5b 5b	5c 5c T5c

Table 9.6. Tally Sheet Grade 4 Class

Name	Grade 5		Grade 4		Grade 3:2		Grade 3:1		Grade 2:2	
	Oral	*Silent*	*Oral*	*Silent*	*Oral*	*Silent*	*Oral*	*Silent*	*Oral*	*Silent*
1. Jim	7	7	3	3			0	0		
2. Doris					3	5	1	2		
3. Joe					5	5	4	3		
4. Bobby			6	4	5	3	2	3		
5. Brady	1	3	0	0			0	0		
6. Joan							5	5	4	3
7. Louise			6	6	3	3	5	3		
8. Fran			4	6	4	3	2	2		
9. Florine							7	3	5	1
10. Jean	4	3	0	0			0	0		
11. Grace			7	7	3	3	2	2		
12. Virginia							6	6	5	3
13. Earl					6	5	5	3		
14. Ed							6	8	3	3
15. Frank					8	0	5	0		
16. Sidney							3	7	3	3
17. Jerry	0	0	1	0			0	0		
18. Larry	0	0	1	0			0	0		
19. Carrie	7	5	5	3	3	2	2	1		
20. George	6	6	3	1	3	2	2	1		
21. Roy	6	4	2	3	2	3	1	1		
22. John					6	6	5	3		
23. Jack					5	5	4	3		
24. Dan					2	7	1	3		
25. Gil					6	6	3	3		

Note: Each oral selection has 100 words. Each silent reading selection is followed by 10 comprehension questions. Numbers shown indicate number of errors.

8. Objective 8. How can achievement level groups be used in a basal reader approach, a language experience approach, and an individualized approach to teaching reading?
9. Objective 9. How can interest groups be used in a basal reader approach, a language experience approach, and an individualized approach to teaching reading?
10. Objective 10. How can needs groups be used in a basal reader approach, a language experience approach, and an individualized proach to teaching reading?
11. Objective 11. How can a child's interests be diagnosed?
12. Objective 12. Describe at least two "substitutes" for the teacher that can be used to facilitate grouping.
13. Objective 13. What are two basic premises involved in teaching peers to help each other?

Chapter 9

Experience 1

Objective

Given a tally sheet of test scores for a class in grades two through six, the participant will divide the class into achievement level groups and plan for a week of instruction.

Activity and Assessment Guide

1. Where did you obtain the tally sheet of test scores?

   ____

2. What assessment instrument was used to determine the reading scores shown on tally sheet? ______________________________

   ____

* 3. Were allowances made for more than one achievement level? (circle one) yes no Briefly describe the number of levels. ______________

   ____

*Asterisked questions may be answered by an observer. See Chapter 1: Experience 1 for further explanation.

* 4. Did you follow all the teaching suggestions for planning for each group found in Table 9.4? (circle one) yes no . If no, briefly describe which ones were not followed and the reasons why. ______________________

____

____

5. Did you use any teacher "substitutes"? (circle one) yes no
Briefly explain the "substitute" if one was used. ______________________

____

* 6. Did the total organization seem feasible in terms of a week's worth of basal reader instruction for the group? (circle one) yes no Briefly explain why or why not. ______________________

____

7. State what you believe to be the significant implications of this experience for you as a future classroom teacher. ______________________

____

____

Chapter 9
Experience 2

Objective

The participant will design and teach a lesson in which pupils are grouped for achievement, interest, or need in a basal reader, language experience, or individualized reading program.

Activity and Assessment Guide

1. Did you design a lesson in which youngsters were grouped by needs, interest, or achievement in a basal reader, language experience, or individualized program? (circle one) yes no Briefly describe the type of group and the type of reading approach. ______________________

____

2. Did you teach the lesson? (circle one) yes no Briefly describe the situation in which the lesson was used. ______________________

____

* 3. Was the objective for which the lesson was intended met? (circle one) yes no Briefly describe why or why not? ______________________

____

*Asterisked questions may be answered by an observer. See Chapter 1: Experience 1 for further explanation.

* 4. Did the children react favorably to the lesson? (circle one) yes no
Briefly describe why or why not? ________________

____

5. Do you have any suggestions for varying the lesson or improving upon the lesson that you taught? (circle one) yes no Briefly describe your suggestions. ________________

____

6. State what you believe to be the significant implications of this experience for you as a future classroom teacher. ________________

____

____

7. Attach a copy of your lesson plan to this sheet.

Chapter 10
Strategies for Classroom Management

Objectives 10.1

On completion of this chapter, the participant should be able to

1. Describe at least three strategies focused upon dealing with behavioral incidences *before* they occur in the reading lesson.
2. Describe at least three questioning strategies designed to increase pupil participation in an elementary reading lesson.
3. Describe at least three pupil-involving strategies for achieving individual participation in a whole-group situation.
4. Describe at least three strategies for dealing with behavioral incidences *after* they occur.

Experiences 1, 2, 3, and 4 extend Chapter 10 with these objectives:

5. Design and teach a lesson that includes at least three strategies focused upon dealing with behavioral incidences *before* they occur in the reading lesson; and/or
6. Design and teach a lesson that includes at least three questioning strategies designed to increase pupil participation in an elementary reading lesson; and/or
7. Design and teach a lesson that includes at least three pupil-involving strategies designed for achieving individual participation in a whole-group situation; and/or
8. Design and teach a lesson that includes at least three strategies for dealing with behavioral incidences *after* they occur.

Information Given 10.2
Strategies for Classroom Management

Beginning teachers frequently complain that the maintenance of discipline takes precedence over the teaching of reading. They state that their knowledge of the reading skills is irrelevant if they must occupy their time in maintaining order instead of teaching their pupils to read. This chapter contains a sampling of several practical strategies that have been used successfully by classroom teachers to help them manage classrooms most conducive to learning.

These strategies are designed to facilitate effective discipline in the classroom by providing some answers to the following questions often asked by beginning teachers:

What can be done by the teacher to prevent misbehavior before it occurs?
Can effective questioning strategies stimulate desirable behavior?
Would 100 per cent participation encourage acceptable behavior?
What recourses are possible after a misbehavior takes place?

HOW TO AVOID MISBEHAVIOR

Behavioral incidences can be precipitated by at least six major causes: (1) surplus energy of pupils, (2) physical discomfort on the part of the pupil, (3) poor curriculum and methods, (4) poor classroom management, (5) desire on the part of the pupil to be noticed, and (6) personality disturbances. Regardless of the cause, many misbehaviors can be prevented by teacher activity both before and during the reading lesson. Several strategies are described here for reducing negative behavior before it occurs.

1. *Motivate the child who has a history of misbehavior before beginning the task.* Find out his or her likes and dislikes and then find out his or her interests. Construct a chart or activity especially designed to interest him or her. For example, if the child likes horses and the story is about a horse, draw an outline of a horse on newsprint. Give the child some periodicals that can be cut up and that contain horse pictures. Let the child make a collage of what he or she thinks the horse might look like in the story that he or she is about to read.

2. *Involve a problem child in the lesson planning.* If the child likes to build things, let him or her make a model of one of the major characters designed to motivate the rest of the children in his or her group to read the story. Develop a set of directions that requires the child to look to the story for specific details so that he or she can construct an accurate model of the character he or she has chosen.

3. *Reward groups of children who exhibit behavior you like.* If the students are working in a manner that conforms with the classroom rules, rein-

force them immediately. Construct a wall chart that has "Johnny's Row," "Susie's Row," and the like across the top. When everyone in the row is doing what you want them to, put a mark such as a star or a flower in the appropriate column. Peer pressure helps shape individual behavior as everyone in the row has to behave properly to get a "mark" on the chart. Here is a sample of such a chart:

Johnny's row	Susie's row	Billy's row	Nancy's row	Bob's row

Each time everyone in the row practices good behavior those children receive a "flower." *Examples:* raising hand before talking; walking instead of running; sharing books and not grabbing books.

4. *Reward individual children who behave in a manner that you find desirable.* If Bobby usually runs around the room, wait until he is walking and tell him so; that is, "Bobby, I like the way you are walking." Construct a chart and put a "star" on the chart by his name when he does walk. Three stars could earn him the privilege of being "race coordinator" on the playground for the next week. Here is a sample of a possible chart for all children and, specifically, Bobby:

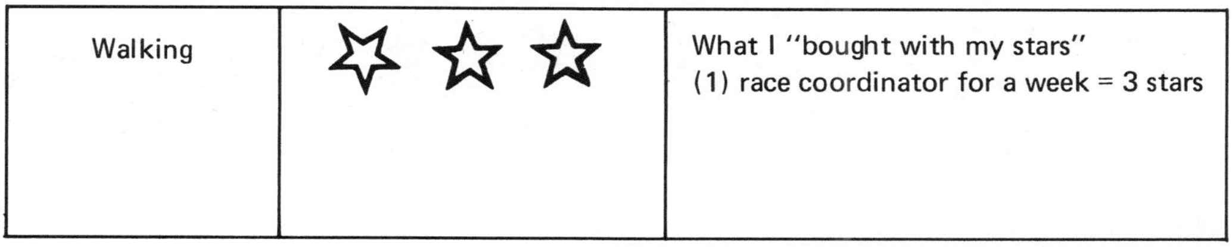

Walking		What I "bought with my stars" (1) race coordinator for a week = 3 stars

HOW TO ENCOURAGE ACCEPTABLE BEHAVIOR THROUGH EFFECTIVE QUESTIONING STRATEGIES

One thing that a classroom teacher can do to encourage acceptable behavior is to keep the pupils highly involved in the reading lesson. The strategy suggested here focuses upon questioning strategies designed to include as many pupils as possible.

Much of the work in reading is done in small, skill-building groups in the classroom. For each student to get maximum benefit, it is important that he or she participate as much as possible. Strategies listed here will improve your discussion skills, increase participation, and facilitate positive behavior.

1. *Call upon a child who doesn't usually volunteer.* Try to do this in such a manner that the child can answer correctly.

Example: A child tells you during lunch that he or she really liked the story this time. When the child is in his or her reading group, ask the child to tell the others what he or she liked about the story.

Cautions: (a) If you call the child's name before you ask the question, other students may stop listening, as they know they won't be put on the spot. (b) Don't call upon a nonvolunteer as punishment for not listening. You know that Johnny is not paying attention, so you ask him a question that he can't possibly answer correctly. This technique tends to cause a dislike for reading and hence decreases participation in the reading group.

2. *Redirect a question so that the child who doesn't usually respond can answer correctly.*

Example 1: "Now that Bobby read the statement that we were looking for in the book, can someone else read it as though the character were angry?" (Jimmy is a nonreader, but he heard Bobby read the statement "Get out!" The sentence is short, and he is able to remember it well enough to "read" it to the rest of the reading group in an "angry voice.")

Example 2: "Who can tell me why the mother spanked the boy in the story we just read?" (Joey gives the correct response, "The boy had run away from home.") "Good, Joey. Now who can find the spot in the book that tells he ran away?" (Johnny heard the correct answer, though he didn't know it originally, and is able to locate the appropriate sentence in the book.)

Merits: (a) This enables the child who never responds or never knows the correct answer to be able to respond correctly. The positive reinforcement caused by giving a correct response should increase the probability that he or she will begin to like to respond. (b) This strategy tends to support increased participation. Even though a question has been asked, the child does not stop listening, as he or she might be asked to elaborate on what another child says. In addition, the added benefits of interaction and listening between learners is encouraged.

3. *Differentially reinforce the acceptable parts of a response.*

Example: "Who can tell me why the main character planted two trees instead of one?" (Ruth responds incorrectly by saying that he likes trees. The answer should be because he was afraid one would die.) "Good point, Ruth. If you look at the page, you will see that he was afraid one would die. He must have really liked trees or he wouldn't have been concerned that one would die."

Suggestion: If possible, redirect the question to another pupil to turn the incorrect response into an acceptable answer. For example, in response to Ruth, say "Good going, Ruth. Can someone tell us why Ruth knew he liked trees?" This cuts down on teacher's monopolizing the discussion and keeps the children's participation high.

Merits: This has the advantage of reinforcing a child who responds to the discussion, whether his or her answer is the response the teacher wanted or not. Pupil participation increases when pupils realize that they are rewarded for trying rather than chastised for responding incorrectly.

4. *Prompt a child so that you get the correct answer.*

Example: "Who can tell me why the boy stopped working on his car?" (Phil responds that he was lazy. The correct answer was that he was discouraged because every time he fixed it something else would go wrong.) "What makes you think he was lazy, Phil?" (Phil replies that he just sat down on the grass by his car and closed his eyes.) "Well, what did he do just before he sat down?" (Phil replies that he had been holding the wrench.) "Look back at that part and see what he did with the wrench." (Phil looks and says that the boy threw the wrench up in the air.) "Does this relate to his sitting on the grass? Have you every thrown anything up in the air and then sat down?" (Phil replies that maybe he was discouraged.) "Good, Phil, he evidently got dejected because nothing seemed to go right. We all feel like that sometimes."

Merits: The child is not chastised for an "incorrect" response. In this case, Phil is directed toward the "answer." The prompting teaches the child how to get to the response sought after. This is better than having the child listen to the correct answer given by someone else and yet still not possess the skills to arrive at the answer on his or her own.

5. *Re-aim a response to reinforce the child who has answered.*

Example: "Who knows why the dog was so important to the boy?" (Answer anticipated was that the boy was an orphan and very lonely; the student responding states that the dog was the only thing the boy owned and that ownership was an important thing.) "Bruce, that is great. I never thought of that angle. What an excellent point! Can someone else tell us why ownership would be so important to an orphan?"

Merits: This gives the creative thinker an opportunity to show the other students a different perspective and interpretation of the story. It also gives the students a chance to practice the critical thinking skills they seldom get to practice because of the predominance of memory-type questions often asked in small reading groups. It has the added advantage of getting children to share their responses and interact with each other. The child who responded becomes the focal point of the discussion; this takes the teacher out of the spotlight and puts him or her in the role of facilitator—where he or she really belongs.

6. *Ask some questions that are not content-tied to the story.*

Example: "The story we just read discussed a funny-looking dog. We said it was funny-looking because it had a big kink in its tail. Has anyone ever seen such a tail on a dog?" (Jane, a nonreader, has seen such a dog; she tells the group about it and contributes much to the discussion.)

Merits: This enables a pupil who can't or didn't read the story to participate in a constructive manner in the classroom.

Caution: Beware of too many of these types of questions. Remember, your purpose for small-group reading discussion is to teach the children to read and interpret the story better. If questions are never content tied, you'll never know if the child can or cannot read.

7. *Ask some questions that relate and elaborate on the first question asked.*

Example: How do we know that the story took place in a large city?" (One child states that there were lots of cars.) "Good example. What other examples like 'lots of cars' tell us that the story took place in a large city?" (Many children respond with such items as "lots of people," "much noise," and "pollution.")

Merits: Often children and teachers play a "guessing game," and the pupils are really not certain what kind of response the teacher is looking for. When the teacher asks related questions, those youngsters who were not sure the first time the question is asked, can have an opportunity to contribute to the discussion.

HOW TO ENCOURAGE ACCEPTABLE BEHAVIOR THROUGH 100 PER CENT PARTICIPATION

Another method of encouraging acceptable behavior by keeping pupils involved in the reading lesson focuses upon strategies that require all pupils to participate individually in a whole-group situation.

1. *Make "yes" and "no" cards for each pupil.* Hold up a word such as "elephant" and its corresponding picture. Ask the children to select the "yes" card if the picture represents the word, and a "no" card if the picture does not represent the word. Sometimes hold up a word like "automobile" and a picture of a kite; sometimes hold up a word such as "dog" and a picture of a dog. As each word and picture are presented, ask the children to select the appropriate "yes" and "no" cards and put them down on their desks. At a given signal have all the children hold up their cards simultaneously so that each pupil's answer cannot be affected by his or her neighbor's card. Those who hold up the incorrect card do not know the word.

2. *Ask a question and direct those who know the answer to pull their right ear with their eyes closed*; next time have them put their hand over their eyes and tap their nose if they know the answer. Change directions each time. This encourages both willingness to respond and following directions.

3. *Ask a question and direct the pupils to confer with one other pupil on the answer.* Then ask each pair to tell the rest of the group their comments.

4. *Read a passage aloud and assign each child in the group a different purpose for listening.* After the passage has been read, ask each child to reveal his or her purpose and his or her findings.

Example: One child listens for how Daddy felt; another child listens for whether Mommy was angry or just excited; still another child listens for places where "mysterious music" would fit in if this were made into a movie. Each child should have his or her own purpose for listening to the story.

5. *Give each child a card with the word "before" and a card with "after" on it.* Then ask questions concerning the sequence of the story. Each child has to decide which of his or her word cards tells the appropriate sequence and put it face down on the desk. At a given signal all children hold up the card they chose. Those who hold up the wrong card probably do not understand the skill "sequence." For example, ask them if Mommy got mad at Bobby *before* or *after* Bobby hit his sister. The correct response is *after* and they should all hold up their "after" cards. Those who hold up the "before" card should be diagnosed further to see why they did not know the answer.

HOW TO DEAL WITH BEHAVIORAL INCIDENCES

Because behavioral incidences that may upset you do occur in the classroom, the following are some activities to help you manage both your own behavior and that of the misbehaving child.

1. Psychologists have discovered that it is better to *concentrate on the act* rather than on the person doing the act when either complimenting or criticizing an action (Ginott, 1973).

Example: If a child who is usually naughty picks up Susie's books when she dropped them, you should say "I like the way you picked up Susie's books" rather than "You are such a good boy today." Johnny can "handle" picking up the books; but being a "good boy" puts him on a pedestal and he's liable to jump off before he falls off. Two minutes after being told he was a "good boy," Johnny might be seen in the back of the room pulling Jane's hair.

One strategy to help you control your own feelings when a child misbehaves is simply to keep a chart.

Did I concentrate on the act and not the child? How? *Example: Yes. I said, "John, you picked up Susie's books. That is good behavior in here." (Don't say, "John, you are such a good boy!)*
1.
2.
3.
4.

2. There are times when it is normal and acceptable for a teacher to get angry or upset with a child. Again psychologists suggest that if you do get angry, it is best to tell the child in a solution-oriented manner. Ginott (1973) suggests (a) describing the act that made you angry, (b) stating how you feel, and (c) stating a solution. The use of a chart such as that shown here might be helpful to the teacher in implementing this strategy.

Did I state to the child what made me angry? How? *Example: Yes. I said, "John, I see milk on the floor." (Don't say, "I see a bad boy.")*	*Did I state to the child how I felt? How?* *Yes. I said, "When I see milk on the floor it makes me angry." (Don't say, "You make me mad.")*	*Did I state a solution? How?* *Yes. I said, "Wipe up the milk." (Don't say, "You nasty boy, get out of my sight.")*
1.	1.	1.
2.	2.	2.

3. *Construct an activity that isolates the child from the cause of the problem.*

Example: Give the child who misbehaves a task to do by himself or herself. The child could listen to a tape recording of a story while the rest of the group works together.

4. *Construct an activity in which the child works with youngsters who aren't conducive to his or her problem.*

Example: If the child always fights with Bobby, have him or her play with other children who dislike fighting.

5. *Construct an activity where the child is satiated with his misbehavior.*

Example: If the child makes spitballs, ask him to illustrate the story by making a collage made out of spitballs.

6. *Construct a log book where you mark down how many times you were able to ignore a behavioral incident.*

Example: If the child who is misbehaving is just seeking attention, it is quite possible that the child will stop if no one notices that he or she is doing it. As soon as possible give the child a chance to get attention through an acceptable activity that you construct for him or her.

7. *Construct an activity in which you pair up a negative situation with a positive one.*

Example: If the child gets into trouble because he or she runs around the room, construct an activity that involves running after the child has participated in an acceptable quiet activity.

SUMMARY

Beginning teachers feel that their knowledge of teaching reading is irrelevant if they must spend their time maintaining order. This chapter contains several specific strategies which have helped teachers maintain order in their classrooms. The first set of strategies include those that are designed to be implemented before any misbehavior has occured and include (a) providing a special motivation for the child who is apt to misbehave, (b) involving a problem child in lesson planning, and (c) rewarding children who follow the classroom rules. The second set of strategies are designed to encourage acceptable behavior during the lesson through the use of effective questioning techniques and include (a) calling upon children who don't usually volunteer, (b) adjusting the difficulty level of questions so that all children are able to give correct responses, (c) reinforcing the acceptable parts of a child's response, (d) asking leading questions, (e) making children's responses the focal points of discussions, and (f) asking a series of related questions which guide students to accurate responses. The third set of strategies are designed to encourage acceptable behavior by involving all the children in the group and includes (a) having pupils use response cards, (b) having pupils "signal" their knowledge of answers, (c) having pupils discuss answers to questions, and (d) assigning individual pupils specific questions to answer. The fourth set of strategies are designed to reduce classroom misbehavior by appropriate handling of behavioral incidences after they occur and include (a) concentrating on the behavior that occured instead of the child who performed it, (b) being angry in a solution-oriented manner, (c) constructing activities that isolate children from situations or other children that provoke their antisocial behavior, (d) satiating responses by requiring repetition of inappropriate activities, (e) keeping anectdotal records of your ignoring provocative behavior, and (f) pairing negative situation with positive ones.

References and Bibliography

Callahan, J., and Clark, L. *Teaching in the Elementary School.* New York: Macmillan Publishing Co., Inc., 1977.

Collier, C., Houston, R., Schmatz, R., and Walsh, W. *Modern Elementary Education: Teaching and Learning.* New York: Macmillan Publishing Co., Inc., 1976.

Dreikurs, R., Grunwald, B., and Pepper, F. *Maintaining Sanity in the Classroom.* New York: Harper & Row Publishers, 1971.

Engleman, S. *Preventing Failure in the Primary Grades.* Chicago: Science Research Associates, 1969.

Ginott, H. *Between Teacher and Child.* New York: Avon Books, 1973.

Glasser, M. D. W. *Schools Without Failure.* New York: Harper and Row, Publishers, 1969.

Musgrave, G. R. *Individualized Instruction: Teaching Strategies Focusing on the Learner.* Boston: Allyn and Bacon, Inc., 1975.

Self-Check 10.3
Strategies for Classroom Management

The following questions are designed to help the participant assess his or her competence on the first four objectives stated at the beginning of this chapter. Although every effort has been made to make the self-check questions comprehensive, participants should remember that they are held responsible for meeting the objectives as stated at the beginning of this chapter.

1. Objective 1. Julianne has a history of misbehavior. She often engages in behavior designed to capture the attention of the teacher and other children. Julianne's major interest is art. Describe at least three strategies focused upon dealing with Julianne's behavioral incidences *before* they occur in the reading lesson.
2. Objective 2. Describe at least three questioning strategies designed to increase pupil participation in an elementary reading lesson. For each strategy listed, include an example based on a familiar children's story.
3. Objective 3. Five strategies for achieving individual participation in a whole-group situation are given in the text. Which three do you believe are preferable? Why? Describe a reading class situation in which each of these three might be used.
4. Objective 4. During clean-up time Paul and Les continue to play with their reading game and refuse to put it away. What strategies described in this chapter could be used to deal with this behavioral incident *after* it occured?

Chapter 10
Experiences 1, 2, 3, and 4

Objective

The participant will do one or more of the following:

1. Design and teach a lesson that includes at least three strategies focused on dealing with behavioral incidences *before* they occur in the reading lesson; and/or
2. Design and teach a lesson that includes at least three questioning strategies designed to increase pupil participation in an elementary reading lesson; and/or
3. Design and teach a lesson that includes at least three pupil-involving strategies designed for achieving individual participation in a whole group situation; and/or
4. Design and teach a lesson that includes at least three strategies for dealing with behavioral incidences *after* they occur.

Activity and Assessment Guide

1. Which one of the following do you intend to incorporate into the lesson?

   _______ strategies focused on dealing with behavioral incidences *before* they occur

   _______ questioning strategies

_______ pupil-involving strategies

_______ strategies for dealing with behavioral incidences *after* they occur

2. Which three strategies do you intend to use?

   a. ____

   b. ____

   c. ____

* 3. Briefly explain why the strategies were successful or not successful in maintaining discipline. ____

____

____

4. Did the children show intended appropriate behavior? (circle one) yes no

   Describe an intended behavior. ____

____

____

* Describe a behavior observed. ____

____

____

5. Did these strategies give you more time to teach reading than the lesson you taught just before this one? (circle one) yes no Briefly explain why. ____

____

____

6. Briefly describe at least one additional management strategy that is related to those you have used in this experience but is not described in this text. ____

____

____

*See Chapter 1: Experience 1 for an explanation of the asterisk.

Part Five
Rounding Out the Reading Program

Chapter 11
Recreational Reading

Objectives 11.1

On completion of this chapter, the participant should be able to

1. Discuss at least one purpose for establishing a recreational reading program.
2. Describe at least three techniques for stimulating interest in a recreational reading program.
3. Describe at least two ways in which a teacher can identify the reading interests of children.
4. Discuss at least four factors that affect a child's interests.
5. List at least five ways in which children can share books or react creatively to what has been read.
6. Identify at least five criteria by which a recreational reading program may be evaluated.
7. Differentiate among the types of recreational reading programs used in a basal reader approach, a language experience approach, and an individualized approach.
8. Discuss the role of a diagnostic-prescriptive teacher in planning a recreational reading program.
9. Given a specific child, discuss how to locate books that he or she could read for recreation.
10. Given a description of a recreational reading program, evaluate it according to criteria discussed in this chapter.

Experiences 1 and 2 extend Chapter 11 with these objectives:

11. Select or design an interest inventory and administer it to a child; and/or

12. Design and teach a lesson in which a child is required to share a book in a creative manner.

Information Given 11.2
Recreational Reading

When Miss Henderson visited Mr. Poindexter's sixth grade class she was amused at the sight of five children dressed up like characters from *Call It Courage* by Armstrong Sperry. The children had made costumes and constructed a canoe out of an old cardboard box. "Mafatu" got into his "canoe" and paddled through the water. He spent the next five minutes facing a storm, fighting a shark, and overcoming an octopus—all portrayed by various sixth graders. Next, Maria went to the front of the room armed with pictures from *National Geographic* to illustrate the setting of her book, *My Name Is Pablo*, by Aimee Sommerfelt. Emmett's turn followed. He got up and showed everyone a drawing of a model engine that he had made and that he felt represented one of the engines described in the book he had read, *Motors and Engines and How They Work*, by H. Weiss.

All these activities represented the book-sharing component of Mr. Poindexter's individualized reading program. Books shared in this activity were of two kinds: (1) books the children had read that they particularly liked and had discussed with Mr. Poindexter and (2) books they had read that they particularly liked but had not discussed with Mr. Poindexter. The second kind could be identified as "recreational reading" books, or books read for no other reason than personal fulfillment. For Mr. Poindexter, his task of setting up a recreational reading component was simple, as his total program was based on books chosen because of interest. However, for Miss Yohannan, the third grade teacher who was using a basal reader approach, the task was not so simple. She had to include recreational reading as an additional component, as books chosen by the children because of interest were not an integral part of her skill-building program. Likewise, Mr. Weather, the first grade teacher using the language experience approach, had to gather a variety of resource materials so that his pupils could extend their reading from their own dictated stories to books read just for pleasure.

THE NEED FOR A RECREATIONAL READING PROGRAM

Regardless of the method of teaching reading used, exposure to instructional reading materials alone does not constitute a total reading program. Although such materials may be useful in systematically developing needed reading skills, they do not always help in developing reading habits and attitudes that stimulate children's interest in reading outside school. A total reading program is one that provides activities above and beyond the skill development program—a reading program in which the children have a chance to practice, in a pleasurable way, the skills that they have learned.

Many capable readers who appear uninterested in reading may be this way because they learned through reading programs that failed to distinguish between activities that build reading skills and activities that build reading habits and attitudes. Habit formation begins in the early formative years, and positive reading environments are built into all reading programs so that reading skills are practiced in personally relevant reading situations. Although a teacher cannot force a child to be interested in reading, a teacher can provide a program of recreational reading that helps make children want to read.

METHODS TO STIMULATE INTEREST IN A RECREATIONAL READING PROGRAM

Mr. Weather used a language experience approach for teaching reading. When Miss Henderson walked into his first grade class, she and Mr. Weather noticed that one of the children was printing a title of a book halfway down the body of a huge paper worm taped to the wall. The name "Jeff" was written on the head of the "book worm," and all the space between the head and halfway down the body, where he was writing, was filled with titles of books. Mr. Weather told the whole class to look at Jeff's worm because it was so long. The youngsters all clapped, and Jeff smiled broadly. The college student looked around the room and noticed that brightly illustrated book covers and the children's stories were taped up in many places around the classroom. There was a section in the back of the room marked with a sign, "Reading Center." A rug was in the center of the area, and several children were lying on the floor reading books. Mr. Weather called to the class, and all the children stopped what they were doing and began to participate in a "show and tell" activity.

Two children went to the front of the room to show the "movie" they had made of *Blackboard Bear* by Martha Alexander. The rest of the children watched as the two "movie producers" rolled the sheet of paper attached to two dowels through a theater constructed from a cardboard box. The sheet of paper contained five or six sentences that summarized their story. Each sentence was illustrated, and sections were taped together to produce their "film."

After they sat down, four other children got up and played a tape recording. They had made up a story about one of the characters in the book that they had just finished reading and had dictated the story into a tape recorder. In addition, each had made several drawings to accompany their story, and as the tape was played the children held up the appropriate illustrations.

Then a group of three children held up a mural of their story for all to see. They had used crayons to draw and color large figures of the main characters on a long piece of brown paper. Cutouts of trees, flowers, and clouds were also pasted to the mural.

As soon as the "show and tell" was over, Mr. Weather told them he was going to read them a story about a ghost. They listened intensely to him as he read the story. At one point he yelled "Boo!" and several of the children squealed and bounced up and down in their chairs. After he finished the story, the children asked if they could read the story again by themselves. Others asked him where to find another "ghost" story. He then sat with one group and helped them dictate a story about a ghost while several others sat down to write their own ghost stories.

Miss Henderson then walked down the hall and into Miss Yohannan's third grade class. Miss Yohannan had stacks of paperback books placed on tables at several different locations around the room. She rang a bell; the youngsters looked up from their perusal of the pile of books in front of them and then moved in small groups counterclockwise to examine a new stack of paperbacks. This movement continued every five minutes. Finally, it became evident that Miss Yohannan was receiving annoyed looks from some of the children. They had found books that they liked and were annoyed that they had to move on. After forty-five minutes of this activity, she rang the bell for the last time and told the class that they could check out any books that they felt were interesting. There was a scramble for books as each youngster rushed over to get the books that he or she had selected before someone else did. After a few minutes of book selecting, the youngsters returned to their seats. There was silence as Miss Yohannan let them read. A glance around the room revealed that most of the books had been checked out. Some youngsters had as many as four books on their desks. Miss Yohannan, in her talk with Miss Henderson, told her that she had often used various such techniques to stimulate her class's recreational reading. In fact, the month before, she had had a "book fair" in which the children were allowed to look at and purchase from a large number of paperback books that had been brought to the school. She felt that their reaction to these types of activities had been very enthusiastic because she had selected books according to their interests, which she continually noted through close observation and individual discussions with each child.

Both Mr. Weather and Miss Yohannan were using techniques to increase children's recreational reading. The classroom teacher can do many things to encourage his students' use of nontextbook materials. Following are some suggestions.

ALLOW THE CHILDREN PLENTY OF TIME TO READ

A successful reading program must provide the youngsters with plenty of time to read. They need to have designated time spans of at least an hour a week for free reading. Although younger children, with their shorter attention spans, need to have shorter time spans—perhaps only ten to fifteen minutes long—they can be more frequent so that the child is provided with at least an hour a week in which to read for pleasure. Free reading is too important to the development of a positive attitude toward reading to be used only for those children who get their work done early, though additional recreational reading time may be accumulated in this fashion. If children are to become avid readers, they need to be provided with large amounts of pleasurable practice in using their reading skills and to react privately to ideas in print for extended periods of time.

PROVIDE A WIDE CHOICE OF BOOKS

A classroom library, the school library, and the municipal library are all sources that provide the youngsters with a great choice of reading materials. Children should be encouraged to develop their own libraries. The book fair held by Miss Yohannan is one example of how children may gain access to books that they wish to purchase.

HELP CHILDREN LOCATE APPROPRIATE BOOKS

Since successful reading depends on the drive that comes from within the child, the material must be written at a reading level that can be easily understood and must contain information that is interesting enough to the child so that he or she is motivated to seek meaning from the printed page. Teachers who read the children's books themselves find this practice helpful in finding books to recommend to children. There are available many resources from which books for children of a particular age and interest can be obtained.

References

The comprehensive bibliography *Books About Children's Books* (White and Schulte, 1979) is an excellent resource for teachers wishing to locate bibliographies on selected topics for children of given ages. The following partial list of references may prove helpful to the elementary school teacher:

Baskin, B. H., and Harris, K. H. *Notes from a Different Drummer: A Guide to Juvenile Fiction Portraying the Handicapped.* New York: R. R. Bowker Co., 1977.

Bernstein, J. E. *Books to Help Children Cope with Separation and Loss.* New York: R. R. Bowker Co., 1977.

Ciancolo, P., ed. *Adventuring with Books.* Urbana, Illinois: National Council of Teachers of English, 1977.

Dill, B. E., ed. *Children's Catalog.* 13th ed. New York: H. W. Wilson Co., 1976.

Fein, R. L., and Ginsberg, A. H. "Realistic Literature About the Handicapped." *The Reading Teacher*, 31 (April 1978): 802–805.

International Reading Association/Children's Book Council Joint Committee. "Children's Choices." *The Reading Teacher* (annual compilation).

Larrick, N. *A Parent's Guide to Children's Reading.* 4th ed. New York: Bantam Books, 1975.

Maring, G. H. "Books to Counter TV Violence." *The Reading Teacher,* 32 (May 1979): 916–920.

Moustafa, M. "Picture Books for Oral Language Development for Non-English Speaking Children: A Bibliography." *The Reading Teacher*, 33 (1980): 914–919.

Reid, V. M., ed. *Reading Ladders for Human Relations.* 5th ed. Washington D.C.: American Council on Education, 1972.

Spache, G. *Good Reading for Poor Readers*, 9th ed. Champaign, Illinois: Garrard Publishing Co., 1974.

SUGGEST BOOKS TO CHILDREN THAT SEEM TO RELATE TO THEIR NEEDS AND INTERESTS

As teachers get to know children's hobbies, favorite television shows, interests, and personal problems, they can then suggest books geared to particular interests or problems that children might have. A systematic study of each child's reading interests should be an important part of the instructional program in reading. This can be facilitated by teacher-made informal inventories, commercially prepared interest inventories, and noting what nonreading materials and interests the children have. For example, when Mr. Poindexter first met his sixth graders in September, he had no idea about what their interests were or what types of books they were interested in. Therefore, he made up a reading interest inventory (Table 11.1) to help him determine their recreational, emotional, and practical interests. Although the format is intended for sixth graders, similar inventories can be made for primary age children. In some cases, the teacher will need to read it to the children to record their responses. In other cases, it can be written simply enough that even beginning readers could respond independently.

In addition to the interest inventory, Mr. Poindexter used several other factors as suggested by Spache (1973) to help him determine what books to obtain and suggest for each child. He knew age and sex had a bearing on the types of books selected. For example, one of the older girls, Elizabeth, had been retained for a year and was a year older than most of the others. Her maturity gave her a different range of interests from that of the rest of the girls. She was interested in reading stories about older girls in dating situations, while the younger girls were still reading nature and animal stories. Likewise, the romance story that appealed to twelve-year-old Elizabeth was not at all interesting to twelve-year-old Ralph. He liked adventure and mystery stories and wanted little to do with "love stories."

Mr. Poindexter also knew that his own attitude affected the children's choice of books. He openly discussed how he liked to read and continually talked about books he had liked. He tried to read many books of sixth grade interest and readability, so that if the children liked something he talked about, they would have the reading skills to understand it.

Environmental factors also had a great deal to do with the type of books that the children liked to read. For example, Bert's parents never read, so it was not too important to Bert to want to learn to read. On the other hand, Betty's parents had been reading to her the Sunday comics since she was old enough to sit on her father's lap. Likewise, Antonio, who was newly arrived from Mexico, was interested in books about his native country. Since he had just learned to speak English, his reading level was grade one. Therefore, Mr. Poindexter tried to find him books about Mexico at a sixth grade interest level but written at a first grade level of reading.

The effect of mass media was also an important factor in the children's choice of reading material. Although Bert's parents did not read, they spent a great deal of their leisure time watching television. Mr. Poindexter found out that Bert's favorite shows were mysteries. By careful selection of materials, he was able to find books on the right reading level that appealed to

TABLE 11.1 Reading Interest Inventory

Name ______________________ Age __________

School ______________________ Date __________

Grade ______________________

Directions: Below is a list of topics that some boys and girls find interesting. Some of these are things that you can actually do. Others can be watched on television or read about in books, magazines, or newspapers. Put one check if the topic is somewhat interesting to you; put two checks if the topic is very interesting to you. Leave a blank if the topic does not interest you at all.

fairy tales, myths, and legends __________
animal stories __________
nature stories __________
adventure stories __________
stories about boys your age __________
stories about girls your age __________
science __________
travel __________
geography __________
history __________
inventions __________
mechanics __________
biographies __________
sports __________
historical fiction __________
manners, customs __________
love stories __________
mystery stories __________
electricity __________
aircraft __________
exploration __________
comic books or cartoons __________
home life __________
social problems __________
career stories __________
music __________
science fiction __________
westerns __________
detectives __________
cars __________
drawing and painting __________
cooking __________
fishing __________
dancing __________
sewing or knitting __________
hunting __________
repairing things __________
games __________

Bert and that Mr. Poindexter was able to get Bert to read. At first he had problems because Bert's attitude was one of "Why read? I can watch it on TV." However, Bert soon became aware of the fact that books did not have commercials, did not have to be read only at certain hours, and the boring parts could be skimmed through and ignored.

An extremely important factor was that of accessibility. If books were there and attractively packaged, the children would pick them up, look through them, and often read them. Therefore, Mr. Poindexter tried to obtain fresh material by borrowing books from the local library and changing the selection frequently.

ESTABLISH A MEANS OF SHARING BOOKS OR REACTING CREATIVELY TO WHAT HAS BEEN READ

This type of activity is particularly effective in the upper grades where what children's peers feel about what they read has a great deal of influence over the books that the children choose to read.

Book reports are not new concepts to a teacher. Many times book reviews have been only oral or written summaries of the plot. Teachers can do much with book report techniques to stimulate critical reading and avoid asking the children to merely retell the story. Some of the major guidelines that can be used are as follows (Harris and Smith, 1972):

1. *Teach some interpretative and creative level comprehension skills.* After a story has been read to a group, the teacher can encourage critical thinking through higher-level questioning; for example, "Is Jane the same at the end of the story as she is at the beginning? See if the character in the story you are reading changes in any way." In later discussions the children can compare the changes made in the characters in the different books that were read.

2. *Give the child options of which books he or she chooses to report on.* Do not always require a report on every book. For some books, just recording the name of the author and the title of the book should suffice.

3. *Try to allow each child's response to a book to be as individualized as possible.* Avoid standardized book report forms; rather, allow the child to write book reports, each in his or her own style.

4. *Encourage reporting on books through a variety of means.* By establishing a pleasurable means for sharing books or reacting creatively to them, the teacher can promote the reading of other books while measuring the one that has just been read. However, teacher guidance is a key factor in making book projects interesting and worthwhile to the children. Often merely discussing a book that has been read by the teacher with the children will encourage them to want to read the same one. If children prefer to share a book alone with the teacher, this should be allowed. The teacher can occasionally meet with a child for a few minutes of discussion about a book that the child has just finished reading. They might discuss ways of sharing it with the rest of the class, and hence the teacher can carefully guide the child in his or her choice of method of telling his or her peers about his or her book. One extremely effective method of guidance is for the teacher to read a children's book and then carry on one of the creative book reports that he or she wants them to try. For example, one of the activities in the following list is "construct a revolving diorama that represents several scenes in the book." If Mr. Poindexter did this with a book he had read, it would provide a model for future reports as well as encourage the children in his class to share their

books in a similar manner. There are many creative projects that can be used to stimulate interest in further reading while reviewing a book that has been read. The children can be asked to do one or more of the following.

1. Make a *peep show* of one scene in your book. Construct objects out of clay, pipe cleaners, papier mache, or any other materials and arrange them in a small enclosed box. Admit light through a small opening cut across the box lid covered with tissue paper. In the end of the box, cut a peephole for viewing the scene.
2. Construct a *revolving diorama* that represents several scenes in the book. Divide a cardboard box into three or four sections and use that as background for the scene. Make objects and people out of paper cutouts, papier mache, clay, pipe cleaners, or any other material and arrange these in front of the scenic background.
3. Make up a *riddle* about one of the characters. Place it on the back of a cutout of the character and try to present it to the class in such a manner that they will want to know more about the character.
4. Make some *paper bag puppets* of several of the characters. Present a scene from the book that will make others want to read it.
5. Construct a *mobile* about the book you just read. Cutouts or objects representing themes or characters can be balanced and suspended on thread or fine wire attached to rods. Tell the class what each piece of the mobile represents.
6. Retell an exciting part of the story using *characters* that you have *cut out of felt.* Place the accompanying illustrations on a felt board as you describe what happens.
7. Cut out a *life-size drawing* of one of the main *characters.* Pretend that you are that character and stand behind the cutout as you describe yourself and one or two things that you do in the story. If others have read the story, ask them to guess who you are.
8. Construct a *mask* out of a *large paper bag* that represents the face of a person or animal from the book. Wear the mask and present the character to the class.
9. Make a *talking character* by drawing, coloring, and cutting out a large head of the main character. Construct the mouth with strips of paper in such a way that the lips can move. Pretend to be that character and tell about the book.
10. *Pantomime a scene* from the book. Plan so that you and some of your friends read the same book. Then prepare and present a skit on part of the book. Have the class guess what you are doing. Tell them only enough to get them interested in the book.
11. Make your *hand* into a *puppet* that represents your favorite character in the book. Use yarn, crayon, and makeup to illustrate how you think he looked. Tell the class in the puppet's words why he looks like he does.
12. Create a *box movie* of one scene in your book. Attach rods to either side of an enclosed cardboard box. On a long sheet of paper,

draw a sequence of several pictures. Fasten each end of the strip of paper to a rod. Ask the viewer to unroll the strip of paper by turning a rod as you describe the scene to him.

13. Make a collage of one scene in the book. Use bits of paper, cloth, or any other available material.
14. Construct a *jacket* for the *book*. Make appropriate illustrations and label the jacket with the title of the book and the name of the author.
15. Request an *individual conference* with your teacher. Tell your teacher why you did or did not like the book.
16. Draw a *picture* of the *main character*. Tell about an adventure that you had that was similar to the one that the characters in the book had.
17. Draw an *important object* from the book you just read. Have the class guess what it is and why it might be important in the story. Give them a few hints, but don't tell them. Let them guess.
18. *Tape-record* a *dramatization* of the book presented as a *radio show*. Play the recording for a small group of class members who might want to read about that topic.
19. Create a *picture* that shows the saddest, funniest, or *most exciting incident* in the book. Use charcoal, crayons, cloth, paper, or whatever else is available. Explain to the class the reason for drawing what you did.
20. *Dress up as a character* in the story and tell about yourself or one of the adventures that you had.
21. Meet in *small groups* and *discuss* the books you have read.
22. Make up a *game* about the *story*. Use the characters and events in the book for playing "Twenty Questions," "Bingo," "checkers," or other similar type activities.
23. Construct a *map* of the *location* of the story. Use this to illustrate the book as you tell the class the importance of the story's taking place where it did.
24. Pretend to be a *television* or *radio* personality and *interview* one of the main characters. Ask the character why he does what he does in the book.
25. Take the role of a *book salesperson* and *sell* the book to the class.
26. Retell the *story in poetry*.
27. Assume that you are the main *character* but be ten years *older*. Tell what happened during your life.
28. Design a *radio* or *television commercial* in which you tell the high points of the book in an effort to *sell* it.

Many, many more such activities can be designed for use with children. On the whole, youngsters who participate in fun ways to report in books that they have read are encouraged to continue to tell others about their books. The teacher who wishes to use this technique can easily think of other ways.

Sometimes tangible rewards can be used to help children get into the habit of reading. These can include giving the child symbolic tokens, such as stars, for each book read; helping the child develop his or her own means of record-keeping, which becomes rewarding in itself, such as Jeff's "book worm" seen in Mr. Weather's first grade class; and praising the children verbally each time they complete a book, as Mr. Weather praised Jeff in front of the class when Jeff added another title to his "book worm."

Motivating children to read for their own enjoyment is a major objective of reading instruction at all levels. In an effort to discover different ways to motivate students to read, Roeder and Lee (1973) conducted a survey to ascertain which techniques teachers have found most effective in encouraging students to read for their own enjoyment. Some of the techniques they found useful include (1) *Auction*—Paperbacks were brought in by students, and children bid on them with play money. Student auctioneers encouraged the bidding. (2) *Reading*—Each child selected a partner. Specific times were set aside for partners to read to each other. (3) *Promotional Campaign*—The children staged a sales campaign for promoting books. They acted like advertising executives and tried to "sell books." (4) *Topic of the Month*—Colorful posters were made to advertise a specific topic such as "nature stories" for each month. (5) *Quotations*—Direct quotations from famous figures in history on the value of books were mounted in conspicuous places around the room. (6) *Series*—Children were encouraged to read a book from a series or to read a book by an author who had written several similar books. (7) *Home Library*—Children were encouraged to start libraries of their own. The teacher helped them to get started with a list of "musts." (8) *Write Books*—The children wrote, illustrated, and bound their own books. "Pen names" were encouraged, and the books were circulated around the classroom and the school. (9) *Book Clubs*—A classroom book club was formed with specific book-reading quotas and activities for members. (10) *Thought-Provoking Objects*—Thought-provoking objects were brought in that motivated children to read books on specific topics. (11) *Community Members*—Members of the community were invited to speak to the class on their special interests. A link between the presentation and the reading activity was provided.

CRITERIA FOR EVALUATING THE RECREATIONAL READING PROGRAM

However, for Mr. Poindexter to make certain that his recreational reading program was doing what it was supposed to be doing, it was important that he evaluate the program. Since reading is a receptive activity, one way in which he knew he could have evaluated the success of the program was simply to observe the children as they read and see how they were receiving the ideas in the book. He could walk around the room and, by noticing the looks on the faces of the youngsters, evaluate their enjoyment of reading. However, he felt that he could use more concrete criteria than the nonverbal reactions of the children as they read. He looked at each child's book report as a means for evaluating the child's reading growth. The child's tastes, interests, understanding, and appreciation were revealed in the types of books he or she had selected and the way in which the child reviewed them. Mr. Poindexter knew that he could use the book reports to evaluate his recreational program in terms of (1) the number of books that a child had read, (2) the growth that the child demonstrated in the quality of the literature that the child selected to read, (3) the enjoyment that the child experienced, (4) the effect of recreational reading on the child's attitude toward reading in general, (5) the information that the child accumulated, (6) the progressive growth in the length of time that a child could spend at recreational reading at one sitting (sustained silent reading), or (7) the effect that the recreational reading had on the child's overall achievement.

Mr. Poindexter felt that each of these criteria, and many others, could be used to assess the success of a recreational reading program. There were many strengths and weaknesses in using the various criteria, and he knew that the classroom teacher must decide his or her priorities in his or her evaluation. One teacher's primary goal might be to let the child read so that the child may practice his or her reading skills in a pleasurable way, and hence the teacher's priority might be on the criteria that have to do with improvement of reading skills and academic achievement. Another teacher might be primarily interested in developing the attitude of the children in such a way that they will become avid readers; as such, that teacher's emphasis would be on criteria that measure enjoyment of what has been read.

RECREATIONAL READING IN THE VARIOUS APPROACHES TO TEACHING READING

There are several ways in which to set up a recreational reading program. Descriptions of different kinds of recreational reading programs that have been used successfully by the classroom teacher follow.

RECREATIONAL READING IN A BASAL READER PROGRAM

Helen Yohannan had taught for three years. Although her reading program centered around several basal reader series, she used many teacher-made materials in addition to some of the supplementary material supplied with the basal series. She had read most of the new children's books and subscribed to a paper that gave a review of children's books every Sunday. She was also beginning to build up a classroom library of a substantial size. She scheduled recreational reading into her program in two basic ways. First, whenever a child had finished his or her skills assignment, the child was encouraged to read for pleasure. Second, since she knew time should be set aside specifically for this purpose, she scheduled a half hour two afternoons a week when children were given time to read just for fun.

Mr. Deck's third graders also participated in a recreational reading program that was part of a total basal reading program. However, he was a brand-new teacher who felt somewhat overwhelmed by the massive amount of coordination and planning needed to establish both a skill-building and a recreational reading program. The basal series that he had been using was a revision of an older series. In addition to the total skills development program and structure that it gave him, the series had an optional strand that provided for an extensive recreational reading program. His particular series did this in several ways:

1. *Provided books that extended concepts touched upon in the basal reader stories.* For example, one of the stories in the 3:1 reader dealt with a boy and his Shetland pony. Two different supplementary stories provided by the publishers centered on stories about Shetland ponies. Furthermore, one of the stories was written for the good reader, and the other was written for the youngster who was not reading up to grade level.

2. *Extended some of the stories into other media.* Filmstrips and recordings that provided background music and dramatizations of many of the stories had been developed by the publisher. Thus, if a youngster particularly liked a story, the child could either enjoy it again in another form or, if he or she were a poor reader, the child could enjoy it for the first time in that form. The filmstrips and recordings did not just retell the original story but, rather, extended some of the concepts, much like the supplementary books about the Shetland pony.

3. *Provided read-by-yourself books.* These were library-type books especially suitable for independent reading and keyed in with words already presented in the basal stories.

4. *Provided supplementary paperbacks centered around special topics that the publisher's research had indicated was of special interest to third grade youngsters.* Each book was accompanied by a teacher's guide that contained suggestions for teaching and presenting the book, as well as a study guide designed to tell the reader something about the author, the artist, and the format of the book. The study guide also provided the reader with questions to be answered both before and after he or she read the book, as well as creative suggestions for telling his or her classmates about the book. Follow-up activities and books that were suggested if the reader liked the book that he or she read were also part of the student guide. The subjects provided were written to include a broad range of designated reading levels, and topics included (a) folk tales, myths, legends, and fantasy; (b) humor; (c) historical stories and tales of other lands; (d) biographies of famous men and women; (e) animal stories; (f) realistic stories, adventure stories; (g) multicultural-focused stories designed to give pupils a better understanding of the multicultural society in which they live and a constructive view of their role in it; (h) scientific stories; and (i) poetry of all kinds—modern verse, nursery rhymes, and pop rock lyrics.

5. *A bibliography of correlated books.* At the end of each basal reader lesson, the authors listed recommended books that correlated with the topic of the basal reader story. Most of these recommended books were well-known

favorites that had been used for years with great success with children of the same age group. For example, one story in the third grade reader had to do with a child who was trying to keep a little brother from taking newly made toys. The bibliography in the teacher's manual recommended several books on the same topic. One of these books was *Best Friends for Frances* by Russell Hoban. Therefore, Mr. Deck located a copy of that book and recommended it to his third graders for recreational reading purposes (Evertts, et al., 1973).

Mr. Deck's program was set up so that the students followed the basal reading lesson plan from 9 to 10 every day. However, for one half hour every Monday and Friday afternoon, the youngsters had a chance to "free read." As the basal reader publishers had provided Mr. Deck with a teacher's guide for each of the "supplementary texts," he was able to use the suggestions and the summary of the book found there to help his students in the selection of their materials. He placed each child in a "recreational reading" program according to the following procedures: (1) He used a record-keeping system that gave him information on each child's skill development, interests, and basal reading levels. (2) As children read their basal readers, he noted their skills and interest in the topic of concern. (3) During individual conferences, which were set up while the children were free reading on Monday and Friday afternoons, he helped each child to select books that he thought the child would like and could read. (4) In addition, during the "extension portion" of each basal reading lesson, he tried to provide the youngsters with time to read their recreational books.

RECREATIONAL READING IN A LANGUAGE EXPERIENCE PROGRAM

Since Mr. Weather was using a language experience approach, he did many different things to encourage reading. He knew that, if his first graders were to expand their backgrounds and learn to enjoy reading, they needed to come into contact with "good literature." Obviously, this meant that he had to supplement their own dictated stories with well-written materials that they would find exciting and relevant. Therefore, whenever his children wrote about topics, he would assume they were interested in the topic and would recommend books that related to the subject. For example, when one little girl wrote a story all about her kitty, Mr. Weather showed her *The Cat in the Hat* by Dr. Seuss. Her enthusiasm in reading the book encouraged other children to want to read it also.

Another way in which Mr. Weather expanded the children's recreational reading was to help them bind and illustrate the stories that they had written and put them in the "reading center" to share with others. This not only inspired the children to take great care with their illustrations so that others would understand their drawings, but also stimulated ideas for future stories that the young authors wanted to write for others.

RECREATIONAL READING IN AN INDIVIDUALIZED READING PROGRAM

Mr. Poindexter did not set aside any special time for his students to do recreational reading but, rather, let them participate in this program whenever they completed their assigned work.

On the other hand, Mrs. Gonzales, a second grade teacher who also taught reading in an individualized manner, set aside her afternoon reading time for recreational purposes. She would begin with a "buzz session" in which all the recommended recreational activities for the day were listed on the chalkboard. The children then came up and signed up for the activity in which they wished to participate. On some days, she divided the class into squads and assigned each to an activity. On Friday, the children would give book reports on the books they had read.

Since her purpose was to provide the children with material that they liked to read, she planned her activities so that children could participate in reading situations that were enjoyable to them. In some cases, this might mean reading library books; in other cases, it might mean reading directions to games. Some of the activities that she used to do this included (1) "Listening tapes" or stories that had been recorded on audiotape. (2) "Guess the answer," in which children were given riddles to read. When they figured out the riddle, they would draw a picture of the answer. (3) "Read to the kindergarten," in which the children would take a favorite story and go to Mrs. Hamblen's class, where they would spend time reading the book aloud to a younger child while pointing out appropriate pictures in the book to the child. (4) "Games" that required some reading to play and that could be played alone or with other children depending on the rules of the game. (5) "Library Corner," where Mrs. Gonzales had placed a variety of books, magazines, and newspapers that the children could read on their own.

RECREATIONAL READING IN A DIAGNOSTIC-PRESCRIPTIVE APPROACH

The teachers described who tried to assess the recreational interests as well as the emotional and practical interests of each of their pupils were using a diagnostic-prescriptive approach to setting up a recreational reading program. However, in such a case, the scope and sequence of skills would be compared with the scope and sequence of interests of individual children. Such a source of interests can be located in many of the references listed earlier in this chapter. However, as in any facet of reading, the child himself or herself should be the final determiner of what he or she likes to read. References can help in the selection of books that appeal to students typically in the age group involved. The diagnostic-prescriptive teacher should, however, construct an interest inventory and keep careful records of the interests of each child to help him or her learn to find reading both relevant and enjoyable.

SUMMARY

Regardless of the method of teaching reading used, exposure to instructional materials alone does not constitute an adequate reading program. Although such materials may be useful in systematically developing needed reading skills, they do not always help in developing reading habits and attitudes that establish a lifelong interest in reading. The recreational reading program is designed to foster such an interest as well as to provide children with a pleasureable chance to practice the reading skills that they have learned. A recreational reading program might include the teacher's allowing the children plenty of time to read, providing a wide choice of books, helping children locate appropriate books, suggesting books to children that seem to relate to their needs and interests, establishing a means of sharing books or reacting creatively to what has been read, as well as using specific motivational devices to encourage reading. Recreational reading programs may be assessed effectively through the use of a variety of criteria and should be established to enhance all methods of teaching reading.

References and Bibliography

Alexander, M. *Blackboard Bear.* New York: The Dial Press, 1969.

Carlson, R. K., ed. *Literature for Children: Enrichment Ideas,* 2nd ed. Dubuque, Iowa: Wm. C. Brown Company, 1976.

Evertts, E. L., Hunt, L. C., Weiss, B. J., and Cruikshank, S. B. *Never Give Up: Teacher's Edition.* New York: Holt, Rinehart and Winston, 1973.

Greenbaum, J., Varas, M., and Markel, G. "Using Books About Handicapped Children." *The Reading Teacher,* 33 (January 1980): 416-418.

Harris, L. A., and Smith, C. B. *Reading Instruction Through Diagnostic Teaching.* New York: Holt, Rinehart and Winston, 1972.

Hoban, R. *Best Friends for Frances.* New York: Harper & Row Publishers, 1969.

Huck, C. S. *Children's Literature in the Elementary School,* 3rd ed. New York: Holt, Rinehart and Winston, 1976.

National Geographic Magazine. Washington, C.D.: National Geographic Society (periodical).

Roeder, H. H., and Lee, N. "Twenty-Five Teacher Tested Ways to Encourage Voluntary Reading." *The Reading Teacher,* 27 (October 1973): 48-50.

Sebesta, S. L., and Iverson, W. J. *Literature for Thursday's Child.* Chicago: Science Research Associates, 1975.

Seuss, Dr. *The Cat in the Hat.* New York: Random House Inc., 1957.

Sommerfelt, A. *My Name is Pablo.* New York: Criterion Press, 1966.

Spache, G. D., and Spache, E. B. *Reading in the Elementary School.* 3rd ed. Boston: Allyn & Bacon, 1973.

Sperry, A. A. *Call It Courage.* New York: Macmillan Publishing Co., Inc., 1969.

Tiedt, I. M. *Exploring Books with Children.* Boston: Houghton Mifflin Co., 1979.

Weiss, H. *Motors and Engines and How They Work.* New York: Thomas Y. Crowell Company, 1969.

White, V. L. and Schulte, E. S. *Books About Children's Books: An Annotated Bibliography.* Newark, Delaware: International Reading Association, 1979.

Self-Check 11.3
Recreational Reading

The following questions are designed to help the participant assess his or her competence on the first ten objectives stated at the beginning of this chapter. Although every effort has been made to make the self-check questions comprehensive, participants should remember that they are held responsible for meeting the objectives as stated at the beginning of this chapter.

1. Objective 1. Why should a recreational reading program be established?
2. Objective 2. What are three techniques for stimulating interest in a recreational reading program?
3. Objective 3. Describe two ways in which a teacher can identify the reading interests of children.
4. Objective 4. Discuss four factors that affect a child's interests.
5. Objective 5. List at least five ways in which children can share books or react creatively to what has been read.
6. Objective 6. What are five criteria by which a recreational reading program may be evaluated.
7. Objective 7. Differentiate among the types of recreational reading programs used in a basal reader approach, a language experience approach, and an individualized approach.
8. Objective 8. What is the role of a diagnostic-prescriptive teacher in planning a recreational reading program?
9. Objective 9. Donny is in fifth grade. Although he has excellent reading skills, he rarely reads unless he "has to." Donny's major interest is in the snakes and insects that inhabit the creek behind his home. What resources might Donny's teacher use to find books that would be of interest to Donny?
10. Objective 10. The first grade library at Sugarland School includes highly recommended books purchased with school funds on each child's birthday. The birthday child's name is subsequently written on a bookplate placed inside the front cover. Volunteer mothers come to the school regularly to read the books to small groups of first grade children. During the day, children are allowed to go to the library and read books of their choice. Critique this program according to the criteria discussed in this chapter.

Experiences 11.4
Recreational Reading

Chapter 11
Experiences 1 and 2

Objectives

The participant will do one or more of the following:

1. Select or design an interest inventory and administer it to a child; and/or
2. Design and teach a lesson in which a child is required to share a book in a creative manner.

Activity and Assessment Guide

Special Instructions for Objective 1

To complete this objective, you need to have an interest inventory that is appropriate for the child being assessed. The inventory given in this text is appropriate for intermediate grade children. If you intend to assess the interests of a primary grade child, you will have to adapt the inventory to meet his or her maturity level and reading skills. The younger child's attention span is shorter, and the inventory should not take more than ten minutes. Portions of the inventory may be read aloud to the younger child to procure needed information, or the inventory may be rewritten to reflect the needs of the first, second, or third graders.

Note: Questions 1–3 refer to objective 1; questions 4–6 refer to objective 2.

* 1. Was an inventory used that was appropriate to the age and reading skills of the child? (circle one) yes no Briefly explain why or why not. ____

____

* 2. Was the inventory administered in a manner appropriate to the age and reading skills of the child? (circle one) yes no Briefly describe his or her manner of administration. ____

____

* 3. Was the inventory administered in a manner that established rapport with the child? (circle one) yes no Briefly describe the child's reaction. ____

____

* 4. Was a lesson planned that required a child to share a book in a creative manner? (circle one) yes no Briefly describe the lesson. ________

____

* 5. Was a lesson taught in which the child presented a creative report? (circle one) yes no Briefly describe the report. ________________

____

* 6. Was the report appropriate to the book? (circle one) yes no Briefly identify the book. ____

____

7. Did this lesson give you any more ideas for assessing a child's interests or presenting book reports in a creative manner? (circle one) yes no Briefly describe your idea(s). ____

____

8. Describe your interpretation of the child's reading interests and/or his or her understanding of the book on which he or she reported. __________

____

*Asterisked questions may be answered by an observer. See Chapter 1: Experience 1 for a complete explanation.

9. Write a brief summary about the child's reaction toward this experience and the amount of learning that took place.________________________

____

____

10. State what you believe to be the significant implications of this experience for you as a future classroom teacher.________________________

____

____

11. Attach a copy of your interest inventory or lesson plan to this sheet.

Chapter 12
Content Area Reading

Objectives 12.1

On completion of this chapter, the participant should be able to

1. Describe at least four reading problems associated with teaching the content area subjects.
2. Differentiate between reading skills that are needed by specific content areas and reading skills that are needed by all content areas.
3. Discuss at least one major problem associated with a great many content area textbooks.
4. Describe how a diagnostic-prescriptive teacher would teach the content area subject matter.
5. Describe at least one method for identifying reading skills needed in a particular content area.
6. Describe two major components involved in designing instructional strategies for the content areas.
7. Discuss the purpose for and construction of a differentiated guided reading sheet.
8. Discuss at least three ways in which content area materials may be differentiated to meet the reading needs of a variety of children.
9. Given a description of a specific child and a specific content area, discuss how to design content area instruction appropriate for his or her reading level.
10. Given a description of a specific content area reading program, evaluate it according to the criteria discussed in this chapter.

Experiences 1 and 2 extend Chapter 12 with these objectives:

11. Construct, administer, score, and interpret a diagnosis for a student on a content area textbook.
12. Design and teach a content area lesson according to the following criteria:
    a. Select a specific content area lesson and identify one reading skill particularly needed to understand the lesson.
    b. Design a guided reading sheet on this specific reading skill for a child who is reading above grade level, a child who is reading at grade level, and a child who is reading below grade level.

Information Given 12.2 Content Area Reading

When the teacher education major walked into the first grade class, Miss Daisy had just instructed the children to put away their readers and get out their science books. She pointed to a photograph in the attractively illustrated book of a small girl building a snowman. She asked one of the children to read the title of the story for her. The other children listened as a little girl read aloud "What Makes Snow." The rest of the pictures in the lesson consisted of children involved in a variety of activities with snow. Under each picture were two or three sentences that asked the children simple questions about the snow. For example, under a picture of a boy with a sled were the questions:

> "How is snow made?"
> "Why is the boy dressed warmly?"
> "What makes snow stay?"

Miss Daisy used other similarly carefully worded questions to guide the children through the remaining three pictures of the lesson.

The teacher education major then left the room and went down the hall to the fourth grade class. Mr. Rough was in the process of concluding his basal reader lesson. The group he was with had just read a story about grasshoppers and was learning to use chapter subheadings as an aid to locating specific information. Mr. Rough had listed six headings on the chalkboard, and the children were to determine which heading they would look under to find the answers to some specific questions he was asking them. They finished the exercise and then regrouped for social studies. Mr. Rough spent several minutes with the children discussing what they were going to read. Their particular assignment had to do with early American history, and Mr. Rough was asking the children to describe the principle of "compromise" during the first winter that the Pilgrims spent in America. The teacher education major noticed that many of the children seemed to be having trouble understanding what Mr. Rough was talking about, and the discussion was primarily being carried on by two girls in the front row. Shortly thereafter the children were given time to read the appropriate chapter in their social studies textbook. The two girls who had participated in the discussion read avidly. Several of the other children were just staring into space. One of the boys moved his lips as he read silently and was obviously struggling with the material.

Mr. Rough interrupted the two girls reading and asked them if they could locate the section of the chapter where an incident requiring compromise first took place. One of the pair flipped through the pages of her textbook looking at the headings; the other girl put her finger on the pages and began moving it rapidly down the print. Although Mr. Rough had just finished showing the two girls how chapter headings reflected the organization of science texts, he did not directly instruct the fourth graders to use the headings to find the answer to the question he asked. One of the girls was able to transfer the skill from her reading lesson to her history lesson; the other girl did not make the necessary connection.

READING PROBLEMS IN TEACHING CONTENT AREAS

The observations described illustrate four main problems associated with teaching the content areas: (1) While direct instruction in using reading skills is given during the reading lesson, direct instruction in using reading skills during the content area lesson seldom occurs. Mr. Rough's failure to remind the students that subheadings could be used as an aid to locating specific information in social studies is typical of the way in which reading is approached in the content areas. (2) The concepts and vocabulary in the content areas are more difficult than the concepts and vocabulary found in the reading lesson material. The principle of compromise discussed in the fourth grade social studies text was not easy for all the youngsters to understand immediately. (3) The thrust of instruction in the intermediate grades is different from the thrust in the primary grades. While the emphasis in Miss Daisy's program was on teaching reading skills, Mr. Rough spent the majority of his instructional focus on teaching the content area subjects. Heilman (1972) expresses this concern by stating, ". . . there is a diminished emphasis upon teaching the language tools which are needed for 'mining' all the subjects, and an air of urgency about having pupils accumulate facts in various subject areas" (p. 416). (4) Often, the content area subject is taught through the use of one primary textbook that is not appropriate for the reading levels of all the children.

READING SKILLS INVOLVED IN THE CONTENT AREAS

Each discipline has its own language and concepts that emphasize certain reading skills to achieve understanding of the material. The knowledge explosion and rapid development of technology have caused the constant creation of new vocabulary (astronaut, sputnik, skylab, stratified-charge engine). Some words are unique to science (gamma ray, isotope), and others are hard to understand because they have special meaning in science (module, culture, work, energy). Reading in science requires the ability to follow a sequence of events. If a student can't follow a set sequence, his or her plant may die because he or she watered it before he or she planted it.

Reading in social studies requires that pupils learn new vocabulary (peninsula), common vocabulary with special meaning (plain, range), and many words that describe difficult-to-understand abstract concepts (democracy, communism). The reader must also learn how to read new symbols such as those found on maps, charts, diagrams, and graphs. The interpretation of relationships, especially cause–effect, can cause difficulty in comprehending the content materials.

Reading in mathematics introduces some new words (divisor, dividend, multiplicand). Other terms are confusing because they take on new meaning (product, set, prime). It also puts the youngster in contact with numerical concepts that are expressed by new sets of symbols. Comprehension is sequential, and one concept is built on another. If a pupil does not understand a first concept, his or her understanding of all else based on that concept is also affected.

All the other content area skills also emphasize the use of certain reading skills to be understood.

However, although the various disciplines require certain reading skills that are more identifiable with them than with others, reading ability requires the synthesis of all the reading skills, and reading skills cannot really be divided along content area lines. Although "following directions" may be a skill that is particularly needed in understanding science, it is a skill required by all the other subject matter areas. Likewise, although "tone" and "mood" usually may be identified with literature, they also arise in descriptive materials in science (the effects of pollution on the world's future), social studies (the soldiers saw the awful destruction of the bomb blast), and math ("How many suns light up the day to chase the shadows of night away?") (Adler and Adler, 1969, p. 46). Whether the teacher is working with what is meant by "oblique parallel lines" in math or "minutemen" in history, the reading skill that needs to be stressed is still word meanings.

READING PROBLEMS INVOLVED WITH CONTENT AREA TEXTBOOKS

The problem with content area texts is not that they introduce unique reading skills but, rather, that they introduce new vocabulary and complex concepts. In basal reader texts, the vocabulary is carefully controlled and introduced. This is not the case in content area texts. A student who may be bored with the repetitious vocabulary in one text may be overwhelmed by the rate of new vocabulary in the content area text. Hildreth (1958) writes, "The middle-grade pupil can now expect to meet new words he has never seen before in the proportion of about 1 to 10, even in material prepared for his age group. . .".

Textbook Readability

Readability refers to the ease with which a book can most likely be read by a particular population. For example, a book labeled *grade three* would be read comfortably by a child with an instructional reading level of grade three. The same book would be extremely difficult for a child with an instructional reading level of grade one and extremely easy for a child with an instructional reading level of grade five. Klare (1974–1975) discusses several ways in which readability may be assessed. One way is to construct a comprehension test covering the material to find out how well it has been understood by persons of varying ages and reading abilities. This technique was discussed in Chapter 5. A second possible means is to use a readability formula. A third technique is for writers and teachers to make estimates of readability based on the ease with which former students have read the material to be assigned (Dillner and Olson, 1977, p. 117).

Assessment through Readability Formulas

A readability formula measures some of the language variables in a piece of writing to estimate the probable readability level. The language variables include assessments of the difficulty of words and sentences. Several readability formulas have been developed including those by Fry (1972, 1976, 1977), Flesh (1948), and Dale and Chall (1948). Fry's graph has been validated on both primary and secondary materials, and the scores derived from it correlate highly with those from several well-known formulas. This graph will be explained in detail in the next section (Dillner and Olson, 1977, p. 118).

Use of Fry's Readability Formula

The 1972 version of Fry's graph directed the teacher to skip all proper nouns when calculating the readability level. However, in 1976, Fry revised his graph to include the use of proper nouns in performing the calculations. He states that his reason for making this change is that "Proper nouns do contribute to the difficulty of the material. It is easier for a child to read 'Joe' than 'Joseph,' and children or adults certainly do not skip proper nouns in most reading" (Fry, 1977, p. 244).

To use the 1977 version of the Fry graph, seven basic steps should be completed. These steps are given on the bottom of the graph shown in Figure 12.1. Three one-hundred-word passages, randomly selected from a fifth grade social studies textbook, are shown in Figures 12.2, 12.3, and 12.4. The syllables per one hundred words, the number of sentences, and the approximate grade levels have been calculated. The estimated readability of the book based on the average of the three calculations is plotted on the graph in Figure 12.1.

Figure 12.1. Graph for Estimating Readability—Extended

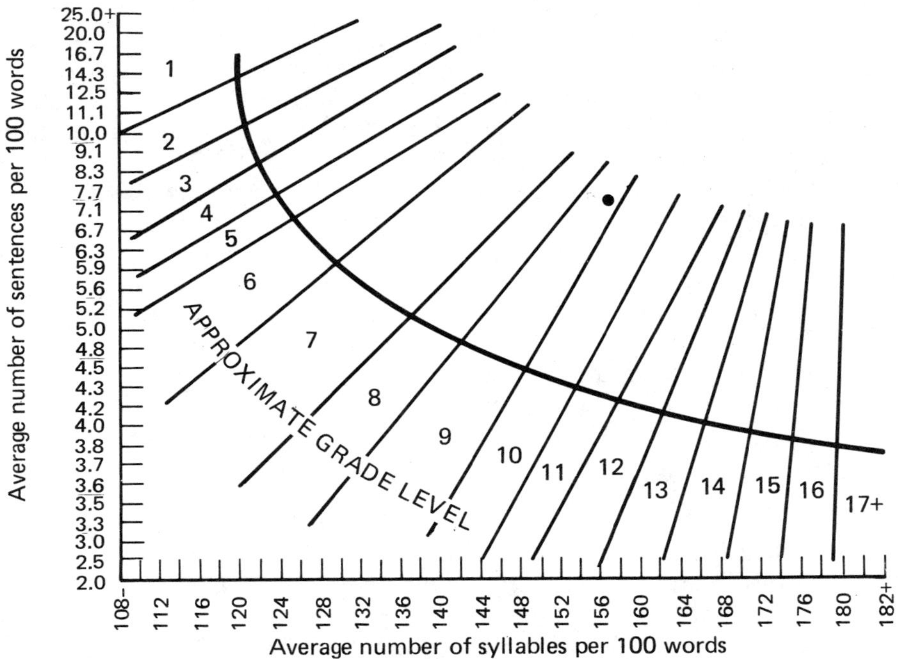

Example:

	Sentences	*Syllables*
1st hundred words	9.0	139
2nd hundred words	7.3	156
3rd hundred words	5.4	175
Average	7.2	157

Readability ninth grade (see dot plotted on graph)

Expanded Directions for Working Readability Graph

1. Randomly select three sample passages and count out exactly one hundred words each, beginning with the beginning of a sentence. Do count proper nouns, initializations, and numerals.
2. Count the number of sentences in the hundred words, estimating length of the fraction of the last sentence to the nearest one tenth.
3. Count the total number of syllables in the one hundred-word passage. If you don't have a hand counter available, an easy way is to simply put a mark above every syllable over one in each word; then, when you get to the end of the passage, count the number of marks and add one hundred. Small calculators can also be used as counters by pushing numeral 1, then push the + sign for each word or syllable when counting.
4. Enter graph with *average* sentence length and *average* number of syllables; plot dot where two lines intersect. Area where dot is plotted will give you the approximate grade level.

5. If a great deal of variability is found in syllable count or sentence count, putting more samples into the average is desirable.
6. A word is defined as a group of symbols with a space on either side; thus, *Joe*, *IRA*, *1945*, and *&* are each one word.
7. A syllable is defined as a phonetic syllable. Generally, there are as many syllables as vowel sounds. For example, *stopped* is one syllable and *wanted* is two syllables. When counting syllables for numerals and initializations, count one syllable for each symbol. For example, *1945* is five syllables, *IRA* is three syllables, and *&* is one syllable.

Note: This "extended graph" does not outmode or render the earlier (1968) version inoperative or inaccurate; it is an extension. (Reproduction permitted—no copyright.)

Landforms are one kind of resource. We use the various kinds of landforms differently. Most people of the United States and Canada live on plains land. In these lands are the biggest cities and the best farmland. But mountains and plateaus are useful in other ways. Most mountains contain rocks that once were buried deep in the earth's crust. As the mountains were pushed up, these rocks came close to the earth's surface. Today men can mine the rocks that contain useful minerals. Most mountain and plateau regions are covered with dense forests, useful for timber, lumber, plywood, and paper./The rivers in many mountain areas can be dammed to produce electricity. The rivers and forests of most mountain areas contain game and fish, which attract sportsmen. Mountains are great recreation areas. People like to go to them to ski in the winter and to camp during the summer.

Number of sentences:	9
Number of syllables:	139
Approximate grade level:	6

Figure 12.2. Social Studies Excerpt (From *Lands of Promise* by M. Prunty and E. B. Fincher, p. 8. Copyright 1971, Macmillan Publishing Co., Inc.)

But average rainfall figures can be misleading. The average rainfall of a place may be 17 inches a year. This does not mean that 17 inches is received *each* year. The 17 inches is based upon the records of many years that have been averaged. For example, the amount of rainfall received each year of a five-year period may be 23, 24, 11, 9, and 18 inches. Added together, these figures total 85 inches, the rainfall for the entire five-year period. The average for the five-year period (85 divided by 5) is 17 inches.

The average yearly rainfall on the/ Great Plains, while low, is sufficient for the production of some crops, such as wheat. However, it is the *average* rainfall that is sufficient, not the amount that is received each year. On the Great Plains, a few wet years are followed by a few dry years. This is a variable pattern of rainfall. To understand the natural environment and the history of the Great Plains, it is necessary to be aware of this variation.

Number of sentences:	7.3
Number of syllables:	156
Approximate grade level:	9

Figure 12.3. Social Studies Excerpt. (From *Lands of Promise* by M. Prunty and E. B. Fincher, p. 295, Macmillan Publishing Co., Inc.)

French Canadians make up about 30 percent of the total population of Canada. They are almost all descendants of the original French settlers you read about in an earlier chapter. You will recall that they came to New France in the 1600's and 1700's and settled along the St. Lawrence River. Quebec, founded by Champlain in 1608, and Montreal, settled in 1642, are among the oldest cities on the continent. Among the French who came to North America in that period were many fishermen, explorers, missionaries, fur trappers, and traders. The majority, however, were farmers, called habitants in New France,/whose lives revolved around their farms, their families, and their church, which was Roman Catholic.

Number of sentences:	5.4
Number of syllables:	175
Approximate grade level:	15

Figure 12.4. Social Studies Excerpt (From *Lands of Promise* by M. Prunty and E. B. Fincher, p. 439, Macmillan Publishing Co., Inc.)

Readability of Content Area Textbooks

Because of the formidable vocabulary, grammatical intricacies, and concept complexity, content area textbooks at any grade level tend to be much more difficult than the material used in reading class at the same level. For example, one study indicated that a popular science text designed for fifth graders had a readability of 9:1 as assessed by the Dale–Chall readability formula (Smith, 1969).

Another study used several different readability formulas to evaluate the reading levels of sixty-eight social studies textbooks for grades one through six. Their conclusion was that only some of the textbooks are appropriate for the average reader and that most will require students to be above-average readers. None are for the slow or low-achieving child (Johnson and Vardian, 1973).

PROCEDURES FOR DESIGNING INSTRUCTION

Research has indicated that there is a need for specific instruction in dealing with the type of concepts found in reading in the content area materials (Serra, 1953; Johnson, 1952). Furthermore, there is not necessarily a transfer of reading skills from general instruction in reading improvement to the specific problems inherent in content area reading without further instructional implementation (Gray, 1960).

Both Miss Daisy and Mr. Rough can help their students to understand the material in the content areas by including direct instruction in the reading of each.

One of the fifth grade teachers in the school had solved the problem through a variety of means. Miss Ankele used an individualized approach in her reading program but still used content area textbooks to teach the children the other subjects in the curriculum. However, she knew that she had a reading range in her classroom from grade two to grade nine. Since she was a diagnostic–prescriptive teacher, she used the same techniques to teach the content area subjects as she used to teach reading—but she reversed her emphasis.

TASK 1: ASCERTAINING A SCOPE AND SEQUENCE OF SKILLS

In reading, Miss Ankele would look at the individual child and determine what reading skill he or she needed to learn because her focus was on teaching the skill of reading. However, in the content areas, she looked first at the material to determine what reading skills were most needed to understand the content. For example, in the reading class, if Chris needed to learn the skill "making inferences" as revealed in his individual conference, she would develop lessons on that skill in his self-selected reading book. However, if Chris were reading in a social studies book, and the purpose of the lesson were to teach the reader to "identify six characteristics of the Old South," she would ascertain what reading skills Chris would particularly need to understand this concept. In this case, the reading skill needed to understand the concept would probably be the cause-effect relationships between the characteristics of the Old South and the effect that they had upon its future in American history. Restated, this means that Miss Ankele used the books in the reading class to reinforce a specifically needed reading skill but used reading skills in the content area class to reinforce a specifically needed concept.

Identification of Reading Skills Needed in Content Areas

Many of the problems with vocabulary and concepts in the content areas have been anticipated by the textbook authors; hence their organizational formats reflect this. Therefore, each time Miss Ankele presented a lesson to the students, she pointed out aspects of the book that she felt would help the children identify and retain important aspects of what was to be read.

A number of strategies designed to enhance this objective have been developed by reading authorities. The forerunner of most of these study techniques was the SQ3R method developed by Robinson (1970). Although this strategy was discussed more extensively in Chapter 4, under the heading "Using a Study Technique," it will be reviewed here in terms of Miss Ankele's specific content area lesson.

SQ3R is an acronym for survey, question, read, recite, and review, which provides the student with a mnemonic device to remember both the steps and the order in which they occur. In this method, the students are encouraged to do the following: (1) The survey step directs the student to look over his or her text to obtain a general idea of the material to be explicated. He or she is encouraged to look at the length, main headings and subheadings, italicized portions, final summaries, and other facilitative aids to organization and emphasis found within most academic reading. (2) The question step involves looking through the text again and formulating questions about what is to be read. The reader is encouraged to change main headings, subheadings, and topic sentences into questions to narrow the focus and add specific purposes to reading. (3) The read step is the student's third look at the material. He or she is directed to read the text in such a manner that he or she can answer the questions about the data that has been formulated. (4) The recite stage instructs the reader to go back to the questions he or she made up about the chapter to see if he or she can answer them. (5) The last step is one of review and suggests that the reader take a second look at the chapter at some later time to gain new insights into the material.

Most reading authorities agree that, even if the material to be read is written in such a manner as to lend itself easily to study strategies, the student will not utilize these aids without specific instruction. Robinson (1961) stresses that children may not be able to read better when they are given well-organized and facilitative material *unless they are given special instructions.*

Miss Ankele used the surveying aspect of the SQ3R study strategy designed by Robinson (1970) each time she presented her class with a new textbook. She would do this by asking them to do the following with her:

Surveying a Book

1. Read preface (to note purpose of book).
2. Read table of contents (to note what book contains).
3. Leaf through book glancing at headings and reading occasional sentences under them.
4. Read summaries of chapters.

Each time the children were introduced to a new chapter in a textbook, she asked them to do the following with her:

Surveying a Chapter

1. Read headings (to note organization of material—how topics go together and follow each other—and determine what the main subject of each section is).
2. Pay attention to order of headings (main headings and subheadings: such arrangements or order tell what topics are subordinate to the main topics; note headings: they are the key to the structure of the subject you are studying).
3. Skim some of the sentences at certain points within the chapter (look at pictures and charts).
4. Read summary (to obtain most important points of the chapter).

Since Miss Ankele began the study of the content area reading with this strategy, the first skills she identified from the list of skills located in Chapter 15 of this text were the study skills that were needed to complete this process. Therefore, her sequence of skills in all content areas began with the skills needed to preview, or "Using a Study Technique" and "Skimming" (see Chapter 4, study skills 3 and 4). Other study skills that became important in using the textbook most efficiently were "using glossaries," "reading tables," and "reading graphs" (see Chapter 4, skills 5 and 6).

Another important skill was the variety of signaling devices that children can use to help them realize that important information is being given. These include italicized words, boldface type, parentheses around words, and words in colored print. Since Miss Ankele found that a number of her fifth graders did not realize the purpose of these signaling devices, she included that instruction (see Chapter 4, skill 5).

In addition to identifying these study skills as being particularly important in all the content areas, Miss Ankele also looked at each content area lesson before she presented it to the children to see what word recognition or comprehension skills might be most needed to understand the subject matter. In this manner, she identified skills such as identifying cause–effect relationships (see Chapter 3, skill 5) in the "Old South" social studies lesson discussed earlier in this chapter.

In each case, she would look at the objective she had set for the content area lesson and determine what reading skills would be most needed to understand that content area lesson.

TASK 2: DIAGNOSING BEFORE INSTRUCTION

Each time Miss Ankele gave the children new material in a content area, she diagnosed their ability to read that material. Her procedure for doing this was similar to the administration of the IRI described in Chapter 5, except that for short-cut purposes, she reversed her order and administered the silent reading portion first. She would select a passage of about one hundred words from the content area textbook. Then she would design ten comprehension questions to accompany the material. She would type the questions on a ditto and ask the children to read the passage and answer the questions exactly as she would the silent portion of the IRI discussed in Chapter 5. If the pupils could answer seven out of ten questions on the silent reading, she assumed that they could read the content area. If they could not, she asked them to come to her desk one at a time to read another passage of one hundred words aloud to her. In this manner, she determined whether or not they could understand the text and if the procedure for teaching that she had outlined would be appropriate for them. As the science books differed in difficulty from the social studies books, which likewise differed in difficulty from other content area textbooks, she tested each child in each content area before prescribing instruction for him or her in the area.

TASK 3: KEEPING RECORDS

As Miss Ankele had records on each child from the reading class, she knew that she didn't have to duplicate all the records for the content areas. However, she did know that not all children read all content areas alike. For example, Chris read on the fifth grade level in reading class. However, the social studies book designed for the fifth grade was written at the seventh grade level, and Chris had difficulty in reading it. On the other hand, the science book, also designed for fifth grade level, was written at an eighth grade level, but Chris had no difficulty whatsoever with that text. The reason for his ability to cope with one area text and not the other was his high interest in science, which had caused his knowledge of the vocabulary and concepts involved to extend well above grade level. Therefore, Miss Ankele knew that there was not always a direct relationship between reading level and content area understanding. Her records for the content areas were carefully kept and similar to the ones she kept in reading class (see Table 12.1).

TABLE 12.1
Science Checklist

Objective Name	*Objective Number*	*Chris*	*Reta*	*Betty*	*Art*	*Emmy*	*Dave*	*Nancy*	*Joe*	*Fred*	*Margie*	*Janie*	*Fritz*	*Bruce*
		Students												
Skimming	Study skill #3	√	√	○	√	√	√	√	○	√	√	○	○	√
Previewing	Study skill #4	√	○	○	√	√	√	√	○	√	√	○	○	√
Using glossaries	Study skill #5	√	√	√	○	○	○	○	○	○	√	○	○	√
Reading tables	Study skill #6	√	√	√	○	√	√	○	○	○	√	○	○	√
Applying morphemic analysis	Word identification skill #6	√	√	○	√	√	○	√	○	√	√	○	○	√

TABLE 12.1 (cont'd)
Social Studies Checklist

Objective Name	*Objective Number*	*Chris*	*Reta*	*Betty*	*Art*	*Emmy*	*Dave*	*Nancy*	*Joe*	*Fred*	*Margie*	*Janie*	*Fritz*	*Bruce*
		Students												
Identifying cause-effect relationships	Comprehension skill #5	○	√	○	○	○	○	○	○	√	√	○	√	√
Skimming	Study skill #3	○	√	√	√	√	√	√	○	√	√	○	√	○
Previewing	Study skill #4	○	○	√	√	√	○	√	○	○	○	○	√	√
Using glossaries	Study skill #5	○	○	○	○	√	√	○	○	√	√	○	√	○
Using illustration clues	Study skill #5	○	○	○	○	○	○	√	○	√	○	○	√	√

Blank Not assessed
√ Passed preassessment
○ Did not pass preassessment; needs instruction
(√) Did not pass preassessment; has received instruction and completed postassessment satisfactorily.

TABLE 12.1 (cont'd)
Math Checklist

Objective Name	*Objective Number*	*Students:* *Chris*	*Reta*	*Betty*	*Art*	*Emmy*	*Dave*	*Nancy*	*Joe*	*Fred*	*Margie*	*Janie*	*Fritz*	*Bruce*
Skimming	Study skill #3	○	√	○	√	√	√	√	○	√	√	○	√	○
Previewing	Study skill #4	√	√	√	√	√	√	√	○	√	√	○	√	√
Using glossaries	Study skill #5	○	√	√	√	√	√	√	○	√	√	○	√	√
Using illustration clues	Study skill #5	○	√	√	√	√	√	√	○	√	√	○	√	√
Reading tables	Study skill #5	√	√	√	√	√	√	√	○	√	√	○	√	√

Blank Not assessed
√ Passed preassessment
○ Did not pass preassessment; need instruction
(√) Did not pass preassessment; has received instruction and completed postassessment satisfactorily

It is interesting to note that, in the records, Miss Ankele used the survey technique in *all* three content areas. As stated previously, children do not necessarily make a transfer of a reading skill from one content area to another without direct instruction. Therefore, Miss Ankele emphasized this skill in all three areas, as she felt it was important in understanding the content.

In addition, she discovered that the skill "applying morphemic analysis" became extremely important in science, as there were a large number of compound words and words with foreign roots. Some of the words the children were required to read to understand that particular lesson were *biomedical*, *sunshade*, *airlock*, *telescope*, and *cosmonaut*.

In math, the children had great trouble "reading tables," so she emphasized that particular skill before assigning them the lesson.

TASK 4: DESIGNING INSTRUCTIONAL STRATEGIES

Once Miss Ankele had determined which materials the children could read and which they couldn't she designed her instructional strategies accordingly. The two main components of her instructional strategies were (1) develop methods of guiding the student's reading and (2) select appropriate materials.

Develop Methods of Guiding the Student's Reading

Donald Durrell (1956), in his book *Improving Reading Instruction*, recommends that teachers make reading and reasoning guides to help readers of different abilities to do their assignments. He suggests that differences among pupils in their need for study guides of different levels is greater than their need for materials written on different reading levels. If the teacher can provide the right kind of help, materials of the same reading level can be used for the entire class. Herber (1970) has written an entire textbook in which his thrust is upon the concept expressed by Durrell. Therefore, Miss Ankele modeled her lessons after those suggested by Herber in his book, *Teaching Reading in Content Areas.*

Since Miss Ankele always had an objective when presenting a content area lesson, she used that objective to help her make up a differentiated assignment sheet on the content area lesson. When she looked over the next chapter in the social studies book, she read the accompanying teacher's manual and the follow-up questions designed for her pupils. Five questions were located under a section marked "Arriving at Understandings." One of the questions asked the pupil to discuss the relationship between Whitney's cotton gin and the development of the Inland South (Prunty and Fincher, 1971, p. 166). She knew that her poorest readers would have great difficulty in answering the question. In addition, she knew that the reading skill of "identifying cause–effect relationships" was particularly important in this assignment. Therefore she did several things. (1) When she introduced the chapter, she reviewed the skills of cause and effect with the children. (2) She gave them a guided reading sheet before they were asked to read the assignment. The poorest readers needed the most guidance, so Miss Ankele gave them a specific description of the cotton gins in the past and asked them to match these with a specific list of possible effects. The average readers needed less guidance and were simply given a list of pages in the text on which the descriptions of the cotton gin and possible effects were located. They were then asked to discuss the relationship between the development of the cotton gin and the development of the Inland South. The superior readers could have been given the question as stated and asked to answer it; however, Miss Ankele reworded it to focus more upon cause–effect relationships.

The assignment sheets for the different pupils looked like this:

Excerpt from Assignment Sheet for Poor Readers

Directions: Given below are some descriptions of cotton gins as found in your textbook on pp. 150–153. In each case the first event has caused a second event to take place. Draw a line from each cause to its effect. The page number on which each description is located is given in () next to the description so that you may check with Chapter Seven to match the cause with the effect correctly.

Cause	*Effect*
1. The Industrial Revolution in England made production of huge quantities of cloth available at low prices. (p. 151)	1. There was a great demand in Britain for a cotton crop. (p. 151)
2. Sea Island cotton could be separated with a cotton gin, but Upland cotton could not be separated with a gin. (p. 152)	2. Sea Island was more profitable to the grower. (p. 151)
3. Sea Island cotton could not grow in the Inland South but Upland cotton could. (p. 151)	3. The Inland South could not benefit from the great demand for cotton in England. (p. 152)
4. Eli Whitney invented a new cotton gin that could separate Upland cotton from fiber. (p. 152)	4. Upland cotton could be grown profitably to supply the demand for cotton. (p. 152)

Excerpt from Assignment Sheet for Average Readers

Directions: In each of the following sentences about the "Old South," the incident described has been caused by another incident that took place first. Look in your textbook on page 151-152 to find the event that caused the second event to occur. The first one has been done for you.

Event 1 (Cause)	*Event 2 (Effect)*
1. The Industrial Revolution occurred in England.	1. Production of hugh quantities of cloth were available at low prices.
2.	2. Sea Island cotton was more profitable to the grower.
3.	3. The Inland South could not benefit from the great demand for cotton in England.
4.	4. Upland cotton could be grown profitably to supply the demand for cotton.

Excerpt from Assignment Sheet for Superior Readers

Directions: In real life, certain events happen that cause other events to occur. Look in your textbook on pages 150-151 and locate at least five events concerning cotton that caused other events to happen in the "Old South." Put the first event in the first column (cause) and the resulting event in the second column (effect) as shown below. The first one has been done for you.

Cause *Event 1 (Cause)*	*Effect* *Event 2 (Effect)*
The Industrial Revolution occurred in England.	Production of huge quantities of cloth were available at low prices.

Selection of Materials

Miss Ankele relied upon three major techniques for teaching reading in the content areas: (1) the single materials approach, (2) the multilevel materials approach, and (3) the multiple, multilevel materials thematic approach.

The Single Materials Approach: In this approach she used the fifth grade text or texts as her major resource. When she first began to teach, this was her basic approach to teaching in the content areas. However, she did not just assign the materials, but treated them in much the same manner as Mr. Rough treated his basal reader material. Before beginning reading, she introduced the new concepts and words and thoroughly discussed them in an attempt to build up the children's background for their reading assignment. Then, before she asked the children to read their lesson, she gave them a purpose for reading by giving them the guided reading sheet shown earlier and asked them to read silently to look for the answers. Following the silent reading, she had oral reading of the text. Most of her oral reading requirements were of the type, "Prove the statement that Whitney's cotton gin changed the fortune of the Inland South." However, Miss Ankele knew that this method was only satisfactory for those children who could read the text on an instructional or independent level. For those children who could not read the text, the method was unsatisfactory.

The children who could not read the textbook were taught in a variety of ways. She usually used at least one or more of the following alternatives throughout the year, but she did not do each with every lesson.

1. She would read the textbook to the group of children who could not read the text while the rest of the youngsters were doing the silent reading already discussed. Although she was doing the reading, the youngsters were asked to follow along in their books. This helped them increase their reading skills, as they saw the words in print when she pronounced them. In addition, since they were listening for the purpose described on their differentiated guided reading sheet, they were able to locate many of the answers when she read the appropriate portions of the chapter. They were included in the follow-up discussion in much the same manner as the students who had read the material independently.

2. As the oral reading method took up her teaching time with the rest of the students, she taped her own summary of some of the lessons and let small groups listen to the chapter while she was working with other groups. As she had used that same textbook several times, she made a point to tape several lessons a year so that eventually she would have the entire book summarized on audiotape.

3. In addition, she had talked with the sixth grade teacher, Mr. Poindexter, who felt that some of his students needed help in oral interpretation. And he had some of his sixth graders, who were reading on a fifth grade level, tape the fifth grade content area lessons. In that way the sixth grade youngsters got needed practice with oral reading.

4. Another strategy used by Miss Ankele was to pair the children in her own fifth grade and have the better reader read to the weaker one. This had some social implications, as some parents didn't like their child always being helped by someone else's child. Therefore, she established a routine where every youngster helped every other youngster in some way. (See Chapter 9 for more ideas on ways in which peers can help each other.)

Using Multilevel Materials: In addition to the methods described for teaching the content area subject matter through the use of one major text or set of materials, Miss Ankele also employed a system in which she used materials of different instructional levels. For example, Joe read on the third grade level, and she obtained a third grade social studies book for him to use instead of the fifth grade social studies book. Since her objectives for the unit in social studies focused upon knowledge of the "Old South," she had to look very carefully to locate a third grade textbook on the "Old South." When she did discover one, she found that he had already read it. Therefore, she also relied upon reference lists, such as those suggested in Chapter 11 on recreational reading, to locate materials on the "Old South" that were written on a third grade reading level. However, as in all situations dealing with children who were reading below grade level, she tried to be very careful that the books he read did not appear to be written for a much younger child because she did not want to embarrass him in front of his friends. In some cases, she was able to find materials especially written for fifth grade interests and third grade reading levels. Joe was able to participate in the broad discussion and keep up with the content of the rest of the children. In addition, Miss Ankele made a "guided reading sheet" for Joe much as though he were in the same text as everyone else.

Another source for multilevel material on the same topic was for Miss Ankele to rewrite the material on the child's reading level. Dallmann et al. (1974) suggest that material in the textbook can be rewritten so that the child can read it independently. In this manner the children were able to participate in the activities preceding and following the silent reading. While the rest of the children read their texts, the children reading below grade level would read their rewritten versions. In all cases, differentiated guide sheets were constructed to go along with their rewritten materials.

Using Multiple, Multilevel Materials in a Thematic Approach: Another technique that Miss Ankele found particularly effective was to use a "thematic approach" to teaching her content areas. To do this, she would look at the fifth grade objectives for social studies and then select a variety of materials on many grade levels that could be used by the youngsters to meet the objectives. Using the curriculum guide and the textbook, she ascertained the objectives of the fifth grade social studies program. She knew one way to meet those objectives was through the textbook itself. However, a variety of other means existed for meeting the objectives. For example, the "Old South" unit might have as one of its objectives "The student will be able to identify at least five cause-effect relationships between the growing of cotton and the growth of the economy of the Inland South." Youngsters could be given a wide list of resources in which they could find the material needed to meet each objective listed at the beginning of each unit. Some could use the textbook; others could use magazines, reference books, other textbooks, filmstrips, audiotapes, and the like.

In some cases, she combined subjects and taught science and social studies together. In such instances, her objectives broadened, and, instead of asking children to find the cause-effect relationship of the growing of cotton in the "Old South," she might ask them to research reasons why cotton of all types could not grow in the "Old South" and what kinds of plants could be grown there. The task of the science thrust might be to examine what types of conditions would cause cotton to grow well. Soil conditions, weather, and periods needed for dormant growth could all be investigated. If Miss Ankele wanted to stress concepts involved in physics along with the study of the "Old South," the children could examine the construction of simple machines, such as the cotton gin, and the type of work required and energy needed to harvest it by hand. Math could be brought in, for example, to estimate the number of work-hours saved by the cotton gin and the total number of calories expended. Health could be related to the topic in terms of the foods that people ate at that time. A literature unit could include stories and poems written by authors living in those times. Art class could be used to portray the type of art that flourished in that era or as a medium to express a particular aspect of the "Old South" that a student wanted to portray.

In all cases, Miss Ankele relied on the differentiated guided reading sheets to make the objectives clear to the students at a level appropriate to their achievement ability. The superior reader might be asked to relate the climatic conditions needed to grow cotton to the economic growth of the South. The average reader might be given the following set of guides: (1) read science text, pp. 60-70, social studies text, pp. 51-65, and *National Geographic*, pp. 25-35, and list six characteristics of the climate in the South that affected its economic growth. The weak readers' directed reading guide would be even more structured: (1) Read text (below grade level, simply written science text), page 42, column 1, and match the conditions listed for growing cotton located there with the mimeo list of climatic conditions of the "Old South" located below. Make a statement about the South's ability to grow cotton based on your two lists.

Extension Activities: Regardless of the technique used, Miss Ankele always developed extension activities that helped provide for the wide range of achievement levels found in her fifth grade classroom. Sartain (1973) suggests that projects can be used to stimulate study of any content area. Some of the activities he suggested that Miss Ankele adapted for her classes included (1) English—diaries of main characters, authors' fan clubs, family tree of some of the characters; (2) social studies—souvenir exhibit of costumes, postcards with paragraph labels on life and institutions represented, reproduced historical documents supplemented with background information, historical songs representative of the era; (3) mathematics—class business organization including money made from grass cutting and babysitting, selection of recipes and recomputed measurements of ingredients to fit different family sizes; (4) science—conservation or recycling campaign, mock-up exhibits of a cotton gin, raising plants such as cotton in class; (5) fine and applied arts—home decorating book, home repair book, personal storage chest.

TASK 5: DIAGNOSING AFTER INSTRUCTION

As with all her teaching, Miss Ankele always gave children tests on the content after they had been guided through it. In the case of the content area, her test matched the skills that the children had been asked to complete in their assignments. For example, since Joe was reading on the third grade level, he had been given the very carefully constructed guide sheet shown on page 331 of this chapter. Since he could not read it by himself, he had listened to an audio recording of the chapter that Miss Ankele had made for him. Joe's test asked him to match some causes with some effects; Fred was an average reader, so his test asked him to identify some effects of several causes that were listed; and Margie, a superior reader, was asked to discuss the cause-effect relationships between six major events.

TASK 6: ORGANIZING INSTRUCTION

As discussed earlier, Miss Ankele varied her instructional techniques during the year. Although she always used a guided assignment sheet for the pupils, in some cases she would use a multiple-materials combined content area unit approach; in other cases she would adapt a single textbook to meet the needs of all her students. Her instructional technique determined her class organization. When she combined two contents in the unit approach, she had an hour block for the subject and planned her time accordingly. When she used the single textbook or multilevel single subject approach, she planned a half hour a day for each content lesson.

FACILITATING INDIVIDUALIZATION OF INSTRUCTION

The task of making out differentiated assignment sheets for each child was a massive one that Miss Ankele developed over a period of years. The first year she taught, she made differentiated assignment sheets only for the poorest readers, as she felt they needed the most help. The following years, she built up assignment sheets for the other pupils. In addition, she let her pupils help her. For example, the assignment prepared for the superior readers could become a guide sheet for the next group of average readers. Likewise, the assignment completed by the average students could become the basis for a guide sheet for the poor readers. The guided reading sheet designed for superior readers shown on page 332 of this text was subsequently used by Miss Ankele as a guided reading sheet for her next year's group of average fifth grade readers. Likewise the guided reading sheet for the average reader shown on page 332 of this text was used for her next year's group of weak fifth grade readers.

Furthermore, as mentioned previously in this text, when she used children to help each other, she was extremely conscious of using them in such a way that *all* children were helpers at some time during the year. Joe couldn't help anyone in social studies, but he was the expert in math. Fritz didn't know a thing about science, but he was extremely knowledgeable about American history. Even Janie, whose achievement level was low, was able to help others in science when they discussed growing plants, as her hobby was collecting flowers.

When graphs confused everyone else in class when studying climatic conditions, Bruce designed a lesson in interpreting baseball scores and told them how simple it was to read graphs.

By teaching her content area subjects as she did, Miss Ankele was able to help all the pupils learn something about the content area subject matter in a manner commensurate with their ability.

SUMMARY

This chapter has shown that reading class is not the only time that children are required to read in school. Reading is also done in arithmetic, science, social studies, health, and other such "content area" subjects. Since the focus in teaching the content areas is different from the focus in teaching reading, special provisions must be made for reading in these areas. This chapter has acquainted the participant with reading problems that occur in the content areas as well as with techniques for teaching reading skills particularly needed in each content area.

References and Bibliography

Adler, Irving and Ruth. *Sets and Numbers for the Very Young.* New York: The John Day Co., Publishers, 1969, p. 46.

Bond, Guy L., and Wagner, Eva Bond. *Teaching the Child to Read.* New York: Macmillan Publishing Co., Inc., 1966.

Dale, E. and Chall, J. S. "A Formula for Predicting Readability." *Educational Research Bulletin* 27 (21 January 1948), pp. 11-20 and (15 February 1948), pp. 37-54.

Dallmann, Martha, Rouch, Roger L., Char, Lynnette Y. C., and DeBoer, John. *The Teaching of Reading.* 5th ed. New York: Holt, Rinehart and Winston, 1978.

Dillner, Martha, and Olson, Joanne. *Personalizing Reading Instruction in Middle, Junior, and Senior High Schools.* New York: Macmillan Publishing Co., Inc., 1977.

Durrell, D. D. *Improving Reading Instruction.* New York: Harcourt Brace Jovanovich, Inc., 1956, p. 288.

Flesch, R. "A New Readability Yardstick." *Journal of Applied Psychology* 32 (June 1948): 221-233.

Fry, Edward. "Fry's Readability Graph: Clarifications, Validity, and Extension to Level 17." *The Journal of Reading* 21 (December 1977): 242-251.

Fry, Edward. *Reading Instruction for Classroom and Clinic.* New York: McGraw-Hill Book Company, 1972.

Fry, Edward, *Fry Readability Scale.* Providence, R.I.: Jamestown Publishers, 1976.
Gray, William S. "Reading," in Chester W. Harris, ed., *Encyclopedia of Educational Research.* 3rd ed. Macmillan Publishing Co., Inc., 1960, p. 1092.
Guszak, Frank J. *Diagnostic Reading Instruction in the Elementary School.* 2nd ed. New York: Harper & Row, Publishers, 1978.
Harris, Larry A., and Smith, Carl B. *Reading Instruction: Diagnostic Teaching.* New York: Holt, Rinehart and Winston, 1976.
Heilman, Arthur W. *Principles and Practices of Teaching Reading.* 4th ed. Columbus, Ohio: Charles E. Merrill Publishing Company, 1977.
Herber, Harold L. *Teaching Reading in Content Areas.* Englewood Cliffs, N.J.: Prentice-Hall, Inc., 1970.
Hildreth, Gertrude. *Teaching Reading.* New York: Holt, Rinehart and Winston, 1958.
Johnson, Mary E. "The Vocabulary Difficulty in Content Subjects in Grade Five." *Elementary English* 29 (May 1952): 277-280.
Johnson, Roger E., and Vardian, Eileen B. "Reading, Readability, and Social Studies." *The Reading Teacher* 25 (Feb. 1973): 483-488.
Klare, G. R. "Assessing Readability." *Reading Research Quarterly* X (1974-1975): 62-102.
Olson, Joanne, and Dillner, Martha. *Learning to Teach Reading in the Elementary School.* New York: Macmillan Publishing Co., Inc., 1976.
Prunty, Merle, and Fincher, E. B., *Lands of Promise. Western Hemisphere: Setting and Settlement.* New York: Macmillan Publishing Co., Inc., 1971.
Robinson, Francis P. "Study Skills for Superior Students in Secondary School." *The Reading Teacher* 15 (Sept. 1961): 29-33, 37.
Robinson, Francis P. *Effective Study.* 4th ed. New York: Harper & Row, Publishers, 1970.
Sartain, Harry. "Content Reading—They'll Like It." *Journal of Reading* 17 (Oct. 1973): 47-51.
Serra, Mary, C. "The Concept Burden of Instructional Materials." *Elementary School Journal* 53 (May 1953): 508-512.
Smith, Carl. "Tadpoles Make the Nicest Frogs." *Bulletin of the School of Education* (Indiana University), 45 (Dec. 1969): 113-125.
Spache, George D. and Evelyn, B. *Reading in the Elementary School.* 3rd ed. Boston: Allyn & Bacon, Inc., 1973.
Zintz, Miles V. *The Reading Process: The Teacher and the Learner.* 3rd ed. Dubuque, Iowa: William C. Brown Company, Publishers, 1979.

Self-Check 12.3
Content Area Reading

The following questions are designed to help the participant assess his or her competence on the first ten objectives stated at the beginning of this chapter. Although every effort has been made to make the self-check questions comprehensive, participants should remember that they are held responsible for meeting the objectives as stated at the beginning of this chapter.

1. Objective 1. Describe at least four reading problems associated with teaching the content area subjects.
2. Objective 2. Differentiate between reading skills that are needed by specific content areas and reading skills that are needed by all content areas.

3. Objective 3. Discuss at least one major problem associated with a great many content area textbooks.
4. Objective 4. Describe how a diagnostic–prescriptive teacher would teach the content area subject matter.
5. Objective 5. Describe at least one method for identifying reading skills needed in a particular content area.
6. Objective 6. Describe two major components involved in designing instructional strategies for the content areas.
7. Objective 7. Discuss the purpose for and construction of a differentiated guided reading sheet.
8. Objective 8. Discuss at least three ways in which content area materials may be differentiated to meet the reading needs of a variety of children.
9. Objective 9. Jim is a third grade child who reads well in the 3.1 basal reader, but has trouble reading his math book. Discuss how to design a content area lesson which would help him understand his math word problems.
10. Objective 10. Ms. Reynolds teaches science for all the fourth and fifth grade students in her elementary school. She has asked the school to purchase supplementary science texts designed for children who read below third and fourth grade reading levels. She intends to assign each child a text according to reading ability and construct assignment sheets telling each child in what order to read each section of his or her own textbook. Her rationale for the assignment sheets is based on her intention to have all children read about the same topic at the same time so that she can conduct large group discussion on the topic. What other things can Ms. Reynolds do to help her students read their science texts? Evaluate her program according to criteria discussed in this chapter.

Experiences 12.4
Content Area Reading

Chapter 12
Experience 1

Objective

During this experience, the participant will construct, administer, score, and interpret a diagnosis for a student on a content area textbook.

Activity and Assessment Guide

1. State the name, age, grade, and content area for the child you worked with. ____________________

   ____

2. Briefly describe the diagnostic instrument that you constructed to measure this child's reading skill (or attach a copy of the instrument to this sheet). ____________________

   ____

   ____

3. Write the results of your testing below:

   a. Errors on silent reading ____________________

   b. Errors on oral reading ____________________

* 4. Can this child read in that textbook? (circle one) yes no

Briefly explain why or why not ______________________________

____

____

* 5. Briefly describe a procedure for teaching this child the material contained in the textbook you used for diagnosis. ______________________________

____

____

* 6. State what you believe to be the significant implications of this experience for the classroom teacher. ______________________________

____

____

*See Chapter 1, Experience 1 for explanation of the asterisk.

Chapter 12
Experience 2

Objective

During this experience, the participant will design and teach a content area lesson according to the following criteria:

1. Select a specific content area lesson and identify one reading skill particularly needed to understand the lesson.
2. Design a guided reading sheet on this specific reading skill for a child who is reading above grade level, a child who is reading at grade level, and a child who is reading below grade level.

Activity and Assessment Guide

1. Give the name, age, and reading level for three children: one who reads at grade level, one who reads above grade level, and one who reads below grade level.

   a. Child one: ____________________

   b. Child two: ____________________

   c. Child three: ____________________

* 2. Briefly describe your rationale for selecting the reading skill that you did. Support with examples from the textbook why you think this reading skill is particularly needed in this content area lesson. ____________

   ____

   ____

   ____

   ____

3. Did you notice any children whom you taught previously who seemed to learn more because of the differentiated guided reading sheet? (circle one) yes no

Briefly explain your answer.____

* 4. How was your lesson for the children who read *above* grade level different from your other lessons? Attach a copy of your lesson to this sheet and then briefly explain the difference.__________________________________

* 5. Did you gain any more ideas about how to construct another lesson on the same lesson you taught for the children who read *above* grade level? (circle one) yes no

Briefly describe your idea. ____

* 6. How was your lesson for the children who read *at* grade level different from your other lessons? Attach a copy of your lesson to this sheet and then briefly explain the difference.__________________________________

* 7. Did you gain any more ideas about how to construct another lesson on the same lesson you taught for the children who read *at* grade level? (circle one) yes no

Briefly describe your idea.____

* 8. How was your lesson for the children who read *below* grade level different from your other lessons? Attach a copy of your lesson to this sheet and then briefly explain the difference.__________________________________

* 9. Did you gain any more ideas about how to construct another lesson on the lesson you taught for the children who read *below* grade level?

(circle one) yes no

Briefly describe your idea.____

____

* 10. State what you believe to be the significant implications of this experience for the classroom teacher.______________________________________

____

____

*See Chapter 1, Experience 1 for explanation of the asterisk.

Part Six
Teaching Reading to Special Groups

Chapter 13
Teaching Reading to the Diverse Learner

Objective 13.1

On completion of the chapter, the participant should be able to

1. Differentiate among the terms "culturally different," "culturally disadvantaged," "economically different," "economically disadvantaged," "linguistically different," "nonstandard speaker of English," and the like.
2. Describe at least three traits related to language and experiential background that are characteristic of the culturally different learner.
3. Identify the roles that language and experiential background play in hindering a culturally different child's ability to read when given a description of a specific child.
4. Design a lesson using the aural-oral procedure for teaching standard English to a speaker of nonstandard English when given a specific group of learners.
5. Describe how instruction for the culturally different may be individualized in a basal reader program, in a language experience program, and in an individualized program.
6. Describe at least one technique that a monolingual teacher can use to teach reading to a second language speaker of English.
7. Give an example of how a diagnostic-prescriptive teacher can adapt and utilize a scope and sequence of reading skills chart for the culturally different learner.
8. Describe at least one way in which a peer may be used to help provide reading instruction for the culturally different learner.

9. Identify the two major types of "exceptional" children.
10. Differentiate among and list traits of three different types of "handicapped" children.
11. Differentiate between and list traits of two different types of "gifted" children.
12. Describe at least one teaching technique that a teacher can use to design a lesson for the "exceptional" child.

Experiences 1 and 2 extend Chapter 13 with these objectives:

13. During this experience, the participant will research various resources and then design a lesson particularly relevant to a specific type of "diverse" learner.
14. During this experience, the participant will teach one reading skill to a "diverse" learner in a manner that includes a preassessment, an introductory lesson, two reinforcement lessons, and a postassessment.

Information Given 13.2
Teaching Reading to the Diverse Learner

Mrs. Fontaine's third grade class was composed of children with a diversity of backgrounds. She used an individualized reading approach and often set up small skill-building groups for children with similar reading problems. As her student observer entered the classroom, he heard her call for Tommy Carver, George Parsons, John Gonzalez, Lorelei Kang, and Mark Anderson to join their skill-building group. Tommy Carver was a black child from the ghetto area of the inner city; Lorelei Kang was a Chinese girl from a Chinese-speaking family; John Gonzalez was a Chicano from a Spanish-speaking environment; Mark Anderson and George Parsons were recent arrivals in the area—Mark from southern Minnesota and George from the Appalachian mountain area.

The group observed the following sentence that was written for them on a sentence strip: "The horse was helped by the strap guard." Each child looked at the sentence and used his or her word recognition skills to pronounce some words in the sentence correctly. However, none of the five children was able to interpret the correct meaning of the sentence.

All the youngsters could be considered "culturally different." All except Mark could be considered as speakers of "nonstandard" English. They were experiencing reading difficulties either because of their variant pronunciations of the English language or because their native tongues were languages other than English. For the native speakers of English, the discrepancies between their usual pronunciation of the words in the subject sentence and what each heard as he or she listened to himself or herself say the words in "standard English" caused problems in comprehension.

George Parsons was familiar with horses and was easily able to visualize a horse and a strap. However, he had no idea what the word "guard" represented, and the context of the sentence provided him with no clue to the meaning, although his experiential background did include the use of a small woolen pad that slipped between a strap and the horse's body to prevent pinching and to which he referred to as a "strap god." Tommy Carver had similar problems because of his pronunciation. He typically pronounced "guard" like "god," "helped" like "hep," and "strap" like "scrap." The varied pronunciation of "help" did not affect his understanding of the sentence at all, as he was able to identify the word correctly and to pronounce it in "standard English" in the reading situation. However, like George Parsons, his usual pronunciation of "guard" and "strap" did affect his understanding. When he referred to the mounted policeman's "strap guard" on his horse, Tommy called it a "scrapgod." Had he seen "scrapgod" in print, or had the context of the sentence given him more clues, he would have had no problem understanding the sentence. John Gonzalez and Lorelei Kang had a different problem, as they were not native speakers of English and could barely understand the language. John and Lorelei could only pronounce "the" and "was." While Mark Anderson had no language problem, his cultural background varied greatly from that of the average American youngster. He had grown up on a small farm in southern Minnesota and had seldom seen a horse except on television. His father grew corn and had a highly mechanical means of farming. His problem was one of concept development rather than of speaking pattern.

CHARACTERISTICS OF THE CULTURALLY DIFFERENT LEARNER

The children just discussed have been described by a diversity of terms. They have been labeled as "culturally disadvantaged," "culturally deprived," "economically disadvantaged," "economically deprived," "linguistically different," and "speakers of nonstandard English."

Each of these "labels" refers to the learners who have problems in school because their backgrounds differ from that to which most of the instructional materials and techniques have been traditionally geared. As more and more attention has been focused on this type of learner, the "label" that describes him or her has gone through changes that reflect the expanded knowledge on this topic. The gain in information has made educators realize that "culturally disadvantaged" and "culturally deprived" imply a negative connotation about the learner's background and that his or her culture should not be considered less good than other cultures—merely different. The terms "economically disadvantaged" and "economically deprived" are not always accurate, as some culturally different learners come from homes with more than adequate financial means. The terms "linguistically different" and "speaker of nonstandard English" cannot be applied to those children who speak standard English but whose environments differ sharply from the average American pupil's background. Children who were originally classified correctly as "speakers of nonstandard English" and who have since learned to speak in standard English are still products of the experiential background that produced the nonstandard speech pattern. To reflect these concerns, the term "culturally different" will be used in this text as an overall description of the group of learners described. The remainder of this section will be devoted to two major aspects that should be considered when teaching the "culturally different" child: (1) the speaking pattern and (2) the concept development.

THE SPEAKING PATTERN

"Standard English can be defined as the dialect accepted by the majority of the population because of the social and political positions of the people who speak it (Ruddell, 1974). Some variation in dialect, due to geographical differences, is present and is considered acceptable as "standard English." If the speech varies too much from the norm, it is considered "nonstandard."

One predominant characteristic of the culturally different learner is that his or her speech pattern is usually considered nonstandard. The nonstandard English speaker may be of two types: (1) a native speaker of English whose difficulties occur because he or she uses a nonstandard dialect or (2) a second language speaker of English. In either situation, some of the learners included in this description are black children in urban or rural ghetto areas; Chicano, Puerto Rican, and Cuban youngsters from Spanish-speaking homes; Chinese children from Chinese-speaking homes; Caucasian youngsters from the Appalachian area of the United States; speakers of pidgin English from Hawaii; and Indian and Eskimo children who speak a variant English or whose first language is not English.

Nonstandard speaking patterns do not indicate that the speaker lacks language competence; rather, it means that the speaker has learned his or her language in an environment that uses this language for communication purposes (Ruddell, 1974). Furthermore, just because a dialect is nonstandard does not mean that it follows an erratic phonological, grammatical, or syntactical pattern. The nonstandard dialects used by the group of learners designated as culturally different in this text contain consistent and regular deviations from standard English dialect.

A close look at these dialects as such can help the teacher to understand and recognize that variations from standard English do occur in a systematic manner. This knowledge can subsequently aid him or her in distinguishing between "errors" in speech and "consistent" language usage. Essentially, the relationship between language development and academic achievement may be looked at in terms of three basic dialectical differences: *phonological differences*, *grammatical and syntactical differences*, and *vocabulary differences.*

Phonological differences refer to differences in speech sounds within words. For example, Tommy usually said "hep" for "helped" and "god" for "guard" in the classroom situation discussed earlier in this chapter. If the words "helped" and "guard" were included in an IRI, it is likely that Tommy would pronounce them as he did in everyday speech. This could lead to the teacher's mistakenly interpreting these pronunciations as errors. Morever, in other oral reading situations, if Tommy were compelled to insert phonemes that were ignored in his phonological system, the results could be pronunciations that were unfamiliar and meaningless to him. These pronunciations could prove to be barriers to his progress in getting meaning from the printed page.

Grammatical and syntactical differences refer to inflectional changes, verb forms, verb auxiliaries, and the order in which words are placed in phrases and sentences. For example, Tommy, who spoke in a black dialect, might tell the teacher, "He be good" (change and omission of verb form); "He saw three dog" (omissions of *s* in plurals and possessives); and "He fill the bowl" (omission of *ed* ending). These grammatical divergencies are often substituted in the child's oral reading of the text and can help the teacher to identify the existing grammatical and syntactical differences.

Vocabulary differences refer to word meanings and connotations unique to a specific dialect. Tommy's black dialect would be filled with such differences. He might use such slang terms as "ace" for "close friend," "tote" for "carry," "gig" for "party," and "vamp" for "leave." In many cases, variations in the meanings of words between the language of the teacher and the language of the learner can inadvertently cause unexpected negative reactions. The most obvious example of this type of miscommunication occurs when the teacher calls the young blacks "boys," meaning male children. The young blacks react negatively, for to them the word "boy" is a derogatory term meaning a subservient person.

Differences in Speaking Problems between Second Dialect Speakers and Second Language Speakers of English

Both types of culturally different learners have difficulties due to language variations such as omission, substitution, or simplification of sound system components. However, the second dialect speaker can usually understand the standard English speaker, whereas the second language speaker is often unable to understand the standard English speaker. For certain foreign language speakers, the problem is unusually complex. For example, a Chinese student learning English must not only learn a different sound and intonation system, but also a different set of language structure. Additionally, the tone level has much more significance in distinguishing individual words in Chinese than it does in English (Ruddell, 1974).

Because the differences are more pronounced for the second language speaker, the teacher is usually aware of the problem that exists. The second dialect speaker's problems are not as pronounced and, therefore, are sometimes forgotten or neglected (Ruddell, 1974).

CONCEPT DEVELOPMENT

One frequent comment on the culturally different learner is that of a "lack of experiences from which language may be developed." This is a presumptuous statement, as these children obviously have backgrounds quite sufficient for them to cope with their home environments. This statement would have some validity if they were restated as follows: "The culturally different learner has a lack of language activities of the type ordinarily expected of the population toward which most traditional teaching materials are directed." In other words, the information that the culturally different child possesses may be quite remote from the information that the teacher, with his cultural background, possesses. Because the background of the culturally different learner may vary greatly from the one on which the usual school program is apparently based, he or she may encounter communication difficulties. For example, if a child has never seen a dishwasher or a television, any class discussion on these topics would make little sense to him or her. Likewise, if the child's parents have migrated to many places across the United States, he or she may have seen a great deal of this country but knows little about it because aspects that were not relevant to his or her parents were not pointed out to him or her. The child may know a great deal about weather conditions, farm equipment, and harvesting methods and nothing whatsoever about the great art centers in the area in which he or she formerly resided. If the teacher views the learner in terms of "the nature of his or her background," rather than in terms of his or her "lack of experiential background," some of the experience that the child already possesses can be utilized to reduce the number of "unknown quantities" confronting him or her when he or she is learning to read. The child who understands the content and the concepts of a story has a great advantage over the child who has no idea what message is intended by the story, even if his or her participation in the reading experience is that of listening to the teacher read the story.

Type of Motivation

To some children, learning to read is a low-priority item. If the child's parents do not read and do not value reading, the child may be unmotivated to learn how to read. In such an instance, the teacher's task is twofold; not only must the teacher teach the child to read, the teacher must also motivate the child to learn to read. The typical motivational devices that work with the standard speaker of English may or may not be motivating to the nonstandard speaker of English. For example, telling a child who comes from a noncompetitive society that he or she needs to learn his or her sight words so that he or she will have more on his or her list than anyone else is not particularly meaningful to that child. A better motivational device for this child might be to learn words relevant to his or her own heritage.

Allen (1971), who has had a great deal of success with teaching Indian students to read, stresses that the most essential step in making reading meaningful to students is to make it interesting. The student must be gradually brought to the point where he or she wants to read. Allen suggests methods such as class discussions, peer group writing, and reading materials written by and about Indians.

Differences in Concept Development Problems between Second Dialect Speakers and Second Language Speakers of English

Often the second language speaker of English comes from a background so different from that of the author of a story that the student would fail to understand the concept stressed by the author even if he or she could read all the words. For example, if a Navajo youngster read a story about a pet who had a humanlike personality, the reader would find that illogical, as to a Navajo pets would be distinctly different from humans (Evvard and Mitchell, 1966).

Another major difference between the second dialect speaker and the second language speaker relates to student motivation. Most second dialect speakers can comprehend standard forms when they hear them and can successfully communicate with those who use them. Therefore, they may not appreciate the advantage of learning another dialect. The second language speaker, however, must learn standard English to comprehend and communicate. He or she usually knows exactly why he or she needs to learn English (Ruddell, 1974).

EFFECT UPON READING INSTRUCTION

These two major characteristics of the culturally different learner—speaking pattern and concept development—provide major roadblocks in the child's learning process. While his or her language is adequate at home and in his or her social settings, it is less helpful to him or her at school because most reading material in the elementary schools tends to portray the life of "middle-class" boys and girls. These textbooks may use words and concepts foreign to a child with a nonmiddle-class background. In addition, the language of the textbook may seem stilted and the content cold and uninteresting to the culturally different child. There may also be a factor of emotional stress experienced by the child when he or she is deprived of the comfortable language familiar to him or her in his or her home environment and is exposed to the unfamiliar language pattern encountered in the school environment (Dallmann, 1974).

From an instructional standpoint, the teacher should be able to identify language deviations that interfere with the child's ability to comprehend oral and written language and to communicate with the teacher in spoken form. Recent research suggests that there is little comprehension interference for the second dialect child as a consequence of the differences in the sound and grammatical systems of nonstandard English, provided that there is sufficient context to resolve such meaning problems (Ruddell, 1974).

In designing instructional procedures for the second dialect speaker of English, it is probably best to focus initially on those differences in language and background that affect his or her ability to understand standard English and to stress reasons why he or she needs to learn some variations from his or her dialect, rather than to attempt to force him or her to change his or her entire speech pattern to standard English.

On the face of it, there is no reason why a person cannot learn to read standard English texts quite well in a nonstandard pronunciation. Eventually the school may wish to teach the child an alternative system of pronunciation. But the key to the situation in the early grades is for the teacher to know the system of homonyms of nonstandard English, and to know the grammatical differences that separate her own speech from that of the child. (Labov, 1967, p. 25)

Words that the standard English speaker considers homonyms are words such as "bore" and "boar," which are pronounced exactly alike but have entirely different meanings. However, for some nonstandard English speakers, the words "toll" and "toe" are pronounced in the same way and, for them, can also be considered as homonyms. Because of the meaning difficulties that may be caused by such pronunciation, the classroom teacher should be aware that homonyms of this type exist in nonstandard English.

A second language speaker of English must be taught enough English so that he or she can communicate with the teacher and the English-speaking children in his or her room. Vocabulary should be taught and practiced in a context that reinforces and clarifies the meaning. New patterns of language can then be introduced with vocabulary that is already known.

The instruction needed to teach children who have standard English as a second dialect is often similar to that used to teach children who speak English as a second language. Both groups of learners have similar needs in instructional techniques. Whether a child is a second dialect speaker or a second language speaker, the techniques of mimicry, repetition, and substitution can be effective tools in helping the students listen to model patterns, respond to the patterns by repeating them, and replace words in the pattern with words of their own choosing (Marquardt, Miller, and Hosman, 1970).

TECHNIQUES FOR TEACHING READING

Mrs. Fontaine knew that as a diagnostic-prescriptive teacher she should use a scope and sequence chart to help her plan instruction for the culturally different children. Therefore, she did two things: (1) She looked over her scope and sequence chart of skills to ascertain whether or not it contained anything that would be particularly helpful to the culturally different. (2) She researched the available literature to find characteristics of the speech and backgrounds of the culturally different learners. With these two resources she was able to concentrate on factors she thought might be most needed by these students.

She had discovered that, in black dialect, there was a general tendency to weaken the final consonant. Words such as *tool* and *boot* become *too* and *boo* (final *l* and *t* disappear) (Labov, 1967). Since there was no suitable objective on the scope and sequence chart, she added a skill objective called "locating final consonants." When Sally came in for her individual conference, Mrs. Fontaine looked in Sally's book for words ending in *l*, *t*, and *d* and asked her to read aloud the following sentences: "The men asked a large toll. A few who could not meet the demand went home." Sally was able to say the words in the sentences correctly, and ordinarily Mrs. Fontaine would have preassessed Sally as having mastered this skill. Since there was a known phonological variable, she asked Sally what the sentences meant. Sally was unable to interpret the sentences correctly. The context of the sentences gave her sufficient clues to understand words such as "meet" and "went," but she did not have enough information to interpret "toll." When Mrs. Fontaine explained what the word meant, Sally responded with the statement, "Oh, is that how you say that?" Therefore, Mrs. Fontaine knew that Sally understood the concepts, but her variant pronunciation had impeded meaning for her. Mrs. Fontaine then assigned Sally a series of lessons on locating final consonants.

The next child with whom Mrs. Fontaine had a conference was Roberto, a Chicano who was progressing well with his reading. His family spoke fluent English and he was a speaker of standard English. She decided to assess him on the skill "identifying inferences." The story that Roberto was reading concerned baseball. One of the characters in the story, in a fit of temper, threw the baseball down on the ground. When his coach ran out to see what he had done, the boy had been too angry to look at his coach and had stared at the ground. Mrs. Fontaine asked Roberto this inference question: "Why do you think the boy looked at the ground when his coach asked him a question?" Roberto replied, "Because he was the coach." Instead of assuming that Roberto did not know how to make inferences, she wondered what aspect of the story had made Roberto give her that answer. She remembered that in Roberto's culture humility in the presence of adults was a sign of respect and that Roberto would probably have looked at the ground if his own baseball coach had come over to speak to him. Mrs. Fontaine decided that Roberto might already know how to make inferences but was hindered in this case from making a correct inference because of his cultural background. Instead of giving him a set of lessons on making inferences, she discussed with him the intended inference in terms of differences in cultures. She then assigned him to a research project on cultural differences that exist between the Chicanos and the Anglo-Americans.

After preassessing all the students in her class, she decided to group George, Tommy, John, and Lorelei together for the skill instruction on "distinguishing between homonyms." This skill was not listed on her scope and sequence chart, but she felt that it was a primary problem for the culturally different and she added it as a major skill for development rather than subsuming it under the more general category of "gaining word meaning," which did appear on her existing chart.

INSTRUCTIONAL PRIORITIES

SKILLS SELECTION

To teach the culturally different child to read, Mrs. Fontaine did not want to change his or her entire language pattern. Rather, she focused on language and concept differences that would interfere with meaning. One reason for her adding the skill of homonyms to the chart was that she knew that a large number of homonyms occurred in nonstandard speech that differed from the homonyms she used in her own speech. For example, in one black dialect "log" is said "law," "wind" is said "wine," and "holes" is said "hose"; in one Spanish dialect "hat" is said "hot," "shut" is said "shot," "dug" is said "duck," "yes" is said "jes"; in one Chinese dialect "have" is said "half," "thank" is said "tank," "rib" is said "rip," and "she" is said "see" (Ruddell, 1974).

As a result, many speakers of nonstandard English encounter difficulty in recognizing words in their standard spellings (Labov, 1967). As long as the nonstandard use of language did not hinder Tommy's reading, Mrs. Fontaine left it alone. However, in the case of the words "strap" and "guard," it did make a difference. For example, if she had told Tommy that "The horse was helped by the scrap god (meaning that the horse was being assisted by deity who reigned over trash), Tommy would be likely to visualize a horse wearing a cushioned strap. Therefore, Tommy needed to learn these homonyms.

TEACHING STRATEGIES

Mrs. Fontaine knew that the children would make many more errors than the one upon which she was presently focusing, but she decided that their feelings of self-worth were more important than the speedy acquisition of a particular skill. She designed her instruction so that each child would have a maximum chance for success. A successful performance in an academic situation would strengthen a child's self-confidence. She would, therefore, concentrate on only one skill at a time. If a child made other errors that did not impede his or her understanding, she would ignore them at this time. When she called on individual children to respond, she would begin with those whom she felt had the greatest chance of success. In this way, a child like Lorelei, who spoke almost no English, would have an opportunity to hear words correctly pronounced many times before she would have to pronounce them.

The Aural-Oral Procedure

The aural-oral procedure is based on the premise that language was speech before it was reading or writing. In this method of learning standard English, emphasis would initially be placed on hearing and speaking the new form. The learners would only say what they had heard and understood and read what they had said. Therefore, Mrs. Fontaine's first task in teaching them standard English was to see that the children had aural-oral control of the aspects of standard English material that they would be expected to read in the lesson being taught to them.

The group contained both second dialect speakers and second language speakers, but her basic approach was the same with all members of the group. At step 1 she held up a concrete object representative of the word or words being taught; at step 2 she pointed to the written word and pronounced it for them; at step 3 she asked the group to pronounce the words in a response-type situation; at step 4 individuals pronounced the word in a response-type situation; at step 5 the group members pronounced the words to each other in a response-type situation (Marquardt et al., 1970).

Her procedure for one day in class is as follows.

Step 1: Mrs. Fontaine held up a picture of a horse wearing a bridle containing a strap guard.

Step 2: She pointed to the sentence strip containing the words "The horse was helped by the strap guard" and then pronounced each word in her normal speaking pattern. She did not overenunciate or draw out sounds, as she wanted to provide them with a speech pattern that was representative of standard English.

Step 3: She asked the children a question that required them to use the words on the sentence strip to answer. She said, "The horse was helped by what kind of guard?" The children responded in unison with, "The horse was helped by a strap guard." (Note that "strap" was chosen for focus as it is a homonym often pronounced as scrap, a word with an entirely different meaning.)

Step 4: She asked an individual child a question that required that he use the words on the sentence strip in meaningful context. In this case she asked George, "What kind of guard was the horse helped by?" he responded, "The horse was helped by the strap guard." Each youngster in turn responded to the same question. Tommy responded; he said "da" for "the" and "scrap" for "strap." Mrs. Fontaine was very very careful in correcting Tommy's errors. She said, "Do you know what the word 'scrap' means? Do you know why we need to know the difference between how we say both words? Tommy, can you say 'strap' with the sound of 'stra' as in 'straggle'?" There was a short exchange when they said "strap" back and forth to each other. (Note that she ignored "da" as it was not a homonym and did not impede meaning.)

Step 5: Mrs. Fontaine instructed the group members to ask each other questions about the sentence. George asked Tommy, "What kind of guard was the horse helped by?" Tommy responded by reading the sentence. In turn, Tommy asked John the same question. The procedure continued until each child had an opportunity to respond as well as to ask another child to respond.

Since Tommy had understood how to pronounce the homonyms as soon as he had been corrected by the teacher, she made him group leader for the rest of the lesson. There were three more sentences, each containing the homonyms "strap" and "guard," extending the topic of horse equipment. Each sentence represented a concrete situation and was accompanied by a picture representative of its meaning. In addition, Mrs. Fontaine had read each sentence into the tape recorder and left it with the group so that they could make certain their pronunciation was correct.

Mrs. Fontaine used other similar types of drills to teach her pupils standard English. Sometimes her strategies included formal lessons like the one just discussed; other times her lessons were much less structured. Basically she felt that the more experience these children had with standard oral English, the more they would be able to build a bond of common vocabulary.

Grouping the Children by Reading Tasks

Mrs. Fontaine liked to use group work in her individualized program. The children enjoyed group work and had been members of many other groups during the year. In addition, each had been, at various times, in the "Living Language Research Group." This was actually a standing committee with rotating membership that researched and compared different regional dialects that existed in the United States. She had encouraged the formation of such a group early in the school year under the premise that all youngsters should know that a variety of dialects exists and that some are more advantageous than others in certain social and economic situations. In this manner the entire class became aware of language differences and were very much interested in each variety of dialect. One of their research activites had included making a scrapbook of the Appalachian area of the United States. Mrs. Fontaine had located many magazine articles included a photographic essay done by *National Geographic.* George served as resource person and pointed out the mountain range near his previous home. In addition, several members of the class had gone with George to interview his parents so that the listener might hear "real Appalachian speech" while flipping through the scrapbook the group had constructed to illustrate the terrain of the area.

When Roberto had been in the group, he encouraged the other members to study the particular dialects found among Spanish-speaking Americans in his community. One of the other members of the group, Phil, was not a speaker of nonstandard English, but he was a real geography buff. At his suggestion, the group decided to compare some of the traditions common to the Spanish-speaking Americans in various parts of the southwestern United States. They made a scrapbook of customs common to all Spanish-speaking Americans. It contained pictures clipped from magazines and newspapers as well as brochures gathered from the travel agencies on various cities in the Southwest, which contained a large number of Spanish-speaking Americans. Roberto, a Chicano who did not live in the Chicano neighborhood near the school, had gone with the group that had walked through that neighborhood taking appropriate photos. Roberto helped to interview some of the people and was made aware of many aspects of his own Chicano culture that were previously unknown to him.

From time to time the research group reported on their projects to the rest of the class. Mrs. Fontaine made certain that they not only discussed the variety of dialects in the United States but also the appropriateness of dialect versus standard English to place, time, and people involved. One of the groups had focused on "appropriateness" as a topic and had presented their topic in a "quiz show" format. They cut out figures and placed three on each child's desk. One figure represented the teacher, one a close friend, and the third an employer at a job interview. Members of the research group would say sentences using variations of dialects. Then the pupils chose the figure who spoke, closed their eyes, and held up the chosen figure. Upon a given signal, the students would open their eyes. Each child who was holding up the correct figure was given a point. If a pupil had chosen a figure other than the one intended, he or she was given a chance to explain his or her choice. If the child gave an explanation that satisfied the rest of the class, the child was also awarded a point. At the end of the game, the child with the most points was permitted to keep all three figures, while the others were allowed to keep the one of their choice.

In essence, Mrs. Fontaine was concerned that the children understood that varieties of language did exist and that each was acceptable in the proper situation. She also knew that the best way to teach the children how to speak and read standard English was to develop their listening and articulation skills. The five-step group procedure utilized with Tommy, George, Lorelei, and John, as outlined, as well as the research group served as drills on the use and appropriateness of language.

TECHNIQUE FOR FACILITATING INSTRUCTION

The use of teacher substitutes, discussed more thoroughly in Chapter 12, is an effective way for the classroom teacher to give individualized help to those students who need it. The use of the tape recorder to give the speaker of nonstandard English an immediate check on his or her pronunciation is an obviously helpful tool. The use of peer tutors can prove effective with a second language speaker of English. Frequently one of the class members is bilingual and can be of invaluable assistance.

The same principles discussed in Chapter 12 for helping peers learn to help each other should be followed when pairing pupils for bilingual work. The teacher can often place a non-English-speaking student in the role of "helper" by asking him or her to teach other children some words in his or her language and by assigning him or her tasks that require little verbal exchange. Some of these assignments are checking answers to multiplication problems, cutting pictures from magazines for a group bulletin board, drawing pictures to illustrate a dictionary used to teach the standard English speaker foreign words, growing plants for science class, or making models and puppets to illustrate a story.

The cross-age tutoring mentioned in Chapter 12 can prove beneficial to both the older and the younger culturally different child. The younger child gets specific help in learning to read; the older child gains a sense of worth that he or she may not have had before because of academic failures due to his or her cultural background. Furthermore, in teaching another child that it is important to know that the word "Carol" has an "r" sound, the tutor may even convince himself or herself of the worth of learning individual sounds.

Other resource people useful to the classroom teacher are volunteer workers such as high school students, parents, and senior citizens who want to become involved in community work. Some schools have available teacher aides, usually adults, college students, and high school students, who are paid minimum amounts to assist the teacher.

TEACHING THE CULTURALLY DIFFERENT LEARNER THROUGH THE DIFFERENT APPROACHES TO TEACHING READING

USING THE BASAL READER APPROACH

In the past, the culturally different have been treated in the basal reader, as well as literature in general, in several different ways. Often, the minority character just didn't exist. At other times he or she was pictured as a simple, rugged person who lived close to nature, a buffoon, a menial worker, or as the representative of a stereotyped cultural belief. More recently, basal readers have attempted to change their content to include more direct involvement of believable minority characters. For example, inner-city life, with its family hardship, racial conflict, and discrimination are all shown in a manner devoid of moralizing.

Miss Daisy was using a basal reader approach to the teaching of reading to her first graders. When her class entered in September, she knew that about one fourth of the pupils could be categorized as "culturally different." She investigated the commercially written materials to ascertain what was available for her to teach her children. Several companies had published "dialect" readers that contained words in the dialect of the speaker under the premise that the transition to traditional textbook materials could be more gradual for the beginning reader. Her reaction was negative, as she felt that these readers would perpetuate dialectical differences and reinforce language patterns that might otherwise be neutralized through time and exposure. Furthermore, she felt that the readers did not actually reflect the pronunciations in dialect used by the children in her class. Her own basal reader series had books available written in standard English, but the content focused upon the minority child. She looked through this material as well as material available from other basal reader companies. Since she was not a member of a minority group, Miss Daisy decided to try out some of this multiethnic material on her culturally different learners. As is typical of the basal reader approach, this material was accompanied by a teacher's guide, a student storybook, and a student workbook. She felt that this structure would be most helpful to her in relating to the needs of the children, as she herself felt that she didn't really know much about the culturally different.

On the other hand, Mr. Rough, also not a member of a minority group, preferred to use the new version of the same basal reader he had always used. He felt that his fourth graders could relate well to the characters, as there were children of all cultural backgrounds in the new series. Furthermore, Mr. Rough felt that he could teach the culturally different child by using any basal reader program, but by modifying the existing program a bit. He would use the same five-step basal reader lesson plan, but his supplementary and extension activities would encourage the children to focus in upon cultural and language differences. He felt that he could teach the children to respect each other's dialect, to recognize that differences did exist between dialects, and to know the reasons why the children were being asked to use a different language pattern.

Mr. Rough knew that, with second dialect speakers of English, the differences in pronunciations among American dialects seldom impeded communication. The mass media and mass transit promoted uniformity and understanding in even the most out-of-the-way places. In other words, as long as the dialect did not interfere with communication, Mr. Rough ignored it. Because many of his extension activities concerned language and dialectical differences, Mr. Rough fostered a free atmosphere in which the children became vitally interested in how the other children would pronounce the same word.

In a like manner, Mr. Rough extended and adapted all basal reader stories to suit the needs of each type of learner. For example, one of the basal reader stories that the children were reading had to do with a family that was preparing to move to another part of the United States. Although the series presented a variety of different cultures in its stories, the family focused upon happened to be a white middle-class one. Mr. Rough knew that some of the children in his class had never been outside the immediate neighborhood in their lives. The concept of moving to another geographic part of the country was understandable, but not really relevant to them. Therefore, his extension activities concentrated on what he felt was a "universal concept" not foreign to their needs and interests—that of friendship. The children were involved with tasks that centered around the question "If I moved, which people would I most want to take with me and why?"

USING THE LANGUAGE EXPERIENCE APPROACH

A heavy reliance upon the language experience method is often suggested for the teacher of the culturally different. Since this approach uses child-dictated or child-written experiences as the major instructional tool for reading instruction, the pupil automatically uses the language with which he or she is familiar rather than a textbook language that may be alien to him or her. However, culturally different children should be encouraged not only to write about experiences already known to them in their own culture, but also about new experiences that take place under the guidance of their classroom teacher. In this manner, the background becomes a standard one, and the communication barrier breaks down. The teacher can take the children to the zoo, for walks around the school, or just bring in to the classroom objects so that the children can "experience" something in common with the teacher that they can write down and later read about.

For example, Mr. Weather brought in a top for his second grade class. He showed them how it worked and then asked them to spin themselves just like the top. As a result of the experience, the following story was written together:

Our Top

This is our top.
It is red and white.
It spins.
We can spin like a top.

While the story was being written together, Mr. Weather was aware of two things about the culturally different children: (1) their concept development would not hinder their learning, as they were participating in a common experience to which they could relate—that of being a top—and (2) they were seeing their dialect written in standard English. Therefore, when one of the children read a sentence back to Mr. Weather and said "It spin," the teacher knew that the child understood what the top did but was merely automatically translating the idea into his own dialect. Because Mr. Weather was sure that the boy understood the word, he made no effort to correct him. Instead, he gave him credit for the correct reading, and then continued on to the next line.

Another activity that Mr. Weather liked to use with all children, including the culturally different, was that of asking each child to write an illustrated story about his or her life. Each child, regardless of his or her background, seemed to know a lot about himself or herself and liked to tell that information. One day Mr. Weather brought in his Polaroid camera and took pictures of each child. Some of the children were from economically impoverished backgrounds and had never seen a photograph of themselves before. As soon as he took each child's picture, Mr. Weather would sit down with each and help him or her dictate the story of his or her life. While this was being done, Mr. Weather made no attempt to correct the English or transform it into standard format. After all the stories were written and illustrated, they were placed on the bulletin board for all to read. This stimulated an outgrowth of activity, where the children wanted to write biographies of all their friends and relatives. Mr. Weather followed the same procedure as when writing the autobiographies. He wrote down the story each child dictated without changing it into standard English. One of the boys wrote a story about his sister. When Mr. Weather copied the story for him, he did not change the content or the wording, but he did put the story into traditional spelling. He changed words such as "wanna" to "want to," "Ah" to "I," and "on" to "don't." In other words he changed the phonological variables that could not be translated into traditional spelling. He had reviewed the literature and found no authority suggesting that nonstandard spellings be used. It was quite obvious to him that, were they used, confusion in learning sight words and word attack skills would result (Heilman, 1972).

Essentially, he was most interested in making reading meaningful to the culturally different by enabling them to see that reading was really just talk written down. He wanted the children to feel as comfortable as possible before making the transition to traditional English. He, therefore, tried to accept each child and his or her language as it existed at present and only changed what he had to so to retain traditional spellings. He knew that eventually the child would have to learn to cope with standard English to make progress in the typical school curriculum. He decided that, as soon as the child began to feel comfortable with him, he would begin to transcribe the experience stories into traditional English format by making immediate corrections in grammatical structures and other divergencies.

USING THE INDIVIDUALIZED READING APPROACH

This approach has proved quite useful with speakers of nonstandard English. As it is based on the self-selection of materials, and self-paced instruction, many materials designed to be of special interest to the culturally different child can be made available to that child. Reading material of this nature can be gleaned from basal readers, supplementary readers, experience stories, content area books, magazines, newspapers, or almost anything in print. After the children read the material by themselves, they meet with their teacher about once a week to discuss the material and read it aloud (see Chapter 7). Both child and teacher keep track of the reading; the teacher should have a system for diagnosing the word recognition and comprehension skills that takes the child's language and cultural background into consideration. Then the teacher should prescribe instruction according to those needs at the end of each conference.

Mr. Poindexter found that his sixth grade culturally different youngsters liked to read books and magazines that focused upon their cultural background. Carol, one of the more mature girls, had already decided she wanted to be a model. Therefore, all her spare time was spent in locating fashion magazines and books on make-up and drama. In the individual conferences, Carol simply read her magazines to Mr. Poindexter and answered all word recognition, comprehension, and study skills questions he asked through the medium of the magazine. He used the scope of skills found in Chapter 15 of this text. He sequenced the skills in much the same order as they are presented in that chapter under the rationale that they seem to progress from simple to more complex. When preassessing the skill "naming consonant blends and digraphs" (see Chapter 2, skill 5), he gave Carol the following words out of her *Ebony* magazine.

> The past performance of the dressmakers has meant that women must learn to mend at home.

Since he was interested in consonant blends and digraphs, he determined that, if she could pronounce all three of the final consonant blends in the underlined words correctly, she knew the skill. Carol pronounced *past* as *pass*, *meant* as *men*, and *mend* as *men*. Mr. Poindexter knew that a tendency to simplify consonant clusters at the ends of words was characteristic of a black dialect, so he did not immediately assume that she did not know the skill (Labov, 1967). He asked her the meaning of the sentence. She paraphrased it correctly, so he determined that she understood the meaning of the underlined words. Furthermore, although she pronounced "meant" and "mend" alike, she obviously recognized them as two different words when she saw them in print or heard them in standard form. Therefore, Mr. Poindexter determined that she had passed the preassessment on that skill and proceeded to preassess her on another.

The Second Language Speaker Who Reads Another Language

One of the boys in Mr. Poindexter's class had recently arrived from Mexico. His knowledge of English was minimal. Additionally, Mr. Poindexter was not certain whether he could read in Spanish. He knew that this could make a great deal of difference in terms of Antonio's reading instruction. If he knew how to read in Spanish, Antonio would be familiar with the Roman alphabet as well as with the concept of translating abstract written symbols into their auditory representations. His instruction in written English could begin as a translation of Spanish to English rather than having to first learn that written words are only a symbolic representation of the spoken language. As Mr. Poindexter had no material written in Spanish, he was not certain how he could determine whether or not Antonio could read in Spanish. It occurred to him, however, that if Antonio could write, he could read. Through much body language he finally was able to communicate to Antonio what he wanted him to do. At that point, Antonio picked up the pencil and wrote a few words in Spanish.

Once Mr. Poindexter determined that Antonio was fluent in written Spanish, he decided that he would try to use the same scope and sequence chart he had been using with the rest of the children. Since Antonio knew no English, he would start at the beginning reader level, so he looked at the chart to see if there were any skills that he could teach to the boy. The first skill he saw that he felt would be useful to Antonio was that of using pictures clues (see Chapter 3, skill 2). He located pictures of an ax, a tree, and a Mexican boy and labeled them in English "ax," "tree," and "Antonio." He pointed to each word and motioned to Antonio to pronounce it. Antonio was able to say his name but was unable to pronounce the other two words. From his reaction Mr. Poindexter knew that Antonio knew how to use picture clues and tried to communicate to him how each picture was related to the written word. It finally struck Mr. Poindexter that the picture of the tree might not mean "tree" but "branches" and the picture of the "ax" might not mean "ax" but "tool" to Antonio. Therefore, since he knew Antonio could read in Spanish, he bought an English-Spanish dictionary and looked up the words. As soon as Antonio saw the Spanish equivalent, his eyes lit up and he nodded his head. When he felt that Antonio understood the meaning of the English words, Mr. Poindexter gathered pictures of more objects that he felt would be familiar to Antonio. To assure himself that he and Antonio were always talking about the same object, Mr. Poindexter wrote the Spanish equivalent of the English word on the back of the picture. He then recorded each word onto a tape recorder and coordinated the tape with the pictures.

Antonio was to listen to the English pronunciation, look at the word and accompanying picture, pronounce it in English, then write down the word in English.

Another skill that Mr. Poindexter decided he could teach Antonio was the use of morphonic analysis. He had discovered that there were many words in Spanish similar to words in English. For example, Antonio easily learned the word "gallop" because it looked very much like the Spanish word he knew for "running." Through the use of concrete objects, pictures, and structural analysis, Antonio soon began to gather an English vocabulary of words that he recognized readily. Mr. Poindexter used these as base words for extending Antonio's word attack skills to more unfamiliar English words. In the meantime, Mr. Poindexter had located several books and magazines on a beginning reader level that Antonio could use as reading material. Mr. Poindexter also asked Antonio to teach the rest of the class Spanish. So every week when the book sharing went on between group members, Antonio would hold up his pictures and tell the class the Spanish word for the picture. This technique encouraged sharing, and the rest of the class members were constantly bringing pictures to Antonio so that he could tell them the Spanish words for them. They used the English-to-Spanish dictionary to make certain the word was spelled correctly and, more important, that they were both speaking of the same word.

When Mr. Poindexter preassessed Antonio on the naming of consonant blends and digraphs, he anticipated that he might have trouble with the *ch* sound. It was a peculiarity of the American Spanish speaker of English to pronounce the *ch* sound in words such as *chicken, chap,* and *chalk* like the *sh* sound of *ch* in *champagne.* When Antonio read the sentence "The pupil took the chest," he pronounced the *ch* like the *sh* sound for *ch* in *champagne.* When Mr. Poindexter asked him to explain the sentence, Antonio was unable to do so because it didn't sound like any word he had ever heard any English speaker pronounce. However, when Mr. Poindexter read the sentence to Antonio, the boy was able to tell him the meaning of the sentence. Mr. Poindexter determined that in this case the digraph sound of *ch* was interfering with his comprehension, and he therefore needed work in this digraph. He asked him to pronounce the name of a well-known local restaurant. When Antonio said "Chico's" with the *ch* sound of *child,* he understood what had been wrong with his pronunciation of the word *chest.* Mr. Poindexter located several books at the first grade level, where Antonio was now reading, and let him choose the material that most appealed to him. Then he designed instruction on this *ch* sound around the material selected by the child.

Other activities that Mr. Poindexter had Antonio do were look through magazines and catalogues for particular pictures that he would cut out and place on index cards. Then Mr. Poindexter or another "student helper" would assist Antonio in writing the English word on the index card and, in some cases, pronounce the word for him into a tape recorder. Often, Mr. Poindexter asked him to locate pictures representing particular categories, as he felt that a logical organization would help Antonio to learn more quickly. As such, Antonio had a file of pictures that belonged to the following categories: animals, transportation, tools, clothes, food, seasons of the year, and occupations.

It is important to note at this point that, if Antonio had not been able to read in Spanish, Mr. Poindexter would have had to change his procedure. There is currently much controversy about whether a second speaker of English should be taught to read in his or her own language before being taught to read in English. Since one speaks before he reads and writes, some authorities feel that the same sequence should be followed in learning a second language. In fact some educators firmly believe that a language can't be read until it can be spoken and understood orally. Finocchiari (1968) states that learners should be able to speak about a topic with reasonable fluency before they are permitted to look at written material about it.

On the other hand, Doman (1971), in *Teaching Your Baby to Read*, states that children can learn to read earlier than they learn to speak. Likewise, other authorities feel that reading instruction in a second language can speed up the mastery of that language (Hughes, 1971). Although it would undoubtedly reduce the number of unknowns to have the child learn to read his or her own language first, the adversaries of this position oppose it for several reasons: (1) They feel that if the child lives in this country the child needs to learn English. They fear that by teaching the child to read first in his or her own language, the child may never progress to the state where he or she ever learns to read in English. (2) They know that there are very few bilingual teachers available who can teach the child to read first in his or her own language and then in English.

In Mr. Poindexter's case, as in the case of many middle-class, monolingual teachers, he had no choice in deciding his strategies for teaching Antonio. Since he could not speak Spanish, he either had to ignore Antonio completely, or send him to a "special bilingual class," or provide him with some sort of "teacher substitute" such as programmed audio material, that could teach Antonio how to read in Spanish. However, there were many things that Mr. Poindexter could do to teach Antonio, though he did not speak his language. He could have been quite helpful to Antonio by adapting the same strategy of matching pictures, English words, and audio-recorded renditions of the English words as mentioned. Since Antonio could understand spoken Spanish, Mr. Poindexter could have located another bilingual child or adult to pronounce the Spanish equivalent of the English word on to the tape recording. Mr. Poindexter would not have to show Antonio the Spanish word in written form but would have to explain on the audiotape in Spanish what the English word and its accompanying picture meant. In this manner, the child would be learning to speak English and read it simultaneously.

However, Mr. Poindexter would have to be aware of the fact that Antonio might be confused when he encountered English and was suddenly given twelve new vowel sounds, a handful of consonants he had never been taught to pronounce, new sentence structures, and told that some phonemes of Spanish could not be transferred to English. To help him identify such differences between the languages, Mr. Poindexter would be wise to refer to a resource book that delineates all the differences and then try to adapt them to his scope and sequence of reading charts. Even though most scope and sequence of reading charts that he would use would have been originally intended for the speaker of standard English, they do provide a systematic approach to teaching any sound-symbol relationship. In the case of Antonio, Mr. Poindexter would identify some of the variations between Spanish and English and then place them on his chart. For example, the Spanish speaker may substitute these sounds in his language: /v/ vest; /th/ this; /z/ zoo; /sh/ ship; /j/ jump. Therefore, Antonio might say "vest" like "best"; "this" like "dis"; "zoo" like "sue"; "ship" like "sip" and "jump" as "yump." These differences could be added to a scope and sequence chart as a subcategory of naming consonant sounds. By writing this down, the teacher is assured of a systematic approach to providing instruction for the culturally different learner (Zintz, 1970).

Furthermore, if the child had been unable to read in any language, the child, like readiness readers of any language, would first have to be shown that there was a sound-symbol relationship between the spoken language and its written equivalent. In such cases, the teacher would have to look at the skills on any readiness level scope and sequence chart and adapt the teaching procedures for the child who could not speak English. For example, to teach the readiness skill of "using left-to-right progression," Mr. Poindexter could have learned the Spanish equivalent of the words first, second, third, fourth, and fifth in a matter of minutes. Then he could proceed to show Antonio a page with five pictures and ask him to determine which comes "primero, segundo, tercero, cuarto, quinto."

Likewise, the procedures for teaching the other readiness skills could be adapted for the Spanish-speaking child. As American English is really a mixture of many different languages, one of the easiest ways for Mr. Poindexter to do this would be to look for words and sounds in English that are similar in Spanish. For example, the words *radio*, *gala*, and *telefono* mean the same in both Spanish and English and are similar enough in sound to be understood by speakers of either language. In this manner Antonio would be learning English words and sounds that would not be foreign to him, and Mr. Poindexter would be using what knowledge he possessed of the language as a common basis for communication. For example in teaching "recognizing letter sound," the child is supposed to learn to match pictures with the appropriate beginning consonants. Mr. Poindexter should first check his references to identify consonants that are similar in Spanish and in English. Then he could simplify and obtain a list of nouns that are similar in Spanish and in English and match the picture of a "taco" with the consonant "t," "California" with the consonant "c," and so forth.

In a like manner, most of the readiness and beginning level skills can be adapted and taught by a monolingual classroom teacher. This process can enable the child to build up a basic sight vocabulary that the child can then use in conjunction with the other word recognition skills for learning more words.

THE EXCEPTIONAL CHILD

Mrs. Fontaine considered the culturally different child to be a "diverse" learner because she felt that this type youngster required distinctive variations in the instructional process from the "average" child. Other children whom she placed in the "diverse" category included five children in her class whom the school had designated as "exceptional." Anita Rodriquez was a brilliant child who could always find something to do when she finished her assigned work. Fred Gaines was equally as intelligent but tended to be a discipline problem if not given enough challenging assignments. Sue Henderson was a "slow learner" and needed much repetition on a skill to learn it. Paul Snider was "emotionally disturbed" and frequently caused chaos in the classroom for no apparent reason. Joe Poluski was considered "legally blind" and could only read with the help of an enormously powerful magnifying glass. Characteristics of these two types of exceptional children—that is, "gifted," such as Anita and Fred, and "handicapped" such as Sue, Paul, and Joe—will be discussed briefly in the following paragraphs.

CHARACTERISTICS OF THE HANDICAPPED CHILD

The three kinds of handicapped children whom the regular classroom teacher is most likely to encounter are (1) the educable mentally retarded, (2) the emotionally disturbed, and (3) the learning disabled (Ransom, 1978).

The *educable mentally retarded* is usually defined in terms of quantifiable mental abilities such as IQ. In general, children with an IQ of between 50 and 75 are labeled as "educable mentally retarded," between 75 and 90 as "slow learner," and between 90 and 115 as "average." In most school situations, children whose IQ scores are less than 75 are considered to be "retarded." However, educable mentally retarded children vary widely in intellectual, educational, social, physical, and emotional characteristics, and often children whose IQ scores place them within the retarded range can learn in school without any special help (Ransom, 1978).

The *emotionally disturbed* child may be an extremely aggressive child who lacks self-control or a completely withdrawn child who causes no trouble but is unable to participate in class activities. Diagnosis of emotional disturbance is usually left to the mental health professional, although many referrals to counselors originate with the classroom teacher. A list of behaviors that indicate potential problems are (1) *indications of low self-concept* (e.g., speaks disparagingly of self, has extremely negative reactions to minor failures), (2) *disturbed relations with peers* (e.g., has no close friends, is avoided by peers in games and activities), (3) *inappropriate relationships with teachers, parents, and other authority figures* (e.g., refuses reasonable requests, steals, lies), (4) *other signs of social-emotional problems* (e.g., is easily distracted, makes meaningless or "animal" noises, has violent outbursts of emotions) (Wallace and Kaufman, 1973).

The child who is *learning disabled* may be so for a variety of reasons. Although there are many disabilities, the most commonly seen by the average classroom teacher are visual, auditory, speech, and coordination.

Another disability that should be noted, because poor readers are too often mislabeled with this term, is "dyslexia." The Research Group on Developmental Dyslexia of the World Federation of Neurology in 1968 recommended two definitions of the term: (1) *dyslexia*, "a disorder in children who, despite conventional classroom experience, fail to attain the language skills of reading, writing, and spelling commensurate with their abilities" and (2) *specific developmental dyslexia*, "a disorder manifested by difficulty in learning to read despite conventional instruction, adequate intelligence, and socio-cultural opportunity. It is dependent upon cognitive disabilities which are frequently of constitutional origin" (Critchley, 1970, in Harris and Sipay, 1979, pp. 435-436).

Both definitions suggest a neurological inability to read "despite conventional" classroom instruction. Misconceptions of the term "specific developmental dyslexia" and inadequacy of available diagnostic tools and procedures yield spuriously high estimates of its incidence, which are believed to be approximately 2 per cent of the normal child population (Eichenwald, 1967, esp. p. 1098). Since such a small percentage of the population can be assumed to be dyslexic, the classroom teacher should carefully analyze the adequacy of a child's instructional experiences and the expertise of those who labeled him or her as dyslexic before accepting the child as such (Money, 1962, esp. p. 1101).

The Classroom Teacher and the "Handicapped" Child

Until quite recently, many handicapped children were not in the regular classroom. However, in 1975, the federal government mandated the inclusion of "special" children in the regular classroom with the enacting of PL 94-142, the Education for All Handicapped Children Act. This law provides special funds for the education of exceptional children. A major provision of this act is that handicapped children be placed in a "least restrictive environment." This least restrictive environment has, in many cases, been interpreted to be the regular classroom. Placement of students in this environment has been referred to as "mainstreaming." As a result many children who were segregated in the past are being placed in the regular classroom, and this puts the responsibility upon the classroom teacher to provide reading instruction for the handicapped child (Rupley and Blair, 1979.)

Mangieri and Readence (1977) suggest that the teaching of reading will be greatly affected by mainstreaming and recommend that teachers place increased emphasis upon (1) diagnostic-prescriptive reading, (2) heterogeneous grouping plans, (3) differentiated and interdisciplinary staffing, (4) trained paraprofessionals, (5) positive reading self-concepts, and (6) recreational reading (Rupley and Blair, 1979).

CHARACTERISTICS OF GIFTED CHILDREN

The earliest definition of gifted children was in terms of IQ derived from an intelligence test. More recently, the advisory panel to the U.S. Commissioner of Education established a broader definition for the purpose of establishing federal aid to such educational programs. The federal government suggests six general kinds of giftedness: (1) general intellectual aptitude, (2) specific academic aptitude, (3) creative or productive thinking, (4) leadership ability,

(5) visual and performing arts, and (6) psychomotor ability (*Education of the Gifted and Talented*, 1972).

More than one type of giftedness may be found in a child, and giftedness in any one of these areas does not necessarily mean that the child is "gifted" in reading. Gifted in reading refers to those children who, according to achievement tests and other identification measures, seem to be intellectually and/or academically gifted and who read with comprehension at an advanced level (Trezise, 1978).

A comparison of gifted and creative children with other children of their same age shows that gifted children tend to have a longer attention span, a persistent curiosity, a desire to learn rapidly, a good memory, an awareness and appreciation of people and things, a wide range of interests, and the ability to solve many of the problems confronting society (Labuda, 1974).

The Classroom Teacher and the Gifted Child

Although the gifted child is not ordinarily thought of as a "problem" child, these children need to be kept challenged and motivated. Although high-IQ children are typically found to be well-adjusted socially and get along well with their peers, creative pupils have been found to be less well-adjusted and to have difficulties in peer relationships. Torrence (1971) states

> Many of the highly creative individuals are disturbing elements in classroom groups in elementary schools. The problem of teachers and guidance workers resolves itself into one of helping highly creative individuals maintain those characteristics which seem essential to the development of creative talent and, at the same time, helping them to acquire skills for avoiding, or reducing to a tolerable level, the peer sanctions.

Similarly, the intellectually gifted child may experience difficulties because of inappropriate instruction. In some cases, he or she may become an underachiever in reading, which goes unnoticed because, although reading far below his or her ability, the child does read on grade level. In other cases, the intellectually gifted child may become restless and disruptive in class or may withdraw into fantasy to escape boredom (Witty, 1971).

Labuda (1974) suggests that the reading needs of the gifted and the creative differ in many respects from those of other groups. The gifted child needs to be taught to think and act in a creative manner. Strict regimentation is not conducive to creative thinking and reading. The child must be encouraged to express himself or herself freely and not feel restrained because of nonconformity or divergent thinking. This can best be accomplished in a classroom atmosphere that has the freedom to permit the child to accomplish his or her learning task at his or her own level and rate. The classroom teacher needs to help the gifted and creative child advance at his or her own rate. In addition, these children need extra enrichment activities that carry them beyond the scope of the normal classroom experience.

Both the handicapped and the gifted child need "special" attention by the classroom teacher. The slow and/or mentally retarded child needs a very slow learning pace with much repetition of instruction, In some cases, the teacher will not be able to move to higher-level thinking skills but, rather, should emphasize understanding of relatively simple material. As much of the material as possible should be related to real-life situations (Ransom, 1978).

Comprehensive reading programs seldom take into account the needs of the gifted. Simply creating a "top" group and then using basically the same kind of reading instruction is not an adequate response to the needs of the gifted (Trezise, 1978). Gifted children need creative reading assignments. They should be asked to do reading tasks in which they are to originate, evaluate, and apply new ideas. Divergent and varied responses, rather than one "right" answer, should be encouraged (Torrence, 1965; Russell, 1956; Jarolimek, 1962).

The integration of the "diverse" learner into the regular classroom demands both instructional and organizational accommodations in the reading program. The mainstreaming of the handicapped and providing for the gifted may add other dimensions to the regular classroom organization and management system, but they do not change the basic nature of the task.

The diagnostic-prescriptive technique can be used to individualize instruction for both the handicapped and the gifted. In some cases, the same materials used with the "average" child may be appropriate for the handicapped child. In other cases, the lessons need adaptation or must be designed specifically with a particular child's handicap in mind. For example, the visually handicapped child would require a much different type of lesson than would the mentally retarded child. Hence, when a classroom teacher has a handicapped child in his or her classroom, he or she should consult appropriate resources and design lessons that are most conducive to the learning of that specific child's needs.

Gifted children are usually ready for certain kinds and levels of instruction earlier than the average child and typically are able to move more rapidly through materials. Hence the classroom teacher must design lessons to accommodate this advanced timing and pacing. In addition, because of their cognitive abilities and frequent interest in ideas, theories, and the whole realm of the abstract, intellectually gifted children are likely to want to go deeper into ideas and talk longer and in great depth about what they are learning (Trezise, 1978). Hence response to what is presented in class may be so different from the typical response that the whole learning situation may have to be restructured to appropriately accommodate these responses (Trezise, 1978). The encouragement of originality, creativity, curiosity, and fluency in solving problems should be a primary objective in teaching the gifted child (Swiss, 1976).

For example, Mrs. Fontaine determined that Sue, who was a "slow learner," Fred, who was "intellectually gifted," and Joe, who was "visually handicapped," all needed help in learning to take notes. Sue was given very concrete lessons (e.g., she was asked to construct a grocery list). Fred's lessons encouraged creativity (e.g., he was asked to take notes from his science textbook from three different points of view—one as a teacher who wanted to purchase a science text, one as an author looking for ideas for a textbook of his own that he wanted to write, and one as a gatherer of material for a debate on a particular topic). Joe's lessons were constructed so that his poor eyesight would not prevent him from completing them (e.g., one lesson was written in huge type so that he could read it; a second lesson was accompanied by an audiotape).

Although good teachers should always try to individualize their instruction for all children, they need to realize that the individualization needed for the diverse learner sometimes requires more careful planning and research. An awareness of the needs and characteristics of the various types if diverse learner should help the classroom teacher to locate and design appropriate lessons when such children are placed in the regular classroom situation.

SUMMARY

This chapter has discussed children who are somewhat different from those children for whom most instructional materials have been written. The "diverse" learner has been defined as one who usually should be given instruction that has been somewhat adjusted from that given in the regular classroom to derive maximum benefit from the lesson. Children who may be considered diverse include the culturally different, the handicapped, and the gifted. Each category has been defined to help the teacher obtain an overview of the type and range of individual differences that are likely to be found in the regular classroom. In designing lessons, the teacher must respond to each child's individual needs, not to the category in which the child is placed.

Some very general teaching procedures that emphasize the diagnostic-prescriptive approach have been suggested. However, the teacher should research specific techniques that are most appropriate for each individual child when designing lessons. These specific techniques are best determined when the teacher encounters a "diverse" learner who has been placed in his or her classroom.

References and Bibliography

Allen, T. D. "Reading as a Life Style." *English for American Indians.* A newsletter of the Office of Education Programs, Bureau of Indian Affairs, University of Utah (Spring 1971).

Baratz, J. "The Relationship of Black English to Reading: A Review of Research" in J. Laffey and R. Shuy, eds., *Language Differences: Do They Interfere?* Newark: International Reading Association, 1973.

Bereiter, K. and Englemann, S. *Teaching Disadvantaged Children in the Preschool*, Englewood Cliffs, N.J.: Prentice Hall, 1966.

Bond, Guy L., and Wagner, Eva Bond. *Teaching the Child to Read.* New York: Macmillan Publishing Co., Inc., 1966.

Bryen, Diane, Hartman, Cheryl, and Tait, Pearl. *Variant English: An Introduction to Language Variation.* Columbus, Ohio: Charles E. Merrill Publishing Company, 1978.

Burling, R. *English in Black and White.* New York: Holt, Rinehart and Winston, 1973.

Burns, Paul, and Roe, Betty. *Teaching Reading in Today's Elementary Schools.* Chicago: Rand McNally & Company, 1976.

Critchley, Macdonald. *The Dyslexic Child.* London: W. Heinemann Limited, 1970.

Dallman, Martha, Rouch, Roger, Char, Lynette, and DeBoer, John. *The Teaching of Reading.* 5th ed. New York: Holt, Rinehart and Winston, 1978.

Doman, Glenn. *Teach Your Baby to Read.* London: Jonathan Cape Ltd., 1971.

Education of the Gifted and Talented. Report to Congress by the U.S. Commissioner of Education and background papers submitted to the U.S. Office of Education. (72-502-0). Washington, D.C.: Government Printing Office, 1972.

Eichenwald, Heinz, "The Pathology of Reading Disorders: Psychological Factors," in Marjorie Johnson and Roy Kress, eds., *Corrective Reading in the Classroom.* Newark, Dela.: International Reading Association, 1967, pp. 31-43.

Evvard, Evelyn, and Mitchell, George C. "Sally, Dick, and Jane at Luckachukai." *Journal of American Indian Education* 5 (May 1966).

Finocchiaro, Mary. *Teaching English as a Second Language in Elementary and Secondary Schools.* Rev. ed. New York: Harper & Row, Publishers, 1968.

Fry, Edward. *Reading Instruction for Classroom and Clinic.* New York: McGraw-Hill Book Company, 1972.

Gallagher, James. "Gifted Children," in Robert Ebel, Victor Noll, and Roger Bauer, eds., *Encyclopedia of Educational Research.* 4th ed. New York: Macmillan Publishing Co., Inc., 1969, pp. 537-544.

Guszak, Frank J. *Diagnostic Reading Instruction in the Elementary School.* 2nd ed. New York: Harper & Row, Publishers, 1978.

Harris, A. J. and Sipay, E. R. *How to Teach Reading.* New York: Longman Inc., 1979.

Harris, Larry A., and Smith Carl B. *Reading Instruction: Diagnostic Teaching.* New York: Holt, Rinehart and Winston, 1976.

Harris, Theodore. "Reading," in Robert Ebel, Victor Noll, and Roger Bauer, eds. *Encyclopedia of Educational Research.* 4th ed. New York: Macmillan Publishing Co., Inc., 1969, pp. 1069-1104.

Heilman, Arthur W. *Principles and Practices of Teaching Reading.* 4th ed. Columbus, Ohio: Charles E. Merrill Publishing Company, 1977.

Hughes, Felicity. *Reading and Writing Before School.* London: Jonathan Cape Ltd., 1971.

Jarolimek, John. "The Taxonomy: Guide to Differentiated Instruction." *Social Education* 25 (Dec. 1962): pp. 445-447.

Johns, Jerry L., ed. *Literacy for Diverse Learners: Promoting Reading Growth at All Levels.* Newark, Dela.: International Reading Association, 1974.

Labov, William. *Some Sources of Reading Problems for Negro Speakers of Nonstandard English.* Champaign, Ill.: National Council of Teachers of English, 1967.

Labov, William. *The Study of Nonstandard English.* Champaign, Ill.: National Council of Teachers of English, 1970.

Labuda, Michael. "Gifted and Creative Pupils: Reasons for Concern," in Michael Labuda, ed., *Creative Reading for Gifted Learners: A Design for Excellence.* Newark, Dela.: International Reading Association, 1974, pp. 2-7.

Mangieri, John, and Readence, John. "Mainstreaming Implications for the Teaching of Reading." *Reading Improvement* (Winter 1977): pp. 165-167.

Marquardt, William F., Miller, Jean H., and Hosman, Eleanore. *English Around the World, Level 1 Guidebook.* Glenview, Ill.: Scott, Foresman and Company, 1970.

Masland, Susan. "Black Dialect and Learning to Read: What Is the Problem?" *Journal of Teacher Education* 30 (March-April 1979): pp. 41-44.

Money, John, ed. *Reading Disability: Progress and Research Needs in Dyslexia.* Balti-More: The Johns Hopkins University Press, 1962.

Ransom, Grayce. *Preparing to Teach Reading.* Boston: Little, Brown and Company, 1978.

Ruddell, Robert B. *Reading Language Instruction: Innovative Practices.* Englewood Cliffs, N.J.: Prentice-Hall, Inc., 1974.

Rupley, William, and Blair, Timothy. "Mainstreaming and Reading Instruction." *The Reading Teacher* (March 1979): 762-765.

Russell, David. *Children's Thinking.* Boston: Ginn and Company, 1956.

Savage, John, and Mooney, Jean. *Teaching Reading to Children with Special Needs.* Boston: Allyn & Bacon, Inc., 1979.

Spache, George D. and Evelyn B. *Reading in the Elementary School.* 3rd ed. Boston: Allyn & Bacon, Inc., 1973.

Swiss, Thom, and Olsen, Turee. "Reading and Gifted Children." *The Reading Teacher* 29 (January 1976): 428-431.

Terman, L. M., and Oden, Melita. *Genetic Studies of Genius.* Vol. 5. *The Gifted Group at Mid-Life.* Palo Alto, Calif.: Stanford University Press, 1959.

Torrence, E. Paul. "Are the Torrence Tests of Creative Thinking Biased Against or in Favor of Disadvantaged Groups?" *Gifted Child Quarterly* 15 (Summer 1971): pp. 75-80.

Torrence, E. Paul. *Gifted Children in the Classroom.* New York: Macmillan Publishing Co., Inc., 1965.

Trezise, Robert L. "What about a Reading Program for the Gifted?" *The Reading Teacher* 31 (April 1978): 742-747.

Wallace, G., and Kauffman, J. M. *Teaching Children with Learning Problems.* Columbus, Ohio: Charles E. Merrill Publishing Company, 1973.

Witty, Paul A. "Rationale for Fostering Creative Reading in the Gifted and Creative," in Michael Labuda, ed., *Creative Reading for Gifted Learners: A Design for Excellence.* Newark, Dela.: International Reading Association, 1974, pp. 8-24.

Witty, Paul A., ed. *Reading for the Gifted and The Creative Student.* Newark, Dela.: International Reading Association, 1971.

Zintz, Miles V. *The Reading Process: The Teacher and the Learner.* 3rd ed. Dubuque, Iowa: William C. Brown Company, Publishers, 1979.

Self-Check 13.3
Teaching Reading to the Diverse Learner

The following questions are designed to help the participant assess his or her competence on the first twelve objectives stated at the beginning of this chapter. Although every effort has been made to make the self-check questions comprehensive, participants should remember that they are held responsible for meeting the objectives as stated at the beginning of this chapter.

1. Objective 1. Differentiate among the terms "culturally different," "culturally disadvantaged," "economically different," "economically disadvantaged," "linguistically different," "nonstandard speaker of English," and the like.
2. Objective 2. Describe at least three traits related to language and experiential background that are characteristic of the culturally different learner.
3. Objective 3. Freddie is newly arrived from Mexico. He is in the third grade and reads well in Spanish. His speaking and reading ability in English is quite limited and his vocabulary consists of about

fifty "essential" words. Identify possible differences in his language and experiential backgrounds which may interfere with his ability to read English.

4. Objective 4. Design a lesson using the aural-oral procedure for teaching Freddie (described in "Self-Check" question 3) standard English.
5. Objective 5. Describe how instruction for the culturally different may be individualized in a basal reader program, in a language experience program, and in an individualized program.
6. Objective 6. Describe at least one technique that a monolingual teacher can use to teach reading to a second language speaker of English.
7. Objective 7. Give an example of how a diagnostic-prescriptive teacher can adapt and utilize a scope and sequence of reading skills chart for the culturally different learner.
8. Objective 8. Describe at least one way in which a peer may be used to help provide reading instruction for the culturally different learner.
9. Objective 9. Identify the two major types of "exceptional" children.
10. Objective 10. Differentiate among and list traits of three different types of "handicapped" children.
11. Objective 11. Differentiate between and list traits of two different types of "gifted" children.
12. Objective 12. Describe at least one teaching technique that a teacher can use to design a lesson for the "exceptional" child.

Chapter 13
Experience 1

Objective

During this experience, the participant will research various resources and then design a lesson particularly relevant to a specific type of "diverse" learner.

Activity and Assessment Guide

1. For what type of "diverse" learner do you intend to design a lesson? Be specific, for example, a first grade girl who is intellectually gifted.______

   ____

2. What reading skill do you intend to teach? Be specific, for example, inference skills.________________________________

   ____

3. What resources do you intend to use as the basis of your lesson planning? For example, use correct bibliographical references if you use texts or periodicals; cite names and professional occupations if you interview resource persons. Attach a list of all resources to this sheet.

* 4. Write out how you think this lesson is different from one taught to the "average" child, for example, must allow and encourage much creative thinking.

* 5. Design a lesson using the appropriate lesson plan format and attach it to this sheet. For example, include behavioral objectives, list of materials, preassessment, description of procedure, and postassessment.

* 6. Briefly summarize what you have learned about the type of child for whom this lesson is intended during your research and lesson planning.

* 7. State what you believe to be the significant implications of this experience for the classroom teacher.

*See Chapter 1, Experience 1 for explanation of the asterisk.

Chapter 13
Experience 2

Objective

During this experience, the participant will teach one reading skill to a "diverse" learner in a manner that includes a preassessment, an introductory lesson, two reinforcement lessons, and a postassessment.

Activity and Assessment Guide

1. What type of "diverse" learner do you intend to teach? Be specific, for example, a fourth grade boy who is mentally retarded. ______________

____

2. What reading skill do you intend to teach? Be specific, for example, context clues. ______________________________________

____

3. What resource person or material do you intend to use as the basis of your lesson planning, for example, name of author, title of work, date of publication, and exact page numbers used. ______________________

____

* 4. Explain how you think this lesson is different from one on the same skill that would be taught to an "average" child, for example, must provide a great deal of direct help and practice. ______________________

____

____

5. Briefly describe your preassessment (or attach a copy of the preassessment to this sheet). ____

____

____

____

6. Briefly describe your introductory lesson (or attach a copy of your lesson plan to this sheet). ____

____

____

7. Briefly describe your first reinforcement lesson (or attach a copy of your lesson plan to this sheet). ____

____

8. Briefly describe your second reinforcement lesson (or attach a copy of your lesson plan to this sheet). ____

____

____

____

9. Briefly describe your postassessment (or attach a copy of the postassessment to this sheet). ____

____

____

10. Write our the child's responses to the lessons that you gave:
    a. Child's performance on the preassessment: ____

    ____

    b. Child's performance and reaction to the introductory lesson: ________

    ____

    ____

    c. Child's performance and reaction to the first reinforcement activity:

    ____

    ____

    d. Child's performance and reaction to the second reinforcement activity: ____

    ____

e. Child's performance on the postassessment: ______________________

____

____

* 11. Write a brief summary of your feelings about the child's reaction toward this lesson and the amount of learning that took place. ______________

____

____

____

* 12. State what you believe to be the significant implications of this experience for the classroom teacher. ______________________________

____

____

*See Chapter 1, Experience 1 for explanation of the asterisk.

Chapter 14
Reading Readiness

Objectives 14.1

On completion of this chapter, the participant should be able to

1. Describe educators' common perceptions of reading readiness prior to 1920, between 1920 and 1960, and currently.
2. State the importance of assessing and prescribing instruction for each of the following basic learning skills: visual acuity, auditory acuity, general health, visual discrimination, visual memory, auditory discrimination, auditory memory, visual-motor skills, left-right progression, individual work habits, interest in books, and group work habits.
3. State the importance of assessing and teaching each of the following word identification skills: sight word skills, configuration clues, picture clues, context clues, identifying graphemes and pronouncing phonemes, and blending.
4. State the importance of assessing and teaching each of the following comprehension skills: gaining word meaning, identifying details, identifying main ideas, identifying sequence, making inferences, identifying characterization, and identifying fact, fiction, and opinion.
5. State the importance of assessing and teaching each of the following study skills: following directions, using the table of contents, classifying, and memorization.
6. Describe two types of scores that can be derived from a standardized reading readiness test and state how each might influence instruction.

7. Describe three procedures other than a standardized test that may be used to assess reading readiness skills.
8. List three reasons why the language experience approach is an excellent strategy to use at the reading readiness level.
9. Given a description of a readiness activity or program, state whether it is valuable and give the reasons for your answer.
10. Describe how the following may be assessed and taught: (a) any two basic learning skills, (b) any two word identification skills, (c) any two comprehension skills, (d) any two study skills.
11. Describe a parent-child activity designed to strengthen the child's ability to perform: (a) any one basic learning skill, (b) any one word identification skill, (c) any one comprehension skill, (d) any one study skills.

Experience 1 extends Chapter 14 with this objective:

12. The participant will assess and teach a minimum of one skill on the readiness level.

Information Given 14.2
Reading Readiness

In preparation for setting up a reading readiness program for her kindergarten class, Miss Hamblen has observed her students and has recognized within each several strengths that will aid as well as several weaknesses that will hinder the children's learning to read. Therefore, Miss Hamblen has decided to base her reading readiness program on these strengths and weaknesses to better prepare her students for reading instruction when they begin their formal schooling.

For example, one of Miss Hamblen's pupils, Jonathan, can already read many words. However, his inability to work independently and to draw circles and lines will hinder him in a first grade reading program, which requires both independent work and printing. Thus, as part of her reading readiness program, Miss Hamblen will attempt to increase Jonathan's independent work habits and fine motor coordination. Karen is a healthy child who appears to be able to learn both independently and in groups. However, Karen has not been taught left-right progression, how to print, or how to recognize words or sounds. Therefore, Miss Hamblen will include these skills as part of Karen's instruction.

As an aid to other teachers who, like Miss Hamblen, must design and implement a reading readiness program, this chapter will discuss educators' historical and current perceptions of reading readiness, assessment and teaching procedures for the reading readiness skills, and activities that parents may use to enhance their children's reading readiness.

HISTORICAL AND CURRENT PERCEPTIONS OF READING READINESS

It was originally thought that children possessed the ability to learn to read upon reaching the age of six years, when they were therefore allowed to begin school. However, as early as 1908, Huey noted the high degree of failure in first grade as proof that this theory is not valid. That is, not every six-year-old is ready for reading instruction.

During the 1920s educators espoused a new theory (Arthur, 1925) that maintained that children were ready to receive reading instruction when they reached a *mental* age of six-and-one-half (6.5) years. Mental age is computed in the following manner: chronological age × (IQ/100) = mental age. Therefore, if a child had just celebrated his or her sixth birthday and his or her IQ measured 110, the child's mental age was calculated as 6.6 years—6.0 × (110/100)—and was said to be ready for reading instruction. However, if a child with an IQ of 100 had just turned six, then his or her mental age—6 × (100/100) = 6.0—would be below the required 6.5 and reading instruction would be withheld.

Some educators today still use mental age as one indicator of reading readiness (Fowler, 1971). However, due to several trends that emerged during the 1960s and 1970s, this theory is no longer adhered to rigidly. The major trends that tended to discredit complete reliance upon the mental age concept of reading readiness include

1. Inadequacies of intelligence tests. During the early 1960s educators recognized that intelligence test results did not necessarily indicate a child's intelligence. For example, many IQ tests were found to be culturally biased, giving accurate results for white, middle-class children only. Therefore, because it was based upon the false assumption that intelligence tests always gave accurate IQ scores, the mental age theory of reading readiness became less respected.

2. Positive response to preschool education of children with mental ages of less than 6.5. During the 1960s research became available that evaluated the worth of preschool education toward readiness for reading instruction (Coltheart, 1979). Data indicated that those children who had received training in the skill prerequisite to reading (reading readiness skills) were ready for formal reading instruction at an earlier age than were children who had received no such instruction. Therefore, educators often became unwilling to withhold a child's reading instruction until he reached a mental age of 6.5 years.

3. Introduction of formal reading instruction in the preschool. Many preschools are now offering reading instruction as part of the curriculum, and many children with mental ages of less than 6.5 appear to be profiting from such instruction.

4. Assessing and teaching cognitive skills. The theories of the Swiss psychologist Piaget have recently begun to be related to reading instruction. Piaget's greatest contribution appears to be his theory that children must understand certain concepts, such as conservation, before they are able to

profit from reading instruction (Kirkland, 1978). An example of a child's mastery of the concept of conservation is his or her ability to recognize that a volume of water stays constant whether the water is in a tall, thin container or in a long, wide container. Research indicates that concepts such as conservation should be developed before reading instruction begins, and researchers believe that such concepts can be assessed and taught (Pulaski, 1971; Roberts, 1976; Kirkland, 1978).

5. Integrating language arts and reading programs. Based on psycholinguistic theory, which has reemphasized reading as part of language, efforts are being made to integrate all learning related to reading with the child's existing language. Therefore, today's reading readiness programs tend to coordinate oral language, listening, handwriting, spelling, and reading.

6. Increased emphasis upon diagnostic-prescriptive instruction. During the 1960s and 1970s instruction based on children's assessed needs—diagnostic-prescriptive instruction—has come to the fore. The major results of this current emphasis on diagnostic-prescriptive instruction are (a) recognition that there is no single agreed-upon set of readiness skills. However, although it is unlikely that any two educators would agree on an identical list of skills, a great deal of overlap can be found among lists. For example, *using a table of contents* may appear on some lists but not others, whereas *recognizing consonant sounds* appear on most lists. (b) the development of assessment procedures to test a variety of skills relating to the reading readiness program. That is, instead of assessing readiness as a unitary skill, assessment could be made of specific subskills. (c) the development of a great number of programs to teach beginning reading, each requiring a different pattern of subskills for success.

All these trends have resulted in changing educators' views of reading readiness from global to specific, so that today reading readiness may be considered as preparation for success in a specified reading instruction program. Such a program will probably implement a comprehensive approach to reading readiness, including all the language arts skills as well as selected cognitive skills (such as conservation). These readiness skills will probably be taught to all children, regardless of chronological or mental age, and skill instruction will be based upon a diagnosis of the specific child's needs.

SCOPE AND SEQUENCE OF READINESS SKILLS

As stated in the previous section, a particular readiness skill will be included in a child's curriculum according to his or her need for that skill. A list of fundamental readiness skills is presented in Table 14.1, and the rationale for teaching these skills is presented in the following section.

A RATIONALE FOR TEACHING THE READINESS SKILLS

During the readiness phase, children are prepared for ease and success in beginning reading instruction by being evaluated and then instructed in the

TABLE 14.1 Skills to Be Mastered by Children with Readiness Instructional Levels

	Basic Learning Skills
	Physical skills
1	Demonstrating visual acuity
2	Demonstrating auditory acuity
3	Demonstrating general health
	Perceptual skills
4	Demonstrating visual discrimination
5	Demonstrating visual memory
6	Demonstrating auditory discrimination
7	Demonstrating auditory memory
8	Demonstrating visual-motor skills
9	Using left-right progression
	Emotional skills
10	Using individual work habits
11	Showing interest in books
	Social skills
12	Using group work habits
	Word Identification Skills
13	Using sight word skills
14	Using configuration clues
15	Using picture clues
16	Using context clues
	Using phonic clues
17	Identifying graphemes and pronouncing phonemes
18	Blending
	Comprehension Skills
19	Gaining word meaning
20	Identifying details
21	Identifying main ideas
22	Identifying sequence
23	Making inferences
24	Identifying characterization
25	Identifying fact, fiction, and opinion
	Study Skills
26	Following directions
	Using aids within books
27	Using the table of contents
	Organizing information
28	Classifying
	Recalling information
29	Memorization

basic learning skills needed to learn to read, as well as in word identification, comprehension, and study skills. The skills to be mastered during this phase and a rationale for teaching each of them will be discussed in the following section under four main headings: "Basic Learning Skills," "Word Identification Skills," "Comprehension Skills," and "Study Skills."

BASIC LEARNING SKILLS

Successful beginning reading instruction requires not only that the child have some ability in word identification, comprehension, and study skills but also that the child possess some basic learning skills, including physical, perceptual, emotional, and social skills.

Physical skills required for reading readiness include visual acuity, auditory acuity, and good health. The child with good *visual acuity* can see clearly because he or she has good eyesight, naturally or corrected. Learning to read becomes an extremely difficult task for the child whose eyesight is inadequate. *Auditory acuity* refers to the child's ability to hear distinctly. If the child cannot, his or her language skills will develop slowly and therefore adversely affect his or her reading progress. Learning to read requires energy, which the ill child may not have. *Good health* is therefore also essential to reading readiness. Moreover, the chronically ill child may miss much beginning reading instruction, further retarding his or her progress.

Perceptual skills allow the use of visual and auditory acuity. Therefore, even though a child may have excellent acuity, he or she may exhibit poor perceptual skills because he or she has not learned to use these physical abilities to best advantage. Perceptual skills include visual discrimination (the ability to distinguish among shapes), visual memory (the ability to remember shapes), auditory discrimination (the ability to distinguish sounds), auditory memory (the ability to remember what has been heard), visual-motor skills (the ability of the eye and hand to work together), and left-right progression (the ability to read from left to right and top to bottom). If a child is to have a successful beginning reading experience, he or she must be able to distinguish shapes and to visually remember words. Thus, *visual discrimination and memory* are essential to reading readiness. Furthermore, since virtually all methods of reading instruction require distinguishing sounds and include periods of listening, the development of *auditory memory and discrimination* becomes worthwhile. *Visual-motor skills* are important because most programs use writing as a means of learning to read, teaching children to read and to write letters at the same time. If little writing is used in the instruction, then the skill is less important. Finally, all children should master *left-right progression* before beginning reading instruction. Until a child begins to read, it may not matter whether he or she views a form from bottom to top or in a circular motion. However, to read successfully, the child must learn to observe the print from left to right and from the top to the bottom of the page.

Emotional skills include the child's *individual work habits* and *interest in books.* To the extent that beginning reading students are required to work individually, an effort must be made to develop their independent behavior. Additionally, learning to read involves a great deal of work for first graders. To put sufficient effort into learning, they must be motivated. Therefore, interest in books is important for the beginning reader.

Social skills are necessary to reading readiness because much beginning reading is taught in groups, making the ability to work and learn with other children present a necessary skill. If a child were to be tutored in reading on a one-to-one basis, then *group skills* would not be a necessary prerequisite for reading instruction.

WORD IDENTIFICATION SKILLS

Sight word skills help a child immensely during beginning reading instruction. The fact that there are a few words in a book or on a page that are known to the child will help him or her to begin reading more easily. For this reason a small core of sight words should be introduced into the readiness program.

Configuration clues are helpful to children in preparation for formal reading instruction, because their use encourages visual scrutiny of words for distinguishing characteristics that aid in recognizing a particular word.

Picture clues are introduced verbally to readiness level children when the teacher shows them a card containing a word and a picture and asks the children what the word is. This technique encourages children to use pictures to figure out unknown words when they actually begin reading.

Context clues are introduced verbally. The teacher may say a sentence, leaving out one word, such as "The ________________ is red," encouraging the children to respond with any suitable word. This skill is later transferred to a reading situation in which the child encounters an unknown word in a sentence such as "________________ dog jumped." Although the child does not recognize the first word in the sentence, he or she might assume that it is "the" because "the" is a word that fits the context.

Locating graphemes and pronouncing phonemes is introduced at the readiness level by the teaching of initial consonants. Some programs also suggest instruction in the short and long vowel sounds. Recognizing these graphemes is important in beginning reading, as children can combine this skill with configuration, picture, and context clues to help decipher an unknown word.

Blending is also introduced at the readiness level. As soon as children have mastered a few consonant and vowel sounds, they can pronounce words by blending them.

COMPREHENSION SKILLS

Each of the comprehension skills outlined in Chapter 3 is important to the accomplished reader. However, because some are too complex, all these skills cannot be introduced at the readiness level. Therefore, although these skills will be used collectively throughout a reading lifetime, it is essential that the comprehension skills introduced to beginning readers be simple enough for young children to understand. For this reason, at the readiness level the comprehension skill to be learned is applied in listening situations so that the pupil will have developed the skill auditorially before encountering its need visually in a reading situation. The wide range of comprehension skills discussed in the following paragraphs may be instructionally presented in this manner to provide an initial and basic introduction to the comprehension skills as a whole. A brief rationale for teaching each of these skills at the readiness level follows.

Gaining Word Meaning: Since this skill involves the determination of the writer's intended meaning, without it reading would become not only laborious but also nonsensical.

Identifying Details and Identifying Main Ideas: These objectives are often the purposes of reading. Therefore, development of each of these skills is important.

Identifying Sequence: Determining the order in which components occur or are placed helps children to understand the relationship between time and space and the meaning of what has occurred.

Making Inferences: Often, the major purpose of reading is to respond to a question whose answer is not specifically written within the reading material and is, therefore, inferred by formulating images not directly presented.

Identifying Characterization: Determining the personality traits and feelings of a character in a selection aids the young child in identifying with and understanding the actions of characters in stories.

Identifying Fact, Fiction, and Opinion: Children at the readiness level are normally very interested in what is real and not real. Therefore, this is an ideal time at which to introduce them to the concepts of fact and fiction by teaching them to distinguish passages that represent actual conditions and passages that reflect the personal feelings of the author or of the character who is speaking.

STUDY SKILLS

Although all study skills are important, small children have not yet gained the maturity required to understand or the prerequisite skills needed to master all of them. Therefore, these skills are introduced at only the most basic level. *Following directions* is essential for the beginning reader who will be doing independent as well as group work while learning to read. *Using a table of contents* increases the child's awareness of nontextual parts of books that are of value when locating materials within them. Therefore, instruction in this basic study skill introduces the beginning reader to the more comprehensive skill *using aids within books.* Likewise, *classifying* introduces the children to an important, but elementary, method of organizing information. *Memorization* is basic to the entire reading process when it is necessary to be able to recall (*recalling information*) the "gist" of what has been read.

ASSESSING READINESS SKILLS FOR READING

A pupil's reading readiness skills may be assessed by evaluating his or her performance on standardized reading readiness tests as well as on other measures designed to assess pupil performance on specific skills.

STANDARDIZED READING READINESS TESTS

Standardized reading readiness tests are used in most schools and are administered to students at the end of kindergarten or the beginning of grade one to assess their readiness for reading instruction. Commonly used readiness tests include the Gates-MacGinitie Readiness Skills Test (1968), the Lee-Clark Readiness Test (1962), the Metropolitan Readiness Tests (1976), and the Macmillan Reading Readiness Test (Harris and Sipay, 1970).

Each of these readiness tests assesses several skills. Basic learning skills assessed may include auditory discrimination, visual discrimination, and visual-motor skills; word identification skills assessed may include using picture clues and blending phonic elements; comprehension skills may include gaining word meaning and identifying sequence; and study skills may include following directions. For example, the Macmillan Reading Readiness Test includes assessment of visual discrimination, auditory discrimination, vocabulary and concepts, letter names, and visual-motor skills.

The Macmillan test (Harris and Sipay, 1970)* measures visual discrimination by asking the child to match the item in the box at the beginning of a row to the appropriate item within the row. For example,

top	man top went run

Auditory discrimination is assessed by asking the child to indicate the pictured item that starts with a given consonant. For example, using the pictures, the teacher might say, "Put an X on the picture that starts like 'pen.' "

Assessment of vocabulary and concepts is made by having the child indicate a named item within a series of pictures. For example, using the following series the teacher might say, "Put an X on the boat."

A child's skill in naming letters is measured by asking him or her to indicate the letter that has been named. For example, the teacher might show the student the following examples and say, "Put an X on the letter 'O,' "

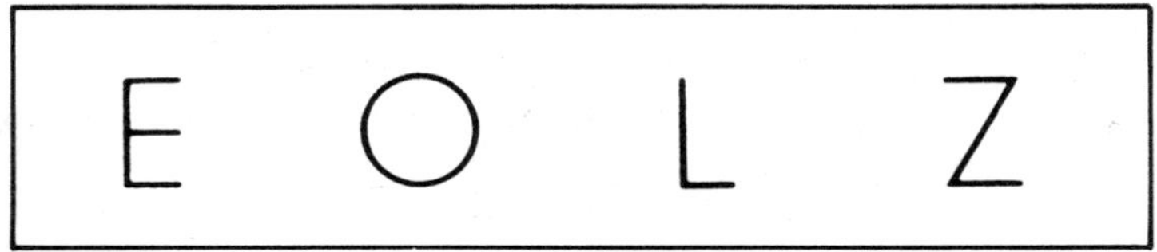

or "put an X on the letter 'e.' "

Visual-motor skills are measured by asking the child to draw a series of designs such as the one shown here:

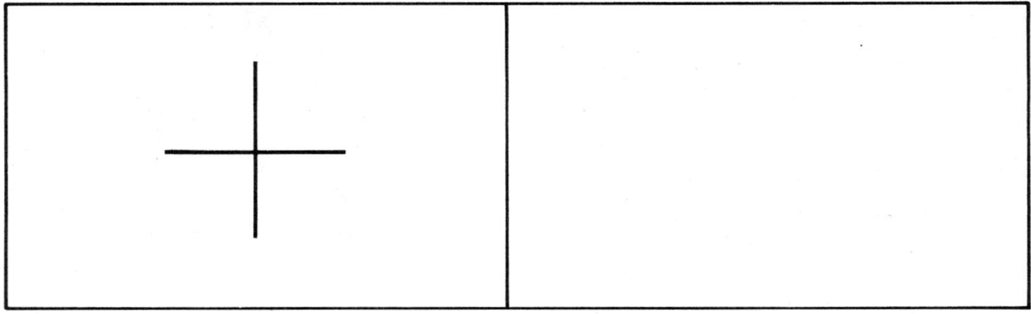

Deriving Scores from Standardized Reading Readiness Tests

Two scores may be derived from readiness tests: one for each skill tested and one for total readiness. The individual score for each skill may be interpreted in descriptive terms. For example, a child's performance on the auditory discrimination portion may be rated as outstanding, superior, good, fair, or poor. The total readiness score may also be interpreted in descriptive terms, indicating, for example, that the child is very ready, ready, or not ready for reading instruction.

*The examples on these pages are taken from A. J. Harris and E. R. Sipay, *The Macmillan Reading Readiness Test* (New York: Macmillan Publishing Co., Inc., 1970).

Disadvantages of Standardized Reading Readiness Tests

Although standardized reading readiness tests may be very valuable indicators of a pupil's preparedness for formal reading instruction, these tests do have the following disadvantages (Rude, 1973):

1. Authors of reading readiness tests often disagree about which skills comprise the readiness skills. For example, most readiness tests assess letter recognition, whereas only some measure vocabulary or eye–hand coordination.

2. Reading readiness tests are predictive in nature. That is, by indicating skill weaknesses, the tests may identify those students who will or will not succeed with reading instruction. However, it does not necessarily follow that training in these skills will increase a child's chances of learning to read. For example, if a child's score is low in letter names, teaching him or her the letter names will not necessarily increase the child's reading ability.

OTHER PROCEDURES FOR ASSESSING READINESS SKILLS

Assessment procedures other than standardized reading readiness tests may prove valuable to the teacher as valid supplementary alternatives to standardized testing. For example, several readiness tests include as supplements observational checklists that are valuable guides in the teacher's evaluation of skills that are not actually measured on the formal test, such as physical, emotional, and social skills. For instance, the Macmillan Reading Readiness Test (Harris and Sipay, 1970) includes checklists in the areas of intellectual development, language development, physical development, home background, emotional and social development, and interest development. The teacher rates each item on the checklists on a five-point scale ranging from 1 (low) to 5 (high). The checklists for emotional and social development and interest development are shown here:

CHARACTERISTIC	RATING				
	Low		Average		High
	1	2	3	4	5
Emotional and Social Development					
Self-reliance and independence	____	____	____	____	____
Emotional maturity, self-control	____	____	____	____	____
Group participation	____	____	____	____	____
Interest Development					
Attention during story reading	____	____	____	____	____
Expressed desire to read	____	____	____	____	____
Expressed desire to write	____	____	____	____	____

Another procedure for assessing reading readiness involves the child's knowledge of the alphabet. Research has indicated that knowledge of the alphabet correlates highly with readiness test scores and success in beginning reading instruction (Durrell and Murphy, 1978). However, this finding does not mean that knowledge of the alphabet will necessarily provide readiness for reading. Rather, it simply reflects the fact that the child probably comes from a background that provides the conditions allowing for the learning of such readiness skills (Lapp and Flood, 1978).

Teachers can also use informal tests to measure readiness skills. Suggestions for such tests of each skill listed in the preceding "Scope of Readiness Skills" (Table 14.1) may be found in Chapter 15. "Teaching Word Identification, Comprehension, Study, and Readiness Skills."

CONCLUSION

Research has indicated that the best method for determining reading readiness is eclectic, involving the use of a variety of assessment procedures (Harris, 1974). Thus, standardized readiness tests should be used in conjunction with other sources of information on the child's readiness level, such as observational checklists, knowledge of the alphabet, and informal tests.

TEACHING READINESS SKILLS FOR READING

Today, most authorities (LaConte, 1969; O'Donnell and Raymond, 1972; Silberberg, Silberberg, and Iverson, 1972; Seaton and Smith, 1977; Strickland, et al., 1977; Kirkland, 1978; Blachowicz, 1978) agree that kindergarten reading instruction should be implemented using a broadly based program that includes listening, speaking, writing, and other cognitive skills. A joint statement issued by several professional organizations, including the American Association of Elementary/Kindergarten/Nursery Educators, the Association for Childhood Educational International, the International Reading Association, and the National Council of Teachers of English, provides the following guidelines for preschool reading programs by stating that they should

> Provide reading experiences as an integrated part of the broader communication process that includes listening, speaking, and writing.
>
> Provide for a broad range of activities both in scope and in content. Include direct experiences that offer opportunities to communicate in different settings with different persons.
>
> Foster children's affective and cognitive development by providing materials, experiences, and opportunities to communicate what they know and how they feel.
>
> Plan activities that will cause children to become active participants in the learning process rather than passive recipients of knowledge.
>
> Provide opportunities for children to experiment with language and simply to have fun with it. (Strickland et al., 1977, p. 780)

Additionally, the kindergarten reading readiness program might include the following strategies:

1. Individualizing instruction to meet the needs of each learner. Readiness programs that assess each child's individual needs and then develop activities that enable the child to learn the needed skills are generally more effective than are programs that do not (Paradis and Peterson, 1975).

2. Including on a daily basis many activities designed to enhance the child's reading readiness. For example, the children should be read to daily (McDonnell, 1975).

3. Designing instructional activities so that they reinforce as many readiness skills as possible. For example, readiness skill lessons should be conducted with letters rather than with nonreading objects (e.g., a sorting task might be performed with letters instead of with colored beads) (Hall, 1976). Additionally, activities such as the one following can reinforce several skills simultaneously, such as knowledge of initial consonants (which letter represents the first sound in rabbit?), following directions (circle the correct answer), and fine motor skills (trace the letters and color the picture).

METHODS FOR TEACHING GENERAL READINESS SKILLS

Readiness programs may be based upon any of several approaches to the teaching of reading. For instance, a basal reader series readiness program prepares the child for that specific series and normally uses a total language approach to the teaching of the readiness skills by incorporating reading, writing, speaking, and listening skills into the program. For example, one such program (Smith and Wardhaugh, 1978) includes instruction in such basic learning skills as auditory skills, visual skills, and visual-motor skills; such word identification skills as sight vocabulary, context, and phonic skills; such comprehension skills as oral language development, predicting story outcomes, recognizing the main idea, and recognizing sequence; and such study skills as classifying and following directions.

Another technique for teaching readiness skills involves the language experience approach, an ideal method for teaching reading-related skills at the kindergarten level (Armstrong, 1974; Strickland et al., 1977; Kirkland, 1978). For example, normally an experience story is based on an experience, integrates the communication skills of listening, speaking, and writing, and involves the listeners as active participants.

The language experience approach can also be used to foster the development of specific skills. For example, the teacher can encourage the development of left-right progression by swooping her arm under the words as she reads the story to the children. Visual discrimination can be stressed by having the children match word cards with identical words on a chart. Sight word skills can be developed by using the same word several times on the story chart. Enhancement of phonic skills may be accomplished by having the children locate words that contain a given grapheme ("Find two words that start like ball"). Instruction in vocabulary and language skills can be provided through the introduction of new words and new sentence structures. For example, the teacher might have one of the children dictate the sentence, "The secretary stood up and smiled." Because the word secretary might be new to several children, the teacher might attempt to teach them the new word by discussing the duties of a secretary. Furthermore, the teacher could show the children how two actions (stood up, smiled) by one person may be combined in one sentence. Other comprehension skills can be developed through the use of questions such as, "Was Johnny happy when he was invited to the birthday party?" (identifying characterization). Study skills may be incorporated through activities such as having the children group together all words that begin with a given initial consonant (classifying). And memory skills can be developed by having the children retell the story in their own words.

METHODS FOR TEACHING SPECIFIC READINESS SKILLS

This section, which may be found in Chapter 15, includes a method of assessment and teachings for each of the readiness skills listed in Table 14.1. One basic teaching procedure and two or more reinforcement activities are presented for each skill, with the exception of those, such as demonstrating visual acuity, that do not lend themselves to this format.

ACTIVITIES FOR PARENTS TO DO WITH READINESS LEVEL CHILDREN

The following text lists a series of activities that a teacher might provide to parents who wish to help their readiness level children but do not know how to do so. Included with each sample activity is the specific skill that the activity is designed to encourage.

1. Be sure that the child is physically healthy. If any signs of visual, auditory, speech, or health problems exist, try to obtain appropriate medical help (demonstrating visual acuity, auditory acuity, and general health).
2. Ask the child to find matching letters in magazine or newspaper headlines. Say, "This is an *M*. Can you find another letter just like it?" (demonstrating visual discrimination).
3. During tidy-up time, show the child several items on a shelf or on the floor. Then put some of the things away and ask the child, "What's missing?" (demonstrating visual memory).
4. Play word games with the child. For example, say, "I see Matt and he wears a hat." Or say, "Can you think of two words that start like forty" (demonstrating auditory discrimination).
5. Give the child a list of things to remember to buy at the store. Start with one item, and then have the child remember two, three, and so on (demonstrating auditory memory).

6. Provide the child with craft activities such as coloring, painting, and bead stringing. When the child shows proficiency in these activities, provide more advanced ones such as letter tracing (demonstrating visual-motor skills).

7. When reading to the child, move your hand in a constant motion under the words as you read them. Show where you start and finish each line (using left-right progression).

8. Require your child to work independently. Begin with one brief activity that you know that the child can perform, such as taking the garbage to the can. Reward the child for doing the task alone and correctly. Extend this activity by asking the child to do increasingly more complex tasks properly. Your goal is for the child to be able to complete a ten-minute activity correctly and independently (using individual work habits).

9. Take your child to the library and have him or her check out books that you can read together on a daily basis at home. Also, take the child to the library during its planned story hours (showing interest in books).

10. Encourage working with others in group situations by enrolling your child in activities such as Sunday school, vacation church school, or a YMCA or YWCA (using group work habits).

11. During rides and walks, help your child to recognize familiar advertising signs and street signs, such as "HILL," "STOP," and "SPEED LIMIT 30" (using sight word skills).

12. Show the child how words differ. For example, say, "This word is look. This word is book. The first letter in look is different from the first letter in book" (using configuration clues).

13. When reading to the child, discuss the pictures that accompany the story. For example, say, "This story is about an opossum. Can you find the opossum in this picture?" (using picture clues).

14. Play "I Spy." For example, say, "I spy with my little eye something that is tall and skinny, made of black metal, and has a light on top. What is it?" (using context clues).

15. Allow the child to watch "Sesame Street" once daily. Most experts agree that this television program does an excellent job of teaching the basic phonic sounds and blending skills. However, evidence indicates that watching "Sesame Street" excessively, that is, several times a day, is not desirable. Therefore, if the child is to watch more than one television program, "Sesame Street" should be supplemented by other slower-moving children's programs such as "Mister Rogers" (locating graphemes, pronouncing phonemes, and blending).

16. When reading or watching television with your child, ask questions such as "Do you know what a native is?" (gaining word meaning); "What did the little boy look like?" (identifying details); "What happened first? Next? Last?" (identifying sequence); "What do you think will happen next in this program?" This question can be asked during an advertisement (making inferences); "Would you like the boy in the story to be your friend? Why?" (identifying characterization); "Do you think that the story in this program could really happen? Why or why not?" This question is particularly good for use following Saturday morning cartoons (identifying fact, fiction, and opinion).

17. Play the directions game. Begin by giving your child one simple direction, such as "Put your shoes in the closet." Continue by issuing more complex instructions, such as "Put the blue block in the yellow basket," as well as more than one direction at once, such as "Put the beanbags in the closet and the giraffe on the shelf" (following directions).

18. When the child wants you to read a favorite story, poem, or nursery rhyme that happens to be contained in a book with a table of contents, use the table of contents to locate the selection and explain to the child what you are doing (using the table of contents).

19. Allow your child to help put away the dishes and explain that the flatware, for example, is put away so that all the spoons are together, all the forks are together, and all the knives are together (classifying).

20. Encourage the child to retell a story. When difficulty is encountered, refer to the pictures and/or ask appropriate questions. For example, if the child has trouble remembering while retelling "The Three Bears," you might ask questions such as "What is Goldilocks doing now?" while pointing to a picture of Goldilocks walking in the woods; "Now what is she doing?" while pointing to a picture of Goldilocks going into the bears' house; "Whose porridge did Goldilocks eat first? Next? Last?" and "What did she do with Baby Bear's porridge?" Continue in this manner until the child has finished by telling the complete story. Some children require fewer questions than others. Therefore, ask as few questions as possible (recalling information).

SUMMARY

Early in the twentieth century, readiness to learn to read was thought to be a global factor coincidental with a chronological age of six years. By the 1920s, readiness to learn to read was still viewed globally, but was thought to coincide with a mental age of six and one-half years. Today, readiness is viewed as an aggregate of skills necessary for success in a specified reading program. The readiness skills may include specified basic learning skills, word identification skills, comprehension skills, and study skills. A pupil's readiness for reading may be assessed by evaluating his or her performance on standardized reading readiness tests. Additionally, the results of teacher observation of pupil characteristics, knowledge of the alphabet, and the results of informal tests of specific skills may be used as measures of reading readiness. Research has indicated that the best method for determining reading readiness is eclectic, involving the use of a variety of assessment procedures. Readiness skills should be taught as part of a language program which is sufficiently flexible to meet the learning needs of all children. Parents are encouraged to provide experiences for their children which will enhance the readiness program of the school.

References and Bibliography

Armstrong, M. K. "First Grade Lift-Off with Library Books and Lots of Energy." *The Reading Teacher* 27 (May 1974): 778-786.

Arthur, G. "A Quantitative Study of the Results of Grouping First Grade Children According to Mental Age." *Journal of Educational Research* 12 (October 1925): 173-185.

Bader, L. A. *Reading Diagnosis and Remediation in Classroom and Clinic.* New York: Macmillan Publishing Co., Inc., 1980.

Blachowicz, C. L. Z. "Metalinguistic Awareness and the Beginning Reader." *The Reading Teacher* 31 (May 1978): 875-876.

Coltheart, M. "When Can Children Learn to Read—And When Should They Be Taught?" in T. G. Waller and G. E. MacKinnon, eds., *Reading Research: Advances in Theory and Practice,* 1. New York: Academic Press, Inc., 1979, p. 1-30.

Cox, M. B. "The Effect of Conservation Ability on Reading Competency." *The Reading Teacher* 30 (December 1976): 251-258.

Diaz-Guerrero, R., and Holtzman, W. H. "Learning by Televised 'Plaza Sesamo' in Mexico." *Journal of Educational Psychology* 66 (October 1974): 623-643.

Durrell, D., and Murphy, H. "A Prereading Phonics Inventory." *The Reading Teacher* 31 (January 1978): 385-390.

Fowler, W. A. "A Developmental Learning Strategy for Early Reading in a Laboratory Nursery School." *Interchange* 2 (Winter 1971): 106-125.

Gates, A. T., and MacGinitie, W. H. *Gates-MacGinitie Readiness Skills Test.* New York: Teacher's College Press, 1968.

Hall, M. "Prereading Instruction: Teach for the Task." *The Reading Teacher* 30 (October 1976): 7-9.

Harris, A. J. *How to Increase Reading Ability.* 5th ed. New York: David McKay, Co., Inc., 1974.

Harris, A. J., and Sipay, E. R. *The Macmillan Reading Readiness Test.* New York: Macmillan Publishing Co., Inc., 1970.

Huey, E. B. *The Psychology and Pedagogy of Reading.* New York: Macmillan Publishing Co., Inc., 1908.

Kirkland, E. R. "A Piagetian Interpretation of Beginning Reading Instruction." *The Reading Teacher* 31 (February 1975): 497-503.

LaConte, C. "Reading in Kindergarten." *The Reading Teacher* 23 (November 1969): 116-120.

Lapp, D., and Flood, J. *Teaching Reading to Every Child.* New York: Macmillan Publishing Co., Inc., 1978.

Lee, J. M., and Clark, W. W. *Lee-Clark Readiness Test.* Monterey: California Test Bureau, 1962.

McDonnell, G. M. "Relating Language to Early Reading Experiences." *The Reading Teacher* 28 (February 1975): 438-444.

Menlove, C. K. *Ready, Set, Go!* Englewood Cliffs, N.J.: Prentice-Hall, Inc., 1978.

Metropolitan Readiness Tests. New York: Harcourt Brace Jovanovich, Inc., 1976.

Nurss, J. R. "Assessment of Readiness," in T. G. Waller and G. E. MacKinnon, eds., *Reading Research: Advances in Theory and Practice.* 1. New York: Academic Press, Inc., 1979, pp. 31-62.

O'Donnell, C. M., and Raymond, D. "Developing Reading Readiness in the Kindergarten." *Elementary English* 49 (May 1972): 768-771.

Paradis, E., and Peterson, J. "Readiness Training Implication from the Research." *The Reading Teacher* 28 (February 1975): 445-448.

Perney, J., Freund, J., and Barman, A. "TV Viewing and Early School Achievement." *Phi Delta Kappan* 59 (May 1978): 637-638.

Pulaski, M. A. *Understanding Piaget.* New York: Harper and Row, Publishers, 1971.

Roberts, K. P. "Piaget's Theory of Conservation and Reading Readiness." *The Reading Teacher* 30 (December 1976): 246-250.

Rude, R. T. "Readiness Tests: Implications for Early Childhood Education." *The Reading Teacher* 26 (March 1973): 572-580.

Sawyer, D. J. "Readiness Factors for Reading: A Different View." *The Reading Teacher* 28 (April 1975): 620-624.

Seaton, H. W., and Smith, S. D. "The Use of Receptive and Expressive Language Development for Improving Students' Reading Achievement," in P. David Pearson, ed., *Reading: Theory, Research, and Practice.* 26th Yearbook. Clemson, S.C.: National Reading Conference, 1977, pp. 82-87.

Silberberg, N. E., Silberberg, M. C., and Iverson, I. A. "The Effects of Kindergarten Instruction in Alphabet and Numbers on First Grade Reading." *Journal of Learning Disabilities* 5 (May 1972): 254-261.

Smith, C. B., and Wardhaugh, R. *Reading Readiness.* New York: Macmillan Publishing Co., Inc., 1978.

Sprigle, H. A. "Can Poverty Children Live on Sesame Street?" *Young Children* 25 (March 1971): 202-216.

Strickland, D., et al., "Reading and Pre-First Grade: A Joint Statement of Concerns about Present Practices in Pre-First Grade Reading Instruction and Recommendations for Improvement." *The Reading Teacher* 30 (April 1977): 780-781.

Weimer, W. and Weimer, A. *Reading Readiness Inventory.* Columbus, Ohio: Charles E. Merrill Publishing Company, 1977.

Self-Check 14.3
Reading Readiness

The following questions are designed to help the participant assess his or her competence on the first eleven objectives stated at the beginning of this chapter. Although every effort has been made to make the self-check questions comprehensive, participants should remember that they are held responsible for meeting the objectives as stated at the beginning of this chapter.

1. Objective 1. Describe one perception relative to reading readiness that was commonly held prior to 1920, one perception relative to reading readiness that was commonly held between 1920 and 1960, and six perceptions relative to reading readiness that developed between 1960 and the present time.
2. Objective 2. What is the importance of assessing and teaching each of the following basic learning skills at the readiness level: visual acuity, auditory acuity, general health, visual discrimination, visual memory, auditory discrimination, auditory memory, visual-motor skills, left-right progression, individual work habits, interest in books, and group work habits.
3. Objective 3. What is the importance of assessing and teaching each of the following word identification skills at the readiness level: sight word skills, configuration clues, picture clues, context clues, identifying graphemes and pronouncing phonemes, and blending.
4. Objective 4. What is the importance of assessing and teaching each of the following comprehension skills at the readiness level: gaining word meaning, identifying details, identifying main ideas, identifying sequence, making inferences, identifying characterization, and identifying fact, fiction, and opinion.
5. Objective 5. What is the importance of assessing and teaching each of the following study skills at the readiness level: following direc-

tions, using the table of contents, classifying, and memorization.

6. Objective 6. Describe two types of scores that can be derived from a standardized reading readiness test and state how each might influence instruction.
7. Objective 7. Describe three procedures other than a standardized test that may be used to assess reading readiness skills.
8. Objective 8. List three reasons why the language experience approach is an excellent strategy to use at the reading readiness level.
9. Objective 9. At Happy Valley Nursery School for four and five-year-olds, the children have been divided into two groups. One group copies words such as Kip, bun, and mat from the chalkboard. The second group is involved in a learning activity in which each child moves a tiny toy animal from space to space on a game board on which the consonants have been printed. As the toy touches the letter, the children pronounce the letter sound. What (if anything) is valuable in this program? What (if anything) is not valuable? Give reasons for your answer.
10. Objective 10. Describe how to assess and teach: (a) any two basic learning skills, (b) any two word identification skills, (c) any two comprehension skills, and (d) any two study skills.
11. Objective 11. Describe a parent-child activity designed to strengthen the child's ability to perform: (a) any one basic learning skill, (b) any one word identification skill, (c) any one comprehension skill, and (d) any one study skill.

Chapter 14
Experience 1

Objective

The participant will assess and teach a minimum of one skill on the readiness level.

Activity and Assessment Guide

Write "yes" or "no" in the blanks preceding each statement.

Plan

1. Does the lesson plan include
   _______ Objective?
   _______ Preassessment?
   _______ Instructional strategies?
   _______ Postassessment?

Selection of Objective

* 2. _______ Does objective selected appear to be on the correct instructional level for the subjects? Why or why not?________________

____

Preassessment Design

* 3. _______ Does each test question appear to assess the behavior described in the objective? If no, why not?________________

____

* 4. _______ Are there at least three items for the objective being assessed?

* 5. _______ Does each test question appear to be on the correct level of difficulty? If no, why not?________________

____

6. _______ General comments:________________

____

Instructional Strategies

* 7. _______ Are the instructional activities appropriate for the objective? If no, why not?________________

____

* 8. _______ Are the instructional activities appropriate for the children's level of skill development? If no, why not?________________

____

* 9. _______ General comments:________________

____

Postassessment

* 10. _______ Did each test question appear to assess the behavior described in the objective? If no, why not?________________

____

* 11. _______ Are there at least three test questions for the objective?

*Asterisked questions may be answered by an observer. See Chapter 1: Experience 1 for further explanation.

* 12. _______ Did each test question appear to be at the correct level of difficulty? Explain: ____

____

* 13. _______ General comments: ____

____

After you have completed this activity, answer the following:

14. _______ Do you believe that your preassessment was valid? Why or why not? ____

15. _______ Do you believe that you taught your subjects a skill? Why or why not? ____

____

16. _______ Do you believe that your subjects felt that they had learned? Why or why not? ____

____

17. _______ General comments: ____

____

18. Write a brief summary of your feelings about the child reaction toward this experience. ____

____

19. State what you believe to be the significant implications of this experience for the classroom teacher. ____

____

____

20. Attach a copy of your lesson plan to this sheet.

Part Seven
Practicing Teaching Reading

Chapter 15
Teaching Word Identification, Comprehension, Study, and Readiness Skills

Elementary reading instruction should be looked upon as a growth process where in new skills are mastered and formerly learned skills are refined and applied to more difficult material. One of the most efficient ways for elementary teachers to overview the reading skills and to select those to be mastered and refined is to look at all the reading skills and how to teach them. This chapter provides the participant with several teaching techniques for each reading skill presented in Chapter 2, "Word Identification Skills," Chapter 3, "Comprehension Skills," Chapter 4, "Study Skills," and Chapter 14, "Reading Readiness." Additionally, assessment procedures are given for each skill described in Chapters 2 and 14. Assessment procedures for skills presented in Chapters 3 and 4 are given in those chapters.

This chapter differs from Chapters 1-14 in that there are no objectives or experiences. However, several of the objectives and experiences in Chapters 1-14 require the participant to use the material presented in Chapter 15.

An overview of the skills in this chapter is given in Table 15.1. Each skill is presented in the order in which it is listed in this table. Therefore, the participant may wish to use Table 15.1 as a table of contents for the teaching techniques that follow. For example, if the participant wished to find teaching techniques for the skill "identifying details," he or she would look in the "comprehension skills" section for skill 2, "identifying details." In addition, if the participant were teaching young children, he or she might also look in the "readiness skills" section for skill 20, "identifying details," for ways in which to teach this skill to young children.

In addition, it should be noted that the teaching strategies discussed in this chapter are basically made up of two types: (1) introductory activities and (2) reinforcement activities. In Chapter 8, "Diagnostic-Prescriptive Teaching," the concept of initial teaching lessons and reinforcement lessons was discussed. The introductory strategies presented in this chapter can be

TABLE 15.1 Skills Presented in Chapter 15 in Order of Their Presentation

Word Identification Skills

1. Using sight word skills
2. Using configuration clues
3. Using picture clues
4. Using context clues
5. Using phonic clues
6. Using morphemic clues
7. Using the dictionary
8. Using word identification skills in combination

Comprehension Skills

1. Gaining word meaning
2. Identifying details
3. Identifying main ideas
4. Identifying sequence
5. Identifying cause-effect relationships
6. Making inferences
7. Making generalizations and conclusions
8. Identifying tone and mood
9. Identifying theme
10. Identifying characterization
11. Identifying fact, fiction, and opinion
12. Identifying propaganda

Study Skills

1. Following directions
2. Scheduling time
3. Adjusting rate to purpose
4. Using a study technique
5. Using aids within books
6. Using maps, graphs, and tables
7. Using locational aids in the library
8. Using reference material
9. Using materials appropriate to purpose
10. Organizing information
11. Recalling information
12. Evaluating information

Readiness Skills

1. Demonstrating visual acuity
2. Demonstrating auditory acuity
3. Demonstrating general health
4. Demonstrating visual discrimination
5. Demonstrating visual memory
6. Demonstrating auditory discrimination
7. Demonstrating auditory memory
8. Demonstrating visual-motor skills
9. Using left-right progression
10. Using individual work habits
11. Showing interest in books
12. Using group work habits
13. Using sight word skills
14. Using configuration clues
15. Using picture clues
16. Using context clues
17. Identifying graphemes and pronouncing phonemes
18. Blending
19. Gaining word meaning
20. Identifying details
21. Identifying main ideas
22. Identifying sequence
23. Making inferences
24. Identifying characterization
25. Identifying fact, fiction, and opinion
26. Following directions
27. Using aids within books (using the table of contents)
28. Organizing information (classifying)
29. Recalling information (memorization)

used as part of the initial teaching lesson. An introductory activity usually explains to the child what the skill is and then gives the child a chance to practice that skill. A reinforcement activity may or may not reexplain the skill, but it does require the child to use that skill in a practice situation. For example, if a teacher explained to a child that the letter g had two sounds and then gave examples of the two sounds, the lesson would qualify as an introductory activity or an initial teaching lesson. On the other hand, if the teacher assigned the child a tic-tac-toe game in which the child could only make a move if he or she could supply a word beginning with soft g, the teacher would be presenting a reinforcement activity. The child would have to have some idea of the two sounds of g before he or she could play the tic-tac-toe game.

In many cases, the introductory activity and the reinforcement activity are exactly the same. In other cases, the assessment procedure may also be used to introduce a new skill. Hence, although the activities in this chapter have been labeled as "introductory" or "reinforcement" or "assessment," in many cases, they may be used in ways other than those labeled. The labels are intended as guidelines, but the teacher is encouraged to use and adapt each activity in the way that best suits his or her purposes.

WORD IDENTIFICATION SKILL 1: USING SIGHT WORD SKILLS

ASSESSMENT

To determine whether a word is part of a child's sight vocabulary, display the written word and ask the pupil to say it. If the child responds accurately within a few seconds, give credit for a correct response and assume that the word is part of the pupil's sight vocabulary. When simultaneously assessing several children's knowledge of many words, use a multiple-choice format requiring the pupils to mark a specific given word in each row of an individual answer sheet containing several rows with about four words written in each. This method involves much less teacher time than the individual assessment procedure just described. However, although correct choice indicates that the word is in the child's sight vocabulary, results of a multiple-choice evaluation may not be totally accurate due to the possibility of the children's making accurate guesses.

TEACHING PROCEDURES

Introductory Activities

1. Tell the children the word to be learned; then use picture, context, configuration, phonic, and morphemic clues to help them learn the word; follow with copious reinforced practice. For example, begin by showing the

class an illustration of a pig and then discuss it (picture clues). Next, identify the word pig in a sentence on the chalkboard such as "The pig lived on a farm." Then, discuss the general configuration of the written word pig by posing questions such as the following (configuration clues). "Is pig a long word or a short word? Are there any tall letters in pig? Are there any letters that go below the line in pig? What are they?" Finally, draw the children's attention to any phonic or morphemic features of the word with which they might be familiar. For example, point out initial and final consonants by asking, "What word does pig start like?" and "What word does pig finish like?" (phonic and morphemic clues). Require the children to recognize the word immediately in a variety of situations, such as locating the word on a page of a book or reading it from a flashcard.

2. Require pupils to use their decoding skills to read the word and then provide practice in a variety of situations. Begin this activity by writing the new word on the board in a sentence that relates to the children's interests and that contains, except for the word to be learned, only words that are in the children's sight vocabularies. For example, when introducing the word bicycle, the teacher might use the sentence, "Bill likes to ride his bicycle." If possible, also provide an appropriate picture. Next, have the children independently use their skills with picture clues, configuration clues, context clues, phonic clues, and morphemic clues to read the new word. If they are unable to do so without teacher aid, ask helpful questions such as "Using the picture, what do you think the word might be?" (picture clues); "What word makes sense in this sentence?" (context clues); "With what affix does the word begin? End?" (morphemic clues). After the word has been accurately identified, draw the children's attention to it in a variety of new situations. For example, have some of the pupils use the word in an original sentence, divide the word into syllables, identify the accented syllable, or discuss the meanings of its affixes or root words.

3. Write the word to be learned on the chalkboard in a sentence that relates to the child's interests. Then have the pupil trace over the word on the board. Next, write the word on a 3″ X 5″ card (which may also be used for a variety of reinforcement activities) and, again, have the pupil trace over the letters on the card. Continue until the child is able to write the word from memory. Pupils may be encouraged to form word banks (as described in Chapter 7) showing the words that they have learned. This activity is particularly useful for children who have difficulty learning sight words.

Reinforcement Activities

4. So that the pupil's phrase reading may be enhanced, teachers are encouraged to use phrases in addition to single words in some of the following activities. For example, instead of simply using the word up, alternate with phrases that also include known words, such as up the hill, and up the stairs.

5. Encourage copious reading materials that are easy for the pupil. (See Chapter 11, "Recreational Reading," for numerous suggestions for motivating children to read.)

6. Play "Around the World." Have the class form a circle in which all sit down, except one child who stands behind the first one sitting in the circle. Show a card containing the sight word to all the children. If the child standing says the word first, he or she moves behind the next child in the circle. But, if the child sitting says the word first, he or she stands behind the next child sitting in the circle and the child who was standing sits in his or her place. Play is continued in this manner. Each player's objective is to go around the circle without sitting down.

7. Play "Fishing." Write the word to be reinforced on colored pieces of paper cut to look like fish. Attach a paper clip to each and place the "fish" in a "fishbowl." Construct a fishing pole by tying to a stick a short piece of string with a small magnet attached. Have the children take turns using the fishing pole to "catch" the fish. When the pupils catch a fish, they try to read the word written on it. If they are able to do so, they keep their catches. If they cannot correctly pronounce the word, they must return their fish to the bowl. The child with the most fish at the end of the game is the winner.

8. Play "Bingo," using sight words on the "Bingo" cards.

9. Play "Old Maid" with cards constructed using new sight words.

10. Play "Concentration" with a deck containing several pairs of new sight word cards.

WORD IDENTIFICATION SKILL 2: USING CONFIGURATION CLUES

ASSESSMENT

To assess skill configuration clues, ask the reader to tell how he or she identifies a given word. For example, show the child the word basket. If the pupil says that the word is basket because it contains three tall letters, then configuration clues were used to recognize the word.

TEACHING PROCEDURES

Introductory Activity

1. When introducing a new word, carefully indicate important aspects of its physical configuration such as its length, shape, double letters, capital letters, hyphens, apostrophes, and/or repetition of letters. For example, the word vacuum is easily recognizable because it includes two consecutive letter u's.

Reinforcement Activities

2. Have the pupil match configuration clues to appropriate words (Ives, Bursuk, and Ives, 1979). This activity could be set up using a lacing board

in which the child places the lace in the hole beside the appropriate response. Or the items to be matched could be written on a piece of colored paper that has been covered with clear plastic so that the children may respond by drawing lines with erasable felt-tip pens or crayons. A third alternative might include providing a duplicate copy of the exercise for each pupil, who may then use pen or pencil to complete the exercise.

Example: Matching Words with Configuration Clues

Fred	__ __ __ ‾ __ __ __
daddy	M __ __ __
bow-wow	__ __ __
Ted	⊔
Mike	d __dd__

3. Provide pupils with worksheets containing several scrambled words written on illustrations and have them complete the activity by unscrambling the words. This activity can be made easier by listing the unscrambled words elsewhere on the worksheet.

Example: Winter Word Scramble

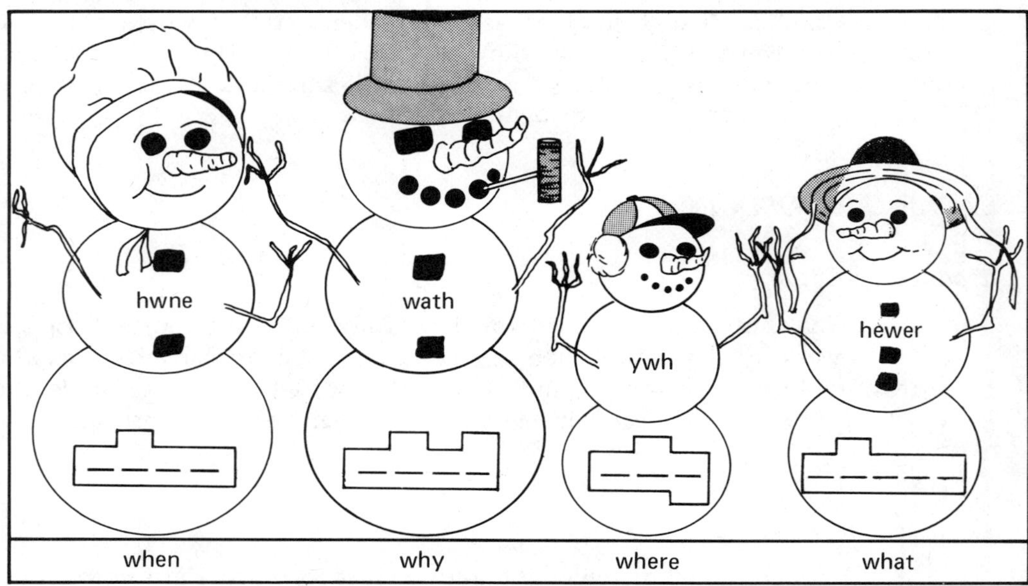

WORD IDENTIFICATION SKILL 3: USING PICTURE CLUES

ASSESSMENT

Ask the children to read a brief passage that is accompanied by a relevant picture. (Part of almost any story from a child's reader or textbook is satisfactory, providing that it includes a picture.) After reading the selection, have the children close their books and then assess their use of picture clues by asking them several questions whose answers are based upon observing the picture rather than reading the text.

TEACHING PROCEDURES

Introductory Activity

1. Explain to children that sometimes authors use illustrations to clarify or expand an idea. Go through a content area textbook with the children and show them photographs, cartoons, line drawings, and other illustrations that appear in the book. Select a simple illustration and explain that "one picture is worth a thousand words." Direct each child to describe one of the illustrations in writing.

Reinforcement Activities

2. Before the pupils begin a reading assignment, draw their attention to any pictures that may accompany the text, discussing terminology or concepts illustrated.

3. Encourage pupils to use pictures when they are in their reading materials.

4. Have the pupils choose unusual objects with which they are familiar. Then, ask them to write definition of their items and to exchange these definitions with classmates, who attempt to draw the objects using only the clues provided by the definitions. Then, show the drawings and discuss them with the pupils who wrote the definitions. Follow up this activity with a teacher-led discussion about how pictures can clarify definitions.

WORD IDENTIFICATION SKILL 4: USING CONTEXT CLUES

ASSESSMENT

The cloze procedure, originated by Bormuth (1968), is one of the methods used to both teach and assess the use of context clues. This technique involves the use of a teacher-selected reading passage of one or more paragraphs in which words have been deleted at regular intervals and replaced with blanks of a uniform size. Usually, no more than every fifth or less than every tenth word is deleted. Pupils are asked to complete the activity by filling in the blanks with appropriate words.

For example, the teacher may assess the pupils' use of context clues by having them complete a cloze passage such as the one given here. Credit should be given for any sensible response.

> Rachel Stewart. That is (my) name, and today I (am) eight years old. I (am) writing this in my (diary) that was a birthday (present) from my mother. It's (strange) to look and (see) nothing but blank pages.*

TEACHING PROCEDURES

The cloze procedure may be used as an instructional as well as an assessment technique. However, in instructional cloze passages, words may be deleted at the teacher's discretion and not necessarily at regular intervals. Each activity presented here is a variation of the cloze procedure, and pupils should be given credit for any sensible responses.

Introductory Activity

1. Write on the chalkboard sentences with one word missing and ask pupils to contribute words that make sense. Discuss the pupil's word choices. Explain how to use context clues to find the correct word.

Reinforcement Activities

2. Prepare worksheets containing paragraphs in which words have been omitted and replaced by blanks. Below each blank write several words and have the pupils fill in the blanks with the most appropriate choice.

Example:

Scooter was a furry, black dog. He liked to lie in the ____________________.
(road, off, roof)
Cars coming down the street drove around ____________________ al-
(them, those, him)
though he ____________________ like a big, black mop.
(ate, looked, sang)

This activity may be made self-correcting by writing in the correct responses and then covering them with small flaps of paper attached with a single piece

*Reprinted by permission of the publishers from Dorothy and Thomas Hoobler, *Frontier Diary*, New York: Macmillan, 1975.

of tape so that they may be lifted. After the students select their answers, they lift the "flaps" to see if they are correct.

3. Prepare worksheets containing paragraphs in which words have been omitted and have pupils fill in the blanks with words that fit the context.

4. Prepare worksheets containing sentences or short paragraphs including one word that the pupil does not recognize as a sight word. Have the child choose from four alternatives the word that most closely matches the meaning of the unknown word.

Example:

The butterfly *hovered* over the doorway.

_______ a. ran　　　　_______ c. shouted

_______ b. fluttered　　　　_______ d. cried

This exercise may be made self-correcting by using flaps as in the first reinforcement activity.

5. Remove a story from an about-to-be discarded book or a children's magazine so that some of the words (such as those against the binding) are deleted. Paste the story to a file folder and cover it with clear plastic. Have the children attempt to reconstruct the story by writing words that fit the context in the blanks that replace the deleted words.

Example: Torn Story

Stranger in the City*

Peggy Peters was a stranger in the _______
She was not used to tall buildings and _______
walks and faces of people she didn't _______
The Peters family had always lived on a _______
They had just moved to the city, and life _______
very different here.

*Reprinted by permission of the publishers from A. J. Harris and M. K. Clark, *Better Than Gold*, New York: Macmillan, 1965, p. 25.

Word Identification Skill 4: Using Context Clues

In addition to using the cloze procedure, the teacher may use a variety of other strategies to teach context clues to children.

6. Show the children a new word and encourage them to read the entire sentence and then come back and try and guess the meaning of the word. Discuss the five types of clues, that is, *definition*, *implication*, *example*, *contrast*, and *expectancy* (see Chapter 2). Then introduce more new words in sentences that give the meanings of the words.

7. Give the children a list of sentences in which the meanings of new words can be determined. List the five types of context clues in a column below the sentences. The children are to guess the meaning of the new word and then match the sentence with the type of context clue that they used to determine meaning.

WORD IDENTIFICATION SKILL 5: USING PHONIC CLUES

Using phonic clues includes assessment of sound-symbol correspondence, teaching procedures for sound-symbol correspondence, assessment of syllabication skills, and teaching procedures for syllabication skills.

ASSESSMENT OF SOUND-SYMBOL CORRESPONDENCE

When assessing skill in the use of sound-symbol correspondence as a tool for decoding unrecognized words, evaluation must be made of the reader's proficiency in the two separate skills: (1) identification of graphemes and pronunciation of phonemes and (2) blending of phonemes.

Assessing Identifying Graphemes and Pronouncing Phonemes

To test an individual child's ability to identify graphemes and pronounce phonemes, display a word that is not in the pupil's sight vocabulary. Then ask the child to pronounce the word and evaluate this pronunciation on the basis of knowledge of sound-symbol correspondence. For example, ask the child to pronounce the word each. If the response pronunciation correctly treats the graphemes e and a as the vowel digraph ea and the graphemes c and h as the consonant digraph ch, then the teacher may assume that the child possesses skill in identifying the graphemes and pronouncing the phonemes ea and ch. However, if the pronunciation incorrectly treats these graphmes as the singular phonemes e, a, c, and h, then it must be assumed that the pupil lacks this skill.

Group assessment of identification of graphemes and pronunciation of phonemes may be accomplished through the following procedure. Provide each child with a test sheet containing rows of words not in the pupil's sight vocabularies and have the child mark the word containing the appropriate grapheme as you designate its corresponding phoneme through sentences such as "Circle the word that begins like shine." (It should be noted that the teacher should not say, "Circle the word with the sh sound," as pronouncing isolated phonemes sometimes results in sound distortion.)

Assessing Blending of Phonemes

Assessment of a child's ability to blend word parts may be accomplished by saying a word slowly and then by having the child attempt to pronounce the word. For example, say "hat" very slowly (h-a-t) and then ask the pupil to repeat the word "hat."

TEACHING PROCEDURES FOR SOUND-SYMBOL CORRESPONDENCE

The following techniques for developing skill in using sound-symbol correspondence as a phonic clue are presented under the headings "Teaching Identifying Graphemes and Pronouncing Phonemes," "Teaching the Rules for the Use of Long and Short Vowel Sounds," and "Teaching Blending."

Teaching Identifying Graphemes and Pronouncing Phonemes

Introductory Activity

1. Show the class several objects or pictures whose names contain the grapheme and/or phoneme to be learned. For example, a chick, a chair, and a cherry may be used to introduce the consonant digraph ch. While displaying these objects or pictures, pronounce the name of each and then ask the pupils to identify the phoneme common to all three. Next, write the grapheme ch on the chalkboard, appropriately label each picture or object with its written name, and have the children pronounce each word. Finally, have the pupils think of other words that contain the phonemes ch and write these words on the chalkboard, underlining the grapheme ch in each.

a. Tell aloud a story in which there are many words containing the grapheme and phoneme ch. Ask the pupils to name these words. Then write them on the chalkboard and have the children underline the grapheme ch within each word.

Example:

Story	*Grapheme/Phoneme*	
"Charlies cheered for each church team. He choked when he jumped and bumped his chin on the bench."	Charlie cheered each church	choked chin bench

b. Give each child two pieces of paper, one blank and one with the grapheme ch written on both sides. Then call out a series of words or show a series of pictures, including some whose names contain the phoneme ch. Ask the students to hold up the marked card when you say a word or hold up a picture whose name contains ch and to hold up the blank card when a word that does not contain ch is indicated.

Of course, this activity and its extensions may be used to introduce any grapheme or phoneme. However, each lesson in which a grapheme or phoneme is introduced should end with an exercise requiring the children to use their new knowledge to decode a word with which they are not familiar. For example, the children might be asked to read sentences containing an unfamiliar word, such as "John chose a big dog. Jerry chose a little cat."

Reinforcement Activities

2. Give the children a worksheet containing several pictures and multiple-choice answers and instruct them to circle the answer that indicates the word part appropriate to the picture.

Example: Initial Consonant Circle

Word Identification Skill 5: Using Phonic Clues

Extend this activity by asking the children to write the correct grapheme beside an illustration of an object whose name contain it.

Example: Initial Consonant Write

3. Provide children with a worksheet with a column of pictures and a column of graphemes to be matched.

Example: Initial Consonant Match

4. Have the children draw or cut from magazines pictures of objects whose names contain the letter or letter group under study.

5. Design a colorful bulletin board containing envelopes labeled with graphemes (such as d, oy, ph, and ea). Instruct the children to collect pictures of objects whose names contain the specific word parts (such as dog, boy, phone, and meat) and to file the pictures in the appropriate envelopes.

6. Have the children play "Bingo" on cards labeled with graphemes with which they are familiar. As the "caller" pronounces words, the players cover the graphemes on their cards.

Example: Bingo Card

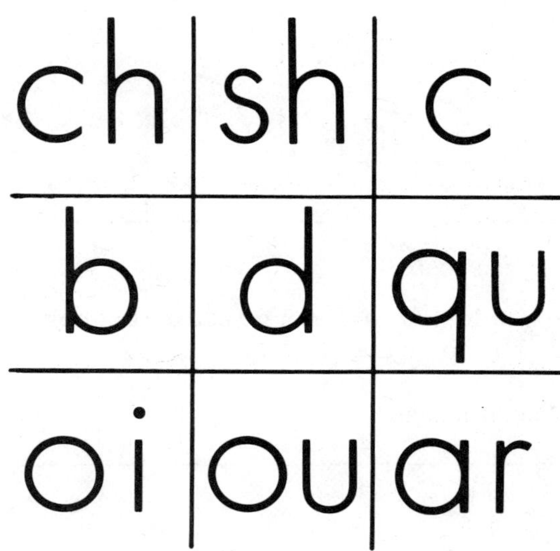

7. Label the inner bottoms of plastic cups with graphemes to which the children have been introduced. Then have the children sort into these cups pictures of objects whose names contain the phonic element indicated.

Teaching the Rules for the Use of Long and Short Vowel Sounds

The rules for the use of long and short vowel sounds, as stated previously, are that (1) short vowel sounds usually occur in accented syllables and one-syllable words ending in a consonant, and (2) long vowel sounds usually occur in accented syllables and one-syllable words ending in the vowel itself, ending in silent e, or containing a vowel digraph. When introducing these rules, the teacher should discuss them one at a time and should begin with a review of common long and short vowel sounds.

Word Identification Skill 5: Using Phonic Clues

Introductory Activity

1. Write on the chalkboard a list of words that are in the children's sight vocabularies and that follow the rule being introduced. For example, when introducing the rule that vowels normally have a short sound when followed by a consonant in an accented syllable or a one-syllable word, list words such as and, help, in, not, and up on the board and have the class determine that the vowel sound is short. Then ask the pupils to make up the rule for knowing if the vowel sound is short, leading them to realize that each word has only one syllable and that the vowel in each is followed by a consonant. Have the pupils think of several one-syllable words that have short vowel sounds and discuss whether the rule holds true for these words. Then divide the class into small groups of two or three students and ask the members of each group to take from their reading book a list of one-syllable words that contain a single vowel followed by a consonant. At the end of a five-minute period, have each group write its words on the chalkboard. Discuss the word lists, looking for exceptions to the rule. Conclude the lesson by having the children read sentences containing words that are not in their sight vocabularies and that follow the rule learned.

Reinforcement Activities

2. Children complete worksheets requiring them to fill in blanks and words meeting specified criteria relating to the use of long and short vowel sounds.

Example:

Mother said, "I see the ________________________." (short a)
(man, rain, milk)

3. Have the class play the game "Postman." Give several children "mailboxes," each with a label indicating one of the rules under study. For example, one box may be labeled "cat—short vowel sound." Give the remaining children cards that serve as letters, each with a word written on it. Instruct the children to mail their "letters" in the correct "mailbox." For example, the letter with the word them would be placed in the mailbox labeled "cat—short vowel sound" as both words follow the same rule.

4. Construct an activity board that shows a small terrier, labeled *short*, and a dachshund, labeled *long*. Provide the pupils with bone-shaped cards containing single words, some with short vowel sounds and some with long

vowel sounds. Have the children "Give the dog a bone" by sorting the cards according to the rules for use of vowel sounds.

Example: Give a Dog a Bone

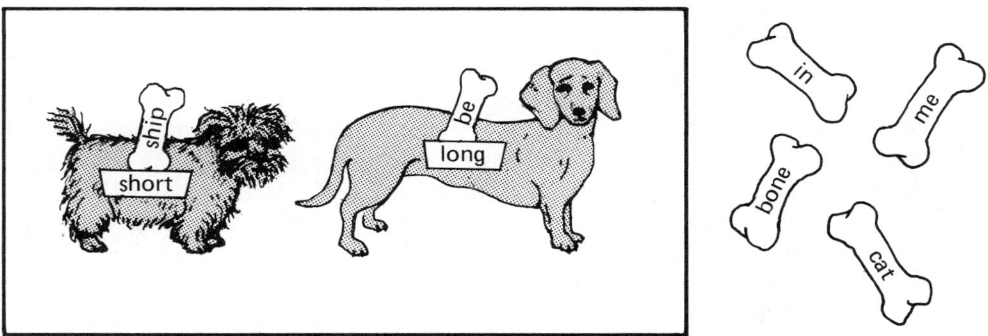

5. Instruct the class to build a bulletin board that has words with short vowel sounds on one side and words with long vowel sounds on the other. Then ask the children to explain why the vowel sounds are long or short in specific words.

Teaching Blending

Introductory Activity

1. Write on the chalkboard a simple three-letter word that is not in the children's sight vocabulary. Then ask the children to use letter cards to construct the word at their desks in individual pocket charts.

Example: Individual Pocket Chart

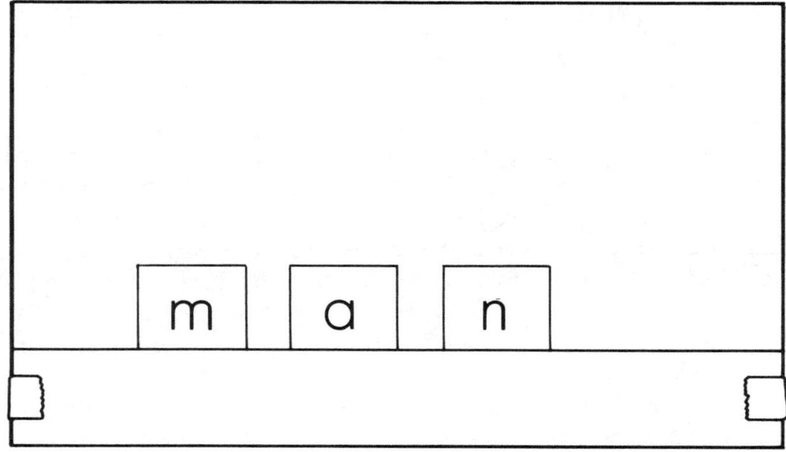

Next have the class say the word as you slowly blend its letters. Conclude the lesson by asking the children to read two- and three-letter words that are not in their sight vocabularies.

Reinforcement Activity

2. Provide the pupils with simple blending devices, such as those shown, that have strips that are inserted into and pulled through slots, forming words as they appear. This activity can be made more interesting by constructing the blending devices so that they match the children's interests or reflect the season.

Example: Blending Devices

ASSESSMENT OF SYLLABICATION SKILLS

To assess pupils' skill in using syllabication to decode unrecognized words, show them nonsense words such as those in the sample following and ask them to (1) divide the words into syllables, (2) indicate the accented syllables, (3) mark each vowel sound as short, long, or schwa, and (4) pronounce the words.

Sample: Instructions to the student

1. Divide the following words into syllables. The first one has been done for you.

   dabbad ______dab/bad______

   rashape ____________________

   sitlo ____________________

   loka ____________________

   presorting ____________________

2. Mark the accented syllable (') in each word. Example: dab'/bad.
3. Mark the vowels in each of the above words as short (˘), long (-), or schwa (ə). Example: dăb/bəd.
4. Read each of the words to your teacher.

TEACHING PROCEDURES FOR SYLLABICATION SKILLS

The following techniques for developing skill in using syllabication skills as a phonic clue are presented under the headings "Teaching Definition of a Syllable," "Teaching Generalizations for Dividing Words into Syllables and Accenting Syllables," "Teaching Generalizations for Pronouncing Syllables," and "Teaching Syllabication As a Decoding Skill."

Teaching Definition of a Syllable

Introductory Activity

1. Demonstrate to the class the correlation between the number of vowel sounds in a word and its number of syllables. For example, list on the board familiar multisyllabic words that contain several vowels. Then, divide the words into syllables and point out that, even though a syllable may contain more than one vowel, it has only one vowel sound.

Example:

dou/ble
pleas/ant
through/out

Word Identification Skill 5: Using Phonic Clues

Reinforcement Activities

2. Have the children place their hands on their chins while saying a multisyllabic word. Each time that a syllable is said, their chins will drop one time.

3. Provide each student with three cards: one with one colored dot, another with two colored dots, and a third with three colored dots. Then call out words and have the children hold up the cards with the number of dots corresponding to the number of syllables in the words.

4. Play "Buttons on the Snowmen." Draw several snowmen on the chalkboard. When the leader says a word, the player draws as many buttons on a snowman as there are syllables in the word. This lesson may be adapted as a flannel board activity or as a worksheet.

Teaching Generalizations for Dividing Words Into Syllables and Accenting Syllables

Introductory Activities

1. Write on the chalkboard at least three words that follow the rule to be taught and that are familiar to the children. Have the children attempt to name the rule demonstrated by all the words (e.g., list mommy, winter, and accent). Then divide the first word into syllables, using colored chalk to identify the breaking point (mom/my) and verbalize the reason for dividing the word in such a manner (when two consonants occur between two vowels the word is divided between the two consonants). Next, have the pupils divide the remaining words and verbalize the appropriate rule. Finally, have the children think of or locate in their textbooks examples of words that follow the rule and have them practice the rule by dividing the words.

2. Use the same instructional procedure presented in activity 2; that is (1) present known words that exemplify the rule being introduced, (2) have the pupils attempt to name the rule demonstrated by the words, (3) accent one of the sample words and explain the rule for doing so, (4) have the pupils accent the remaining words and state the rule, (5) have the pupils think of or locate words that follow the rule, and (6) provide practice applying the rule.

Reinforcement Activities

3. Construct word or picture word cards and cut them between syllables. Then have the children match card pieces and tell the generalization for dividing words into syllables exemplified by each word.

Example:

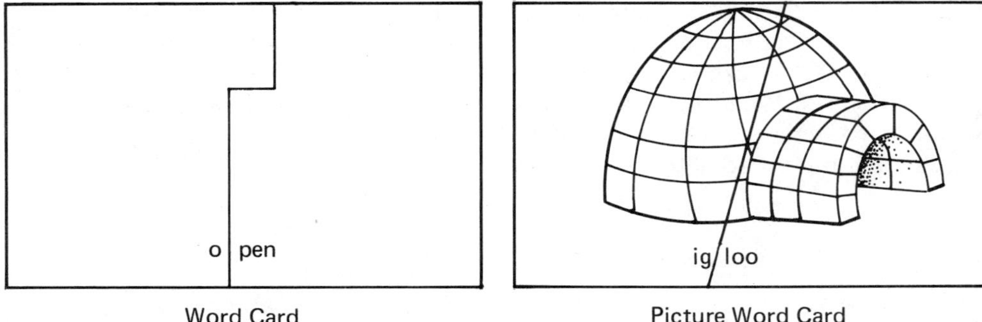

Word Card

Picture Word Card

4. Within the classroom hang key word charts such as the ones shown that present words exemplifying generalizations for dividing words into syllables and accenting.

Example:

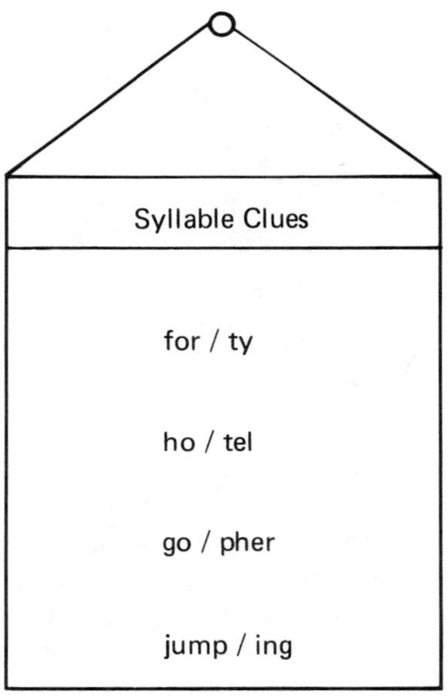

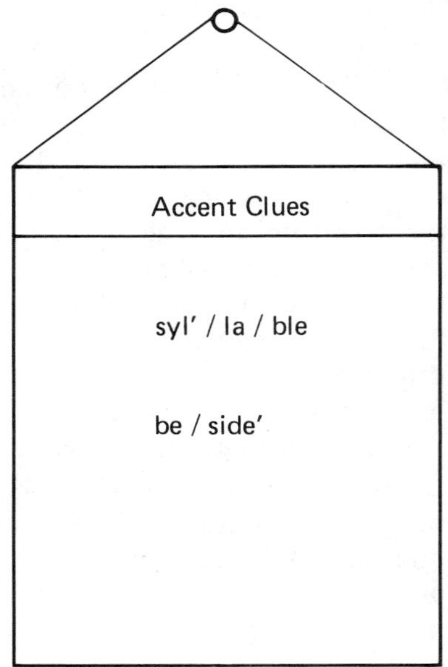

5. Play a game in which the children divide into syllables and properly accent the names of the pupils in the class.

6. Have a "Syllable Bee" during which opposing teams attempt to divide words into syllables, place accents, and state the generalizations for both. If the first team's player is not successful, the second team's first player is given a try with the same word. This procedure continues until the word is correctly divided and accented and the generalizations have been cited. When a team is successful, his or her team receives one point. The team with the most points at the end of the game wins.

Teaching Generalizations for Pronouncing Syllables

Introductory Activity

1. Use word cards as blending devices. For example, write common initial syllables (such as per, con, in, and trans) on a strip to be inserted into the slit on a card containing a second syllable (such as form) to make various words (such as perform, conform, inform, and transform).

Example: Blending Device

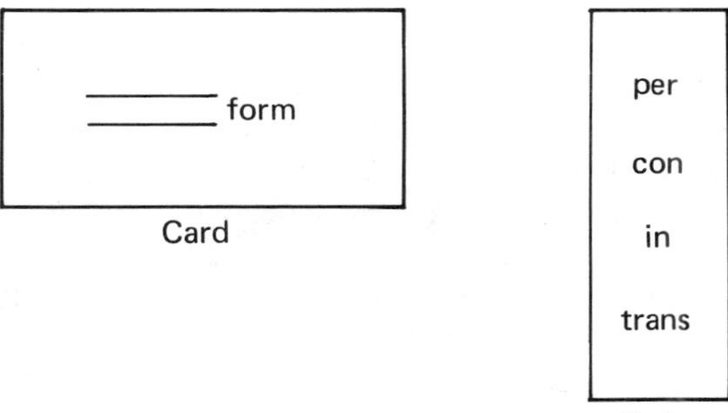

Reinforcement Activity

2. Play the game "Syllable Move" in which the pupils take turns attempting to pronounce multisyllabic words. Pupils are allowed to mark syllable divisions and accents. If a player is successful, he or she moves his or her marker as many spaces on the gameboard as there are syllables in the word.

Teaching Syllabication As a Decoding Skill

Introductory Activity

1. Hold a class discussion during which it is explained to the pupils that they should use syllabication when they come to a word that they do not

recognize immediately only if they are unable to identify the word using other decoding skills. Then, discuss the four steps in using syllabication as a phonic clue: (1) divide the word into syllables, (2) identify the accented syllables, (3) pronounce each syllable, and (4) blend the syllables to pronounce the word. Continue the discussion by asking leading questions to elicit the information that the goal of syllabication is to be able to pronounce the word accurately enough that its spoken counterpart can be brought to mind.

Following the class discussion, present the pupils with a few multisyllabic words and have them practice the syllabication sequence. Or divide the class into teams of two or three members and instruct each team to locate five terms believed to be unknown in the printed form to another team. Then have the teams exchange lists and use syllabication to discern the correct pronunciation of the words. The group with the highest number of correct responses wins.

Reinforcement Activities

2. Present words with which the pupils are familiar and have them (a) divide the words into syllables, (b) place the accent, (c) pronounce the syllables, and (d) blend the syllables to pronounce the words.

3. Present the class with a few sentences containing words that the pupils do not recognize in print. Some of these words should follow the generalizations for syllabication, and some should not. Have the children try to pronounce the words.

Sample: Exception to the rule

The lemon was in the bowl.

Following the generalizations for dividing words into syllables, the pupils should divide lemon as le/mon. However, since this division, with the first syllable rhyming with me, does not provide a pronunciation allowing for recognition of the spoken word, pupils should try the alternate division lem/on to correctly pronounce and, thus, identify the word.

This reinforcement activity should be used only after the pupils are well acquainted with the phonic generalizations necessary to the syllabication procedure. Pupils should be instructed to attempt to decode an unfamiliar word by first following the rules, but to consider the exceptions when the rules prove unsuccessful before giving up on the syllabication procedure.

WORD IDENTIFICATION SKILL 6: USING MORPHEMIC CLUES

ASSESSMENT

Assess the pupil's ability to recognize and interpret the meanings of the various types of morphemic clues through exercises such as the following.

Root Words

Have the pupil circle the roots of familiar words.

Example:

helping helps called graphic enlarge telegraph

Prefixes

Have the child circle the prefix in each of a list of words and then draw a line from the word to the correct meaning of its prefix.

Example:

(bi)cycle ———	not
nonsense	——— two
remind	one
uniform	again

Suffixes

Have the pupil circle the suffix in each of a list of words and then draw a line from the word to the correct meaning of its suffix.

Example:

play(er) ———	one who
friendless	worthy of
milky	like
respectable	without

Inflectional Endings

Show the child a sentence containing a blank to be filled in with a word with an inflectional ending provided as a multiple-choice answer. Have the child write the correct word in the blank and then circle the word's inflectional ending.

Example:

Mary has two doll(s) ____________.
(doll, dolls, doll's)

____________ truck is green.
(Howard, Howard's, Howards)

Betty ____________ her head yesterday.
(bumping, bumped, bumps)

Matt is ____________ than Pete.
(shortly, shorter, shorts)

Contractions

Have the pupil draw a line from a contraction to the two words that express its meaning.

Example:

can't	will not
won't	cannot
I'm	you are
you're	I am

TEACHING PROCEDURES

Introductory Activity

1. Show students known words that contain an example of the type of morphemic clue under study. For example, if the class is learning to use an inflectional ending such as the morpheme 's, house's and Billy's might be used. Have the pupils pronounce the words and use them in sentences. Provide example if necessary. Next, have the class divide the base words from the morphemic clue (dog/'s, house/'s, Billy/'s). Continue the exercise by asking the children to name or locate in their text other words that contain the specified morpheme. Write their choices on the chalkboard and write the morpheme in each word. The meaning of the morpheme may then be deduced by the class through a teacher-led discussion that elicits the understanding that, because the morpheme always bears the same meaning, it is a useful tool in decoding unrecognized words. Ask the pupils to demonstrate their understanding by decoding words that incorporate the newly acquired morpheme.

Word Identification Skill 6: Using Morphemic Clues

Reinforcement Activities

2. Declare a "Morpheme of the Day" and have the pupils think of words that contain this morpheme (Kaufman, 1974).

3. Provide the children a reading selection such as a short paragraph and have them underline examples of a specified type of morphemic clue.

Example:

Baby Joe walked slowly toward the stairs. Acting quickly, Joe's older sister caught him before he reached the highest step. Otherwise, Baby Joe would have fallen.

4. Develop a crossword puzzle that requires the children to identify morphemes. For example, to complete the puzzle shown, pupils would identify the suffixes and inflectional endings and write them in the correct place.

Example: Morpheme Crossword

Across	*Down*
1. respectful	2. slowly
3. tempted	3. bushes
5. former	4. grantor

5. Show the pupils a sentence in which a contraction is used. Together with the teacher, children identify the contraction and its meaning, carefully noting the apostrophe and its purpose.

6. Play "Concentration," using pairs of cards, one of which contains the contraction and the other its corresponding words.

7. Play "Rummy" and "Old Maid" using cards such as those prepared for "Concentration" in activity 6.

8. Play "Tagboard Baseball." Draw a baseball field on a piece of tagboard and cut out small circles of paper that look like baseballs. On one side of the "baseball" write the contraction. On the other, write its correspond-

ing words. Place the baseballs on home plate, either side up. Proceed as in regular baseball with the "batter" required to tell what is written on the opposite side of his or her baseball.

9. Present the pupils with a word (such as aquamarine) and have them (a) divide the word into morphemes (aqua/marine), (b) examine the morphemes for meaning (aqua meaning water, and marine meaning sea), and (c) interpret the meaning of the word (seawater).

WORD IDENTIFICATION SKILL 7: USING THE DICTIONARY

ASSESSMENT

Each of the assessment procedures described here requires the teacher to work with a small group of pupils, all of whom are holding identical dictionaries.

Assessing Locating Words in the Dictionary

To test the pupils' skills in locating words in the dictionary, write a main entry word on the chalkboard and ask the children to find it in the dictionary. While the pupils are completing this task, note their abilities to turn to the appropriate part of the dictionary (first, middle, last), use guide words, and find the main entry word noted.

Assessing Using Diacritical Markings to Pronounce a Word

The pupils' skills in using diacritical markings to ascertain the pronunciation of a word may be evaluated by asking them to find the pronunciation of a word that they are unable to pronounce without using the dictionary. First, reveal the location of the word in the dictionary. Then, ask each child to pronounce the word, repeating this procedure until all have had an opportunity to pronounce at least one word. Give credit for correct pronunciations.

Assessing Finding the Appropriate Meaning of the Word

Evaluate the pupils' skills in ascertaining the appropriate meaning of a word from those listed by using a word that has more than one definition in a sentence within whose context the meaning of the word is not recognized by the children; for example, "The sled's left runner fell off." Show the pupils the location of the word in the dictionary and give them credit for locating its appropriate meaning.

Word Identification Skill 7: Using the Dictionary

TEACHING PROCEDURES

Teaching the Dictionary Skills in General

Introductory Activity

1. Ask each child for his or her favorite word. Construct a list of all the words given and duplicate copies for every child. Explain to the children that a dictionary is a source that they can use to find the meaning of each word. Show them how the dictionary arranges words in alphabetical order so that each word can be found easily. Then place the children in small groups and ask them to cut out the list of "favorite" words and place them in alphabetical order so that they can make a classroom dictionary. Use these words to teach children how to alphabetize by the first two and three letters of each word. Explain guide words to children and have each group look up the first word on the "favorite" word list. Help the children to determine if any more of the words would use those same two guide words. Eventually, the children should each be helped to construct their own dictionary of the favorite words from the class. Each dictionary should contain guide words and definitions. Throughout the year, the dictionary should be individualized by asking each child to add weekly at least one word that he or she wants to "know."

Reinforcement Activities

2. Divide the class into teams of two and make certain that each pair has a dictionary. Give the children a list of words and ask them to locate aspects such as the following concerning each word: (a) guide words on the page, (b) accent, (c) syllabication, (d) phonetic spelling, (e) any cross-references, (f) the plural form, (g) the part of speech, and (h) the tense. After each pair has finished its list, compare their responses with the other pairs of children. Discuss any aspects that the children may not have known. Finally, summarize the type of things that can be found in a dictionary.

3. Ask the children to watch television and look for three new words shown on the screen for which they are not sure of the meaning. They are to look up the words in the dictionary and then compare words that they have found with those located by other class members.

4. Give each child a dictionary and a list of questions. The winner is the first one to get all the items correct. Use questions that force them to use many parts of a dictionary: for example, "How many numbered definitions are there for the word fuzz? How many ways to correctly pronounce the word "horrid"? In what year was Einstein born? Where is Transylvania? Is the rattlesnake native to the United States?"

Teaching Locating Words in the Dictionary

Introductory Activity

1. Provide each child with a copy of the particular dictionary to be used for this lesson. First, explain that the dictionary can be divided into three

parts: the first (A–G), the middle (M–P), and the last (Q–Z). Next, write a word on the chalkboard and ask the children to name the part of the dictionary in which the word would be located. For example, boy would be in the first part, joke would be in the middle, and snake would be in the last. Practice with several words, having the children turn to the appropriate part of the dictionary for each word given.

Continue this lesson by explaining the location and use of guide words. Write on the chalkboard the two guide words located on a page of the dictionary being used. Have the pupils think of as many words as they can that might appear on that page. Then have the class turn to the page on which the given guide words are located and check to see how many of their choices actually appear on that page. During this activity, ask leading questions that help the children to realize that using guide words will allow them to locate words in the dictionary more quickly.

As the next part of this activity, explain how and why the words on each page of a dictionary are alphabetized. Next, have the class alphabetize a given list of words, all of which are located on the same dictionary page, and then open their dictionaries and locate these words on the page indicated.

Finally, provide practice in combining all the newly acquired skills to locate words in the dictionary by (a) turning to the appropriate part of the dictionary, (b) using guide words, and (c) using alphabetization to locate the word on the page.

Reinforcement Activities

2. *Parts of the dictionary:* Mark three boxes, one "First (A–G)," another "Middle (H–P)," and the third "Last (Q–Z)." Then provide the children with word cards and instruct them to place the cards in the appropriate boxes.

3. *Guide words:* Prepare a folder containing (a) three envelopes, each of which has written on it a pair of guide words from the pupils' dictionary, and (b) cards printed with words taken from the appropriate dictionary pages. Have the children first file the word cards in the correct envelopes and then check their own responses by turning to the appropriate page of the dictionary to verify the presence of each word.

Example:

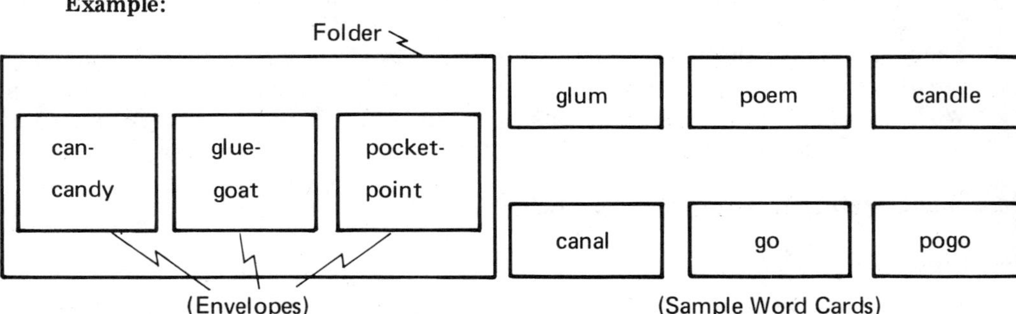

4. *Alphabetization:* Punch holes in several colorful word cards and have the pupils string the cards in alphabetical order.

5. *Alphabetization:* After discussing vocabulary words taken from a story in the pupils' reader or from a spelling lesson, have the children alphabetize the words.

6. *Alphabetization:* Have each child cut out five words from the newspaper and exchange them with a partner who pastes the words in alphabetical order on notebook paper. Each partner checks the other for accuracy before turning in the lists.

Teaching Using Diacritical Marking to Pronounce a Word

Introductory Activity

1. Show the pupils the pronunciation key in their dictionaries and then discuss facets of the key by asking questions such as "How is the short sound for each vowel shown? How is the long sound for each vowel shown? How many sounds are shown for each consonant? each vowel? the silent letters? the schwa? the hard c? the hard g? the soft c? soft g? How are primary accents shown?" Next tell the children that they are going to be detectives and crack a secret code. Then show several words written according to the pronunciation key and ask them to pronounce each. Continue by having the children locate words in the dictionary. Show them how and where the words are written with diacritical markings and have them pronounce the words.

Reinforcement Activities

2. Rewrite a paragraph using diacritical markings and have the pupils attempt to transcribe the paragraph into normal English, using the dictionary when necessary. Discuss the childrens' answers.

3. Write on the chalkboard a list of words that the children are unable to pronounce. Allow the pupils to attempt to pronounce the words. Then have them look up the words in the dictionary and write their diacritical transcriptions beside the original words on the chalkboard. Then ask the children to try again to pronounce the words.

4. Play "Dictionary Bingo." Equip all pupils with markers and playing cards that contain words written in regular script. Proceed as in regular "Bingo." When the leader writes the phonetic transcription of a word on the chalkboard, those players who have that word on their cards cover it. The first player to cover five spaces in a row wins.

Word Identification Skill 7: Using the Dictionary

Teaching Finding the Appropriate Meaning of the Word

Introductory Activity

1. Choose a word that is in the pupils' dictionaries, has a minimum of two meanings listed, and whose meaning is unknown to the pupils. Write on the chalkboard a sentence containing the word, underline the word, and below it provide several of its meanings that are listed in the dictionary. Have the pupils select the meaning that they believe to be correct and to then locate the word in the dictionary. Point out to the children the multiple meanings of the word. Help them to select the one that is appropriate for the sentence and compare it with their original choice. Repeat this procedure with several words.

Example:

The hobo kept his clothes in a poke.
(jab, sack, dawdle)

Reinforcement Activities

2. Give the pupils a worksheet containing words underlined in sentences and instruct them to look up the words in the dictionary, to choose their correct meanings from those listed, and to write the appropriate meanings on lines preceding the sentences.

3. Have each pupil locate in the dictionary an unfamiliar word. Then, ask the pupil to pronounce the word (using diacritical markings), to choose one of the word's meanings, and to use the word in a sentence. Next, have the individual children present their sentences to the class and ask the other pupils to guess the meaning of the word and to verify their guesses by using the dictionary.

4. Play "Dictionary Old Maid." Write out sentences containing underlined vocabulary words on separate index cards, making duplicates of each card. Also make one card that reads, "Old Maid." To play the game, all the cards are dealt, and play proceeds exactly as in regular "Old Maid" except that a player wishing to put down a matching set must correctly pronounce and define the underlined word. (Dictionaries may be used.) The player who fails in this task must relinquish the pair in exchange for the "Old Maid." If the player already holds the "Old Maid," the pair must be awarded to the next player on the right.

WORD IDENTIFICATION SKILL 8: USING WORD IDENTIFICATION SKILLS IN COMBINATION

ASSESSMENT

To test the pupils' abilities in using the word identification skills in combination, present them with a sentence and note the skills that they use to read the sentence.

TEACHING PROCEDURES

Introductory Activity

1. Help pupils to develop a technique, or sequence, for identifying unfamiliar words. For example, pupils may be taught to first "look around" when they encounter an unknown word, examining the words that precede and follow it for possible context clues and/or picture clues that may allow them to make an educated guess at the word. They can be taught next to attempt to verify this guess by using configuration, phonic, and morphemic clues. Pupils should be taught to use the dictionary, but only as the last resort in the decoding process.

Reinforcement Activities

2. Develop exercises that encourage pupils to use more than one decoding strategy simultaneously. Samples are given.

Sample 1: Context and phonic clues

Grass is gr____________.

Billy's bicycle has two wh_______________.

Sample 2: Context and configuration clues

Put the eggs in the Easter ____________________.

3. As is true with any skill, reading, as a process of using the identification skills collectively, will develop only with much practice. Therefore, encourage children to read copiously as the best way to develop strong reading skills.

COMPREHENSION SKILL 1: GAINING WORD MEANING

Introductory Activity

The questioning strategy following is designed to teach word meaning by relating an unknown word to the background of the child.

Example:

Step 1 1. What does the word *pronto* mean?

Step 2 2. In this sentence from *Josita's Dancing Cleaners*, what does the word *pronto* mean?

Step 3 3. In this sentence from *Josita's Dancing Cleaners*, does the word *pronto* mean (a) quickly, (b) with enthusiasm, or (c) very clean? Yes, *pronto* does mean quickly. How did you know that? You probably figured that out because of the surrounding words. See, here is the word *quick* and here is the word *on time.*

Step 4. 4. If you picked up a hot coal, you would probably drop it *pronto.* What does the word *pronto* mean? Good, *pronto* does mean quickly. How did you know that? You probably figured that out because of the surrounding words. Anyone who would *pick up* a *hot coal* would most likely drop it quickly. Now can you tell me what *pronto* means in the story *Josita's Dancing Cleaners*?

Step 5. 5. In the sentence about a hot coal, *pronto* means quickly. You can tell that because of the way in which it is used in the sentence. Since we know how most people would react to *pick up* and *hot coal*, these words give us clues to the meaning of the word *pronto.* Anyone who would pick up a *hot coal* would most likely drop it quickly. Now can you make up a sentence in which you use the word *pronto*? Good, now look for the word *pronto* in *Josita's Dancing Cleaners* and see if there are any clues that can tell you if the word means the same thing there.

Note: In steps 3–5, the teacher explains how to use context clues to obtain the exact word meaning. If the word had lent itself better to another word attack strategy, such as structural analysis, the teacher would have taught the child that strategy.

Reinforcement Activities

The use of games for reinforcing the skill can make learning word meaning fun for children. The following list of activities attempts to reinforce word meaning through enjoyable activities that are intended to help the child make an association between the new word and his background experiences.

1. Ask each child to cut out a paragraph or cartoon from any part of the newspaper and substitute as many synonyms as possible for existing

words. The child who is able to substitute the most in his or her selection during a given time period is the winner. An example appears in Figure 15.1.

find dog food quickly

Dogs ~~discover Pooch flakes in a hurry~~!

Figure 15.1 Using the Newspaper to Reinforce the Teaching of Synonyms

2. Use the same teaching strategy as in activity 1 but ask the child to substitute antonyms.

3. Give each child a newspaper and see who can locate the most antonyms, metaphors, hyperboles, similes, or idioms in a given time limit. They may be asked to look for one type of word or several different types simultaneously.

4. Ask the children to use the newspaper to cut out synonyms, homonyms, or acronyms around a central theme to construct a collage. For example, if a child were focusing on homonyms around the theme of "winning," his or her collage might contain the following words and pictures: (a) the word *tackle*, with lines connected to pictures of fishing gear and a football play; (b) the word *running back*, with lines connected to pictures of a jogger and a football player; and (c) the word *pace*, with lines connected to a harness horse in a race and a coach walking in a circle while waiting for an umpire's decision.

5. Ask children to make their own dictionaries by finding words that fit into a certain category. For example, words for dogs include puppy, cocker spaniel, canine, litter. The words are gathered through interview, listening, reading, or just "thinking" about words already known that fit the category. The child with the most words in a certain category could be asked to share his or her list with other students.

6. Children can collect or construct words that are written in a manner that depicts their meaning. Several examples which might be constructed by children are presented here.

7. Ask children to make up riddles that can only be answered by using a pair of homonyms. For example, "What is double good to eat?" Answer: "A pair of pears."

8. Ask the children to locate pairs of antonyms, synonyms, homonyms, or other similar word forms. Write the pairs out on index cards and place them face down on the table. Each child, in turn, flips over a pair of cards. If the cards match (if they are antonyms, synonyms, etc.), the child keeps the cards and turns over another pair. The child with the most cards at the end of the game is the winner.

COMPREHENSION SKILL 2: IDENTIFYING DETAILS

Introductory Activity

The questioning strategy following is designed to teach identifying details by relating important details that are to be located to the background and interests of the child.

Example:

Step 1 1. What was the name of the street toward which Josita was walking?

Step 2 2. Read the first sentence and see if you can tell me the name of the street toward which Josita was walking.

Step 3 3. Was the name of the street toward which Josita was walking called (a) Mango Street, (b) Palm Street, or (c) Cleaning Shop Street? Fine. How did you know that? You probably knew that because it is directly stated in the first sentence.

Step 4 4. If I told you that "My address is 604 Elm Street," what is the name of the street on which I live? Nice. How did you know that? You probably knew that because I told you directly when I said, "address is . . . Elm." Now look back at the first sentence in the story and see if you can tell me the name of the street toward which Josita was walking.

Step 5 5. In the sentence about my address, the name of the street on which I live is Elm Street. You know this because I directly stated "address is . . . Elm." Can you use the name of the street on which you live in a sentence so that I can know the name of your street? Great. Now go back to the story and see if you can tell me the name of the street toward which Josita was heading.

Reinforcement Activities

1. Put a spinner on a round board with the following questions in pie-shaped sections: "Where did the event take place? What was the name of the event? Were there any animals or people in the story? What happened in the event? Did the event have a happy ending? Who were the main characters in the event? At what time of year do you think that this event took place? What was the most exciting part of the event?" Then ask the children to locate a selection from any section of the newspaper. After they have cut out their selection, they are to use the spinner game to answer questions about it.

2. Locate a short story on the child's reading level. Construct questions that measure the child's knowledge of specific details from the story and write them on the yellow side of petal-shaped pieces of posterboard that look like a daisy. Write the answers on the back (the white side of the petal). Have the pupils place all the petals yellow side up and then read the story. They answer the questions and turn the petals over to see if their answers are correct.

3. After children have read a story silently, divide them into two teams and ask them questions from the board game discussed in strategy 1. If any team member responds to a question incorrectly, a member of the other team is given a chance to answer the question. As long as a team member is responding correctly, he or she may continue to spin the dial and answer more questions from the game board. After all the questions on the board have been answered correctly, the team with the highest score wins.

4. Give each child a picture. The child is allowed to look at it for a specified period of time. Then the child must turn it over and list as many details as possible within a certain time limit. The child with the most details is the winner.

5. Tell the children a story. Then ask them to draw a picture depicting as many details as they can remember.

Comprehension Skill 2: Identifying Details

6. Ask students to cut out short articles from the newspaper. They glue these articles to worksheets that contain the labels *who*, *what*, *when*, *where*, and *how*. They are then to underline the correct responses in the articles and draw a line from the underlined response to the corresponding label.

7. Ask the children to look through their current assignments in science or social studies and construct at least five questions that require location of specific details. The class then divides into two teams. Each team member is given a chance to answer at least one of the questions constructed by the children. The team that is able to answer the most questions correctly makes up five questions for the teacher. As the teacher responds to each of the five questions, the rest of the class members use their textbooks to verify the correctness of the answers.

COMPREHENSION SKILL 3: IDENTIFYING MAIN IDEAS

Introductory Activity

The questioning strategy following is designed to teach identifying main ideas by relating techniques to the background and interests of the child.

Example:

Step 1 1. What is the main idea of the story?

Step 2 2. Read the last two paragraphs of *Josita's Dancing Cleaners* and see if you can tell me the main idea of the story.

Step 3 3. Is the main idea of the story (a) Josita's parents owned a cleaning shop, (b) Josita's father operated a clothes presser, or (c) Josita was sorry about being late to work? Nice. How did you know that? You probably knew that because of details such as "you are late" and "I'm sorry." These words give us clues that she is late and is sorry about it. Since all the details support this notion, this is called the main idea.

Step 4 4. In the sentence, "Johnny jumped out of bed, turned off his alarm clock, threw on his clothes, and ran in a hurry toward school," what is the main idea? Fine. How did you know that? You probably knew that because of the words "jumped," "threw," "ran," and "hurry" that support the notion that Johnny was in a hurry. Since all the details support this idea, this is called the main idea. Now go back to the story and see if you can tell me the main idea.

Step 5 5. The main idea of the sentence about Johnny is that Johnny was in a hurry to get to school. You can tell this because of details such as "jumped," "threw," "ran," and "hurry." Main idea means the most central idea in the sentence, paragraph, or story. One good way to find the main idea is to pretend that you are sending a telegram. Read the sentence about Johnny again and underline the words that would have to be included so that your telegram could be understood. Since you do not want to spend a lot of money, use the least number of words that you can and still get your message across. Great. The words "Johnny hurry school" would do it. Now can you tell me something that happened to you? Nice. Now what is the main idea? Good. Now read the *Josita's Dancing Cleaners* again and see if you can find the main idea.

Note: It is usually easier for children to identify directly stated main ideas than inferred ones. If the child has trouble with this skill, a technique such as the "telegram technique" is a good beginning point.

Reinforcement Activities

1. Read a story aloud to the children. Discuss what the story is about and, as a group, write the main idea and a title for the story. Then ask the children to read a short selection to themselves. After all have read the selection, they are to pick out the best main idea from three given choices.
2. Ask the students to read a selection from a content area textbook and then write subheadings for each paragraph.
3. Cut out articles from the newspaper without headlines. Ask the children to make up headlines for the articles. These might be exchanged with a buddy to check to see if the headline seemed appropriate to the buddy. The actual headlines could be pasted on the back of the articles as a self-checking key.
4. Explain the concept of topic sentences to the children. Have them work in groups to examine topic sentences in their content area textbooks. They are then to compare their responses; for example, did they all agree that paragraph 3 had no topic sentence and that the main idea was inferred? and so on.
5. Group the students into threes and assign each group to look for the topic sentences in different content area textbook (science, social studies, math, health, etc.). After about fifteen minutes stop the groups and ask them to share what type of paragraph pattern they have the most in their content area; for example, science often gives the topic sentence first and then supports it with many examples, whereas social studies often places the topic sentence last.
6. Ask the children to read and cut out at least three different articles from the newspaper. They are then to trade articles with and match their partner's articles with the appropriate headlines. They should then check each other's responses and discuss why they chose the headline that they did. They then are to place the articles and headlines in an envelope and turn it in.
7. Children are asked to clip out a picture from the newspaper and make up a title. If there is an accompanying article, the child should attach that to the picture, underlining any key words that helped him or her to make up his or her title.

8. Clip out an article, cartoon, or advertisement from the newspaper. Ask children to tell in their own words the main idea of the selection. Then have children compare their responses with a partner. If there are differences of opinion about the main idea, they should discuss why they think that those differences have occurred. The teacher can then discuss the "correct" main idea and the reason for this with the whole group.

9. Children are asked to cut out their own selections from the newspaper and then write what they think is the main idea. Then they trade articles with group members and write the main idea of each other's article. This process is repeated until each article has been read by each group member. Then the children compare their responses on each and come up with a main idea from the group.

10. Read a story to the children and then ask each child to draw a picture of the main idea of the story. Select the pictures that seem to best reflect the main idea and show them to the entire class. Elicit comments on why the pictures depicts the main idea and what details in the story were most helpful in drawing the picture.

11. Read a story to the children without telling them the title. After they have heard the story, ask them to write a title for the story. Discuss why various titles represent the main idea of the story and why they are the most appropriate titles for the story.

COMPREHENSION SKILL 4: IDENTIFYING SEQUENCE

Introductory Activity

The questioning strategy following is designed to teach sequence by relating time and spatial order to the background of the child.

Example:

Step 1 1. What is the first thing that Josita does in the story? the second? the third?

Step 2 2. What does Josita do in the first sentence? What does she do in the fifth sentence? What does she do in the ninth sentence? Now, what is the first thing she does? the second? the third?

Step 3 3. In the story, which of the three events happened first? second? third? (a) Josita looked in the window; (b) Josita said, "Lo siento"; (c) Josita walked to the dry cleaning store. Great. How did you know that? You probably knew that because of the order in which the details are presented in the story. The first paragraph tells us that Josita walked to the cleaning shop. The second paragraph tells us that she stopped and looked in the window. The third paragraph tells us she said "Lo siento." This order is called sequence. Sequence helps us to understand a story by presenting it to us in an orderly manner.

Step 4 4. If I tell you to go home, get your bike, and come back to school, what would be the first thing that you would do? the second? the third? Fine. How did you know that? You probably knew that because of the order in which I told you to do something. That is, first, I told you to go home, second, I told you to get your bike, and, third, I told you to come back to school. This order is called sequence. Sequence helps us to understand a story by presenting it to us in an orderly manner. Now, can you look back at *Josita's Dancing Cleaners* tell me what Josita did first? second? third?

Step 5 5. In the sentence just given, the first thing that you would do would be to go home; the second thing would be to get your bike; the third thing would be to come back to school. Sequence refers to the order in which events occur. Clue words such as *first*, *second*, and *finally* help us to determine that order. Can you make up a sentence in which you tell me the order in which you have done something? For example, can you tell me what you did when you first woke up this morning? Then, what did you do next. Then, after that what did you do. Good. Now look back at *Josita's Dancing Cleaners* and tell me what Josita did first. second? third?

Reinforcement Activities

1. Have children bring in their favorite cartoons. Then ask the children to cut the cartoons apart but number the order on the back of each section. The children then trade cartoons and attempt to identify the original order.

2. Cut a story into paragraphs and paste each paragraph on cardboard. The children are to read the paragraphs and place them in proper sequence. A self-checking key should be on the back of the paragraphs.

3. Keep a time line that correlates the historical events discussed in social studies. Use a long roll of newsprint or butcher paper and hang the time line on the wall for use throughout the year. The children should illustrate the time line by drawing in clothing worn, food eaten, and any television shows that depict events happening during the period being studied.

4. Ask children who have difficulty with sequence to help you dramatize a story such as "The Three Little Pigs." Three children can act as the pigs and say their lines as the events occur in the story.

5. Give the children a story with several "sequence signals": *first*, *then*, *next*, *finally*, and so on. Have the children circle the words in the story.

6. Use a flannel board and tell a story, such as "Little Red Riding Hood." Ask the children to participate with questions such as "What happened first? What happened next?" and so on.

7. Use the children's social studies text and give children examples of sequences of time and space. For example,

Time: Christopher Columbus, Benjamin Franklin, Andrew Jackson, ____________

____

Space: California, Arizona, Texas, ____________________________

8. Give students a map and have them find various locations. Based on this map, have them write directions for getting from one place to another.

9. Assign a paragraph in the student's content area textbook and have each student list the sequence indicators.

COMPREHENSION SKILL 5: IDENTIFYING CAUSE-EFFECT RELATIONSHIPS

Introductory Activity

The questioning strategy given is designed to teach the skill of identifying cause-effect relationships.

Example:

Step 1 1. Why did Josita's father look up from his work?

Step 2 2. Read the third paragraph and tell me why you think Josita's father looked up from his work.

Step 3 3. Did Josita's father look up from his work because (a) a customer came into the shop, (b) a little bell rang over the door, or (c) Josita waved. Fine. Now, can you tell me how you knew that? You probably knew that because it says in the story that a little bell rang over the door and her father looked up from his work. We can tell that the first event (bell ringing) probably caused the second event (looked up) to occur. This is called a cause-effect relationship because one event causes a specific effect upon another.

Step 4 4. In the sentence, "Bobby dropped the brick on his toe and then jumped in pain," can you tell me why Bobby was jumping? Good. Now, can you tell me how you knew that? You probably knew that because you recognized that the first event (dropping the brick) caused the second event (jumping) to occur. This is called a cause-effect relationship. Now look back at *Josita's Dancing Cleaners* and see if you can tell me why Josita's father looked up from his work.

Step 5 5. In the sentence about Bobby, the brick caused Bobby to jump in pain. The first event (dropping the brick) caused the second event (jumping in pain) to occur. This is called a cause-effect relationship because one event causes a specific effect upon another. Words such as "because," "on account of," and "then" as well as the order in which events are presented can help to locate the cause-effect relationships. Now, can you tell me something you did which caused something else to happen? Have you ever eaten too much and gotten a stomachache? O.K. That is a cause-effect relationship because one event (ate too much) caused the second event (stomachache). Can you tell me another one? Good. Now, look back at the story and tell me why Josita's father looked up from his work.

Comprehension Skill 5: Identifying Cause-Effect Relationships

Reinforcement Activities

1. Show two newspaper pictures depicting cause-effect relationships. Ask the children to tell what is happening in the pictures and why they think the situation is occurring. Restate the observations made in terms of cause-effect relationships.

2. Give examples of key words that indicate the presence of a cause-effect relationship, for example, "because," "therefore," and "consequently." Hand out list of effects and key words. Ask the children to circle the key words and to supply the causes.

3. Ask children to locate cartoons that illustrate cause-effect relationships. They are to bring them in and trade with friends.

4. Construct a folder game in which children can advance along the game board as they correctly identify cause-effect relationships.

5. Group the students by threes or fours and ask them to open content area textbooks to preselected pages. They are to locate cause-effect relationships. Each group writes out the cause part of various paragraphs. They present these to other groups and see if they can supply the correct effects.

6. Ask the children to locate a cause-effect sentence in the newspaper. They are to underline all clue words that helped them identify the relationship. If there is no clue word, they should write in the inferred word.

COMPREHENSION SKILL 6: MAKING INFERENCES

Introductory Activity

The questioning strategy given is designed to teach inference skills.

Example:

Step 1 1. What country do you think Josita lived in?

Step 2 2. Read the first paragraph of the story and tell me in which country you think Josita lived.

Step 3 3. In which of these countries do you think Josita lived: (a) the United States, (b) Mexico, (c) Greenland. Good. How did you know that? You probably knew that because of certain clue words such as "palm tree," "two-story building," and "Pronto Cleaner" (written in English on the sign in the story.) These words tell us that the story is in a warm, English-speaking country that has some modern conveniences.

Step 4 4. In the sentence "Bobby picked up his rope, spurred his horse, and tried to catch the calf," what do you think Bobby's job was? Good. How did you know that? You probably knew that because of key words such as "horse," "rope," and "calf." When an author doesn't tell us directly that a person is a cowboy, but makes us guess with the help of clue words, this is called inference. Now can you look back at the story and tell me in which country you think Josita lived?

Step 5 5. In the sentence about Bobby, Bobby was probably a cowboy. We know this because of clue words such as "horse," "rope," and "calf." When an author doesn't tell us directly that a person is a "cowboy" but makes us guess with the help of clue words, this is called inference. Can you make up a riddle about a person and give me clues to what he or she does without directly telling me? Good. Now read the story again and tell me in which country you think Josita lived. Be sure to look for words that give you clues to the meaning.

Reinforcement Activities

1. Ask children to cut out an article of their choice from the newspaper. They are to underline the first sentence and then to list at least three possible outcomes. Then they read the rest of the article to verify their inferences. They may be asked to trade articles with a partner and repeat the process.

2. Ask children to cut out their favorite comic strip and bring it to class. They are to cut off the last picture in the strip and paste it on the back. Then they trade comic strips with a partner and see if they can make inferences about the missing picture. If they make an incorrect inference, they should discuss the reasons for their inferences with partners.

3. Cut out stories from old basal readers and put them in manila folders. Give each child a story to read that is on his or her reading level. The story should have the last paragraph cut out and put in an envelope pasted to the back of the manila folder. The child makes up his or her own last paragraph and then compares it with the original. After many children have made up many different endings, a child who has not read the story should be asked to select the original one. That child then tells why he or she thinks that the ending he or she has selected is probably the original ending to the story.

5. The teacher reads part of a story aloud to the children. The children then draw a picture of what they think will happen next. The teacher then asks the children to share their pictures and describe why they think that their pictures correctly depicts the next event. After all pictures have been shown, the teacher reads the correct ending and discusses why the author used that as the ending.

6. Each child is asked to make up a riddle, collage, mobile, pantomine, and puppet show in which they reflect traits of someone they read about. The rest of the children must infer from the child's project what type of person is being described and what they used as clues to make their inferences.

7. Ask the children to bring their content area textbooks to reading group. They are to meet in groups of three and look at various chapter headings and make inferences about what information they think will be contained in that section of the textbook. They then compare their inferences and read the section to determine whose inference was the closest to that of the textbook.

Example:

Heading: "The Prairie Provinces"

Possible inferences: "This section is probably going to describe the historical development of this area" or
"This section is probably going to describe the current economic conditions" or
"This section is probably going to compare these provinces with the eastern provinces."

8. Ask children to look for pictures in their textbooks that they think will be a major topic for a particular chapter. Discuss why they selected the pictures that they did. Have them compare their selections with those of a partner. Then after they have read the chapter determine which children made the inferences that seemed closest to the actual information contained in the chapter. For example, child infers "sugar and its effect on the human body" will be the focus of the chapter because the child has found two pictures of various types of sugar in the science textbook.

COMPREHENSION SKILL 7: MAKING GENERALIZATIONS AND CONCLUSIONS

Introductory Activity

Another example of Fraenkel's technique (discussed in depth in Chapter 3) is illustrated in step 5 of the questioning strategy described here.

Example:

Step 1 1. Do you know what I mean why I say "generalization"? Good. Can you make a generalization about owning a cleaning shop?

Step 2 2. Read the third and fourth paragraphs and see if you can make a generalization about owning a cleaning shop.

Step 3 3. Read these three statements and tell me which one is most correct according to what we read in *Josita's Dancing Cleaners*: (a) owning a shop would be fun; (b) owning a shop would be a lot of work; (c) owning a shop would make you rich. Good. Can you tell me how you knew that? You probably knew that because of certain facts such as "behind the counter," "working the big clothes presser," and "carefully pressed." When we can gather together a set of facts and they all add up to the same thing, we call this a generalization.

Step 4 4. If I tell you that my dog bit Sandy, clawed Bruce, and ripped off Susie's sleeve, what can you tell me about my dog? Great. How did you know that? You probably knew that because of the facts "bit Sandy," "clawed Bruce," and "ripped off Susie's sleeve." Whenever you can take a set of statements like that and make a series of inferences, it is called a generalization. Now, reread the story and tell me if you can make a generalization about owning a cleaning shop.

Step 5 5. From the sentence about my dog, we can say that my dog is mean. That is called a generalization and is based on a set of facts. I don't have to tell you that my dog is mean because, when you hear the words "bit," "clawed," and "ripped," you can make that generalization. Can you give me an example of a generalization? O.K. Let's do one together.

a. What is your favorite food? What is your brother's favorite food? (Fraenkel's first strategy: Reader is asked to describe aspects of two different situations.)
b. What differences are there between the foods you like and the foods your brother likes? (Fraenkel's second strategy: Reader is asked to describe any differences between the two situations.)
c. Why do you think that you and your brother like almost the same foods? (Fraenkel's third strategy: Reader is asked to account for why there are *no* differences.)
c. Do people who live in the same family or grow up together often like the same types of food? (Fraenkel's fourth strategy: Reader is asked to describe other situations that support the differences that have been pointed out. In this case, there are no differences, so the reader would be asked to look for situations that support his or her generalization that people in the same family learn to like the same types of food.)

That's great. Now read back over the story about Josita and see if you can make a generalization about owning a cleaning shop.

Note: As the reading skills become more sophisticated, the teacher must make certain that the child understands what he or she is being asked to do. Hence in step 1 the teacher made certain that the child understood the term "generalization" before requiring that the child respond to the question.

In step 5 the teacher very carefully led the student through Fraenkel's questioning strategy. As reading skills become more complex, the components become more complex and it takes more time and explanation to help the child become an independent user of that skill.

Reinforcement Activities

1. Ask the children to cut out their favorite cartoons for a week. Then they should make some generalizations about the type of information that they feel the cartoonist wants the reader to receive. Some generalizations that might be made could include "Ziggy as always the fall guy"; "Lucy in 'Peanuts' as not very nice"; "Crime doesn't pay" as shown in "Dick Tracy."

2. Tie in content area material whenever possible. For example, when studying the various types of animal life in science, ask the children to list a group of animals in a variety of ways. The children might decide to group animals by color, types of food that they eat, defenses that they have, and

size. They should be asked to list animals by the traits that they have generated. Generalizations about which way to group animals for scientific classification could be made. Children would have to support their generalizations by showing how "inclusive" their grouping system was.

3. Ask children to collect pictures of the effects of some disaster, such as a hurricane. They are to list all the effects shown in the pictures and make a generalization about the effects of a hurricane upon people and property involved.

4. Ask the children to locate as many words as they can that deal with the American cowboy. After collecting words such as "lariat," "lasso," and "corral," have them make a generalization about what nationality probably influenced the growth of the American West the most.

COMPREHENSION SKILL 8: IDENTIFYING TONE AND MOOD

Introductory Activity

In the questioning strategy illustrated, the alternative responses given in step 3 are easily distinguishable from one another.

Example:

Step 1 1. How do you think the author wanted you to feel after you read the story?

Step 2 2. Look at the last two paragraphs and then tell me how you think the author wanted you to feel after you read the story.

Step 3 3. After you read the story, do you think the author wanted you to feel (a) mad, (b) happy, (c) serious? Very nice. How did you know that? You probably knew that because of certain actions in the story. Josita's father told her to "get here on time"; that would indicate that he was probably unhappy with her. Since she then told him, "Lo siento," she probably felt a little ashamed of spending so much time talking with her friends. Since most of us take lectures from our fathers seriously, the author probably wanted us to feel serious when reading about the lecture. This feeling is called mood and is created on purpose by the author to help us understand his or her message.

Step 4 4. If I said "Susie ran down the stairs and saw a bike with a brand new basket under the Christmas tree," how would you feel? Right. How come you felt that way? You probably felt that way because of certain words such as "bike," "new basket," and "Christmas tree." When authors use words like these to create certain feelings in their readers, this is called mood. Now, look back at the story and see if you can find any words that give you clues as to how the author wanted you to feel after you read about Josita.

Step 5 5. In the sentence about Christmas, I wanted you to feel joyful and happy. I did this by providing you with an event that would make most people happy. Words that helped to picture this event as happy were "bike," "new basket," and "Christmas tree." Authors often use this same technique when they write their stories. Whenever an author tries to make a reader feel a certain way, the author is creating a "mood." Moods can be happy, sad, angry, funny, and more. Can you give me an example of something that would make you feel happy? sad? Great. You felt happy or sad because of certain events that you described to me. Now, look back at the story and see if you can find any words or events that give you clues as to how the author wanted you to feel after you read about Josita.

Reinforcement Activities

1. Ask the students to select an article or cartoon from the newspaper and underline the words that helped to set the tone and mood. They are to think of three synonyms for each underlined word and determine if the synonym changes the tone and mood of the original passage.

2. Give the children a sentence with a word left out and ask them to think of as many words as they can that would fit in the blanks. Then ask them to meet in small groups and discuss the varying tones and moods created by the different words selected to fill in the blank.

3. Ask the students to look for all the words they can find in a newspaper that reflect a certain tone and/or mood and construct a collage. For example, a student wants to express the feeling of "victory" and locates words such as "rushing," "exploding," and "big play."

4. Ask the students to locate a cartoon strip from the daily paper and remove all the words from one of the characters. They are to replace the original words with other words, but keep the original tone and/or mood intact. They then find a partner and trade cartoons. The partner is to guess the original tone and/or mood. If the partner is unable to do this, the team should discuss why or why not this was accomplished.

5. Ask children to bring in copies or recordings of their favorite songs. They are to identify how that song makes them feel and isolate words in the songs that contribute to the tone or mood.

6. Ask the children to locate pictures of people in magazines, textbooks, or newspapers that illustrate a particular mood. Then they make a collage of those pictures and identify the mood.

7. Assign the children a content area passage and ask them to rewrite it to reflect a different tone. For example, a passage on air pollution might be rewritten to reflect a light and happy tone. Discuss how the tone and mood changes the reader's reaction toward the topics. This exercise is also an excellent introduction to the topic of satire, as it brings out the relationship of appropriateness of tone and mood toward given aspects of life.

COMPREHENSION SKILL 9: IDENTIFYING THEME

Introductory Activity

This strategy illustrates how children may be taught to identify theme.

Example:

Step 1 1. Do you know what I mean when I ask you to tell me the theme of a story? Great. What is the theme of the story?

Step 2 2. Read the fourth paragraph again and then tell me what you think the theme of the story might be.

Step 3 3. Do you think the theme of the story might be (a) an ounce of prevention is worth a pound of cure, (b) you ought to live up to your name, (c) carelessness can cause a lot of trouble? Very nice. How did you know that? You probably knew that because of certain words and actions in the story. When Josita's father says "This is not called Pronto Cleaners for nothing!," we know that he is concerned that his cleaning shop will do what it is supposed to do, that is, clean clothes quickly. The main idea of this story is that Josita is late and is sorry about it. The theme or lesson to be taught from this main idea is that Josita is particularly sorry about her lateness because of the emphasis that her father places on promptness. We know this because of the name of his shop. If he had not placed so much emphasis on promptness he would have named the shop "Dependable Cleaner" or "Thorough Cleaners."

Step 4 4. In the story of King Midas, we learn of a king who loved gold more than anything else in the world. He was given a chance to have any wish he wanted granted so he asked to have everything that he touched turn to gold. However, when he tried to eat his food or touch his daughter, he found that both his food and his daughter turned to gold. He eventually asked that this wish be taken away and his world was returned to normal. What would the theme of that story be? Yes. Now, can you tell me how you knew that? You probably knew that because of details that reflected his unhappiness when he had the power to turn everything into gold. Theme means the lesson that a story is trying to teach or the moral of the story. It is usually not directly stated, but you can figure it out by paying attention to the details and looking at the main idea in terms of "What is this trying to tell me?" or "Why is the author trying to tell me this?" Now, look back at *Josita's Dancing Cleaners* and see if you can tell me if the author wanted you to learn any lessons when he tells you of Josita's lateness.

Step 5 5. In the story about Midas, the theme was that money is not everything, that there are many things much more important. A theme is a lesson, or a moral, or a "universal message" that the author is trying to get across to the reader. Sometimes the author tells us this message directly, but, usually, we have to use our imagination to guess what it means. Can you tell me a story in which you teach a lesson? Yes, the story of the rabbit and the turtle does tell us that persistence pays off. Now, go back to the story and see if you can figure out what the author wanted us to learn when he told us about Josita's lateness.

Reinforcement Activities

1. Place a group of popular expressions or proverbs on the chalkboard and ask the students to choose one to illustrate with an original story and/or an original work of art. Examples of expressions include

Haste makes waste.
Time heals all wounds.
A stitch in time saves nine.

2. Ask the children to list as many expressions or proverbs as they can think of on a sheet of paper. The one who lists the most in a given time slot wins the prize.

3. Ask the children to bring in copies or recordings of their favorite popular songs. Discuss the fact that many songs and stories contain messages or themes about life. Ask them to write down what they think the "theme" of their song is. They then trade songs with a partner and repeat the procedure. Finally, they compare the themes to see if their responses are the same. If the responses differ, they should discuss why they each stated that the songs had differing themes.

COMPREHENSION SKILL 10: IDENTIFYING CHARACTERIZATION

Introductory Activity

This questioning strategy is designed to teach characterization.

Example:

Step 1 1. What type of person do you think Josita's father was?

Step 2 2. Read the fourth paragraph and tell me what type of person you think Josita's father was.

Step 3 3. Which of the following statements might describe Josita's father: (a) he never got upset with her, (b) he liked to live up to his word, (c) he was an extremely mean person? How did you know that? Great. You probably knew that because of what Josita's father said. We can usually tell what type of person someone is by what they say, by what they do, by what others say about them, or by what the author says about them.

Step 4 4. If I told you that I gave a lot of money to charity, what kind of person would you think I was? Nice. How did you know that? You probably knew that by what I did. You can usually tell what type of person someone is by what he says, what he does, what others say about him, or what the author says about him. Now, look back at the story and see if you can tell what type of person Josita's father is. Look to see if you can find any of the four basic types of clues.

Step 5 5. In the example about giving to charity, I would probably be described as a kind or generous person. You can tell this by what I did; that is, I gave money to charity. You can usually tell what type of person someone is by what they say, what they do, what others say about them, and what the author says about them. Can you describe a person to me and let me figure out what type of person he or she is. Good. I knew that you described a mean person to me by what he did. Mean people kick dogs. Now, look back at the story and see if you can tell me what type of person Josita's father is. Look to see if you can find any of the four basic types of clues to help you interpret his character.

Reinforcement Activities

1. Ask the children to collect newspaper articles about someone they like. They are to cut out the articles and underline the words or statements that describe the things that they like about the person. They are then to make a list of the things that they like and compare their list of "likes" with those of other children. If any children have picked the same person, they should compare their lists to see if they liked the person for the same reasons.

2. Ask the children to clip cartoons out of the newspaper for a week. Then ask them to cut out the dialogue of one of the characters in the last strip. Then they select partners and try to fill in what they think the character in the last strip said. After they have made their interpretation, they compare their responses with the actual cartoon dialogue (Verner, 1978).

3. Ask the children to locate a comic strip with at least two characters who speak. They are to cut one picture of each character from the comic strip and paste it on a blank sheet of paper. Then they cut the other pictures from the dialogue and place the dialogue in an envelope. They are to pick a partner and have the partner match each section of the dialogue with the picture of the character whom they think is talking. They should discuss how they know the correct answer or why they think they did not get the correct answer (Verner, 1978).

4. Children are asked to clip out problems from the advice column and draw a picture of the person with the problem. They are to underline clue words that made them draw the character as they did.

5. Give each child a sock and help the child make a puppet. The children are then to pick a character from their favorite story and have the puppet speak the character's dialogue. If the character has no dialogue in the story, the children should convert the action to dialogue. After they have practiced their dialogue, they present it to the rest of the class.

6. Ask the children to make up a riddle about one of the interesting people they have read about. They are not to tell the person's name, but they are to give clues to other classmates according to the following se-

quence: (a) help others guess what the character is like by something he or she does; (b) help others guess what the character is like by something he or she says; (c) help others guess what the character is like by what someone else says about him or her; (d) help others guess what the character is like by telling others something that the author stated directly about the character.

7. Ask the children to select one of the persons about whom they have read in their social studies or science book as a potential "friend." They are to look for traits about that person that helped them to determine why they wanted him or her as a "friend." Then they are directed to sit in pairs and compare their choices and their reasons for selection. Children who have selected the same persons should be given a chance to compare character traits.

COMPREHENSION SKILL 11: IDENTIFYING FACT, FICTION, AND OPINION

Introductory Activity

The questioning strategy described here illustrates how the child's own background can be utilized to introduce and reinforce the ability to identify and discriminate among fact, fiction, and opinion.

Example:

Step 1 1. Do you know what I mean when I say the word "opinion"? Great. Now look at the story and see if you think there are any opinions expressed.

Step 2 2. Look at the statement made by Josita's father and tell me whether you think he gives any of his opinions.

Step 3 3. Which of the following things that might be said by Josita's father would be an opinion: (a) "Josita, you knocked on the window"; (b) "Josita, I think that you are a silly girl"; or (c) "Josita, you work in my shop". Right. How did you know that? You probably knew that because of the words, "I think." An opinion means that someone is telling us how he or she thinks or feels about something. Additionally, the other two statements tell about things that we know actually happened. Now, look at the statements really made by Josita's father and tell me if you think that he is giving any opinions. Great. You probably knew that because the facts in the story substantiate all his statements.

Step 4 4. If I said "I think that pizza tastes awful," would this be fact, fiction, or opinion? Good. How did you know that? You probably knew that because of the clue words "I think." Words such as this indicate that I am expressing my own feelings or my opinion. Now, look back at the story and express an opinion about it. Can you find a sentence in the story in which Josita's father expresses an opinion?

Step 5 5. In the sentence about pizza, an opinion is given. We can tell this because I directly state my own feelings about pizza. Opinions are directly stated or implied statements that reflect a person's own feelings. Can you give me your opinion on something? For example, can you tell me what your favorite food is? Very nice. That expresses your personal feelings about that food. What words did you use that let me know that what you said is your opinion and not a fact? Now, look back at the story and see if you can express an opinion about it. Can you find a sentence in the story in which Josita's father expresses an opinion?

Reinforcement Activities

1. Ask the children to locate an article from the newspaper. They are to underline sections that are facts and circle sections that are opinions. Then they are to select partners and discuss why they underlined or circled the sections that they did.

2. Ask the children to locate two differing opinions on the same topics in the newspaper. Then they are to select a partner and discuss which point of view they believe is closest to their own.

3. Ask the children to locate a fact article and an opinion article from the newspaper. Then they are to select partners and discuss why they think that the articles they selected are facts or opinion. Then they are to make a summary statement about where facts and where opinion accounts are ordinarily located in the newspaper.

4. The teacher writes the words *fact*, *fiction*, and *opinion* on the chalkboard. The children look up the meanings for all three words in the dictionary. After a group discussion on the meanings, the teacher reads selections to illustrate each concept. Each student is then given a card with a reading selection pasted on it. They are to read their respective cards and identify the selection as fact, fiction, or opinion. A key is on the back of each card so that the child can self-check his or her responses. The children then read their selections to partners to determine if the partners can correctly identify the selection as fact, fiction, or opinion.

5. Ask the children to list some events that have happened recently in their lives. Show how one of those real events can be changed so that it is no longer fact and how it can be made into an opinion. Each child then takes one of the events and illustrates to a partner how it might be made into a fictional account and how it might be changed to an opinion.

6. Ask the children to locate statements made by persons in their social studies or science textbook. They are to then discuss whether the statement is fact, fiction, or opinion. Use, for example, Neil Armstrong's statement as he stepped on the moon, "This is one small step for man but one giant step for mankind." Children should be aware of aspects such as (a) the statement was made by Neil Armstrong (fact) and (b) the statement reflects Neil Armstrong's feelings about the importance of the event in history (opinion).

COMPREHENSION SKILL 12: IDENTIFYING PROPAGANDA

Introductory Activity

This questioning strategy is designed to teach children how to recognize propaganda by relating the persuasive devices often used by propagandists to the background of the child.

Example:

Step 1 1. Do you know what I mean by propaganda? Can you find an example of propaganda in the story?

Step 2 2. Read the fourth paragraph of the story and tell me if you can find an example of propaganda in the story.

Step 3 3. Which of the following statements might be considered to contain language that attempts to make the reader feel or think in a certain way: (a) two-story, (b) palm tree, (c) Pronto Cleaners. Great. How did you know that? You probably knew that because the word "Pronto" means "quick." When Josita's father named his cleaners "Pronto Cleaners," he wanted customers to think that his service was extremely quick. This is called a "transfer" technique for persuading a person to perform a certain action.

Step 4 4. When I tell you that my dog is named "Killer," what do I want you to believe about my dog? Great. How did you know that? You probably knew that because you knew what the word "Killer" meant. If I named my dog that, I would want you to believe he exhibited those traits. Now, look back at the story and see if you can find an example of propaganda. Be sure to look for words such as "killer" that persuade us to think a certain way by the use of "transfer."

Step 5 5. When I tell you that my dog's name is "Killer," I want you to think of him as a vicious animal. If he is a watchdog, this will help persuade anyone knowing his name not to break into my house. When I give something a name that conveys an image like that, I am using a propaganda technique called "transfer." Can you give me an example of "transfer"? Very good. Your brother's little league team is called the "Giants" to indicate that they are undefeatable. Now, look at the story and see if you can find an example of propaganda.

Reinforcement Activities

1. Discuss the seven types of propaganda strategies and then focus on one. For example, discuss how "transfer" is often used by advertisers to persuade consumers to associate love of country with a product. Children could be asked to look for advertisements in the newspaper that contain patriotic symbols (e.g., the American flag, Uncle Sam).

2. Ask students to bring advertisements from various magazines and newspapers and make a "propaganda mural."

3. Ask students to use one or more of the propaganda techniques in making a book report to the rest of the class members.

4. Rewrite the same advertisement so that the product would appeal to various types of buyers. For example, locate an advertisement for a townhouse and rewrite the advertisement so that it would appeal to a young, single adult, a teenager, and a retired school teacher.

5. Ask the children to list "jingles" from commercials that they have heard on the radio or television. Then divide the class into teams. Read a commercial to the first team. If that team can correctly identify the propaganda technique used, they get a point. The same team continues to answer the jingles until they incorrectly answer the question. Then, the other team attempts to identify the technique. Play is continued in this manner until all jingles have been discussed. The team with the most points wins.

6. Ask the children to locate as many examples of each of the seven types of propaganda as possible. The children then bring their examples to class and see if a partner identifies each in the same way as the person who originally clipped out the advertisement.

7. Ask the children to look in their social studies book for a description of one of the English generals during the Revolutionary War. Have them underline any words that they feel contain negative connotations. Then have them rewrite the description of the battle from the viewpoint of a British journalist.

STUDY SKILL 1: FOLLOWING DIRECTIONS

Introductory Activity

1. The teacher should explain to the children the importance of following directions carefully. Examples of what could happen by not following directions may be elicited from the children. Teachers can generate questions such as "What would happen if your mother didn't read the directions and put salt instead of sugar in the fudge? What would happen if you didn't follow instructions and found the paint store instead of the ice cream store?"

Reinforcement Activities

2. Write directions for making a paper-folding activity, such as a paper airplane. Each child should read the directions independently and follow the stp-by-step instructions. If the children have trouble, place the children in pairs and have them help each other to follow the directions.

3. Ask the children to write directions for a game they like to play. They are then to trade directions with a partner and see if the partner is able to play the game.

4. Ask the children to write directions for locating some object in the classroom. The children then place all directions in an envelope and take

turns drawing them out. The child drawing the direction is to follow it to find the object. If the child is unable to do so, the teacher reads the direction aloud while another child attempts to follow the directions. If the second child is unable to do this correctly, the class discusses how the direction might be improved so that it could be followed correctly.

5. Ask the students to go through their daily newspapers to locate one or more coupons. Direct them to paste them on a sheet of paper and then fill them out. They are then directed to meet in small groups to compare coupons and to make certain that all students filled out their coupons correctly (Verner, 1978, p. 41).

6. Place various sets of directions on index cards. Each child draws a card and then must act out the directions. For example, "Pretend that you have just found a dollar. You pick it up and then go to the store. You buy a candy bar and a bottle of something to drink."

7. Print directions for playing a new game on a poster. The children read the directions silently and then tell their partner how the game is played. If the two do not agree, they reread the directions again to verify their answers.

8. Direct the children to construct sets of directions concerning one of their content area texts. For example, in social studies, the following set of directions might be made. (a) Read the title of chapter. (b) Write down the first word in the second paragraph on a sheet of paper. (c) Write the date of the Declaration of Independence directly underneath the word in step b. (d) Count the number of words in bold print on page 62 and write it on top of the word in step b. (e) Point to the map of New England and then, with your finger on the map, turn the book in a circle. The children then draw slips of paper upon which the directions have been written. Next, the children take turns reading their directions orally and completing the instructions.

9. Construct a board for tic-tac-toe but place directions for information contained in one of the content area texts on index cards on the board. To make a move, the child must correctly follow the directions on the card; for example, "Open your science book to the graph on weather conditions in various parts of the United States. Put your left hand on the coldest city in the country and your right hand on the warmest."

STUDY SKILL 2: SCHEDULING TIME

Introductory Activity

1. Write a time table on the board that includes one-hour time slots beginning at 6:00 A.M. and ending at 10:00 P.M. Ask the children to list the type of things they usually do around 9:00 A.M. Compare answers and then ask children to make a list of the things they usually do around 5:00 P.M. Again compare answers. Tell them that they have made what is called a "schedule" and that this can help them keep track of how they spend their

time. Explain that sometimes they do not get as much of their homework done as they ought to because they waste a lot of time. Ask each child to keep track of his or her schedule for the following day. To help the child do this, send a note home with each child requesting parental assistance. A sample of a typical note is

> Dear Parent,
>
> Please help (child's name) write his or her schedule for one typical day of the week. This day's memo need cite no more than eight activities with scheduled hours from rising until bedtime. Thank you for your cooperation.
>
> Your truly,
>
> (your signature)

When the schedules come back, ask the children to share them with other members of the group (adapted from Evertts et al., 1973).

Reinforcement Activities

2. Have the children imagine that they are reading the television schedule in their daily newspapers. Write the following on the chalkboard.

12:00 News
12:30 "Popeye"
1:00 Bowling
1:30 Movie

Ask a child to read the schedule. Help the children see that the colon separates the hour and the minutes. Give each child a paper and pencil and ask the child to write his or her television-viewing schedule for one afternoon. Help each use the colon in writing the times in his or her schedule (Evertts et al., 1973).

3. Some children profit from cooperative planning with their teacher. Each day, just before the children go home, set aside some time to write a schedule or contract with the group or individual children. Let the children share in the planning of the schedule for the coming day. This may be posted for the group or kept in separate notebooks for individual children (Evertts et al., 1973).

4. The teacher requires each child to keep a study card such as that shown here. The cards may be turned in to the teacher at the end of each week for about a month, so that the teacher may assess the children's progress in time scheduling (Dillner and Olson, 1977).

Planned Time			*Actual Time*		
Mon.	Sept. 19	7:00-7:45 P.M.	Mon.	Sept. 19	7:00-7:50 P.M.
	home-work	7:00-7:30		home-work	7:00-7:50
	review	7:30-7:45			
Wed.	Sept. 21	7:00-7:45 P.M.	Wed.	Sept. 21	7:00-7:30 P.M.
	home-work	7:00-7:30		home-work	7:15-7:30
	review	7:30-7:45			
Sat.	Sept. 24	10:00-10:45 A.M.	Sat.	Sept. 24	10:00-10:45 A.M.
	home-work	10:00-10:30		home-work	10:00-10:15
	review	10:30-10:45		review	10:15-10:45

5. If a teacher notes that a particular child seems to waste a lot of time, the teacher might ask one of the child's peers to take notes on the child's behavior. After twenty minutes, the child who wastes time is given the notes. A short conference between the child and the teacher can focus on ways in which the child can make more efficient use of his or her available time. The child then may be asked to construct a study schedule for a week. At the end of the week, the child can compare the planned schedule with the one actually completed.

6. Have children keep a diary of activities. After a week ask them to summarize the amount of time spent in various activities. Discuss ways in which they might want to rearrange their activities to be more efficient. For example, a child who spent a lot of time making book covers as well as watching television might combine these two activities to give himself or herself more time to study.

STUDY SKILL 3: ADJUSTING RATE TO PURPOSE

OVERVIEW

Introductory Activity

1. Put transparencies of three different textbook excerpts on an overhead projector. Ask the students to read the first one to locate a specific de-

tail, the second one to locate the main idea, and the third one to apply the information to a homework assignment to be given at the end of the period. As soon as the first student finishes the task, turn off the overhead and ask him or her to tell the class his or her answers. If the child is correct, ask him or her to explain how he or she was able to finish so quickly. Explain to the class the the first passage could be scanned, the second passage could be skimmed, and the third passage had to be read carefully. Then explain the relationship among the three techniques.

Show the students how to locate the answers to the questions by searching for key words that relate to a specific question. Demonstrate the procedure using several textbook passages that have been placed on transparencies.

Select several pages from the content area textbook that require slow, careful reading as well as some passages that may be read at a faster rate (e.g., mathematics—an introductory paragraph about the nature of sets, followed by a word problem requiring the application of mathematical concepts concerning sets). Tell the students that they will be expected to know all the relevant details in the assigned reading and that they will be given a time limit for completing their reading. At the end of the time limit, give the students a quiz in which they are to close their textbooks and list the relevant details that they found in the assignment. Then place a transparency of the textbook pages on the overhead and demonstrate to the students clue words that should have helped them determine the pace at which they were to read the materials. Point out that words in italics or boldface are usually considered important and that the reader should slow down and carefully read such portions of the text. Also explain that some material does not have to be read so slowly and should be read at a faster pace. Show them that words in very tiny type are usually minor details about some subtopic and can be skimmed unless the student's purpose for reading is one that requires that they learn those details (Dillner and Olson, 1977).

Reinforcement Activities

2. Tell the students that they are to read several pages in their textbook to locate most of the relevant details. Before they read, give them a few minutes to look over the pages and place an "S" by those portions that they think should be read at a slow, careful rate, an "M" by those portions that they think should be read at a moderate rate, and an "F" by those portions that they think could be read at a fast rate. At the end of the time limit, assemble the students in small groups and ask them to compare their markings with those of their peers. After several minutes, ask a member of each of the small groups to report any differences of opinion. Discuss with the whole class how the purpose relates to the rate and what the rates of each of the portions of the textbook should have been.

Give the students a new purpose for reading the pages (e.g., identify main ideas) and repeat the procedures just outlined (Dillner and Olson, 1977).

3. Place the children in groups of two and give them a list of problems that can be solved by referring to the newspaper. The problems should be such that the efficient reader would use a variety of rates in looking for the answer. For example, "Locate a current movie featuring an English actress"; "Find the name of a recipe that contains coriander"; "Locate an advertisement for something being sold because children no longer use it"; "Find an article written by someone who is trying to make you laugh." The children use their newspapers to locate the answers. They time how long it took them to answer each question and note the strategy they used. The teacher should then hold a large-group discussion summarizing the "best" reading rate for solving each problem.

SKIMMING

Introductory Activity

1. Hold a class discussion on how skimming can be beneficial to the child. Explain that skimming is primarily a means to get the "gist" of the information presented. Have them open one of their content area textbooks to a simple passage. Give them one minute to read the passage and then tell them to stop reading and close their books. Ask them to share what they think the main idea was with a partner. If the two children agree upon the main idea, they share it with the class. If they disagree, they team up with another pair and try to get a concensus of opinion. The teacher then asks the children to tell what key words they used to help them locate the "gist." Illustrate to the class, by reading aloud only the "key words," the words that the children should have used to get the main idea. Reinforce the purpose of skimming and then give the children more easy passages to practice with. Repeat the procedure of sharing main ideas with partners until the majority of the children seem to understand the major purposes and strategies involved in skimming.

Reinforcement Activities

2. Give each child a page from the daily newspaper. The children are directed to glance over the page for one minute. Then they are to turn over the page and jot down as many different facts as they can remember. Continue this same activity a few times a week for a month. Require the children to keep a chart of the number of items recalled. At the end of the month, the children should use the graph to assess their progress.

3. Photostat and cut out several paragraphs from at least three different textbooks. Make sure that each paragraph contains a clue as to which textbook it came from. Mix all the paragraphs together and place them in an envelope. Write the names of the textbooks on the outside of the envelope. Give the children these envelopes and have them sort through them rapidly,

putting each paragraph in one of three or more piles to match the textbook titles. When a child has finished sorting these, give the child a key to check his or her work.

4. Ask one child to find a part of the story that represents some action. Tell the child to pantomime this action while the rest of the children skim rapidly to try to find the sentence in the story that describes the action of the child doing the pantomiming (Ekwall, 1970).

SCANNING

Introductory Activity

1. Hold a class discussion on how scanning can be beneficial to the child. A list of times when scanning may be appropriate could include when

a. looking for a name in a telephone book
b. looking for a date in a history book
c. looking for a certain number of factors to solve a problem
d. reading the newspaper and searching for a certain article
e. wanting an idea of what an article or book will be about
f. looking for a word in a dictionary (Ekwall, 1970)

Reinforcement Activities

2. Explain to the children that this is a technique to locate specific information. The scanning should be done so rapidly that no other information is retained. Using transparencies of paragraphs related to course content, show children how to scan for target words. Ask specific questions and demonstrate what words or phrases they should look for to find answers to the questions.

Then use the content area textbook and ask specific questions that students may answer by scanning. For example, in science, "What are fossils?"; in history, "When was Washington elected president?"; in mathematics, "Tell me the formula for finding the area of a triangle" (Dillner and Olson, 1977).

3. Play the "I Spy Game" by selecting words from a content area textbook. Announce page numbers and give clue to the various words. For example, "I spy the word with three p's and two e's (pineapple)" or "that would interest a cow (hay)." The children race to see who can find the word first.

RAPID READING

Introductory Activity

1. Explain to the children that they can read faster if they read for ideas rather than word by word. Place an easy-to-read passage on the over-

head projector and ask the children to locate the key words and phrases. Underline the key phrases as they are identified by the children. Then illustrate, by reading aloud, how the children should use the key phrases to read the passage rapidly.

Give each child another easy to read passage and request that each child underline the words that represent key idea. Next, conduct a large-group discussion summarizing key ideas that they should have identified. Finally, give them another easy-to-read passage and ask them to read it as rapidly as possible. After they have finished, they are to tell a partner what they understood from the passage. Then together they carefully examine the passage and identify the key ideas that each used to read the passage rapidly.

Reinforcement Activities

2. Select a passage from a content area textbook and retype it so that the words are in "clumps" of thought units. The student is directed to read the passage in these thought units rather than word by word. A sample is given:

Example:

Energy   is also needed   to make food.   The plant   gets its energy
from sunlight.   What happens   to the plant   in the dark?

The game may be varied by asking children to construct their own "clumps" of words from content area materials. After the children have constructed their own, they can meet in small groups and discuss why they clumped the words as they did. If certain passages have been agreed upon as correct by all team members, groups may trade with each other and try to read the "clumps" as rapidly as possible.

3. Photostat a number of short selections from old readers or easy-to-read textbooks. Put each selection along with approximately ten comprehension questions in an envelope. Develop time limits for each story; for example, a certain selection may be labeled as a five-minute story. Label the envelopes under headings such as "Dog Stories," "Family Life Stories," "Science Stories." Let the children choose the stories that they want to read. From the labeling, the children will know that they should read the story in a certain number of minutes. This is a change from the timed test in which each student is reading the same subject matter. It also avoids having the faster readers waiting for the slower readers; that is, when a child finishes a story, that child can get another envelope and begin another story. Have the children keep a record of the stories they have read and their percentage of comprehension on each story (Ekwall, 1970).

STUDY SKILL 4: USING A STUDY TECHNIQUE

Introductory Activity

1. Explain the SQ3R study strategy to the children. Illustrate each step with material from one of their content area textbooks. As each step is discussed, elicit responses from the children about the purpose of each step. Assign the children to small groups and ask for volunteers from each group to prepare the strategy for the upcoming lesson. The next day each volunteer goes over the SQ3R technique with members of his or her group. A teacher-led discussion can be held to compare the steps of the SQ3R used by each volunteer.

Finally, ask for new volunteers from each group and repeat the process until each child has had a chance to present the SQ3R strategy to his or her group members.

Reinforcement Activities

2. Construct a checklist that contains the letters S, Q, R, R, R. Each time that the children are given an assignment, the teacher reminds them to check off the steps as they proceed through the material.

3. Ask the children to complete the first two steps of the SQ3R study technique. Then ask them to select a partner and compare questions that they have made up. Point out that the type and number of questions depends on the reader's familiarity with the topic and his or her purpose for reading it. For example, a child reading about "electric circuits" for the first time might construct a question such as "What is an electric circuit?" The child familiar with the topic might construct a question such as "Is this going to discuss a series type of electrical circuit?"

STUDY SKILL 5: USING AIDS WITHIN BOOKS

OVERVIEW

Introductory Activity

1. Use the table of contents from a textbook available to all children and the tables of contents from several other course-related materials. Design questions in which students must use the tables of contents to answer the questions; for example, "In which source would you find information about the stars?"

After the children have had time to answer the questions, discuss the correct answers with them. Show them that the purpose of a table of contents is merely a guide as to the kind of material contained in the book. After the children understand the use of the table of contents, show them how headings and subheadings may be used to locate information. Explain to them that, by using the table of contents to locate a general topic, they may skim through the portion of the chapter looking at headings and subheadings to determine whether or not the information contained therein is related to the topic in which they are interested. For example, if they were looking for information on the Big Dipper, they could look in the table of contents to determine where the topic was discussed. The chapter heading "Stars—Day and Night" might indicate to the children to turn to that chapter. Instead of reading the entire chapter, they could then look through headings and subheadings until they found the heading "Pictures in the Sky." Then they could look through the subheadings until they found the topic "Constellations."

Tell the children to turn to a given page in the index and ask them to locate the answers to the questions that they cannot answer from the table of contents alone; for example, "What is the name of the constellation that looks like a lion? After they locate the answer, explain that (a) all topics in an index are in alphabetical order, (b) pages on which the information related to the topic may be found are given in the index, (c) topics are arranged in the index according to key words (i.e., the key words for the "brightness of stars" would be "stars, brightness of"), and (d) commas often separate topics and page numbers. Demonstrate the four rules by showing students several examples in their own textbooks. Explain to the class that the primary technique in using an index is in determining the key words to locate a topic. Present a list of topics from the content area and ask the students to identify the key words that they would use to find the topic in the index. An example from science follows:

a. motion of waves
b. noise pollution
c. voluntary muscles
d. mechanical energy
e. red blood cells

After the students locate the correct key words, discuss some of the problems with locating key words. For example, if the topic cannot be located, try to find a (a) synonym for the key word—for example, the windpipe may be listed as trachea; (b) more general term for the key word—for example, windpipe may be listed under respiration; (c) more specific term for the key word—for example, throat may be listed under windpipe; (d) related term—for example, windpipe may be listed as cartilage tissue (Dillner and Olson, 1977).

Reinforcement Activities

2. Construct a list of questions that may be answered from the textbook. Ask the students to locate the answers and then state whether they

used the table of contents, the headings and subheadings, the index, or all three. Later discuss the most efficient source that should have been used. Point out the questions that obviously could be located only through the use of the index and explain to students why they should not use all three aids if they do not have to. Likewise, explain that some of the questions would best be answered by reference to the table of contents because the index would be too narrow to give the general response required. Questions of this type include the following: "What is the author's order of presentation of topics in this text? Why do you think that the author presents them in this order?" (Dillner and Olson, 1977).

3. Give children a list of topics and see how many key words they can make up that relate to the topics. They are to use their knowledge of synonyms, specific terms, general terms, and related terms to make their lists of key words as expansive as possible. Have them indicate which terms they think would be the ones actually used in the index (Dillner and Olson, 1977).

4. Make up a "Concentration" game. One card contains a key word; its match contains a broader term, narrower term, related term, or synonym. Let children play the game in pairs. Encourage them to make up more cards so that the game may be played with different topics (Dillner and Olson, 1977).

5. Time the children on the speed with which they can locate a list of topics in the text. Let the child who finishes first explain why he or she was able to locate the correct information so quickly (Dillner and Olson, 1977).

6. Have the children sit in pairs and open their science, health, math, and social studies texts. They are to list the differences in each text between the table of contents and the indexes. The team that comes up with the longest list gets to read it to the rest of the class. Other class members listen to see if they can add to the list.

7. Photostat a variety of paragraphs from a content area textbook. Use paragraphs that give a clue that can be found in the table of contents, index, or another of the textbook's locational aids. Each of these paragraphs is placed in an envelope along with a blank sheet of paper. Every child is given an envelope, and the assignment to find where the paragraph came from by using one of the book's locational aids. When the child finds the same paragraph in the textbook, the child writes the information on the blank piece of paper and hands it back to the teacher. Number the envelopes and have the children keep records on which envelopes they have done (Ekwall, 1970).

8. Generate a list of presents that the children would like to give to a friend. Then have the children meet in small groups and arrange the terms as they would be found in an index. They repeat the task by rearranging the terms as though they were in a table of contents. Have them share their indexes and tables of contents with each other and compare how the various groups have arranged the items.

9. Divide the class into teams. Each team is to construct a list of questions from a different content area. All questions should be answerable by

use of the index, table of contents, or other locational aid found in the textbook. While they complete their task, they are to underline the key words in each question. They also tell which locational aid they used to answer the question.

10. Construct a set of questions and definitions that match each question concerning various parts of books; for example, "List part and chapter titles and page numbers" (Answer card: table of contents). Turn all question cards upside down. Children draw one card at a time. If they are able to correctly match question with correct part of book, then they get to continue to draw cards. If they answer incorrectly, they lose their turns. The child with the most cards at the end of the game is the winner.

FOOTNOTES

Introductory Activity

1. Ask children why they think that authors include footnotes. Elicit answers that footnotes include explanatory notes and references to material in another source. Have children turn to several footnotes of the reference type in their text. Make certain that children can understand how the number in the text refers to the footnote number, the type of information included (i.e., author, title, place of publication, publisher, and date of publication), and any abbreviations used (Dillner and Olson, 1977).

Next have students turn to footnotes that contain explanatory notes. Have them analyze the type of information included. Complete the lesson by having children read material in their texts using a guided reading sheet that requires them to use information contained in the footnotes (Dillner and Olson, 1977).

Reinforcement Activities

2. Design a treasure hunt by developing questions that children must answer by referring to footnotes. Divide the class into teams of four or five. The team finding the correct answers to all the questions first wins (Dillner and Olson, 1977).

3. Ask children to locate a footnote that contains a reference to a topic in which they are particularly interested. Then have children locate the book or periodical in the library (Dillner and Olson, 1977).

GLOSSARY

Introductory Activity

1. Discuss with the children the purpose and location of the glossary. Ask them to locate a few words. Have them compare the glossary with the

dictionary in terms of scope and function. Assign the children a lesson to read with one or more terms that they may need to look up in the glossary. Discuss the use of the glossary following the reading of the selection (Dillner and Olson, 1977).

Reinforcement Activities

2. Divide the class into teams of four. Give each team six words whose meanings are to be found by using the glossary. Each team has fifteen minutes to locate the meanings of the words and to practice a method of presenting the meanings in some novel form. Children then present their word meanings (adapted from Bergman 1976, p. 98).

3. Have children make a glossary of words that they encounter in their text and whose meanings they do not know. This exercise is particulary profitable when the text that the student is using does not include a glossary (adapted from Bergman 1976, p. 113).

4. Have children use the glossary to play charades with partners. Each team selects a word from a content area textbook glossary and acts it out. The rest of the class members try to decide which word is being acted out.

TYPOGRAPHICAL AIDS

Introductory Activity

1. Have the children open a content area textbook to a predetermined chapter. Point out such typographical aids as words in italics and boldface. Then place the children in groups of five and ask each team to locate as many typographical aids in the chapter that they can. The team that finds the most at the end of a given time period tells the rest of the class the words and terms that its members have located. The rest of the class adds to the list until the teacher feels that all typographical aids have been located. Next, each group is to make a summary statement about why its members feel that certain ideas have been placed in a particular typographical format. The teacher lets each group tell its summary and adds any points that the group members feel may not have been covered.

Reinforcement Activities

2. Construct a tic-tac-toe board with terms that have been placed in different typographical formats by the author. To make a move, the child must look at the term and state why he or she thinks that it has been emphasized. A key to possible responses should be on the back of each term. Children who enjoy the game can be encouraged to make up more cards for future game playing. However, if a card has been made up by a child, the correct response to each term should be validated by a teacher. Such validation may

be done before the cards are used or when there is a dispute among pupils who disagree with the child who constructed the card.

ILLUSTRATIONS

Note: Strategies for introducing and reinforcing this skill are very similar to those discussed with word identification skill 3, "Using Picture Clues." However, illustration clues can provide meaning for more than just words and, in many cases, help a child to understand whole concepts that can not be explained adequately in words. For example, a flow chart illustrating electrical current is more than a representation of a single word. The teacher is encouraged to adapt the ideas presented with word identification skill 3 as well as the ones here to teach concepts to children.

Introductory Activity

1. Explain to the children that many ideas cannot be adequately expressed in words and are more concisely understood if done in terms of an illustration. Show the children an illustration from one of their content area textbooks and ask them to discuss how it simplifies the idea that the author is presenting. For example, a diagram of the flow of blood through the body helps to explain the process of the circulatory system. Show the children other similar illustrations and ask the child to describe the illustration in words. The child who describes it in the fewest words reads his or her description to the rest of the class. The teacher should then summarize the purposes for which authors use illustrations and demonstrate ways in which the different types of illustrations must be read; for example, a flow chart requires the use of sequence, whereas an editorial-type cartoon requires careful attention to details about which the reader must make references.

Reinforcement Activities

2. Photostat simple descriptive paragraphs from one of the content area texts. Ask the children to draw a picture of the main idea. Then ask them to draw a picture of one of the details that they feel is extremely important. Have the children compare pictures and see if they all drew similar illustrations of the main idea. Discuss why the main idea pictures may differ. Next compare their pictures of the important details. Discuss how and why different details have been drawn by the various class members.

3. Photostat and cut out illustrations and portions of the text that relate to the illustrations. Mix them together and place them in an envelope. The children are to sort through the material in the envelope and match the illustrations with the appropriate portion of the text. A key should be provided so the children can check their own answers. This process should be re-

peated for several different content area texts. If enough photostats are made, this activity can be made into a game, and teams of children can race to see which team can match the illustrations with the text materials in the least amount of time. If children have trouble matching the correct illustrations with the written text, point out clues that can be helpful. Team a good reader with a poor one and then have the team explain to other class members the clues that they used to match the illustrations with the written text.

ORGANIZATION OF PARAGRAPHS

Introductory Activity

1. Explain to the children that ideas are often arranged in patterns and that, if they learn to recognize the pattern and use it when they study, they will have an easier time remembering what they read or hear. Place on the overhead a transparency of content-related paragraphs that provide examples of the following types of paragraph organization: (a) cause–effect, (b) comparison–contrast, (c) enumerative, and (d) chronological. Go through the paragraphs one at a time and underline the key words that the reader may use as clues to help him or her understand the pattern used. Once the children understand how to identify the various patterns, tell them that they should always ask themselves the following questions about the patterns that they have identified: (a) What caused the effect to occur? (b) What is being compared or contrasted? (c) What types of things are listed? (d) What is the time order? (Dillner and Olson, 1977).

Reinforcement Activities

2. Select several paragraphs from the content area textbook or from other content-related materials and ask students to identify the paragraph pattern (Dillner and Olson, 1977).

3. Group children into threes and give each group a different type of paragraph pattern to look for in their textbooks. After ten minutes, ask members of each group to identify the paragraphs that they have located. Compare the number of each type of paragraph found in the text and discuss why the author would tend to use one type of paragraph more than another. For example, in history, the chronological pattern would probably prevail; in mathematics, the pattern would be enumerative (Dillner and Olson, 1977).

4. Group the children into pairs and give the groups the task of locating one specific type of paragraph pattern. After ten minutes, find out which pair has located the most. If the paragraphs located by the pair are the correct pattern, ask them to tell the remainder of the class what clue words they used to locate the paragraphs so quickly. Then discuss how these same clue words should give the children aids to interpreting the meanings of the paragraphs (Dillner and Olson, 1977).

STUDY SKILL 6: USING MAPS, GRAPHS, AND TABLES

OVERVIEW

Introductory Activity

1. Locate a map, graph, or table in content-related materials and ask the child to listen as you read the information contained (e.g., science—the path blood takes from the heart to the thumb; history—growth of the population in the United States from 1860 to 1900; mathematics—ordered pairs.)

Then give the children a quiz on the materials that you read aloud to them. Explain to them that words alone are often inadequate to clearly communicate some concepts. Show them the map, graph, or table that you read to them and discuss its worth in helping the reader to understand the message intended by the author.

Explain to the class that diagrams usually contain information to help the reader to understand an object, a process, or an operation. Give the children a diagram that they have not seen before and ask them to answer specific questions about it. Discuss the correct answers to the questions and the procedure that should have been followed to locate the correct answers. Finally, explain how to use the following graphic aids that are relevant to your content area: maps, graphs, tables.

Maps: Show the child maps that all have *legends.* Demonstrate the meanings of the symbols on various legends. Give them a map that they have not seen before and ask them to locate answers to several questions that require them to use its legend correctly. Discuss the correct answers to the questions and the procedure that should have been followed to locate the correct answers.

Graphs: Tell the child that several different kinds of graphs exist. Explain that *pictorial graphs, bar graphs, line graphs,* and *circle graphs* all contain similar elements. The children should always (a) read the title to get an idea of what the graph is about; (b) look for the scale of measure or legend (e.g., a picture of a school may represent a university or a figure of a man may represent two thousand people); (c) note what types of relationships are being presented (e.g., relationships of objects, places, or ideas); (d) identify the relationships shown by the graph (e.g., comparison of change in rate of population growth from 1860 to 1900, comparison of functional relationships between number of calories consumed and gain in weight). Give the children a graph that they have not seen before and ask them to answer specific questions about it. Discuss the correct answers to the questions and the procedure that should have been followed to locate the correct answers.

Tables: Explain to the class that a table is usually a listing of facts and information. It is helpful in showing comparisons of facts as well as in helping the reader to locate specific facts. The approach to reading a table is similar to that of reading a graph. Children should follow the succeeding steps: (a) Read the title to determine the contents of the table. (b) Look at the headings of the various columns; note any subheadings. (c) Read the details along the vertical and horizontal columns of the chart. (d) Begin to draw some conclusions about the information contained. Give students a table that they have not seen before and ask them to follow the four steps given to answer specific questions. Discuss the correct answers to the questions and the procedures that should have been followed to locate the correct answers (Dillner and Olson, 1977).

Reinforcement Activities

2. Ask the children to construct a map, graph, or table of something in their content area textbook that is not already in such a format. Then ask the students to share their illustrations with the remainder of the class. Discuss whether the map, graph, or table makes the original idea of the author any clearer (Dillner and Olson, 1977).

3. Place the children in pairs. Ask them to sit back to back. One child is to read from a map the directions for getting from one place to another. The second child is to draw a map of the oral directions and then compare the actual map with the one that he or she drew. Then the children switch roles and repeat the process. Examples from several content areas follow: science—one child describes the Great Lakes while the other fills in a map; language arts—one child describes the route of Huckleberry Finn and Jim down the Mississippi while the second fills in a map; social studies—one child describes the discovery of North America by the various explorers while the second child fills in a map (Dillner and Olson, 1977).

4. Group the children into threes and give them a set of questions concerning maps, graphs, and tables. The group that finishes first should compare answers with the other groups and then discuss the procedures that the winning three used to locate the information so quickly (Dillner and Olson, 1977).

5. Construct a game using index cards that have words such as "two-lane highway," "river," and "university" written on them. Each child has his or her own road map and plays the game by drawing a card. If the child is able to locate the symbol on his or her map for the word on his or her card, the child gets to keep his or her card. If the child is not able to do so, he or she loses a turn. The child with the most cards at the end wins the game.

6. Construct a "Bingo" game in which each child has a board containing symbols for objects such as "mountain," "river," and "university." A caller is chosen and draws similar symbols from an envelope. Each time that a term is drawn and read aloud, children who have that symbol on their playing

board can look for a similar symbol on their road map. If they have the symbol on their map, they can place a marker on their board. The winner is the first person who is able to cover a row of terms. Very young children can play the game by simply placing a marker over a symbol if it appeared on their "Bingo" board.

MAPS

Introductory Activity

1. Construct simple maps for first grade children that they can use to locate objects in the classroom. Use symbols such as pictures of windows and chairs so that they can learn how objects are represented on maps. Define "maps" in terms of these concrete activities.

Reinforcement Activities

2. Ask the children to construct maps of the journey taken by one of the persons in the social studies or science text. Show them how to use symbols to represent aspects from the real environment. For example, one inch could represent one hundred miles, five inches five hundred miles.

3. Show the children how to make maps of their own classroom. They could use string to divide their classroom into sections. Then they could give directions to each other by stating such things as "Would the student in grid B-6 wearing a blue shirt move forward one step" (Otto, Rude, and Spiegel, 1979, p. 211).

4. Use an overhead projector and a transparency of a city map to "find the teacher." The game is played like "Twenty Questions." Each child asks a question such as "Is the teacher in the northern part of the city? Is the teacher near a river?" The child who finds the teacher gets to decide where to hide the teacher for the next time that the game is played.

GRAPHS

Introductory Activity

1. Illustrate the purposes of various different types of graphs to the children. Make classroom graphs with the children. Show them how to use the necessary symbols by helping them to decide on the symbol to use for such graphs as (a) how to represent the number of books read by the children, (b) how to represent which rows of children have remembered to raise their hands when called upon, and (c) how to represent how many pets are owned by each child.

Reinforcement Activities

2. Older children can be asked to make circle graphs of the amount of time that they have spent in various activities throughout the previous day. This activity can be integrated with "scheduling time" discussed previously. For example, children can graphically represent what part of their time was spent in completing their homework. Discussion concerning how to make more efficient use of that time should follow.

3. Children can be encouraged to make bar graphs representing the amount of time spent each day on homework on several different subjects. For example, red could be math, blue could be science, and orange could be social studies. At the end of the week, the children could compare the difference in the amount of time spent by each in the various content areas. A graph comparing their grades to the amount of time spent could then be constructed.

TABLES

Introductory Activity

1. Illustrate the purposes of various different types of tables to the children. Children can be shown how to construct a table and then instructed to make one of their own on a topic of their own choosing. Possible topics might include (a) the time each day at which several of their friends ate breakfast, lunch, and dinner over a period of a week; (b) the temperature of five of their favorite cities over a week-long period of time; and (c) the passes completed by several of their favorite quarterbacks during the last five football games.

Reinforcement Activities

2. Ask for volunteers to watch the weather forecaster on the nightly television news. They are to report and discuss symbols or pictures used by the weatherman. The volunteers are to use the information from the television to keep a daily up-to-date classroom weather chart for several designated cities.

STUDY SKILL 7: USING LOCATIONAL AIDS IN THE LIBRARY

OVERVIEW

Introductory Activity

1. The first lesson on this topic may be carried out in the classroom. Using the overhead projector, show children facsimiles of title, subject, and

author cards. Briefly note that the call number occurs on each as does the author, title, publisher, place of publication, and date of publication. Describe sample situations in which various types of references should be used. For example, ask "If you wish to locate a book entitled *Wild Horses of America*, what type of card should you use?"

Using the overhead projector, show the children a page of the *Reader's Guide to Periodical Literature*. Study the format with the children carefully. Project the key that interprets the symbols used. Discuss with the children the information that is contained in the *Readers' Guide* but not in the card catalogue. A brief discussion of other indexes—such as *Who's Who*, dictionaries, and *Roget's International Thesaurus*—and their purposes might follow.

Give children a subject that they might need to research in the library and ask them to decide which topics they might look under to find information. For example, children might be asked under which topics they might look to find information on the first horse in North America.

The last step in this lesson would be to take children to the library and have the librarian show them the location of the card catalogue, the indexes, and the encyclopedias. A natural follow-up activity would be to have children find several references on a topic using the card catalogue, indexes, and encyclopedias (Dillner and Olson, 1977).

Reinforcement Activities

2. Write topics on slips of paper, place them in a hat, and ask each child to draw one. The child is to make up two cards: (a) a title card in which the child makes up the name of a book that fits the topic and (b) an author card in which the child is the author. All the title cards are then gathered and shuffled. The class is divided into small groups, and the title cards are divided among the groups. Children are instructed to make subject cards from the title cards. As soon as the groups finish making the new subject cards, they locate the original author to check their answers (Dillner and Olson, 1977).

3. Give the children a list of questions that requires them to look in the card catalogue, indexes, and encyclopedias to find the answers (Bergman, 1976, p. 234).

4. Near the beginning of the year, arrange the classroom books on tables. Discuss procedures with the children for creating a library from the stacks of books. Plan the work and assign tasks, such as classifying, arranging within categories according to author, numbering, creating a card catalogue, and devising a lending system. The resulting classroom library should be used as much as possible by children and teacher (Indrisano, 1976).

READER'S GUIDE

Introductory Activity

1. Ask each child to list at least three topics in which he or she is interested. Put the topics given by each child on the board. Select one of the

most current topics and elicit suggestions from the children as to how they could find out more about that topic. Explain that the material on the most up-to-date information is likely to be found in magazines rather than in books. Have them compare a card from the card catalogue with a photostated copy of a page from the *Reader's Guide*. Show how each type of reference aid contains an author and subject heading. Ask them questions that can be answered by reference to their photostated copy of the page from the *Reader's Guide*. For example, how many current articles are there on the topic of "football"? How many of the articles on "football" are fiction? List the titles of the magazines that contain the articles about "football." What other magazine articles related to the topic of "football" are found on the same page? Why would the index include the heading of "Football Fields" and "Football Players" as well as just the heading "Football"? Finally, ask each child to use the *Reader's Guide* to look up one of the topics that he or she listed at the beginning of the discussion. Let the children use a copy of the guide borrowed from the library and give them a day or two to complete the assignment unless the school happens to have enough guides so that each child or pair of children can have one to use.

Reinforcement Activities

2. Construct a "Treasure Hunt" game in which assorted pages from the *Reader's Guide* are photostated. Each participant is given a different page and a list of symbols and abbreviations used in the *Reader's Guide* that he or she must locate. If the abbreviation or symbol is not on his or her page, the child crosses the item off his or her list. If it is there, the child circles the item. The first child to complete his or her list is the winner.

THE CARD CATALOGUE

Introductory Activity

1. Bring the following to class: (a) five shoe boxes with the labels A—E, F—J, K—O, P—T, and U—Z on the front, (b) six index cards for each child, and (c) a different book for each child. Use one of the children's content area textbooks to illustrate the three types of cards that are found in a card catalogue. Then hold up a second content area textbook and ask each child to make three cards for the text. If the children seem to understand as evidenced by the cards that they make, ask them to make three more cards on the library book that they are given. Walk around the room while the children are making their cards and locate any children who seem to be having trouble. Further instruction should be given to those who seem to need it.

Study Skill 7: Using Locational Aids in the Library (Card Catalogue) (Library Call System)

Reinforcement Activities

2. Locate as many paperback books as possible. Have the children use index cards to make sets of library cards for a classroom card catalogue.

3. Divide a worksheet into five sections to correspond with card catalogue drawers: A—E, F—J, K—O, P—T, U—Z. Give the children the names of several different books. They are to indicate in which drawer they would need to look to locate the book by title, author, and subject.

LIBRARY CALL SYSTEM

Introductory Activity

1. A lesson on the library call system should be conducted in the library. The teacher or librarian should explain that books in the library are shelved according to the organizational system used in that library, be it the Dewey decimal system or the Library of Congress system. The general classes of the systems should be explained. The children should be shown how to locate books using the call numbers found on the cards in the card catalogue. Children should be given the call numbers and titles from five books and asked to locate them. Discussion of any difficulties should follow.

The teacher should show children reference cards for magazine articles made from the *Readers' Guide to Periodical Literature* and should instruct the children in the location of periodicals. Similarly, children should be shown reference cards for books based on materials taken from bibliographies in an encyclopedia. Children should be questioned as to how they would locate the books. The teacher should elicit the answer that children should look up the title or author card for each book in the card catalogue (Dillner and Olson, 1977).

Reinforcement Activities

2. Divide the class into teams. Give each team a list of books and journal articles. The teams must use the library reference tools to decide whether the materials are in the library and, if so, to locate them. The first team to correctly finish wins (Bergman, 1976, p. 14).

3. Provide a box with book catalogue cards. Divide the class into teams of five. The first member of each team chooses a card from the box and goes to find the book. When he or she finds it, the next member of the team repeats the procedure. This system is followed until all the members of one team have found a book (Bergman, 1976, p. 224).

STUDY SKILL 8: USING REFERENCE MATERIALS

OVERVIEW

Introductory Activity

1. Borrow a variety of reference materials from the library. Include a dictionary, several volumes from an encyclopedia, an atlas, an almanac, a yearbook, a directory, a *Reader's Guide*, a thesaurus, and a list of audiovisual recordings and microfilmed information. Explain to the children that each reference has a different purpose. Then place the children in small groups and give them a list of problems that may be solved by referring to one or more of the references. After a given time limit, have the groups compare their solutions to the problems and the resources that they used to find their answers. Discuss why some children used different sources to find answers to the same problem. If any of the reference materials were not used by the children, make a point of explaining the purpose of that particular reference.

Reinforcement Activities

2. Develop a "Scavenger Hunt" in which teams of children are to locate answers to questions by using a variety of reference materials. The team that finds the most answers in the shortest amount of time gets to make up questions for future "Scavenger Hunts."

3. Construct two kinds of index cards. The first kind contains the names of various reference materials; the second kind contains a list of questions. The child is to pick the most likely source in which to find the answer to each question (e.g., almanac, telephone book, encyclopedia, atlas, *Guiness Book of Records*). Possible question: "Where would you locate the largest hamburger ever eaten by anyone?"

Extend the game by giving children the list of references and having them construct questions for other children to react to.

4. Design motivating activies to correlate with content area studies. For example, if the children are studying research about food in science, draw a picture of an old wooden ice box on the outside of a manila folder. The open folder would look like the inside of an old-time refrigerator. On the "shelves" inside place question cards that the children are to use as the basis of an individual research project that requires them to use a variety of reference materials. For example (a) List at least ten different types of your favorite food; choose one for further study. (b) Use the encyclopedia to find out what makes popcorn pop; prepare a report to present to the class; be creative when presenting it. (c) Who invented peanut butter? Use the library to find out more about it; write a short biography about the inventor and present it to the class. (d) Write a story about the origin of all the food you ate at your last meal. Tell me what you ate, what part of the country each edible portion came from, and what means you used to eat it. (e) Make a

scrapbook about your favorite foods; some picture sources are advertisements in newspapers and magazines, consumer booklets from state and local governments, and original drawings. (f) Preview films, filmstrips, or slides about food products. Choose one to share with the class. Make up some questions to ask after the presentation.

5. With the help of the teacher, young children prepare a class chart of all the sources and resources that provide information at their level. The chart is an ongoing activity; new entries are made as children discover new ways to know. A rebus may be used to assist children who are not yet able to read (Indrisano, 1976).

6. Each child selects a topic of special interest and becomes an expert on the sources of information about that subject. Through a class scrapbook, each child shares his or her expertise with others who are interested in the topic. To assist the process, the children may first discuss the available sources and resources (Indrisano, 1976).

DICTIONARIES

Note: Dictionary skills are presented in this text as a reference tool as well as a means of helping children to expand their vocabularies. The following activities emphasize the dictionary as a reference tool. For more specific techniques on using the dictionary to increase word identification skills, turn to word identification skill 7, "Using the Dictionary."

Introductory Activity

1. Explain to the children that the word "dictionary" may be used to describe a wide variety of reference works. Typically, a dictionary contains a list of words with information about each word. If the list is short and is found in the back of a book, it is usually called a "glossary" instead of a dictionary. If the list contains only geographical names, it is called a "gazetteer." In some cases, reference books that list specific entries in alphabetical order are also labeled as dictionaries (e.g., a list of famous people included in a "dictionary of biography"). Ask the children to each locate a dictionary and do the following: (a) Write down the first entry. (b) Write down the last entry. (c) Write down the total number of pages in the dictionary. After the children have completed this task, compare the differences in the various dictionaries used and discuss why those differences probably exist.

Reinforcement Activities

2. Explain to the children that most dictionaries only list words that they think will be used by their readers rather than every word in existence. Ask each child to select three words that he or she has heard on television and that he or she thinks will probably not be in the dictionary. Point out

that the reasons why words are not placed in the dictionary include (a) slang, (b) newness, and (c) a word not typically needed by the reader (e.g., the word "perianth" is not in every dictionary). After the task has been completed, have the children verify their word selections by looking them up in the dictionary. Each child should then turn in his or her words to the teacher so that the teacher can make a master list of words that were and were not found in the dictionary. The master list can be used as the focus of a class discussion illustrating reasons why some of the words were not in the dictionary.

3. Show the children how dictionaries may be used as a quick reference for locating information about certain geographical locations. Most dictionaries contain geographical entries that contain the names of countries, states, important cities, lakes, mountains, and the like. Help the children to generate a list of questions about geographical locations that they believe might be answered by use of the dictionary. Have the children try to locate the answers to such questions.

4. Show the children how dictionaries can be useful in finding out certain information about a limited number of people. Show them how biographical entries include the years of a person's birth and death, his or her nationality, and a phrase or two describing the person's occupation or main area of contribution. Ask each child to list three people whom they feel will probably be listed in their dictionaries. Each child then verifies his or her choices by looking in the dictionary. Those children who locate persons on their list share the names with the rest of the class members. A summary discussion should focus on why some people were or were not in the dictionary.

5. Explain to the children that a word's *etymology*, or history, may be found in the dictionary. Give them a list of words with interesting origins and ask them to look up each. Then ask the children to select words that they feel are of "foreign" origin and verify the origin in the dictionary. The children then share their words and the origin of each with the rest of the class.

DIRECTORIES

Introductory Activity

1. Explain to children that usually the purpose of a directory is to make available the names and residences of (a) the inhabitants of a particular place or (b) those engaged in a particular profession or business. Point out that most of them should already be familiar with the telephone directory. Give each child a telephone directory and ask him or her to list at least five facts that can be found there. After a set period of time, summarize the responses of the children. Make certain that all are aware of aspects such as the name of a person, his or her address, his or her telephone number, the occupation of selected individuals, and area codes for towns and cities in the area.

After the discussion, place the children in pairs and give them a list of names to look up. The pair who completes its list first wins the round and is asked to construct a list of new names for future playing.

Reinforcement Activities

2. Obtain a zip code directory for each child. Divide the class into teams and give each team a list of cities. The children use a relay race to locate the zip code for each city. The team that finishes first wins the game.

3. Make a telephone directory containing just the names of the children in class. Extend the task by asking each child to describe something that he or she does well and construct a "Yellow Pages" to go along with each child's area of expertise; headings might include "Bicycle Repair," "Newspaper Delivery," "Snow Shoveling," and "Baby Sitting."

4. Make up a list of fictitious emergencies. Have the children respond to each by locating appropriate phone numbers as rapidly as possible.

ENCYCLOPEDIAS

Introductory Activity

1. Use the overhead projector to compare treatment of a content area topic in the encyclopedia with its treatment in other books. For example, "South America" might be discussed for two pages in the encyclopedia, for two sentences in the dictionary, in map form only in the atlas, and for several hundred pages in a book entitled *South America: Its Land and Its Peoples.*

Explain to the children that the purpose of an encyclopedia is to present a summary of knowledge about a variety of topics. Explain that efficient use of the encyclopedia requires that they use their knowledge of such previously learned skill as key words, cross-referencing, alphabetizing, and guide words.

Reinforcement Activity

2. Ask each child to select a different content area topic to research. The child is to locate the topic in an encyclopedia as well as in at least two other sources. The children are asked to bring photostats of the various references to class. The children then are placed into groups. Each child shares his or her photostats with other group members without telling the source of each photostat. The other group members read the photostats and attempt to determine which one came from the encyclopedia. The group members then discuss clues that helped them to identify the resource. Finally, the group summarizes the differences between material typically found in the encyclopedia and that found in other resources.

Study Skill 8: Using Reference Materials (Atlases)

ATLASES

Introductory Activity

1. Ask each child to write down the name of his or her favorite television character. The teacher collects all the names and compiles them into a list made available to all the children. The teacher then asks the children if they know where each of their favorite characters lives. As geographical locations are mentioned by either the teacher or the children, they are placed on the board. Then the teacher gives each child a copy of an elementary level atlas. The children are shown how to look up the location of several of their favorite television characters. Explain to the children that an atlas is simply a collection of maps bound together and is an excellent source for finding information about geographical locations rapidly.

Reinforcement Activity

2. Ask children to prepare a scrapbook of places that they would like to visit. Suggest that they cut out pictures from magazines or newspapers to illustrate their scrapbook. Construct a map of the world on the floor of the classroom. Each child is to locate the place that he or she would like to visit and to put his or her scrapbook on the proper spot on the map. The class members then take a "trip around the World" by walking from spot to spot on the map and looking at each other's scrapbooks.

STUDY SKILL 9: USING MATERIALS APPROPRIATE TO PURPOSE

Introductory Activity

1. The teacher brings in a group of picture books on the same topic. The children are asked to give ideas about what they might learn from the books. The teacher writes down all responses on the board in one of three columns: (a) to find the answer, (b) to do, and (c) to solve a problem. For example, if children were shown picture books about dogs, the following responses might be given:

a. To find the answer: "What is the color of the dog? What is the dog doing? Who is following the dog?"
b. To do: "This story makes me laugh. The dog's friend is scary to read about. I would like to show this book to my little brother."
c. To solve a problem: "I would like to try to teach my dog that trick; he doesn't know anything" (adapted from Indrisano, 1976).

Study Skill 9: Using Materials Appropriate to Purpose

Reinforcement Activities

2. Read two stories on the same topic aloud to the class. Ask the children to work in pairs and list as many problems as they can think of that might be solved by the information given in each story. Then ask the pairs to compare the ways in which the two stories might help them to solve each of the problems. For example, a teacher might read two stories about a pet that died. One could be from a health book, the other from a science book. Typical problems that might be solved include

How can you make someone feel better if their pet dies? Do most people who have pets feel the same way when they lose a pet? Is it normal to feel sad about the death of a pet? What causes pets to die? At what age do pet dogs typically die? How sick must a pet be before the veterinarian "puts him to sleep?" Is it best to let a pet die naturally or should he be "put to sleep?"

A comparison of the two sources should indicate that the health book is appropriate for gathering information about feelings and emotions about death and that the science book is appropriate for gathering information about causes and types of deaths. Finally, the teacher should discuss why some sources are more appropriate for particular purposes than others. A list of purposes for reading and materials appropriate for each could be generated and used as a summary for the class session.

3. List several purposes for which books may be read. Then make up a list of fictitious book titles accompanied by author, author's qualifications, and copyright dates. Illustrate to the children how each of these traits affects the purpose. Then make a second worksheet and have the children match the purpose of each book with the correct title.

4. A box is placed in the classroom into which a child may place a picture of something that arouses his or her curiosity. As a small-group activity, the box is opened and the children help the curious child define his or her curiosity as objectives—things to find out, activities to do, questions to answer. Possible types of books to answer each objective are discussed (Indrisano, 1976).

5. The children write problems or questions on individual cards or slips of paper. In a discussion group (and later in teams), the cards are read and sorted into two categories: those that will have many right solutions or answers and those that will have only one. For example, "How many children have a birthday in March?" will have one answer; "What is the best birthday present you can give to a friend?" will have many. Sources for the answer to each are discussed (Indrisano, 1976).

6. The teacher notes the ideas that the children question. On separate cards, several possible patterns of questions are listed. The children discuss the questions and choose the one that will be most effective in guiding a search for answers. Questions about rain, for example, might include "What about rain?" and "Why does it rain?" The types of books that can best an-

swer each question are discussed (adapted from Indrisano, 1976).

7. A unit in a content area book is selected. The children skim the material and set out their purposes for reading the content. The aim is to state *specifically* problems, purposes, and questions. A list is made and checked off as the purposes are realized (adapted from Indrisano, 1976).

8. Each youngster makes a personal list of problems, objectives, and/or questions related to an area of interest. The list is used to guide personal reading, project planning, and independent research activites (Indrisano, 1976).

9. Select from a collection of pictures the ones that contribute to the topic under investigation (adapted from Indrisano, 1976).

10. Create a bibliography of sources and resources for a given topic, including all possible types. Later the sources may be rank ordered according to their potential value for the specific purpose (adapted from Indrisano, 1976).

11. List all the possible uses for which one source or resource might be used, for example, *The Junior Book of Authors* (adapted from Indrisano, 1976).

12. Give the students a problem and ask them to figure it out using all the materials located on the table. The team that finishes first tells which materials they used and why.

STUDY SKILL 10: ORGANIZING INFORMATION

OVERVIEW

Introductory Activity

1. The teacher empties a bag on the floor containing twenty or more different objects. He or she asks for a volunteer to find three or four of the objects as rapidly as possible. Afterward, the teacher should ask questions such as "Can anyone think of ways in which to make the objects easier to locate? Is there a way in which these objects on the floor could be rearranged so that they would be easier to find?" After some questioning, the teacher should illustrate a variety of organizational procedures that could be used to rearrange the objects on the floor. These might include placing together by size, shape, or function (classifying); drawing a diagram that pictures the location of each item (preliminary note-taking); subdividing the position of objects within the various categories, for example, placing all coins in the same category but arranging them from the smallest in value to the largest (preliminary outlining); and placing objects in related categories closest to each other, for example, placing real-life objects such as coins near the items categorized together as "tools." Play items such as "plastic animals" could be placed near "toy building blocks" (compare and contrast). The merits of each organizational format should be discussed through ques-

tions such as "Is it harder to place objects that are alike together than to just draw a diagram?" Afterward, the children decide how they think that the objects should be organized, and a volunteer completes the task.

Reinforcement Activity

2. The class can visit a place of interest in or near their school. During the visit each member organizes the information that he or she obtains. The teacher can instruct students to (a) take notes, (b) classify information under the headings "What I Saw," "What I Heard," and "What I Smelled," or (c) compare and contrast. When the children return to the classroom, the teacher may request that they write a summary paragraph based on their written notes (adapted from Bergman, 1976, p. 19).

NOTE-TAKING

Introductory Activity

1. Show the children short paragraphs on chart paper or with an overhead projector. After they have had a chance to read the paragraph, remove it from their view and have them tell or write down one or two important ideas from their paragraph in their own words. They need not use complete sentences but, rather, should be encouraged just to note the most important details (Fisher and Terry, 1977).

Reinforcement Activities

2. From a simple nonfiction account, such as an article in a children's newspaper, the children write three important ideas to remember (Indrisano, 1976).

3. The children preview a taped selection of an expository piece and decide the important ideas and details. The tape is played again and the children take notes. Later they compare their notes with a written version of the material. As proficiency grows, the preview may be unnecessary (Indrisano, 1976).

4. Note-taking skills can be presented to older children as a technique to be used when a more structured outline is not needed. The teacher can show children various types of notes including single-word notes, incomplete sentence (phrase) notes, and complete sentence notes. Then the teacher might ask children to take notes on a paragraph and follow this activity with a discussion.

For example, the teacher might instruct children to read the following paragraph from the health book to be able to name some foods rich in fat:

Foods rich in fat are better than others in giving you energy. Some of these foods are margarine, butter, and nuts. Other energy foods are bread, potatoes, rice, meat, milk, and cheese. (Richmond and Pounds, 1977, p. 102)

One child's notes might be

Foods rich in fats: margarine, butter, nuts, bread, potatoes, rice, meat, milk, cheese

Following this activity, children's notes could be evaluated by discussing the following:

a. Is the information appropriate for the purpose?
b. Are the author's points restated in child's words?
c. Are all important points recorded?
d. Were any shorthand techniques used to increase speed of note-taking?
e. Will the notes be readable at a later date? (Dillner and Olson, 1977)

5. Write the following steps concerning note-taking on posterboard: (a) Read all of the story to get a good idea of what it is all about. (b) Reread the story. (c) Underline the main ideas. (d) Write down the main ideas in your own words. Discuss each of the four steps with the children. Then pass out comic strips from the newspaper. Each child is to select a comic strip and follow the four steps. However, the child is directed to write notes concerning the comic strip in his or her own words on an index card. Children trade comic strips with a partner and repeat the process. After each has read and taken notes on the two comic strips, they compare their notes. Any wide discrepancies should be discussed and shown to the teacher for clarification.

6. Ask the children to take notes from the information given on a nonfiction television show and then give a class report. They should note the source of the direct quotes and specific information (Adams and Harrison, 1975).

7. Ask children to take notes on words or phrases on products being advertised but not said out loud in the commercial. Note the words are seen in print only. Discuss possible reasons for such discrepancies in class (Adams and Harrison, 1975).

CLASSIFYING

Introductory Activity

1. Construct a shopping bag from the lower portion of a grocery bag. Attach handles and paste pictures of various foods on the sides. Direct the children to find more pictures of food and put them in the shopping bag. Have each child tell what he or she brought. Then dump the bag and tell

the children to place the food into various categories, such as they might find in the grocery store. Ask them to find a particular picture. Discuss how grouping by categories can help them to locate specific items more quickly.

Reinforcement Activities

2. Ask the children to divide all the words seen on television commercials into categories such as glad words (good, tasty), bad words (germs, disease), emotional words, or names of famous people. They may add other categories if they wish (Adams and Harrison, 1975).

3. Ask the children to look in the newspaper for words that fit together; for example (a) color words—brown, black, red, (b) animal words—dog, cat, horse, (c) transportation words—car, boat, bicycle, (d) food words—meats, vegetables, fruits (Verner, 1978).

4. Ask the children to use the newspaper to organize topics representing (a) things that you like and things that you don't like, (b) cars that are older or younger than three years, and (c) a variety of pets.

5. Ask the children to look in a content area textbook for items that fit predetermined categories; for example (a) famous men, (b) acts of conflict, and (c) foods that contain starches.

6. Classifying can be taught to older children by assigning them questions to which the answers can best be found by classifying. For instance, students might be asked to answer the question, "Which of the cities that we've read about manufacture machinery? clothes? glass? iron and steel?" After reading a selection that answers this question and then listing which cities belong in each category, formats for classifying could be discussed. One format that may be used is the following:

	New York	*Pittsburgh*	*Atlanta*	*Dallas*
Manufactures machinery				
Manufactures clothing				
Manufactures glass				
Manufactures iron, steel				

(Adapted from Dedrick et al., 1979)

7. Construct a "Bingo" game that children can use while watching television. The board should contain such terms as "a villain is on the screen," "a cowboy is on the screen," "an animal hero is on the screen," "a commercial is on the screen," "a detective is on the screen," "a doctor is on the screen." Whenever the action on television reflects a term on the board, a marker is placed over that item. When enough spaces are filled to make a straight line, the child wins the "Bingo" game. Children who have trouble with classifying information can play this game for homework with the help of a parent.

SUMMARIZING

Introductory Activity

1. Explain to the children that when they summarize something they are really locating the main ideas. Place a transparency of a simple passage from a content area textbook on the overhead projector. Show the children how to revise the passage, capturing the main points but using only one third to one fourth as many words. Show them how quotes, illustrations, minor details, and unnecessary words should be eliminated when making a summary. Illustrate how to reword sentences and make nouns and verbs do most of the work. Then give each child a copy of another content area passage. Ask them to see who can summarize it in the least amount of words. Have the children compare their summaries of the passage with a partner. Read aloud those passages written by children that seem to summarize the passage well. Point out words that were omitted and phrases that were rewritten to say the same thing more concisely.

Reinforcement Activities

2. Ask the first graders to write an experience story together after telling about an activity or completing a field trip. As they construct the story, show them how to express ideas concisely. Help them to summarize and clarify their ideas as they express them.

3. Suggest to the children that they prepare a book jacket for a favorite book that they have just read. The front flap should contain a summary of the story; the back flap should contain a summary of the author's life (Indrisano, 1976).

4. Suggest to the children that they each select a topic of particular interest and research the topic. Then they summarize their finding in a format that can be published in a class newspaper or given as an oral report to selected classmates (Indrisano, 1976).

Study Skill 10: Organizing Information (Outlining)

OUTLINING

Introductory Activity

1. An outline of a favorite story is shown. The relative importance of each detail as shown by its place on the outline is discussed. An outline of a second story is done together. A third story is done individually and assessed by the teacher.

Reinforcement Activities

2. The class makes a mural to depict a favorite story. Class discussions precede the activity as children decide the most important scenes and later what will be included in each scene. A popular variation is the dramatization of a story using the same procedure (Indrisano, 1976). After discussing the form of an outline, the children arrange a cut-up outline, comparing their version with the original. The outlines used for this practice should be very simple, including only a limited number of items in each category (Indrisano, 1976).

3. Crossley (1957)* has suggested a highly effective procedure for teaching outlining:

1) Present a skeletal outline, including the main topics. The child reads to fill in the minor ideas.

The Colonists Sail for America

I. The countries they came from

A. . . . .

B. . . . .

C. . . . .

II. The reasons they left for America

A. . . . .

B. . . . .

C. . . . .

2) Provide the minor ideas. The child reads to fill in the major ideas.

The Colonists Sail for America

I. . . . .

A. England

B. Germany

C. Africa

*Crossley, B. A., "Can We Help Children Write?" *Journal of Education* 139 (1957); 10-11. Copyright by the Trustees of Boston University.

II. . . . .

A. Religious freedom

B. Ownership of land

C. Indentured servants

3) Present the structural organization. The child reads to fill in the parts of the outline.

I. . . . .

A. . . . .

B. . . . .

C. . . . .

4) Finally the child writes an original outline.

Each step represents the culmination of several practice sessions, using increasingly detailed material. The final step may not come until after several months of concentrated discussion and practice.

4. Discuss with students the role of outlining. Stress that this technique should be used when children need to note main ideas and details in relationship to a specific purpose. Show children a completed outline. Discuss placement of heading and details. Some of the important rules that might be brought out are that (a) the size of the indentation and the notation used are determined by the importance of the ideas; (b) all ideas of the same importance should have equal indentation; (c) items may be written in either phrases or sentences, but the entire outline should be one or the other; (d) the first word of each item in an outline should be capitalized; (e) a period is always placed after each notation symbol (numbers and letters) in an outline.

5. Ask the children to watch their favorite television show. They are to make a simple outline of the movie and determine if the show breaks for commercials at key points of the plot (Adams and Harrison, 1975).

6. Give the children a list of topics and ask them to identify the key word that summarizes the list (e.g., cocker spaniel, Scottish terrier, collie, and Doberman would be summarized by the word "dog"). After they can do this, give them a list of items that can be outlined into three levels of indentation. They are to read the words and then place them into outline format. For example, the words sugar, starch, carbohydrates, candy, potato would be outlined as

Carbohydrate

Sugar

Candy

Starch

Potato

7. Give the children a skeleton of an outline and list of terms that fit into the skeleton and ask them to fill in the blanks. For example, sugar, starch, carbohydrates, candy, potato

I. ____________________

A. ____________________

1. ____________________

B. ____________________

1. ____________________

COMPARING AND CONTRASTING INFORMATION

Introductory Activity

1. Give the children newspapers and scissors and ask them to cut out pictures of as many different types of animals as they can find. The teacher collects all the pictures. The children are shown the pictures one at a time and must look for "things that are alike" about each animal (e.g., all eat, all breathe, all can move). As similarities are noted, the teacher writes them on the board. The process is repeated, but children are to look for "things that are different" (e.g., some eat only plants, some don't have legs). As differences are noted, the teacher writes them on the board. Finally, the relationship between similarities and differences and the purpose for each are discussed. Then children are given new newspapers and are asked to cut out more animals and group them by similarities. Later they repeat the task but regroup by differences.

Reinforcement Activity

2. Divide the class into teams of five students. Ask students to compare two objects not usually compared. For example, the teacher might say, "A book is like a pencil." The teams are given five minutes to compare the objects. Each team reads its comparisons aloud. The entire class then votes for the best comparisons (class members cannot vote for their own team's contribution) (adapted from Bergman, 1976, p. 18).

STUDY SKILL 11: RECALLING INFORMATION

Introductory Activity

1. Empty a bag of assorted items related to content area studies on the teacher's desk (e.g., a picture of Winnie the Pooh). Direct the children to look at the items and try to remember them. At the end of two minutes, cover the items and tell each child to list as many items as he or she can. Ask the child who remembered the most how he or she did it. Next empty a second bag of objects on the table. This time, rearrange the objects into categories. At the end of a given time limit, cover the objects and ask the children to name as many of the objects as possible. Discuss the relationship between organization and memory. Illustrate by helping them outline a current chapter from one of their content area texts.

Reinforcement Activities

2. Give each child a list of unrelated events or objects from one of the content areas (e.g., the names of twenty famous americans). Each child is told to look at his or her list and try to remember as much as he or she can. At the end of a given time limit, the children turn their papers over and write down as many items as they can recall. Ask the child who remembers the most how he or she was able to do so. Show the children how organization can help them to remember more easily. Go over the list and help them organize it in some order (e.g., chronological). Then give them a similar list and repeat the task. Encourage them to organize the material as they are trying to remember it. Assign the students the task of organizing their current homework assignment in any manner they see fit. The next day compare ways in which the children organized to best remember.

3. Group the children into pairs and direct them to open up one of their content area textbooks to a predetermined page. The children read the passage and then one of the children tells the other child what he or she read. The second child verifies the information, and both children reread the same passage to see if any important details were missed. A second paragraph is assigned and the process is repeated. After each child has had a turn, the teacher asks the children to discuss what effects the telling aloud had upon their ability to remember the given information. The teacher should explain that the children have been involved in a "recitation" process and that this process can be used to help them remember better. Assign them the task of reciting at least three passages to themselves on the next homework assignment. The next day, have the pair of children share with each other the passages that they recited and how they felt about their ability to remember them. Each day for the next few weeks ask the children to spend a moment or two sharing the information that they have recited for homework with their partner.

4. Young children love rhymes and teachers should use them to help

the children use the repetition of and association between the rhyming words to remember better. For example, if a child is having trouble with the alphabet, he or she might be paired with a child who knows the alphabet song. The children practice the song together until they can present it, as a puppet show, to the rest of the class members.

5. Ask the children to list the times or events that they have trouble remembering. Use some of the items to illustrate how they can use repetition to help them remember. Suggest that for some items, such as spelling words, index cards can be made and used as "flash cards." Explain that another means for studying some concept repetitiously is to simply reread the material. Help the children to generate purposes for rereading that would make the task more interesting, for example, to locate specific facts, to look for biases in the text, to visualize the events that are occurring, to construct background music if the event were dramatized.

6. Children can be taught to increase their visual memory with the aid of a teacher-made tachistoscope. Words are printed on long strips of paper that the child places in the device. As the child pulls the shutter, the word "flashes" and the child is to recite it aloud. The child should repull the shutter to verify the word (see Figure 15.2).

Figure 15.2 Tachistoscope

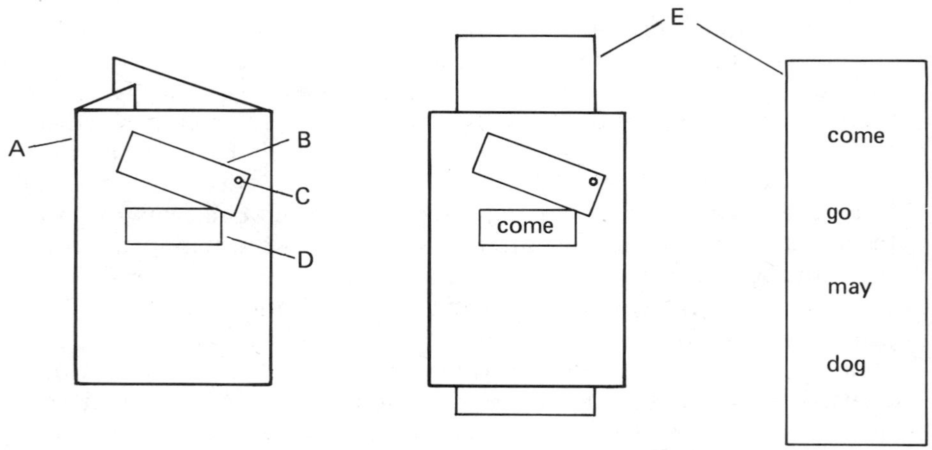

A = folded poster board
B = shutter
C = brass paper fastener
D = opening
E = card board containing list of words

7. Children enjoy increasing their auditory memory through games such as "Gossip." The teacher tells the children that they are going to be told a piece of information and that it will be whispered from person to person. The last child repeats the message aloud and a comparison with the actual message aloud and a comparison with the actual message is made. This may be played in teams, with the team that finishes first with the "correct" message being the winner.

8. When presenting mnemonic devices to the children, make them aware of the principles behind the strategies and help them to create their own. For example, in social studies the children might be told that one way to remember that Abraham Lincoln's first vice president was Hamlin would be to look at the name Abraham Lincoln and remember the underlined cues. This cue utilizes the principle of association; that is, the learner makes a visual connection between the name of the president and his first vice president.

9. Explain to the children that associations with things already known can help them to remember new information. Give them an example from a current content area assignment; for example, the events discussed in social studies during "the cattle drive to the railroads" might be remembered by thinking about the song "The Old Chisholm Trail." Tell each child to open his or her content area text to a given page. Arrange the class into small groups and ask them to make as many associations about the topic as they can. After a given amount of time, have each group list the associations that they have made. Compare the associations and discuss which ones would be most helpful in remembering the current lesson. For the next few weeks require each child to make at least one association on predetermined content area lesson daily. These associations should be shared with the total class immediately before that lesson is discussed.

10. Construct a game board similar to "Concentration" in which pictures of objects from various content areas are placed on index cards and put face up in the middle of the table. The child is instructed to look at the objects and try to remember as many of them as possible. After a given time limit, the child turns the cards face down and tries to see how many pairs he or she can turn over and match up. A typical example of pairs might be pictures representing "Huck" and "Jim" from *Huck Finn*; "light bulb" and "electrical current" from science; "cattle" and "Chisholm Trail" from social studies. As children become proficient at the game, they can make up their own pairs for use in future games.

11. If the children are to take a standardized test accompanied by an answer sheet, give them practice using answer sheets before they are required to take the actual test. Copies of the answer sheets similar to the ones that they will be asked to use can be made. Adapt questions from some of the content lessons to match the format on the answer sheet (e.g., make multiple-choice responses for three of four questions located at the end of the social studies chapter). Show the children how to mark a sample answer sheet and then tell them to complete the rest independently. If this process

is repeated daily a week or two before the test, some failure due to incorrectly marking the answer sheet should be prevented.

12. If possible, obtain old copies of a test similar to the one that children are going to be asked to take. Go over suggestions for taking standardized test, for example, "follow directions" and "read all multiple-choice alternatives before selecting the one best answer." Administer the test in the same manner as the actual test will be administered. After the test has been scored, do an item analysis and find questions missed by many children. Go over these specific questions with the children, showing them the answer intended and the types of things that they have done that prevented them from making the correct response (e.g., didn't read the question carefully and overlooked the word *not*; read too much into the question and got the wrong answer). Review the type of things that testmakers are usually after and help the children to respond to the items in this manner.

STUDY SKILL 12: EVALUATING INFORMATION

Introductory Activity

1. Present the children with a simple piece of writing, such as a two- or three-paragraph description of a product that relates to something that they are reading about in one of their content areas. Tell them that the piece was written by the president of the company promoting the product and ask them to judge the authenticity of the paragraphs. Then inform the students that you made an error and that the ad was actually written by an objective consumer agency. What changes do they now make in their evaluation of the ad?

Explain to the students that our view of written material changes drastically when it is based on the author's purpose for writing, as has just been demonstrated. Explain further that all responsible writing has a purpose and ask leading questions to elicit some of the purposes—for example, to entertain, to inform, to persuade.

With the children, analyze the purposes of a few short selections. Then ask them to work in small groups to ascertain the purposes of some other selections. For example, students could analyze their science textbook author's purpose (to inform); the purpose of the writer of an article concerning prejudice in sports (to persuade); a short story about a pet kangaroo (to entertain) (Dillner and Olson, 1977).

Reinforcement Activities

2. Each child chooses a topic in which he or she is interested that appears in the newspaper. The child is to cut out all articles that he or she can find on the topic. At the end of two weeks, the child should evaluate the articles in the following manner: (a) Rank order each according to the

amount of facts given about the topic. (b) Categorize each according to purpose of the author (e.g., to inform, to entertain, to persuade). (c) Rank order each in terms of his or her personal feelings about each (i.e., which one he or she liked the best, giving several reasons for choosing the order that he or she did).

3. Ask each child to bring in a newspaper or magazine article related to a topic discussed in one of the content area textbooks. For example, if the children were studying "noise pollution," articles brought in could include an article concerning how loud music is affecting the hearing of teenagers, a picture of a traffic jam in which everyone was honking their car horns, a complaint written by a person living near the airport, and an advertisement for earphones. The teacher should select one of the articles, make duplicate copies, and ask the children to meet in small groups and react to the article using the following questions: (a) How do I personally feel about noise pollution? What do I know about this topic? What are my personal experiences with noise pollution? (b) Who is the author? What is his or her background? What was the author's purpose in writing this article? (c) How complete is the author's discussion of the topic? Are there any facts that I know about the topic that the author should have mentioned and did not? How true are the author's facts? Does the author support his or her facts with references? Are there words in the article that might indicate bias on the part of the author? (d) How well written is the article? Does the author's word choice help convey his or her meaning? Does the author make himself or herself understood?

After each group has had a chance to answer the questions, they are to rate the articles brought in by each group member on the same criteria as they rated the first article. The teacher checks each group to ascertain whether or not they understand how to evaluate information adequately.

4. Read a passage from a content area textbook that you know will be disliked by some of the children, for example, "electrical circuits." Ask the children to tell reasons why they like or dislike the topic. Responses should be written on the board in either the "Like" or "Dislike" column. After all the statements have been made, underline any facts that were given. Ask for additional facts that concern the topic. Then ask the children to tell how much they already know about the topic. Place these responses on the board. Children who might not like the topic might include those who have had adverse experiences with the topic already or those who have had no experience and found the terminology and concepts difficult. The teacher should then discuss ways in which each child's personal feeling toward and experiences with affect his or her interest in a topic.

5. Ask the children for the names of their favorite television shows. Responses should be written in one of three columns written on the board: (a) to entertain, (b) to inform, (c) to persuade. Explain to children that the purposes that authors have for writing may also be grouped into one of these three major categories. Pass out short selections on the same topic (e.g.,

tooth care) and ask the children to identify which of the three purposes they think applies to each selection. Finally, ask the children to suggest types of materials that they think would most probably fit into each of the categories (e.g., "advertisements" usually persuade). These should be written on the board under the appropriate column. As a follow-up exercise, ask the children to locate examples of the three types of materials in the newspaper.

6. Copy passages from content area texts, newspapers, magazines, and other types of written materials. Cut each apart and paste on an index card. The correct answer should be on the back of the card. Children are to read the passages and group them by purpose into three piles: (a) to inform, (b) to entertain, (c) to persuade. These cards may also be used with a tic-tac-toe board. Each child can make a move only if he or she is able to correctly identify the purpose.

7. Photostat a factual account of some event from one of the content area textbooks. Locate both an extended and an abbreviated version of that same event in two other sources. For example, a description of a "tepee" might be found in the textbook, a dictionary, and a book entitled *American Indians of the Southwest.* Make copies of all three passages for each child in the class. Have the children compare the articles and determine which one they think is "best." Explain that the completeness of an article affects its worth to the reader. Have them underline the facts given in each of the passages. Help them to determine differences in the three accounts because of the differences in the number of facts given. Explain that their textbooks are basically a summary of facts that contains information that they can usually believe. However, they should realize that for some purposes more or less information is appropriate. Each source should be evaluated for completeness in light of the purpose for which the material was intended and is needed.

8. Ask children to collect articles or advertisements that mention "research." They are to note whether any facts are given about the research or if the article merely states that "research proves." An alternative technique is to ask children to take notes on television commercials to determine whether or not facts are given when reference to research is made. The ensuing class discussion should focus on the completeness and accuracy of the information presented.

9. Locate two selections on the same topic. One should be of high literary quality, the other of poor literary quality. For example, the teacher might locate a poem by Carl Sandburg and then purposely construct a poorly written poem on the same topic. Copies of each are given to the children who work in pairs to determine which poem they think is best. The teacher then directs the children to tell their choices and their reasons for choosing as they did. As responses are given, the teacher writes them on the board. Comparisons between such aspects as imagery created and word choice should be mentioned. Finally, the teacher summarizes the types of traits that make one piece of writing of higher quality than another.

Readiness Skill 1: Demonstrating Visual Acuity
Readiness Skill 2: Demonstrating Auditory Acuity
Readiness Skill 3: Demonstrating General Health

READINESS SKILL 1: DEMONSTRATING VISUAL ACUITY

Visual acuity, which refers to the child's ability to see clearly, is usually measured in schools by the use of a Snellen chart, which contains rows of letters of decreasing size to be read by the child from a distance of twenty feet. However, the Snellen chart does not test many facets of visual acuity that may affect a child's reading ability, such as his or her ability to see an object held fourteen inches from the eyes (the normal distance between the child's eyes and the page of a book) or to coordinate his or her eyes (binocular fusion). Therefore, the wise teacher will not rely entirely upon Snellen chart assessments to identify students with unsatisfactory visual acuity, but will remain alert to other signs of visual difficulty such as crossed eyes, holding a book too close or too far away, rubbing of the eyes, or squinting. If any of these signs is present, the teacher should report them to the school nurse so that the child may be given further testing.

READINESS SKILL 2: DEMONSTRATING AUDITORY ACUITY

Auditory acuity, which refers to the child's ability to hear distinctly, is normally tested through the use of an audiometer. Usually, all children in a given grade level are tested twice during the elementary school years by a trained audiometer technician. However, teachers should always remain alert to any student symptoms of auditory difficulties such as little or no speech, turning the head to hear, poor attention to auditory stimuli, daydreaming, frequent need for questions to be repeated, speaking in an unnatural voice tone, and frequent colds or congestion. If any of these symptoms is present, the teacher should make a referral to the school nurse or speech therapist, so that the child may be given further testing.

READINESS SKILL 3: DEMONSTRATING GENERAL HEALTH

Few school districts provide routine medical checkups for children. Therefore, the teacher must be aware of symptoms of poor health, including frequent absences, excessive fatigue, and inadequate energy. If any of these signs is present, the teacher should refer the child to the school nurse whose duty is to provide parent guidance in appropriate medical care.

READINESS SKILL 4: DEMONSTRATING VISUAL DISCRIMINATION

ASSESSMENT

Visual discrimination, the ability to discriminate shapes, can be assessed by having the child select the one out of any four pictures, letters, or words that is different from the remaining three. Research (Paradis and Peterson, 1975) has demonstrated that children normally find it more difficult to discriminate words than to discriminate pictures or letters. Therefore, a test of visual discrimination, such as the one presented here, might require that the child first distinguish pictures, then letters, and then words.

Example: Visual Discrimination Assessment Question

TEACHING PROCEDURES

As preparation for reading readiness, children should be taught only letter and word discrimination skills. Picture discrimination should be used only as a method of assessment, to motivate children, or to introduce the concept of same and different (Paradis and Peterson, 1975).

Introductory Activity

1. The teacher may give instruction in visual discrimination skills by holding up two letters or letter cards, asking the class if the letters are the same or different, and then discussing the reasons for the correct answer. When the children have thoroughly mastered distinguishing two letters, the teacher may extend the activity by using groups of three, and then four, letters. When the students have mastered letter discrimination, the teacher should progress to word discrimination activities, again beginning with two words and then extend the activity using first three and then four words.

Readiness Skill 4: Demonstrating Visual Discrimination

Reinforcement Activities

Activities such as the following may be used to reinforce visual discrimination skills.

2. *Help the bunny find the carrot game:* For each word on the game board, four matching cards are constructed and then stacked face (word) down in a pile at the start of the game. To begin, any of the two, three, or four players selects the top card from the pile. If the word on the card matches the first word on the board, then the first player places the card on the first square. If it does not match, the player places his or her card face up in a discard row. The next player continues the game by choosing a card from either the face-down card pile or the face-up discard row. After all the squares on the board have, in correct succession, been matched and covered, the player who chooses the card that matches the last square on the game board wins. Note: This game can be constructed using words or letters and can also be adapted to children's current interests, such as Halloween ("Help the Ghost Find the Jack-o-Lantern").

Example

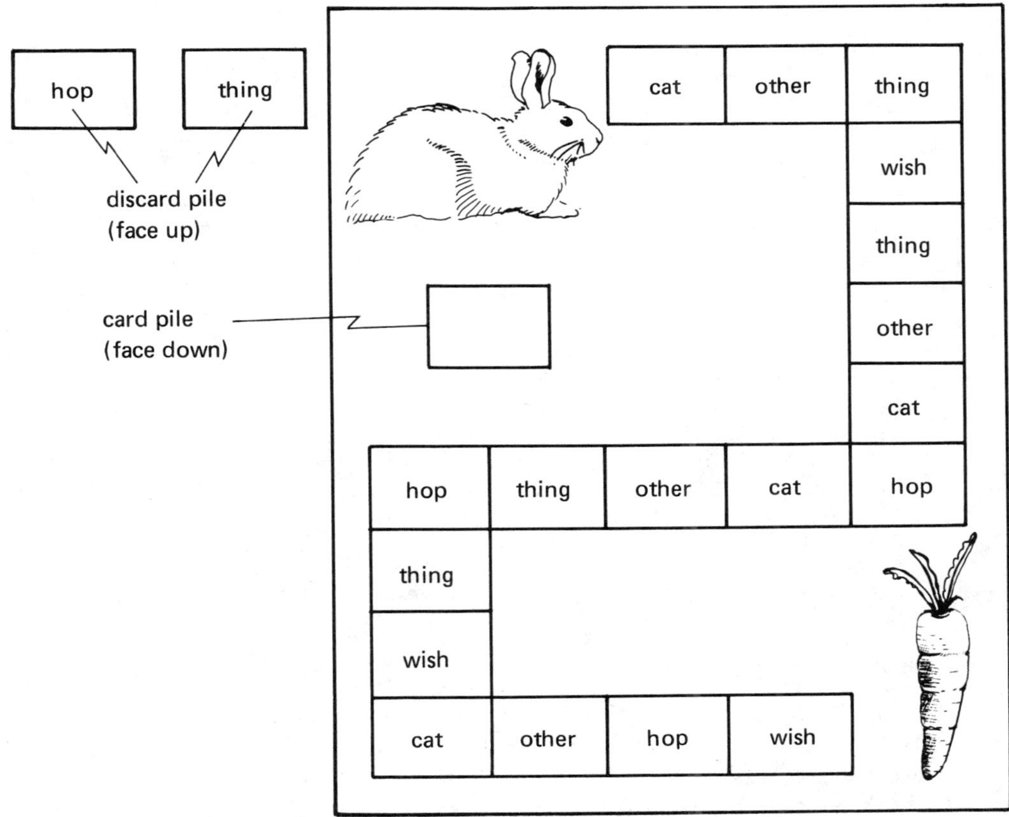

3. *Pipe cleaner words and letters:* Have the children use pipe cleaners to construct words or letters.

4. *Sorting:* Have the students sort letters or words by placing them into containers. Example: Give a child several letters A, B, C, and D and four paper cups. Place a letter A in one cup, a letter B in the second cup, and so on, and then have the child continue the activity by sorting all the remaining letters.

READINESS SKILL 5: DEMONSTRATING VISUAL MEMORY

ASSESSMENT

The teacher may assess visual memory, the ability to remember what has been seen, by showing pupils a picture, letter, or word card (stimulus card) and asking them to identify from memory this same item on a test sheet. For example, the teacher might hold up the letter C for a few seconds and then put it out of the children's sight. About ten seconds later the teacher has the children try to find the same letter in a group of letters on their sheets. The teacher repeats this process using several different letters and then with two- and three-letter words.

Example:

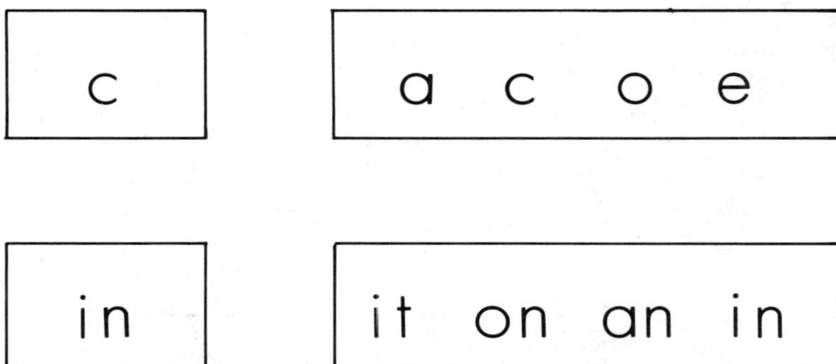

TEACHING PROCEDURES

Introductory Activity

1. To begin teaching visual memory for letters and words, the teacher tells the children that they are about to become "memory whizzes." Then the teacher holds up a stimulus card with one letter on it and tells the pupils to look at it carefully. After putting away the stimulus card, the teacher dis-

plays two others, one of which is identical to the stimulus card, and asks the pupils to tell which is the matching letter. When the pupils have decided which letter is correct, the teacher once again shows the original card and allows the children to check their responses. This activity may be repeated several times with different stimulus cards. When the students demonstrate proficiency in remembering a single letter, the process is repeated with two-letter words and then with words containing three and four letters. Visual memory instruction may be varied by giving the child four cards, each marked with a letter or letter group. The child holds the cards down until the appropriate card is presented by the teacher or another student. Then, after the stimulus card is removed, the pupil turns his or her cards face up, chooses the matching card, and holds it up.

Reinforcement Activities

Visual memory skills can be reinforced by activities such as the following.

2. *Memory wizard box:* Place a few letter or word cards on a desk and cover them with a box. Then show the pupils the cards by lifting the box for about three seconds. Cover the cards again and have the children select from another set of cards those that match the stimulus cards. Check responses by lifting the box. The number of letters can be increased as the children develop greater skills.

3. *Concentration game:* Prepare about eight different pairs of letter or word cards. Mix the cards up and place all of them face down, no two cards touching. The first player turns over two cards. If they match, the player keeps them. If they do not match, they are shown to the other players and returned face down to the exact place where they were found. The player with the most pairs at the end of the game wins.

4. *Mail memory:* For each child prepare one envelope with a word printed on the outside. Inside the envelope place a separate letter card for each letter in the word. Have the child look carefully at the word on the front of his or her envelope and then turn the envelope face down, take out the letters, and try to duplicate the word from memory.

READINESS SKILL 6: DEMONSTRATING AUDITORY DISCRIMINATION

ASSESSMENT

Auditory discrimination refers to the ability to discriminate sounds. The teacher may assess this skill by instructing the pupil to turn his or her back to the teacher and then pronounce about twenty pairs of words, including identical words or words differing only in initial sound ("man," "can"), medial sounds ("step," "stop"), or final sound ("star," "start"). The child responds by indicating whether the words in each pair are the same or different.

TEACHING PROCEDURES

Introductory Activity

1. To introduce the skill of auditory discrimination, show the pupils pairs of picture cards that depict two words that are the same or that differ in their beginning, medial, or ending sounds. For example, use a picture of a can and a picture of a man. Have the children tell the name of the first picture, the name of the second, and then the names of both. Then discuss whether the words pictured sound the same or different. Repeat this procedure several times with other appropriate pairs of picture cards. This instructional procedure may be varied by the teacher's saying a word and the pupil's selecting the matching picture card.

Reinforcement Activities

Reinforcement activities for the development of auditory discrimination include the following.

2. *Go:* Begin this game by having all the children stand on one side of the room. Then assign each child one word and tell him or her to listen for it and to take one step forward each time that he or she hears it. Warn the child that, if he or she moves at an incorrect time, the child must take one step backward. (The child may hold a card with his or her word printed on it.) Next, say several words, encouraging the children to move each time that they hear their words. The child who crosses the room first wins the game.

3. *Picture card display:* To begin this activity, the teacher should display one set of several picture cards and then provide each child a card of his or her own from a separate set. Then the teacher asks each pupil, in turn, to come up to the display and identify these pictures, showing objects whose names begin with the same sound as the one naming the picture in his or her card.

4. *Traffic light:* The teacher gives each child a small (2″ x 2″) piece of red paper and a small piece of green paper. He/she says two words, which may or may not be identical or may or may not contain the same initial, medial, or final sound. The children hold up their pieces of green paper if the words match and the pieces of red paper if they do not.

READINESS SKILL 7: DEMONSTRATING AUDITORY MEMORY

ASSESSMENT

The teacher may assess a child's auditory memory, the ability to remember what one has heard, by telling the child that he/she is going shopping and needs his or her help in remembering to buy crayons, tape, and glue. Fifteen minutes later, the teacher gives the child a sheet with many store items pictured on it and asks the child to circle the three objects mentioned previously. The child is given credit for a correct response if he or she circles the pictures of the crayons, tape, and glue.

TEACHING PROCEDURES

Introductory Activity

1. A child's auditory memory may be strengthened by the use of activities such as the one here, which involves the step-by-step development of the ability to remember and follow successfully more complex directions. For example, first ask the child to follow a simple direction such as "Walk to the door." When the child has shown proficiency with such simple directions, extend the activity by making the directions increasingly more complex. For example, next tell the child to "Walk to the door and put your hands on your head." When the child has demonstrated ability at this level, proceed to more difficult directions such as "Walk to the door, put your hands on your head, and come to me."

Reinforcement Activities

Other activities that may be used to reinforce auditory memory include the following.

2. *Head, shoulders, knees, toes:* Begin by having the leader, who may be the teacher or a child, name three body parts. Then have the children touch the three parts of their bodies in the order named. On each succeeding round of the game, increase the number of parts listed.

3. *Flannel board:* The teacher or leader, places pictures of three items on a flannel board that only the teacher/leader can see. Then the teacher names the items and, after twenty seconds, has the children try to recall them. The flannel board can be exposed to check the accuracy of responses. Extend the activity by using larger numbers of pictures, numerals, letters, or words.

4. *In the future:* Tell the children that you want them to do something, such as drawing a picture of a traffic signal, in about fifteen minutes. Engage them in other activities until the time period has elapsed. When the time is

up ask the children to do the required activity. Extend this learning experience by increasing the complexity of the activities recalled.

READINESS SKILL 8: DEMONSTRATING VISUAL-MOTOR SKILLS

ASSESSMENT

Visual-motor skills involve eye-hand coordination, the ability for the eye and the hand to work together. These skills can be assessed by having children trace simple line drawings with their crayons.

Example:

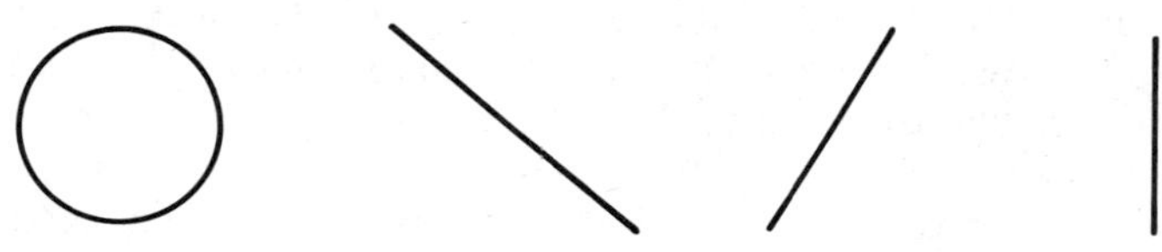

Children who can trace within 1/8″ of the original probably have sufficient skills to begin writing.

TEACHING PROCEDURES

Introductory Activity

1. Connect-the-dot activites are very effective in the development of visual-motor skills (eye-hand coordination). For example (Spache, 1973), the teacher could have the pupils connect the dots in the following sequence: (a) horizontal lines, (b) vertical lines, (c) oblique lines, and (d) a combination of horizontal, vertical, and oblique lines. The child should master all preceding steps before being allowed to attempt succeeding ones.

Readiness Skill 8: Demonstrating Visual-Motor Skills

Connect-the-dot activities can be made more interesting by using pictures instead of letters.

Example: Help the Boy Find His House

Reinforcement Activities

Visual motor skills can be reinforced by use of activities such as the following.

2. String beads.

3. Using cardboard templates to trace inner and outer shapes on the chalkboard.

4. Tracing over broken-line outlines, such as the one below on the chalkboard or on paper.

Example: Broken-Line Outline

5. Tracing with a crayon on a worksheet. Like those below, thse outlines might stress the basic shapes for writing.

Example: Solid-Line Outline

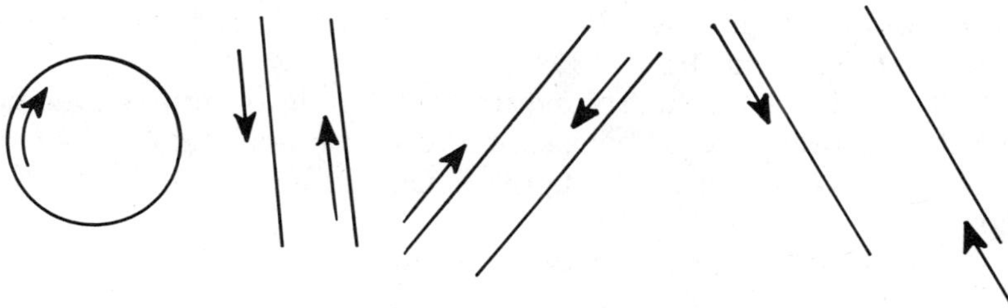

READINESS SKILL 9: USING LEFT-RIGHT PROGRESSION

ASSESSMENT

The child's knowledge of left-right progression, the ability to read from left to right and from top to bottom, can be easily assessed through the use of a simple, two-line story such as the one here.

Example:

Kristen has a new doll.
The doll has a pink dress.

Show the child the story and then ask him or her to answer questions such as "Which word should I (the teacher) read first?" "Next?" "Which word should I read after I read this word?" (Point to the final word in the first line.)

TEACHING PROCEDURES

Introductory Activity

1. Direct instruction in the skill of left-right progression may begin by showing children a storybook while you read it to them. First, point out the word with which you start (the first word of the first line), and then show which word you move to next. Then, show the last word in the first line and the starting point (the first word) of the next line. Next, have the children show you where to start reading on a page, which word to read next, and which word to move to when you come to the end of a line.

Reinforcement Activities

Left-right progression can be reinforced throughout the day with activities such as the following.

2. *Follow the leader.* The leader, who may be a teacher or a child, stands with his or her back toward a group of children. Then the leader turns at intervals. If the leader turns to his or her right, the children slap their right thighs and shout, "Right." If the leader turns to his or her left, the children slap their left thighs and shout, "Left."

3. Cut out from magazines pictures of people or animals facing left or right. (Pictures should be of back of person or animal.) Have the child identify all the pictures in which the figure is facing left and all in which it is facing right.

4. When using numbers, show the children how they, like words and letters, are also read from left to right.

READINESS SKILL 10: USING INDIVIDUAL WORK HABITS

ASSESSMENT

Using individual work habits refers to the child's ability to work independently. The teacher may assess development of this skill by assigning simple activities to be completed independently and without teacher help. Sample assignments include puzzles, alphabet or number copying, matching, or cutting selected pictures from a magazine. The teacher should be sure that the child understands the task, knows what to do if he or she has difficulty, and knows what to do when he or she finishes. If a child can work independently for at least ten minutes, that child's individual work habits are probably sufficiently developed for beginning reading instruction.

TEACHING PROCEDURES

Introductory Activity

1. The teacher can encourage the development of individual work habits through reinforced practice. At some time during each day have a "work alone" time. At first, this period should be so brief that all the children can succeed. Later, extend the activity by gradually increasing the length of the "work alone" time and use a reward system to encourage those who succeed.

Reinforcement Activities

The skill of using individual work habits may be reinforced through the use of the following activities.

2. Praise children who show progress in performing independent activities, even if they are nonacademic tasks such as placing one's coat on the appropriate hook.

3. Make class visits to classrooms where children are working independently. Show your class how pencils, books, and other necessary materials are arranged and ready for use during independent work time.

4. Using a language experience chart, formulate rules for independent work time. Review the chart when necessary as an aid in reminding children what is expected of them.

READINESS SKILL 11: SHOWING INTEREST IN BOOKS

ASSESSMENT

The child who is ready to learn to read will show an interest in books by exhibiting behaviors that may be used as an assessment of this skill. Such behaviors include asking to be read to, looking at books, and "reading with" an adult by saying an occasional word as the adult reads. To encourage and reinforce children's interest in books, many activities can be integrated into the curriculum. Examples of such activities follow.

TEACHING PROCEDURES

Introductory Activity

1. Have the child write an original book, using the language experience approach and featuring the pupil as the star. The first page of the book might include a self-portrait and the teacher's recording of the child's self-description. The book can be extended with pictures and sentences relating to the child. For example, the child could draw three favorite objects, a family portrait, or some favorite foods. Books can be shared with the entire class and can also be taken home for family appreciation.

Reinforcement Activities

2. Have the children construct bulletin boards featuring book covers.
3. Hold daily story times during which the teacher reads or tells a story. Follow-up activities may include discussion or art work.
4. Plan regular library days during which the teacher or librarian reads a story to the children and each child borrows a book to take home.
5. Have the class visit the public library during story time.

READINESS SKILL 12: USING GROUP WORK HABITS

ASSESSMENT

A child's ability to work in a group can be assessed on a day-to-day basis as the pupil participates in teacher-led groups. The child with satisfactory group work habits will be attentive and will share, neither dominating the group nor withdrawing from it.

TEACHING PROCEDURES

The development of group work habits can be encouraged through reinforced practice. Each day the teacher should provide the class some group work, being sure that each child knows the rules, such as answering questions so that others can hear, and rewarding the pupils who follow them. Group work habits can be reinforced through the use of activities such as the following.

Readiness Skill 12: Using Group Work Habits

Introductory Activity

1. Discuss with the children the role of group members by examining questions such as "What should the teacher do?" "Should boys and girls wait until their names are called before speaking?" Discuss how such behavior can help us live happily together.

Reinforcement Activities

2. Give each child the responsibility for certain activities within the group. For example, each pupil might be responsible for bringing his or her own pencil, and individual children could be given the responsibility for bringing books or other learning aids to the group.

3. Praise children for assuming group responsibility and for abiding by decisions that are made by and for the group.

READINESS SKILL 13: USING SIGHT WORD SKILLS

ASSESSMENT

The ability to immediately recognize a few words on sight can be most helpful to the beginning reader. This skill can be assessed by showing a child a word printed on a 3″ x 5″ card. If the pupil can say the word, then it is in his or her sight vocabulary.

TEACHING PROCEDURES

Words to be taught as sight words should ideally be those that the child will learn in his or her beginning reading program. However, if this information is unavailable, the teacher should choose words from a basic sight word list, supplemented by nouns such as the child's name, names of brothers and sisters, and number and color words. (See Chapter 2 for a basic list.)

Introductory Activity

1. The teacher should introduce sight words one at a time in a context that is meaningful to the pupils. For example, the teacher might say, "This word is hat. Peter has a blue hat today. Nicky has a green hat. Who else has a hat?" While the teacher speaks, the children's attention should be directed to the word hat written on the chalkboard. Next, the teacher should ask questions that require the child to observe the word closely, such as "With what letter does the word begin?" "With what letter does the word stop?" Next the teacher should hold up a word card containing the word hat and ask, "What is this word?"

When the children appear to have mastered the word hat, the teacher might hold up other word cards and ask, "Is this the word hat?" The teacher might then extend this activity by giving each child a blank piece of paper and a picture of a hat. Each time that the teacher holds up the word hat, the children show their hat pictures. Each time that the teacher holds up a different word, the children show their blank papers.

Reinforcement Activities

Activities such as the following may be used to reinforce the development of sight word skills.

2. *Picture word cards, method 1:* On one side of the picture word card, print only the word. On the other side, put both the word and a picture of the object that it names. Have the children, working singly or in pairs, read from the word-only side of the card and check their accuracy by turning the card over to the picture word side.

3. *Picture word cards, method 2:* Have the children make up sentences using the words on the cards.

4. *Stories:* Using sight words that the children know, the teacher may write brief stories (fifty words or less) for the children to read. For example, a brief story might read

Mommy Is in Trouble

Mommy is in trouble. "Help, Alan, help!"
Here comes Alan. Alan rescues Mommy.
"Thank you, Alan, thank you."

5. *Magic sentence:* The teacher should teach the words *the, on,* and *is* and then introduce new nouns by using the following format.

The______________ is on the______________.

6. *Word writing:* If the children demonstrate sufficient manual dexterity, have them write words in salt or sand or make them with modeling clay. Alternately, they may spell out words using paper or plastic letters.

READINESS SKILL 14: USING CONFIGURATION CLUES

ASSESSMENT

Many times, words can be recognized due to their distinctive shapes or configurations. Ives, Bursuk, and Ives (1979) include word length, word shape, double letters, capital letters, hyphens, apostrophes, and repetition of letters in words as visual configuration clues.

Readiness Skill 14: Using Configuration Clues

A child's skill in using configuration clues can be assessed by showing the child three words and three shapes and asking him or her which word shape fits which word.

Example: Configuration Assessment Question

summer is chair

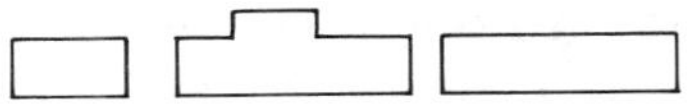

The teacher may further assess this skill by showing children words and asking how they identified them. Many responses will indicate that the pupils used configuration clues such as "short word" or "two m's in middle."

TEACHING PROCEDURES

Introductory Activity

1. The teacher may strengthen the use of configuration clues by pupils who already have a well-developed use of this skill as well as by those who do not by pointing out features that distinguish words and by having children compare words (Ives, Bursuk, and Ives, 1979). For example, the teacher can write three words on the chalkboard and point out their distinguishing features. Then the teacher and pupils can play "what word am I thinking of?," in which a visual configuration clue card is shown and the pupils match the appropriate card to the word on the chalkboard.

Example:

Words Printed on Chalkboard	*Visual Configuration Clue Card*
to	
we	
will	

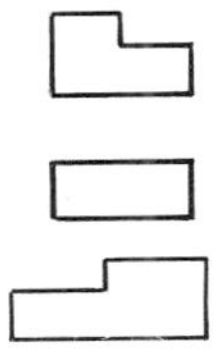

Reinforcement Activities

The use of configuration clues can be reinforced through activities such as the following.

2. *Puzzles:* Cut out words and matching configuration cards and have the child try to find the matching pieces.

3. *Draw around:* Have the child draw the configuration of a word.

4. *Match-up:* Have the child select from two configurations the one that matches a given word.

READINESS SKILL 15: USING PICTURE CLUES

ASSESSMENT

The skill of using picture clues to identify unknown words can be most helpful to the beginning reader and can be assessed easily. First, show the pupil the unknown word bicycle. Next, display a picture in which a bicycle (labeled) is the main feature and then determine whether or not the pupil now knows the word.

TEACHING PROCEDURES

Introductory Activity

1. The teacher can provide instruction in the use of picture clues while reading a story to the children by viewing and discussing the pictures accompanying the story with the objective of predicting what the story is about. Then, after the teacher has read the story to the class, the similarities between the prediction and the text are compared. For example, the teacher might say, "We were right! The story is about a red wagon."

Reinforcement Activities

Activities such as those following might be used to reinforce the use of picture clues.

2. *Picture word cards:* Provide picture word cards that have only the word on one side and both the picture and the word on the other side. Have the children use the pictures to check their accuracy in recognizing the words.

3. *Story time:* When reading to the children, the teacher should relate the story to the pictures. That is, the teacher might say, "The story is about a beaver and a platypus. Which animal in the picture is a beaver? What is a platypus?"

4. *Pictures:* The teacher shows a simple picture to the children and then asks a related questions.

Example: Illustration for Question

"Is the doll under the chair?"

5. *Picture stories:* The teacher shows the children a picture and, after giving them a few minutes to study it, asks them to tell what is happening. Questions that help the children to correlate their ideas with the picture may be asked. For example, the teacher might say, "If the two boys are going for a walk together, why is one hiding behind the dog house?"

READINESS SKILL 16: USING CONTEXT CLUES

ASSESSMENT

The use of context clues involves employing surrounding known words as aids in determining the meaning of an unknown word and is one of the most helpful reading skills at not only the readiness level but at all levels. This skill may be assessed by presenting a sentence in which a word has been deleted and asking the pupil to provide a word that fits. For example, the teacher might say, "The car was parked on the ______________." Children whose use of context clues is well-developed should be able to respond with an appropriate answer such as "road" or "street."

TEACHING PROCEDURES

Introductory Activity

1. At the readiness stage, context clues can be taught through the use of oral language activities such as reading a story in which some of the words are omitted. That is, the teacher can begin reading a story in the normal manner and then omit words that the children try to supply orally. For example, the teacher might read, "The bear cub and its mother walked slowly. Then the mother bear ran. The bear cub ran after its ______________." The pupils try to guess the missing word (mother).

Reinforcement Activities

The use of context clues can be further encouraged by reinforcement activities such as the ones given here.

2. *What's missing:* The teacher reads a simple sentence and the children supply the missing word: "Pears grow on ______________."

3. *Riddles:* The teacher, or leader, describes an object and has the pupils guess what has been described.

READINESS SKILL 17: IDENTIFYING GRAPHEMES AND PRONOUNCING PHONEMES

ASSESSMENT

A pupil's skill in locating graphemes and pronouncing phonemes may be assessed in the following manner. For example, evaluate knowledge of consonant sounds by showing the child a series of pictures such as the one here.

Example: Illustration for Assessment of Readiness Skill 17

Next, name the pictures in the series (telephone, house, book, saw). Then, display a consonant letter (h, for example) and have the child circle the picture in the row whose name starts with this letter. Repeat this process with different letters and several appropriate rows of pictures.

TEACHING PROCEDURES

Introductory Activity

Initial consonants and the short and/or long vowel sounds are usually taught as part of most readiness programs. The progression of skills in teaching both the consonant and vowel sounds follows. First, have the children identify the sound when they hear the spoken word ("Do book, bat, and ball begin with the same sound?") and name both the upper- and lowercase forms of each letter ("Whose letter pile has little d? Whose letter pile had big D?"). Next, teach the children to associate the sound with the correct written letter ("With what letter do book, bat, and ball begin? Who can point to that letter on the chalkboard?") Finally, have the child give a word starting with a given initial consonant or containing a given vowel sound.

The following are teaching strategies for each of the steps in this progression. Although these strategies use as examples consonant sounds, the same techniques are applicable to the teaching of vowel sounds.

Activities That Encourage Children to Identify Words with with Similar Initial Consonants

Reinforcement Activities

1. *Consonant stories:* The teacher tells a story to the children and asks them to raise their hands each time that they hear a given sound. For example, the consonant j might be taught with the sample story: "Jo was a girl. She jumped for joy."

2. *Toy store:* The teacher says, "I am thinking of a toy whose name begins like barn (or dot or window)." The children take turns going to the toy shelf to select a toy whose name begins with the specified consonant sound.

3. *Key words:* Children are given key words and told to listen for their initial consonants. The teacher shows and names an object or a picture of an item whose name begins with the given consonant. The child whose key word starts with the same letter identifies that object as his or hers. For example, one child is given the key word home (h) and another king (k). When the teacher holds up a picture of a horse, the child with the key word home claims the picture.

Activities That Encourage Children to Name Upper- and Lowercase Alphabet Letters

Reinforcement Activities

1. To introduce each letter, the teacher displays a card portraying its uppercase form and a card portraying its lowercase form and says the letter name. Next, the teacher shows how the letter is formed and the children, using the correct strokes, trace the upper- and lowercase forms of the letter on worksheets at their desks. As tactile reinforcement, the children can glue beans or bottle caps to both the upper- and lowercase letters.

A second worksheet with rows of letters can provide practice in distinguishing the upper- and lowercase forms of letters as well as in distinguishing a particular letter to be learned from other letters when the teacher asks the pupils to mark the appropriate letter or form on the worksheet.

2. The teacher provides worksheets with upper- and lowercase forms of each letter and the children draw lines matching the two letter forms.

Example: Letter Matching

A	B	D	Q
b	a	q	d
L	M	i	j
m	l	j	I

3. Using magnetic or paper letters, children match upper- and lowercase forms.

4. Children construct the upper- and lowercase forms of letters from modeling clay, pipe cleaners, or toothpicks.

5. Children listen to a tape that instruct them to identify either the

upper- or lowercase form of a specific letter in a given row of letters on a worksheet.

Activities That Encourage Children to Associate Sounds with Given Letters

Reinforcement Activities

1. To introduce this concept, the teacher reads from a chart showing an initial consonant with a key word and a picture depicting that consonant. Then the teacher shows the children a series of pictures and has them name each one and then state which begins with the consonant being introduced.
2. The teacher provides the pupil with a lacing board containing a printed consonant and pictures of items whose names begin with that consonant. Next, the teacher names, or has the child name, the letter and the pictures on the board. Then the pupil uses the lacing board to match the consonant with the pictures that begin with its sound.
3. Have the children call out the names of the initial consonants on sandpaper letter cards, trace the letters, and then select pictures or objects that begin with each letter's sound.
4. Give each child a letter to pronounce and then hold. When a picture or object beginning with that letter is shown and named by the teacher or student leader, have the child holding the letter collect the picture or object.
5. Have the children sort small pictures or toys into plastic pint-sized fruit baskets or boxes labeled with a given consonant.

Activities That Require Children to Name Words That Contain Specific Letters or Letter Groups

Reinforcement Activities

1. Give the pupil a worksheet, such as the one shown, that contains printed letters. Have the children draw pictures or paste magazine pictures of objects whose names contain the sounds of the letters printed on the worksheet.

Example: Stimulus Letters for Pictures

b	r
m	h

2. Using masking tape, attach to the floor a letter card with a specified letter or letter group written on it. Then have the children throw beanbags

onto the card and name as many words as they can that contain the specified word part. The player who can name the most words wins.

READINESS SKILL 18: BLENDING

ASSESSMENT

A child's ability to blend the phonic elements of words can be measured in the following way. The teacher pronounces the parts of a word phonetically ("m"—"an") and then asks the child, "What did I say?" If the pupil is able to identify a series of words in this manner, he or she probably has sufficient blending skills to begin reading instruction.

TEACHING PROCEDURES

Introductory Activity

1. Children can be taught blending skills through the use of activities such as the following. Write a simple word such as man on the chalkboard and help the children to spell out the word with plastic or paper letters so that a space is left between m, a, and n. Then instruct the children to push the word parts together as you say the word. This activity can be repeated with other short words.

Reinforcement Activities

Examples of reinforcement activities for the skill of blending follow.

2. *Word puzzles:* The child forms words by joining puzzle pieces containing consonants and phonograms that he or she knows.

Example: Word Puzzle for Word Sink

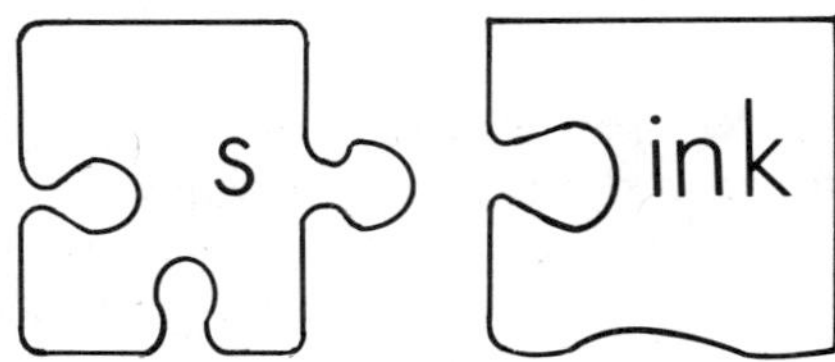

This activity may be self-correcting if an appropriate picture is included on the back of the puzzle.

3. *Hand games:* The teacher and the children begin this activity by placing their hands several inches apart on a table. Then the teacher says a word slowly, with a break between the initial consonant and the final sound (b—e).

Readiness Skill 18: Blending

As the initial consonant is said, the table is patted with the left hand. As the phonogram is said, the table is patted with the right hand. The next time that the word is said, the break is shorter and the hands are brought closer together. When the hands finally touch, the word is said normally. Children bring their hands together as the teacher does. This activity can be extended by marking the back of the children's hands, one with a given consonant and the other with a final sound.

READINESS SKILL 19: GAINING WORD MEANING

ASSESSMENT

Developing language at the readiness level through the gaining of word meaning is one of the major tasks of the preschool and, as such, is an integral part of the activities of the school day. This skill may be assessed by reading a story aloud to a child. If his or her answers reflect knowledge of the word meanings, the child should be given credit for knowing this skill. Specific vocabulary may be assessed by showing the child a series of pictures and asking the child to name the objects shown. For example, show the child a picture of a dog and ask the child to name what he or she sees. If the child says that the picture is of a dog, a puppy, or a collie, or if the child gives a similar response, the child's vocabulary includes the concept of dog.

The child's vocabulary should also be informally assessed by listening to the words that he or she uses when talking with others. For example, a child who says, "It was incredible, I couldn't believe it," would have an exceptionally good vocabulary for a preschooler.

TEACHING PROCEDURES

Introductory Activity

1. Since the most basic of all comprehension skills is associating the correct meaning of a word with its printed symbol, it is essential to include a systematic study of words in the reading program. The first step in enriching the word meanings of children is to teach them to attend to words and understand that words have precise meanings. Most words that are first introduced should have one primary meaning. Material that is highly related to experiences common to all children should be presented (e.g., all children sleep, have birthdays, see the moon). Motivation is one of the most important aspects in teaching new words. Words that make a child feel successful because he or she knows their meanings (such as "birthday") and words that interest a child (such as ones the teacher mentions after all the children have made a trip to the zoo) encourage and motivate the child to want to learn.

Readiness Skill 19: Gaining Word Meaning

Reinforcement Activities

Reinforcement activities for helping children in gaining word meaning follow:

2. The teacher should be sure that the children know the meanings of all the words that occur in stories and in classroom activities. For example, do the children know the meaning of "tic-tac-toe" or "stalk of celery."

3. The teacher should give the children something to talk about and time to do so. For example, the children could be encouraged to bring interesting items for show and tell. Arrowheads, for instance, might spark an interest in Indians, leading to the development of such concepts as "wigwam," "teepee," "tribe," "wampum," and "papoose."

4. Plan walks through the room, school, or school yard that involve one observational task. For example, a color walk could involve looking for items of a specific color. Similarly, circle, rectangle, or triangle walks could be held.

5. Developing an awareness of the concept of multiple word meanings. For example, teach two meanings of words such as "run" and "stalk."

6. Use various kinds of centers within the classroom. For instance, a nature center could help to develop concepts such as "cotton ball" and "pumpkin seed" and a housekeeping center, "kettle," "cup," and "glass."

READINESS SKILL 20: IDENTIFYING DETAILS

ASSESSMENT

The teacher can assess the ability to identify details by asking children a question such as "How old is Johnny?" and then telling them to listen for the answer while a short selection in which this information is contained is read to them.

TEACHING PROCEDURES

Since skill in the ability to answer detail questions in listening situations is a positive step toward the development of this ability in reading situations, a child's readiness level expertise in this skill can be developed through the use of listening exercises, such as those presented here.

Introductory Activity

1. Each day during story time, the teacher should encourage the children to listen for the answer to a specific question requiring listening for detail. For example, the teacher might say, "Listen to find out what Scooter ate for breakfast."

Reinforcement Activities

2. Ask children to listen for the answers to who, what, when, where, and why questions such as "Whom is the story about?," "Where does the story take place?," and "What time of day is it?"

3. Have the children attempt to identify incorrect details mentioned by the teacher while orally telling a story and displaying a picture about it. For example, while telling the story the teacher mentions a boy in a green shirt even though the pictures shows a boy in a red shirt, and the children identify the detail that does not match.

READINESS SKILL 21: IDENTIFYING MAIN IDEAS

ASSESSMENT

The skill identifying main ideas can be assessed by having the children select an appropriate title from a group of three for a story that has been read to them.

TEACHING PROCEDURES

At the readiness level, identifying main ideas, like most of the other comprehension skills, can be taught in listening situations such as the assessment exercise just presented. Further development of this skill may be achieved through the use of activities such as the following.

Introductory Activity

1. *Identifying the main idea of a picture:* Show the children a major action picture such as the one here and ask them what the picture is about.

Example: Stimulus Picture for Identifying Main Idea

Readiness Skill 21: Identifying Main Ideas

Provide the children with copious practice by using various pictures. Discuss their answers, attempting to lead them to perceive the main idea of the picture rather than a detail. That is, the main idea in the picture is "playing baseball," not "a baseball bat."

Reinforcement Activities

2. *Classifying related pictures:* Show the children pictures of several objects, all of which belong to the same class (dog, cat, rabbit, mouse). Then have the pupils identify the pictures common element (animals).

3. *Producing story titles:* Read a story to the children without telling them its title. At the end of the story, suggest one possible title and ask the children to state their reasons for thinking that it would be a good one. Alternately, offer them three titles and let them choose the best one. Make this activity more difficult by having the children produce their own title for the story.

READINESS SKILL 22: IDENTIFYING SEQUENCE

ASSESSMENT

A child's ability to identify sequence—to determine the order of objects or events—may be assessed by giving the pupils a series of four pictures and asking them to put the pictures in correct order.

Example: Pictures for Sequencing

Readiness Skill 22: Identifying Sequence

TEACHING PROCEDURES

Introductory Activity

1. The teacher can introduce the skill of identifying sequency by holding discussions about events that happen in sequence. For example, the teacher could ask questions pertaining to the child's first activity upon arising in the morning: Did the child eat breakfast first, or did the child dress first? Did the child awake before he or she went to school? Questions pertaining to well-known children's stories could also be asked after the story has been read in class. For example, the teacher could ask, "Whose porridge did Goldilock eat first? Next? Last?"

Reinforcement Activities

Sequencing skills can be reinforced by activities such as

2. *Sequencing picture cards that tell a story:* Provide pupils with picture cards constructed from illustrations of children's stories. Have the children first sequence two picture cards, then progress to three, then four, and so on.

3. *Sequencing picture cards that show a series of events:* Provide pupils with picture cards that depict an order of events and ask them to put the cards in the correct sequence. For example, a series of picture cards might show a small tree, a slightly larger tree, and a fully grown tree.

READINESS SKILL 23: MAKING INFERENCES

ASSESSMENT

The ability to infer—to deduce nonexplicitly stated information—can be assessed by reading the child a story and then asking the pupil a question that is based on the story but is not overtly stated in the text. If the child can answer several such questions accurately, the child's ability to make inferences is probably developed sufficiently for beginning reading instruction.

TEACHING PROCEDURES

Introductory Activity

1. Skill in making inferences can be introduced through classroom activities that include reading part of a short story to the children and then showing them two pictures from which they choose the one that best shows the story ending. Activities such as the one following will also aid in the development of this skill.

2. Show the children a picture depicting an action and ask them to predict what will happen next.

3. Pose to the pupils simple riddles such as "What is white, has four legs, and says 'Baa'?"

READINESS SKILL 24: IDENTIFYING CHARACTERIZATION

TEACHING PROCEDURES

ASSESSMENT

Introductory Activity

1. Identifying characterization—determining the personality traits and feelings of a character in a reading selection—can be both assessed and taught at the readiness level by reading the children a story and then asking them questions leading to the interpretation of its characters. For example, after reading "Little Red Riding Hood" to the class, the teacher could have the pupils answer such questions as "How do you think that Little Red Riding Hood felt when she saw the wolf? Would you like to be Red Riding Hood's friend? Why?" Further improvement of this skill may be accomplished through discussions of the story's characters begun by the teacher's asking leading questions such as "Did you like the Grandma? Why?"

Reinforcement Activities

Other activities designed to increase the child's ability to identify characterization include

2. *Dramatic play:* Read a story to the children and then have them act it out using minimal props. For example, in dramatizing a story about a cowboy's losing his hat, use a child's cowboy hat or a box for the hat and the classroom as the countryside in which the children search for it.

3. *Role playing:* Have the children act out such feelings as "skipping with joy," "smiling broadly," and how friends feel when they are happy and when they argue.

READINESS SKILL 25: IDENTIFYING FACT, FICTION, AND OPINION

ASSESSMENT

Identifying fact, fiction, and opinion refers to the ability to determine reality (fact), fantasy (fiction), and theory (opinion). At the readiness level children are required to distinguish fact from fiction. The child's development in this skill may be assessed by the teacher's reading a selection and then asking the children to decide which of the events presented could really happen.

TEACHING PROCEDURES

Introductory Activity

2. The idea of discriminating fact from fiction can be introduced by discussing what is real and not real in each story read. For example, the teacher might read a story concerning a rabbit and a mouse who built a house and then ask the following questions. "What is real about this story?" (rabbits, mice, and houses). "What is not real?" (animals wearing clothes, animals building houses, animals behaving like people).

Reinforcement Activities

Activities such as the following can also be used to develop this skill:

2. Hold discussions centering on what really happens in the classroom and what might happen in the classroom but does not.

3. Discuss obvious fiction such as nursery rhymes and fairy tales. Compare what happens in these stories with what happens in reality. For example, examine the idea that a pig could not really build a house of bricks.

READINESS SKILL 26: FOLLOWING DIRECTIONS

ASSESSMENT

Children at the readiness level and at all levels will have developed a useful skill if they can follow verbal directions. Assess this skill by giving the child a set of three oral directions, such as "walk to the window, pick up the books, and bring them to me." If the children have already developed some ability in this skill, they should be able to carry out such a set of directions easily.

TEACHING PROCEDURES

Introductory Activity

1. The teacher can help to prepare children for reading instruction by first giving them one direction at a time and later two directions at the same time. That is, at first, the teacher might instruct the children to draw lines between matching balloons. Then, after the pupils have drawn the lines, the teacher might tell them to color the matching balloons the same color. However, later in the school year, the teacher might give the two directions to-

gether. That is, the children would be told to first draw a line between the matching balloons and, second, to color the matching balloons the same color. This activity may be extended by giving the instructions and then having the children participate in an intervening activity before carrying them out.

Reinforcement Activities

Techniques such as those given here can also be used to encourage the skill of following directions.

2. Give the children one set of directions to be followed on all multiple-choice activities. For example, the children could be taught to always underline the correct answer.

3. Give directions carefully so that the children are able to follow them more easily. That is, be sure that the children understand the basic concepts necessary to correctly perform the activity.

4. Have all the children's attention before giving any directions.

5. Give directions one time only.

READINESS SKILL 27: USING AIDS WITHIN BOOKS (Using the Table of Contents)

ASSESSMENT

Because tables of contents are widely used in children's books of stories, poems, and nursery rhymes, this nontextual aid within books is one of the most easily introduced to children at the readiness level. The teacher may assess this skill by asking the children to use the table of contents to locate a story or poem within a book with which they are familiar.

TEACHING PROCEDURES

Introductory Activity

1. The skill—Using a Table of Contents—can be introduced informally during story, poetry, or music time by the teacher's showing the children a familiar book and asking them which story, poem, or song they wish to hear. When the selection is made, the teacher can display the book's table of contents and show how it indicates the number of the page on which the selection is located. When the children's number-reading ability is sufficiently advanced, this activity can be extended by having the pupils themselves read and locate the page numbers.

Readiness Skill 27: Using Aids Within Books (Using the Table of Contents)

Reinforcement Activities

Reinforcement activities for the skill of using a table of contents might include the following.

2. Each child selects two books from the classroom and library and looks for tables of contents in them. Following this activity the teacher holds a class discussion focusing upon whether all books contain tables of contents and the types of books that do contain them.

3. Children make tables of contents for their own experience stories that have been stapled or tied together to form a book.

READINESS SKILL 28: ORGANIZING INFORMATION (CLASSIFYING)

ASSESSMENT

Readiness level children can be taught to organize information by developing their skill in classifying or identifying similar objects and assigning them to a common category.

Skill in classifying may be assessed by providing a set of beads and a set of baskets (or boxes) and asking the child to place all the beads of one color into one basket and all the beads of another color into a second basket.

TEACHING PROCEDURES

Introductory Activity

1. Classifying activities can be included throughout the school day. For example, toys may be classified and stored according to given properties. In September they could be shelved according to color. That is, red toys would be placed on the shelf labeled with the word "red" and a red square. Later in the school year the same toys could be shelved according to a different classification system. The entire toy shelf could become an imaginary "city" and the toys available could suggest the classifications or parts of the city to be used. For instance, one section could be the "zoo," where the stuffed animals would be kept, another a "parking lot," where the cars and trucks would be stored, and another the "fire station," where the fire trucks would be shelved.

Reinforcement Activities

Classifying can be reinforced through activities including the following.

2. Place one bead of a given color into each of three boxes, for example, a red bead into one box, a yellow bead into a second box, and a blue bead into a third box. Then have the children place the remaining beads into the appropriate boxes. Extend this activity by including blocks, sorting by

shape, and sorting by shape and color and involving wider concepts, such as sorting animals, birds, and fish.

3. During cleanup time instruct the children to place, for example, all the chips into one container, all the sticks into a second container, and all the beads into a third container.

READINESS SKILL 29: RECALLING INFORMATION (MEMORIZATION)

ASSESSMENT

The ability to recall information can be assessed by reading aloud a short story and asking the pupil to retell it. If the child can repeat the essence of the story, the ability to recall information is probably sufficiently developed for beginning reading instruction.

TEACHING PROCEDURES

Introductory Activity

1. One of the best ways to begin teaching this skill is to say a sentence to the class and then have one child retell what you said. After the children have become proficient in retelling one sentence, gradually increase the number of sentences until the children can retell an entire short story.

Reinforcement Activities

Memorization can be reinforced by using the following activities.

2. Show the children a series of pictures and have them select those that best illustrate a story that has been read to them.

3. Have the children dramatize a simple story that has been read to them. Assign parts to the pupils and encourage them with questions such as "How did the rabbit feel when his friend fell into the water?"

References and Bibliography

Aaron, Ira, David, Charles, and Schelley, Joan. *Flying Hoofs.* Glenview, Ill.: Scott, Foresman and Company, 1978.

Adams, Anne, and Harrison, Cathy. "Using Television to Teach Specific Reading Skills." *The Reading Teacher* 29 (October 1975): 45-51.

Anastosio, Dina. "Mary of Valley Forge," in *Never Give Up.* New York: Holt, Rinehart and Winston, 1973, pp. 194-207.

Barrett, Thomas C. "Taxonomy of Reading Comprehension." *Reading 360 Monograph.* Lexington, Mass.: Ginn and Company, 1972.

Beery, Althea. "Clustering Comprehension Skills to Solve Problems," in *Forging Ahead in Reading.* Newark, Dela.: International Reading Association, 1958, pp. 109-111.

Bergman, F. L. *The English Teacher's Activities Handbook: An Idea Book for the Middle and Secondary Schools.* Boston: Allyn & Bacon, Inc., 1976.

Bond, G. L., and Tinker, M. A. *Reading Difficulties: Their Diagnosis and Correction.* 3rd ed. New York: Appleton-Century-Crofts, 1973.

Buck, Pearl. *The Big Wave* (1947 reprint). New York: Scholastic Book Service, 1976.

Burns, Paul C., and Roe, Betty. *Teaching Reading in Today's Elementary School.* Chicago: Rand McNally & Company, 1976.

Carver, Ronald. "Reading as Reasoning: Implications for Measurement," in W. MacGintie, ed., *Assessment Problems in Reading.* Newark: Dela.: International Reading Association, 1973.

Clark, E. V. "On the Acquisition of the Meaning of 'Before' and 'After.' " *Journal of Verbal Learning and Verbal Behavior* 10 (1971): 266–275.

Crossley, B. A. "Can We Help Children Write?" *Journal of Education* 139 (1957): 10–11.

Dahl, Roald. *Charlies and the Chocolate Factory*, New York: Knoff, 1964.

Dedrick, Nelle, Lindop, Ester, Tiegs, Ernest, and Adams, Fay. *Our People Workbook.* Lexington, Mass.: Ginn and Company, 1979.

Dillner, Martha, and Olson, Joanne. *Personalizing Reading Instruction in Middle, Junior, and Senior High Schools.* New York: Macmillan Publishing Co., Inc., 1977.

Ekwall, Eldon. *Locating and Correcting Reading Difficulties.* Columbus, Ohio: Charles E. Merrill Publishing Company, 1970.

Evertts, Eldonna, Hunt, Lyman, Weiss, Bernard, and Bartlett, Elsa. *People Need People.* New York: Holt, Rinehart and Winston, 1973.

Fisher, Carol, and Terry, Ann. *Children's Language and the Language Arts.* New York: McGraw-Hill Book Company, 1977.

Fraenkel, J. R. *Helping Students Think and Value: Strategies for Teaching the Social Studies.* Englewood Cliffs, N.J.: Prentice-Hall, Inc., 1973.

Gerhard, Christian. *Making Sense: Reading Comprehension Improved Through Categorizing.* Newark, Dela.: International Reading Association, 1975.

Harris, A. J., and Clark, M. K. *Better Than Gold.* New York: Macmillan Publishing Co., Inc., 1965.

Herr, Selma. *Learning Activities for Reading.* 2nd ed. Dubuque, Iowa: William C. Brown Company, Publishers, 1973.

Hoobler, D. and T. *Frontier Diary.* New York: Macmillan Publishing Co., Inc., 1975.

Indrisano, Roselmina. "Reading: Specialized Skills," in Pose Lamb and Richard Arnold, eds., Calif.: Wadworth Publishing Co., Inc., 1976, pp. 419–431.

Ives, J., Bursuk, L. Z., and Ives, S. *Word Identification Techniques.* Chicago: Rand McNally & Company, 1979.

Kaufman, B. B., ed. "EJ Workshop," *English Journal*, May 1974, p. 71.

Mallison, George C., Mallison, Jacqueline B., and Feravolo, Rocco. *Science: Understanding Your Environment—Level Three.* Dallas: Silver Burdett Company, 1975.

Menlove, C. K. *Ready, Set, Go!* Englewood Cliffs, N.J.: Prentice-Hall, Inc., 1978.

Nichols, Eugene, Anderson, Paul, Dwight, Frances, Flournoy, Frances, Kalin, Robert, Schuep, John, and Simon, Leonard. *Holt School Mathematics.* New York: Holt, Rinehart and Winston, 1974.

Otto, Wayne, Peters, Nathaniel, and Peters, Charles. *Reading Problems: A Multidisciplinary Perspective.* Reading, Mass.: Addison-Wesley Publishing Co., Inc., 1977.

Otto, Wayne, Rude, Robert, and Spiegel, Dixie Lee. *How to Teach Reading.* Menlo Park, Calif.: Addison-Wesley Publishing Co., Inc., 1979.

Paradis, E., and Peterson, J. "Readiness Training Implications from the Research." *The Reading Teacher* 28 (February 1975) 445–448.

Parker, Dorothy. "News Item," (1924) *The Oxford Book of American Light Verse.* New York: Oxford University Press, 1979.

Pearson, David, and Johnson, Dale. *Teaching Reading Comprehension.* New York: Holt, Rinehart and Winston, 1978.

Piltz, Albert, and Van Bever, Roger. *Discovering Science 5.* Columbus, Ohio: Charles E. Merrill Publishing Company, 1970.

Prunty, Merle, and Fincher, E. B. *Lands of Promise: Western Hemisphere: Setting and Settlement.* New York: Macmillan Publishing Co., Inc., 1971.

Richmond, Julius B., and Pounds, Elenore. *You and Your Health.* Glenview, Ill.: Scott, Foresman and Company, 1977.

Rockcastle, Verne, Salamon, Frank, Schmidt, Victor, and McNight, Betty. *STEM: Elementary School Science.* Menlo Park, Calif.: Addison-Wesley Publishing Co., Inc., 1975.

Spache, G. D. and E. B. *Reading in the Elementary School.* 3rd ed. Boston: Allyn & Bacon, Inc., 1973.

Thomas, E. L., and Robinson, H. A. *Improving Reading in Every Class.* Boston: Allyn & Bacon, Inc., 1972.

Verner, Zenobia. *Newsbook of Reading Comprehension Activities.* Houston: Clayton Publishing Company, 1978.

Walborn, Maria. *Josita's Dancing Cleaners.* New York: Macmillan Publishing Co., Inc., 1975.

Additional References

"Beetle Bailey"
"Charlies Brown"
"Dick Tracy"
"Fred Bassett"
"King Midas"
"Marmaduke"
"Three Little Pigs"
"Sleeping Beauty"

Appendixes

Appendix A: Teacher's Copy of Oral Reading Selections

Appendix B: Student's Copy of Oral Reading Selections

Appendix C: Teacher's Copy of Silent Reading Selections and Comprehension Questions

Appendix D: Student's Copy of Silent Reading Selections and Comprehension Questions

Appendix E: Sample Lesson Plans

Appendix A
Teacher's Copy of Oral Reading Selections

Contents:

1. Selections to be used for oral reading from each level: primer-grade 6.
2. Instructions to be given to the pupil.
3. Directions for scoring the test.

Primer Level—Oral Reading Selection

The teacher should say to the student: "This story is about Mary (point to the word Mary), Jeff (point to the word Jeff), and Bolo (point to the word Bolo). Please read it aloud to me."

"Come here, Mary," said Jeff.
"Bolo knows something new.
He has a new trick."

What is the trick?" asked Mary.

Jeff said, "I bounce the ball.
Then Bolo jumps up and gets it.
Look at him do it."

Bolo did the trick.

"Oh," said Mary.
"That's a good trick.
Bounce the ball again.
See if Bolo can do it again."

Instructional level: 95% or max. of 3 errors.

Selection from Macmillan Reading Program, *Worlds of Wonder* (Primer Level), edited by Albert J. Harris and Mae Knight Clark. New York: Macmillan Publishing Co., Inc., 1965. Used by permission.

First Reader—Oral Reading Selection

The teacher should say to the student: "This story is about a boy named Tommy. This word is Tommy (point to the word Tommy). *Please read the story aloud to me."*

Tommy went into the barn.
The mother cow was there.
Both her twins were with her.
The little twin looked
like the big twin.
It was just not as big
as the big calf.

Tommy loved the little twin
right away.
He wanted her for his own calf.
Tommy asked, "Daddy, may I have
the little twin for my own?
May I show her at the fair?"

His father said, "No, Tommy.
You are not big enough
to take care of a calf.
You are not old enough
to show a calf at the fair.
You can show a calf there
when you are as old as Ben is now."

Instructional level: 95% or max. of 5 errors.

Selection from Macmillan Reading Program, *Lands of Pleasure* (First Reader), edited by Albert J. Harris and Mae Knight Clark. New York: Macmillan Publishing Co., Inc., 1965. Used by permission.

Grade 2:1—Oral Reading Selection

The teacher should say to the student: "This story is about some boys and girls who are playing together. Please read it aloud to me."

One morning David was looking at the others play. He was wishing his wish as one of the girls came up.

"David," said Sue, "I want to talk to you about our next Hobby Time. Five of us had to plan our next show at school. We know what we are going to do. We are going to have a magic show."

"A magic show!" said David. "We can't do any magic."

"Oh, it won't be real magic," Sue answered. "It will just be make-believe. We can do any trick that the others don't know about. It will look like magic because they won't know how to do it."

Instructional level: 95% or max. of 5 errors.

Selection from Macmillan Reading Program, *Enchanted Gates* (Grade 2:1), edited by Albert J. Harris and Mae Knight Clark. New York: Macmillan Publishing Co., Inc., 1965. Used by permission.

Grade 2:2—Oral Reading Selection

The teacher should say to the student: "This story is about a boy. Please read it aloud to me."

Tommy stood very still and listened. He heard the rustle again. He started to get down to look under the bushes. When he moved, a little squirrel jumped out. It ran off through the woods.

Tommy stared at it until it was out of sight. Then he walked on and on through the woods. He hoped he would see another squirrel. He had forgotten that he should be on his way to the lake to learn to swim.

When he got home he told about the squirrel. "You should have seen it run," he said. "Tomorrow I'll learn to swim."

Instructional level: 95% or max. of 5 errors.

Selection from Macmillan Reading Program, *Shining Birdges* (Grade 2:2), edited by Albert J. Harris and Mae Knight Clark. New York: Macmillan Publishing Co., Inc., 1965. Used by permission.

Grade 3:1—Oral Reading Selection

The teacher should say to the student: "This story is about a boy called Rikki (point to the word Rikki*). Please read it aloud to me."*

The one thing Rikki most wanted was to go fishing with his father. "You are much too little," his father always said. "Wait until you have grown as big as your brother Joe."

Joe was eleven years old and almost a man. This summer Joe had gone with his father every morning, just like a real fisherman. Every afternoon, when the boat returned, he would tell Rikki the size of the day's catch. Sometimes he would toss in a story of some danger that he had escaped.

Rikki always listened with wide eyes and said, "I want to go, too."

Instructional level: 95% or max. of 5 errors.

Selection from Macmillan Reading Program, *Better Than Gold* (Grade 3:1), edited by Albert J. Harris and Mae Knight Clark. New York: Macmillan Publishing Co., Inc., 1965. Used by permission.

Grade 3:2—Oral Reading Selection

The teacher should say to the student: "This story is about a group of boys and girls who are doing something together. Please read the story aloud to me."

Twenty pairs of shoes clattered along the hard, wooden floor. Here and there Miss Ryan would hold up her hand, and the class would stand still. Then she would tell the children about a picture.

One time Miss Ryan stopped the class before a picture of a basket of fruit on a table. Right at one side of the picture on the wall was another picture on an easel. It was an exact copy of the picture on the wall. . . .

The class went on but Mary Ann stood before the easel and looked from one picture to the other. Maybe the paint was still wet on the copy, she thought.

Instructional level: 95% or max. of 5 errors.

Selection from Macmillan Reading Program, *More Than Words* (Grade 3:2), edited by Albert J. Harris and Mae Knight Clark. New York: Macmillan Publishing Co., Inc., 1965. Used by permission.

Grade 4—Oral Reading Selection

The teacher should say to the student: "This story is part of a fairy tale. Please read it aloud to me."

"In a forest not far from here," he told the tailor, "live two giants so fierce that no one will go into that part of my kingdom. If you can destroy these giants, I will let you marry my daughter and half my kingdom will belong to you. You shall have a hundred soldiers with spears to help you."

The tailor rode off to the forest, the hundred soldiers following after him. When they reached a cottage at the edge of the forest, he asked them to stay behind while he looked for the giants. This they were quite willing to do.

Instructional level: 95% or max. of 5 errors.

Selection from "The Brave Little Tailor" by Wilhelm and Jacob Grimm, reprinted from the Ginn Basic Readers, *Roads to Everywhere* (Grade 4), edited by David H. Russell and others. Boston: Ginn and Company, 1964.

Grade 5—Oral Reading Selection

The teacher should say to the student: "This story is about a group of boys and girls in school. Please read it aloud to me.

Miss Curtis was about to start class when she noticed the fairly large brown wooden box on the floor beside the new boy. It looked a little too mysterious to be a homemade lunch box.

"Melvin, we do not keep our belongings in the classroom," she said. "Would you put your box with your wraps, please?"

Mel tucked the box under his arm and started toward the cloakroom. He could almost feel the curious eyes following him—and the box. He knew he would be stopped before he could get very far. And he was!

Instructional level: 95% or max. of 5 errors.

Selectionfrom "Mel's Magic Brain," by William Gustus, *Instructor*, Copyright © March 1955 by The Instructor Publications, Inc., used by permission.

Grade 6—Oral Reading Selection

The teacher should say to the student—"This story is about a boy who lives very far North. Please read it aloud to me."

Mark McRoy came out of his father's trading post and quickly skirted the sod Eskimo houses. Sled dogs tied nearby sniffed and eyed him with suspicion. He passed the frame schoolhouse, where his mother taught school, and hurried west across the flat toward the frozen river.

Mark, who was thirteen, remembered how excited he and his mother had been about coming way up here to the Arctic. His father called it the last great frontier in America. They had been here two years, and Mark hoped this would always be his home.

When Mark reached the river, Oka was waiting with a loaded supply sled. It was Friday afternoon, and the two boys were heading up the river for their hunting camp.

Oka had been Mark's first really close friend among the Eskimo boys.

Instructional level: 95% or max. of 5 errors.

Appendix B
Student's Copy of Oral Reading Selections

Contents:

1. Reading selections identical to those found in Appendix A, "Teacher's Copy of Oral Reading Selections." Information regarding grade level, administration, and scoring is omitted on the student's copy.

"Come here, Mary," said Jeff.
"Bolo knows something new.
He has a new trick."
"What is the trick?" asked Mary.
Jeff said, "I bounce the ball.
Then Bolo jumps up and gets it.
Look at him do it."
Bolo did the trick.
"Oh," said Mary.
"That's a good trick.
Bounce the ball again.
See if Bolo can do it again."

— — — — — — — — — — — — — Fold— — — — — — — — — — — — — —

Tommy went into the barn.
The mother cow was there.
Both her twins were with her.
The little twin looked like the big twin.
It was just not as big as the big calf.
Tommy loved the little twin right away.
He wanted her for his own calf.
Tommy asked, "Daddy, may I have the little twin for my own?
May I show her at the fair?"
His father said, "No, Tommy.
You are not big enough to take care of a calf.
You are not old enough to show a calf at the fair.
You can show a calf there when you are as old as Ben is now."

One morning David was looking at the others play. He was wishing his wish as one of the girls came up.

"David," said Sue, "I want to talk to you about our next Hobby Time. Five of us had to plan our next show at school. We know what we are going to do. We are going to have a magic show."

"A magic show!" said David. "We can't do any magic."

"Oh, it won't be real magic," Sue answered. "It will just be make-believe. We can do any trick that the others don't know about. It will look like magic because they won't know how to do it."

— — — — — — — — — — —Fold— — — — — — — — — — — —

Tommy stood very still and listened. He heard the rustle again. He started to get down to look under the bushes. When he moved, a little squirrel jumped out. It ran off through the woods.

Tommy stared at it until it was out of sight. Then he walked on and on through the woods. He hoped he would see another squirrel. He had forgotten that he should be on his way to the lake to learn to swim.

When he got home he told about the squirrel. "You should have seen it run," he said. "Tomorrow I'll learn to swim."

The one thing Rikki most wanted was to go fishing with his father. "You are much too little," his father always said. "Wait until you have grown as big as your brother Joe."

Joe was eleven years old and almost a man. This summer Joe had gone with his father every morning, just like a real fisherman. Every afternoon, when the boat returned, he would tell Rikki the size of the day's catch. Sometimes he would toss in a story of some danger that he had escaped.

Rikki always listened with wide eyes and said, "I want to go, too."

— — — — — — — — — — — Fold — — — — — — — — — — — — — — —

Twenty pairs of shoes clattered along the hard, wooden floor. Here and there Miss Ryan would hold up her hand, and the class would stand still. Then she would tell the children about a picture.

One time Miss Ryan stopped the class before a picture of a basket of fruit on a table. Right at one side of the picture on the wall was another picture on an easel. It was an exact copy of the picture on the wall. . . .

The class went on but Mary Ann stood before the easel and looked from one picture to the other. Maybe the paint was still wet on the copy, she thought.

"In a forest not far from here," he told the tailor, "live two giants so fierce that no one will go into that part of my kingdom. If you can destroy these giants, I will let you marry my daughter and half my kingdom will belong to you. You shall have a hundred soldiers with spears to help you."

The tailor rode off to the forest, the hundred soldiers following after him. When they reached a cottage at the edge of the forest, he asked them to stay behind while he looked for the giants. This they were quite willing to do.

— — — — — — — — — — Fold — — — — — — — — — — — —

Miss Curtis was about to start class when she noticed the fairly large brown wooden box on the floor beside the new boy. It looked a little too mysterious to be a homemade lunch box.

"Melvin, we do not keep our belongings in the classroom," she said. "Would you put your box with your wraps, please?"

Mel tucked the box under his arm and started toward the cloakroom. He could almost feel the curious eyes following him—and the box. He knew he would be stopped before he could get very far. And he was!

Mark McRoy came out of his father's trading post and quickly skirted the sod Eskimo houses. Sled dogs tied nearby sniffed and eyed him with suspicion. He passed the frame schoolhouse, where his mother taught school, and hurried west across the flat toward the frozen river.

Mark, who was thirteen, remembered how excited he and his mother had been about coming way up here to the Arctic. His father called it the last great frontier in America. They had been here two years, and Mark hoped this would always be his home.

When Mark reached the river, Oka was waiting with a loaded supply sled. It was Friday afternoon, and the two boys were heading up the river for their hunting camp.

Oka had been Mark's first really close friend among the Eskimo boys.

Appendix C
Teacher's Copy of Silent Reading Selections and Comprehension Questions

Contents:

1. Silent reading selections and accompanying comprehension questions appropriate for each level of a basal reader series: primer-grade 6.
2. Information regarding the grade level, administration, and scoring for each selection.

Primer Level—Silent Reading Selection

The teacher should give the copy of the selection (see Appendix D) folded on the "fold line" to the student with instructions to read the story carefully and then answer the questions on the bottom of the sheet in writing without looking back at the story.

Bolo ran up and down the bus.

"Stop, Bolo!" said Jeff.
"You can't run in the bus.
The busman will put you off
if you do!
Come here, Bolo!"

Bolo didn't come to Jeff.
He didn't stop.
But the busman did.

The busman said, "Boy!
Take that dog off the bus.
We don't let dogs ride."

"I put him in that," said Jeff.

The busman said,
"He is not in it now.
Take him off!"

"We can't get off!" said Jeff.
"If we do, how will we get
to the dog show?"

Choose the best word from the list at the bottom of the page and write it in the blank.

1. Bolo ran up and down the ______________________.
2. Jeff told Bolo, "______________________."
3. Did Bolo stop? ______________________
4. The ______________________ told Jeff, "We don't let dogs ride."
5. Bolo and Jeff were going to the ______________________.

busman	bus	yes	no
Jeff	dog show	stop	

Instructional level: 70% or max. of 1 1/2 errors on answers to questions.

Selection from Macmillan Reading Program, *Worlds of Wonder* (Primer Level), edited by Albert J. Harris and Mae Knight Clark. New York: Macmillan Publishing Co., Inc., 1965. Used by permission.

First Reader Level—Silent Reading Selection

The teacher should give the copy of the selection (see Appendix D) folded on the "fold line" to the student with instructions to read the story carefully and then answer the questions on the bottom of the sheet in writing without looking back at the story.

Tommy lived on a farm.
He had a big brother.
His brother's name was Ben.

One morning Ben ran into the house.
"Mother! Mother!" he yelled.
"The black and white cow has twins.
One of the twins is little
and one is big.
Daddy said I could have
the big twin for my calf!"

Tommy looked at his mother.
"I want a twin, too," he said.

"You are too little," said Ben.
"You have to be big like me
to take care of a calf.
I will take good care of my calf.
I will show him at the fair."

Choose the best word from the list at the bottom of the page and write it in the blank.

1. Tommy lives on a ________________.
2. Ben is Tommy's ________________
3. The story takes place in the ________________
4. Ben yelled to his ________________
5. Ben was ________________

brother	friend	morning	farm
Mother	happy	sad	

Instructional level: 70% or max. of 1 1/2 errors.

Selection from Macmillan Reading Program, *Lands of Pleasure* (First Reader Level), edited by Albert J. Harris and Mae Knight Clark. New York: Macmillan Publishing Co., Inc., 1965. Used by permission.

Grade 2:1—Silent Reading Selection

The teacher should give the copy of this selection (see Appendix D) folded on "fold line" to the student with instructions to read the story carefully and then answer the questions on the bottom of the sheet in writing without looking back at the story.

The blast-off had come!
The rocket was up and away!
The men looked up at the rocket as long as they could see it. They knew that it would go far up into outer space. There the nose cone would come off the rocket. It would fall back to earth with the monkeys in it! Would they be alive?
If the nose cone came down right, it would fall into the water. Then men would hurry to get it. Some Navy ships were far out on the water. Men on one of them were ready to get the nose cone.

Choose the best words from the list at the bottom of the page and write them in the blanks.

1. The rocket went into____________________.
2. The__________looked at the rocket for as long as they could see it.
3. The____________________would come back to earth.
4. The nose cone would fall into the____________________.
5. Some____________were on the water.

ships	children
outer space	men
nose cone	water

Instructional level: 70% or max. 1 1/2 errors.

Selection from Macmillan Reading Program, *Enchanted Gates* (Grade 2:1), edited by Albert J. Harris and Mae Knight Clark. New York: Macmillan Publishing Co., Inc., 1965. Used by permission.

Grade 2:2—Silent Reading Selection

The teacher should give the copy of this selection (see Appendix D) folded on "fold line" to the student with instructions to read the story carefully and then answer the questions on the bottom of the sheet in writing without looking back at the story.

Mark wanted to be a cowboy. He wanted to show Mr. Langford that he was learning the work of a cowboy quickly. Mr. Langford was the owner of the ranch where Mark was staying. He might send Mark away if Mark didn't show him he would make a good cowboy. Mark wanted to stay.

Mark liked Shag best of all the cowboys on the ranch. Shag was teaching him the things that mattered to a cowboy.

"Now we're going to round up the cattle," Shag told him. "The cowboys will ride two by two. We will make what is called a circle. We will listen to Old Roan and do as he says."

---

1. Mark wanted to be a ____________________
2. Mr. Langford was the ____________________ of the ranch.
3. Mr. Langford would send Mark away if he weren't a good __________
4. Mark liked Shag better than any other ____________________
5. Did Mark like the ranch? ____________________
6. The cowboys were going to round up the ____________________

Instructional level: 70% or max. of 1 1/2 errors.

Selection from Macmillan Reading Program, *Shining Bridges* (Grade 2:2), edited by Albert J. Harris and Mae Knight Clark. New York: Macmillan Publishing Co., Inc., 1965. Used by permission.

Grade 3:1—Silent Reading Selection

The teacher should give the copy of this selection (see Appendix D) to the student with instructions to read the story carefully and then answer the questions on the following page in writing without looking back at the story.

Pierre Pidgeon was seven years old, waiting to be eight. He lived near the sea.

His father sailed out in his boat every day to catch fish. He usually left early in the morning when Pierre was still asleep.

Every afternoon Pierre went down to the dock. He watched his father's boat come in and he helped unload the fish.

Fishing didn't bring in much money, so Pierre's mother worked, too. She baked bread in an outdoor oven and sold it to town people and visitors. Pierre liked to help her.

Pierre liked to do lots of things. He liked to drive a dogcart and to sail on his father's boat. Most of all he liked to make ship models.

---

1. What was the name of the little boy in the story? ______
2. How old was he? ______
3. What kind of work did his father do? ______
4. He went to the ______ every afternoon.
5. What type of work did his mother do? ______
6. What did he do to help his father? ______
7. What did he like to do the most? ______
8. When did his father leave to go to work? ______
9. Where did he live? ______
10. Did he like to help his mother? ______

Instructional level: 70% or max. of 3 errors.

Selection from Macmillan Reading Program, *Better Than Gold* (Grade 3:1), edited by Albert J. Harris and Mae Knight Clark. New York: Macmillan Publishing Co., Inc., 1965. Used by permission.

Grade 3:2—Silent Reading Selection

The teacher should give the copy of this sheet (see Appendix D) folded on "fold line" to the student with instructions to read the story carefully and then answer the questions on the bottom of the sheet in writing without looking back.

Mary Ann pressed her finger against the picture on the easel. Oh, dear! It *was* wet. She felt the paint slide a little under her finger. She was sorry she had touched the picture. It had left a mark right in the middle of the basket.

Mary Ann hurriedly caught up with Frances and stepped along beside her.

"I looked back and I saw you," whispered Frances. "You shouldn't have done that. Miss Ray wouldn't have given you permission to touch a picture in the museum."

---

1. ______________________ touched the picture.
2. She touched the picture in the ______________ of the basket.
3. The picture was sitting on the ______________ when it was touched.
4. Was the picture wet? ______________
5. How did she know the picture was or was not wet? ______________
6. Who saw her touch it? ______________
7. She felt ______________ after touching the picture.
8. Would the teacher have given her permission to touch the picture? ______________
9. What was her teacher's name? ______________
10. Where was the art class? ______________

Instructional level: 70% or max. of 3 errors.

Selection from Macmillan Reading Program, *More Than Words* (Grade 3:2), edited by Albert J. Harris and Mae Knight Clark. New York: Macmillan Publishing Co., Inc., 1965. Used by permission.

Grade 4—Silent Reading Selection

The teacher should give the copy of this selection (see Appendix D) to the student with instructions to read the story carefully and then answer the questions on the following page in writing without looking back at the story.

The Merry Widow was no longer young, but she was still lively. For years she had taken Doctor Brown on his rounds through the city to visit his sick patients. She waited quietly outside the houses, trying to swish the flies off her back with her short tail. You see, the Merry Widow was not a lady but a horse, and not a black one but a white one.

On Sunday afternoons the whole Brown family always went to drive in the buggy. Little Susan sat on the seat between Doctor and Mrs. Brown. Mrs. Brown held Baby Brown on her knee, and Samuel sat on the floor and helped his father with the driving. So they drove happily along the quiet country roads.

---

1. The Merry Widow was a ____________________.
2. For what did the Merry Widow's owner use her? __________
3. To whom did the Merry Widow belong? __________
4. What did the Merry Widow do with her tail? __________
5. What color was the Merry Widow? __________
6. Who was Samuel Brown? __________
7. On what day of the week did the Brown family always go for a drive? __________
8. Where did Susan sit in the buggy? __________
9. How did Samuel help his father when the family went for a drive? __________
10. What is a buggy? __________

Instructional level: 70% or max. of 3 errors.

Grade 5—Silent Reading Selection

The teacher should give the copy of this sheet (see Appendix D) folded on the "fold line" to the student with instructions to read the story carefully and then answer the questions on the bottom of the sheet in writing without looking back at the story.

"Well, it proves what you can do if you think you can. But listen, Davey, we won't let on to the others that the brain machine is a fake, will we? Let's keep them guessing."

"But it isn't a fake!" Davey shouted. "It made me work harder. It made me think I could do better, and it made me get eight words out of ten right. That's twice as many as I ever got right before. Why I even spelled *abbreviation* right!"

Mel sat down to think that one over. For all he knew, he might be another Thomas Edison!

---

1. Write two words that describe the machine.__________ and __________.
(2 points)
2. The names of the two boys in the story were __________ and __________.
(2 points)
3. What did the boy mean when he said, "Let's keep them guessing?"
____
4. What word was the boy able to spell?____________________
5. The boy got____________________words out of ten right, which was
____________ as many as before.
(2 points)
6. How did the machine make the boy work harder?____________________
____
7. The moral of the story is______________________________
____

Instructional level: 70% or max. of 3 errors.

Appendix D
Student's Copy of Silent Reading Selections and comprehension Questions

Contents:

1. Silent reading selections and comprehension questions identical to those found in Appendix C, "Teacher's Copy or Silent Reading Selections and Comprehension Questions." Information regarding grade level, administration, and scoring is omitted on the student's copy.

Bolo ran up and down the bus.
"Stop, Bolo!" said Jeff.
"You can't run in the bus.
The busman will put you off if you do!
Come here, Bolo!"
Bolo didn't come to Jeff.
He didn't stop.
But the busman did.
The busman said, "Boy!
Take that dog off the bus.
We don't let dogs ride."
"I put him in that," said Jeff.
The busman said,
"He is not in it now.
Take him off!"
"We can't get off!" said Jeff.
"If we do, how will we get to the dog show?"

— — — — — — — — — — - Fold — — — — — — — — — —

Choose the best words from the list at the bottom of the page and write them in the blanks.

1. Bolo ran up and down the ________________.
2. Jeff told Bolo, "________________________."
3. Did Bolo stop? ________________________
4. The ________________ told Jeff, "We don't let dogs ride."
5. Bolo and Jeff were going to the ________________.

busman	bus	yes	no
Jeff	dog show	stop	

Tommy lived on a farm.
He had a big brother.
His brother's name was Ben.

One morning Ben ran into the house.
"Mother! Mother!" he yelled.
"The black and white cow has twins.
One of the twins is little
and one is big.
Daddy said I could have
the big twin for my calf!"

Tommy looked at his mother.
"I want a twin, too," he said.

"You are too little," said Ben.
"You have to be big like me
to take care of a calf.
I will take good care of my calf.
I will show him at the fair."

— — — — — — — — — — — · Fold — — — — — — — — — — —

Choose the best words from the list at the bottom of the page and write them in the blanks.

1. Tommy lives on a ____________________.
2. Ben is Tommy's ____________________.
3. The story takes place in the ____________________.
4. Ben yelled to his ____________________.
5. Ben was ____________________.

brother	friend	morning	farm
Mother	happy	sad	

The blast-off had come!
The rocket was up and away!

The men looked up at the rocket as long as they could see it. They knew that it would go far up into outer space. There the nose cone would come off the rocket. It would fall back to earth with the monkeys in it! Would they be alive?

If the nose cone came down right, it would fall into the water. Then men would hurry to get it. Some Navy ships were out on the water. Men on one of them were ready to get the nose cone.

— — — — — — — — — — — — -Fold — — — — — — — — — — — —

Choose the best words from the list at the bottom of the page and write them in the blanks.

1. The rocket went into ____________________.
2. The ________ looked at the rocket as long as they could see it.
3. The ________________ would come back to earth.
4. The nose cone would fall into the ______________.
5. Some ____________________ were on the water.

ships	children
outer space	men
nose cone	water

Mark wanted to be a cowboy. He wanted to show Mr. Langford that he was learning the work of a cowboy quickly. Mr. Langford was the owner of the ranch where Mark was staying. He might send Mark away if Mark didn't show him he would make a good cowboy. Mark wanted to stay.

Mark liked Shag best of all the cowboys on the ranch. Shag was teaching him the things that mattered to a cowboy.

"Now we're going to round up the cattle," Shag told him. "The cowboys will ride two by two. We will make what is called a circle. We will listen to Old Roan and do as he says."

— — — — — — — — — — — — Fold — — — — — — — — — — — — —

1. Mark wanted to be a ______________________.
2. Mr. Langford was the ______________ of the ranch.
3. Mr. Langford would send Mark away if he weren't a good ______________________________________.
4. Mark liked Shag better than any other __________.
5. Did Mark like the ranch?______________________
6. The cowboys were going to round up the ________.

Pierre Pidgeon was seven years old, waiting to be eight. He lived near the sea.

His father sailed out in his boat every day to catch fish. He usually left early in the morning when Pierre was still asleep.

Every afternoon Pierre went down to the dock. He watched his father's boat come in and he helped unload the fish.

Fishing didn't bring in much money, so Pierre's mother worked, too. She baked bread in an outdoor oven and sold it to town people and visitors. Pierre liked to help her.

Pierre liked to do lots of things. He liked to drive a dogcart and to sail on his father's boat. Most of all he liked to make ship models.

— —

1. What was the name of the little boy in the story?

____

2. How old was he? ________________________
3. What kind of work did his father do? __________

____

4. He went to the ______________ every afternoon.
5. What type of work did his mother do? __________

____

6. What did he do to help his father? ___________

____

7. What did he like to do the most? ____________

____

8. When did his father leave to go to work? _______

____

9. Where did he live? ______________________
10. Did he like to help his mother? _____________

Mary Ann pressed her finger against the picture on the easel. Oh, dear! It *was* wet. She felt the paint slide a little under her finger. She was sorry she had touched the picture. It had left a mark right in the middle of the basket.

Mary Ann hurriedly caught up with Frances and stepped along beside her.

"I looked back and I saw you," whispered Frances. "You shouldn't have done that. Miss Ryan wouldn't have given you permission to touch a picture in the museum."

— — — — — — — — — — — — -Fold- — — — — — — — — — — — —

1. ________________________ touched the picture.
2. She touched the picture in the ______ of the basket.
3. The picture was sitting on the __________ when it was touched.
4. Was the picture wet? ____________________
5. How did she know the picture was or was not wet?
   ____
6. Who saw her touch it? ____________________
7. She felt ________________________________ after touching the picture.
8. Would the teacher have given her permission to touch the picture? ____________________
9. What was her teacher's name? ______________
10. Where was the art class? __________________

The Merry Widow was no longer young, but she was still lively. For years she had taken Doctor Brown on his rounds through the city to visit his sick patients. She waited quietly outside the houses, trying to swish the flies off her back with her short tail. You see, the Merry Widow was not a lady but a horse, and not a black one but a white one.

On Sunday afternoons the whole Brown family always went to drive in the buggy. Little Susan sat on the seat between Doctor and Mrs. Brown. Mrs. Brown held Baby Brown on her knee, and Samuel sat on the floor and helped his father with the driving. So they drove happily along the quiet country roads.

— —

1. The Merry Widow was a ______________________.
2. For what did the Merry Widow's owner use her?

____

3. To whom did the Merry Widow belong? __________

____

4. What did the Merry Widow do with her tail? ______

____

5. What color was the Merry Widow? ____________
6. Who was Samuel Brown? ___________________

____

7. On what day of the week did the Brown family always go for a drive? ______________________
8. Where did Susan sit in the buggy? ____________

____

9. How did Samuel help his father when the family went for a drive? ______________________
10. What is a buggy? ________________________

____

"Well, it proves what you can do if you think you can. But listen, Davey, we won't let on to the others that the brain machine is a fake, will we? Let's keep them guessing."

"But it isn't a fake!" Davey shouted. "It made me work harder. It made me think I could do better, and it made me get eight words out of ten right. That's twice as many as I ever got right before. Why I even spelled *abbreviation* right!"

Mel sat down to think that one over. For all he knew, he might be another Thomas Edison!

— — — — — — — — — — — — —Fold— — — — — — — — — — — — —

1. Write two words that describe the machine. ______ and ____________
2. The names of the two boys in the story were ______ and ____________.
3. What did the boy mean when he said, "Let's keep them guessing?" ______________________________

    ____
4. Which word was the boy able to spell?____________
5. The boy got ________words out of ten right, which was ____________________ as many as before.
6. How did the machine make the boy work harder?

    ____
7. The moral of the story is ______________________

    ____

Pecos Bill was the greatest cowboy of all time. In fact, before Pecos Bill became foreman of the I. X. L. Ranch, there was no real cowpunching. Pecos Bill invented the lasso and taught the I. X. L. boys how to use it. He next invented branding and the roundup, which made it simplier to keep track of the cattle.

The thing which most surprised the cowhands, however, was the way Bill conquered the weather. One summer when drought dried up the range grass, Bill dug a canal, but no water flowed into it. Then Bill took his lasso and roped a ten-mile piece of the great river—the Rio Grande—enough to last the ranch a day.

— — — — — — — — — — — — —Fold— — — — — — — — — — — — —

1. What is cowpunching? ____________________
2. What kind of job did Bill have at the I.X.L. Ranch?

   ____
3. What did Pecos Bill invent? ____________________
4. What surprised the cowhands most about Pecos Bill? ____________________
5. What is a drought? ____________________
6. What river did Bill rope? ____________________
7. Name one thing Pecos Bill invented to keep track of the cattle. ____________________
8. Why did Pecos Bill rope a river? ____________________
9. What is a canal? ____________________
10. Why did Pecos Bill dig the canal? ____________________

Appendix E
Sample Lesson Plans

Appendix E presents sample lesson plans for teaching specific reading skills. The format in the following lessons is the same as that described in Chapter 6 under the heading *Teacher's Lesson Plans.* Each plan below contains a. a behavioral objective, b. a preassessment, c. a list of materials needed, d. a procedure for teaching the lesson, and e. a postassessment. The *behavioral objective* describes what the pupils should be able to do after they complete the lesson. The *preassessment* is used to determine what the pupils already know about the skills to be taught. The *materials* section lists the materials that are necessary for the lesson. The *procedures* section describes how the instructor intends to teach the skill. The *postassessment* completes the lesson and is indicative of the pupils' knowledge of the skill at the conclusion of the lesson.

Sample Lesson Plan 1

Objective: Upon successful completion of this lesson, the children will be able to identify at least five multi-syllabic words and count their syllables.

Preassessment: Give a list of words, the students will be asked to identify the multi-syllabic words and to indicate the number of syllables in each.

Materials: Coffee can with plastic lid (one for every other child), small stick or pencil, and copy of first reader for every child.

Procedure: Say a word and beat out the syllables on the coffee can. You might also say a child's name and beat out the syllables. After the children are fully prepared (Do they know what syllables are?), pair off the children and assign each pair a page from the basal reader. Give them one coffee can and a drumstick or ask them to use their pencils or their hands for "drumsticks." Have one child from each pair find a word with more than one syllable; he is to pronounce the word, circle it, and then write the number of syllables next to the word. Pausing between syllables, he then reads the word to his partner, who taps out the syllables on the coffee can. Switch this procedure and let the second child find a word. When the group has worked on this for ten minutes, let each child beat out his favorite word.

Postassessment: Given a different list of words from those used in the preassessment, the students will be asked to identify the multi-syllabic words and to indicate the number of syllables in each.

Sample Lesson Plan 2

Objective: Upon successful completion of this lesson, the pupil will be able to discriminate fact from fiction when presented with three pictures from *The Little Wooden Farmer.*

Preassessment: Show each child three pictures from *The Little Wooden Farmer* and ask them to identify factual and fictional aspects.

Materials: One copy of *The Little Wooden Farmer* by Alice Dalgliesh for each child, poster board, scissors, paste, and pictures from the story.

Procedure: Show pictures of real objects and pictures of imaginary objects to the group. Encourage the pupils to discuss things they are able to do and tasks that are impossible to perform. Divide the class into pairs and ask each to look for at least three different pictures concerning characters in the story. The pair are to separate the pictures into fact and fiction categories. When the children have finished separating the pictures, have them draw a picture of the most improbable thing that could ever happen to them.

Postassessment: Those children who can identify pictures of real situations or objects and also pictures of fictional or imaginary objects or situations have met the objective for this lesson.

Sample Lesson Plan 3

Objective: Given a consonant letter of the alphabet, the child will give an example of a word beginning with that sound.

Preassessment: Say a consonant to the child and ask him to say a word that begins with it. Repeat with three different consonants.

Materials: Newspapers; crayons; pre-constructed box with sturdy cutout letters of the alphabet inside; and pre-constructed Bingo boards.

Procedure: Pull out a consonant letter from the box, have children name the letter, locate and circle a word beginning with that letter in the mimeo of the story they had previously written together. Then have children draw that letter on a large sheet of paper, using large arm strokes. Repeat several times using different letters. Give out Bingo boards. Pass the box around to each child. Have him reach inside and "feel" a consonant. After which, without looking, he guesses what it is. If he is right he says a word that begins with that sound and then locates that letter on the Bingo board and marks an "x." If he is wrong, no marks are made. First one to "bingo" wins the game.

Postassessment: Those children who can give examples of words beginning with a consonant sound when given a specific consonant at least two out of three times have met the objective for this lesson.

Sample Lesson Plan 4

Objective: Upon successful completion of this lesson, the child will be able to identify at least five words that help him interpret the feelings of a character.

Preassessment: Given a list of words that includes five words which describe Goldilocks' feelings, students will be asked to circle those words.

Materials: One copy for each child of *Where the Wild Things Are*, by Maurice Sendak.

Procedure: Discuss words that express feelings. Divide the class into pairs and have each pair go through their books to find words that express Max's feelings. Have the children discuss the words with each other. Have one of the children in each pair identify the words selected as expressive of Max's feelings and give his reasons for those selections. This should be done in front of the whole group and discussion concerning various pair choices should be encouraged.

Postassessment: Those children who can correctly identify at least five words that help them to interpret Max's feelings have met the objective for this lesson.

References

Dalgliesh, A. *The Little Wooden Farmer.* New York: Macmillan Publishing Co., Inc., 1968.
Sendak, M. *Where the Wild Things Are.* New York: Harper & Row Publishers, Inc., 1963.

Index

2867

HIEBERT LIBRARY
3 6877 00124 5900